W9-CUV-400

MAINE COAST
1ST EDITION

Where to Stay and Eat
for All Budgets

Must-See Sights
and Local Secrets

Ratings You Can Trust

Fodor's Travel Publications   New York, Toronto, London, Sydney, Auckland
www.fodors.com

FODOR'S MAINE COAST

Editors: Amanda Theunissen, Mark Sullivan

Editorial Contributors: Stephen and Neva Allen, Lelah Cole, Sherry Hanson, Mary Ruoff, Laura V. Scheel

Editorial Production: Jenna L. Bagnini

Maps: David Lindroth, *cartographer;* Bob Blake and Rebecca Baer, *map editors*

Design: Fabrizio La Rocca, *creative director;* Guido Caroti, *art director;* Moon Sun Kim, *cover designer;* Melanie Marin, *senior picture editor*

Production/Manufacturing: Robert B. Shields

Cover Photo (Isle au Haut Light): Peter Guttman

COPYRIGHT

Copyright © 2005 by Fodors LLC

Fodor's is a registered trademark of Random House, Inc.

All rights reserved under International and Pan-American Copyright Conventions. Published in the United States by Fodor's Travel Publications, a unit of Fodors LLC, a subsidiary of Random House, Inc., and simultaneously in Canada by Random House of Canada Limited, Toronto. Distributed by Random House, Inc., New York.

No maps, illustrations, or other portions of this book may be reproduced in any form without written permission from the publisher.

ISBN 1–4000–1466–2

SPECIAL SALES

This book is available for special discounts for bulk purchases for sales promotions or premiums. Special editions, including personalized covers, excerpts of existing books, and corporate imprints, can be created in large quantities for special needs. For more information, write to Special Markets/Premium Sales, 1745 Broadway, MD 6-2, New York, New York 10019, or e-mail specialmarkets@randomhouse.com.

AN IMPORTANT TIP & AN INVITATION

Although all prices, opening times, and other details in this book are based on information supplied to us at press time, changes occur all the time in the travel world, and Fodor's cannot accept responsibility for facts that become outdated or for inadvertent errors or omissions. So **always confirm information when it matters,** especially if you're making a detour to visit a specific place. Your experiences—positive and negative—matter to us. If we have missed or misstated something, **please write to us.** We follow up on all suggestions. Contact the Maine Coast editor at editors@fodors.com or c/o Fodor's at 1745 Broadway, New York, New York 10019.

PRINTED IN THE UNITED STATES OF AMERICA

10 9 8 7 6 5 4 3 2 1

ON THE ROAD WITH FODOR'S

A trip takes you out of yourself. Concerns of life at home completely disappear, driven away by more immediate thoughts—about, say, what marvels will beguile the next day or where you'll have dinner. That's where Fodor's comes in. We make sure that you know all your options, so that you don't miss something around the next bend just because you didn't know it was there. With Fodor's at your side, serendipitous discoveries are never far away.

Our success in showing you every corner of the Maine Coast is a credit to our extraordinary writers. Although there's no substitute for travel advice from a good friend who knows your style, our contributors are the next best thing—the kind of people you would poll for travel advice if you knew them.

In addition to writing for Fodor's, Stephen and Neva Allen have written extensively about travel for many newspapers and magazines. They moved to the Mid-Coast of Maine five years ago and are devoted to the beautiful area they've come to call home.

Lelah Cole grew up on Mount Desert Island and presently resides in Bar Harbor. When she's not gardening or writing, she enjoys hiking Acadia's mountains, biking, and cross-country skiing its carriage roads, and learning French.

Twelve years ago, Sherry Hanson packed up her home in Illinois and moved to the Mid-Coast of Maine, a place she has loved since childhood. Sherry has written for many magazines, newspapers, and online publications. She has also worked on special projects for organizations such as Habitat for Humanity. When she's not writing, she can be found hiking, biking, kayaking, skiing, watching ocean storms, or walking on the beach.

As a Maine-based freelance writer, Mary Ruoff has enjoyed writing articles about Maine travel and other topics. A graduate of the University of Missouri School of Journalism, she previously worked as a newspaper reporter. Mary is married to a Mainer, Michael Hodsdon, and spends as much time as she can at their family land "Way Down East," where Michael's grandfather was a fisherman.

Laura V. Scheel has spent a good portion of her years in Maine driving and exploring her adopted home state's numerous back roads and small towns. She has written frequently for Fodor's, including the Maine chapter in *The Thirteen Colonies,* part of Fodor's recent Travel Historic America series. History and travel are just two of her favorite things.

CONTENTS

ABOUT THIS BOOK

The best source for travel advice is a like-minded friend who's just been where you're headed. But with or without that friend, you'll be in great shape to find your way around your destination once you learn to find your way around your Fodor's guide.

SELECTION

Our goal is to cover the best properties, sights, and activities in their category, as well as the most interesting communities to visit. We make a point of including local food-lovers' hot spots as well as neighborhood options, and we avoid all that is touristy unless it's really worth your time. You can go on the assumption that everything in this book is recommended wholeheartedly by our writers and editors. Flip to On the Road with Fodor's to learn more about who they are. It goes without saying that no property pays to be included.

RATINGS

Orange stars ☆ denote sights and properties that our editors and writers consider the very best in the entire book. These, the best of the best, are listed in the Fodor's Choice section in the front of the book. Black stars ★ highlight the sights and properties we deem Highly Recommended, the don't-miss sights within any region. Sights pinpointed with numbered map bullets ❶ in the margins tend to be more important than those without bullets.

SPECIAL SPOTS

Pleasures & Pastimes and text on chapter title pages focus on experiences that reveal the spirit of the destination. Also watch for Off the Beaten Path sights. Some are out of the way, some are quirky, and all are worthwhile. When the munchies hit, look for Need a Break? suggestions.

TIME IT RIGHT

Check chapters' Timing sections for weather and crowd overviews and best days and times to visit.

SEE IT ALL

Use Fodor's exclusive Great Itineraries as a model for your trip. Either follow those that begin the book, or mix regional itineraries from several chapters. In cities, Good Walks guide you to important sights in each neighborhood; ▶ indicates the starting points of walks and itineraries in the text and on the map.

BUDGET WELL

Hotel and restaurant price categories from ¢ to $$$$ are defined in the opening pages of each chapter—expect to find a balanced selection for every budget. For attractions, we always give standard adult admission fees; reductions are usually available for children, students, and senior citizens. Look in Discounts & Deals in Smart Travel Tips for information on destination-wide ticket schemes.

BASIC INFO

Smart Travel Tips lists travel essentials for the entire area covered by the book; city- and region-specific basics end each chapter. To find the best way to get around, see the Transportation section; see individual modes of travel ("By Car," "By Train") for details.

ON THE MAPS	Maps throughout the book show you what's where and help you find your way around. Black and orange numbered bullets ❶ ➊ in the text correlate to bullets on maps.
FIND IT FAST	Within the book, chapters are arranged geographically from south to north. All regional chapters are divided geographically; within each area, towns are covered in logical geographical order and with attractive routes, and interesting places between towns are flagged as En Route. Heads at the top of each page help you find what you need within a chapter.
DON'T FORGET	Restaurants are open for lunch and dinner daily unless we state otherwise; we mention dress only when there's a specific requirement and reservations only when they're essential or not accepted—it's always best to book ahead. Unless we say otherwise, hotels have private baths, phone, TVs, and air-conditioning and operate on the European Plan (aka EP, meaning without meals). We always list facilities but not whether you'll be charged extra to use them, so when pricing accommodations, find out what's included.

SYMBOLS

Many Listings

★ Fodor's Choice
★ Highly recommended
⊠ Physical address
✢ Directions
⌕ Mailing address
☏ Telephone
🖷 Fax
⊕ On the Web
✉ E-mail
💲 Admission fee
🕘 Open/closed times
► Start of walk/itinerary
▭ Credit cards

Outdoors

🏌 Golf
⛺ Camping

Hotels & Restaurants

🏨 Hotel
🛏 Number of rooms
♿ Facilities
🍴 Meal plans
✕ Restaurant
☙ Reservations
👔 Dress code
✕🏨 Hotel with restaurant that warrants a visit

Other

☕ Family-friendly
🔢 Contact information
⇨ See also
⊠ Branch address

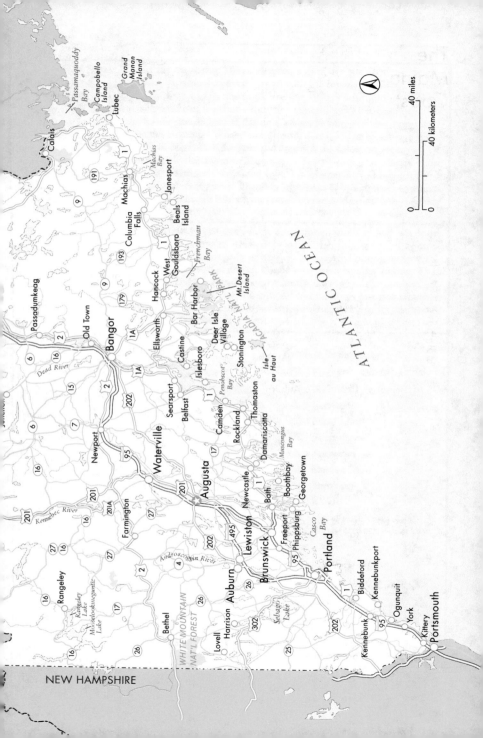

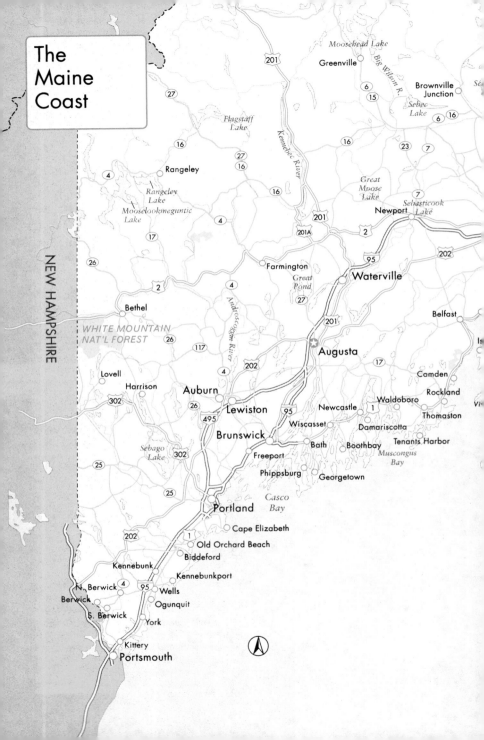

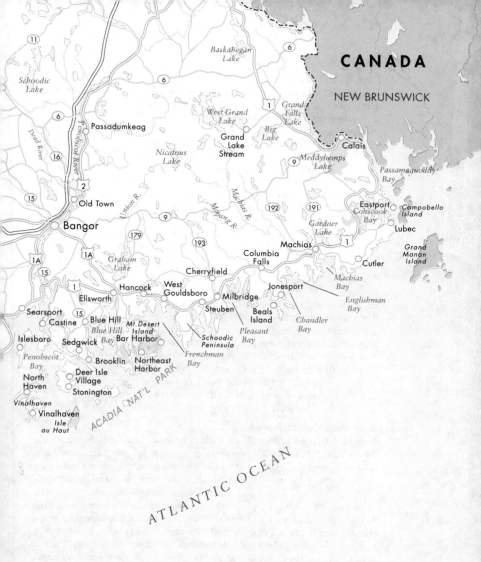

WHAT'S WHERE

(1) The Southern Coast

The Southern Coast is Maine's most visited region, stretching north from Kittery to just outside Portland. Despite the very chilly waters of the Atlantic, beachgoers are enamored with the area's miles and miles of sandy expanses, which invite long walks along the shore and offer sweeping views of lighthouses, forested islands, and the wide open sea. The towns along the shore cater to summer visitors with shops, restaurants, and numerous lodging establishments that range from full-service resorts to impeccably restored B&Bs. Kittery, the Yorks, and the Kennebunks have much to offer of historical interest, while the boisterous towns of Old Orchard Beach and York Beach throw in a heady serving of Coney Island–like amusements, cotton candy, blinking neon, and carnival rides. In contrast to all the man-made fun, the region is also home to many thousands of acres devoted to conservation and the preservation of wildlife.

(2) Greater Portland

Maine's largest and most cosmopolitan city, Portland, deftly balances its historic role as a working—and still-thriving—harbor with its new identity as a center of sophisticated shopping, innovative restaurants, and stylish accommodations. The city is blessed with an active and varied cultural scene, brimming with talent in the form of strong local music, numerous theater groups, dozens of impressive art galleries and venues, and a grand art museum. In the warmer months the city really comes alive, with a full schedule of outdoor concerts, performances, blooming garden parks, and a twice-weekly farmers' market. While Portland is a popular destination in itself, its nearness to more rural and coastal areas makes it a perfect beginning point from which to wander.

(3) The Mid-Coast Region

North of Portland, from Brunswick to Monhegan Island, is the state's Mid-Coast region. This is where the geography begins to truly defy traditional compass point parameters. The coastline swirls and winds its way around pastoral peninsulas, sheltering harbors and waterways from the severity of the open ocean. Dozens of lighthouses stand watch atop rock-strewn bluffs, while calm waters welcome pleasure boats, sailing sloops, and solitary kayakers. Historically, the area prospered in maritime trade; today it's best known as a prime resort area. The bustling coastal villages in the region boast rich maritime museums, a great wealth of antiques shops, and plenty of places to dine and stay amid the region's beauty.

(4) Penobscot Bay

The Penobscot Bay region combines lively and heavily traveled (for good reason) coastal towns with dramatic natural scenery. Camden, the anchor of the region, is one of Maine's most picture-perfect towns, with its skyward church steeples, manicured antique homes, and the blue, blue harbor moving in the perpetual sway of boats of all sizes. With nearby Rockland, the two towns make up the general headquarters of the famed historic windjammer fleet. These dramatic wooden schooners with their multimasted sails humming in the wind are a common sight in the bay and offer cruises of various lengths. For an even more remarkable (and more solitary) glimpse into the sheer beauty of the region, head to the top of Camden's Mount Battie where you can gaze at the dramatic hills that twist and tumble down, eventually merging with the sea. Farther up the coast, Belfast stands out with its beautiful waterfront, Searsport is known as the "Antique Capital of Maine," and a little inland, Bangor—Maine's second largest city—offers easy access to the region via its international airport.

5 The Blue Hill Peninsula

While the pace of life and commercial development on the Blue Hill Peninsula is significantly less vigorous than on other parts of the coast, in no way is the sheer drama of its natural scenery lessened. Life here is decidedly more peaceful, driven not by the thrust of tourist attractions and activities but by the sheer natural wonder of the place itself. Much of the treasure of the Blue Hill area is found by the inquisitive explorer who seeks entertainment and enchantment in the physical environment. Artists and art lovers have long been attracted to the area for that very reason, and galleries are far more plentiful than shops selling lobster T-shirts and lighthouse curios. The entire region is ideal for the more solitary pursuits of biking, hiking, kayaking, or boating. For many, the Blue Hill Peninsula defines the silent beauty of the Maine Coast.

6 Mount Desert Island & Acadia National Park

Mount Desert Island is home to Acadia National Park—Maine's most heavily visited attraction. Travelers come by the millions to climb (mostly by car) the miles of 19th-century carriage roads leading to the stunning peaks and vistas of the island's mountains. Each curve of the road reveals breathtaking scenes of cliff and rock set amid the sparkling waters of the surrounding bays. Hikers and cyclists enjoy a less crowded experience on off-road jaunts and trails. Like other regions in Maine, the island has many different flavors—in the Northeast quadrant is Bar Harbor, filled with tourists and all the accompanying attractions; the quieter side exists in the smaller towns of Southwest Harbor, Bass Harbor, and other outlying small islands. Wherever you go, ever-present is the massive peak of Cadillac Mountain, heralded as the best—and first—place in the nation to see the sun rise up over the water.

7 Way Down East

Many, many people will tell you that the *real Maine* exists only in the areas above Mount Desert, up past the heavily trod tourist meccas of the south. Way Down East unfurls in thousands and thousands of acres of wild blueberry barrens, congestion-free coastlines, and a tangible sense of rugged endurance not found elsewhere. Outdoor enthusiasts can amble or paddle through pristine expanses of numerous wildlife refuges, state parks, and preservation lands. The impact of nature's hand is felt strongly and it is the vulnerability of the land here to the winds, the winters, and the immense tides that makes the area so strikingly beautiful.

Highlights of the Maine Coast
10 to 12 days

Much of the appeal of the Maine Coast lies in its geographical contrasts, from its long stretches of swimming and walking beaches in the south to the cliff-edged, rugged rocky coasts in the north. And not unlike the physical differences of the coast, each town along the way reveals a slightly different character. This sampler tour will provide you with a good taste of what the Maine Coast offers; allow the individual chapters to invite you along other trails on the way.

THE YORKS **1 day.** Start your trip in York Village with a leisurely stroll through the seven buildings of the Old York Historical Society, getting a glimpse of 18th-century life in this gentrified town. Spend time wandering amid the shops or walking the nature trails and beaches around York Harbor. There are several grand lodging options here, most with views of the harbor. If you prefer a livelier pace, continue on to York Beach, a haven for families with plenty of entertainment venues. Stop at Nubble Light for a seaside lunch or dinner. *Chapter 1*

OGUNQUIT **2 days.** For well over a century, Ogunquit has been a favorite vacation spot for those looking to combine the natural beauty of the ocean with a sophisticated environment. Take a morning walk along the Marginal Way to see the waves crashing on the rocks. In Perkins Cove, have lunch, stroll the shopping areas, or sign on with a lobster boat cruise to learn about Maine's most important fishery—the state's lobster industry supplies over 90% of the world's lobster intake. See the extraordinary collection at the Ogunquit Museum of American Art, take in a performance at one of the several theater venues, or just spend time on the beach. *Chapter 1*

THE KENNEBUNKS **1 day.** Head north to the Kennebunks, allowing at least two hours to wander through the shops and historic homes of Dock Square in Kennebunkport. This is an ideal place to rent a bike and amble around the back streets, head out on Ocean Avenue to view the Bush estate, or ride to one of the several beaches to relax awhile. *Chapter 1*

PORTLAND **2 days.** You can easily spend several days in Maine's largest city, exploring its historic neighborhoods, shopping and eating in the Old Port, or visiting one of the several excellent museums. A brief side trip to Cape Elizabeth takes you to Portland Head Light, Maine's first lighthouse, which was commissioned by George Washington in 1790. The lighthouse is on the grounds of Fort Williams Park and is an excellent place to bring a picnic. Be sure to spend some time wandering the ample grounds. There are also excellent walking trails (and views) at nearby Two Lights State Park. If you want to take a boat tour while in Portland, get a ticket for Casco Bay Lines and see some of the islands that dot the bay. *Chapter 2*

BATH TO CAMDEN **1 day.** Head north from Portland to Bath, Maine's shipbuilding capital and spend some time touring the Maine Maritime Museum or have lunch on the waterfront. There is a nice area for shopping, with boutiques and antiques shops, and plenty of beautiful homes to view. Continue on U.S. 1 north, through the towns of Wiscasset and Damariscotta, where you may find yourself pulling over frequently for outdoor flea markets or any number of intriguing antiques shops. This stretch of road is filled with such treasures. *Chapter 3*

CAMDEN **2 days.** Camden is the picture-perfect image of a seaside tourist town: hundreds of boats bobbing in the harbor, immaculately kept antique homes, streets lined with boutiques and specialty stores, and restaurants serving lobster at every turn. The modest (by Maine standards, anyway) hills of nearby Mount Battie offer good hiking and a great spot from which to picnic and view the surrounding area. Camden is one of the hubs for the beloved and historic windjammer fleet—there is no better way to see the area than from the deck of one of these graceful beauties. If you're an art lover, save some time for Rockland's Farnsworth Art Museum and the Wyeth Center. *Chapter 4*

MOUNT DESERT ISLAND/ACADIA NATIONAL PARK **2 days.** From Camden, continue north along U.S. 1, letting your interests dictate where you stop. Once you arrive on the island, you can choose to stay in Bar Harbor, the busiest village in the area, or in the quieter Southwest Harbor area; either way, the splendor of the mountains and the sea are all around you. Several days are easily spent exploring Acadia National Park, boating or kayaking in the surrounding waters, and simply enjoying the stunning panorama. *Chapter 6*

Maine Maritime History Tour
5 to 7 days

Maine's maritime leanings extend well back into the early 17th century, and while many things have changed, the sea—via lobstering, fishing, and tourism—is still the backbone of the state's economy and culture. This tour gives the traveler a glimpse of how the sea has influenced the people, towns, and industries along the coast of Maine to create the delightful and diverse region it is today.

PORTLAND **2 days.** A thriving, working harbor since the 17th century, Portland has maritime history written all over it. Take a step back in time at the Fish Exchange, where the day's catch is unloaded and auctioned off to worldwide markets just as it was centuries ago. For a more refined maritime experience, head to the Portland Museum of Art to see the impressive collection of sea-inspired art by such greats as Edward Hopper and Winslow Homer. Lighthouses once played an integral role in keeping Maine's coasts safe and navigable. Take a trip to Fort Williams Park and Two Lights State Park, in Cape Elizabeth, to see the area's most famous lighthouses. For a more intimate view of the sea, try a boat cruise from Portland to the nearby islands in Casco Bay. *Chapter 2*

BATH TO ROCKLAND **1 to 2 days.** From Portland, head north to Bath, Maine's present shipbuilding capital. The Bath Iron Works, which once built tall-masted wooden schooners, now engineers immense, powerful freighters and fighters for the U.S. Navy. Spend some time at the Maine Maritime Museum and Shipyard to get a sense of the area's previous prowess in the shipping industry. Wander the streets of Bath to see the grand mansions of 19th-century sea captains (many of which are now elegant B&B's).

Head north on U.S. 1 to Wiscasset, a village that gained great wealth in the shipbuilding industry as evidenced by its stunning array of grand sea captains' and merchants' homes. Tour the Nickels-Sortwell house (1807) to get a glimpse of the wealth these seafaring businessmen enjoyed. Continue on to Damariscotta, another town that found its wealth in shipbuilding. From here, take a detour down Route 130 to the Pemaquid Peninsula. At the end of Route 130, Pemaquid Point Lighthouse has stood watch over the water since 1827. Adjacent to the light is the Fishermen's Museum, which has a fascinating display illustrating Maine's 400-year-old fishing industry. *Chapters 3 and 4*

ROCKLAND/CAMDEN **2 days.** Make your way north from Damariscotta to Rockland, where you can tour the Farnsworth Art Museum and Wyeth Center, an excellent place to see maritime-inspired artworks. The fascinating Maine Lighthouse Museum, also in Rockland, displays many lighthouse and Coast Guard artifacts as well as other maritime memorabilia. You can—and should—take a one-day or overnight cruise on a historic windjammer from either Rockland or nearby Camden. Time spent aboard one of these graceful schooners is the ideal way to see the coast. *Chapter 4*

SEARSPORT **1 to 2 days.** Farther up U.S. 1 is the town of Searsport, Maine's second largest deepwater port and a haven for both maritime history buffs and antique treasure hunters. The relationship between the two is not accidental—world-traveling 19th-century sea captains, a good many of whom made their homes here, constantly brought back goods and gifts from Europe to fill their houses. You never know what kind of gem you can find in one of the multitude of antiques shops and outdoor flea markets. A treasure of another sort exists here as well: the Penobscot Marine Museum is a multibuilding complex brimming with fascinating sea history. Several hours can be easily spent here. *Chapter 4*

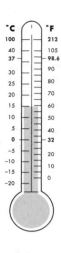

°C		°F
100		212
40		105
37		98.6
30		90
25		80
20		70
15		60
10		50
5		40
0		32
−5		20
−10		10
−15		0
−20		

Despite the long and often frigid winters that make even the locals shudder, Maine is truly a year-round destination. The state's dramatic coastline, impressive and expansive mountains and trails, fiery autumn foliage, and pure natural beauty welcome visitors of all tastes throughout the seasons. Be aware that black-fly season (many jokingly refer to the detested insect as Maine's state bird), from mid-May to mid-June, can rile even the most seasoned outdoorsfolk. It's also important to know that many smaller museums and attractions are open only for high season—from Memorial Day to mid-October—as are many of the waterside attractions and eateries.

Memorial Day is the start of the migration to the beaches and the mountains, and summer begins in earnest on July 4. Weekend traffic heading to the Maine Coast along its feeder roads, I–95 and U.S. 1, can be brutally frustrating, especially at the toll booths. Midweek travelers won't find themselves nearly as stymied, nor will those who travel outside of the peak season.

Fall is the most colorful season in Maine, a time when many inns and hotels are booked months in advance by foliage-viewing visitors. The state's dense hardwood forests explode in color as the diminishing hours of autumn daylight signal trees to stop producing chlorophyll. As green is stripped away from the leaves of maples, oaks, birches, beeches, and other deciduous species, a rainbow of reds, oranges, yellows, purples, and other vivid hues is revealed. The first scarlet-and-gold colors emerge in mid-September in northern areas; "peak" color occurs at different times from year to year. Generally, it's best to **visit the northern reaches in late September and early October** and move southward as October progresses.

All leaves are off the trees by Halloween, and hotel rates fall as the leaves do, dropping significantly until ski season begins, just around Thanksgiving. November and early December are hunting season, when hunters from many outside states come to try their luck at bringing home one of the plentiful deer or moose; those who venture into the woods should wear bright orange clothing.

Winter (November–April) is the time for downhill and cross-country skiing. Maine has several major ski resorts as well as numerous smaller mountains; all seem to be less burdened by crowds than places such as Vermont and are well equipped with snowmaking equipment if nature falls short. Along the coast, bed-and-breakfasts that remain open will often rent rooms at far lower prices than in summer.

In spring, despite mud season, maple sugaring goes on in earnest. The third Sunday in March is designated as Maine Maple Sunday and farms throughout the state open their doors to visitors not only to see the steamy process of turning sap into golden syrup but to sample the intensely sweet results.

Climate

In winter coastal Maine is cold and damp; inland temperatures may be lower, but generally drier conditions make them easier to bear. Snowfall is heaviest in the interior mountains and can range up to several hundred inches per year in the northern portion of the state. Spring is often windy and rainy; in many years it appears as if winter segues almost immediately into summer. Coastal areas can be quite humid in summer, making even moderate temperatures uncomfortable, though the sea breeze is ever present. Even after a steamy summer day, nights are often cool, requiring a sweatshirt over those sunburned shoulders. Autumn temperatures can be quite mild in more southerly areas well into October, but northern portions of the region can be quite cold by Columbus Day. In some years, a period of unseasonably mild weather occurs in late October and early November.

🎦 Forecasts **Weather Channel Connection** ☎ 900/932-8437 95¢ per minute from a Touch-Tone phone ⊕ www.weather.com.

The following are the average daily maximum and minimum temperatures for Portland.

Jan.	31F	− 1C	May	61F	16C	Sept.	68F	20C
	16	− 9		47	8		52	11
Feb.	32F	0C	June	72F	22C	Oct.	58F	14C
	16	− 9		54	15		43	6
Mar.	40F	4C	July	76F	24C	Nov.	45F	7C
	27	− 3		61	16		32	0
Apr.	50F	10C	Aug.	74F	23C	Dec.	34F	1C
	36	2		59	15		22	− 6

PLEASURES & PASTIMES

Bicycling Long-distance cyclists have long favored Maine's byways for their terrain, stunning vistas, and ease of navigation. Biking in Maine is especially scenic in and around Kennebunkport, Camden, Deer Isle, the Penobscot Bay area, and the Schoodic Peninsula. The carriage paths in Acadia National Park are ideal, with many miles of off-road trails providing finer and more intimate views than the roads open to traffic. For more adventurous riders, many ski resorts allow mountain bikes during the summer months. The Maine government publishes many maps and routes for cyclists; printable versions of these maps are available on the Web at ⊕ www.exploremaine.org.

Fishing Anglers will find sport aplenty throughout the region—surf-casting along the shore; deep-sea fishing in the Atlantic on party and charter boats; fishing for trout in streams; and angling for bass, landlocked salmon, and other fish in freshwater lakes. Sporting-goods stores and bait-and-tackle shops are reliable sources for licenses—necessary in fresh waters—and for leads to the nearest hot spots.

Golf Courses Golf caught on early in New England. The region has an ample supply of public and semiprivate courses, many of which are attached to distinctive resorts or even ski areas. One dilemma facing golfers is keeping their eyes on the ball instead of the scenery. During prime season, make sure you reserve ahead for tee times, particularly near urban areas and at resorts.

Kayaking More than 5,000 mi of meandering coastline have made Maine a premier destination for kayakers. The sport has caught on tremendously, and with that popularity, many local businesses have sprung up (several had been steadfastly operating long before the recent trend) offering instruction, rental equipment, and guided tours ranging from half-day to several-day jaunts. Paddlers have tremendous options, regardless of salt or freshwater preference, and the sheer vastness of the waterways allow for uncrowded and unhurried explorations amid harbors, marshes, tidal rivers, and hundreds of islands. Be aware that tides may be turbulent, the water is always cold, and you should never venture out onto the water alone. Kayak rental shops can provide safety tips, tidal information, and good maps.

Lighthouses With its many thousands of miles of jagged coastline, it's no wonder that Maine is home to well over 60 lighthouses, perched high on rocky ledges or on the tips of wayward islands. While modern technology in navigation has made many of the lights obsolete, preservationist and lighthouse enthusiast groups expressed enough fervent interest in the keeping of this maritime history to catch the eye of the U.S. government: A law signed by former President Bill Clinton transferred ownership of nearly 40 lighthouses from the Coast Guard (which likely would have torn them down) to nonprofit groups who restore and maintain them, and often make them accessible to the public. Some of the state's more famous lights include Portland Head Light, commissioned by President George Washington in 1790, and Quoddy Head, farther up the coast. Some lighthouses are privately owned and others are accessible only by boat, but plenty are within easy reach and are open to the public with museums and tours.

National & State Parks

Maine's National and State parks and forests provide myriad activities and facilities, including campgrounds, picnic grounds, hiking trails, nature walks, boating, and ranger programs. The state's most famous—and most visited—park is Acadia National Park, which covers much of Mount Desert Island and more than half of Isle au Haut and Schoodic Point on the mainland. The grand drama of well over a dozen mountains seemingly springing directly from the ocean's depths, combined with forested lakeshores, a great range of wildlife, and a network of roads ideal for biking, hiking, and driving makes Acadia National Park the destination of choice for more than 2 million visitors a year. The 6,700-acre Moosehorn National Wildlife Refuge, in the eastern quarter of Maine near the New Brunswick border, is bounded by Cobscook Bay and the mouth of the Dennys and Whiting rivers. This park is best known for birding and wildlife spotting. A number of state parks line Maine's fabled rock-bound coast. One of these, Camden Hills State Park, has an auto road that winds to the top of Mount Battie for spectacular views of Penobscot Bay.

Windjammers

Maine's maritime history is rich, going back nearly 400 years, and a good portion of the early colony's wealth came from its prowess in shipbuilding. Before the advent of steam engines, tall, graceful, and speedy wooden schooners were built to transfer goods for trade throughout the seas of the world markets. These ships were strong yet lightweight, and relied on the power of the winds and the sharp eye of the sailors who guided them. Though modern technology put an end to the building of these beauties for commerce, the advent of recreational boating gave windjammers an entirely new purpose. The Penobscot Bay region (Chapter 4) is famous for its mighty fleet of windjammers—a good portion of them original, aged, and retired from their 19th-century workloads. The drama of their majestic sails unfurled in the wind is a common sight in the harbors of the area. Their hulls have been redesigned to house passengers for overnight trips; the cruising season starts in mid-May and continues into fall foliage season. Each year in late June, Windjammer Days, a weeklong festival in Boothbay, brings dozens of members of the fleet to gather for a floating parade in the harbor. A cruise on one of these elegant vessels is an ideal way to truly appreciate the beauty of the Maine Coast. Some day trips are also available; check with the Maine Windjammer Association (800/807–9463; www.sailmainecoast.com) for details.

Fodor'sChoice
★

The sights, restaurants, hotels, and other travel experiences on these pages are our editors' top picks—our Fodor's Choices. They're the best of their type in the area covered by the book—not to be missed and always worth your time. In the destination chapters that follow, you can find all the details.

LODGING

$$$$	**The Colony,** Kennebunkport. Maine's first environmentally responsible hotel is grand, white, and set majestically atop a rise overlooking the ocean.
$$$$	**Captain Lord Mansion,** Kennebunkport. Built in 1812, this stately inn is sumptuously appointed with gas fireplaces, whirlpool tubs, and elegant furnishings.
$$$$	**Inn at Ocean's Edge,** Lincolnville. Old-fashioned New England elegance prevails at this beautiful white inn on 7 acres. With heavy forest on one side and the ocean on the other, this is one of the loveliest settings on the coast.
$$$–$$$$	**Black Boar Inn,** Ogunquit. Wine and hors d'oeuvres are served in the afternoon at this exquisite inn. The interior is stunning with wide-pine floors and fireplaces in every room.
$$$–$$$$	**Chapman Cottage,** York Harbor. Built in 1899 this inn has been impeccably restored and indulges its guests with spacious rooms, antique furnishings, and sumptuous breakfasts.
$$$–$$$$	**Log Cabin Inn,** Brunswick area. Every room has a view in this luxurious lodging. Take a dip in the pool or enjoy a glass of wine on your private deck.
$$$–$$$$	**Norumbega,** Camden. Housed in an actual castle, this B&B is filled with antiques, in-room fireplaces, and private balconies that overlook the bay.
$$$–$$$$	**Pomegranate Inn,** Portland. Vivid hand-painted walls, floors, and woodwork adorn this handsome inn in the architecturally rich Western Promenade area.
$$$–$$$$	**Ullikana,** Bar Harbor. Within this traditional Tudor-style cottage, you can find an eclectic blend of color and art. The elaborate breakfast is a real treat.
$$–$$$$	**Castine Inn,** Castine. This simple but charming inn offers bright rooms with ocean views and an excellent on-site restaurant.
$$–$$$$	**Haven by the Sea,** Kennebunkport. Once a seaside church, this unusual inn still boasts its original cathedral ceilings and stained-glass windows.

$$–$$$$	**Lucerne Inn,** Bangor. On a hilltop overlooking Phillips Lake, this stunning inn is a perfect getaway spot. Every room is furnished with antiques and has a view of the surrounding mountains and lake.
$$–$$$$	**Samoset Resort,** Rockport. This 230-acre, all-encompassing, ocean-side resort offers luxurious rooms and suites, an 18-hole championship golf course, and three excellent restaurants.
$$–$$$	**Oceanside Meadows Inn,** Schoodic Peninsula. A must for nature lovers, this inn is set amid a 200-acre preserve at the head of Sand Cove. The entire inn is furnished with antiques; guest rooms are sunny and inviting.
$$–$$$	**Watchtide . . . By the Sea,** Searsport. This lovely inn was built in 1794 and is listed on the National Register of Historic Places.
$$–$$$	**Youngtown Inn and Restaurant,** Lincolnville. Inside this white Federal-style farmhouse you can find a French-inspired country retreat and a well-respected French restaurant.
$–$$$	**Welch House,** Boothbay. This 1889 shipbuilder's house has been converted into a charming inn. From the shared third-floor deck, you can take in 180-degree views of the water.
$–$$	**Craignair Inn,** Tenants Harbor. Sitting on 4 waterfront acres, this inn was originally built to house granite workers from nearby quarries. Most rooms have views of the water. The creative cuisine in the dining room is stupendous.
$–$$	**Harpswell Inn Bed & Breakfast,** Harpswell. The smell of the salt air greets you each morning at this charming B&B. Rooms are furnished with antiques, and many have fireplaces and balconies with views of Middle Bay.
$	**Weston House,** Eastport. A Federal-style home built in 1810, this antique-filled inn overlooking Passamaquoddy Bay is comfortably elegant. Naturalist John James Audubon once slept here.

RESTAURANTS

$$$–$$$$	**Marcel's,** Rockport. One of the finest restaurants in Maine, Marcel's will wow you with its near-perfect continental cuisine and extensive wine list, not to mention the views of the bay.
$$$–$$$$	**Café Brio,** South Berwick. This jazzy little café offers an interesting mix of Mediterranean and New Mexican spice.
$$–$$$$	**Cook's Lobster House,** Brunswick area. The delectable haddock sandwich here is among the best in Maine, as is the lobster casserole. Located on Bailey Island, this is a great spot to dine while watching the bay.

$$–$$$$	Primo, Rockland. The cuisine here combines fresh Maine ingredients with Mediterranean influences. The menu changes weekly and much of the food is grown in an extensive organic garden.
$$–$$$$	Street and Co., Portland. Enjoy some of the freshest seafood around at this cozy spot in Portland's Old Port district.
$$$	Arborvine, Bluehill. Crackling fireplaces, period antiques, and exposed beams create an elegant atmosphere in the candle-lit dining rooms of this renovated Cape Cod–style house. The food is simply outstanding.
$$$	Burning Tree, Bar Harbor. Local art adorns the walls at this charming restaurant. The ever-changing menu emphasizes freshly caught seafood and always includes vegetarian options.
$$–$$$	Broad Arrow Tavern, Freeport. Organically grown local ingredients make up the sumptuous menu at this rustic tavern in the Haraskeet Inn.
$–$$$	Lobster Pound Restaurant, Lincolnville. This summertime favorite offers Maine's traditional Shore Dinner: chowder, steamed mussels or clams, a fresh boiled lobster, and corn.
$–$$$	Rockland Cafe, Rockland. Though it doesn't look like much, this is one of the most popular restaurants in town. The giant breakfasts are famous.
$–$$$	Young's Lobster Pound, Belfast. It may resemble a corrugated steel fish cannery, but this restaurant is pure Maine. Lobster doesn't get any better than this.

HISTORIC BUILDINGS

Hamilton House, South Berwick. This palatial Georgian-style mansion and its spectacular grounds were part of author Sarah Orne Jewett's Revolutionary War novel *The Tory Lover*.

Old Port, Portland. A working harbor since the early 17th century, Portland's Old Port district is today a bustling center of shops, galleries, and restaurants.

Portland Head Light, Cape Elizabeth. Immortalized in one of Edward Hopper's paintings, this white stone tower is one of the most picturesque lighthouses in Maine.

MUSEUMS

Downeast Heritage Center, Calais. With interactive exhibits and a wealth of information on the area, this three-level center is a great spot to start your visit Way Down East.

Farnsworth Art Museum and Wyeth Center, Rockland. This small but fascinating museum includes works by Andrew Wyeth, Fitz Hugh

Lane, George Bellows, Frank W. Benson, Edward Hopper, Louise Nevelson, and Fairfield Porter.

OUTDOOR ATTRACTIONS

Acadia National Park, Schoodic Peninsula. This is the only part of Acadia National Park that sits on the mainland. Hike up Schoodic Head for panoramic views up and down the coast, or drive the 6-mi loop along the coast.

Reid State Park, Bath. Come here to enjoy the 1½ mi of sand split between three beaches. There's also a great viewpoint for lighthouse enthusiasts.

Popham Beach State Park, Bath. The vista near the entrance to this park is known as the "Million Dollar View." At low tide you can walk to a nearby island and explore tide pools.

SHOPS & BOUTIQUES

Enchantments, Boothbay. Windchimes and streamers greet you at the door of this spiritual retreat filled with magical gifts such as cards, carvings, mobiles, and jewelry.

Island Artisans, Bar Harbor. All of the jewelry, pottery, and other creative pieces for sale at this charming shop were dreamed up and produced by Maine-based artisans.

TOURS & FESTIVALS

American Folk Festival, Bangor. Thousands of people come to this three-day event that includes traditional folk performers, a rich array of music, storytelling, parades, craft exhibits, and tons of food.

Ghostly Tours, York Village. A hooded guide leads you on a candlelit walking tour of the town, with tales of witches, ghosts, and other peculiar history.

SMART TRAVEL TIPS

Finding out about your destination before you leave home means you won't squander time organizing everyday minutiae once you've arrived. You'll be more streetwise when you hit the ground as well, better prepared to explore the aspects of the Maine Coast that drew you here in the first place. The organizations in this section can provide information to supplement this guide; contact them for up-to-the-minute details, and consult the A to Z sections that end each chapter for facts on the various topics as they relate to the state's many regions. Happy landings!

AIR TRAVEL

AIRPORTS

The two primary airports serving the Maine Coast area are Portland International and Bangor International. Logan International in Boston is the closest major international airport; Boston is about 65 mi (three hours' driving time) from the southern end of the Maine Coast. Manchester Airport, in New Hampshire, is only 45 mi from the beginning of the Maine Coast and is becoming an increasingly popular airport because of the number of discount airlines, such as Southwest, which fly there.

🛈 Airport Information **Logan International (BOS)** ✉ 600 Tower Rd., East Boston, MA ☎ 800/235-6426 ⊕ www.massport.com/logan. **Portland International (PWM)** ✉ 1001 Westbrook St., Portland, ME ☎ 207/774-7301. **Bangor International (BGR)** ✉ 287 Godfrey Blvd., Bangor, ME ☎ 207/947-0384. **Manchester International** ✉ 1 Airport Rd., Manchester, NH ☎ 603/624-6539 ⊕ www.flymanchester.com.

BOOKING

When you book, look for nonstop flights and remember that "direct" flights stop at least once. Try to avoid connecting flights, which require a change of plane. Two airlines may operate a connecting flight jointly, so ask whether your airline operates every segment of the trip; you may find that the carrier you prefer flies you only part of the way. To find more booking tips and to check prices and make online flight reservations, log on to www.fodors.com.

CARRIERS

Portland International and Bangor International airports are both served by American, American Eagle, Delta, Northwest, and US Airways. Portland is also served by United Airlines.

🚹 Airlines **American (800/433-7300). American Eagle (800/433-7300). Delta (800/221-1212). Northwest (800/225-2525). United (800/241-6522). US Airways (800/428-4322).**

CHECK-IN & BOARDING

Always **find out your carrier's check-in policy.** Plan to arrive at the airport about two hours before your scheduled departure time for domestic flights and 2½ to 3 hours before international flights. You may need to arrive earlier if you're flying from one of the busier airports or during peak air-traffic times.

To avoid delays at airport-security checkpoints, try not to wear any metal. Jewelry, belt and other buckles, and steel-toe shoes are among the items that can set off detectors.

Assuming that not everyone with a ticket will show up, airlines routinely overbook planes. When everyone does, airlines ask for volunteers to give up their seats. In return, these volunteers usually get a several-hundred-dollar flight voucher, which can be used toward the purchase of another ticket, and are rebooked on the next flight out. If there are not enough volunteers, the airline must choose who will be denied boarding. The first to get bumped are passengers who checked in late and those flying on discounted tickets, so get to the gate and check in as early as possible, especially during peak periods.

Always **bring a government-issued photo ID** to the airport; even when it's not required, a passport is best.

CUTTING COSTS

The least expensive airfares are priced for round-trip travel and must usually be purchased in advance. Airlines generally allow you to change your return date for a fee; most low-fare tickets, however, are nonrefundable. It's smart to call a number of airlines and check the Internet; when you are quoted a good price, book it on the spot—the same fare may not be available the next day, or even the next hour. Always check different routings and look into using alternate airports. Also, price off-peak flights, which may be significantly less expensive than others. Travel agents, especially low-fare specialists (⇨ Discounts & Deals), are helpful.

Consolidators are another good source. They buy tickets for scheduled flights at reduced rates from the airlines, then sell them at prices that beat the best fare available directly from the airlines. (Many also offer reduced car-rental and hotel rates.) Sometimes you can even get your money back if you need to return the ticket. Carefully read the fine print detailing penalties for changes and cancellations, purchase the ticket with a credit card, and confirm your consolidator reservation with the airline.

🚹 Consolidators **AirlineConsolidator.com** 📞 888/468-5385 ⊕ www.airlineconsolidator.com, for international tickets. **Best Fares** 📞 800/880-1234 or 800/576-8255 ⊕ www.bestfares.com; $59.90 annual membership. **Cheap Tickets** 📞 800/377-1000 or 800/652-4327 ⊕ www.cheaptickets.com. **Expedia** 📞 800/397-3342 or 404/728-8787 ⊕ www.expedia.com. **Hotwire** 📞 866/468-9473 or 920/330-9418 ⊕ www.hotwire.com. **Now Voyager Travel** ✉ 45 W. 21st St., Suite 5A, New York, NY 10010 📞 212/459-1616 📠 212/243-2711 ⊕ www.nowvoyagertravel.com. **Onetravel.com** ⊕ www.onetravel.com. **Orbitz** 📞 888/656-4546 ⊕ www.orbitz.com. **Priceline.com** ⊕ www.priceline.com. **Travelocity** 📞 888/709-5983, 877/282-2925 in Canada, 0870/876-3876 in U.K. ⊕ www.travelocity.com.

ENJOYING THE FLIGHT

State your seat preference when purchasing your ticket, and then repeat it when you confirm and when you check in. For more legroom, you can request one of the few emergency-aisle seats at check-in, if you're capable of moving obstacles comparable in weight to an airplane exit door (usually between 35 and 60 pounds)—a Federal Aviation Administration requirement of passengers in these seats. Seats behind a bulkhead also offer more legroom, but they don't have under-seat storage. Don't sit in the row in front of the emergency aisle or in front of a bulkhead, where seats may not recline.

Ask the airline whether a snack or meal is served on the flight. If you have dietary concerns, request special meals when booking. These can be vegetarian, low-cholesterol, or kosher, for example. It's a good idea to pack some healthful snacks and a small (plastic) bottle of water in your carry-on bag. On long flights, try to maintain a normal routine, to help fight jet lag. At night, get some sleep. By day, eat light meals, drink water (not alcohol), and **move around the cabin** to stretch your legs. For additional jet-lag tips consult *Fodor's FYI: Travel Fit & Healthy* (available at bookstores everywhere).

FLYING TIMES

Flying time from New York City to Portland is 1½ hours; from New York City to Bangor it's 2½ hours. Flying time from Boston to Portland is less than an hour, as is the time from Portland to Bangor.

HOW TO COMPLAIN

If your baggage goes astray or your flight goes awry, complain right away. Most carriers require that you **file a claim immediately.** The Aviation Consumer Protection Division of the Department of Transportation publishes *Fly-Rights,* which discusses airlines and consumer issues and is available online. You can also find articles and information on mytravelrights.com, the Web site of the nonprofit Consumer Travel Rights Center.

Airline Complaints **Aviation Consumer Protection Division** ✉ U.S. Department of Transportation, Office of Aviation Enforcement and Proceedings, C-75, Room 4107, 400 7th St. SW, Washington, DC 20590 ☎ 202/366-2220 ⊕ airconsumer.ost.dot.gov. **Federal Aviation Administration Consumer Hotline** ✉ For inquiries: FAA, 800 Independence Ave. SW, Washington, DC 20591 ☎ 800/322-7873 ⊕ www.faa.gov.

RECONFIRMING

Check the status of your flight before you leave for the airport. You can do this on your carrier's Web site, by linking to a flight-status checker (many Web booking services offer these), or by calling your carrier or travel agent.

BIKE TRAVEL

Despite the fact that U.S. 1, the major road that travels along the Maine Coast, is only a narrow two-lane highway for most of its route, it is still one of America's most historic highways, a sort of Appalachian Trail on a highway. As a result, this road is very popular in spring, summer, and fall with serious long-distance bike riders. As always, bicyclists should ride carefully and look out for motorists who may be looking out for a glimpse of the sea.

There are a number of bicycle rental places in towns along the coast (see individual chapters), but the best place to rent a bike for a long period of time and for distance traveling is Portland.

BIKES IN FLIGHT

Most airlines accommodate bikes as luggage, provided they are dismantled and boxed; check with individual airlines about packing requirements. Some airlines sell bike boxes, which are often free at bike shops, for about $20 (bike bags can be considerably more expensive). International travelers often can substitute a bike for a piece of checked luggage at no charge; otherwise, the cost is about $100. Most U.S. and Canadian airlines charge $40–$80 each way.

BOAT & FERRY TRAVEL

Maine State Ferry Service provides ferry service to the islands of Monhegan, Mantinicus, Vinalhaven, North Haven, and Islesboro. The *Scotia Prince* is a beautiful seven-deck cruise ship that goes from Portland harbor to Yarmouth, Nova Scotia, on overnight or three- or four-day trips. The Cat is a swift catamaran ferry that goes between Bar Harbor, on Mount Desert Island, and Yarmouth, Nova Scotia. You can bring your car on the *Scotia Prince,* The Cat, and the ferries to Islesboro, Vinalhaven, North Haven, and Mantinicus. The Monhegan Island ferry is passenger-only.

Boat & Ferry Information **The Cat** ☎ 888/249-7245 ⊕ www.fun.catferry.com. **Maine State Ferry**

Service ⊠ Box 207, Rockland, ME 04841 ☏ 207/ 596-2202 or 800/491-4883. *Scotia Prince* ☏ 866/ 574-8250 ⊕ www.scotiaprince.com.

BUSINESS HOURS
In general, banks are open from 9 to 4; post offices from 8 to 5. Most large grocery stores or supermarkets are open from 9 AM to 9 PM. Some convenience stores, such as the Irving chain, where you also can get gas, are open 24/7.

MUSEUMS & SIGHTS
Most museums in Maine are open from 9 to 5, some close on Sunday, and many of them, such as the Penobscot Marine Museum in Searsport, close during the off-season, mid-October to mid-May.

SHOPS
Most shops are open from 9 to 5, seven days a week. Those that cater to the tourism business, in Camden for example, are often open until 9 PM in the high season but close down completely between mid-October and mid-May.

BUS TRAVEL
There is a luxury bus service (including snacks, drinks, and an "in-flight" movie) operated by Concord Trailways that travels the length of the coast from Orono (not far from Bangor), all the way to Logan International Airport in Boston. The bus stops in every major town along the way. Greyhound and Vermont Transit also operate bus services from the terminal in Bangor.

🚌 **Concord Trailways** ☏ 207/945-4000 or 800/ 639-3317 ⊕ www.concordtrailways.com. **Greyhound** ☏ 207/873-5000. **Vermont Transit** ☏ 207/ 945-3000.

CAMERAS & PHOTOGRAPHY
The *Kodak Guide to Shooting Great Travel Pictures* (available at bookstores everywhere) is loaded with tips.

🚌 Photo Help **Kodak Information Center** ☏ 800/ 242-2424 ⊕ www.kodak.com.

EQUIPMENT PRECAUTIONS
Don't pack film or equipment in checked luggage, where it is much more susceptible to damage. X-ray machines used to view checked luggage are extremely pow-erful and therefore are likely to ruin your film. Try to ask for hand inspection of film, which becomes clouded after repeated exposure to airport X-ray machines, and keep videotapes and computer disks away from metal detectors. Always keep film, tape, and computer disks out of the sun. Carry an extra supply of batteries, and be prepared to turn on your camera, camcorder, or laptop to prove to airport security personnel that the device is real.

CAR RENTAL
A car is essential in most parts of the Maine Coast. All the major car rental agencies have counters at the airports. Rental rates average about $38 per day, or $175 per week, for a compact car. Most towns also have at least one car rental firm, often independently owned, but don't expect more than one; and often, they are not open weekends.

To rent a car at most agencies, you have to be at least 21 years of age and have a major credit card.

🚌 Major Agencies **Alamo** ☏ 800/327-9633 ⊕ www.alamo.com. **Avis** ☏ 800/331-1212, 800/ 879-2847, 800/272-5871 in Canada, 0870/606-0100 in U.K., 02/9353-9000 in Australia, 09/526-2847 in New Zealand ⊕ www.avis.com. **Budget** ☏ 800/ 527-0700, 0870/156-5656 in U.K. ⊕ www.budget. com. **Dollar** ☏ 800/800-4000, 0800/085-4578 in U.K. ⊕ www.dollar.com. **Enterprise Rent-a-Car** ☏ 800/736-0822 **Hertz** ☏ 800/654-3131, 800/263-0600 in Canada, 0870/844-8844 in U.K., 02/ 9669-2444 in Australia, 09/526-8690 in New Zealand ⊕ www.hertz.com. **National Car Rental** ☏ 800/227-7368, 0870/600-6666 in U.K. ⊕ www. nationalcar.com.

CUTTING COSTS
For a good deal, book through a travel agent who will shop around. Also, price local car-rental companies—whose prices may be lower still, although their service and maintenance may not be as good as those of major rental agencies—and research rates on the Internet. Consolidators that specialize in air travel can offer good rates on cars as well (⇨ Air Travel). Remember to ask about required deposits, cancellation penalties, and drop-off charges if you're planning to pick up the

car in one city and leave it in another. If you're traveling during a holiday period, also make sure that a confirmed reservation guarantees you a car.

INSURANCE

When driving a rented car you are generally responsible for any damage to or loss of the vehicle. You also may be liable for any property damage or personal injury that you may cause while driving. Before you rent, see what coverage you already have under the terms of your personal auto-insurance policy and credit cards.

For about $9 to $25 a day, rental companies sell protection, known as a collision- or loss-damage waiver (CDW or LDW), that eliminates your liability for damage to the car; it's always optional and should never be automatically added to your bill. In most states you don't need a CDW if you have personal auto insurance or other liability insurance. However, **make sure you have enough coverage to pay for the car.** If you do not have auto insurance or an umbrella policy that covers damage to third parties, purchasing liability insurance and a CDW or LDW is highly recommended.

SURCHARGES

Before you pick up a car in one city and leave it in another, ask about drop-off charges or one-way service fees, which can be substantial. Also inquire about early-return policies; some rental agencies charge extra if you return the car before the time specified in your contract while others give you a refund for the days not used. To avoid a hefty refueling fee, fill the tank just before you turn in the car, but be aware that gas stations near the rental outlet may overcharge. It's almost never a deal to buy the tank of gas that's in the car when you rent it; the understanding is that you'll return it empty, but some fuel usually remains. Surcharges may apply if you're under 25 or if you take the car outside the area approved by the rental agency. You'll pay extra for child seats (about $8 a day), which are compulsory for children under five, and usually for additional drivers (up to $25 a day, depending on location).

CAR TRAVEL

GASOLINE

There are numerous gas stations along the Maine Coast, but many close at 6 PM. Irving stations are open 24 hours, have a convenience store, and pride themselves on the cleanliness of their restrooms. Nearly all gas stations in Maine are self-service, and allow you to pay with a credit card right at the pump. As of this writing, gas was more than $2 a gallon.

ROAD CONDITIONS

Most principal roads in Maine are well maintained, and plowed and graveled in winter. Secondary roads are another matter; beware of potholes and frost heaves. Watch out for deer and moose on the road; the number of accidents caused by moose is astonishingly high.

U.S. 1 is a well-paved and maintained highway, but it's only two lanes wide for much of its distance and can be quite slow. If you need to make faster time to a destination such as Bar Harbor, take Interstate 95.

RULES OF THE ROAD

The speed limit on the Maine Turnpike or the Interstate is 65 mph. The speed limit on secondary roads is 35 to 50 mph.

Maine has zero tolerance for driving under the influence of alcohol—the legal limit is .08—and penalties are severe. Car radars are legal, as are right turns on a red light. Although you are not required by law to stop and get off the road when using a cell phone, Maine State Police suggest that it is a good practice to do so. Pedestrians have the right of way at all marked crossings; you have to stop for them. Always strap children under age four or under 40 pounds into approved child-safety seats.

CHILDREN IN MAINE

If you are renting a car, don't forget to arrange for a car seat when you reserve. For general advice about traveling with children, consult *Fodor's FYI: Travel with Your Baby* (available in bookstores everywhere).

FLYING

If your children are two or older, ask about children's airfares. As a general rule, infants under two not occupying a seat fly at greatly reduced fares or even for free. But if you want to guarantee a seat for an infant, you have to pay full fare. Consider flying during off-peak days and times; most airlines will grant an infant a seat without a ticket if there are available seats.

Experts agree that it's a good idea to use safety seats aloft for children weighing less than 40 pounds. Airlines set their own policies: if you use a safety seat, U.S. carriers usually require that the child be ticketed, even if he or she is young enough to ride free, because the seats must be strapped into regular seats. And even if you pay the full adult fare for the seat, it may be worth it, especially on longer trips. Do **check your airline's policy about using safety seats during takeoff and landing.** Safety seats are not allowed everywhere in the plane, so get your seat assignments as early as possible.

When reserving, request children's meals or a freestanding bassinet (not available at all airlines) if you need them. But note that bulkhead seats, where you must sit to use the bassinet, may lack an overhead bin or storage space on the floor.

LODGING

Most hotels in Maine allow children under age 12 to stay in their parents' room at no extra charge, but some charge for them as extra adults; be sure to ask about your hotel's policy when booking your room.

SIGHTS & ATTRACTIONS

Places that are especially appealing to children are indicated by a rubber-duckie icon (🐤) in the margin.

CONSUMER PROTECTION

Whether you're shopping for gifts or purchasing travel services, **pay with a major credit card** whenever possible, so you can cancel payment or get reimbursed if there's a problem (and you can provide documentation). If you're doing business with a particular company for the first time, contact your local Better Business Bureau and the attorney general's offices in your state and (for U.S. businesses) the company's home state as well. Have any complaints been filed? Finally, if you're buying a

package or tour, always consider travel insurance that includes default coverage (⇨ Insurance).

🔳 **BBBs Council of Better Business Bureaus** ✉ 4200 Wilson Blvd., Suite 800, Arlington, VA 22203 ☎ 703/276-0100 🖷 703/525-8277 ⊕ www. bbb.org.

CUSTOMS & DUTIES

When shopping abroad, keep receipts for all purchases. Upon reentering the country, **be ready to show customs officials what you've bought.** Pack purchases together in an easily accessible place. If you think a duty is incorrect, appeal the assessment. If you object to the way your clearance was handled, note the inspector's badge number. In either case, first ask to see a supervisor. If the problem isn't resolved, write to the appropriate authorities, beginning with the port director at your point of entry.

IN AUSTRALIA

Australian residents who are 18 or older may bring home A$400 worth of souvenirs and gifts (including jewelry), 250 cigarettes or 250 grams of cigars or other tobacco products, and 1,125 ml of alcohol (including wine, beer, and spirits). Residents under 18 may bring back A$200 worth of goods. Members of the same family traveling together may pool their allowances. Prohibited items include meat products. Seeds, plants, and fruits need to be declared upon arrival.

🔳 **Australian Customs Service** 🕮 Regional Director, Box 8, Sydney, NSW 2001 ☎ 02/9213-2000 or 1300/363263, 02/9364-7222 or 1800/020-504 quarantine-inquiry line 🖷 02/9213-4043 ⊕ www. customs.gov.au.

IN CANADA

Canadian residents who have been out of Canada for at least seven days may bring in C$750 worth of goods duty-free. If you've been away fewer than seven days but more than 48 hours, the duty-free allowance drops to C$200. If your trip lasts 24 to 48 hours, the allowance is C$50. You may not pool allowances with family members. Goods claimed under the C$750 exemption may follow you by mail; those claimed under the lesser exemptions must accompany you. Alcohol and tobacco products may be included in the seven-day and 48-hour exemptions but not in the 24-hour exemption. If you meet the age requirements of the province or territory through which you reenter Canada, you may bring in, duty-free, 1.5 liters of wine *or* 1.14 liters (40 imperial ounces) of liquor *or* 24 12-ounce cans or bottles of beer or ale. Also, if you meet the local age requirement for tobacco products, you may bring in, duty-free, 200 cigarettes and 50 cigars. Check ahead of time with the Canada Customs and Revenue Agency or the Department of Agriculture for policies regarding meat products, seeds, plants, and fruits.

You may send an unlimited number of gifts (only one gift per recipient, however) worth up to C$60 each duty-free to Canada. Label the package UNSOLICITED GIFT—VALUE UNDER $60. Alcohol and tobacco are excluded.

🚩 **Canada Customs and Revenue Agency** ✉ 2265 St. Laurent Blvd., Ottawa, Ontario K1G 4K3 ☎ 800/461-9999 in Canada, 204/983-3500, 506/636-5064 ⊕ www.ccra.gc.ca.

IN NEW ZEALAND

All homeward-bound residents may bring back NZ$700 worth of souvenirs and gifts; passengers may not pool their allowances, and children can claim only the concession on goods intended for their own use. For those 17 or older, the duty-free allowance also includes 4.5 liters of wine or beer; one 1,125-ml bottle of spirits; and either 200 cigarettes, 250 grams of tobacco, 50 cigars, *or* a combination of the three up to 250 grams. Meat products, seeds, plants, and fruits must be declared upon arrival to the Agricultural Services Department.

🚩 **New Zealand Customs** ✉ Head office: The Customhouse, 17–21 Whitmore St., Box 2218, Wellington ☎ 09/300–5399 or 0800/428–786 ⊕ www.customs.govt.nz.

IN THE U.K.

From countries outside the European Union, including the United States, you may bring home, duty-free, 200 cigarettes, 50 cigars, 100 cigarillos, or 250 grams of tobacco; 1 liter of spirits or 2 liters of fortified or sparkling wine or liqueurs; 2 liters of still table wine; 60 ml of perfume; 250 ml of toilet water; plus £145 worth of other goods, including gifts and souvenirs. Prohibited items include meat and dairy products, seeds, plants, and fruits.

🚩 **HM Customs and Excise** ✉ Portcullis House, 21 Cowbridge Rd. E, Cardiff CF11 9SS ☎ 0845/010–9000 or 0208/929–0152 advice service, 0208/929–6731 or 0208/910–3602 complaints ⊕ www.hmce.gov.uk.

IN THE U.S.

U.S. residents who have been out of the country for at least 48 hours may bring home, for personal use, $800 worth of foreign goods duty-free, as long as they haven't used the $800 allowance or any part of it in the past 30 days. This exemption may include 1 liter of alcohol (for travelers 21 and older), 200 cigarettes, and 100 non-Cuban cigars. Family members from the same household who are traveling together may pool their $800 personal exemptions. For fewer than 48 hours, the duty-free allowance drops to $200, which may include 50 cigarettes, 10 non-Cuban cigars, and 150 ml of alcohol (or 150 ml of perfume containing alcohol). The $200 allowance cannot be combined with other individuals' exemptions, and if you exceed it, the full value of all the goods will be taxed. Antiques, which U.S. Customs and Border Protection defines as objects more than 100 years old, enter duty-free, as do original works of art done entirely by hand, including paintings, drawings, and sculptures. This doesn't apply to folk art or handicrafts, which are in general dutiable.

You may also send packages home duty-free, with a limit of one parcel per addressee per day (except alcohol or tobacco products or perfume worth more than $5). You can mail up to $200 worth of goods for personal use; label the package PERSONAL USE and attach a list of its contents and their retail value. If the package contains your used personal belongings, mark it AMERICAN GOODS RETURNED to avoid paying duties. You may send up to $100 worth of goods as a gift; mark the package UNSO-

LICITED GIFT. Mailed items do not affect your duty-free allowance on your return.

To avoid paying duty on foreign-made high-ticket items you already own and will take on your trip, register them with Customs before you leave the country. Consider filing a Certificate of Registration for laptops, cameras, watches, and other digital devices identified with serial numbers or other permanent markings; you can keep the certificate for other trips. Otherwise, bring a sales receipt or insurance form to show that you owned the item before you left the United States.

For more about duties, restricted items, and other information about international travel, check out U.S. Customs and Border Protection's online brochure, *Know Before You Go.*

U.S. residents who have been out of the country for at least 48 hours may bring home $600 worth of foreign goods duty-free, as long as they have not used the $600 allowance or any part of it in the past 30 days.

🏛 **U.S. Customs and Border Protection** ✉ For inquiries and equipment registration, 1300 Pennsylvania Ave. NW, Washington, DC 20229 ⊕ www.cbp. gov ☎ 877/287-8667 or 202/354-1000 ✉ For complaints, Customer Satisfaction Unit, 1300 Pennsylvania Ave. NW, Room 5.2C, Washington, DC 20229.

DISABILITIES & ACCESSIBILITY

General information for travelers with disabilities visiting Maine can be obtained from the Committee for Accessible Leisure, Arts & Recreation. Most hotels, motels, and restaurants are reasonably accessible to those in wheelchairs. B&Bs are another matter. Many of them are in historic homes in which the owners cannot violate the integrity of the property by adding something like a ramp. Best to call first.

🏛 Local Resources **Committee for Accessible Leisure, Arts & Recreation** ⊕ www.maine.gov/portal/accessibility.html.

LODGING

Despite the Americans with Disabilities Act, the definition of accessibility seems to differ from hotel to hotel. Some properties may be accessible by ADA standards for people with mobility problems but not for people with hearing or vision impairments, for example.

If you have mobility problems, ask for the lowest floor on which accessible services are offered. If you have a hearing impairment, check whether the hotel has devices to alert you visually to the ring of the telephone, a knock at the door, and a fire/emergency alarm. Some hotels provide these devices without charge. Discuss your needs with hotel personnel if this equipment isn't available, so that a staff member can personally alert you in the event of an emergency.

If you're bringing a guide dog, get authorization ahead of time and write down the name of the person with whom you spoke.

RESERVATIONS

When discussing accessibility with an operator or reservations agent, ask hard questions. Are there any stairs, inside *or* out? Are there grab bars next to the toilet *and* in the shower/tub? How wide is the doorway to the room? To the bathroom? For the most extensive facilities meeting the latest legal specifications, opt for newer accommodations. If you reserve through a toll-free number, consider also calling the hotel's local number to confirm the information from the central reservations office. Get confirmation in writing when you can.

🏛 Complaints **Aviation Consumer Protection Division** (⇨ Air Travel) for airline-related problems. **Departmental Office of Civil Rights** ✉ For general inquiries, U.S. Department of Transportation, S-30, 400 7th St. SW, Room 10215, Washington, DC 20590 ☎ 202/366-4648 🖶 202/366-9371 ⊕ www.dot. gov/ost/docr/index.htm. **Disability Rights Section** ✉ NYAV, U.S. Department of Justice, Civil Rights Division, 950 Pennsylvania Ave. NW, Washington, DC 20530 ☎ ADA information line 202/514-0301, 800/514-0301, 202/514-0383 TTY, 800/514-0383 TTY ⊕ www.ada.gov. **U.S. Department of Transportation Hotline** ☎ For disability-related air-travel problems, 800/778-4838 or 800/455-9880 TTY.

TRAVEL AGENCIES

In the United States, the Americans with Disabilities Act requires that travel firms serve the needs of all travelers. Some agencies specialize in working with people with disabilities.

⧉ Travelers with Mobility Problems **Access Adventures/B. Roberts Travel** ✉ 206 Chestnut Ridge Rd., Scottsville, NY 14624 ☎ 585/889-9096 ⊕ www.brobertstravel.com ✍ dltravel@prodigy. net, run by a former physical-rehabilitation counselor. **Accessible Vans of America** ✉ 9 Spielman Rd., Fairfield, NJ 07004 ☎ 877/282-8267, 888/282-8267, 973/808-9709 reservations ⎙ 973/808-9713 ⊕ www.accessiblevans.com. **CareVacations** ✉ No. 5, 5110-50 Ave., Leduc, Alberta, Canada, T9E 6V4 ☎ 780/986-6404 or 877/478-7827 ⎙ 780/986-8332 ⊕ www.carevacations.com, for group tours and cruise vacations. **Flying Wheels Travel** ✉ 143 W. Bridge St., Box 382, Owatonna, MN 55060 ☎ 507/451-5005 ⎙ 507/451-1685 ⊕ www. flyingwheelstravel.com.

⧉ Travelers with Developmental Disabilities **Sprout** ✉ 893 Amsterdam Ave., New York, NY 10025 ☎ 212/222-9575 or 888/222-9575 ⎙ 212/222-9768 ⊕ www.gosprout.org.

DISCOUNTS & DEALS

Be a smart shopper and compare all your options before making decisions. A plane ticket bought with a promotional coupon from travel clubs, coupon books, and direct-mail offers or purchased on the Internet may not be cheaper than the least expensive fare from a discount ticket agency. And always keep in mind that what you get is just as important as what you save.

DISCOUNT RESERVATIONS

To save money, look into discount reservations services with Web sites and toll-free numbers, which use their buying power to get a better price on hotels, airline tickets (⇨ Air Travel), even car rentals. When booking a room, always **call the hotel's local toll-free number** (if one is available) rather than the central reservations number—you'll often get a better price. Always ask about special packages or corporate rates.

⧉ Airline Tickets **Air 4 Less** ☎ 800/AIR4LESS; low-fare specialist.

⧉ Hotel Rooms **Accommodations Express** ☎ 800/444-7666 or 800/277-1064 ⊕ www.acex.net. **Hotels. com** ☎ 800/246-8357 ⊕ www.hotels.com. **Quikbook** ☎ 800/789-9887 ⊕ www.quikbook.com. **Steigenberger Reservation Service** ☎ 800/223-5652 ⊕ www.srs-worldhotels.com. **Turbotrip.com** ☎ 800/473-7829 ⊕ www.turbotrip.com.

PACKAGE DEALS

Don't confuse packages and guided tours. When you buy a package, you travel on your own, just as though you had planned the trip yourself. Fly/drive packages, which combine airfare and car rental, are often a good deal. In cities, ask the local visitor's bureau about hotel and local transportation packages that include tickets to major museum exhibits or other special events.

EATING & DRINKING

The restaurants we list are the cream of the crop in each price category. Properties indicated by an ✕⊡ are lodging establishments whose restaurant warrants a special trip.

The one signature dinner on the Maine Coast is, of course, the Lobster Dinner, or as some restaurants call it, the Shore Dinner. The Shore Dinner generally includes boiled lobster, a clam or seafood chowder, corn on the cob, and perhaps a salad. Lobster prices vary from day to day; most restaurants list "Market Price" next to the lobster dinners on their menus. Generally, a full lobster dinner should cost around $25, without all the add-ons, about $18.

MEALTIMES

Unless otherwise noted, the restaurants listed in this guide are open daily for lunch and dinner. Lunch generally runs 11–2:30; dinner is usually served 5–9. Only in the larger cities will you find full dinners being offered much later than 9, although you can usually find a bar or bistro serving a limited menu late into the evening in all but the smallest towns.

Many restaurants in Maine are closed on Monday, though this is never true in resort areas in high season. However, resort-town eateries often shut down completely in the off-season.

Credit cards are accepted for meals throughout Maine in all but the most modest establishments. The major acceptable credit cards are American Express, Diners Club, Discover, MasterCard, and Visa.

RESERVATIONS & DRESS

Reservations are always a good idea; we mention them only when they're essential or not accepted. Book as far ahead as you can, and reconfirm as soon as you arrive. (Large parties should always call ahead to check the reservations policy.) We mention dress only when men are required to wear a jacket or a jacket and tie.

WINE, BEER & SPIRITS

The drinking age in Maine is 21, and a photo ID must be presented to purchase alcoholic beverages. Most bars and taverns are open until 2 AM. Beer and wine are sold at convenience stores, and hard alcohol is available at the large supermarkets, generally from 9 AM to 9 PM. There are a number of good local microbreweries along the Maine Coast, a couple of them in the Camden area.

No matter what you might see in the local parks, drinking alcohol in public parks or on the beaches is illegal. It is also illegal to have open containers of alcohol in motor vehicles.

HEALTH

Maine seems to have more doctors than most states, but if you have an emergency, there are four hospitals on the Maine Coast, one near Camden, one in Belfast, and two in Bangor.

PESTS & OTHER HAZARDS

Maine is famous during the late spring and summer for its black flies, and the farther inland you go, the worse they seem to get. Packing a good insect repellent is recommended if you are going to be outside. For some reason, they are not as bothersome along the coast as they are inland. An old salt told us: "The flies don't like the salt air." Maybe he's right.

Maine's other greatest insect pest is the mosquito. Mosquitoes can be a nuisance just about everywhere in summer—they're at their worst following snowy winters and wet springs. The best protection against both pests is repellent containing DEET. A particular pest of coastal areas, especially salt marshes, is the greenhead fly. Their bite is nasty, and they are best re-

pelled by a liberal application of Avon Skin So Soft.

SHELLFISHING

Coastal waters attract seafood lovers who enjoy harvesting their own clams and mussels; permits are required, and casual harvesting of lobsters is strictly forbidden. Amateur clammers should be aware that Maine shellfish beds are periodically visited by red tides, during which microorganisms can render shellfish poisonous. To keep abreast of the situation, inquire when you apply for a license (usually at town halls or police stations) and pay attention to red tide postings as you travel.

HOLIDAYS

Major national holidays are New Year's Day (Jan. 1); Martin Luther King Day (3rd Mon. in Jan.); Presidents' Day (3rd Mon. in Feb.); Memorial Day (last Mon. in May); Independence Day (July 4); Labor Day (1st Mon. in Sept.); Columbus Day (2nd Mon. in Oct.); Thanksgiving Day (4th Thurs. in Nov.); Christmas Eve and Christmas Day (Dec. 24 and 25); and New Year's Eve (Dec. 31).

INSURANCE

The most useful travel-insurance plan is a comprehensive policy that includes coverage for trip cancellation and interruption, default, trip delay, and medical expenses (with a waiver for preexisting conditions).

Without insurance you'll lose all or most of your money if you cancel your trip, regardless of the reason. Default insurance covers you if your tour operator, airline, or cruise line goes out of business—the chances of which have been increasing. Trip-delay covers expenses that arise because of bad weather or mechanical delays. Study the fine print when comparing policies.

U.K. residents can buy a travel-insurance policy valid for most vacations taken during the year in which it's purchased (but check preexisting-condition coverage).

Always **buy travel policies directly from the insurance company**; if you buy them from a cruise line, airline, or tour operator that goes out of business, you probably won't be covered for the agency or operator's default, a major risk. Before making any purchase, review your existing health and home-owner's policies to find what they cover away from home.

🇫 Travel Insurers In the U.S.: **Access America** ✉ 2805 N. Parham Rd., Richmond, VA 23294 ☎ 800/284-8300 🖷 804/673-1491 or 800/346-9265 ⊕ www.accessamerica.com. **Travel Guard International** ✉ 1145 Clark St., Stevens Point, WI 54481 ☎ 715/345-0505 or 800/826-1300 🖷 800/955-8785 ⊕ www.travelguard.com.

FOR INTERNATIONAL TRAVELERS

For information on customs restrictions, see Customs & Duties.

CAR RENTAL

When picking up a rental car, non-U.S. residents need a reservation voucher for any prepaid reservations that were made in the traveler's home country, a passport, a driver's license, and a travel policy that covers each driver.

CAR TRAVEL

Interstate highways—limited-access, multilane highways whose numbers are prefixed by "I–"—are the fastest routes. Interstates with three-digit numbers encircle urban areas, which may have other limited-access expressways, freeways, and parkways. Tolls may be levied on limited-access highways. U.S. highways and state highways are not necessarily limited-access but may have several lanes.

Along larger highways, roadside stops with restrooms, fast-food restaurants, and sundries stores are well spaced. State police and tow trucks patrol major highways and lend assistance. If your car breaks down on an interstate, pull onto the shoulder and wait for help, or have your passengers wait while you walk to an emergency phone. If you carry a cell phone, dial *55, noting your location on the small green roadside mileage markers.

Driving in the United States is on the right. Do obey speed limits posted along roads and highways. Watch for lower limits in small towns and on back roads. Maine requires front-seat passengers to wear seat belts.

Bookstores, gas stations, convenience stores, and rest stops sell maps (about $3) and multiregion road atlases (about $10). The Irving stations along the coast of Maine are always good choices, since they include a convenience store, often a restaurant, clean restrooms, and are open 24/7.

CURRENCY

The dollar is the basic unit of U.S. currency. It has 100 cents. Coins are the copper penny (1¢); the silvery nickel (5¢), dime (10¢), quarter (25¢), and half-dollar (50¢); and the golden $1 coin, replacing a now-rare silver dollar. Bills are denominated $1, $5, $10, $20, $50, and $100, all mostly green and identical in size; designs and background tints vary. In addition, you may come across a $2 bill, but the chances are slim. The exchange rate at this writing is US $1.83 per British pound, .77 per Canadian dollar, .75 per Australian dollar, and .67 per New Zealand dollar.

ELECTRICITY

The U.S. standard is AC, 110 volts/60 cycles. Plugs have two flat pins set parallel to each other.

EMERGENCIES

For police, fire, or ambulance, **dial 911** (0 in rural areas).

INSURANCE

Britons and Australians need extra medical coverage when traveling overseas.

🇫 Insurance Information In the U.K.: **Association of British Insurers** ✉ 51 Gresham St., London EC2V 7HQ ☎ 020/7600-3333 🖷 020/7696-8999 ⊕ www.abi.org.uk. In Australia: **Insurance Council of Australia** ✉ Insurance Enquiries and Complaints, Level 12, Box 561, Collins St. W, Melbourne, VIC 8007 ☎ 1300/780-808 or 03/9629-4109 🖷 03/9621-2060 ⊕ www.iecltd.com.au. In Canada: **RBC Insurance** ✉ 6880 Financial St., Mississauga, Ontario L5N 7Y5 ☎ 800/668-4342 or 905/816-2400 🖷 905/813-4704 ⊕ www.rbcinsurance.com. In New Zealand: **Insurance Council of New Zealand** ✉ Level 7, 111-115 Customhouse Quay, Box 474, Wellington ☎ 04/472-5230 🖷 04/473-3011 ⊕ www.icnz.org.nz.

MAIL & SHIPPING

You can buy stamps and aerograms and send letters and parcels in post offices.

Stamp-dispensing machines can occasionally be found in airports, bus and train stations, office buildings, drugstores, and the like. You can also deposit mail in the stout, dark blue, steel bins at strategic locations everywhere and in the mail chutes of large buildings; pickup schedules are posted. You can deposit packages at public collection boxes as long as the parcels are affixed with proper postage and weigh less than one pound. Packages weighing one or more pounds must be taken to a post office or handed to a postal carrier.

For mail sent within the United States, you need a 37¢ stamp for first-class letters weighing up to 1 ounce (23¢ for each additional ounce) and 23¢ for postcards. You pay 80¢ for 1-ounce airmail letters and 70¢ for airmail postcards to most other countries; to Canada and Mexico, you need a 60¢ stamp for a 1-ounce letter and 50¢ for a postcard. An aerogram—a single sheet of lightweight blue paper that folds into its own envelope, stamped for overseas airmail—costs 70¢.

To receive mail on the road, have it sent c/o General Delivery at your destination's main post office (use the correct five-digit ZIP code). You must pick up mail in person within 30 days and show a driver's license or passport.

PASSPORTS & VISAS

When traveling internationally, carry your passport even if you don't need one (it's always the best form of ID) and **make two photocopies of the data page** (one for someone at home and another for you, carried separately from your passport). If you lose your passport, promptly call the nearest embassy or consulate and the local police.

Visitor visas aren't necessary for Canadian or European Union citizens, or for citizens of Australia who are staying fewer than 90 days.

▞ Australian Citizens **Passports Australia** ☏ 131-232 ⊕ www.passports.gov.au. **United States Consulate General** ✉ MLC Centre, Level 59, 19–29 Martin Pl., Sydney, NSW 2000 ☏ 02/9373-9200, 1902/941-641 fee-based visa-inquiry line ⊕ usembassy-australia.state.gov/sydney.

▞ Canadian Citizens **Passport Office** ✉ To mail in applications: 200 Promenade du Portage, Hull, Québec J8X 4B7 ☏ 819/994-3500, 800/567-6868, 866/255-7655 TTY ⊕ www.ppt.gc.ca.
▞ New Zealand Citizens **New Zealand Passports Office** ✉ For applications and information, Level 3, Boulcott House, 47 Boulcott St., Wellington ☏ 0800/22-5050 or 04/474-8100 ⊕ www.passports.govt.nz. **Embassy of the United States** ✉ 29 Fitzherbert Terr., Thorndon, Wellington ☏ 04/462-6000 ⊕ usembassy.org.nz. **U.S. Consulate General** ✉ Citibank Bldg., 3rd fl., 23 Customs St. E, Auckland ☏ 09/303-2724 ⊕ usembassy.org.nz.
▞ U.K. Citizens **U.K. Passport Service** ☏ 0870/521-0410 ⊕ www.passport.gov.uk. **American Consulate General** ✉ Danesfort House, 223 Stranmillis Rd., Belfast, Northern Ireland BT9 5GR ☏ 028/9032-8239 🖷 028/9024-8482 ⊕ usembassy.org.uk. **American Embassy** ✉ For visa and immigration information or to submit a visa application via mail (enclose SASE), Consular Information Unit, 24 Grosvenor Sq., London W1 1AE ☏ 09055/444-546 for visa information (per-minute charges), 0207/499-9000 main switchboard ⊕ usembassy.org.uk.

TELEPHONES

All U.S. telephone numbers consist of a three-digit area code and a seven-digit local number. Within many local calling areas, you dial only the seven-digit number. Within some area codes, you must dial "1" first for calls outside the local area. To call between area-code regions, dial "1" then all 10 digits; the same goes for calls to numbers prefixed by "800," "888," "866," and "877"—all toll free. For calls to numbers preceded by "900" you must pay—usually dearly.

For international calls, dial "011" followed by the country code and the local number. For help, dial "0" and ask for an overseas operator. The country code is 61 for Australia, 64 for New Zealand, 44 for the United Kingdom. Calling Canada is the same as calling within the United States. Most local phone books list country codes and U.S. area codes. The country code for the United States is 1.

For operator assistance, dial "0." To obtain someone's phone number, call directory assistance at 555–1212 or occasionally 411 (free at many public phones). To have the person you're calling foot the bill, phone collect; dial "0" instead of "1" before the 10-digit number. At pay phones, instructions often are posted. Usually you insert coins in a slot (usually 25¢–50¢ for local calls) and wait for a steady tone before dialing. When you call long-distance, the operator tells you how much to insert; prepaid phone cards, widely available in various denominations, are easier. Call the number on the back, punch in the card's personal identification number when prompted, then dial your number.

LODGING

Beachfront motels and historic-home B&Bs make up the majority of accommodation options along the Maine Coast. There are a few large luxury resorts, such as the Samoset Resort in Rockport or the Bar Harbor Inn in Bar Harbor, but most accommodations are simple and relatively inexpensive. Many properties close completely during the off-season, from mid-October until mid-May; those that stay open drop their rates dramatically. There is a 7% state hospitality tax on all room rates.

The lodgings we list are the cream of the crop in each price category. We always list the facilities that are available, but we don't specify whether they cost extra; when pricing accommodations, always ask what's included and what costs extra. Properties are assigned price categories based on the range between their least and most expensive standard double rooms at high season. Lodgings are indicated in the text by a house icon, 🏠 ; properties marked ✕🏠 are lodgings whose restaurants warrant a special trip.

Assume that hotels operate on the European Plan (EP, with no meals) unless we specify that they use the Continental Plan (CP, with a continental breakfast), Breakfast Plan (BP, with a full breakfast), Modified American Plan (MAP, with breakfast and dinner), or the Full American Plan (FAP, with all meals).

APARTMENT & HOUSE RENTALS

If you want a home base that's roomy enough for a family and that comes with cooking facilities, consider a furnished rental. These can save you money, especially if you're traveling with a group. Home-exchange directories sometimes list rentals as well as exchanges.

Seasonal apartments and houses for rent are common along the coast of Maine, but they are also popular and expensive. You can find out about them by picking up one of the local weekly newspapers or by contacting a real estate agent. The following are some of the best property rental agencies along the coast.

🔲 **Local Agents** All of Maine Coast: **Cottage Connection of Maine** ☎ 800/823-9501 ⊕ www. cotttageconnection.com. **Find Vacation Rentals** ⊕ www.findvacationrentals.com. **Great Rentals** ⊕ www.greatrentals.com. **A1 Vacations** ⊕ www. A1vacations.com. **Vacation Rentals by Owner** ⊕ www.vrbo.com. Mid-Coast area: **Jaret and Cohn** ⊕ www.jaretcohn.com. Camden area: **Camden Real Estate** ☎ 207/236-6171. **Camden Vacation Rentals** ⊕ www.camdenac.com. Belfast area: **Green-Keefe** ☎ 207/338-3500. Mount Desert Island: **Hinckley Real Estate** ☎ 207/244-7011.

BED & BREAKFASTS

The B&Bs of Maine offer some of the region's most distinctive lodging experiences. Many are in historic homes, have beautiful views of the ocean, and provide full American-style breakfasts, often with homemade pastries. For more information contact the Maine State Tourism office. For reservations log onto Bed & Breakfast Inns Online at ⊕ www.bbonline.com/me.

🔲 **Bed & Breakfast Inns Online** ⊕ www.bbonline. com/me. **Maine State Tourism Office** ✉ 325B Water St., Hallowell, ME 04347 ☎ 207/623-0363 ⊕ www.maintourism.com.

HOME EXCHANGES

If you would like to exchange your home for someone else's, join a home-exchange organization, which will send you its updated listings of available exchanges for a year and will include your own listing in at least one of them. It's up to you to make specific arrangements.

🔲 **Exchange Clubs** HomeLink International ⚲ Box 47747, Tampa, FL 33647 ☎ 813/975-9825 or 800/638-3841 🖶 813/910-8144 ⊕ www.homelink. org; $110 yearly for a listing, online access, and catalog; $70 without catalog. **Intervac U.S.** ✉ 30 Corte San Fernando, Tiburon, CA 94920 ☎ 800/756-4663 🖷 415/435-7440 ⊕ www.intervacus.com; $125 yearly for a listing, online access, and a catalog; $65 without catalog.

HOSTELS

No matter what your age, you can save on lodging costs by staying at hostels. In some 4,500 locations in more than 70 countries around the world, Hostelling International (HI), the umbrella group for a number of national youth-hostel associations, offers single-sex, dorm-style beds and, at many hostels, rooms for couples and family accommodations. Membership in any HI national hostel association, open to travelers of all ages, allows you to stay in HI-affiliated hostels at member rates; one-year membership is about $28 for adults (C$35 for a two-year minimum membership in Canada, £14 in the U.K., A$52 in Australia, and NZ$40 in New Zealand); hostels charge about $10–$30 per night. Members have priority if the hostel is full; they're also eligible for discounts around the world, even on rail and bus travel in some countries.

🖪 Organizations **Hostelling International–USA** ✉ 8401 Colesville Rd., Suite 600, Silver Spring, MD 20910 ☎ 301/495-1240 🖷 301/495-6697 ⊕ www. hiusa.org. **Hostelling International–Canada** ✉ 205 Catherine St., Suite 400, Ottawa, Ontario K2P 1C3 ☎ 613/237-7884 or 800/663-5777 🖷 613/ 237-7868 ⊕ www.hihostels.ca. **YHA England and Wales** ✉ Trevelyan House, Dimple Rd., Matlock, Derbyshire DE4 3YH, U.K. ☎ 0870/870-8808, 0870/ 770-8868, or 0162/959-2600 🖷 0870/770-6127 ⊕ www.yha.org.uk. **YHA Australia** ✉ 422 Kent St., Sydney, NSW 2001 ☎ 02/9261-1111 🖷 02/9261-1969 ⊕ www.yha.com.au. **YHA New Zealand** ✉ Level 1, Moorhouse City, 166 Moorhouse Ave., Box 436, Christchurch ☎ 03/379-9970 or 0800/278-299 🖷 03/365-4476 ⊕ www.yha.org.nz.

HOTELS

The Maine Coast is liberally supplied with small, independent motels, which run the gamut from the tired to the tidy. Don't overlook these mom-and-pop operations; they frequently offer cheerful, convenient accommodations at lower rates than the chains. If you stay at a motel located di-

rectly on U.S. 1, request a room in the back to avoid noise caused by traffic. Keep in mind that many motels along the coast of Maine shut down from mid-October until mid-May.

While reservations are always a good idea, they are particularly recommended in summer and winter resort areas; in college towns during September and at graduation time in the spring; and at areas renowned for autumn foliage.

Most hotels and motels will hold your reservation until 6 PM; **call ahead if you plan to arrive late.** All will hold a late reservation for you if you guarantee your reservation with a credit-card number.

MONEY MATTERS

Figure on paying about $1 for a cup of coffee in Maine, $2–$3 for a draft beer, and $4 for a ham sandwich with a few pickles and chips.

Prices throughout this guide are given for adults. Substantially reduced fees are almost always available for children, students, and senior citizens. For information on taxes, *see* Taxes.

ATMS

Automatic teller machines (ATMs) are available at all banks and many convenience stores throughout the Maine Coast area. If you are using a bank other than your own, expect to pay a $1 to $2 surcharge.

CREDIT CARDS

Most major credit cards are accepted throughout the coast; some restaurants and accommodations do not accept American Express or Diners Club.

Throughout this guide, the following abbreviations are used: **AE**, American Express; **D**, Discover; **DC**, Diners Club; **MC**, MasterCard; and **V**, Visa.

🖪 Reporting Lost Cards **American Express** ☎ 800/992-3404. **Diners Club** ☎ 800/234-6377. **Discover** ☎ 800/347-2683. **MasterCard** ☎ 800/ 622-7747. **Visa** ☎ 800/847-2911.

NATIONAL PARKS

Look into discount passes to save money on park entrance fees. For $50, the National Parks Pass admits you (and any passengers in your private vehicle) to all national parks, monuments, and recreation areas, as well as other sites run by the National Park Service (NPS), for a year. (In parks that charge per person, the pass admits you, your spouse and children, and your parents, when you arrive together.) Camping and parking are extra. The $15 Golden Eagle Pass, a hologram you affix to your National Parks Pass, functions as an upgrade, granting entry to all sites run by the NPS, the U.S. Fish and Wildlife Service, the U.S. Forest Service, and the Bureau of Land Management. The upgrade, which expires with the parks pass, is sold by most national-park, Fish-and-Wildlife, and BLM fee stations. A major percentage of the proceeds from pass sales funds National Parks projects.

Both the Golden Age Passport ($10), for U.S. citizens or permanent residents who are 62 and older, and the Golden Access Passport (free), for persons with disabilities, entitle holders (and any passengers in their private vehicles) to lifetime free entry to all national parks, plus 50% off fees for the use of many park facilities and services. (The discount doesn't always apply to companions.) To obtain them, you must show proof of age and of U.S. citizenship or permanent residency—such as a U.S. passport, driver's license, or birth certificate—and if requesting Golden Access, proof of disability. The Golden Age and Golden Access passes are available only at NPS-run sites that charge an entrance fee. The National Parks Pass is also available by mail and via the Internet.

🔁 **National Park Foundation** ✉ 11 Dupont Circle NW, 6th fl., Washington, DC 20036 ☎ 202/238–4200 ⊕ www.nationalparks.org. **National Park Service** ✉ National Park Service/Department of Interior, 1849 C St. NW, Washington, DC 20240 ☎ 202/208–6843 ⊕ www.nps.gov. **National Parks Conservation Association** ✉ 1300 19th St. NW, Suite 300, Washington, DC 20036 ☎ 202/223–6722 ⊕ www.npca.org.

🔁 Passes by Mail & Online **National Park Foundation** ⊕ www.nationalparks.org. **National Parks Pass** National Park Foundation ⬩ Box 34108, Washington, DC 20043 ☎ 888/467-2757 ⊕ www.nationalparks.org; include a check or money order payable to the National Park Service, plus $3.95 for

shipping and handling (allow 8–13 business days from date of receipt for pass delivery), or call for passes.

PACKING

The principal rule on weather in Maine is that there are no rules. A cold foggy morning in spring can and often does become a bright, 60°F afternoon. A summer breeze can suddenly turn chilly, and rain often appears with little warning. Thus, the best advice on how to dress is to **layer your clothing** so that you can peel off or add garments as needed for comfort. Showers are frequent, so **pack a raincoat and umbrella.** Even in summer you should bring long pants, a sweater or two, and a waterproof windbreaker; evenings are often chilly and sea spray can make things cool.

Casual sportswear—walking shoes and jeans or khakis—will take you almost everywhere, but swimsuits and bare feet will not: shirts and shoes are required attire at even the most casual venues. Dress in restaurants is generally casual, except at some of the distinguished restaurants. Upscale resorts will, at the very least, require men to wear collared shirts at dinner, and jeans are often frowned upon.

In summer **bring a hat and sunscreen.** Remember also to **pack insect repellent** to protect you from black flies and mosquitoes. To prevent Lyme disease, you need to guard against ticks from early spring through the summer (⇨ Health).

In your carry-on luggage, pack an extra pair of eyeglasses or contact lenses and enough of any medication you take to last a few days longer than the entire trip. You may also ask your doctor to write a spare prescription using the drug's generic name, as brand names may vary from country to country. In luggage to be checked, **never pack prescription drugs, valuables, or undeveloped film.** And don't forget to carry with you the addresses of offices that handle refunds of lost traveler's checks. Check *Fodor's How to Pack* (available at online retailers and bookstores everywhere) for more tips.

To avoid customs and security delays, carry medications in their original packaging. Don't pack any sharp objects in your carry-on luggage, including knives of any size or material, scissors, nail clippers, and corkscrews, or anything else that might arouse suspicion.

To avoid having your checked luggage chosen for hand inspection, don't cram bags full. The U.S. Transportation Security Administration (TSA) suggests packing shoes on top and placing personal items you don't want touched in clear plastic bags.

CHECKING LUGGAGE

You're allowed to carry aboard one bag and one personal article, such as a purse or a laptop computer. Make sure what you carry on fits under your seat or in the overhead bin. Get to the gate early, so you can board as soon as possible, before the overhead bins fill up.

Baggage allowances vary by carrier, destination, and ticket class. On international flights, you're usually allowed to check two bags weighing up to 70 pounds (32 kilograms) each, although a few airlines allow checked bags of up to 88 pounds (40 kilograms) in first class. Some international carriers don't allow more than 66 pounds (30 kilograms) per bag in business class and 44 pounds (20 kilograms) in economy. On domestic flights, the limit is usually 50 to 70 pounds (23 to 32 kilograms) per bag. In general, carry-on bags shouldn't exceed 40 pounds (18 kilograms). Most airlines won't accept bags that weigh more than 100 pounds (45 kilograms) on domestic or international flights. Expect to pay a fee for baggage that exceeds weight limits. Check baggage restrictions with your carrier before you pack.

Airline liability for baggage is limited to $2,500 per person on flights within the United States. On international flights it amounts to $9.07 per pound or $20 per kilogram for checked baggage (roughly $640 per 70-pound bag), with a maximum of $634.90 per piece, and $400 per passenger for unchecked baggage. You can buy additional coverage at check-in for about $10 per $1,000 of coverage, but it often excludes a rather extensive list of items, shown on your airline ticket.

Before departure, itemize your bags' contents and their worth, and label the bags with your name, address, and phone number. (If you use your home address, cover it so potential thieves can't see it readily.) Include a label inside each bag and **pack a copy of your itinerary.** At check-in, make sure each bag is correctly tagged with the destination airport's three-letter code. Because some checked bags will be opened for hand inspection, the U.S. Transportation Security Administration (TSA) recommends that you leave luggage unlocked or use the plastic locks offered at check-in. TSA screeners place an inspection notice inside searched bags, which are resealed with a special lock.

If your bag has been searched and contents are missing or damaged, file a claim with the TSA Consumer Response Center as soon as possible. If your bags arrive damaged or fail to arrive at all, file a written report with the airline before leaving the airport.

🔻 Complaints **U.S. Transportation Security Administration Contact Center** ☎ 866/289–9673 ⊕ www.tsa.gov.

SENIOR-CITIZEN TRAVEL

To qualify for age-related discounts, mention your senior-citizen status up front when booking hotel reservations (not when checking out) and before you're seated in restaurants (not when paying the bill). Be sure to have identification on hand. When renting a car, ask about promotional car-rental discounts, which can be cheaper than senior-citizen rates.

🔻 Educational Programs **Elderhostel** ✉ 11 Ave. de Lafayette, Boston, MA 02111-1746 ☎ 877/426–8056, 978/323–4141 international callers, 877/426–2167 TTY ᕈ 877/426–2166 ⊕ www.elderhostel.org.

STUDENTS IN MAINE

Most major attractions throughout the region offer discount admissions to students.

🔻 IDs & Services **STA Travel** ✉ 10 Downing St., New York, NY 10014 ☎ 212/627–3111, 800/777–0112 24-hr service center ᕈ 212/627–3387 ⊕ www.sta. com. **Travel Cuts** ✉ 187 College St., Toronto, Ontario M5T 1P7, Canada ☎ 800/592–2887 in U.S., 416/979–2406 or 866/246–9762 in Canada ᕈ 416/979–8167 ⊕ www.travelcuts.com.

TAXES

Maine state sales tax is 5% and applies to all purchases except prepackaged food. Maine's hospitality tax is 7%, and applies to all lodging and restaurant prices.

TIME

Maine is in the Eastern Standard time zone; the state does observe daylight saving time. The difference in time between Maine and the West Coast is three hours.

TIPPING

At restaurants, a 15% tip is standard for waiters; up to 20% is expected at more expensive establishments. The same goes for taxi drivers, bartenders, and hairdressers. Coat-check operators usually expect $1; bellhops and porters should get $1 per bag; hotel maids should get about $1.50 per day of your stay. Hotel concierges should be tipped if you utilize their services; the amount varies widely depending on the nature of service. On package tours, conductors and drivers usually get $10 per day from the group as a whole; check whether this has already been figured into your cost. For local sightseeing tours, you may individually tip the driver-guide $1–$5, depending on the length of the tour and the number of people in your party, if he or she has been helpful or informative.

TOURS & PACKAGES

Because everything is prearranged on a prepackaged tour or independent vacation, you spend less time planning—and often get it all at a good price.

BOOKING WITH AN AGENT

Travel agents are excellent resources. But it's a good idea to collect brochures from several agencies, as some agents' suggestions may be influenced by relationships with tour and package firms that reward them for volume sales. If you have a special interest, find an agent with expertise in that area; the American Society of Travel Agents (ASTA; ⇨ Travel Agencies) has a database of specialists worldwide; you can log on to the group's Web site to find one near you.

Make sure your travel agent knows the accommodations and other services of the place being recommended. Ask about the hotel's location, room size, beds, and whether it has a pool, room service, or programs for children, if you care about these. Has your agent been there in person or sent others whom you can contact?

Do some homework on your own, too: local tourism boards can provide information about lesser-known and small-niche operators, some of which may sell only direct.

BUYER BEWARE

Each year consumers are stranded or lose their money when tour operators—even large ones with excellent reputations—go out of business. So check out the operator. Ask several travel agents about its reputation, and try to **book with a company that has a consumer-protection program.** (Look for information in the company's brochure.) In the United States, members of the United States Tour Operators Association are required to set aside funds ($1 million) to help eligible customers cover payments and travel arrangements in the event that the company defaults. It's also a good idea to choose a company that participates in the American Society of Travel Agents' Tour Operator Program; ASTA will act as mediator in any disputes between you and your tour operator.

Remember that the more your package or tour includes, the better you can predict the ultimate cost of your vacation. Make sure you know exactly what is covered, and beware of hidden costs. Are taxes, tips, and transfers included? Entertainment and excursions? These can add up.

🖪 **Tour-Operator Recommendations American Society of Travel Agents** (⇨ Travel Agencies). **National Tour Association** (NTA) ✉ 546 E. Main St., Lexington, KY 40508 ☎ 859/226–4444 or 800/682–8886 🖷 859/226–4404 ⊕ www.ntaonline.com. **United States Tour Operators Association** (USTOA) ✉ 275 Madison Ave., Suite 2014, New York, NY 10016 ☎ 212/599–6599 🖷 212/599–6744 ⊕ www.ustoa.com.

TRAIN TRAVEL

Amtrak's *Downeaster* connects Portland with Boston. The train makes four runs to and from Boston each day and makes seven stops along the way.

🚆 Train Information **Amtrak** ☎ 800/872-7245 ⊕ www.amtrak.com.

TRANSPORTATION AROUND MAINE

If you plan to travel along the coast of Maine, a car is a *must*. Rail connections exist only along Amtrak's Downeaster line from Portland to Boston, and regional travel by air is expensive. Concord Trailways runs a luxury bus several times a day from Orono, near Bangor, to Logan International Airport, in Boston, and makes stops at major towns along the way, but schedules are often inconvenient. Since one of coastal Maine's primary attractions is its picturesque countryside and innumerable small villages, only the automobile traveler (or bicyclist) can really appreciate all the region has to offer.

TRAVEL AGENCIES

A good travel agent puts your needs first. Look for an agency that has been in business at least five years, emphasizes customer service, and has someone on staff who specializes in your destination. In addition, **make sure the agency belongs to a professional trade organization.** The American Society of Travel Agents (ASTA) has more than 10,000 members in some 140 countries, enforces a strict code of ethics and will step in to help mediate any agent-client disputes involving ASTA members. ASTA also maintains a Web site that includes a directory of agents. (If a travel agency is also acting as your tour operator, *see* Buyer Beware *in* Tours & Packages.)

🚆 Local Agent Referrals **American Society of Travel Agents (ASTA)** ✉ 1101 King St., Suite 200, Alexandria, VA 22314 ☎ 703/739-2782 or 800/965-2782 24-hr hotline ♠ 703/684-8319 ⊕ www.astanet.com. **Association of British Travel Agents** ✉ 68-71 Newman St., London W1T 3AH ☎ 020/7637-2444 ♠ 020/7637-0713 ⊕ www.abta.com. **Association of Canadian Travel Agencies** ✉ 130 Albert St., Suite 1705, Ottawa, Ontario K1P 5G4 ☎ 613/237-3657 ♠ 613/237-7052 ⊕ www.acta.ca. **Australian Federation of Travel Agents** ✉ Level 3, 309 Pitt St., Sydney, NSW 2000 ☎ 02/9264-3299 or 1300/363-416 ♠ 02/9264-1085 ⊕ www.afta.com.au. **Travel Agents' Association of New Zealand** ✉ Level 5, Tourism and Travel House, 79 Boulcott St., Box 1888, Wellington 6001 ☎ 04/499-0104 ♠ 04/499-0786 ⊕ www.taanz.org.nz.

VISITOR INFORMATION

Contact the Maine Tourism Association for additional information about the state.

🚆 Tourist Information **Maine Tourism Association** ✉ 325-B Water St. ✆ Box 2300, Hallowell, ME 04347 ☎ 207/623-0363 or 888/624-6345 ⊕ www.mainetourism.com.

WEB SITES

Do check out the World Wide Web when planning your trip. You can find everything from weather forecasts to virtual tours of famous cities. Be sure to visit Fodors.com (⊕ www.fodors.com), a complete travel-planning site. You can research prices and book plane tickets, hotel rooms, rental cars, vacation packages, and more. In addition, you can post your pressing questions in the Travel Talk section. Other planning tools include a currency converter and weather reports, and there are loads of links to travel resources.

THE SOUTHERN COAST

1

STEP BACK IN TIME
at the Hamilton House ⇨*p.10*

DIG INTO MAINE'S BEST DOUGHNUTS
at Congdon's ⇨*p.29*

GIVE YOURSELF A FRIGHT
on a Ghostly Tour ⇨*p.15*

LAY ON THE LUXURY
at the Chapman Cottage ⇨*p.17*

CHOMP INTO A FAMOUS FRANKFURTER
at Flo's Steamed Hot Dogs ⇨*p.22*

RIDE THE RAILS
at the Seashore Trolley Museum ⇨*p.38*

By Laura V.
Scheel

Maine's southernmost coastal towns—Kittery, the Yorks, Ogunquit, the Kennebunks, and the Old Orchard Beach area—reveal a few of the many stunning faces of the state's coast, ranging from miles and miles of inviting sandy beaches to beautifully kept historic towns to carnival-like attractions. There is something for every taste here, whether you're seeking solitude in a kayak or prefer the infectious spirits of fellow vacationers. The Southern Coast towns are highly popular in summer, an all-too-brief period. Crowds converge and gobble up rooms and dinner reservations at prime restaurants. You'll have to work a little harder to find solitude and vestiges of the "real" Maine here. Still, even day-trippers who come for a few fleeting hours will appreciate the magical warmth of the coast.

North of Kittery, the Maine Coast has long stretches of hard-packed white-sand beach, closely crowded by nearly unbroken ranks of beach cottages, motels, and oceanfront restaurants. The summer colonies of York Beach and Wells have the crowds and ticky-tacky shorefront overdevelopment, but quiet wildlife refuges and land reserves promise an easy escape. York's historic district is on the National Register of Historic Places. Ogunquit is more upscale and offers much to do, from shopping to taking a cliff-side walk.

More than any other region south of Portland, the Kennebunks—and especially Kennebunkport—provide the complete Maine Coast experience: classic townscapes where white clapboard houses rise from manicured lawns and gardens; rocky shorelines punctuated by sandy beaches; quaint downtown districts packed with gift shops, ice-cream stands, and visitors; harbors where lobster boats bob alongside yachts; lobster pounds and well-appointed dining rooms. As you continue north, the scents of french fries, pizza, and cotton candy hover in the air above Coney Island–like Old Orchard Beach, known for its amusement pier and 7-mi-long shoreline. These towns are best explored on a leisurely holiday of two days—more if you require a fix of solid beach time.

Exploring the Southern Coast

While the Southern Coast makes up just a mere portion of Maine's many thousands of miles of shoreline, it offers an incredible variation of sights to discover. The best way to explore the region is by car—taking the time to sidetrack on inviting byways. Summer traffic may be demanding and an inconvenience, but the beauty and diversity of Maine is worth a little patience.

This chapter begins just across from the New Hampshire border in Kittery, the "Gateway to Maine," and heads in a general northward direction. Many of the sites and towns are off the main thoroughfares of U.S. 1 and I–95; you can decide how quickly you want to pass from one town to the next. From Kittery, a brief northwestward trip will bring you to pastoral South Berwick, then back to the coastal towns of the Yorks, Ogunquit, and Wells. The town of Kennebunk is slightly inland, while its sister town of Kennebunkport is right on the water. Old Orchard Beach is a quintessential frolicking beach town.

Numbers in the text correspond to numbers in the margin and on the Southern Coast map.

If you have 3 days

A three-day trip to the Southern Coast can give you a good taste of the different flavors of the region. Start your trip in **South Berwick ❷**. Here you can tour the historic home of author Sarah Orne Jewett and the grand Hamilton House. From South Berwick, follow Route 236 east to Route 91, back to U.S. 1 in York. Take Route 1A and explore the historic sites of **York Village ❸**. Continue the few miles to **York Harbor ❹**, a good place to spend the night. On your second day, follow the Shore Road (Route 1A) and stop in lively **York Beach ❺**, where you can swim, bowl, or play arcade games until after dark. Continue north on Route 1A and spend the night and the next day in **Ogunquit ❼**. Here you can walk the Marginal Way, and spend several hours perusing the shops of both Perkins Cove and the village of Ogunquit. If you're visiting in summer, save some time to relax at Ogunquit Beach.

If you have 7 days

Start your first day in **Kittery ❶**, an area rich in history and natural beauty, as well as a shopper's mecca. If the weather cooperates, bring a picnic, a kayak, or your walking shoes for a full day of enjoying the vistas and trails of Fort Foster. From here, follow the three-day itinerary above. On Day 5, leave Ogunquit, and continue on U.S. 1 into **Wells ❽**, a town known for its 7-mi stretch of pristine beaches. There are several opportunities for bird and nature watchers at Beach Plum Farm as well as the Wells Reserve and the Rachel Carson National Wildlife Refuge. Follow scenic Route 9 to the Kennebunks, a good place to spend the night. Spend the sixth day visiting historic homes and museums, as well as shopping in **Kennebunkport**'s ❿ busy Dock Square. If you like the sights and sounds of a carnival-on-the-beach atmosphere, take coastal Route 9 north from the Kennebunks to **Old Orchard Beach ⓬**. You'll be trading in the Kennebunks' quaintness for the chintzy playfulness of this lively beachfront community with an amusement park, pier, and plenty of fried food and entertainment to keep you sated. There is more than enough here to keep you occupied for the final night of your trip. If peaceful pursuits are more your style, opt instead to skip the neon and rent a canoe or take a guided trip through Scarborough Marsh, Maine's largest salt marsh.

1

For many visitors, the miles of beaches along the Southern Coast are the main attraction. But there is much more to see in the area's history and culture. Each town has its own rich personality just waiting to be discovered.

About the Restaurants

Maine produces well over 90% of the world's lobsters, so it's no surprise that a good portion of its restaurants boast the state's mascot on their menus. Creative chefs have gone well beyond the traditional steamed variety with seemingly endless ways to prepare the dish. Fortunately, the area's restaurants, while almost always giving a nod to the famous crustacean, do not limit themselves to it. Many places specialize in local seafood, and given that Maine has more than 5,000 mi of shoreline, there is plenty of it to choose from. Restaurants along the coast range from the casually eclectic to the formal prix fixe—and naturally there's everything in between. Although you won't find many international restaurants (though there are many Asian restaurants), most menus make explorations into the flavors of other cultures.

About the Hotels

The variation in lodgings along the Maine Coast has a lot to do with individual zoning laws. Towns like the Kennebunks, York Harbor, and Ogunquit have a much higher number of carefully restored B&Bs and small inns, while York Beach, Old Orchard Beach, Wells, and Kittery seem to be filled with one hotel–motel complex after another. U.S. 1 is famous (or infamous, depending on how you look at it) for its rampant commercialism, and its lodging options usually show it. The lovingly restored mansions will cost you quite a bit more than the sprawling hotels but almost all lodging establishments offer off-season price reductions, and special package rates. Minimum stay requirements are very common for weekends and the peak months of July through Labor Day. Expect to pay the highest rates in Kennebunkport, Ogunquit, and the Yorks.

WHAT IT COSTS					
	$$$$	$$$	$$	$	¢
RESTAURANTS	over $25	$18–$25	$11–$17	$7–$10	under $7
HOTELS	over $200	$150–$200	$100–$150	$60–$100	under $60

Restaurant prices are for a main course at dinner, excluding 7% tax. Hotel prices are for two people in a standard double room in high season, excluding service charges and 7% tax.

Timing

July, August, and September are the best months for a vacation in Maine. The weather is warmest in July and August; September is still on the warm side and much less crowded. During these months, most roads are extremely busy (don't expect speedy jaunts down U.S. 1), campgrounds are filled to capacity, and hotel rates are high. Every town has its share of summer festivals, outdoor concerts, and gatherings. Midweek tends to be a little quieter than weekends.

The brilliance of fall foliage brings another round of visitors to the state; often the off-season rates revert back to their summer heights, but even then, it's not quite as crowded as the summer. The prime viewing dates for foliage in Southern Maine are usually within the first week of October (check the state's weekly updated foliage Web site: www.mainefoliage.com).

In years past, most of the coastal towns practically folded up in the winter. Nowadays, many lodging places and restaurants stay open throughout the year, just with limited hours. Rates are lower, and you definitely won't be waiting in line anywhere.

Antiques The north–south corridor of U.S. 1 may be irritatingly slow moving for some in the summertime, but if you're more interested in moseying and poking in and out of antiques shops, then you won't mind the traffic a bit. The stretch of U.S. 1 from just north of Kittery all the way to Scarborough, just south of Portland, is so packed with antiques shops that it would take days for scrutinizing shoppers to make the trip. There are antiques "malls," abrim with the offerings of many dealers; towering and often tipping aged barns filled with all manner of items, right up into the haylofts; individual shops with particular specialties; and several outdoor flea markets that fill parking lots in summer. You can find everything from retired lobster traps (it is Maine, after all) to European furniture, maritime antiques, quilts, kitsch, glass, and probably just about anything else you're interested in. Prices may vary with the seasons as well as the strength of your bargaining prowess.

Beaches Few places can boast of mile after mile of smooth sandy beaches, ideal for walking, sunbathing, or contemplating life's mysteries, the way the Southern Coast of Maine can. This is a haven for beachgoers, provided you don't mind cooler-than-average water temperatures (it's fine after you get in, really). Punctuated by harbors, the occasional rocky ledge, and the distant views of lighthouses and islands, the beaches of this region are grand and plentiful.

SOUTHERN & INLAND YORK COUNTY

Kittery

1 *55 mi north of Boston, 5 mi north of Portsmouth, New Hampshire.*

One of the earliest settlements in the state of Maine, Kittery suffered its share of British, French, and Indian attacks throughout the 17th and 18th centuries, yet rose to prominence as a vital shipbuilding center. The tradition continues; despite its New Hampshire name, the Portsmouth Naval Shipyard is part of Maine and has been one of the leading researchers and builders of U.S. submarines since its inception in 1800. The shipyard has the distinction of being the oldest naval shipyard continuously operated by the U.S. government and is a major source of local employment. While not open to the public, those on boats can pass by the area and get a glimpse of its national significance.

Known as the "Gateway to Maine," Kittery has come to more recent light as a major shopping destination thanks to its complex of factory outlets. Flanked on either side of U.S. 1 are more than 120 stores, which attract hordes of shoppers year-round. For something a little less commercial, head east on Route 103 to the hidden Kittery most people miss: the lands around Kittery Point. Here you can find hiking and biking trails and, best of all, great views of the water. Pepperell Cove, the har-

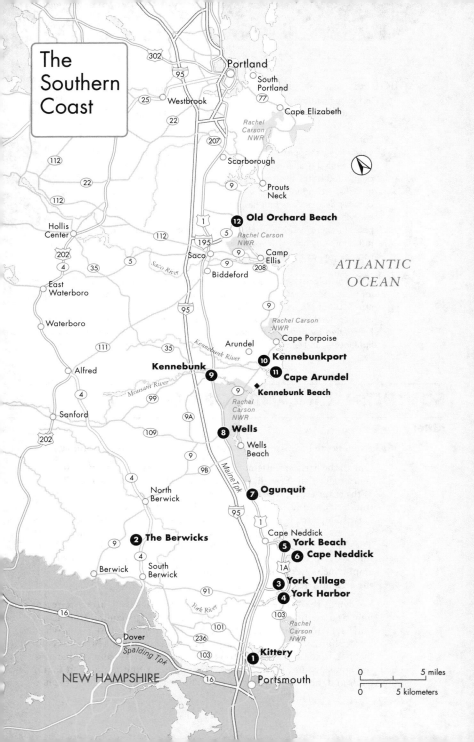

The Southern Coast

ATLANTIC OCEAN

NEW HAMPSHIRE

12 Old Orchard Beach
9 Kennebunk
10 Kennebunkport
11 Cape Arundel
Kennebunk Beach
8 Wells
7 Ogunquit
2 The Berwicks
5 York Beach
6 Cape Neddick
3 York Village
4 York Harbor
1 Kittery

Portland
South Portland
Cape Elizabeth
Westbrook
Rachel Carson NWR
Scarborough
Prouts Neck
Saco
Camp Ellis
Biddeford
Rachel Carson NWR
Hollis Center
East Waterboro
Waterboro
Arundel
Cape Porpoise
Rachel Carson NWR
Alfred
Sanford
Wells Beach
North Berwick
Berwick
South Berwick
Cape Neddick
Dover
Portsmouth

302
95
25
22
207
112
22
112
1
5
195
112
208
202
4
35
5
9
9
9
9
95
111
35
99
202
4
9A
109
9
9B
4
202
9
4
91
16
101
236
103
16
103
Maine Tpk.
Kennebunk River
Mousam River
Saco River
York River
Spalding Tpk.
1A
1

0   5 miles
0   5 kilometers

bor at Kittery Point, is said to be the first commercial port in Maine to thrive in the salt cod trade. With Portsmouth, New Hampshire, across the water, Whaleback Ledge Lighthouse, and the nearby Isles of Shoals, the town of Kittery is a truly picturesque and idyllic place to pass some time. Also along this winding stretch of Route 103 are two forts, both open in summer.

Built in 1872, **Fort Foster** was an active military installation until 1949. Now a town park, the 88-acre area is ideal for picnics (barbecue grills are all over) and explorations into the rocky crevices along the beach. There are also numerous walking trails, swimming areas, and special spots from which to windsurf and kayak. ⊠ *Pocahontas Rd., Kittery Point* ☎ *207/439–3800* ⌸ *$10 per car.*

> **need a break?**
>
> Just shy of Kittery Harbor you'll see **Frisbee's** market (⊠ Pepperell Cove, Rte. 103 ☎ 207/439–0014), which has stood proudly in the same spot since 1828. It's heralded as the oldest family-owned market in the country and they've got all kinds of articles and photographs inside showing the family lineage over the years. It's a neat old place with high ceilings, creaky wooden floors (apparently the very same ones that Mark Twain once trod upon), and some pretty good cookies. Pack your picnic for Fort Foster or a boat ride here; there's a produce section, deli, and butcher as well as some baked goods and fresh coffee. Wine, liquor, and beer are also sold.

Built in 1690 to protect the mouth of the Piscataqua River, **Fort McClary** is particularly notable for its 1812 hexagonal blockhouse. The fort, which successfully countered pirates, Native Americans, the French, and the British, sits on a scenic harbor and has ocean views. ⊠ *Rte. 103, Kittery Point* ☎ *207/439–2845* ⊕ *www.state.me.us/doc/parks.*

For a glimpse into Kittery's three centuries of (and continuing) naval history, visit the **Kittery Historical and Naval Museum**, which has a curious exhibit of artifacts and photographs, and even a lighthouse lens on display. ⊠ *U.S. 1 at Rogers Rd.* ☎ *207/439–3080* ⌸ *$3 adults; $6 family* ☉ *June–Oct., Tues.–Sat. 10–4.*

One of the most elegant houses in America, the **Lady Pepperell House** was built in 1760, as it claims above the doorway, which is framed by two glorious two-story fluted pilasters. Set just past Fort McClary, this was meant to be the grandest mansion in the Piscataqua Valley, as befits "a lady." The immensely rich widow of Sir William Pepperell—one of the J. Paul Gettys of his day—Lady Mary retained the honorary title bestowed on her husband's family owing to his great exploits during the French and Indian Wars. While private and not open regularly for tours, the house may be visited a few times during the year—make inquiries in the town. ⊠ *Rte. 103, Kittery Point.*

Where to Stay & Eat

$–$$ ✕ **Cap'n Simeon's Galley.** This restaurant's nautical-theme dining room may have one of the best views in the area. Look out to the pier, nearby lighthouses, islands, and historic forts while you sample any number of fresh seafood or steak options, from fried oysters to boiled lobster, fresh haddock to New York sirloin. It's a good place for a hearty Sunday brunch. There's also live musical entertainment in the lounge on Saturday nights. ⊠ *90 Pepperell Rd. (Rte. 103)* ☎ *207/439–3655* ⌕ *Reservations not accepted* ▭ *D, MC, V* ⊘ *Closed Tues. and Columbus Day–Memorial Day.*

$–$$ ✕ **Chauncey Creek Lobster Pound.** From the road you can barely see the red roof hovering below the trees, but chances are you can see the cars parked here. This popular spot is down amid the high banks of the tidal river. The menu has lots of lobster items and a raw bar. Bring your own beer or wine if you care to make a toast to your lobster. Open daily for lunch and dinner in season. ⊠ *Chauncey Creek Rd., Kittery Point* ☎ *207/439–1030* ▭ *MC, V* ⊘ *Closed Nov.–Apr.*

$–$$ ✕ **Warren's Lobster House.** A local institution, this waterfront restaurant specializes in seafood and has a huge salad bar. The pine-sided dining room leaves the impression that little has changed since the restaurant opened in 1940. In season you can dine outdoors overlooking the water. ⊠ *U.S. 1 and Water St.* ☎ *207/439–1630* ▭ *AE, MC, V.*

$$$ ▥ **Portsmouth Harbor Inn & Spa** (formerly the Inn at Portsmouth Harbor). Renovations have added a bit more decadent luxury to this inn, but the antique beauty of the place remains the same. The brick Victorian was built in 1889 on the old Kittery town green. It overlooks the Piscataqua River and Portsmouth Harbor. An easy walk over the bridge takes you to nearby Portsmouth, New Hampshire. English antiques and Victorian watercolors decorate the inn, and most rooms have water views. Special spa packages are available. ⊠ *6 Water St., 03904* ☎ *207/439–4040* 🖶 *207/438–9286* ⊕ *www.innatportsmouth.com* ⟿ *5 rooms* ⌂ *In-room data ports, cable TV, spa; no children under 16, no smoking* ▭ *MC, V* ⦿ *BP.*

$–$$ ▥ **Enchanted Nights B&B.** This three-story Victorian is about as amply dressed as a painted lady ought to be; sitting rooms and guest rooms are chock full of unusual antique furniture, draped in frilly fabrics and pillows, and adorned with floral wallpaper and bed coverings. Some rooms have painted skylike ceilings, complete with stars, clouds, and a sliver of moon to encourage the kind of respite conjured up by the inn's name. The most unusual (and smallest) room is the Turret, high up on the third floor. Those who want space to spread out will love the finest room of all: the Bella, in the adjacent Carriage House, has vaulted ceilings, a whirlpool tub for two, a fireplace, and lots of privacy. If you love a particular piece of furniture, ask about it: chances are it's for sale. ⊠ *29 Wentworth St. (Rte. 103), 03904* ☎ *207/439–1489* ⊕ *www. enchantednights.org* ⟿ *8 rooms, 1 apartment* ⌂ *Cable TV, some in-room VCRs/DVDs, some refrigerators, some whirlpool tubs, some fireplaces, pets allowed, no smoking* ▭ *AE, D, DC, MC, V* ⦿ *BP.*

Sports & the Outdoors

With all the water around—the Piscataqua River and the Atlantic Ocean meet here—it's no wonder that outdoor recreation in Kittery revolves around marine pursuits.

For a lively historical boat tour narrated by the captain himself, take a trip with **Captain & Patty's Piscataqua River Tours** (⊠ Rte. 103, Kittery

Point ☎ 207/439–8976). The hour-plus-long trips leave the dock seven times daily; get tickets at the dock.

Help hoist the sails if you wish, or simply bring along your own picnic and enjoy the half- or full-day cruises with **Saboutime Sailing** (✉ Pepperell Cove [Rte. 103] ☎ 207/475–6248 ⊕ www.saboutimesailing. com). Routes vary depending on wind direction.

For private off-shore fishing trips, scenic cruises, whale watching, or scuba charters, sign up with **Seafari Charters** (✉ 7 Island Ave. ☎ 207/439–5068 ⊕ www.seafaricharters.com).

Head out on the Piscataqua River and the ocean to find striped bass and bluefish with **Tidewater Fishing Charters** (✉ Pepperell Cove, Kittery Point ☎ 207/439–1914). Half- and full-day charters are available for up to three people.

Shopping

Kittery has more than 120 outlet stores. Along a several-mile stretch of U.S. 1 you can find just about anything, from hardware to underwear. Among the stores are Crate & Barrel, Eddie Bauer, Jones New York, Esprit, Waterford/Wedgwood, Lenox, Ralph Lauren, Tommy Hilfiger, DKNY, and J. Crew.

Find maps, store locations, special discounts, and events within the **Kittery Outlets** (✉ U.S. 1 ☎ 207/439–4367 or 888/548–8379 ⊕ www. thekitteryoutlets.com) by contacting the outlet association; also, look for brochures in nearby restaurants or tourist centers.

Kittery Trading Post (✉ U.S. 1 ☎ 207/587–6246 or 888/587–62463 ⊕ www.kitterytradingpost.com) rivals Freeport's L. L. Bean for camping, fishing, boating, and other types of outdoor accoutrements. In business since 1938, the company continues to grow and offers various outdoor seminars and instruction.

en route To reach the next stop, the Berwicks, take Route 101 north from U.S. 1 and relax amid farmland on your way to the town of South Berwick. Take a right onto Route 236 (approximately 8 mi on Route 101) and continue until the road meets Route 91. Signs will direct you to Vaughn Woods State Park and the Hamilton House. To reach the Sarah Orne Jewett House, follow Route 236 until you reach the center of South Berwick; at the division of Routes 236 and 4, look for signs; the home is right in the center of town.

If you want to stay along the coast, skip the Berwicks and head straight to the Yorks by taking beautiful Route 103 from Kittery Point, a drive of about 6 mi.

The Berwicks

❷ *14 mi northwest of Kittery via Rtes. 236 and 91.*

For a brief stay or just a passing detour westward from the coast in Kittery, the several towns that make up the Berwicks—North Berwick,

South Berwick, and Berwick—reveal many of the pleasant pastoral byways that originally attracted its 17th-century settlers. Most of the activity is in the little town of South Berwick, a somewhat artsy little enclave amid the farmland and just next to the border of New Hampshire (it seems that many of its residents spend more time in nearby Portsmouth than elsewhere in Maine). The main street is a busy thoroughfare and popular travel route for interstate trucks, but its sidewalks are lined with practical shops set in stately brick buildings and there is something quaintly New England about its layout. It's a great place to spend a morning or an afternoon, sampling some of its good restaurant offerings and exploring the nearby attractions of historical homes and a state park.

Fodor's Choice ★ Set on a bluff overlooking the Salmon Falls River, a palatial Georgian Colonial known as the **Hamilton House** was part of author Sarah Orne Jewett's Revolutionary War novel, *The Tory Lover*. The mansion, with four immense chimneys, dormer windows, and a mansard roof, was built in 1785 by shipbuilder Jonathan Hamilton to receive noted guests (including John Paul Jones) in regal splendor. In 1898 Mrs. Emily Tyson and her stepdaughter purchased the home and, with the help of their friend Sarah Orne Jewett, resurrected and decorated the place in a combination of Colonial and Victorian styles. If touring the innards of old homes doesn't interest you, come here to explore the grounds; they're simply spectacular. Beautifully kept gardens look out over the tidal Salmon Falls River below, where first owner Hamilton built ships, filled them with goods, and sailed straight to England from his front yard. The Embargo Act of 1807 ended his trade and, hence, his fortune quite abruptly. Picnickers and hikers are welcome on the grounds free of charge. Held within the formal gardens, **Sundays in the Garden** offers a summer concert series ranging from classical to folk music. ⊠ *40 Vaughn's La., South Berwick* ☎ *207/384–2454* ⊕ *www.spnea.org* ⊠ *$8* ☉ *June–mid-Oct., Wed.–Sun. 11–4.*

The **Sarah Orne Jewett House,** a sturdy Georgian-style home, dates to 1774 and reflects the shipbuilding wealth of its time. Sarah Orne Jewett was born in the house in 1849, lived elsewhere for a time, then came back to her house of birth to reside with her sister for the remainder of her life. The view from her desk in the top floor hall looks down on the town's major intersection, which indeed gave her material for her novels, including *The Country of the Pointed Firs*. Now a museum, the house contains period furnishings. Jewett's bedroom remains as she left it. ⊠ *5 Portland St., South Berwick* ☎ *207/384–2454* ⊕ *www.spnea.org* ⊠ *$5* ☉ *June–mid-Oct., Fri.–Sun. 11–4.*

A 250-acre preserve along the banks of the Salmon Falls River, **Vaughn Woods** is a perfect place for a picnic or a stroll. Its many nature trails wind amid pine and hemlock forests. The river was of prime importance to early settlers and it was here that the nation's first water-powered sawmill was built. Local legend says that among the ships that carried supplies and the harvested timber downriver and to the sea, one called the *Pied Cow* unloaded the first cows to inhabit Maine in 1634. ⊠ *28*

MAINE'S BELOVED SARAH ORNE JEWETT

"TACT IS, AFTER ALL, A KIND OF MIND READING."–Sarah Orne Jewett

Maine has had its share of famous authors, resident and visiting, who have heralded both the natural and the physical spirit of the state itself in their literary works. Horror guru Stephen King makes his home in Bangor and has modeled several of his frightening stories on his Maine experiences; Harriet Beecher Stowe wrote Uncle Tom's Cabin while living in Brunswick; and of course, well-known poet Henry Wadsworth Longfellow grew up in Portland, including his birthplace in many of his writings. But few are as endearingly held among Maine's literary greats as Sarah Orne Jewett, born the daughter of a country doctor and his wife in South Berwick in 1849.

Sarah Orne Jewett grew up privileged yet not out of reach of those within the rural farming community of 19th-century Maine; often she accompanied her father on house calls throughout the area, and many accredit her skills of quiet observation and sensitivity to these trips in the doctor's horse and buggy. Known for her sketches of rural life, Jewett is seen as a true daughter of Maine in the way that she beautifully and lovingly portrayed the intimate and poignant moments of her fellow citizens. Most famous are her novels The Country Doctor (1884) and The Country of Pointed Firs (1896), though she published dozens of short stories and poems throughout her writing career. Nowhere else in literature are there more endearing portraits of small town life as in The Country of Pointed Firs; within her words you can nearly smell the sea air as it mingles with the scent of pines, and clearly visualize the colorful characters that make up the pages within her stories.

After she published her novel The Tory Lover (1901), based on the wealthy Hamilton family who lived in nearby South Berwick, a review in the Lewiston Journal Magazine Section from that year summed up her writing skills aptly: "So strong and true are the pictures drawn of life . . . they come to Maine readers with a sort of familiarity, born of the tales of those troublous times handed down from their forefathers. Her readers feel a nearness to these men and women which makes them forget that more than a century separates them."

Jewett never married though had a long and loving friendship with the widow Annie Fields, with whom she spent many years traveling and socializing with other literary greats of the day, including Willa Cather, William Dean Howells, Henry James, Rudyard Kipling, and Harriet Beecher Stowe. A serious carriage accident in 1902 precipitated the end of her writing career and her eventual death in 1909. Sarah Orne Jewett's writing remains as a picture of the quintessential Maine known in the hearts and minds of Maine residents, both past and present.

Oldsfields Rd., South Berwick ☎ *207/384–5160* ☉ *Memorial Day–Labor Day, daily dawn–dusk.*

Where to Stay & Eat

$$$–$$$$ ✕ **Café Brio.** The inside decor of this funky little café is as creative as
FodorsChoice   the menu. With a jazzy, bistro feel, the place even has a special martini
★   menu; this passion for the beverage is reflected in artwork on both the
walls and even the windows. The menu has an interesting mix of
Mediterranean and New Mexican spice. The chef does some great
things with artichokes. Try the roast pork with a green peppercorn
demiglace or the pumpkin tortellini in a New Mexican chili sauce.
✉ *279 Main St.* ☎ *207/384–5636* ▭ *MC, V* ☉ *Closed Mon. and Tues.*

$$–$$$ ✕ **The Lodge Restaurant at Spring Hill.** With a waterfront seat along-
side Salmon Falls River, this location is hard to beat. The menu mixes
a good amount of land and seafood; there's a bit of everything from
salmon to filet mignon, and haddock to, yes, even Wiener schnitzel.
✉ *117 Pond Rd., South Berwick* ☎ *207/384–2693* ☉ *Closed Mon.
and Tues. No lunch.*

¢–$ ✕ **Flynn's News.** This old-fashioned dinerlike place has been around for
a long time and seems to have developed its own special brand of humor
(the restaurant's motto is "where everyone's out-to-lunch"). Lunch
doesn't venture much beyond grilled cheese and tuna melts—though break-
fast is a bit more sophisticated with orange French toast, huevos
rancheros, and eggs Benedict. The menu is also equipped for vegetari-
ans with veggie burgers and a tofu scramble. With only about six ta-
bles and as many swivel stools at the counter, it fills up fast but the wait
isn't bad—you can easily pass the time in the so-called gift shop . . . some-
one needs to find out if the "sizzling bacon" air freshener really lives
up to its name. ✉ *233 Main St., South Berwick* ☎ *207/384–2602*
▭ *MC, V* ☉ *Closed Mon.*

$ ⌂ **Academy Street Inn.** Antiques, family photos, and a collection of sleds
and snowshoes adorn the interior of this grand 1903 home, within
walking distance of two historic houses, Hamilton House and Sarah Orne
Jewett's home. Its location on the New Hampshire border is convenient
for exploring both southern Maine and New Hampshire. Rates include
big breakfasts served in the formal dining room. Rooms are comfort-
ably furnished and spacious. ✉ *15 Academy St., South Berwick 03908*
☎ *207/384–5633* ⇜ *5 rooms* ⌘ *Some room TVs; no room phones, no
children under 10, no smoking* ▭ *AE, MC, V* ❤ *BP.*

Nightlife & the Arts

On Sundays in July, the Hamilton House presents **Sundays in the Gar-
den** (✉ 40 Vaughan's La. ☎ 207/384–2454 ✉ $6), a series of concerts
ranging from blues to folk and jazz. Picnicking is encouraged on the ample
lawn; concerts begin at 4.

Shopping

Tiny but filled with tempting, bulging shelves to peruse, the **SoBo** (✉ 241
Main St. ☎ 207/384–8300) is a used bookstore–coffee shop. It's defi-
nitely a long way from Manhattan and perhaps that's the point. Pick
up copies of former neighbor Sarah Orne Jewett's famous books to get
you in the mood for further Maine travels.

en route

For an appealing drive back toward the coast and the Yorks, follow Route 236 east out of town until it meets with Route 91, which branches off to the left. The under 10-mi winding road leads you past farmland, exquisite antique homesteads, and marshland views meandering from various tidal rivers. You can end up at U.S. 1; head north to proceed to the York area.

THE YORKS, OGUNQUIT & WELLS

The Yorks—York Village, York Harbor, York Beach, and Cape Neddick—are typical of small-town coastal communities in New England and are smaller than most. Many of their nooks and crannies can be explored in a few hours. The beaches are the big attraction here.

Not unlike siblings in most families, the towns within this region reveal vastly different personalities. York Village and York Harbor abound with old money, picturesque mansions, impeccably manicured lawns, and gardens and shops that cater to a more staid and wealthy clientele. Continue along Route 1A from York Harbor to York Beach and soon all the pretense falls away like autumnal leaves in a storm—it's family vacation time (and party time), with scores of T-shirt shops, ice-cream and fried seafood joints, arcades and bowling, and plenty of motor court–style motels. Left over from earlier days are a surprising number of trailer and RV parks spread across the road from the beach—in prime real estate that must have hotel developers and monied old-timers in pure agony.

North of York Beach, Cape Neddick blends back into more peaceful and gentle terrain, while Ogunquit is elegant high-spirited tourism to the hilt. With its walkable village filled with restaurants, shops, and B&Bs, Ogunquit is a prime resort destination. Continue north on U.S. 1 and you find yourself in Wells, a town seemingly lost in the commercialism of the main route yet blessed with some of the area's best beaches.

York Village

❸ About 6 mi north of Kittery on Rte. 103 or Rte. 1A via U.S. 1.

As subdued as the town may feel today, the history of York Village reveals a far different character. One of the first permanently settled areas in the state of Maine, it was once witness to great destruction and fierce fighting during the French, Indian, and British wars; towns and fortunes were sacked yet the potential for prosperity encouraged the area's citizens to continually rebuild and start anew. Colonial York citizens enjoyed great wealth and success from fishing and lumber as well as a penchant for politics. Angered by the British-imposed taxes, York held its own little-known tea party in 1775 in protest. Then in the late 1700s, the first cries for independent statehood from ruling Massachusetts were heard here, though these would not be answered until the next century.

The actual village of York is quite small, housing the town's basic components of post office, town hall, a few shops, and a stretch of impressive antique homes. It feels more lived in than touristed, though the various museums of the York Historical Society are well worth a visit. Sharp-eyed American history buffs may notice something amiss with York's Civil War Monument. After the war, it was common for towns to erect a statue of a Civil War soldier to honor the local boys who served and died, and York was no exception. The statue sent to York, however, was most likely meant to be shipped much farther south—the image is of a Confederate soldier. Legend says that the citizens of York, acting in accordance with their frugal New England Yankee nature, refused to pay the extra money required to switch the statue for the correct one. That lost Confederate soldier still stands today in York Village, though no one seems to know where the Union statue ended up.

Most of the 18th- and 19th-century buildings within the **York Village Historic District** are clustered along York Street and Lindsay Road; seven are owned by the Old York Historical Society and charge admission. You can buy tickets for all the buildings at the **Jefferds Tavern** (⊠ Rte. 1A at Lindsay Rd.), a restored late-18th-century inn. The **Old York Gaol** (1720) was once the King's Prison for the Province of Maine; inside are dungeons, cells, and the jailer's quarters. Theatrical jailbreak tours are staged Friday and Saturday nights. The 1731 **Elizabeth Perkins House** reflects the Victorian style of its last occupants, the prominent Perkins family. The Historical Society also offers guided walking tours (or simply take the self-guided tour as you go through each of the seven buildings) and a popular Decorator's Show House held each July through August. ☎ 207/363–4974 ⊕ www.oldyork.org ⊠ All buildings $7 ⊙ Mid-June–mid-Oct., Mon.–Sat. 10–5.

In an earnest effort to keep traffic down, ease parking woes, and to keep visitors (and locals) happy, the trolleys of the **York Trolley Company** make daily loops through York Village, York Harbor, out to Nubble Lighthouse, and all the way to Short Sands Beach in York Beach. In addition to regularly scheduled stops, you can take narrated sightseeing tours, trips to Ogunquit and Perkins Cove, and even trips to the shopping outlets in Kittery. Day passes are available for about $5 (cheaper than beach parking!) while tours start at $7. Route maps can be picked up nearly everywhere in York and at the Chamber of Commerce. ☎ 207/748–3030 ⊕ www.yorktrolley.com.

York is the headquarters and processing center of **Stonewall Kitchen.** You've probably seen their smartly labeled jars of gourmet chutneys, jams, jellies, salsas, and sauces in specialty stores back home. The company's attractive complex houses the company store, a bustling café and takeout restaurant, a viewing area of the cooking and bottling processes, and stunning gardens. Café tables are set outside and the store is brimming with wares that would make Martha Stewart proud. Sample all the mustards, salsas, and dressings that you can stand in the store, or have lunch at the café. Takeout is available during store hours; lunch is served daily 11–3; Sunday is brunch day. ⊠ Stonewall La., just off U.S. 1, next to information center ☎207/351–2719 ⊕www.stonewallkitchen. com ⊙ Mon.–Sat. 8–8, Sun. 9–6.

Where to Eat

$–$$ ✕ **Carla's Bakery & Cafe.** This little place on the main street is a great spot for a quick bite while touring the Historic Society's complex. For a morning break, there's a tasty selection of pastries, scones, and breakfast sandwiches (full breakfast is served only on Saturday) as well as a supply of full-bodied coffees. For lunch choose from homemade soups, salads, and sandwiches—a favorite is the chicken salad with red grapes and mango chutney. ⊠ *241 York St.* ☏ *207/363–4637* ▭ *No credit cards* ⊘ *Closed Sun.*

Nightlife & the Arts

☾ For an otherworldly version of York's nightlife, tag along with **Ghostly**

FodorśChoice **Tours** (⊠ 250 York St. [Rte. 1A], down the alley near the laundromat)

★ ☏ 207/363–0000 ☒ $10), for candlelit walking tours through York Village. Your hooded guide leads you through the village as tales of witches, ghosts, and the town's peculiar history are revealed. Tours run from late June through Halloween (of course). Tours meet at the appropriately intriguing shop, Gravestone Artwear (*see* listing under Shopping). Call ahead for tour times; reservations are recommended.

Shopping

Guess the theme at **Gravestone Artwear** (⊠ 250 York St. [Rte. 1A] ☏ 207/363–0000), where you'll find items adorned with Colonial, Victorian, and Celtic gravestone carving designs. There are also crystals, gravestone rubbing supplies, books, and candles.

The two stories of **Hawthorn & Nugent** (⊠ 279 York St. [Rte. 1A]) ☏ 207/351–3327) are filled with all manner of gift items for the home.

With everything from women's apparel to fine art, there's much to browse at **Riverplace** (⊠ 250 York St. [Rte. 1A] ☏ 207/351–3266). There are also plenty of children's toys and books to keep the little ones busy.

Everything is handmade at **Blackbird Design Gallery** (⊠ 273A York St. [Rte. 1A] ☏ 207/361–4304), from wall hangings to jewelry and paintings.

Watercolors, mixed media, oils, photography, and more make up the featured art at **Village Gallery** (⊠ 244 York St. [Rte. 1A] ☏ 207/351–3110). Many local artists are represented here.

Local artists are the focus at the **York Art Association** (⊠ 344 York St. [Rte. 1A] ☏ 207/363–4049), where their work is on display and for sale in originals, prints, and greeting cards.

York Harbor

❹ *Approximately 3 mi north of York Village via Rte. 1A.*

Just a few miles from the village proper, York Harbor opens up to the water and offers many more places to linger and explore. The harbor itself is busy with boats of all kinds, while the Harbor Beach is a good stretch of sand for swimming. Much more formal than the northward York Beach, and much quieter, the area retains a slightly more exclusive air.

The waterfront **Sayward-Wheeler House** was built in 1718. In the 1760s, Jonathan Sayward, a local merchant who had prospered in the West Indies trade, remodeled and furnished the house. By 1860 his descendants had opened the house to the public to share the story of their Colonial ancestors. The house, accessible only by guided tour, reveals both the simple decor of the 18th century and the more opulent and elaborate furnishings of the 19th century. ✉ *79 Barrell La., York Harbor* ☎ *603/ 436–3205* ⊕ *www.historicnewengland.org* 🎫 *$5* ⏱ *June–mid-Oct., weekends 11–5; tours on the hr 11–4.*

Where to Stay & Eat

$$$–$$$$ ✕ **Dockside Restaurant.** On a private island, overlooking York Harbor, this restaurant is ideally situated. With the water in such close proximity, it's no surprise that there's plenty of seafood on the menu, as well as such treats as beef tenderloin and duckling. Start with the rich lobster and scallop crêpe or an order of local Maine oysters. Reservations are recommended. ✉ *Harbor Island Rd., just off Rte. 103* ☎ *207/363– 2722* 🍽 *D, MC, V* ⏱ *Closed Mon. and late Oct.–Apr.*

$$$–$$$$ ✕ **Harbor Porches.** Eating here is actually very much like sitting on someone's porch—assuming that someone has a lot of money and can afford extravagant views over York Harbor. Wicker chairs at linen-covered tables fill the space and are surrounded by large windows. There is a lot of local seafood on the menu, as well as rack of lamb and steak. For lunch try some of their interestingly prepared sandwiches and wraps. The Maine crab cakes appetizer is worth a try, as is the lobster bisque. Jeans and sneakers are not allowed at dinner; reservations are recommended. This is one of the restaurants of the Stage Neck Inn complex and is open for breakfast, lunch, and dinner. ✉ *Stage Neck Rd.* ☎ *207/ 363–3850* 🍽 *AE, D, DC, MC, V* ⏱ *Closed 2 wks in Jan.*

★ $$ ✕🛏 **York Harbor Inn.** A mid-17th-century fishing cabin with dark timbers and a fieldstone fireplace forms the heart of this inn. Wings and outbuildings have been added over the years. The rooms are furnished with antiques and country pieces; many have decks overlooking the water, and some have whirlpool tubs or fireplaces. The nicest rooms are in two adjacent buildings, Harbor Cliffs and Harbor Hill. The dining room ($$$–$$$$; no lunch off-season) has great ocean views. For dinner, start with Maine crab cakes and then try the lobster-stuffed chicken breast, or the scallops Dijon. Ask about various packages and Internet specials. ✉ *Rte. 1A* 🏠 *Box 573, York Harbor 03911* ☎ *207/363–5119 or 800/ 343–3869* 🖨 *207/363–7151* ⊕ *www.yorkharborinn.com* 🛏 *47 rooms, 2 suites* ⚓ *Restaurant, cable TV, in-room data ports, pub, meeting rooms; no smoking* 🍽 *AE, DC, MC, V* 🍴 *CP.*

$$$$ 🛏 **Edward's Harborside.** This turn-of-the-20th-century B&B sits on the harbor's edge and is a two-minute walk from the beach. Rooms have private baths (there are four additional rooms without baths that can be combined to make suites for families), are spacious, and have big windows to take in the water views. One room has a whirlpool tub. There is a very homey feel here; throughout the inn are photos of the various family members' weddings and other gatherings. ✉ *Stage Neck Rd.* 🏠 *Box 866, York Harbor 03911* ☎ *207/363–3037* 🖨 *207/363–1544* ⊕ *www.edwardsharborside.com* 🛏 *7 rooms* ⚓ *Cable TV, dock; no children under 8, no smoking* 🍽 *MC, V* 🍴 *BP.*

$$$$ 🛏 **Stage Neck Inn.** Sitting out on its own little peninsula within York Harbor is this luxury and business-oriented resort. The views are everywhere, as one may expect from the resort's position, though not all rooms face the water directly; some look out to impressive gardens instead. Rooms are tastefully outfitted in a standard hotel style—you won't find the whimsical or personal details you'd get in a smaller inn—and offer either two doubles or a king-size bed. There are plenty of activities on the property to keep you busy. ✉ *Stage Neck Rd.* 🏠 *Box 70, York Harbor 03911* ☎ *207/363–3850 or 800/340–1130* 🖷 *207/363–2221* ⊕ *www.stageneck. com* ⟿ *58 rooms* ⌂ *2 restaurants, refrigerators, in-room CD players and VCRs, golf privileges, 6 tennis courts, indoor pool, outdoor pool, fitness room, hot tub, beach, business services, meeting rooms* ▭ *AE, D, DC, MC, V* �⊙∣ *EP.*

\$\$\$–\$\$\$\$
Fodor'sChoice
★

🖽 **Chapman Cottage.** Set proudly atop a grassy lawn is this impeccably restored inn, named for the woman who had it built as her summer cottage in 1899. The luxuriant bedspreads, antiques, and beautiful rugs only hint at the indulgence found here. Innkeepers Donna and Paul Archibald spoil their guests with sumptuous breakfasts, afternoon hors d'oeuvres, port, sherry, and homemade chocolate truffles, all prepared by Paul, a professionally trained chef. Most rooms have fireplaces and whirlpool tubs; all are spacious, bright, and airy. It's a five-minute walk to either York Village or the harbor, but you may never wish to leave. If you're lucky enough to be here at the end of September, Paul clears out one of the rooms for an off-season restaurant—the three-course meals are decadent and surprisingly reasonable. ✉ *370 York St., 03911* ☎ *207/363–2059 or 877/ 363–2059* 🖷 *207/351–3242* ⊕ *www.ChapmanCottageBandB.com* ⟿ *7 rooms* ⌂ *Internet; no room phones, no room TVs, no children under 12* ▭ *AE, D, MC, V* f⊙∣ *BP.*

\$\$\$–\$\$\$\$

🖽 **Inn at Tanglewood Hall.** Owned by the Dorsey family back in the 1940s, this grand Victorian home was a favorite beachside getaway for future musical greats Tommy and Jimmy. Today it is a haven of elegance and comfort, set back among trees and stunning perennial gardens. Rooms are individually decorated though all share decadently rich coloring and fabrics, high ceilings, and many large windows; some have fireplaces. ✉ *611 York St., 03911* ☎ *207/351–1075* 🖷 *207/351–1296* ⊕ *www. tanglewoodhall.com* ⟿ *6 rooms* ⌂ *No room phones, no room TVs, no children under 12* ▭ *MC, V* ⊙ *Closed Nov.–Apr.* f⊙∣ *BP.*

\$\$–\$\$\$\$

🖽 **Dockside Guest Quarters.** This is the kind of place that people return to year after year. Set on its own private peninsula bordering York Harbor and the ocean, the complex consists of the main inn as well as a series of buildings that house standard rooms and suites. Adirondack chairs are thoughtfully placed by twos around the spacious lawn, with plenty of space for privacy if desired. Many hours could be spent on the wraparound porch enjoying the views. Rooms are adorned with antiques and simple white bedspreads; some have fireplaces and most have outdoor decks. A breakfast buffet is offered for an additional charge. ✉ *Harris Island Rd., 03909* ☎ *207/363–2868 or 800/270–1977* 🖷 *207/ 363–1977* ⊕ *www.docksidegq.com* ⟿ *13 rooms, 5 suites, 6 studios* ⌂ *Cable TV, dock, bicycles, badminton, croquet, shuffleboard* ▭ *D, MC, V* ⊙ *Closed Dec.–Mar.*

Sports & the Outdoors

Take to the water in a guided kayak trip with **Harbor Adventures** (✉ Box 345, York Harbor 03911 ☎ 207/363–8466 ⊕ www.harboradventures.

com). Choose from harbor tours, full-moon paddles, half-day trips, and even a luncheon paddle; prices start around $32. Bicycle tours are also offered—by the hour or for several days touring. Departure locations vary; spots are dotted along the coast.

FISHING **Capt. Tom Farnon** (⊠ Rte. 103, Town Dock No. 2, York Harbor ☎ 207/408–1194) takes passengers on lobstering trips, weekdays 10–2.

Fish Tale Charters (⊠ York Harbor 03911 ☎ 207/363–3874 ⊕ www.maineflyfishing.net) takes anglers on fly-fishing charters out of York Harbor.

Rip Tide Charters (⊠ 1 Georgia St., York 03909 ☎ 207/363–2536 ⊕ www.mainestriperfishing.com) goes where the fish are—departure points vary, from Ogunquit to York and Portsmouth, NH. They specialize in fly-fishing and light tackle for stripers, mackerel, and bluefish.

Seabury Charters (⊠ Town Dock No. 2, York Harbor, York ☎ 207/363–5675 ⊕ www.yorkme.org/seaburycharters) offers two trips daily aboard the *Blackback*. The first trip is from 7:30 AM to noon; the second is from 12:30 to 5 PM. No trips Monday or Thursday. Walk-ons are welcome if space allows.

Shearwater Charters (⊠ Box 472, York Harbor 03911 ☎ 207/363–5324) offers spin or fly-casting charters in the York River and along the shoreline from Kittery to Ogunquit. Bait-fishing trips are also available. Departure spots depend on time and tides.

Tidewater Sportfishing Charters (⊠ Rte. 103, Town Dock, York Harbor ☎ 207/363–6524) specializes in light tackle and fly-fishing for striped bass and bluefish.

HIKING & WALKING For a good beachcombing exploration and a jaunt across York's beloved Wiggly Bridge, take the **Shore Walk.** You can start at various spots—either from Route 103 alongside York Harbor (there is minimal parking here, but you'll know it when you see the bridge), or from the George Marshall Store in York Village (part of the York Historical Society complex, 140 Lindsay Road).

For a peek into the Rachel Carson National Wildlife Refuge, take the 2-mi **Brave Boat Harbor Trail,** which is one of the few walking trails available in the refuge. It's a prime bird-watching area. Look for Brave Boat Harbor Road just off Route 103 for trail access and parking.

en route   Continue along Route 1A from York Harbor to York Beach. The waterfront mansions eventually give way to seaside trailer parks, 1950s-style resort motels, and stunning sections of rocky shores and beaches.

York Beach

❺ *6 mi north of York Harbor via Rte. 1A.*

Like many shorefront towns in Maine, York Beach has a long, long history of entertaining summer visitors. Take away today's bikinis and boom box music and it's easy to imagine squealing bathers adorned in the full-length bathing garb of the late 19th century. Just as they did back then, visitors today come here to eat ice cream, enjoy carnival-like novelties, and indulge in the sun and sea air.

York Beach is a real family destination, devoid of all things staid and stuffy—children are meant to be both seen and heard here, and that's part of what gives the area its invigorating feel. Just beyond the sands of Short Sand Beach are a host of amusements, from bowling to indoor minigolf and the Fun-O-Rama arcade.

Head out a couple of miles on the peninsula to see **Nubble Light,** said to be one of the most photographed lighthouses on the globe. Set out on a hill of rocks, the lighthouse is still in use. Direct access is prohibited, but an informational center shares the 1879 light's history. Find parking at Sohier Park, at the end of Nubble Road, as well as restrooms and plenty of benches. ⊠ *The end of Nubble Rd., off Route 1A.*

Between the zoo and the carnival rides, it's sometimes hard to distinguish the wild animals from the kids at **York's Wild Kingdom.** Combination tickets can be purchased to visit the zoo and the amusement park, and discounts are available for kids under 10. There are extensive picnic areas, paddle boats, elephant shows, and plenty of other amusements. The zoo has an impressive variety of exotic animals and is home to the state's only white Bengal tiger. ⊠ *U.S. 1, also entrance from Short Sands Beach area, York* ☎ *207/363–4911* ⊕ *www.yorkzoo.com* ⌨ *$12.50 zoo only, $16.50 zoo and rides* ☉ *Closed Oct.–late May.*

Where to Stay & Eat

$–$$$$ ✕ **Fox's Lobster House.** This place is a little pricier than your average fried-seafood joint (then again, few are cheap), but its location is ideal—right up by Nubble Light and with grand views of the ocean beyond. The place gets packed, but the scenery should make the wait quite bearable. You can get takeout or dine inside with table service. For the most ambitious appetite, see if you can tackle the 3-pound baked stuffed lobster. In addition to the regular offering of seafood, choose from steaks, chicken, and pasta; save room for the homemade blueberry pie. ⊠ *Nubble Point* ☎ *207/363–2643* ⊟ *MC, V* ⚛ *Reservations not accepted* ☉ *Closed Nov.–Apr.*

$$–$$$ ✕ **Mimmo's.** Water views can be had from some tables at this casual but very busy spot on Long Sands Beach. The menu is Italian, with lots of pastas to choose from and classics such as eggplant parmigiana. If you can't get enough seafood, try the *coastazurro,* with shrimp, haddock, calamari, and mussels sautéed with garlic. There is no liquor service here; diners are welcome to bring their own. If you're going for dinner, reservations are a good idea. ⊠ *Long Beach Ave. (Rte. 1A)* ☎ *207/363–3807* ⊟ *AE, MC, V.*

¢   ✕ **The Goldenrod.** If you wanted to—and you are on vacation—you could eat nothing but the famous taffy here, made just about the same way today as it was back in 1896. The famous Goldenrod Kisses, made to the tune of 65 tons per year, are a great attraction and people line the windows to watch the process. Aside from the famous taffy, this eating place is family oriented, very reasonably priced, and a great place to get ice cream from the old-fashioned soda fountain. Breakfast is served all day while the simple lunch menu doubles as dinner; choose from sandwiches and burgers. There is even penny candy for sale for, yes, a penny a piece. ⊠ *Railroad Ave.* ☎ *207/363–2621* ⊟ *AE, MC, V* ☺ *Closed Columbus Day–late May.*

$$–$$$$ ✕⬚ **The Union Bluff Hotel.** Although this hotel had to be rebuilt after a devastating fire, the face of the massive, turreted structure remains very similar to its mid-19th-century beginnings. Things are quite a bit more modern these days but its original grandeur is still evident. Many of the rooms have endless ocean views from private balconies; those that don't are so close that you can still smell the sea air. Rooms don't have a lot of antique character but they feature all the amenities of contemporary hotels, with standard, comfortable furnishings. You couldn't get much closer to all the activity of Short Sands Beach, which is just steps away. The pub serves lunch and dinner daily and has a late-night menu; the restaurant is open for breakfast and dinner. ⊠ *8 Beach St., 03910* ☎ *207/363–1333 or 800/833–0721* ⊕ *www.unionbluff.com* ↵ *36 rooms and 6 suites in main inn, 21 rooms in adjacent motel* ⚐ *Restaurant, pub, cable TV, some in-room Jacuzzis, some in-room fireplaces, refrigerators* ⊟ *AE, D, MC, V.*

$$$ ✕⬚ **Inn at Long Sands.** You can't stay much closer to the beach than this, and most rooms have private balconies from which to enjoy the view of Long Sands Beach. The inn is in the milder area of York Beach, a mile or so from the downtown action. Rooms are simply decorated and comfortable, with such touches as wallpapered walls and four-poster beds. The front porch is a great place for people-watching. It's worth getting breakfast (not included in the room rate) at the on-site restaurant—try the rum raisin French toast or one of their well-stuffed omelettes. The little café is also open nightly for dessert and coffee. ⊠ *125 Long Beach Ave. (Rte. 1A), 03910* ☎ *207/363–5132 or 800/927–5132* ⊕ *www.innatlongsands.com* ↵ *8 rooms* ⚐ *Restaurant, cable TV* ⊟ *AE, MC, V.*

$–$$ ⬚ **Sand & Surf B&B.** This big farmhouse with its expansive front porch was once a boardinghouse, as is evident by its smallish rooms and shared baths. Despite that, the prices are very reasonable for the area and the rooms are cheery and outfitted with pedestal sinks. The incredible views, location, and giant homemade breakfasts are what keep people coming back year after year. The house sits on a bluff and overlooks the ocean and the fun of nearby York Beach. It's close enough to get there leisurely on foot yet far enough away to be peacefully removed. Sunset from the front porch is sublime. ⊠ *53 Ocean Ave. Ext., 03910* ☎ *207/363–2554* ⊕ *http://sandandsurf.islovely.com* ↵ *11 rooms with shared bath* ⚐ *No room phones, no room TVs* ⊟ *MC, V* ☺ *Closed Columbus Day–Memorial Day* ¶⊙⟨ *BP.*

Nightlife & the Arts

Inn on the Blues (⊠ 7 Ocean Ave., York Beach ☎ 207/351–3221) is a hopping blues club that attracts national bands.

Sports & the Outdoors

Route 1A runs right behind **Long Sands Beach,** a 1½-mi stretch of sand in York Beach that has roadside parking and a bathhouse. **Short Sands**

Beach in York Beach has a bathhouse and is convenient to restaurants and shops.

Rent bikes, scooters, and baby joggers at **Beached Wheels** (✉ 52 Main St. ☎ 207/363–8021).

Shopping

There is no shortage of souvenir shopping here. Be sure to get some Goldenrod Kisses—Maine's famous saltwater taffy, made the same way today as it has been for more than a century—at the Goldenrod (*see* Where to Stay & Eat *above*). If you need new flip-flops, a sweatshirt, or a bathing suit to brave the waters of the ocean, you'll find plenty to choose from. Route 1A is the main drag, with smaller, alley-like streets running perpendicular to it; the center of town is easily walkable.

> en route

Follow Route 1A out of boisterous York Beach into the quieter reaches of Cape Neddick.

Cape Neddick

❻ *4 mi north of York Beach via Rte. 1A, just north of York on U.S. 1.*

Cape Neddick is one of the more peaceful of York's villages, running from the water (and Route 1A), along U.S. 1 between York and Ogunquit. Not heavily developed, there are many modest residential homes here with a sprinkling of businesses catering to both locals and visitors. There are a few restaurants and inns, but no distinct downtown center. The views are a nice combination of water, pastoral, and wooded landscapes.

> off the beaten path

MOUNT AGAMENTICUS PARK – Maintained by the York Parks and Recreation Department, this humble summit of 692 feet above sea level is said to be the highest peak along the Atlantic Seaboard. That may not seem like much, but if you choose to hike to the top, you will be rewarded with incredible views that span all the way to the White Mountains in New Hampshire. If you don't want to hoof it (though it's not very steep), there is parking at the top. The Nature Conservancy has chosen the site as very significant owing to the variety of unusual natural flora and fauna. To get here, take Mountain Road just off U.S. 1 in Cape Neddick (just after Flo's Steamed Hot Dogs) and follow the signs. The area is open daily, with no charge. It's a popular place for equestrians and cyclists as well as families and hikers.

Where to Stay & Eat

$$$–$$$$ ✕ **Frankie & Johnny's Natural Food Restaurant.** If you've had about all the fried seafood and calories you can stand for one day, try this casual little spot that focuses on healthy—but tasty—meals. Choose from a variety of vegetarian dishes as well as seafood, poultry, and meat options. The toasted peppercorn seared sushi-grade tuna, served with coconut risotto on gingered vegetables, is excellent. You're welcome and encouraged to bring your own libations. Dinner is served Thursday through Sunday. ✉ *1594 U.S. 1, Cape Neddick* ☎ *207/363–1909* 🗐 *No credit cards* ⊙ *Closed Dec.–Mar. No lunch.*

★ **$$$–$$$$** ✕ **Clay Hill Farm.** Set on 30 acres of pastoral farmland, this is a popular place for elegant weddings. It has also built a long-standing reputation for excellence. If you can bear to forgo the lobster crêpe—a scallion crêpe wrapped around fresh Maine lobster, caramelized onions, and spinach served over toasted almond rice pilaf and drizzled with Newburg sauce—find out what the intriguing nightly chef's special might be. An extensive wine list complements the menu, and there is a pianist in the dining room Wednesday through Saturday nights in season. Jeans and sneakers are not allowed. ✉ *220 Clay Hill Rd.* ☎ *207/361–2272* ⚓ *Reservations essential* 🗐 *AE, D, MC, V.*

¢–$$$ ✕ **Cape Neddick Lobster Pound.** At this casual harborside restaurant, the nautical decor reflects the menu. All kinds of seafood, including lobster, are served. A children's menu and outdoor dining are available. ✉ *Shore Rd., Cape Neddick* ☎ *207/363–5471* 🗐 *MC, V* ⊙ *Closed Jan.–Mar.*

¢ ✕ **Flo's Steamed Hot Dogs.** Yes, it seems crazy to highlight a hot dog stand, but this is no ordinary place. Who would guess that a hot dog could make it into *Saveur* and *Gourmet* magazines? But there is something grand about this shabby, red-shingle shack that has been dealing dogs since 1959. The line is out the door most days but the operation is so efficient that the wait is not long at all. Flo has passed but her granddaughter keeps the business going, selling countless thousands of hot dogs each year. Be sure to ask for the special sauce—consisting of, among other secret things, hot sauce and mayo (you can even take home a bottle of the sauce, and you'll want to). ✉ *1359 U.S. 1* ⊙ *Closed Wed.*

$–$$ 🏨 **Country View Motel & Guesthouse.** Set back along one of U.S. 1's less hectic sections is this appealing little motel—it looks more like an inn than what you usually envision as a motel. There are a few rooms in the main house and the rest are in the adjacent motel complex. It's clean, pretty, and in a good central location for exploring the Yorks and Ogunquit, which are just miles away. Suites sleep up to four people and have full kitchens. ✉ *1521 U.S. 1, 03902* ☎ *207/363–7160 or 800/258–6598* ⊕ *www.countryviewmotel.com* 🛏 *20 rooms, 4 suites* ᗢ *Some kitchens, some kitchenettes, some microwaves, refrigerators, cable TV, pool, pets allowed (fee)* 🗐 *MC, V* ᠍⃝ *CP.*

Sports & the Outdoors

For a challenging 18-hole round, head to the **Cape Neddick Country Club** (✉ 1480 U.S. 1 ☎ 207/361–2011 ⊕ www.capeneddickgolf.com), where the public is welcome. Greens fees start at $50.

Offering a host of various fishing and kayak guided tours is **Eldredge Bros. Fly Shop** (✉ 1480 U.S. 1 ☎ 207/363–9269 or 207/363–9279 ⊕ www.eldredgeflyshop.com). Fishing trips are in fresh- or saltwater; kayak trips come in all types. Rod-and-reel rentals are also available.

Hop on one of the regularly scheduled guided kayak trips with **Excursions/Coastal Maine Outfitting Co.** (✉ U.S. 1 ☎ 207/363–0181 ⊕ www.excursionsinmaine.com). You can cruise along the shoreline or sign up for an overnight paddle. Reservations are recommended. Prices start around $55 (morning trip includes lunch). Kayaks and other boats are available for rental.

Shopping

Home furnishings with an antique feel are the specialty of **Jeremiah Campbell & Company** (✉ 1537 U.S. 1 ☎ 207/363–8499). Everything here is handcrafted, from rugs, decoys, furniture, and lighting to glassware. The shop is closed Wednesday.

Quilt and fabric lovers will delight in a visit to **Knight's Quilt Shop** (✉ 1901 U.S. 1 ☎ 207/361–2500), where quilts and everything needed to make them—including instructional classes—can be found.

For a huge selection of glassworks, pottery, and jewelry, stop at **Panache Gallery of Fine American Crafts** (✉ 1949 U.S. 1 ☎ 207/646–4878).

en route

If you're already on Route 1A, you have two options when continuing on to Ogunquit: Stay on Route 1A, which will merge with U.S. 1 and take you into downtown Ogunquit. Or, for a slower, more winding scenic jaunt, take a right just out of York Beach onto Shore Road. You'll pass impeccable homes and get frequent glimpses of the rocky coast before ending up just shy of Perkins Cove; continue to the village of Ogunquit by turning left at the end of the road.

Ogunquit

❼ *10 mi north of the Yorks, 39 mi southwest of Portland.*

Probably more than any other Southern Coast community, Ogunquit blends coastal ambience with style. The village became a resort in the 1880s and gained fame as an artists' colony. A mini Provincetown, Ogunquit has a gay population that swells in summer; many inns and small clubs cater to a primarily gay and lesbian clientele. Families love the protected beach area and friendly environment. Shore Road, which takes you into downtown, passes the 100-foot Bald Head Cliff, with views up and down the coast. On a stormy day the surf can be quite wild here.

Perkins Cove, a neck of land connected to the mainland by Oarweed Road and a pedestrian drawbridge, has a jumble of sea-beaten fish houses. These have largely been transformed by the tide of tourism to shops and restaurants. When you've had your fill of browsing and jostling the crowds, ★ stroll out along the **Marginal Way,** a mile-long footpath between Ogunquit and Perkins Cove that hugs the shore of a rocky promontory known as Israel's Head. Benches along the route give walkers an opportunity to stop and appreciate the open sea vistas, flowering bushes, and million-dollar homes.

The small but worthwhile **Ogunquit Museum of American Art,** dedicated to 20th-century American art, overlooks the ocean and is set amid a 3-acre sculpture garden. Inside are works by Henry Strater, Marsden Hartley, Winslow Homer, Edward Hopper, Gaston Lachaise, Marguerite Zorach, and Louise Nevelson. The huge windows of the sculpture court command a superb view of cliffs and ocean. ☒ *543 Shore Rd.* ☎ *207/646–4909* ☜ *$4* ☉ *July–mid-Oct., Mon.–Sat. 10:30–5, Sun. 2–5.*

For a look at Ogunquit's colorful past, including its early days as a thriving art colony as well as its maritime history, visit the **Ogunquit Heritage Museum.** Exhibits in the Winn House, which itself dates to 1785, also focus on colonial architecture. ☒ *86 Obed's La.* ☎ *207/646–0296* ☜ *Donations accepted* ☉ *June–Sept., Tues.–Sat. 1–4.*

The **Ogunquit Trolley** is one of the best things that happened to this area. Parking in the village is troublesome and expensive, beach parking is costly and often limited, and isn't it just easier to leave your car parked at your hotel? The trolley begins operation in May and stays in service until Columbus Day. The fare is a mere $1.50 (at this writing) and kids under 10 ride free with an adult. Stops are numerous along the route that begins at Perkins Cove and follows Shore Road through town, down to Ogunquit Beach, and out along U.S. 1 up to Wells (where a connecting Wells trolley takes over for northern travel). Maps are available wherever you find brochures and at the Chamber of Commerce Welcome Center on U.S. 1, just as you enter Ogunquit from the south. ☍ *Box 2368, Ogunquit 03907* ☎ *207/646–1411.*

Where to Stay & Eat

$$$$ ✕ **Arrows.** Elegant simplicity is the hallmark of this restaurant in an 18th-century farmhouse, 2 mi up a back road. Grilled salmon and radicchio with marinated fennel and baked polenta, and Chinese-style duck glazed with molasses are typical entrées on the daily-changing menu. The Maine crabmeat mousse and lobster risotto appetizers, and desserts such as strawberry shortcake with Chantilly cream, are also beautifully executed. ☒ *Berwick Rd.* ☎ *207/361–1100* ☜ *Reservations essential* ☰ *MC, V* ☉ *Closed Mon. and mid-Dec.–mid-Apr. No lunch.*

★ ✕ **Five-O Shore Rd.** Right on Main Street in the thick of the action, this
$$$–$$$$ place gets really busy, but justly so. Popular with the hip and sophisticated crowd, you're likely to see the signature "cosmotinis" topping nearly every table. The menu is inventive, taking such common things as lobster and swordfish to new heights—like the lobster and scallop ravioli in a lemon tarragon pesto, or swordfish served with a papaya and cabbage slaw. If you're not hungry, just go for the cocktails (a staggering menu to choose from) and the lively atmosphere. There's also a late-night lounge menu. ☒ *50 Shore Rd.* ☎ *207/646–5001* ☜ *Reservations essential* ☰ *AE, D, MC, V.*

★ **$$$–$$$$** ✕ **98 Provence.** Country French ambience provides a fitting backdrop for chef Pierre Gignac's French fare. Begin with the duck foie gras or country-style rabbit pâté, and follow it up with a cassoulet or medallion of veal tenderloin with a wild mushroom cream sauce. ☒ *104 Shore Rd.* ☎ *207/646–9898* ☜ *Reservations essential* ☰ *MC, V.*

$$–$$$$ ✕ **Bintliff's Restaurant.** The lounge is inviting with velvet chairs and couches, but it's the food and the extensive wine list that bring people back again and again. Steaks are a specialty here, but don't overlook the other intriguing entrées. One recommendation is the Eggplant Napoleon, combining crispy eggplant, tomatoes, braised onions, fresh mozzarella, roasted red peppers, and marinated portobello mushrooms. This is also one of the best spots around for Sunday brunch and breakfast. ⊠ *335 Main St.* ☎ *207/646–3111* ⌦ *Reservations essential* ☱ *AE, D, MC, V.*

$$–$$$$ ✗ **Poor Richard's Tavern.** In this 18th-century building, the chef prepares traditional New England cooking with a French flair. Try the pot roast jardinière or the lobster pie. There's a pianist on Friday and Saturday evenings. The casual dining room exudes a tavern-like feel with dark wood throughout and colonial touches in decor. ⊠ *125 Shore Rd.* ☎ *207/646–4722* ⌦ *Reservations essential* ☱ *AE, D, MC, V.*

$$–$$$ ✗ **Gypsy Sweethearts.** The multiethnic fare at this popular bistro ranges from shrimp margarita to chili-crusted rack of lamb to Jamaican jerk-rubbed chicken. In the dining area, cobalt-blue glassware accents the white-draped tables. ⊠ *10 Shore Rd.* ☎ *207/646–7021* ☱ *MC, V* ⊘ *Closed Mon. and Jan.–Apr. No lunch.*

$$–$$$ ✗ **Hurricane.** Don't let the weather-beaten exterior or the frenzied atmosphere inside deter you—this small seafood bar and grill with spectacular views of the crashing surf turns out first-rate dishes. Start with lobster chowder or a chilled fresh-shrimp spring roll. Entrées may include lobster cioppino, rack of lamb, or fire-roasted red snapper. A second Hurricane is on Dock Square, in Kennebunkport. ⊠ *Oarweed La., Perkins Cove* ☎ *207/646–6348 or 800/649–6348* ☱ *AE, D, DC, MC, V* ⊘ *Closed early Jan.*

$$$$ ▥ **Cliff House.** Elsie Jane Weare opened the Cliff House in 1872, and her great granddaughter Kathryn now presides over the sprawling oceanfront resort atop Bald Head Cliff. Those who favor country decor and artsy touches may find the rooms (and the physical complex itself) lack warmth, but the resort's facilities are the best in the region. The resort center is equipped with a full health spa, new pools, and 32 oversize rooms with gas fireplaces and ocean views. This place has a loyal following, so reserve well in advance. ⊠ *2 E. Shore Rd.* ⬠ *Box 2274, 03907* ☎ *207/361–1000* ⎙ *207/361–2122* ⊕ *www.cliffhousemaine.com* ⋗ *194 rooms, 2 suites* ⅋ *Restaurant, in-room data ports, cable TV, 2 tennis courts, 2 pools (1 indoor), health club, hot tub, sauna, spa; no smoking* ☱ *AE, D, MC, V* ⊘ *Closed mid-Dec.–late Mar.*

$$$–$$$$ ▥ **The Black Boar Inn.** The original part of this inn dates to 1674, an
FodorśChoice   era that is reflected in the beauty of the wide-pine floors and the fire-
★   places in every room. A sense of absolute luxury pervades here. The interior is exquisite, with bead board, richly colored rugs and comforters, William Morris–like wallpaper, tiled bathrooms, and many antiques. While the manager wasn't sure where the "wild boar" name originated, evidence of the beast abounds in art and sculpture throughout. Wine and hors d'oeuvres are served in the afternoon and can be enjoyed on the front terrace, overlooking the massive gardens and the world of Main Street beyond. Cottages are rented by the week and are notable for their exposed wood, vaulted ceilings, and full kitchens. ⊠ *277 Main St., 03907* ☎ *207/646–2112* ⊕ *www.blackboarinn.com* ⋗ *6 rooms, 3 cottages* ⅋ *Cable TV, Internet; no TVs in some rooms* ☱ *MC, V* ⑩ *BP.*

$$$–$$$$ ▥ **Ogunquit Resort Motel.** Right along U.S. 1, about 2 mi north of Ogunquit village, sprawls this large complex that is great for families and for those who prefer larger hotels to B&Bs. Boasting the largest pool in Ogunquit, the resort also has an outdoor hot tub. Beachgoers can walk to Footbridge Beach just about a half mile away. Choose from deluxe, superior, and luxury rooms; luxury suites have fireplaces and Jacuzzi tubs. Unusual for hotels of this size is the free continental breakfast laid out each morning. You can leave your car here and hop on the trolley to get around, saving yourself the agony (and expense) of trying to park in town or at the beach. Ask about Internet specials. ⊠ *719 Main St. (U.S. 1), 03907* ☎ *800/893–9098* ⊕ *www.ogunquitresort.com* ⇝ *85 rooms, 8 suites* ⚘ *Refrigerators, cable TV, outdoor pool, gym, outdoor hot tub, video game room* ⊟ *AE, D, MC, V* ⦿⊦ *CP.*

$$$ ⊡ **Rockmere Lodge.** Midway along Ogunquit's Marginal Way, this shingle-style Victorian cottage is an ideal retreat from the hustle and bustle of Perkins Cove. All the rooms have corner locations and are large and airy, and all but one have ocean views. Rooms are fluffed to the hilt with colorful pillows, curtains, antiques, and other objects. You'll find it easy to laze the day away on the wraparound porch or in the gardens. ⊠ *150 Stearns Rd.* ⌖ *Box 278, 03907* ☎ *207/646–2985* ⊞ *207/646–6947* ⊕ *www.rockmere.com* ⇝ *8 rooms* ⚘ *Cable TV, refrigerators; no a/c, no room phones, no children under 16* ⊟ *AE, D, MC, V* ⦿ *Closed late Nov.–mid-Apr.* ⦿⊦ *CP.*

$$–$$$ ⊡ **The Marginal Way House.** This may be the best location in all of Ogunquit if you want to be close to the water. The expansive lawn of the complex stretches down from the main 1880s house right to the banks of the tumbling Ogunquit River just as it breaks from the sea. One apartment sits on that edge, as does another shingled building that houses more rooms with decks atop the raging waters. Rooms have floral wallpaper, lots of wicker, and a curious assortment of attic-styled artwork—unfussy, a bit outdated, but very comfortable. Guests spend a lot of time on the back porch area, where morning coffee is available, or out among the flowers in the yard. It's a two-minute walk to town and five minutes to the beach across the footbridge. Apartments are rented weekly in high season. ⊠ *Wharf La., 03907* ☎ *207/646–8801* ⊕ *www. marginalwayhouse.com.* ⇝ *23 rooms, 7 suites, 1 apartment* ⚘ *Refrigerators, some kitchenettes, some pets allowed; no a/c in some rooms, no room TVs* ⊟ *MC, V* ⦿ *Closed Nov.–Apr.*

$$–$$$ ⊡ **Morning Dove B & B.** Antiques fill most spaces in this grand 1860 home, yet the airy rooms remain uncluttered and comfortable. Many of the four-poster and antique brass beds are covered in crisp white spreads; colorful quilts and some fireplaces provide extra warmth. Many guests request to eat the lavish breakfasts prepared by innkeepers Jane and Fred Garland on the large front porch. The yard is abloom with gardens on this quiet street that is about midway between the center of town and Perkins Cove. Beach chairs and towels are provided if you need them, an example of the good nature that pervades here. The innkeepers accept credit cards but prefer to be paid in cash, or by check. ⊠ *13 Bourne La., 03907* ☎ *207/646–3891* ⊕ *www.themorningdove.com* ⇝ *3 rooms, 2 suites* ⚘ *Cable TV, refrigerators; no room phones, no children under 16* ⊟ *MC, V* ⦿⊦ *BP.*

$$ ⊡ **Yardarm Village Inn.** With stenciling winding up stairs and along many of its walls and tin ceilings, this inn has been lovingly cared for since its construction in the late 19th century. Set near the now de-

funct trolley bed of the same era, the peaceful home is a very short walk from the activity of Perkins Cove. Standard rooms are large and suites have separate sitting rooms—a good spot to enjoy the fruits of the inn's in-house gourmet wine and cheese shop. Those eager to get on the water can cruise with the innkeepers on their 26-foot single sail (about $20 for two hours). A continental breakfast is offered for an extra fee. ⊠ *406 Shore Rd., 03907* ☎ *207/646–7006 or 888/927–3276* 🖷 *207/646–9034* ⊕ *www.yardarmvillageinn.com* ⤴ *5 rooms, 3 suites* ⌂ *Cable TV, refrigerators; no room phones* ⊟ *No credit cards* ⊙ *Closed Nov.–Apr.*

Nightlife & the Arts

Much of the nightlife in Ogunquit revolves around the precincts of Ogunquit Square and Perkins Cove, where people stroll, often enjoying an after-dinner ice cream cone or espresso. Ogunquit is popular with gay and lesbian visitors, and its club scene reflects this.

Bernard's (⊠ 82 Shore Rd. ☎ 207/646–8200) gets loud with live music and dancing, as well as karaoke and comedy. **Jonathan's Restaurant** (⊠ 2 Bourne La. ☎ 207/646–4777) hosts live entertainment—usually blues—during peak season, from June to mid-October. **Maine Street** (⊠ 195 Main St. ☎ 207/646–5101) has live entertainment and is a popular dance spot.

The movies are first-run but that's not the only attraction at **Leavitt Fine Arts Theatre** (⊠ 295 Main St. ☎ 207/646–3213), which has been Maine's summer theater since 1923. Look for the grand architectural elements of that earlier era before the movie starts.

The **Ogunquit Playhouse** (⊠ U.S. 1 ☎ 207/646–5511 ⊕ www.ogunquitplayhouse.org), one of America's oldest summer theaters, mounts plays and musicals with well-known actors of both stage and screen from late June to Labor Day. Ogunquit's summer repertory company, the **Booth Theater** (⊠ 13 Beach St. ☎ 207/646–8142 ⊕ www.bothproductions.com), stages performances nightly in summer, ranging from Neil Simon and Stephen Sondheim to such popular favorites as *School House Rock!*. The season kicks off around mid-June and continues through August.

Sports & the Outdoors

A great spot to stretch your legs and have a picnic is **Beach Plum Farm,** a 22-acre parcel of land with several barns and a house. Maintained by the Great Works Regional Land Trust, the area is open from dawn to dusk and features ocean views and community gardens. Benches and a marked path around the perimeter welcome walkers.

Ogunquit Beach, a 3-mi-wide stretch of sand at the mouth of the Ogunquit River, has snack bars, a boardwalk, restrooms, and changing areas (at the Beach Street entrance). Families gravitate to the ends; gay visitors camp at the beach's middle. The less-crowded section to the north is accessible by footbridge and has portable restrooms, all-day paid parking, and trolley service.

Liquid Dreams Surf Shop (⊠ 731 Main St. ☎ 207/641–2545 ⊕ www.finestkindcruises.com) rents surfing equipment (you will want the wetsuit) and bodyboards, as well as offering bathing suits and other wave-riding supplies.

Anglers can sign on with **Bunny Clark Deep Sea Fishing** (✉ Perkins Cove ☎ 207/646–2214), which leaves the dock twice daily from early April through mid-November.

The long boat ride with **Deborah Ann Whalewatching** (✉ Perkins Cove ☎ 207/361–9501) is worth it to witness humpback and finback whales in their natural habitat out on Jefferies Ledge.

Finestkind (✉ Perkins Cove ☎ 207/646–5227 ⊕ www.finestkindcruises.com) operates cocktail cruises, lobstering trips, and cruises to Nubble Light.

Pack a picnic for a billowy 1½- or 2-hour sail with *The Silverlining* (✉ Perkins Cove ☎ 207/646–9800), a 42-foot wooden sloop. She leaves the dock at Perkins Cove six times daily.

For more deep-sea fishing adventures, climb aboard the *Ugly Anne* (✉ Perkins Cove ☎ 207/646–7202), for half- or full-day trips.

Shopping

Ogunquit Village and Perkins Cove are well stocked with shops, many carrying the ubiquitous supply of Maine lobster T-shirts and tourist-type gadgets. There are also some good galleries and specialty spots, selling everything from artwork and pottery to fine linens and apparel.

More than just an art gallery, the **Barn Gallery** (✉ Shore Rd. and Bourne La. ☎ 207/646–8400) hosts special programs, workshops, and exhibitions by some well-known local artists.

Peruse the possible treasures at the multidealer **Blacksmith's Antique Mall** (✉ 166 Main St. ☎ 207/646–9643), where you probably won't find any bargains; but then again, you might!

Stock up in case of rain at **Books Ink** (✉ Perkins Cove ☎ 207/361–2602), where you'll find an array of toys, games, and puzzles in addition to books.

Forget all the high-tech gadgets and worries of the future at the **History Store** (✉ 6A Shore Rd. ☎ 207/646–1776). All things past are captured in books, music, statuary, and more.

Aside from a good collection of stained glass, the wares at **Out of the Blue** (✉ 19 Perkins Cove Rd. ☎ 207/646–0430) include home and garden accoutrements, jewelry, and all things related to wine.

en route The summer traffic isn't the only thing that may make your northern drive up U.S. 1 from Ogunquit to Wells a slow one—this stretch is an **antique lover's path to paradise.** Individual shops with antiques spilling out into the driveways and lawns are numerous, as are the multidealer and multibuilding shops. You can find quilts, glassware, maritime items, aged books, and hundreds of other unknown things along this route. Wells is also home to a great outdoor flea market, held on weekends and a few other days during the week; you can't miss it, it's on the right side of U.S. 1 as you drive by going north.

Wells

8 *5 mi north of Ogunquit, 34 mi southwest of Portland.*

Lacking any kind of noticeable village center, Wells could be easily over-looked as nothing more than a commercial stretch on U.S. 1 between Ogun-quit and the Kennebunks. But look more closely—this is a place where people come to enjoy some of the best beaches on the coast. Part of Ogun-quit until 1980, this family-oriented beach community has 7 mi of densely populated shoreline, along with nature preserves where you can explore salt marshes and tidal pools, and see birds and waterfowl.

The area is also rich in history; Wells has been a thriving community in one way or another since the mid-1600s. It's actually a little more peaceful now than it was back then—the flocks of tourists that crowd the beaches and roadsides are far friendlier than the Native Americans and French who engaged in near constant warfare and attacks during the 17th century.

In the **Wells Reserve at Laudholm Farm,** extensive trails lace the 1,600 acres of meadows, orchards, fields, and salt marshes, as well as two estuar-ies and 9 mi of seashore. Laudholm Farm, an 18th-century saltwater farm, houses the visitor center, where an introductory slide show is screened and a bookstore is well stocked with publications of local and state history. Within the farmhouse are rooms with historical exhibits and information; outside in the separate ecology center are learning ex-hibits geared mainly for kids. In winter, cross-country skiing is permit-ted. ⊠ *342 Laudholm Farm Rd.* ☎ *207/646–1555* ⊕ *www.wellsreserve. org* ✑ *$2 parking fee* ☉ *Grounds daily 8–5; visitor center May–Dec., Mon.–Sat. 10–4, Sun. noon–4; Jan.–Apr., Sat. 10–4, Sun. noon–4.*

The **Rachel Carson National Wildlife Refuge** (⊠ Rte. 9 ☎ 207/646–9226) has a mile-long-loop nature trail through a salt marsh. The trail bor-ders the Little River and a white-pine forest where migrating birds and waterfowl of many varieties are regularly spotted.

The headquarters for both the Ogunquit and Wells Historical Society, the **Meetinghouse Museum and Library** hosts a series of concerts, pro-grams, tours, and exhibits. The library is a gold mine for those inter-ested in genealogy. ⊠ *983 U.S. 1* ☎ *207/646–4775* ✑ *Donations accepted* ☉ *June–mid-Oct., Tues.–Thurs. 10–4; mid-Oct.–May, Wed. and Thurs. 10–4.*

need a break?

How about a doughnut . . . a really superior one that the same family has been making since 1955. The doughnuts from **Congdon's** (⊠ U.S. 1 ☎ 207/646–4219) easily rival (many say there is no contest) some of those other famous places we won't mention here. Choose from about 30 different varieties, though the plain really gives you an idea of just how good these doughnuts are. There's a drive-through window so you don't have to get out of the car; or you can take a seat inside and have breakfast or lunch with your plain doughnut.

(C) A must for motor fanatics and youngsters, the **Wells Auto Museum** has more than 80 vintage cars, antique coin games, and a restored Model T you can ride in. ⊠ *U.S. 1* ☎ *207/646–9064* 🖾 *$5 adults; $2 kids 12 and under* ⊙ *Memorial Day–Columbus Day, daily 10–5.*

Leave your car at your hotel and take the **Wells Trolley** to the beach or to the shops on U.S. 1. The seasonal trolley makes pickups at the Wells Transportation Center when the Downeaster (the Amtrak train with service from Boston to Portland) pulls in; if you want to continue south toward Ogunquit, the two town trolleys meet at the Wells Chamber of Commerce on U.S. 1; get a route map here. Adult fare is $1; kids under 10 ride free. ☎ *207/646–2451* ⊕ *www.wellschamber.org.*

Where to Stay & Eat

$–$$$ ✕ **Billy's Chowder House.** Locals head to this simple restaurant in a salt marsh for the generous lobster rolls, haddock sandwiches, and chowders. Big windows in the bright dining rooms overlook the marsh. ⊠ *216 Mile Rd.* ☎ *207/646–7558* ⊟ *AE, D, MC, V* ⊙ *Closed mid-Dec.–mid-Jan.*

$–$$$ ✕ **Maine Diner.** It's the real thing here—one look at the nostalgic (and authentic 1953) exterior and you start craving good diner food. You'll get a little more here . . . how many greasy spoons make an award-winning lobster pie? That's the house favorite, as well as a heavenly seafood chowder. There's plenty of fried seafood in addition to the usual diner fare, and breakfast is served all day, just as it should be. Be sure to check out the adjacent gift shop, Remember the Maine. ⊠ *2265 U.S. 1.* ☎ *207/646–4441* ⊕ *www.mainediner.com* ⊟ *D, MC, V* ⊙ *Closed 1 wk in Jan.*

¢–$$ ✕ **The Cafe at Merriland Farm.** There's a lot going on at this 200-year-old working farm and family affair. It's a great place for breakfast—home-grown berries appear in jams, jellies, crêpes, pancakes, spread over Belgian waffles, and any other place they taste good. The menu is quite creative for breakfast and lunch, going well beyond the basics with such treats as portobello Benedict, artful crêpes, grilled sandwiches, wraps, and half-pound burgers. Don't miss the desserts—luscious berries in pie, shortcake, or baked crisp. This farm is a delightful beauty. You may want to hit the on-site golf greens to fight off some of the added calories. Breakfast is served from 8 AM. From late July until the frost hits, you can pick blueberries to take home. ⊠ *545 Coles Hill Rd.* ☎ *207/646–5040* ⊕ *www.merrilandfarm.com* ⊟ *No credit cards* ⊙ *Closed mid-Dec.–Apr.*

$$–$$$ ✕🛏 **Grey Gull Inn.** This Victorian inn, built in 1893, has views of the open sea and rocks on which seals like to sun themselves. Most of the unpretentious, simply furnished rooms have ocean views. Overnight guests have access to nearby pool, golf, and tennis facilities. The restaurant ($$–$$$$) serves excellent seafood dishes such as soft-shell crabs almandine; and regional fare such as Yankee pot roast, and chicken breast rolled in walnuts. ⊠ *475 Webhannet Dr., at Moody Point* ☎ *207/646–7501* 🖶 *207/646–0938* ⊕ *www.thegreygullinn. com* 🛏 *5 rooms, 4 with bath* ⚐ *Restaurant, cable TV; no smoking* ⊟ *AE, D, MC, V* ❚◯❙ *CP.*

$$–$$$$ 🏠 **Haven by the Sea.** Once the summer mission of St. Martha's Church
Fodor'sChoice in Kennebunkport, this stunning inn has retained many of the original
★ details from its former life as a seaside church. The cathedral ceilings
and stained-glass windows remain, all gathering and spreading the
grand surrounding light. The guest rooms are spacious, some with
marsh views. Four common areas, including one with a fireplace, are
perfect spots for afternoon refreshments. The inn is one block from the
beach. ⊠ *59 Church St., 04090* ☎ *207/646–4194* 🖷 *207/646–6883*
⊕ *www.havenbythesea.com* ✍ *6 rooms, 2 suites, 1 apartment* ⟐ *Cable
TV, Internet, meeting rooms; no a/c, no children under 12, no smoking*
🖹 *AE, MC, V* ◐ *BP.*

$–$$ 🏠 **Beach Farm Inn.** Innkeepers Nancy and Craig painstakingly renovated and decorated this 19th-century farmhouse, and its gracious ap-
pointments are a testament to their care and good taste. Craig, also a
woodworker, has made a good portion of the furniture as well as sculptures throughout the home. Decorated with a multitude of antiques,
four-poster beds, ample sitting areas, and artful rugs, the home is a place
of real peace among the general busyness of Wells. The appealing enclosed breakfast area is the stage for Craig's monumental breakfasts
served each morning; if it's nice out, eat on the deck overlooking the
pool and grounds. Winter packages include wreath-making and cooking workshops. The beach is about a half-mile walk down the country road. ⊠ *97 Eldredge Rd., 04090* ☎ *207/646–8493* 🖷 *207/646–
5738* ⊕ *www.beachfarminn.com* ✍ *8 rooms, 3 with bath; 2 cottages*
⟐ *Some a/c, outdoor pool; no room phones, no room TVs, no children under 12* 🖹 *AE, MC, V* ◐ *BP.*

Nightlife & the Arts

The **summer concert series** is held in pretty Wells Harbor Park at the gazebo
(Saturday nights, July through early September). Music ranges from rock
to gospel, reggae to swing; concerts begin around 6:30 and are free. Look
for Harbor Road just off U.S. 1 by the Fire and Police stations; the park
is about 1 mi down Harbor Road.

Aran Irish Pub and Restaurant (⊠ 52 Post Rd. [U.S. 1] ☎ 207/646–1900)
has—you guessed it—live Irish music most Thursday through Sunday
nights in summer.

Sports & the Outdoors

With its thousands of acres of marsh and preserved land, Wells is a great
place for those wishing to spend a lot of time outdoors exploring land
or sea.

Nearly 7 mi of sand stretch along the boundaries of Wells, making
beach going a prime occupation. Tidal pools sheltered by rocks are filled
with all manner of creatures awaiting discovery. Parking is available for
a fee (take the trolley!) at **Crescent Beach**, along Webhannet Drive; **Wells
Beach** (at the end of Mile Road off U.S. 1) has public restrooms and two
parking areas. There is another lot at the far end of Wells Beach, at the
end of Atlantic Avenue. Across the jetty from Wells Harbor is **Drakes Island Beach** (end of Drakes Island Road off U.S. 1), which also has parking and public restrooms. Lifeguards are on hand at all the beaches.

Rent bikes, surfboards, wetsuits, boogie boards, and probably a few other things at **Wheels and Waves** (✉ 578 U.S. 1 ☎ 207/646–5774).

Many fish are bound to be caught by anglers with **Captain Satch and Sons** (☎ 207/337–0716). They offer two trips daily, from Wells Town Dock. In addition to boat trips, a guide can take you fishing from the shore within the Rachel Carson Reserve.

Go fishing along the coast or way out in the deep with **Three Ladies** (☎ 207/337–8800), leaving from Wells Harbor. Non-anglers might enjoy a two-hour scenic coastal cruise.

For smooth sailing on a classic 34-foot sloop, try **The Gift** (☎ 207/646–3758), cruising four times daily on two-hour trips leaving from Wells Town Dock.

Kayaking is popular along the coast, and **World Within Sea Kayaking** (☎ 207/646–0455) conducts guided tours with lessons. Departure points depend on time and tide.

The 9-hole golf course at **Merriland Farm** (✉ 545 Cole Hills Rd. ☎ 207/646–0508 ⊕ www.merrilandfarm.com) is pretty challenging and was built by owner–farmer Jim Morrison amid the blueberry and raspberry patches. The course is open daily (except Tuesday League Day) from April through October, with greens fees of $11. This working, 200-year-old farm also offers blueberry and raspberry picking from late July until the berries run out.

Shopping

Douglas N. Harding Rare Books (✉ 2152 Post Rd. [U.S. 1] ☎ 207/646–8785) has more than 100,000 old books, maps, and prints. **Goose-fare Antiques** (✉ 2232 Post Rd. [U.S. 1] ☎ 207/646–0505) is a group shop specializing in 18th-, 19th-, and early-20th-century antiques. The **Lighthouse Depot** (✉ U.S. 1 ☎ 207/646–0608) calls itself the world's largest lighthouse gift store, with lighthouse-theme gifts and memorabilia. **Reed's Antiques and Collectibles** (✉ 1773 Post Rd. [U.S. 1] ☎ 207/646–8010) is a multidealer shop filled with all manner of antiques, from advertising to glass, tools to toys.

R. Jorgensen (✉ 502 Post Rd. [U.S. 1] ☎ 207/646–9444) stocks 18th-and 19th-century formal and country antiques from the British Isles, Europe, and the United States. Paul McElvain is the master coppersmith of **Weathervanes of Maine** (✉ 1451 U.S. 1 ☎ 207/646–0548), making hundreds of different styles of these roof adornments. Thousands of 18th-and 19th-century antiques are stuffed into a 200-year-old barn at **Wells General Store** (✉ 2023 U.S. 1 ☎ 207/646–5553).

en route Drivers have a multitude of options going north from Wells to the Kennebunks. You can travel along U.S. 1, from Wells to the town of Kennebunk, stopping at every antiques shop along the way. To go directly to Kennebunkport, take Route 9A/35, which is a fairly breathtaking route as far as Colonial and Victorian architecture is concerned.

Another route to take from Wells, especially if you are visiting the Rachel Carson National Wildlife Refuge, is Route 9 toward Kennebunkport. Along this route are beautiful views of salt marshes, farms, and plenty of impressive homes. Route 9 will connect with Route 9A/35; follow the signs to Kennebunkport.

THE KENNEBUNKS

Approximately 6 mi north of Wells via U.S. 1, approximately 8 mi via Rte. 9.

The Kennebunks encompass Kennebunk, Kennebunk Beach, Goose Rocks Beach, Kennebunkport, Cape Porpoise, and Arundel. This cluster of seaside and inland villages provides a little bit of everything, from salt marshes to sand beaches, jumbled fishing shacks to architectural gems.

Handsome white clapboard homes with shutters give Kennebunk, a shipbuilding center in the first half of the 19th century, a quintessential New England look. Kennebunkport attracts visitors with the many boutiques and galleries surrounding Dock Square. People flock to Kennebunkport mostly in summer, but some come in early December when the Christmas Prelude is celebrated on two weekends. Santa arrives by fishing boat, and the Christmas trees are lighted as carolers stroll the sidewalks.

From Kennebunk, Route 35 south leads to Kennebunk's Lower Village. Continue south on Beach Avenue for Kennebunk Beach. To reach Kennebunkport from the Lower Village, head east on Route 9/Western Avenue and cross the drawbridge into Dock Square. Continue east on Route 9, or take scenic Ocean Avenue and Wildes District Road to quiet Cape Porpoise. To access Goose Rocks Beach, continue east on Route 9, which is now called the Mills Road. Arundel is between Kennebunk and Kennebunkport.

Kennebunk

Sometimes bypassed to get to its more touristed sister town of Kennebunkport, **Kennebunk** has its own appeal. In the 19th century the town was a major shipbuilding center; docks lined the river with hundreds of workers busily crafting the vessels that would bring immense fortune to some of the area's residents. While the trade is long gone, the evidence that remains of this great wealth exists in Kennebunk's numerous impressive mansions. Kennebunk is a classic small New England town, with an inviting shopping district, steepled churches, and fine examples of 18th- and 19th-century brick and clapboard homes. There are also plenty of natural spaces for walking, swimming, birding, and biking.

The town of Kennebunk is divided among two villages; the upper extends around the Mousam River on Route 9 while the lower is several miles down Route 35, just shy of Kennebunkport proper. The drive down Route 35 keeps visitors agog with the splendor of the area's mansions, spread out on both sides of the road. To get to the grand and gentle beaches

ALL ABOUT LOBSTERS

JUDGING FROM THE CURRENT PRICE OF A LOBSTER DINNER, it's hard to believe that lobsters were once so plentiful that servants in rich households would have contracts stating they could be served lobster "no more than two times a week."

The going price for lobsters in the 1840s was three cents per lobster—not per pound, per lobster. Today, of course, lobster fishing has become one of Maine's primary industries. You can find old-style, wood-slatted lobster traps in front of nearly every seafood restaurant in the state.

The coast of Maine, which is relatively new geologically speaking, is ideal for the breeding of lobsters. The floor of the ocean here is rocky, not sandy or silty like most ocean floors. This gives the baby lobsters places to hide from predators until they are big enough to fend for themselves.

To make sure the lobsters are not fished out, the state now has strict rules governing their catch. If a lobster is undersized, the fisherman has to throw it back. If it is oversized (and therefore a stud), he has to throw it back. If it's a female, with or without eggs, he has to throw it back. Thanks to these conservation laws—and the overfishing of cod, the baby lobsters' natural predator—the harvest is getting bigger all the time.

Because of the size restrictions, most of the lobsters you find in restaurants weigh 1¼ to 1½ pounds. However, lobsters can actually grow much larger and live to a ripe old age. The largest lobster ever caught off the coast of Maine weighed in at nearly 45 pounds and was more than 50 years old!

For an authentic, Maine-style lobster dinner, you must go to a lobster pound. Generally, these places are rustic and simple—they look more like fish-packing plants than restaurants. Hundreds of freshly caught lobsters of varying sizes are kept in pens, waiting for customers. Service is simple in the extreme. You usually sit at a wooden picnic table, and eat off a thick paper plate. A typical dinner consists of lobster—boiled or steamed—with a cup of clam chowder, and an ear of corn. Most lobster pounds offer beer and wine but usually no hard mixed drinks. The two biggest and best lobster pounds are the Lobster Pound Restaurant, in Lincolnville; and the Lobster Pound, a little north of Belfast. Both are on U.S. 1.

—Stephen Allen

of Kennebunk, go straight on Beach Avenue from the intersection of Routes 9 and 35 in the lower village.

To take a little walking tour of Kennebunk's most notable structures, begin from the Brick Store Museum, on Main Street. Head south on Main Street (turn left out of the museum) to see several extraordinary 18th-century homes, including the Nathaniel Frost House at 99 Main Street (1799) and the Benjamin Brown House at 85 Main Street (1788). When you've had your fill of historic homes, head back up toward the museum, pass the First Parish Unitarian Church (from 1773 with a Paul Revere bell) and turn right onto Summer Street. This street is an architectural showcase, revealing an array of styles from Colonial to Federal. Walking amid these grand beauties will give you a real sense of the economic prowess and glamour of the long-gone shipbuilding industry.

The cornerstone of the **Brick Store Museum,** a block-long preservation of early-19th-century commercial buildings, is **William Lord's Brick Store.** Built as a dry-goods store in 1825 in the Federal style, the building has an open-work balustrade across the roof line, granite lintels over the windows, and paired chimneys. Exhibits chronicle Kennebunk's relationship with the sea. The museum leads architectural walking tours of Kennebunk's historic Summer Street on Wednesday and Friday, from mid-June through late August. ✉ *117 Main St., Kennebunk* ☎ *207/985–4802* ⊕ *www.brickstoremuseum.org* ▣ *Donations accepted; walking tours $5* ☉ *Tues.–Fri. 10–4:30, Sat. 10–1.*

Built in 1773, just before the American Revolution, the stunning **First Parish Unitarian Church** is a marvel. The 1804 Asher-Benjamin-style steeple stands proudly atop the village and the sounds of the original Paul Revere bell can be heard for miles. ✉ *Main St.*

Where to Stay & Eat

$$–$$$ ✕ **Grissini.** This popular trattoria draws high praise for its northern Italian cuisine. Dine by the stone hearth on inclement days or on the patio when the weather's fine. You can mix and match appetizers, pizzas, salads, pastas, and entrées from the menu to suit your hunger and budget. ✉ *27 Western Ave., Kennebunk* ☎ *207/967–2211* ▤ *AE, MC, V.*

$–$$$ ✕ **Federal Jack's.** Run by the Kennebunkport Brewing Company, the complex is housed in an old shipbuilding warehouse right on the water. Many different beers are handcrafted on-site, including such favorites as Blue Fin Stout and Goat Island Light—try the sampler if you can't decide. The food is American pub style with lots of seafood elements; the clam chowder is rich and satisfying. There's also Sunday brunch, and a late-night menu for those who get hungry while playing pool in the back room. Brew tours are available. You can find the restaurant and brewery just before the bridge into Kennebunkport. ✉ *8 Western Ave., Lower Village* ☎ *207/967–4322* ▤ *AE, MC, V.*

$$–$$$ ✕▥ **Kennebunk Inn.** This stately brick building has quite a presence on Main Street in downtown Kennebunk. Rooms have a slight boarding-house feel, arranged astride long, creaky corridors; all are simply decorated with antiques. There's nothing fussy about the place. The real pride here is in the dining room, where the husband and wife chef-owner team do an incredible job with their restaurant and more casual pub.

The bistro-style menu is ambitious, including such treats as sassafras-scented pork chops, crab ravioli, salads, and wraps. The Sunday brunch is a real treat. Live Irish music is performed in the tavern on certain Sunday evenings. ⊠ *45 Main St., Kennebunk 04043* ☎ *207/985–3351* 🖷 *207/985–8865* ⊕ *www.thekennebunkinn.com* 🖙 *21 rooms* ☼ *Restaurant, pub, in-room data ports, some in-room phones, some in-room TVs, some pets allowed.* ⊟ *AE, D, MC, V* ⊟⊙⊟ *CP.*

$$$$ ⊡ **The Beach House.** Gooch's Beach is out the front door of this elegant late-19th-century inn. Rooms are individually decorated, with most colored in shades of beige and accented with country antiques that are comfortable rather than fussy. Feather beds and down comforters and pillows add a luxurious touch. Watch the sunrise from the wraparound porch, or sleep in, lulled by the sounds of the water. You can hunker down by the big stone fireplace on rainy days. ⊠ *211 Beach Ave., Kennebunk 04046* ☎ *207/967–3850* 🖷 *207/967–4719* ⊕ *www.beachhseinn.com* 🖙 *34 rooms* ☼ *Some in-room hot tubs, cable TV, in-room VCRs, beach, boating, bicycles; no smoking* ⊟ *AE, MC, V* ⊟⊙⊟ *CP.*

$$$$ ⊡ **The Seaside.** This handsome seaside property has been in the hands of the Severance family since 1667. The modern motel units, all with sliding-glass doors that open onto private decks or patios (half with ocean views), are appropriate for families; so are the cottages with one to four bedrooms. You can't get much closer to Kennebunk Beach. ⊠ *80 Beach Ave., Kennebunk 04046* ☎ *207/967–4461 or 866/300–6750* 🖷 *207/967–1135* ⊕ *http://kennebunkbeachmaine.com* 🖙 *22 rooms, 11 cottages* ☼ *Refrigerators, cable TV, beach, shuffleboard, croquet, playground, laundry service, Internet; no smoking* ⊟ *AE, MC, V* ⊟⊙⊟ *CP* ⊙ *Cottages closed Nov.–May.*

$$$–$$$$ ⊡ **Bufflehead Cove.** On the Kennebunk River at the end of a winding dirt road, this gray-shingle B&B sits amid quiet country fields and apple trees. Surprisingly, however, it's only five minutes from Dock Square. Rooms in the main house have white wicker furniture and flowers hand-painted on the walls. The Hideaway Suite, with a two-sided gas fireplace, king-size bed, and large whirlpool tub, overlooks the river. The Garden Studio has a fireplace and offers the most privacy. ⊠ *18 Bufflehead Cove Rd.* 🖃 *Box 499, Kennebunk 04046* ☎🖷 *207/967–3879* ⊕ *www.buffleheadcove.com* 🖙 *2 rooms, 3 suites, 1 cottage* ☼ *Dock, boating, Internet; no room phones, no TV in some rooms, no children under 12, no smoking* ⊟ *D, MC, V* ⊟⊙⊟ *BP* ⊙ *Closed Dec.–May.*

$–$$ ⊡ **Waldo Emerson House.** The home itself is a historical gold mine, made grand with unusual, maritime architectural touches by a shipbuilder in 1784 and later home to the great-uncle of beloved poet Ralph Waldo Emerson (the writer spent many youthful summers in the house). It's believed that the house was also a stop on the famed Underground Railroad. Notice the sliding wooden panels in the windows, said to keep inhabitants safe from the soaring arrows of angry Indians. The elegance of the wide pine floors remains, as does some remarkable original tilework around the many fireplaces. Rooms are spacious and filled with antiques and colorful quilts. Innkeepers Kathy and John Daamen provide a shuttle to area beaches and operate the Mainely Quilts gift shop next door. ⊠ *108 Summer St. (Rte. 35), Kennebunk 04046* ☎ *207/985–4250* ⊕ *www.waldoemersoninn.com* 🖙 *6 rooms* ☼ *Bicycles, Inter-*

net, shop; no a/c in some rooms, no room phones, no room TVs, no children under 12 ☐ *AE, D, MC, V* ⦿ *BP.*

Sports & the Outdoors

Kennebunk Beach has three parts: Gooch's Beach, Mother's Beach, and Kennebunk Beach. Beach Road, with its cottages and old Victorian boardinghouses, runs right behind them. Gooch's and Kennebunk attract teenagers; Mother's Beach, which has a small playground and tidal puddles for splashing, is popular with families. For parking permits (a fee is charged in summer), go to the **Kennebunk Town Office** (☒ 1 Summer St. [Rte. 35] ☎ 207/985–2102).

For an unusual exploring treat, visit the **Kennebunk Plains** (☒ Rte. 99 west, a few miles out of Kennebunk ☎ 207/729–5181), an 1,100-acre protected grasslands habitat that is home to several rare and endangered species of vegetation and wildlife. Locally known as the blueberry plains, a good portion of the area is abloom with the hues of ripening wild blueberries in late July; after August 1 visitors are welcome to pick and eat all the berries they can find. The roads take you through vast grasslands and scrub oak woods, and by ponds. The area is maintained by the Nature Conservancy and is open daily from sunrise to sunset.

Three-mile-long **Goose Rocks,** a few minutes' drive north of town off Route 9, has plenty of shallow pools for exploring and a good long stretch of smooth sand; it's a favorite of families with small children. You can pick up a parking permit ($5 a day, $15 a week) at the **Chamber of Commerce** (☒ 17 Western Ave., Lower Village ☎ 207/967–0857).

Shopping

The **Gallery on Chase Hill** (☒ 10 Chase Hill Rd., Kennebunk ☎ 207/967–0049) presents original artwork by Maine and New England artists. **Marlow's Artisans Gallery** (☒ 39 Main St., Kennebunk ☎ 207/985–2931) carries a large and eclectic collection of crafts. **Tom's of Maine Natural Living Store** (☒ 64 Main St., Kennebunk ☎ 207/985–3874) sells all-natural personal-care products.

> **en route**   The drive from Kennebunk to Kennebunkport will take you by the **Wedding Cake House** (☒ 104 Summer St. [Rte. 35], Kennebunk). The legend behind this confection in fancy wood fretwork is that its builder, a sea captain, was forced to set sail in the middle of his wedding; the house was his bride's consolation for the lack of a wedding cake. The home, built in 1826, is not open to the public.

Kennebunkport & Cape Arundel

❿ The area focused around the water and Dock Square in **Kennebunkport** is where you can find the most activity (and crowds) in the Kennebunks. Winding alleys reveal shops and restaurants geared to the tourist trade, right in the midst of a hardworking harbor. Kennebunkport has been a resort area since the 19th century but its most famous residents have made it even more popular—the Presidential Bush family is often in residence in their immense home, which sits dramatically out on Walker's Point. The amount of wealth here is as tangible as the sharp sea breezes and the sounds of seagulls overhead. Newer mansions have sprung up alongside the old; a great way to see them is to take a slow drive out along Ocean Avenue.

The heart and pulse of this busy little area is **Dock Square,** the town center. Boutiques, T-shirt shops, art galleries, crafts stores, and restaurants encircle the square and spread out alongside streets and alleys. Many businesses close in winter, but those that stay open tend to offer nice discounts in December. Walk onto the drawbridge to admire the tidal Kennebunk River.

The **Nott House,** also known as White Columns, is an imposing Greek Revival mansion with Doric columns. The 1853 house is furnished with the belongings of four generations of the Perkins-Nott family. Maintained by the Kennebunkport Historical Society, it is open for guided tours and also serves as a gathering place for village walking tours, offered Thursday and Saturday at 11. The Society also runs the **History Center of Kennebunkport,** a mile away from the Nott House on North Street, which includes several exhibit buildings containing an old school house and jail cells. ⊠ *8 Maine St., Kennebunkport* ☎ *207/967–2751* ⊕ *www.kporthistory.org* ☞ *$5 for house tours; $3 for walking tours; $7 combination ticket* ☉ *Mid-June–mid-Oct., Tues., Wed., Fri. 1–4, Thurs., 10–4, Sat. 10–1.*

❶ Ocean Avenue follows the Kennebunk River from Dock Square to the sea and winds around the peninsula of **Cape Arundel.** Parson's Way, a small and tranquil stretch of rocky shoreline, is open to all. As you round Cape Arundel, look to the right for the entrance to former president George Bush Sr.'s summer home at Walker's Point.

★ ℃ The **Seashore Trolley Museum** displays streetcars built from 1872 to 1972 and includes trolleys from major metropolitan areas and world capitals—Boston to Budapest, New York to Nagasaki, and San Francisco to Sydney—all beautifully restored. Best of all, you can take a trolley ride for nearly 4 mi over the tracks of the former Atlantic Shoreline trolley line, with a stop along the way at the museum restoration shop, where trolleys are transformed from junk into gems. Both guided and self-guided tours are available. ⊠ *195 Log Cabin Rd., Kennebunkport* ☎ *207/967–2800* ⊕ *www.trolleymuseum.org* ☞ *$7.50* ☉ *Early May–mid-Oct., daily 10–4:30; reduced hrs in spring and fall, call ahead.*

Get a good overview of the sights with an **Intown Trolley** tour. The narrated 45-minute jaunts leave every hour starting at 10 AM at the designated stop on Ocean Avenue, around the corner of Dock Square. The fare is valid for the day so you can hop on and off at your leisure. ⊠ *Ocean Ave., Kennebunkport* ☎ *207/967–3686* ⊕ *www.intowntrolley.com* ☞ *$10 all-day fare* ☉ *Late May–mid-Oct., daily 10–5.*

Where to Stay & Eat

★ **$$$$** ✕ **White Barn Inn.** Formally attired waiters, meticulous service, and exquisite food have earned this restaurant accolades as one of the best in New England. Regional New England fare is served in a rustic but elegant dining room. The three-course, prix-fixe menu ($85), which changes weekly, might include steamed Maine lobster nestled on fresh fettuccine with carrots, ginger, and snow peas. ⊠ *37 Beach Ave., Kennebunkport* ☎ *207/967–2321* ⚓ *Reservations essential* 🏛 *Jacket required* ⊟ *AE, MC, V* ☉ *Closed 3 wks in Jan. No lunch.*

$$$–$$$$ ✕ **Seascapes.** The emphasis is on seafood at this pretty harbor-front restaurant where the view takes center stage. You can begin with the smoked chowder, then move on to grilled diver-harvested scallops, or try the ginger-garlic rack of lamb. Accompany it all with a selection from the excellent wine list. ⊠ *77 Pier Rd., Cape Porpoise* ☎ *207/967–8500* ⊟ *AE, D, DC, MC, V* ☉ *Closed late Oct.–Apr.*

$$$–$$$$ ✕ **Windows on the Water.** Almost every window in this airy dining room has a view of Dock Square and the working harbor of Kennebunkport. Lobster ravioli and classic Spanish paella are two noteworthy entrées. Unlike many of the other finer dining establishments in the area, this one pledges in its mission statement to keep prices moderate—something unusual in this part of town, especially with this kind of view. ⊠ *12 Chase Hill Rd., Kennebunkport* ☎ *207/967–3313* ⚓ *Reservations essential* ⊟ *AE, D, DC, MC, V.*

$$–$$$$ ✕ **Mabel's Lobster Claw.** Mabel's has long been serving lobsters, homemade pies, and lots of seafood for lunch and dinner in this tiny dwelling out on Ocean Avenue. With its paneled walls, wooden booths, autographed photos of various TV stars (not to mention several members of the Bush family), and paper placements that illustrate how to eat a Maine lobster, this place is a simple little classic. The house favorite is the Lobster Savannah—split and filled with scallops, shrimp, and mushrooms in a Newburg sauce. Make sure you save room for the peanut butter ice cream pie. Reservations are recommended. ⊠ *124 Ocean Ave., Kennebunkport* ☎ *207/967–2562* ⊟ *AE, D, MC, V* ☉ *Closed Nov.–Apr.*

¢–$$ ✕ **Cape Pier Chowder House.** From this oceanfront lobster shack, you can watch the surf crash in the distance near the Goat Island lighthouse and see lobster boats returning with their day's catch. Seating is on the deck or inside. The fare includes lobster, clams, and fried foods. ⊠ *15 Pier Rd., Cape Porpoise* ☎ *207/967–4268 or 800/967–4268* ⊟ *MC, V* ☉ *Closed early Nov.–mid-Apr.*

$$$$ ✕▦ **Cape Arundel Inn.** This shingle-style inn commands a magnificent ocean view that takes in the Bush estate at Walker's Point. The spacious rooms are furnished with country-style furniture and antiques, and most have sitting areas with ocean views. You can relax on the front porch or in front of the living room fireplace. In the candlelit dining room ($$$–$$$$), open to the public for dinner, every table has a view of the surf. The menu changes seasonally. ⊠ *208 Ocean Ave., Kennebunkport 04046* ☎ *207/967–2125* 🖨 *207/967–1199* ⊕ *www.capearundelinn. com* ➳ *19 rooms, 1 suite* ⚭ *Restaurant, in-room data ports, bicycles; no a/c, no room phones, no TV in some rooms, no smoking* ⊟ *AE, D, MC, V* ⦿ *CP* ☉ *Closed Jan. and Feb.*

$$$$ ✕▦ **The Colony.** You can't miss this place—it's grand, white, and incredibly large, set majestically atop a rise overlooking the ocean. The hotel was built in 1914 (after its predecessor caught fire in 1898), and much of the splendid glamour of this earlier era remains. Many of the rooms in the main hotel (there are two other outbuildings) have breezy ocean views from private or semiprivate balconies. All are outfitted with antiques

FodorsChoice
★

and hardwood floors; the bright white bed linens nicely set off the colors of the Waverly wallpaper. The restaurant ($$–$$$$) features New England fare, with plenty of seafood, steaks, and other favorites. The Colony is also Maine's first environmentally responsible hotel and a member of the Green Hotels Association. ⊠ *Ocean Ave., 04046* ☎ *207/967–3331 or 800/552–2363* 🖷 *207/967–8738* ⊕ *www.thecolonyhotel.com/maine* 🖙 *124 rooms* ⟁ *Restaurant, lounge, room service, putting green, saltwater pool, beach, bicycles, badminton, basketball, croquet, bocce, shuffleboard, volleyball, gift shop, business services, pets allowed (fee); no a/c in some rooms, no TVs in some rooms, no smoking* ⊟ *AE, MC, V* ⊘ *Closed Nov.–mid-May* ⫟○⫞ *BP.*

$$$$ 🖳 **Captain Lord Mansion.** Of all the mansions in Kennebunkport's his-
Fodor'sChoice toric district that have been converted to inns, the 1812 Captain Lord
★ Mansion is the most stately and sumptuously appointed. Distinctive architecture, including a suspended elliptical staircase, gas fireplaces in all rooms, and near-museum-quality accoutrements, make for a formal but not stuffy setting. Six rooms have whirlpool tubs. The extravagant suite has two fireplaces, a double whirlpool, a hydro-massage body spa, a TV/VCR and stereo system, and a king-size canopy bed. ⊠ *Pleasant and Green Sts.* 🕀 *Box 800, Kennebunkport 04046* ☎ *207/967–3141* 🖷 *207/967–3172* ⊕ *www.captainlord.com* 🖙 *15 rooms, 1 suite* ⟁ *In-room data ports, bicycles, Internet, meeting rooms; no room TVs, no children under 12, no smoking* ⊟ *D, MC, V* ⫟○⫞ *BP.*

★ **$$$$** 🖳 **White Barn Inn.** For a romantic overnight stay, you need look no further than the exclusive White Barn Inn, known for its attentive, pampering service. No detail has been overlooked in the meticulously appointed rooms, from plush bedding and reading lamps to robes and slippers. Rooms are in the main inn and adjacent buildings. Some have fireplaces, hot tubs, and luxurious baths with steam showers. The ample breakfast includes quiche and freshly baked pastries. The inn is within walking distance of Dock Square and the beach. ⊠ *37 Beach Ave.* 🕀 *Box 560C, Kennebunkport 04046* ☎ *207/967–2321* 🖷 *207/967–1100* ⊕ *www.whitebarninn.com* 🖙 *16 rooms, 9 suites* ⟁ *Restaurant, in-room data ports, cable TV, in-room VCRs, pool, spa services, bicycles, piano bar, dry cleaning, concierge, Internet, meeting room; no children under 12, no smoking* ⊟ *AE, MC, V* ⫟○⫞ *BP.*

$$$$ 🖳 **The Yachtsman.** Relaxing in one of the handsome rooms—in muted shades of beige, brown, and black—in this riverfront hotel feels like you're aboard an elegant yacht. Down comforters cover the king-size beds, and nautical artwork adorns the walls. French doors open onto private patios overlooking the marina. A hearty continental breakfast and afternoon tea are served on the riverfront patio. The shops and restaurants of Dock Square are a short walk away. ⊠ *Ocean Ave.* 🕀 *Box 2609, Kennebunkport 04046* ☎ *207/967–2511* 🖷 *207/967–5056* ⊕ *www.yachtsmanlodge.com* 🖙 *30 rooms* ⟁ *Refrigerators, boating, bicycles; no smoking* ⊟ *AE, MC, V* ⫟○⫞ *CP* ⊘ *Closed early Dec.–Mar.*

$$–$$$ 🖳 **Rhumb Line.** Although the rooms are standard motel fare, the facilities set this family-friendly motor lodge apart. It's on the trolley line, making getting around Kennebunk-area sites easy. Lobster bakes (extra charge) are held in the evening on weekends from late May through June, and daily from July through August. ✉ *41 Turbats Creek Rd.* ☏ *Box 3067, Kennebunkport 04046* ☎ *207/967–5457 or 800/337–4862* 🖷 *207/967–4418* ⊕ *www.rhumblinemaine.com* ↪ *56 rooms, 3 suites* ♨ *Snack bar, refrigerators, cable TV, 3 pools (1 indoor), health club, indoor and outdoor hot tub, sauna, fitness room, meeting rooms, no-smoking rooms* ▤ *AE, D, MC, V* ⁑ *CP.*

$–$$ ⊡ **St. Anthony's Franciscan Monastery Guest House.** Those in search of a quiet, contemplative retreat may want to choose one of the unadorned, motel-style rooms in this former dormitory on the grounds of a riverside monastery. The guest house is private yet within walking distance of Dock Square and the beach. The landscaped grounds with incredible Frederick Law Olmstead gardens (open to the public) have trails and shrines. The monks live in a Tudor mansion on the property, where Mass is said daily. This place is not recommended for those uncomfortable with Christian symbolism, although no religious participation is required. Exact opening and closing dates depend on the weather—there is no heat in the building. ✉ *28 Beach Ave., Kennebunkport 04043* ☎ *207/967–4865* ⊕ *www.franciscanguesthouse.com* ↪ *57 rooms* ♨ *Cable TV, saltwater pool; no room phones* ▤ *MC, V* ⁑ *BP* ⊗ *Closed mid-Oct.–May*

The Arts

For lively summer theater performances held in a 19th-century barn, visit **The Arundel Barn Playhouse** (✉ 53 Old Post Rd., Arundel ☎ 207/985–5552); shows are held Tuesday through Sunday with some matinees.

Sports & the Outdoors

For a dramatic walk along the rocky coastline and beneath the views of Ocean Avenue's grand mansions, head out on the **Parson's Way Shore Walk,** a paved, 4.8-mi round-trip (shorter if you want to just turn back at Walker's Point). Begin at Dock Square and follow Ocean Avenue along the river, passing the Colony Hotel and St. Ann's Church, all the way to Walker's Point. You can simply turn back from here, or take a left onto Wildes District Road for a walk amid more luxury homes and trees.

Cape-Able Bike Shop (✉83 Arundel Rd., Kennebunkport ☎207/967–4382) rents bicycles of all types for all ages, including trailer bikes and tandems.

BOATING & FISHING ☘ Several two-hour scenic water cruises depart daily aboard the *Atlantic Explorer* (✉ Depart from Nonantum Resort, Ocean Ave. ☎ 207/967–4784 ⊕ www.sceniccruise.com). Underwater cameras add an extra and unusual element to the usual coastline scenery.

To reserve a private sail for up to six people, contact Capt. Jim Jannetti of the *Bellatrix* (✉Kennebunkport ☎207/967–8685 ⊕www.sailingtrips.com), a vintage racing yacht. He'll teach you the ropes if you wish.

Cape Arundel Cruises (✉ Kennebunkport Marina ☎ 207/967–5595) conducts scenic cruises, deep-sea fishing, and whale-watching trips.

Find and catch fish with **Cast Away Fishing Charters,** (☏ Box 245, Kennebunkport, 04046 ☎ 207/284–1740 ⊕ www.castawayfishingcharters.com).

First Chance (⊠ 4-A Western Ave., Kennebunk ☎ 207/967–5507 or 800/967–2628) leads whale-watching cruises and guarantees sightings in season. Daily scenic lobster cruises are also offered aboard *Kylie's Chance.*

For half- or full-day fishing trips as well as discovery trips for kids, book some time with **Lady J Sportfishing Charters** (⊠ Arundel Wharf, Ocean Ave. ☎ 207/985–7304 ⊕ www.ladyjcharters.com).

For two-hour sailing trips along the coastline, sign up with **Schooner *Eleanor*** (⊠ Arundel Wharf, Ocean Ave., Kennebunkport ☎ 207/967–8809), a 55-foot classic wooden boat. Bring your own picnic.

Shopping

Abacus (⊠ 2 Ocean Ave., Dock Square, Kennebunkport ☎ 207/967–0111) sells eclectic crafts and furniture. **Kennebunkport Arts** (⊠ 1 Spring St., Dock Square, Kennebunkport ☎ 207/967–3690) is a contemporary crafts gallery with a good selection of unusual items for the home. **Mast Cove Galleries** (⊠ Mast Cove La., Kennebunkport ☎ 207/967–3453) sells graphics, paintings, and sculpture by 105 artists.

> **en route**
>
> For a rewarding drive that will take you farther into the reaches of the coastline on the way to Old Orchard Beach, head out of Kennebunkport on Route 9. This will take you through the charming resort villages of Camp Ellis and Ocean Park, and allow you to do some beachwalking at Goose Rocks Beach, and Fortunes Rocks Beach. You could also pack a picnic and spend some time at Ferry Beach State Park. The varied landscapes in the park include forested sections, swamp, beach, and lots of dunes, all of which have miles of marked trails to hike.
>
> Past the park, Route 9 continues to wind through wooded areas, heads through the slightly weary-looking old mill town of Biddeford, across the Saco River, and into Saco, a busy town with commerce and its accompanying traffic. Once you get past Saco, Route 9 returns to its peaceful curves and gentle scenery, leaving crowded civilization behind. It's a longer route to Old Orchard Beach but worth it for the gems to be found along the way.

Old Orchard Beach Area

⓬ *15 mi north of Kennebunkport, 18 mi south of Portland.*

Back in the late 19th century, Old Orchard Beach was a classic, upscale, place-to-be-seen resort area. The railroad brought wealthy families who were looking for entertainment and the benefits of the fresh sea air. While a good bit of this aristocratic hue has dulled in more modern times—admittedly, the place is more than a little pleasantly tacky these days—Old Orchard Beach remains a good place for those looking for entertainment and thrills by the sea.

The center of the action is a 7-mi strip of sand beach and its accompanying amusement park, which resembles a small Coney Island. Despite the summertime crowds and fried-food odors, the atmosphere can be captivating. During the 1940s and '50s, in the heyday of the Big Band era, the pier had a dance hall where stars of the time performed. Fire claimed the end of the pier—at one time it jutted out nearly 1,800 feet into the sea—but booths with games and candy concessions still line both sides. In summer the town sponsors fireworks (usually on Thursday night). The many places to stay run the gamut from cheap motels to cottage colonies to full-service seasonal hotels. You won't find free parking anywhere in town, but there are ample lots. Amtrak has a seasonal stop here.

A world away from the beach scene, **Ocean Park** (Ocean Park Association, ☎ 207/934–9068) lies on the southwestern edge of town. Residents and visitors like to keep the separation distinct, touting their area as a more peaceful and wholesome family-style village. This vacation community was founded in 1881 by Free Will Baptist leaders as an interdenominational retreat with both religious and educational purpose, following the example of Chautauqua, New York. Today the community still hosts an impressive variety of cultural happenings, including movies, concerts, recreation, workshops, and religious services, open to visitors and members alike. Most are presented in the Temple, which is on the National Register of Historic Places. While the religious nature of the place is apparent in its worship schedule and some of its cultural offerings, visitors need not be a member of any denomination; all are welcome here in this active community. There's even a public shuffleboard area for those not interested in the neon carnival attractions several miles up the road. Get an old-fashioned raspberry lime rickey at the Ocean Park Soda Fountain; it's also a good place for breakfast or a light lunch.

☺ **Palace Playland,** open from Memorial Day to Labor Day, has rides, booths, and a roller coaster that drops almost 50 feet. ⊠ *1 Old Orchard St.* ☎ *207/934–2001.*

On the quieter end of the street, atop a hill, is the **Old Orchard Beach Historical Society,** a small but very informative little museum dedicated to sharing the area's past. Particularly interesting are the old photographs, revealing the beach's history as a glamorous and sophisticated entertainment hub by the sea. ⊠ *4 Portland Ave.* ☎ *207/934–9319* ✉ *Donations accepted* ☉ *June–Labor Day, Tues.–Sat. 1–4.*

Where to Stay & Eat

$$–$$$$ ✕ **Joseph's by the Sea.** Large windows frame the ocean opening up beyond the dunes at this fine restaurant, which offers outdoor dining in season. Appetizers may include goat cheese terrine and lobster potato pancake. Try the grilled Tuscan swordfish or seared sea scallops for your main course. ⊠ *55 W. Grand Ave., Old Orchard Beach* ☎ *207/934–5044* 🗖 *MC, V.*

★ $$–$$$$ ✕ **The Landmark.** This restaurant almost feels as if it doesn't belong here, at least not in this modern transformation of Old Orchard Beach. Tables are set either on the glassed-in porch or within high, tin-ceiling rooms. Candles and a collection of giant fringed art nouveau lamps provide a warm, gentle light. The menu has a good selection of seafood and meats, many treated with either Asian or Mediterranean flavors; the mahimahi might be seared and served with a coconut cream sauce. It's the kind of menu that encourages you to try new things and you definitely won't be disappointed. The tiramisu is divine. Reservations are recommended. ⊠ *25 E. Grand Ave., Old Orchard Beach* ☎ *207/934–0156* ⊟ *AE, D, MC, V* ⊗ *Closed early Jan.–late Mar.*

¢–$ ✕ **DennyMike's.** In Old Orchard Beach, you can't help but notice the heavenly smells of briskets and ribs wafting down the street from this bold and authentic barbecue joint. If you've had your fill of lobster and fried seafood, bring your appetite here. Owner DennyMike is no Texan, but that's where he learned the secret of his craft. Portions are very generous; dinner feasts come with a choice of two sides—absolutely get the beans. There's also a good selection of giant burgers, specialty barbecue sandwiches, and hand-cut fries that rival any sold on the pier. It just might be the best barbecue in New England. Takeout and delivery are available. ⊠ *27 W. Grand Ave., Old Orchard Beach* ☎ *207/934–2207* ⊟ *MC, V* ⊗ *Closed mid-Oct.–mid-May.*

$$–$$$$ ▦ **Old Orchard Beach Inn.** Dating from 1730, this is Old Orchard Beach's oldest inn. Saved from impending demolition in the late 1990s, the entire place was completely renovated with great care and attention to historic detail. The spacious guest rooms are furnished with antiques, area rugs cover the pine floors, quilts brighten the beds, and lace curtains frame the windows. Many rooms have views over the town and of the shimmering Atlantic beyond. The location is ideal—quiet yet very close to the action in the town center. ⊠ *6 Portland Ave., 04064* ☎ *207/934–5834 or 877/700–6624* 🖶 *207/934–0782* ⊕ *www.oldorchardbeachinn. com* ⇆ *17 rooms, 1 suite* ♿ *In-room data ports, cable TV; no smoking* ⊟ *AE, D, MC, V* ⦿ *CP.*

$$–$$$ ▦ **Billow House Inn.** Right behind the dunes of the beach is this gracious B &B–motel complex. All rooms, whether in the motel-style units or within the main 1881 house, have decks to partake of the views and are attractively adorned with colorful quilts and ample sitting areas. All guests are spoiled with afternoon fresh-baked cookies in their rooms. Hosts Mary and Bill Kerrigan are warm and welcoming. ⊠ *2 Temple Ave., Ocean Park 04063* ☎ *207/934–2333 or 888/767–7776* 🖶 *207/934–1510* ⊕ *www.billowhouse.com* ⇆ *13 rooms, 3 suites* ♿ *Refrigerators, some kitchenettes, beach, Internet; no a/c in some rooms* ⊟ *AE, MC, V* ⦿ *CP.*

Nightlife & the Arts

In season, local performers play everything from country and oldies to reggae and rock in Town Square every Monday and Tuesday night at 7. Fireworks light the sky on Thursday night at 9:30 from late June through Labor Day. Concerts by classically trained musicians and choir groups are held most Sunday evenings in Ocean Park. Several bars in Old Orchard Beach feature live bands, dancing, and karaoke.

The community of **Ocean Park** (⊕ www.oceanpark.org) has a lively and varied cultural scene. Educational lectures, musical programs and concerts, storytelling, dances, and even yoga classes are offered daily throughout the summer. All are welcome; check their Web site or get a copy of their summer program for an event schedule.

The home of Salvation Army Camp Meetings (the Salvation Army has been holding these religious-based meetings in this spot since the late

1800s), the **Old Orchard Beach Pavilion** (⊠ Union Ave. and 6th St., Old Orchard Beach ☎ 207/934–2024 ⊕ www.oobpavilion.org) also hosts classical concerts including choirs, orchestras, and brass bands from throughout the New England area. Free parking is available.

Sports & the Outdoors
Not far from Old Orchard Beach is the Maine Audubon–run **Scarborough Marsh Nature Center** (⊠ Pine Point Rd. [Rte. 9], Scarborough ☎ 207/883–5100 ⊙ Closed Oct.–Memorial Day). You can rent a canoe and explore this natural haven on your own, or sign up with a guided trip. The salt marsh is Maine's largest and is an excellent place for bird-watching and peaceful paddling amid its winding ways. The Nature Center has a discovery room for kids, programs for all ages ranging from basket making to astronomy, birding and canoe tours, and a good gift shop.

THE SOUTHERN COAST A TO Z

To research prices, get advice from other travelers, and book travel arrangements, visit www.fodors.com.

AIR TRAVEL
Portland International Jetport is 35 mi northeast of Kennebunk.
▣ **Portland International Jetport** ⊠ Westbrook St. off Rte. 9 ☎ 207/774–7301 ⊕ www.portlandjetport.org.

BIKE TRAVEL
A bicycle can make it easy to get around the Kennebunks, the Yorks, and the Old Orchard Beach area, but the lack of shoulders on some roads can be intimidating. Ogunquit would seem like a good place for bikes, but traffic is hectic in the high season, making it a bit tricky. Biking around town is better, safer, and far more pleasant in the shoulder seasons (early summer or after Labor Day). Two good resources are the Bicycle Coalition of Maine and the Maine Department of Transportation.
▣ **Bicycle Coalition of Maine** ⊕ Box 5275, Augusta 04332 ☎ 207/623–4511 ⊕ www.bikemaine.org. **Maine Dept. of Transportation Bike and Pedestrian Section** ⊕ www.state.me.us/mdot/biketours.htm.

BUS TRAVEL
The Shuttlebus-Zoom is a localized bus service connecting the communities of Biddeford, Saco, Old Orchard Beach, Scarborough, South Portland, and Portland. The larger Vermont Transit Lines has service from throughout northern New England and within Maine.
▣ **Shuttlebus-Zoom** ☎ 207/282–5408 ⊕ www.shuttlebus-zoom.com. **Vermont Transit Lines** ☎ 800/451–3292 ⊕ www.vermonttransit.com.

CAR RENTAL
Rental car agencies are concentrated at the Portland International Jetport in Portland. *See* Car Rental *in* Smart Travel Tips for national rental agency phone numbers.

CAR TRAVEL

U.S. 1 from Kittery is the shopper's route north; other roads hug the coastline. Interstate 95 is usually a faster route for travelers headed to towns north of Ogunquit. Exits on the turnpike coincide with mileage from the border.

Route 9 goes from Kennebunkport to Cape Porpoise and Goose Rocks. Parking is tight in Kennebunkport in peak season. Possibilities include the municipal lot next to the Congregational Church ($2 an hour from May through October) and 30 North Street (free year-round).

Maine Department of Transportation ☎ Dial 511 or 866/282-7578 out of state ⊕ www.maine.gov/mdot for road conditions throughout the state.

Maine Turnpike Authority ☎ 800/675-7453 ⊕ www.maineturnpike.com.

EMERGENCIES

In an emergency dial 911.

Maine State Police ✉ Gray ☎ 207/793-4500 or 800/482-0730.

Kennebunk Medical Center ✉ 24 Portland St., Kennebunk ☎ 207/985-3726. **Southern Maine Medical Center** ✉ Rte. 111, Biddeford ☎ 207/283-7000, 207/283-7100 emergency room. **Wells Urgent Care** ✉ Rte. 109, Wells ☎ 207/646-5211. **York Hospital** ✉ 15 Hospital Dr., York ☎ 207/351-2157 or 800/283-7234.

LODGING

For home rentals in the Kennebunks, try Port Properties or Sand Dollar Real Estate Sales & Rentals. For rentals on the Southern Coast, try Seaside Vacation Rentals. Garnsey Brothers rents condominiums and housekeeping cottages in Wells, Moody Beach, and Drakes Island. The Wight Agency specializes in waterfront rentals in Old Orchard Beach.

Bayside Rentals ☎ 207/934-9180 ⊕ www.baysiderentals.com. **Garnsey Bros.** ✉ 510 Webhannet Dr., Wells 04090 ☎ 207/646-8301 ⊕ www.garnsey.com. **Maine Innkeepers Association** ☎ 207/865-6100 ⊕ www.maineinns.com. **Maine Vacation. com** ⊕ www.mainevacation.com. **Port Properties** ⊕ Box 799, Kennebunkport 04046 ☎ 207/967-4400 or 800/443-7678 ⊕ www.portproperties.com. **Seaside Vacation Rentals** ⊕ Box 2000, York 03909 ☎ 207/646-7671 or 207/363-1825 ⊕ www.seasiderentals.com. **The Wight Agency** ✉ 125 W. Grand Ave., Old Orchard Beach 04064 ☎ 207/934-4576 ⊕ www.oldorchardbeachvacations.com.

MEDIA

The *Biddeford Tribune* and the *Portland Press Herald,* the state's largest paper, are published daily. The *Maine Sunday Telegram* is the state's only Sunday paper. The *York County Coast Star* is published weekly.

WMEA 90.1 is the local National Public Radio affiliate. WCSH, channel 6, is the NBC affiliate. WMTW, channel 8, is the ABC affiliate. WGME, channel 13, is the CBS affiliate. WCBB, channel 10, or WMEA, channel 26, is the Maine Public Broadcasting affiliate.

TRAIN TRAVEL

Amtrak offers rail service on the Downeaster from Boston to Portland, with stops in Wells and Saco and a seasonal stop in Old Orchard Beach.

Amtrak ☎ 800/872-7245 ⊕ www.thedowneaster.com.

TRANSPORTATION AROUND THE SOUTHERN COAST

Trolleys ($1–$3) serve several areas. A trolley circulates among the Yorks from late June to Labor Day. A trolley fleet serves the major tourist areas and beaches of Ogunquit in July and August. Trolleys circulate in Wells on weekends from Memorial Day to Columbus Day and daily from late June to Labor Day. Trolleys circulate through Kennebunkport to Kennebunk Beach from Memorial Day to Columbus Day; an all-day ticket is $10. Biddeford–Saco–Old Orchard Beach Transit operates a trolley that circulates through Old Orchard Beach and a bus service from Old Orchard to Portland with stops in Scarborough and at the Maine Mall.

VISITOR INFORMATION

🚩 **Gateway to Maine Chamber of Commerce** ⊠ 191 State Rd., Kittery 03904 ☎ 207/439-7574 or 800/639-9645 ⊕ www.gatewaytomaine.org. **Kennebunk-Kennebunkport Chamber of Commerce** ⊡ Box 740, Kennebunk 04043 ☎ 207/967-0857 ⊕ www.visitthekennebunks.com. **Maine Tourism Association & Visitor Information Center** ⊠ U.S. 1 and I-95, Kittery 03904 ☎ 207/439-1319. **Ogunquit Chamber of Commerce** ⊠ U.S. 1 ⊡ Box 2289, Ogunquit 03907 ☎ 207/646-2939 ⊕ www.ogunquit.org. **Old Orchard Beach Chamber of Commerce** ⊠ 1st St. ⊡ Box 600, Old Orchard Beach 04064 ☎ 207/934-2500 or 800/365-9386 ⊕ www.oldorchardbeachmaine.com. **Wells Chamber of Commerce** ⊡ Box 356, Wells 04090 ☎ 207/646-2451 ⊕ www.wellschamber.org. The **Yorks Chamber of Commerce** ⊠ 571 U.S. 1, York 03903 ☎ 207/363-4422 or 800/639-2442 ⊕ www.yorkme.org.

GREATER PORTLAND

2

Updated by
Laura V. Scheel

Portland's role as a cultural and economic center for the region has given the gentrified city of 65,000 plenty of attractions that make it well worth a day or two of exploration. Several distinct neighborhoods reveal the many faces of a city that embraces its history as well as its art, music, and multicultural scenes. A city of many names throughout its history—Casco, Falmouth, and finally, Portland—this area has seen many dramatic transformations. Sheltered by the nearby Casco Bay Islands and blessed with a deep port, Portland was a significant settlement right from its start in the early 17th century. Settlers thrived on fishing and lumbering, repeatedly attempting to build up the area while the British, French, and Indians continually sacked it. The region was viewed as a somewhat dangerous frontier, but its potential for prosperity was so apparent that settlers came, despite the danger, to tap its rich natural resources.

Portland's first home was built on the peninsula now known as Munjoy Hill in 1632. The British burned the city in 1775, when residents refused to surrender arms, but it was rebuilt and became a major trading center. Much of Portland was destroyed again in the Great Fire on July 4, 1866, when a boy threw a celebration firecracker into a pile of wood shavings; 1,500 buildings burned to the ground. Poet Henry Wadsworth Longfellow said at the time that his city reminded him of the ruins of Pompeii. The Great Fire started not far from where people now wander the streets of the Old Port.

Despite all the calamity and destruction, the city of Portland has always had spirit; each time the city has fallen, its residents have rebuilt. The theme of the phoenix rising from the ashes has even been somewhat officially adopted by the city, attesting to a real sense of vigor and diversity beloved by both its residents and visitors.

The city is wonderfully accessible by foot; an able-bodied walker can easily take in the Old Port, the Downtown/Arts District, and the stunningly architectural Western Promenade without exhaustion. Narrated trolley tours are also available.

To discover some of the other areas outlined in the chapter, a car is necessary. A drive to Freeport takes about 20 minutes from Portland; to visit Maine's famous Portland Head Light and continue outward to Cape Elizabeth and Prouts Neck involves some driving as well. A trip to some of the islands in Casco Bay is a simple ticket on one of the many ferries that leave from the Old Port; rent a bike or sign on with an island tour to see the sights.

PORTLAND

Though Portland is considered a small city by national standards—with a population just under 65,000—its character, spirit, and appeal belie its physical size. Within the city itself there are several distinct neighborhoods, each revealing the varied histories and current flavors of their inhabitants. The most visited section, the restored Old Port, is a real working harbor where sea-beaten lobster boats share ports with immense cruise ships and vintage sailing yachts. The nightlife is active here, with numerous clubs, taverns, and bars pouring out the sounds of live music. Exceptional restaurants, shops, and galleries abound here as well. Water tours of the harbor and excursions to the islands of Casco Bay depart from the piers of Commercial Street.

Downtown Portland, in a funk for years, is now a burgeoning Arts District connected to the Old Port by a revitalized Congress Street, which runs the length of the peninsular city from alongside the Western Promenade in the southwest to the Eastern Promenade on Munjoy Hill in the northeast. Congress Street is peppered with interesting shops, eclectic restaurants, and several excellent museums. The arts really come alive here, with numerous venues for the performing arts attracting well-known names from the entertainment world. Nestled in the midst and beyond are residential areas; one of the great aspects of the city is that the business and domestic spheres constantly mingle, giving the area a friendly and approachable character.

Just beyond the Arts District is the Western Promenade, an area of extensive architectural wealth. Predominantly residential, the neighborhood is filled with stunning examples of both the city's historical and economic prominence and its emphasis on preserving this past.

A great advantage of the city of Portland is that it is entirely accessible on foot. You can easily explore the different neighborhoods without a car; in fact, the city is best seen without one. Visitors staying in the downtown area can walk to the Old Port within minutes.

Winters are long in Maine, so when summer arrives, the city celebrates the warmer months with a full schedule of outdoor events that include nighttime movie showings, farmers' markets, concerts, and festivals. The many happenings are testament to this small city's large and lively spirit.

The Old Port

Fodor'sChoice ★ A working harbor since the early 17th century, the Old Port bridges the gap between the city's historical commercial activities and those of today. Still a major international port on the East Coast, the harbor is home to fishing boats docked alongside whale-watching charters, luxury yachts, immense cruise ships, and oil tankers from throughout the globe. Busy Commercial Street parallels the water and is lined with brick buildings and warehouses that were built following the Great Fire of 1866, and were intended to last for ages. In the 19th century, candlemakers and sail stitchers plied their trades here; today, specialty shops, art galleries, and restaurants have taken up residence.

There was a point in the mid-20th century when the city's economy slumped, and the Old Port declined and seemed slated for demolition. Luckily, artists and craftspeople began opening shops in the late 1960s, and restaurants, boutiques, and bookstores followed.

As with much of the city, it's best to park your car and explore the Old Port on foot. You can park at the city garage on Fore Street (between Exchange and Union streets) or opposite the U.S. Customs House at the corner of Fore and Pearl streets. A helpful hint: Look for the PARK & SHOP sign on garages and parking lots and get one hour of free parking

Numbers in the text correspond to numbers in the margin and on the Portland and Around Greater Portland maps.

If you have 3 days

When you arrive in Portland, plan on spending at least one day wandering the streets and shops of the **Old Port.** Take a break with a harborside lunch along Commercial Street, or try one of the quaint pubs here before heading to the Downtown/Arts District. Art lovers will want several hours inside the **Portland Museum of Art ❹**; families should head straight to the **Children's Museum of Maine ❺**. For architectural delights, take an hour or so to walk the neighborhood of the **Western Promenade.** Spend the night in the city. On your second day, take a morning boat ride to **Eagle Island ⓭** or one of the other Casco Bay islands. In the afternoon, take a drive to **Cape Elizabeth ⓮**, and visit Portland Head Light and Two Lights. Return to Portland for the night. On your third day, head north to **Freeport ⓰**, where you can go on a shopping frenzy at L. L. Bean and the area's outlet centers.

2

If you have 5 days

Spend your first two days in Portland, exploring the city and beyond. Be sure to linger in the **Old Port,** take leisurely walks through the architectural splendor of the **Western Promenade,** and catch a baseball game at Hadlock Field. You can leave your car parked at your hotel for the two days and easily get around on foot. A great way to see the surrounding islands in Casco Bay is to take a cruise on the mailboat from Casco Bay Lines; this three-hour cruise will give you a glimpse of the beauty of the nearby shoreline and whet your appetite for an island overnight. Other ways to get out on the water from Portland Harbor include whale-watch cruises, themed scenic cruises, and sportfishing adventures.

On Day 3 take a ferry to **Peaks Island ⓬** and prepare for a much slower, more relaxed pace. You'll have left your car in Portland; rent a bicycle on the island to explore its back roads and byways. On the island, take a guided kayak trip or sign up with a golf cart tour. Spend the night here, taking in the more peaceful atmosphere of island life. On Day 4, return to Portland and head out in your car for several hours of touring, including a visit to nearby **Cape Elizabeth ⓮** to see Portland Head Light. The park is a great place for a picnic lunch (there are barbecue facilities). Continue your scenic drive, stopping at several state parks for hiking and beachcombing, before making your way to **Prouts Neck ⓯**. Here you can stroll along the Cliff Walk and visit Winslow Homer's home and studio. Wind your way back to the interstate and continue north to **Freeport ⓰**. Have dinner here and spend the night—but not before midnight shopping at L. L. Bean if you have the energy. Spend Day 5 perusing the outlets, hiking through Wolfe's Neck State Park, or taking a scenic cruise from the harbor.

for each stamp collected at participating shops. Allow a couple of hours to wander at leisure on Market, Exchange, Middle, and Fore streets. The city is very pedestrian-friendly. Maine state law requires vehicles to stop for walkers in crosswalks, and many benches allow for rest and a grand dose of people-watching.

Greater Portland Landmarks (207/772–5800) leads **guided tours** of the Old Port area Monday through Saturday at 10:30 AM, from mid-June through Columbus Day. Tours meet at the Portland Convention and Visitor's Bureau and cost $8 per person.

Working Waterfront **walking tours** are led by local Angela Clark (207/415–0765). She shares a good deal of uncommon history about the docks and alleys of the Old Port. The hour-long tours meet in front of Union Wharf Market on Commercial Street, weekdays at 11 AM and 2 PM; Saturday at 9 AM and 11 AM. The cost is $10 per person.

❶ **Maine Narrow Gauge Railroad Co. & Museum.** Whether you're crazy about old trains or just want to see the sights from a different perspective, the railroad museum has long been delighting people with its extensive collection of train memorabilia and specialty train tours on original narrow gauge rail cars. Theme weekends include rides with Santa, a Harvest Express (pick your own pumpkin!), and the July 4 fireworks ride. The museum has an extensive collection of locomotives and rail coaches from Maine; there's also a gift shop for souvenir collectors. *Museum* ⊠ *58 Fore St.* ☎ *207/828–0814* ⊕ *www.mngrr.org* ✉ *$6* ⊙ *May 15–Oct. 11, daily trains on the hr 11–4; Feb. 14–May 9 and Oct. 16–Nov. 21, weekend trains on the hr 11–3 PM; Dec. 27–31, daily on the hr noon–5. Museum open mid-Feb.–Dec. 23, daily 10–4; Jan. 2–Feb. 13, weekdays 10–3.*

❷ **Portland Fish Exchange.** For a lively and sensory-filled (you may want to hold your nose) glimpse into the Old Port's active fish business, take a free tour of the Portland Fish Exchange. Watch as the fishing boats unload their daily haul, the catch gets weighed in, and prices are settled through an auction process. It's a great behind-the-scenes view of this dynamic market. Auctions take place Sunday at 11 AM and Monday through Thursday at noon. Guided tours can be arranged by appointment; otherwise visit during regular business hours. ⊠ *6 Portland Fish Pier* ☎ *207/773–0017* ⊕ *www.portlandfishexchange.com* ✉ *Free.*

The Downtown/Arts District

This district starts at the top of Exchange Street, near the upper end of the Old Port, and extends all the way up past the Portland Museum of Art. Congress Street is the district's central artery. Much of Portland's economic heart is here, including several large banking firms. It's also the area where Maine College of Art, the Portland Library, and the Portland Public Market make their homes. Art galleries, specialty stores, and a score of restaurants line Congress Street and its larger intersecting byways of High and State streets. Parking along Congress Street is tricky; two-hour meters line the sidewalks but there are several nearby parking garages.

❸ **Children's Museum of Maine.** Touching is okay at Portland's relatively small but fun Children's Museum where kids can pretend they are lobster fisherman, shopkeepers, or computer experts. The majority of the museum's exhibits, many of which have a Maine theme, are best for children 10 and younger. Camera Obscura, an exhibit about optics, pro-

Boating

Portland is a city surrounded by water, so it's little wonder that boats are more than plentiful in the city. If you prefer to stay on dry ground and watch boats peacefully passing from afar, there is plenty to see, but if you want to feel the waves and the wind, there is even more opportunity. Various companies hug the harborside of the Old Port, offering whale-watch cruises, scenic excursions to lighthouses and islands, puffin- and seal-watching jaunts, lobster cruises (see how they're caught), and sportfishing trips. You can sign on for a dinner-and-dancing cruise, sunset tour, or a sunrise sail for early risers. A great way to see the nearby islands is to get aboard the twice-daily mailboat for a three-hour tour (sound familiar?); or simply take scheduled ferry routes to other islands within Casco Bay. For those who want to navigate the waters themselves, sign on with kayak or canoe outfits that rent equipment and give guidance (these are busy waterways, and the novice should take great care).

Microbreweries

For such a small city, Portland makes and drinks a lot of beer—and good, creative, smooth-tasting brew at that. Perhaps it's a consequence of the long winters here, but the state of Maine is home to more than two dozen breweries, not to mention the countless smaller establishments that also make beer. Beer aficionados will be amply satisfied here, ambling from one brew pub to the next, tasting the ales. Within and near the city are several larger brewing companies (Allagash, Geary, Casco Bay Brewing, and Sebago Brewing, to name a few), each open for tours and tastings, but much of the hidden treasure lies in the smaller brew pubs that make their own beer and serve it fresh from their own taps in the lively and inviting setting of a neighborhood tavern. In the Old Port alone there are several such pubs serving homemade brews that often change with the seasons. Look for special events like the annual Maine Brewer's Festival in November. What better way to experience local color than with a good brew?

Shopping

Both bargain and treasure hunters will have plenty to peruse when visiting the Greater Portland area. Shoppers with a taste for the unusual, not-to-be-found-anywhere-else item will delight in Portland—you won't find the same storefronts that fill space in the malls of America (unless you want to; then head straight to the Maine Mall). Instead are specialty shops selling clothing, pottery, art, housewares, and all manner of items, all shops individually owned and unique in their offerings. You can find antiques shops in the Downtown/Arts District as well as along U.S. 1 on the outskirts of the city. Outlet lovers should beeline to Freeport, where brand-name stores (everything from the Gap to Yankee Candle) sell their wares at reduced prices. And, of course, Freeport is the land of L. L. Bean, which never closes its doors—in fact the doors don't even have locks. Maine sales tax is 5%.

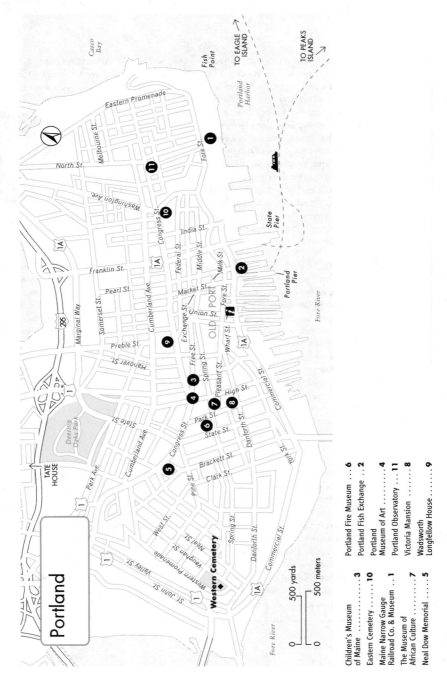

Portland

Casco Bay

Eastern Promenade

Melbourne St.

North St.

Fish Point

TO EAGLE ISLAND →

TO PEAKS ISLAND →

Portland Harbor

Fore St.

1

11

Washington Ave.

Congress St.

10

India St.

State Pier

Franklin St.

1A

Federal St.

Middle St.

Milk St.

Pearl St.

1A

Cumberland Ave.

Market St.

Fore St.

Portland Pier

295

Marginal Way

Somerset St.

Exchange St.

Union St.

OLD PORT

2

7

Fore River

Preble St.

Free St.

9

Wharf St.

1A

Hanover St.

Spring St.

Pleasant St.

3

High St.

Commercial St.

Deering Oaks Park

4

6 **7**

8

State Ave.

Park St.

State St.

Cumberland Ave.

Congress St.

Danforth St.

TATE HOUSE ←

1

5

Brackett St.

York St.

Park Ave.

pine St.

Clark St.

West St.

Spring St.

Neal St.

Danforth St.

Vaughan St.

Western Promenade

Commercial St.

1

St. John St.

Valley St.

Western Cemetery ◆

1

1A

Fore River

⟨ compass ⟩

0	500 yards
0	500 meters

vides fascinating panoramic views of the city. The museum's newest addition, L. L. Bear's Discovery Woods, takes imagination to the great outdoors, with explorations below the sea, up a tree, on top of Maine's tallest mountain, and within a flowing stream. ⊠ *142 Free St.* ☎ *207/828–1234* ⊕ *www.childrensmuseumofme.org* ⊠ *Museum $6; Camera Obscura only, $3* ☉ *Memorial Day–Labor Day, Mon.–Sat. 10–5, Sun. noon–5; early Sept.–Memorial Day, Tues.–Sat. 10–5, Sun. noon–5.*

★ ❹ **Portland Museum of Art.** Maine's largest public art institution has a number of strong collections, including fine seascapes and landscapes by Winslow Homer, John Marin, Andrew Wyeth, Edward Hopper, Marsden Hartley, and other painters. Homer's *Pulling the Dory* and *Weatherbeaten,* two quintessential Maine Coast images, are here; the museum owns 17 paintings by Homer. The Joan Whitney Payson Collection of impressionist and postimpressionist art includes works by Monet, Picasso, and Renoir. Harry N. Cobb, an associate of I. M. Pei, designed the strikingly modern Charles Shipman Payson building. The nearby and entirely renovated McLellan House contains additional galleries housing the museum's 19th-century collection and decorative art as well as interactive educational stations. ⊠ *7 Congress Sq.* ☎ *207/775–6148, 800/639–4067 recorded information* ⊕ *www.portlandmuseum.org* ⊠ *$8, free Fri. 5–9* ☉ *Memorial Day–Columbus Day, Mon.–Thurs. and weekends 10–5, Fri. 10–9; Columbus Day–Memorial Day, Tues.–Thurs. and weekends 10–5, Fri. 10–9.*

❺ **Neal Dow Memorial.** Now the headquarters of the Maine Women's Christian Temperance Union, this majestic 1829 Federal-style home is open for tours. The mansion is filled with the Civil War general's original antiques, personal effects, and papers on prohibition—the mission that gave him fame as the man responsible for Maine's adoption of the anti-alcohol bill in 1851. ⊠ *714 Congress St.* ☎ *207/773–7773* ⊠ *Free* ☉ *Weekdays 11–4.*

↻ ❻ **Portland Fire Museum.** Begun by the Portland Veteran's Firemen's Association in 1891, the Fire Museum is filled with a collection of fire-related art and mementos gathered over generations. Housed in the former fire quarters of Engine 4, the museum has a curious collection of 19th-century firefighting equipment, an old engine, scores of documents and photographs, and even the original stalls of the horses that once pulled the fire wagons. Watch the dramatic silent film footage from 1912 of the horse-drawn fire cart as it heads off to a local fire. The museum is on the National Register of Historic Places. ⊠ *157 Spring St.* ☎ *207/767–3826* ⊕ *www.portlandfiremuseum.com* ⊠ *Free* ☉ *1st Fri. of each month, 6–9, or by appointment.*

↻ ❼ **The Museum of African Culture.** This is the only museum in New England devoted exclusively to Sub-Saharan African tribal arts. There are more than 1,500 pieces in the collection ranging from large-scale, elaborately carved wooden masks to smaller-scale figures, cast copper alloy (bronze) figures, textiles, utilitarian objects, ceramic, bone, ivory, and composite objects. The oldest mask in the collection dates back to 1600 AD. ⊠ *122 Spring St.* ☎ *207/871–7188* ⊕ *www.tribalartmuseum.com* ⊠ *$5 suggested donation* ☉ *Tues.–Fri. 10:30–4, Sat. 12:30–4, or by special appointment.*

THE EASTERN PROM TRAIL

TO TAKE ADVANTAGE OF THE CITY'S BUSY SHORELINE and grand views of nearby islands and an abandoned military fort, head out along the water on the Eastern Prom Trail. Maintained by the Portland Trails organization, this is one of the many routes that are ideal for walkers, cyclists, and even rollerbladers.

Beginning at the intersection of Commercial and India streets, the trail follows the old railroad tracks—still used by the antique trains of the Maine Narrow Gauge Railroad & Museum—and runs right along the water. Watch the sailboats, cruise ships, international freight ships, and ubiquitous Maine lobster trap buoys as you walk along this nicely paved trail. Bring a picnic; there are plenty of places with benches and tables for a break along the way. From the trailhead, it's about 1¼ mi to East End Beach, a busy boat launch and small sandy beach that's not bad for a quick dip in the brisk waters of Casco Bay. It's also a good spot to launch a canoe or kayak.

There are a few options from the beach here. You can continue along the trail, pass underneath busy I–295, and reemerge at Portland's Back Cove on the other side. This trail makes a 6-mi loop around the cove; look for birds and the occasional wayward moose. Your other option is to head back to the Old Port. To do this, you can either backtrack along the paved trail or head straight up the large grassy hill to the Eastern Promenade. Largely residential, grand homes line the road of the same name with inviting balconies and architectural detail. This expanse of green is a popular picnic spot for residents and the place where the city stages its 4th of July fireworks gala; there is also a playground for the little ones.

Head to the left on the Eastern Prom, heading back toward the Old Port.

Starting down the hill, you can see a gazebo and several old cannons to your left. This is the unmarked Fort Allen Park, a small stretch of green with some informative maps and coin-operated viewing scopes. Look out to the tree-topped and lonely Fort Gorges, an imposing military garrison built just before the Civil War yet never put into service.

The Eastern Prom becomes Fore Street; at the intersection, either head straight back into the Old Port or take a left on India Street, which will bring you just about back to where you started.

Allow at least an hour for a good walk on the Eastern Prom Trail to East End Beach and back; certainly if you choose to continue on to the Back Cove Trail, you'll need several hours.

★ ❽ **Victoria Mansion.** The Italianate-style Morse-Libby Mansion (known as Victoria Mansion) was built between 1858 and 1860 and is widely regarded as the most sumptuously ornamented dwelling of its period remaining in the country. Architect Henry Austin designed the house for hotelier Ruggles Morse and his wife, Olive. The interior design—everything from the plasterwork to the furniture (much of it original)—is the only surviving commission of New York designer Gustave Herter. Inside the elegant brownstone exterior of this National Historic Landmark are colorful frescoed walls and ceilings, ornate marble mantelpieces, gilded gas chandeliers, a magnificent 6- by 25-foot stained-glass ceiling window, and a freestanding mahogany staircase; guided tours, running about 45 minutes, cover all the details. The mansion reopens during the Christmas season, richly ornamented and decorated to reveal the opulence and elegance of the Victorian era. ⊠ *109 Danforth St.* ☎ *207/772–4841* ⊕ *www.victoriamansion.org* ⊠ *$10* ⊙ *May–Oct., Tues.–Sat. 10–4, Sun. 1–5. Christmas tours: day after Thanksgiving–Jan. 1.*

❾ **Wadsworth Longfellow House.** The boyhood home of the poet—which is the first brick house in Portland—is particularly interesting because most of the furnishings are original to the house. The late-Colonial-style structure, built in 1785, sits back from the street and has a small portico over its entrance and four chimneys surmounting the roof. The house is part of the Center for Maine History, which includes the adjacent Maine History Gallery and a research library; the gift shop has a good selection of books about Maine. ⊠ *489 Congress St.* ☎ *207/774–1822* ⊕ *www.mainehistory.org* ⊠ *$7, Center $4* ⊙ *House and Maine History Gallery: May–Oct., Mon.–Sat. 10–5, Sun. noon–5; last tour at 4. Nov. and Dec., call for hrs. Library: year-round, Tues.–Sat. 10–3.*

❿ **Eastern Cemetery.** On Congress Street, not far from the Portland Observatory, is this historic mid-17th-century burial ground. Though it's not as well kept as it should be, a stroll through the cemetery nonetheless reveals thousands of enchanting and artfully decorated tombstones of the centuries, carved with winged-skulls, angels, and weeping willows. ⊠ *Congress St. and Washington Ave.*

⓫ **Portland Observatory.** This observatory on Munjoy Hill was built in 1807 by Captain Lemuel Moody, a retired sea captain, as a signal tower. It used lights as both aids for sea navigation and as a warning for the approach of enemy forces. It is the last remaining signal tower in the country and is held in place by 122 tons of ballast. After visiting the small museum at the base, you can climb to the Orb deck and take in views of Portland, the islands, and inland to the White Mountains. ⊠ *138 Congress St.* ☎ *207/774–5561* ⊕ *www.portlandlandmarks.org* ⊠ *$5* ⊙ *Memorial Day–Columbus Day, daily 10–5.*

off the beaten path

TATE HOUSE – This magnificent house fully conjures up the style—even high style—of Colonial Maine. Built astride rose granite steps and a period herb garden overlooking the Stroudwater River on the outskirts of Portland, the 1755 house was built by Captain George Tate. Tate had ★ been commissioned by the English Crown to organize "the King's Broad

Arrow"—the marking and cutting down of gigantic forest trees, which were transported over land to water, and sent to England to be fashioned as masts for English fighting frigates. The house has several period rooms, including a sitting room with some fine English Restoration chairs. With its clapboard still gloriously unpainted, its impressive Palladian doorway, dogleg stairway, unusual clerestory, and gambrel roof, this house will delight all lovers of Early American decorative arts. Guided tours of the gardens are held each Wednesday from mid-June to mid-September, with tea and refreshments served afterward. House tours are offered daily except Monday. ⊠ *1270 Westbrook St., Portland* ☎ *207/774–6177* ⊕ *www. tatehouse.org* ▧ *$5* ⊙ *Mid-June–Sept., Tues.–Sat. 10–4, Sun. 1–4; weekends only in Oct. Christmas tour: end of Nov.–Dec.*

The Western Promenade

A leisurely walk through Portland's Western Promenade, beginning at the top of the Downtown/Arts District, offers a real treat to those interested in historic architecture. Elaborate building began in the mid-1800s, encouraged by both a robust economy and Portland's devastating fire of 1866, which leveled nearly one-third of the city. The neighborhood, on the National Register of Historic Places, reveals an extraordinary display of architectural splendor, from High Victorian Gothic to lush Italianate, Queen Anne to Colonial Revival.

A good place to start is at the very head of the Western Promenade, which has parking, benches, and a great view. From the Old Port, take Danforth Street all the way up to Vaughn Street; take a right and then an immediate left onto Western Promenade. You pass by the Western Cemetery, Portland's second official burial ground laid out in 1829 (tour through here and find the ancestral plot of famous poet Henry Wadsworth Longfellow); just beyond that is the parking area. Once you're on foot, you can happily get lost on sidestreets, each abrim with the statuesque homes of the neighborhood.

You could easily spend an hour or two wandering the back streets of the Western Promenade; longer if you bring a picnic to enjoy in the grassy park at the head of the neighborhood. If you're interested in the particular history of individual homes, pick up a pamphlet from **Greater Portland Landmarks**. A map is included as well as the story of some of the more prominent homes. ⊠ *165 State St.* ☎ *207/774–5561* ⊕ *www. portlandlandmarks.org.*

WHERE TO EAT

Despite its small size, Portland is blessed with a huge variety of restaurants and featured cuisines, many of which are quite exceptional. Part of that quality stems from the fact that large chain restaurants and commercial fast-food joints are nearly nonexistent, making room for chef-owned operations that are willing to experiment.

Seafood, and yes, Maine lobster, certainly hold a significant portion of the offerings, but local chefs have come up with all kinds of unique ways to prepare the beloved crustacean. Many restaurants exclusively utilize local meats, seafood, and produce, and changing menus reflect what is available in the region at the moment. Diners can choose from waterfront seafood shacks, elaborate prix-fixe French dinners, country Italian, Thai, Vietnamese, Japanese, Irish, Mexican, Mediterranean, and a fusion of many different cuisines. As sophisticated as many of these establishments have become, the atmosphere is generally quite casual; with little exception, you can leave your jacket and tie at home.

Keep in mind that as of January 1, 2004, the city of Portland banned smoking in all restaurants, taverns, and bars.

WHAT IT COSTS				
$$$$	**$$$**	**$$**	**$**	**¢**
AT DINNER	over $25	$18–$25	$11–$17	$7–$10	under $7

Restaurant prices are per person for a main course at dinner, excluding 7% tax.

★ **$$–$$$$** ✕ **Cinque Terre.** The passionate and traditional art of Italian dining is celebrated at this Old Port spot, encouraging a long, relaxing eating experience that covers up to five courses and even more Northern Italian flavors. Half portions are available, allowing you to savor more of the many choices. Start with an appetizer such as the pan-roasted clams, mussels, and hot salami on grilled focaccia; move on to salad, pasta, and a main entrée, which could be anything from seafood to veal, quail to venison. Save room for après-dinner cheese and dessert. Reservations are recommended. ⊠ *36 Wharf St.* ☎ *207/347–6154* ⊟ *AE, MC, V* ☉ *No lunch.*

$$–$$$$ ✕ **Katahdin Restaurant.** Long a favorite with both locals and visitors, this small yet comfortable corner restaurant sits nicely amid the Downtown/Arts District. Seafood is the pride here, with an emphasis on the local variety, treated with extra creativity. Imagine the ubiquitous Maine lobster poached in butter with corn risotto, smoked Gouda, and watercress. The menu changes often, keeping favorite staples but reworking them. No matter what the preparation, the Prince Edward Island mussels are always worth a try, as are the Maine crab cakes. Vegetarian dishes are also represented, and a well-rounded wine list complements the menu. ⊠ *106 High St.* ☎ *207/774–1740* ⊟ *AE, MC, V* ⌕ *Reservations not accepted* ☉ *Closed Sun. and Mon.*

$$–$$$$ ✕ **Street and Co.** Fish and seafood are the specialties here, and you **Fodor'sChoice** won't find any better or fresher. You enter through the kitchen, with all ★ its wonderful aromas, and dine amid dried herbs and shelves of staples, at one of a dozen copper-top tables (so your waiter can place a skillet of steaming seafood directly in front of you). Some good choices are lobster diavolo for two, scallops in Pernod and cream, and sole Française. One vegetarian dish is the only alternative to seafood. ⊠ *33 Wharf St.* ☎ *207/775–0887* ⊟ *AE, MC, V* ☉ *No lunch.*

$$–$$$$ ✕ **Uffa!** Though the name means "Oh!" in Italian, this funky place is absolutely French, having imported a genuine French chef, James Tranchemontagne, from overseas. Bringing the richly textured and traditional flavors of his homeland to New England ingredients has resulted in a whole new batch of dedicated diners. A favorite is the seared trout with lobster and leek stuffing, served with herb-scented jasmine rice and a Drambuie creme sauce; or try the nightly "chef's tasting," a changing selection of delights that can be had à la carte or as a complete meal. Sunday brunch is also a treat, served from 9 AM to 1 PM. ⊠ *190 State St.* ☎ *207/775–3380* ⊟ *AE, MC, V* ⊗ *Closed Mon. and Tues. No lunch.*

$$$ ✕ **Hugo's.** Chef-owner Rob Evans has turned Hugo's, always a popular eatery, into one of the city's best restaurants. The subdued yet elegant dining room is a perfect background for Evans' masterful, creative cuisine. The menu, which may include pistachio-crusted lobster or pan-fried Deer Isle scallops, changes weekly. For a splurge, ask for the Chef's Menu: Evans will send out multiple courses of his choosing. ⊠ *88 Middle St.* ☎ *207/ 774–8538* ⊟ *AE, MC, V* ⊗ *Closed Sun. and Mon. No lunch.*

$$–$$$ ✕ **Bella Cucina.** High, painted tin ceilings may seem an unlikely backdrop for a place serving up the wood-fire tastes of country Italian cooking, but the eclectic mix of architecture, colorful paper lanterns, and artwork are a good match for the different flavors you can find on the menu. Despite the oft-changing options of locally procured meats and fish, consistency has kept this restaurant a very good and reasonable choice. Start with the seared calamari and octopus with chipotle, tomatoes, capers, and garlic. If you can't decide on dinner, try the mixed grill of sweet fennel pork sausage, hanger steak, and chicken. Vegetarians will not be disappointed, nor will those who finish with fresh strawberries with a mascarpone custard sauce. Reservations are recommended. ⊠ *653 Congress St.* ☎ *207/828–4033* ⊟ *AE, MC, V* ⊗ *Closed Mon.*

★ $$–$$$ ✕ **Fore Street.** Two of Maine's best chefs, Sam Hayward and Dana Street, opened this restaurant in a renovated, cavernous warehouse on the edge of the Old Port. Every table in the two-level main dining room has a view of the enormous brick oven and hearth and the open kitchen, where creative entrées such as roasted Maine lobster, apple-wood-grilled Atlantic swordfish loin, and wood oven–braised cassoulet are prepared. ⊠ *288 Fore St.* ☎ *207/775–2717* ⊟ *AE, MC, V* ⊗ *No lunch.*

$$–$$$ ✕ **Walter's Cafe.** Brick walls and wood floors in this popular two-story restaurant capture the 19th-century spirit of the Old Port. Begin with lobster bisque or deep-fried lemongrass shrimp sticks; then move on to a shrimp and andouille bake. This casual, busy place in the heart of the Old Port's shopping area manages a good balance of local seafood and meats with Asian and more eclectic flavors. ⊠ *15 Exchange St.* ☎ *207/ 871–9258* ⊟ *AE, MC, V* ⊗ *Closed Sun. and Mon. No lunch.*

$–$$$ ✕ **Ri-Ra.** Whether you're in the mood for a pint of beer and corned beef and cabbage, or a crock of mussels and whole roasted rainbow trout, Ri-Ra delivers. Settle into a comfy couch in the downstairs pub or take a table in the upstairs dining room, where walls of windows overlook the busy ferry terminal. After dinner on weekends, the lower level gets loud with live local bands playing until closing time. ⊠ *72 Commercial St.* ☎ *207/761–4446* ⊟ *AE, MC, V.*

★ $–$$ ✕ **Pepperclub.** A hot spot for vegetarians and a young, casual crowd, this funky little restaurant features its nightly offerings on handwritten, colorful chalkboards propped up about the place. If the portobello pie doesn't tickle your fancy, choose from selections of beef, seafood, pasta, and chicken. Especially tasty is the Middle Eastern–influenced ground lamb with rice and warmly spiced yogurt-based sauce. ⊠ *78 Middle St.* ☎ *207/772–0531* ⊟ *AE, MC, V* ⊗ *No lunch.*

¢–$$ ✕ **Portland Public Market.** Nibble your way through this handsome, airy market where 20 locally owned businesses sell fresh foods, organic produce, and imported specialty items, including fresh-baked goods, soups, smoked seafood, rotisserie chicken, aged cheeses, and free-range meats. The market is open Monday through Saturday from 9 AM to 7 PM, Sunday from 10 AM to 5 PM; some vendors open at 7 AM. ⊠ *25 Preble St.* ☎ *207/228–2000.*

¢–$ ✕ **Becky's.** You won't find a more local or unfussy place than this one, way down on the end of Commercial Street, several blocks beyond the cobblestoned, primly kept streets of the Old Port. Sitting next to you at the counter or in the neighboring booth could be a rubber-booted fisherman back from sea, a college crowd eating off last night's party, or suited business folks with cell phones. The food is reasonably priced, generous in proportion, and has that satisfying, old-time-diner quality. Breakfast is served all day, starting at 4 AM (expect to see a long, bleary-eyed line of people on weekend mornings), with lunch and dinner daily. Nightly specials add to the large menu of fried seafood platters, salads, sandwiches, and yes, meat loaf and mashed potatoes. ⊠ *390 Commercial St.* ☎ *207/773–7070* ⊟ *AE, D, MC, V.*

WHERE TO STAY

As Portland's popularity as a vacation destination has increased, so has its options for overnight visitors. In the past few years, several large hotels—geared toward high-tech, amenity-obsessed guests—have been built in the Old Port. These massive places have in no way diminished the success of smaller, more intimate lodging establishments, of which there are plenty. Inns and bed-and-breakfasts have taken up residence throughout the city, often giving new life to the grand mansions of Portland's 19th-century wealthy businessmen. A few chain hotels have also slipped in, but most of them are clustered near the Interstate and the airport.

You can expect to pay from about $70 a night for a pleasant room (often with complimentary breakfast), all the way up to more than $400 for the most luxurious of suites. In the height of the summer season, many places have minimum stay requirements for weekends and holidays; be sure to make reservations well in advance and inquire about off-season specials.

WHAT IT COSTS				
$$$$	**$$$**	**$$**	**$**	**¢**
over $200	$150–$200	$100–$150	$60–$100	under $60

Hotel prices are for two people in a standard double room, excluding service charges and 7% tax.

$$$$ 🏨 **Portland Regency Hotel.** One of the few major hotels in the center of the Old Port, the brick Regency building was Portland's armory in the late 19th century. Most rooms have four-poster beds, tall standing mirrors, floral curtains, and love seats. You can walk to shops, restaurants, and museums from the hotel. ⊠ *20 Milk St., 04101* ☎ *207/774–4200 or 800/727–3436* 🖷 *207/775–2150* ⊕ *www.theregency.com* 🛏 *87 rooms, 8 suites* ⚐ *Restaurant, in-room data ports, minibars, cable TV, health club, hot tub, massage, sauna, steam room, dry cleaning, Internet, business services, meeting rooms, transportation shuttle, no-smoking rooms* ▭ *AE, D, DC, MC, V.*

$$$–$$$$ 🏨 **Pomegranate Inn.** The classic architecture of this handsome inn in the
Fodor'sChoice architecturally rich Western Promenade area gives no hint of the sur-
★ prises within. Vivid hand-painted walls, floors, and woodwork combine with contemporary artwork, and the result is both stimulating and comforting. Rooms are individually decorated, and five have fireplaces. Room 8, in the carriage house, has a private garden terrace. ⊠ *49 Neal St., 04102* ☎ *207/772–1006 or 800/356–0408* 🖷 *207/773–4426* ⊕ *www.pomegranateinn.com* 🛏 *7 rooms, 1 suite* ⚐ *In-room data ports; no children under 16, no smoking* ▭ *AE, D, DC, MC, V* ⊧ *BP.*

$$$–$$$$ 🏨 **The Portland Harbor Hotel.** One of Portland's newest giant hotels, the Harbor Hotel makes luxury its primary focus and has garnered significant diamond ratings for its efforts. Business travelers favor the hotel for meetings on a more intimate scale, while vacationing guests appreciate the high quality of service and amenities. The location, in the middle of the Old Port, puts you right in the midst of the action. In season, eat on the enclosed peaceful garden patio. ⊠ *468 Fore St., 04101* ☎ *207/775–9090 or 888/798–9090* 🖷 *207/775–9990* ⊕ *www. portlandharborhotel.com* 🛏 *85 rooms, 12 suites* ⚐ *Restaurant, in-room data ports, cable TV, fitness center, dry cleaning, Internet, business services, meeting rooms, valet parking, transportation shuttle, no-smoking rooms* ▭ *AE, D, DC, MC, V.*

★ **$$–$$$$** 🏨 **The Danforth.** This beautiful, 1821 brick home has white columns, a cupola, and a prominent place in the Spring Street historic district. Rooms have fireplaces and are plush with simple Colonial furnishings and couches. Three blocks from the Old Port, the inn overlooks the working waterfront and is also an easy stroll to the downtown area. Other civilized accoutrements include afternoon port, brandy, and a billiard room. Passes to a nearby fitness club are available. ⊠ *163 Danforth St., 04102* ☎ *207/879–8755 or 800/991–6557* 🖷 *207/879–8754* ⊕ *www. danforthmaine.com* 🛏 *10 rooms* ⚐ *In-room data ports, cable TV, some pets allowed (fee)* ▭ *AE, MC, V* ⊧ *BP.*

$$–$$$$ 🏨 **The Percy Inn.** Former travel writer and innkeeper Dale Northrup knows how to welcome guests and keep them happy in this elegantly appointed Federal-style brick row house from 1830. Thoughtful amenities include complimentary in-room soft drinks, 24-hour snacking ability in the well-stocked second-floor pantry, and even summer beach bags complete with blankets, towels, and minicoolers. Each well-sized room is alight with colorful patchwork or flowered quilts, richly painted walls, and queen iron beds. The rooms, named for famed poets, even have books of their namesakes placed about in comfortable sitting areas. Candles, stained glass, a full library of movies, and numerous plants give the inn a generous warmth. Sitting just on the edge of the West End, it's an easy walk to both the Arts District and the Old Port. ✉ *15 Pine St., 04102* ☎ *207/871–7638 or 888/417–3729* ⊕ *www.percyinn.com* ⌨ *8 suites, 4 rooms* ⚭ *Some kitchenettes, refrigerators, cable TV, in-room VCR/ DVD players, parking* ▤ *D, DC, MC, V* ⑩ *CP.*

$$$ 🏠 **Inn at Park Spring.** Comfort and location are paramount at this 1845 home nestled behind the Portland Museum of Art and within a 10-minute walk of the Old Port. Rooms are sizable enough to allow for a generous seating area in addition to queen beds. Some rooms have carpeting; others have beautiful, old wood floors. Choose the Gables Room for its king bed, ample space, and views of the treetops. And don't forget to stay for breakfast: even nonguests have been known to beg for a taste. ✉ *135 Spring St., 04102* ☎ *207/774–1059 or 800/437–8511* ⊕ *www.innatparkspring.com* ⌨ *6 rooms* ⚭ *No smoking* ▤ *AE, DC, MC, V* ⑩ *BP.*

$$$ 🏠 **Inn on Carleton.** After a day of exploring Portland's museums and shops, you can find a quiet retreat at this elegant brick town house on the city's Western Promenade. Built in 1869, it is furnished throughout with period antiques as well as artwork by contemporary Maine artists. A restored trompe l'oeil painting by Charles Schumacher greets you at the entryway, and more of his work is displayed in the back dining room. ✉ *46 Carleton St., 04102* ☎ *207/775–1910 or 800/639– 1779* 🖷 *207/761–0956* ⊕ *www.innoncarleton.com* ⌨ *6 rooms* ⚭ *Internet; no room phones, no room TVs, no children under 9, no smoking* ▤ *D, MC, V* ⑩ *BP.*

$$$ 🏠 **West End Inn.** Set amid the glorious aged homes of the Western Promenade, this 1871 house displays much of the era's Victorian grandeur with high ceilings and a dramatic ruby-red foyer. Spacious rooms are either brightly painted (one a very vivid green) or papered with flowers, and all provide guests with down quilts, thick terry robes, and a complimentary basket of luxury toiletries. It's a short walk to the downtown area. ✉ *146 Pine St., 04102* ☎ *207/772–1377 or 800/338–1377* 🖷 *207/828–0984* ⊕ *www.westendbb.com* ⌨ *6 rooms* ⚭ *Cable TV; no room phones, no smoking* ▤ *AE, MC, V* ⑩ *BP.*

Nightlife & the Arts

Nightlife

Portland has a nicely varied nightlife, with a great emphasis on local, live music. Big, raucous dance clubs are few, but darkened taverns and lively bars (smoke-free by law, as of January 2004) pulse with the sounds of rock, blues, alternative, and folk tunes. Several hip wine bars have cropped up, serving appetizers along with a full array of specialty wines and whimsical cocktails. It's a fairly youthful scene in Portland, but there are plenty of places where you don't have to shout over the bass to be heard.

Acoustic Coffee (✉ 32 Danforth St. ☎ 207/774–0404) serves up organic coffee and vegetarian meals alongside nightly performances of folk music, open mike, or readings of poetry and prose; its walls also showcase local artwork. **Asylum** (✉ 121 Center St. ☎ 207/772–8274) oozes with live entertainment and dancing on two levels and a sports bar; it books local and regional rock, pop, and hip-hop groups. **Brian Boru** (✉ 57 Center St. ☎ 207/780–1506) is an Irish pub with occasional entertainment, ranging from Celtic to reggae, and an outside deck. For nightly themed brew specials, plenty of Guiness, and live entertainment, head to **Bull Feeney's** (✉ 375 Fore St. ☎ 207/773–7210), a lively two-story Irish pub and restaurant. For laughs, head to **Comedy Connection** (✉ 6 Custom Wharf ☎ 207/774–5554). **Gritty's** (✉ 396 Fore St. ☎ 207/772–2739) brews fine ales and serves British pub fare and seafood dishes. For live blues every night of the week, try the **Big Easy Blues Club** (✉ 55 Market St. ☎ 207/871–8817). **Space** (✉ 538 Congress St. ☎ 207/828–5600) sparkles as a unique and alternative arts venue, opening its doors to everything from poetry readings to live music and documentary film showings.

The Arts

Art galleries and studios abound in Portland. Many are concentrated along the Congress Street downtown corridor; others are hidden amid the boutiques and restaurants of the Old Port and the East End. A great way to get acquainted with the city's artists is to participate in the First Friday Art Walk, a self-guided, free tour of galleries, museums, and alternative art venues happening, you guessed it, on the first Friday of each month, from May to December. Brochures are available on the organization's Web site: ⊕ www.firstfridayartwalk.com.

In summer, several organizations sponsor outdoor entertainment venues, including alfresco movies and an outdoor concert series. Portland is also home to a handful of very talented professional and community theater groups that stage performances year-round.

The **Center for Cultural Exchange** (✉ 1 Longfellow Sq. ☎ 207/761–1545 ⊕ www.centerforculturalexchange.org) celebrates world art and cultural diversity with concerts, educational programs, and exhibits by entertainers from around the globe. **Cumberland County Civic Center** (✉ 1 Civic Center Sq. ☎ 207/775–3458) hosts concerts, sporting events, and family shows. **Portland City Hall's Merrill Auditorium** (✉ 20 Myrtle St. ☎ 207/874–8200) hosts numerous theatrical and musical events including performances by the Portland Symphony Orchestra, Portland Concert Association, and Portland Opera Repertory Theater. On most Tuesdays from mid-June to September, organ recitals ($5 donation) are given on the auditorium's huge 1912 Kotzschmar Memorial Organ. **Portland's Downtown District** (☎ 207/772–6828 ⊕ www.portlandmaine.com) plans a host of activities throughout the year, including Portland's beloved Old Port Festival, held the first Sunday in June, a Thursday afternoon outdoor music series in Monument Square, movies in Congress Square, and another outdoor concert series in Post Office Park. There's also the grand tree-lighting ceremony in late November. **Portland Performing Arts Center** (✉ 25-A Forest Ave. ☎ 207/761–0591) presents music, dance, and theater performances. **Portland Stage Company** (✉ 25-A Forest Ave. ☎ 207/774–0465) mounts productions year-round at the Portland Performing Arts Center. Rock concerts and other events are frequently staged at the **State Theatre** (✉ 609 Congress St., Arts District ☎ 207/773–2337).

Sports & the Outdoors

When the weather's good, everyone in Portland heads outside. Some drive out of the city to explore, but many take to the streets and trails with their bikes, their dogs, and/or their kids to enjoy the season. Portland has quite a bit of green space in its several parks and in the heat of the summer these places make for cool retreats with refreshing fountains and plenty of shade.

Baseball

The Class AA **Portland Sea Dogs** (✉ 271 Park Ave. ☎ 800/936–3647 ⊕ www.seadogs.com), an affiliate of the Boston Red Sox, play at Hadlock Field. Tickets cost $4–$6.

Bicycling

For state bike trail maps, club and tour listings, or hints on safety, contact the **Bicycle Coalition of Maine** (✉ 59 Federal St. ☎ 207/774–2933).

Rent bikes right downtown at **Cycle Mania** (✉ 59 Federal St. ☎ 207/774–2933 ⊕ www.cyclemania1.com). They have several models and programs to choose from.

For local biking information, contact **Portland Trails** (✉ 1 India St. ☎ 207/775–2411 ⊕ www.trails.org), a group devoted to blazing (literally) new trails for cyclists and walkers. They can tell you about designated, paved routes that wind along the water, through parks, and beyond. For a map, call, stop in, or get one online.

Summer Feet (☎ 207/828–0342 or 866/857–9544 ⊕ www.summerfeet. net) has both guided and self-guided cycling tours, both in Portland and throughout the state. Trips cover Portland history and last up to four hours; full days and overnights are available in other regions of Maine.

Boat Trips

For tours of the harbor, Casco Bay, and the scenic nearby islands, try **Bay View Cruises** (✉ Fisherman's Wharf ☎ 207/761–0496). For an extra treat, request the Lobster Bake on the Bay—a full meal of chowder, bread, mussels, lobster, and dessert. **Casco Bay Lines** (✉ Maine State Pier, Waterfront ☎ 207/774–7871 ⊕ www.cascobaylines.com) provides narrated cruises and transportation to Casco Bay Islands. **Eagle Island Tours** (✉ Long Wharf ☎ 207/774–6498 ⊕ www.eagleislandtours. com) conducts daily cruises to Eagle Island as well as seal-watching cruises. **Lucky Catch Cruises** (✉ 170 Commercial St. ☎ 207/761–0941 ⊕ www. luckycatch.com) sets out to sea in a real lobster boat so passengers can get the genuine experience, which includes hauling traps and the chance to purchase the catch. There are several itineraries to choose from. **Old Port Mariner Fleet** (✉ Long Wharf ☎ 207/775–0727 or 800/437–3270) leads scenic cruises, whale watching, and fishing trips. **Portland Schooner Co.** (✉ Maine State Pier ☎ 207/766–2500 or 877/724–6663 ⊕ www. portlandschooner.com) offers daily sails aboard a vintage 1924, 72-foot racing schooner. Bring your own food and beverage and help hoist the sails of this beauty.

Hockey

The **Portland Pirates** (⊠ 85 Free St. ☎ 207/828–4665), the farm team of the Washington Capitals, play home games at the Cumberland County Civic Center. Tickets cost $10–$14.

Hot-Air Balloon Rides

Balloon Rides of Portland (☎ 207/761–8373 or 800/952–2076 ⊕ www2. hotairballoon.com/hotairballoon) sets aloft twice daily by reservation, depending on the weather. Flights are $225 per person (for about an hour) and include snacks, champagne, and transportation to your car.

Hot Fun Balloon Rides (☎ 207/799–0193 ⊕ www.hotfunballoons.com) offers mainly sunrise trips and can accommodate up to three people. The price of $250 per person includes a postflight champagne toast, snacks, and shuttle to the liftoff site.

SHOPPING

For a city this size, you can find a plethora of locally owned stores and arts and crafts galleries; trendy Exchange Street is great for browsing. For the souvenir hound, there are plenty of gift shops stretched out along Commercial Street eager to sell nautical, Maine moose, and lobster emblems emblazoned on everything from T-shirts to shot glasses.

In the past few years, several art galleries have opened their doors, offering many alternatives to the ubiquitous New England seaside painting. Modern art, photography, sculpture, pottery, and artful woodwork now fill the shelves of many shops, revealing the sophisticated and avant-garde faces of the city's art scene.

Art & Antiques

Abacus (⊠ 44 Exchange St. ☎ 207/772–4880), an appealing crafts gallery, has unusual gift items in glass, wood, and textiles, plus fine modern jewelry. **Foundry Lane Contemporary Crafts** (⊠ 305 Commercial St. ☎ 207/773–2722) sells plenty of limited-edition glass, home accessories, and jewelry and is Maine's only dealer of famed Marimekko of Finland products. **Greenhut Galleries** (⊠ 146 Middle St. ☎ 207/772–2693) shows contemporary art and sculpture by Maine artists. **F. O. Bailey Antiquarians** (⊠ 141 Middle St. ☎ 207/774–1479), Portland's largest retail showroom, carries antique and reproduction furniture and jewelry, paintings, rugs, and china. The **Institute for Contemporary Art** (⊠ 522 Congress St. ☎ 207/879–5742), at the Maine College of Art, showcases contemporary artwork from around the world. The **Pine Tree Shop & Bayview Gallery** (⊠ 75 Market St. ☎ 207/773–3007 or 800/244–3007) has original art and prints by prominent Maine painters. Representing 100 American artists, the spacious **Stein Gallery** (⊠ 195 Middle St. ☎ 207/772–9072) showcases decorative and sculptural contemporary glass.

Books

Carlson and Turner (⊠ 241 Congress St. ☎ 207/773–4200) is an antiquarian-book dealer with an estimated 70,000 titles. **Cunningham Books**

(⊠ 188 State St. ☎ 207/775–2246) is a grand browsing (and buying) experience for book lovers. Pleasant and knowledgeable owner, Nancy, knows in a moment whether your request is present amid the thousands of titles stacked high on the shelves or along the walls. **Longfellow Books** (⊠ 1 Monument Way ☎ 207/772–4045) is a grand success story of the independent bookstore triumphing over the massive presence of the large chains. They're known for their good service and very thoughtful literary selection. There's also a great selection of greeting cards; author readings are scheduled regularly.

Clothing

The women's clothing at **Amaryllis** (⊠ 41 Exchange St. ☎ 207/772–4439 ⊕ www.amaryllisclothing.com) is as airy, colorful, and sculptured as Maine's wildest beaches. The selection includes great casual wear with some unusual evening choices, not to mention shoes, jewelry, and Maine's new favorite keepsake—the souvenir embroidered pillow.

For boutique-quality women's clothing, jewelry, and other artful accessories, visit **Calypso** (⊠ 2 Milk St. ☎ 207/774–8800). Family-owned **Casco Bay Wool Works** (⊠ 10 Moulton St. ☎ 207/879–9665) sells beautiful, handcrafted wool capes, shawls, blankets, and scarves.

For the style-conscious man, visit **Joseph's** (⊠ 410 Fore St. ☎ 207/773–1274), which features Canali, Tommy Bahama, and more. With a funky combination of good-quality consignment and new clothing for both men and women, **Material Objects** (⊠ 500 Congress St. ☎ 207/774–1241) makes for an affordable and unusual shopping spree. Retro, rockabilly, and suave, **Stitchez** (⊠ 574 Congress St. ☎ 207/780–8340) is a great find for hip male fashions.

Furniture

Maine islander **Angela Adams** (⊠ 273 Congress St. ☎ 207/774–3523 or 800/255–9454 ⊕ www.angelaadams.com) has plunged into the international design scene with her simple but bold geometric designs parlayed into dramatic rugs, handbags, trays, paper goods, and glassware. Her creations are sold in exclusive venues around the globe, but this small shop on Congress Street is her only studio and showroom.

For an international flair for your living quarters, head to **Asia West** (⊠ 219 Commercial St. ☎ 207/775–0066). They offer some beautiful wood work in benches, tables, sculpture, and much more.

Made locally, the handsome cherrywood pieces at **Green Design Furniture** (⊠ 267 Commercial St. ☎ 207/775–4234, 800/853–4234 orders) have a classic feel—somewhat Asian, somewhat Mission; a unique system of joinery enables easy assembly after shipping.

Mall

The **Maine Mall** (⊠ 364 Maine Mall Rd., South Portland ☎ 207/774–0303), 5 mi south of Portland, has 145 stores, including Sears, Filene's, JCPenney, and Macy's.

SIDE TRIPS FROM PORTLAND

Casco Bay Islands

The islands of Casco Bay are also known as the Calendar Islands because an early explorer mistakenly thought there was one for each day of the year (in reality there are only 140). These islands range from ledges visible only at low tide to populous Peaks Island, a suburb of Portland. Some islands are uninhabited; others support year-round communities as well as stores and restaurants. Fort Gorges commands Hog Island Ledge, and Eagle Island is the site of Arctic explorer Admiral Perry's home. The brightly painted ferries of Casco Bay Lines are the islands' lifeline. There is frequent service to the most-populated ones, including Peaks, Long, Little Diamond, and Great Diamond. A ride on the bay is a great way to experience the dramatic shape of the Maine Coast while offering a glimpse of some of its hundreds of islands.

There is little in the way of brief overnight lodging on the islands; while the population swells during the summer months, much of the increase is due to summer-long visitors and part-time residents. Tourism is passive—there are few restaurants or organized attractions other than the natural beauty of the islands themselves. Meandering about by bike or on foot is a good way to explore the islands on a day trip; or you can spend the day viewing the areas from the ferry or mail boat's bow.

⓬ Peaks Island, nearest to Portland, is the most developed of the Calendar Islands, but it still allows you to commune with the wind and sea, explore an old fort, and ramble along the alternately rocky and sandy shore. The trip to the island by boat is particularly enjoyable at or near sunset.

A small museum with Civil War artifacts, open in summer, is maintained in the **Fifth Maine Regiment** building (⌧ 45 Seashore Ave., Peaks Island ☎ 207/766–3330 ⊕ www.fifthmainemuseum.org ☉ Memorial Day–June, weekends 11–5; July–Labor Day, weekdays 1–4, weekends 11–5; Labor Day–Columbus Day, weekends 11–5 pm ☒ $5 suggested donation). When the Civil War broke out in 1861, Maine was asked to raise only a single regiment to fight, but the state raised 10 and sent the 5th Maine Regiment into the war's first battle, at Bull Run. Guidebooks for a two-hour self-guided tour of the World War II Peaks Island Reservation are available. Ask about volunteer reenactment events staged throughout the summer.

⓭ Eagle Island, owned by the state and open to the public for day trips in summer, was the home of Admiral Robert E. Peary, the American explorer of the North Pole. Peary built a stone-and-wood house on the 17-acre island as a summer retreat in 1904 but ended up making it his permanent residence. Filled with Peary's stuffed Arctic birds, the quartz he brought home and set into the fieldstone fireplace, and other objects, the house remains as it was when Peary lived in it. A boat ride here offers a classic Maine experience as you pass by a few of the hundreds of uninhabited, forested islands along the coast. Once you land on Eagle Island, there are plenty of opportunities to explore the rocky

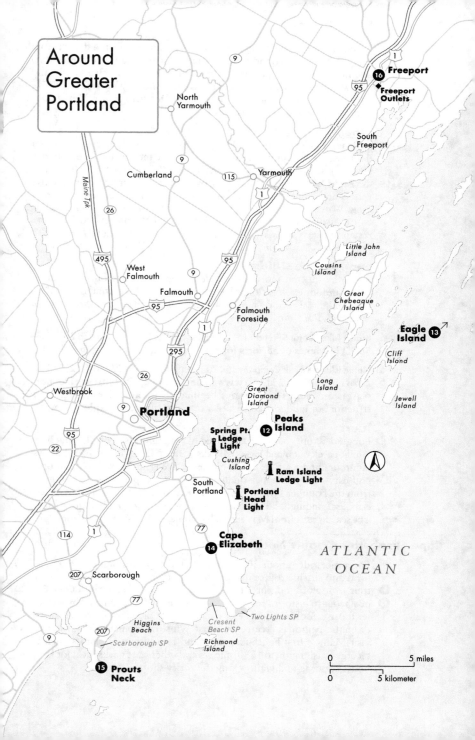

Around Greater Portland

North Yarmouth

Freeport 16

Freeport Outlets

South Freeport

Cumberland

Yarmouth

Maine Tpk

West Falmouth

Falmouth

Falmouth Foreside

Little John Island

Cousins Island

Great Chebeaque Island

Eagle Island 13

Cliff Island

Jewell Island

Long Island

Westbrook

Portland

Great Diamond Island

Peaks Island 12

Spring Pt. Ledge Light

Cushing Island

Ram Island Ledge Light

South Portland

Portland Head Light

Cape Elizabeth 14

Scarborough

Higgins Beach

Cresent Beach SP

Two Lights SP

Richmond Island

Scarborough SP

Prouts Neck 15

ATLANTIC OCEAN

0   5 miles

0   5 kilometer

beach and myriad of trails. The *Kristy K.* and *Fish Hawk* depart from Long Wharf in Portland (you can also visit the island from Freeport) and make four-hour narrated tours; tours of Portland Head Light and seal-watching cruises are also conducted. ⊠ *Long Wharf* ☎ *207/774–6498* ⊜ *$8–$15, depending on tour* ☉ *Departures late May–Labor Day, daily beginning 10 AM.*

Where to Stay & Eat

$–$$ ✕ **Jones' Landing.** Order a lobster sandwich or cold beer on the outdoor deck just steps from the ferry dock. Stay for the live music on Sunday afternoons. ⊠ *Welch St., Peaks Island* ☎ *207/766–5652* ☲ *MC, V.*

$–$$ ▥ **Peaks Island House.** Simplicity by the sea is the motto here; the five rooms are simply decorated yet comfortable, and the views are stunning. Water and city views give one the sense of peace without feeling entirely isolated from Portland's glittering civilization beyond. The inn's restaurant serves breakfast and dinner. ⊠ *20 Island Ave., 04108* ☎ *207/766–4406* ⥼ *5 rooms* ♺ *Restaurant* ☲ *MC, V.*

Sports & the Outdoors

Since the quieter, more independent element of ecotourism endures here, outdoor exploration is best done either by bike, foot, or kayak. If you don't have your own bike or boat, there are a couple of options for rentals and/or tours.

BICYCLING **Brad's Bike Rental & Repair** (⊠ 115 Island Ave., Peaks Island ☎ 207/766–5631) has bikes of all sorts for rent, perfect for exploring the island.

KAYAKING **Maine Island Kayak Company** (⊠ 70 Luther St., Peaks Island ☎ 207/766–2373 or 800/796–2313 ⊕ www.maineislandkayak.com) provides both seasoned paddlers and curious beginners with any necessary gear, instruction, or guidance to ensure a safe and fun water exploration.

Tours

For guided tours of Peaks Island led by longtime residents the MacIsaac family, check out **Island Tours** (⊠ Peaks Island ☎ 207/766–5514 ⊕ http://islandtours.home.att.net). Ramble about the island in style—in an open golf cart—for a very personalized and lively experience. Tours depart from the Founder's Monument at the entrance to the parking lot of Forest City Landing, and include sunset, history, and architecture themes. The season runs from May through October; prices start at $10 for adults.

Cape Elizabeth to Prouts Neck

For a nice ride (about 30 mi or so round-trip) through the more pastoral and seaside routes just out of the city, take the following driving ⑭ tour from Portland, through the upscale Portland suburb of **Cape Eliz-** ⑮ **abeth**, out to historic **Prouts Neck.** This is an area long enjoyed by wealthier tourists looking for quieter escapes, and made famous by a series of dramatic paintings created by artist Winslow Homer. Along the way, visit Maine's first lighthouse, Portland Head Light, commissioned by George Washington in 1790, and several other state parks ideal for lighthouse spotting and walks along the rocky shore.

Take Route 77 southeast from Portland, head over the Casco Bay Bridge, and follow signs for Portland Head Light in Cape Elizabeth. About 2 mi from the beginning of Cottage Road is Fort Williams Park, home of **Portland Head Light.** Stop here to have a picnic, tour the on-site lighthouse museum, and walk the extensive grounds of the park.

Continue by taking a left out of the park; after about 1.5 mi, take a left onto Two Lights Road (you'll see signs for the park) to **Two Lights State Park.** Built in 1828, these were the first twin lighthouses on the coast of Maine. Although not open to the public, the eastern light is an active, automated light station, visible 17 mi at sea. The western light ceased operation in 1924 and is now a private home. One of these towers was the subject of Edward Hooper's famous painting *Lighthouse at Two Lights.* On the grounds of the park you can wander through World War II bunkers in the park and picnic on the rocky coast.

After visiting the park, head back to Route 77. Take a left and continue on about 4 or 5 mi, passing scenic salt marshes, more farmland, and several roadside stands ideal for picking up fresh produce in summer. For another scenic stop, pull into **Crescent Beach State Park,** where you can find miles of hiking trails, beach access, and plenty of picnic facilities.

For another beach experience with lots of sandy spread, waves, and people-watching action, stop at **Higgins Beach,** in the town of Scarborough about 4 mi south. Continue on Route 77 until the junction of Route 207; bear left on Route 207 and head out toward Prouts Neck. On your way is another good beach stop, **Scarborough Beach State Park.**

Parking is nearly nonexistent once you get to **Prouts Neck,** but you may be able to park at the Black Point Inn if you eat there (it's a great place for Sunday brunch). Look for small signs on the road for the Cliff Walk—follow them around the bend until you reach the gated community; there is a small pebbled path that leads to the green house behind the gated community that was once Winslow Homer's home and studio. The studio is open in July and August, daily from 11 AM to 4 PM.

To get back to Portland, backtrack up Route 207. At the junction of Routes 77 and 207, stay straight on Route 207 and it's about 4 mi to U.S. 1. Take a right on U.S. 1 and you'll reach Portland after about 6 mi.

What to See

FodorsChoice
★

Historic **Portland Head Light,** familiar to many from photographs and Edward Hopper's painting *Portland Head-Light (1927),* was commissioned by George Washington in 1790. The towering white stone lighthouse stands over the keeper's house, a white home with a blazing red roof. Besides a harbor view, its park has walking paths and picnic facilities. The keeper's house is now the Museum at Portland Head Light. The lighthouse is in Fort Williams Park, about 2 mi from the town center. *Museum* ⊠ *1000 Shore Rd., Cape Elizabeth* ☎ *207/799–2661* ⊕ *www.portlandheadlight.com* ⊡ *$2* ⊙ *Memorial Day–mid-Oct., daily 10–4; Apr., May, Nov., and Dec., weekends 10–4.*

Two Lights State Park sits on just over 40 acres of Maine's quintessential rocky shoreline. Named for the two lighthouses atop the hill (one is now privately owned, the other still in use since 1828), the park has ample beach access, picnic facilities, and great views of the activities of Portland Harbor. The fee for adults is $3. ⊠ *Rte. 77, Cape Elizabeth* ☎ *207/ 799–5871.*

The 243-acre **Crescent Beach State Park,** about 8 mi south of Portland, has a sandy beach, picnic tables, a seasonal snack bar, and a bathhouse. Miles of nature trails head into the woods beyond the beach, ideal for bird-watching. Popular with families with young children, it charges a nominal fee for admittance ($3.50 for adults). ⊠ *Rte. 77, Cape Elizabeth* ☎ *207/799–5871.*

Higgins Beach is a good-size and very popular sandy beach set amid a little beach colony neighborhood. Parking costs about $4 in several privately owned lots. The beach is popular with surfers and sunbathers. ⊠ *Off Rte. 77 (Spurwink Rd.), Scarborough.*

need a break?
Just off Route 77 (Spurwink Rd.) near Higgins Beach is the **Higgins Beach Market** (⊠ 82 Spurwink Rd. ☎ 207/883–2766), a small wooden barnlike shop filled with surprisingly sophisticated wares. Get the goods for a sunset beach picnic complete with wine or beer, freshly made sandwiches, bakery items, and even prepared cold meals, all to go. The market opens at 6 AM and closes around 6 PM, mid-May through late-October.

Scarborough Beach State Park has a large sandy beach area with ample parking, lifeguards, and lots of people-watching opportunities. There is a parking fee. ⊠ *Rte. 207, Scarborough.*

Where to Stay & Eat

¢–$$ ✕ **Barbara's Kitchen.** The dining room may be small, but its high tin ceilings make the room feel like home—quite comfortable and intimate. The menu is varied and includes creative treatments of pasta, sandwiches, omelets, and seafood. A favorite for dinner is the seared scallops with crab and fresh dill over lemon fettucine, served with a Parmesan cream sauce. The restaurant is open for brunch on Sunday. ⊠ *388 Cottage Rd., South Portland* ☎ *207/767–6313* ⌧ *AE, DC, MC, V* ⊘ *Closed Mon.; no dinner Sun.*

¢–$$ ✕ **The Good Table.** Close to Two Lights State Park, this is a great little place to get weekend breakfast or brunch before visiting the beach. The omelets are big and moist, as is the French toast. The lunch and dinner menu is a bit reminiscent of the old diner days and includes a hot turkey dinner with mashed potatoes and gravy. You'll also find fresh fried seafood and a very tasty lobster roll. Sit under the colorful paper lanterns out on the screened-in porch and enjoy the woodsy view. ⊠ *526 Ocean House Rd., Cape Elizabeth* ☎ *207/799–4663* ▤ *MC, V* ⊘ *Closed Mon.*

¢–$$ ✕ **Lobster Shack.** You can't beat the location—right on the water, below the lighthouse pair that gives Two Lights State Park its name—and the food's not bad either. Just as the name implies, fresh lobster is the watchword here, and you can choose your meal right from the tank. Other menu must-haves include chowder, fried clams, and fish-and-chips.

It's been a classic spot since the 1920s. Eat inside or out. ✉ *225 Two Lights Rd.* ☎ *207/799–1677* ▭ *MC, V* ⊙ *Closed Nov.–late Mar.*

$$$–$$$$ ✕⌧ **Inn by the Sea.** Every unit in this all-suites inn includes a kitchen and a view of the Atlantic. It's a short walk down a private boardwalk to sandy Crescent Beach, a popular family spot. Dogs are welcomed with a room-service pet menu, evening turndown treats, and oversize beach towels. The Audubon dining room ($$$–$$$$), open to nonguests, serves fine seafood and regional dishes. The shingle-style design, typical of turn-of-the-20th-century New England shorefront cottages and hotels, includes a varied roofline punctuated by turretlike features and gables, balconies, a covered porch supported by columns, an open deck, and large windows. ✉ *40 Bowery Beach Rd., 7 mi south of Portland, Cape Elizabeth 04107* ☎ *207/799–3134 or 800/888–4287* 📠 *207/ 799–4779* ⊕ *www.innbythesea.com* ⌁ *43 suites* ♿ *Restaurant, in-room data ports, kitchens, microwaves, refrigerators, cable TV, in-room VCRs, tennis court, pool, croquet, lobby lounge, babysitting, dry cleaning, Internet, meeting rooms; no smoking* ▭ *AE, D, MC, V.*

$$$$ ⌧ **Black Point Inn.** Toward the tip of the peninsula that juts into the ocean at Prouts Neck stands this stylish, tastefully updated historic resort with spectacular views up and down the Maine Coast. The extensive grounds contain beaches, trails, and sports facilities—including use of the tennis courts and golf course at the nearby country club. Finer touches abound, such as nightly turndown service and in-room terry robes. The Cliff Walk, a pebbled path that wanders past Winslow Homer's former studio, runs along the Atlantic headlands that Homer often painted. The inn is 12 mi south of Portland and about 10 mi north of Old Orchard Beach. ✉ *510 Black Point Rd., Scarborough 04074* ☎ *207/883– 2500 or 800/258–0003* 📠 *207/883–9976* ⊕ *www.blackpointinn.com* ⌁ *84 rooms, 12 suites* ♿ *Restaurant, 2 pools (1 indoor), hot tub, boating, bicycles, croquet, volleyball, bar* ▭ *AE, D, MC, V* ⍥ *MAP.*

Sports & the Outdoors

This area is home to several state parks and long stretches of beachfront that are ideal for sunbathing, strolling, and exploring. Routes 77 and 207 are ideal for cyclists who like winding roads and pastoral scenery. Walkers can choose from miles of trails within the state parks, and there are plenty of ideal spots for picnics and oceanside barbecues. This is the region where Portland's city folk come to walk the beach and enjoy the open space.

The **Maine Audubon Society** (✉ Rte. 9, Scarborough ☎ 207/781–2330, 207/883–5100 from mid-June to Labor Day) operates guided canoe trips and rents canoes in Scarborough Marsh, the largest salt marsh in Maine. Programs at Maine Audubon's Falmouth headquarters (north of Portland) include nature walks and a discovery room for children.

Freeport

16 *17 mi northeast of Portland, 10 mi southwest of Brunswick.*

Those who flock straight to L. L. Bean and see nothing else of Freeport are missing out on some real New England beauty. The city's charming backstreets are lined with historic buildings and old clapboard houses, and there's a pretty little harbor on the south side of the Harraseeket River. It's true, many who come to the area do so simply to shop—L. L. Bean is the store that put Freeport on the map, and plenty of outlets and some specialty stores have settled here. Still, if you choose, you can stay awhile and experience more than fabulous shopping; beyond the shops are bucolic nature preserves with miles of walking trails, well-maintained old homes, and plenty of places for leisurely ambling that don't require the overuse of your credit cards.

The **Freeport Historical Society** mounts exhibits pertaining to the town's history. You can also pick up a walking map of the village here. ✉ 45 *Main St.* ☎ 207/865–0477.

♻ At the **Desert of Maine**, a 40-acre natural desert, you can tour the sand dunes in a safari coach, walk nature trails, hunt for gemstones, and watch sand artists at work. Poor agricultural practices in the late 18th century combined with massive land clearing and overgrazing uncovered this desert, which was actually formed by a glacier during the last Ice Age. ✉ I–95, Exit 19 ☎ 207/865–6962 ⊕ www.desertofmaine.com ☜ $7.50 ☺ Early May–mid-Oct., daily.

off the beaten path

PETTENGILL FARM – To escape Freeport's busy outlet scene, take a stroll back in time at this 19th-century farm. Operated by the Freeport Historical Society, the aged and beautiful farm is set on 140 acres of salt marsh, with open fields, exquisite gardens, and an original 1810 saltbox home. It's an excellent spot for nature watching; bring your camera and binoculars to see deer, fox, and a vast array of both migratory and native birds. Tours of the home can be arranged by appointment; otherwise, you're free to wander the grounds. Not too easy to find and with very little parking, the farm is a true hidden treasure. To find the small parking area, head out of Freeport on Bow Street, pass over the Harraseeket River, and look for Pettengill Road on the right. Visitors must walk about a half mile to reach the grounds. It's worth it for the sheer beauty and sense of historic solitude. ☎ 207/865–3170 ⊕ www.freeporthistoricalsociety.org.

Where to Stay & Eat

$$–$$$ ✕ **Broad Arrow Tavern.** On the main floor of the Harraseeket Inn, this
Fodor'sChoice dark-paneled tavern with giant fireplace, mounted moose heads, and other
★ outdoor sporty decor is known for both its casual nature and its sumptuous menu. The chefs use only organically grown food, with a nearly exclusive emphasis on Maine products, to create treats such as wood-fired steaks and seafood. About the only non-Maine ingredient is the farm-raised South Dakota buffalo, though it's a real favorite. For lunch, choose from the ample menu or graze on the well-stocked buffet. The quality is superior. Lunch and dinner are served daily from 11:30 AM. ✉ 162 Main St. ☎ 207/865–9377 ⊘ Reservations not accepted ▭ AE, D, DC, MC, V.

$–$$$ ✕ **Azure Café.** This airy little café right on Main Street provides both an appealing atmosphere and an enticing menu. Local fruits, vegetables, meats, and seafood are all treated to an Italian transformation. Dinner favorites are the Tuscan pork tenderloin and the robust cioppino, a blend of Maine lobster and scallops, shrimp, haddock, and mussels in a spicy broth. With a nod to the state of Maine, the decidedly non-Italian lunch menu offers award-winning clam chowder, steamed lobster, and fish and chips. In summer sit out on the street-side patio, listen to live jazz, savor the tiramisu, and forget about nearby outlet bargains for just a little while. Reservations are recommended. ⊠ *123 Main St.* ☎ *207/ 865–1237* ⊟ *MC, V.*

$–$$$ ✕ **Harraseeket Lunch & Lobster Co.** Seafood baskets and lobster dinners are the focus at this bare-bones place beside the town landing in South Freeport. Order at the counter and find a seat inside or out, depending on the weather. ⊠ *On pier, end of Main St.* ☎ *207/865–4888* ⌔ *Reservations not accepted* ⊟ *No credit cards* ⊙ *Closed mid-Oct.–Apr.*

$–$$$ ✕ **School Street Café.** You won't find a funkier place in Freeport than this, and the food is just as sophisticated and tasty as the streamlined decor. The menu is innovative and full of items not often seen—have you ever tried skate fries on a bed of seaweed? Seafood, meats, grilled gourmet pizzas, and vegetarian dishes make up the changing menu; a favorite is the bacon-wrapped pork medallions with spatzle hash and apple brandy cream. It's amazing what the chefs can do with artichokes, endives, or even grilled salsify. Reservations are recommended. ⊠ *10 School St.* ☎ *207/865–0100* ⊟ *MC, V.*

$$$–$$$$ ✕▥ **Harraseeket Inn.** Despite modern appointments such as elevators and whirlpool baths in some rooms, this 1850 Greek Revival home provides a pleasantly old-fashioned, country-inn experience just a few minutes' walk from L. L. Bean. Guest rooms have print fabrics and reproductions of Federal quarter-canopy beds. Ask for a second-floor, garden-facing room. The formal Maine Dining Room ($$$–$$$$) specializes in contemporary American regional (and organic) cuisine such as green apple and sarsaparilla short ribs and pan-roasted halibut with potato chowder. The casual Broad Arrow Tavern ($–$$$) serves heartier fare and has a charming seasonal patio. ⊠ *162 Main St., 04032* ☎ *207/865–9377 or 800/ 342–6423* ▣ *207/865–1684* ⊕ *www.harraseeketinn.com* ◁ *82 rooms, 2 suites* ⌂ *2 restaurants, in-room data ports, some microwaves, some refrigerators, cable TV, indoor pool, croquet, meeting room, some pets allowed (fee), no-smoking rooms* ⊟ *AE, D, DC, MC, V* ⦿l *BP.*

$$$ ▥ **Atlantic Seal Bed & Breakfast.** The nautical theme of this 1850 waterfront home complements the pleasant water views from all three of its rooms. Owner Capt. Thomas Ring provides homemade quilts, antiques, and down comforters for each room; he also leads scenic boat trips from the nearby harbor (*see* Atlantic Seal Cruises, *below*). ⊠ *25 Main St.* ⎘ *Box 146, South Freeport 04078* ☎ *207/865–6112, 877/285–7325 seasonal* ◁ *2 rooms, 1 suite* ⌂ *Cable TV, in-room VCRs, boating, mountain bike; no smoking* ⊟ *AE, MC, V* ⦿l *BP.*

$$–$$$ ▥ **The James Place Inn.** Set on a quiet side street yet within easy walking distance of shopping paradise, this peaceful inn is tastefully decorated with brightly painted walls, colorful floral bedspreads, hooked rugs, and four-poster beds. Maine-inspired artwork and fresh flowers add to the simple elegance of the place, which serves a full, hot breakfast in a light-dappled sun room. Some marbled bathrooms even provide two-person Jacuzzis. For winter visits, choose the room with a working fireplace. One room has a kitchenette. ⊠ *11 Holbrook St.* ☎ *207/865–4486*

*or 800/964–9086 ⊕ www.jamesplaceinn.com ⇆ 7 rooms ⚬ Cable TV
▭ D, MC, V ▢ BP.*

¢ ▢ **Maine Idyll Motor Court.** The Marsteller family has operated this simple 1932 cottage colony for four generations. The tidy white cabins are shaded by towering pines and popular with families. Wood floors and paneling enrich the rustic interior of each cabin. ⊠ *325 U.S. 1, 04032* ☎ *207/865–4201 ⇆ 20 1- to 3-bedroom cottages ⚬ Some microwaves, refrigerators, cable TV, 2 playgrounds, some pets allowed, no-smoking rooms; no a/c in some rooms ▭ No credit cards ⊗ Closed mid-Nov.–mid-Apr. ▢ CP.*

Nightlife & the Arts

Every Saturday night in July and August, sit outside under the stars for the **L. L. Bean Summer Concert Series** (⊠ Morse St. ☎ 800/559–0747 Ext. 37222 ⊕ www.llbean.com). The free concerts start at 7:30 PM in downtown Freeport at L. L. Bean's Discovery Park. The entertainment ranges from folk, jazz, and country to rock and includes some pretty big names. Bring a blanket and refreshments. Look for special Sunday concert events during the late fall and winter holiday season. Previous summer acts have included Livingston Taylor, zydeco and bluegrass musicians, and the Don Campbell Band.

Sports & the Outdoors

Atlantic Seal Cruises (⊠ South Freeport ☎ 207/865–6112, 877/285–7325 seasonal) operates day trips to Eagle Island and Seguin Island lighthouse, as well as evening seal and osprey watches.

It shouldn't come as a surprise that one of the world's largest outdoor clothing and supply outfitters also provides its customers with instructional adventures to go with their products. L. L. Bean's year-round **Outdoor Discovery Schools** (⊠ Freeport ☎ 888/552–3261 ⊕ www.llbean. com/ods) include half- and one-day classes, as well as longer trips that teach canoeing, shooting, photography, kayaking, fly-fishing, cross-country skiing, and other sports. Classes are for all skill levels; it's best to sign up several months in advance. Check their schedule for special walk-on activities held regularly during the summer months.

STATE PARKS   **Wolfe's Neck Woods State Park** has 5 mi of good hiking trails along Casco Bay, the Harraseeket River, and a fringe salt marsh. Naturalists lead walks in summer and on weekends and holidays in spring and fall; it's an excellent place to view nesting ospreys. The park has picnic tables and grills but no camping. ⊠ *Wolfe's Neck Rd., follow Bow St. opposite L. L. Bean off U.S. 1 ☎ 207/865–4465 ⚐ $2 Memorial Day–Labor Day, $1 off-season (Apr., Oct.) ⊗ Closed Nov.–Mar.*

Bradbury Mountain State Park has moderate trails to the top of Bradbury Mountain. There are lovely views of the sea from the peak. A picnic area and shelter, a ball field, a playground, and 41 campsites are among the facilities. ⊠ *Rte. 9, I–95, 5 mi from Freeport-Durham exit, Pownal ☎ 207/ 688–4712 ⚐ $2 Memorial Day–Labor Day, $1 rest of year.*

Shopping

The *Freeport Visitors Guide* (☎ 207/865–1212, 800/865–1994 for a copy) lists the more than 100 shops and factory outlet stores that can be found on Main Street, Bow Street, and elsewhere, including such big-name designers as Coach, Brooks Brothers, Polo Ralph Lauren, and Cole-Haan. Don't overlook the specialty stores and crafts galleries.

Cuddledown of Maine (⊠ 237 U.S. 1 ☎ 207/865–1713) has a selection of down comforters, pillows, and luxurious bedding. Head upstairs for discounted merchandise. Kids get their chance to shop at the educational toy store **Play and Learn** (⊠ 140 Main St. ☎ 207/865–6434). **Thos. Moser Cabinetmakers** (⊠ 149 Main St. ☎ 207/865–4519) sells high-quality handmade furniture with clean, classic lines.

Founded in 1912 as a mail-order merchandiser of products for hunters, guides, and anglers, **L. L. Bean** (⊠ 95 Main St. [U.S. 1] ☎ 800/341–4341) attracts 3½ million shoppers a year to its giant store (open 24 hours a day) in the heart of Freeport's shopping district. You can still find the original hunting boots, along with cotton, wool, and silk sweaters; camping and ski equipment; comforters; and hundreds of other items for the home, car, boat, or campsite. The **L. L. Bean Factory Store** (⊠ Depot St. ☎ 800/341–4341) has seconds and discontinued merchandise at discount prices. **L. L. Bean Kids** (⊠ 8 Nathan Nye St. ☎ 800/341–4341) specializes in children's merchandise and has a climbing wall and other activities that appeal to kids.

GREATER PORTLAND A TO Z

To research prices, get advice from other travelers, and book travel arrangements, visit www.fodors.com.

AIRPORTS
Portland International Jetport is served by American Airlines, Continental, Delta, Independence Air, Northwest, United, and US Airways.
🖪 **Portland International Jetport** ⊠ Westbrook St. off Rte. 9 ☎ 207/774-7301 ⊕ www.portlandjetport.org.

BIKE TRAVEL
The craggy fingers of land that dominate this part of the coast are fun for experienced cyclists to explore, but the lack of shoulders on most roads combined with heavy tourist traffic can be intimidating. Two good resources are the Bicycle Coalition of Maine and the Maine Department of Transportation, which provide information on trails and bike shops around the state.
🖪 **Bicycle Coalition of Maine** ⌖ Box 5275, Augusta ☎ 207/623-4511 ⊕ www.bikemaine.org. **Maine Dept. of Transportation Bike and Pedestrian Section** ⊕ www.state.me.us/mdot/biketours.htm.

BOAT & FERRY TRAVEL
Casco Bay Lines provides ferry service from Portland to the islands of Casco Bay. The *Scotia Prince* will take you and your vehicle from Portland to Atlantic Canada. Round-trip, 23-hour cruises aboard the ship are also available with live entertainment, casinos, spa treatments, and more.
🖪 **Casco Bay Lines** ☎ 207/774-7871 ⊕ www.cascobaylines.com. **Scotia Prince Cruises** ☎ 866/568-2036 ⊕ www.cruisenovascotia.com.

BUS TRAVEL TO & FROM PORTLAND

Greater Portland's Metro runs seven bus routes in Portland, South Portland, and Westbrook. The fare is $1; exact change ($1 bills accepted) is required. Buses run from 5:30 AM to 11:45 PM.

The Portland Explorer has express shuttle service to the Old Port from the Portland Jetport, the Portland Transportation Center, and Casco Bay Lines terminal. The shuttle runs hourly, 7 days a week, from 6:40 AM to 9 PM.

Long-distance bus travel is available within the state of Maine and neighboring New England states. Concord trailways offers service to Boston's Logan Airport, Boston, and points within coastal Maine. Vermont Transit Company services towns throughout Maine and Northern New England. Portland's Transportation Center is close to downtown and the airport.

🚌 **Greater Portland's Metro** ☎ 207/774-0351. **Portland Explorer** ☎ 207/774-9891 ⊕ www.transportme.org. **Concord Trailways** ☎ 207/828-1151 ⊕ www.concordtrailways. com. **Vermont Transit Co.** ☎ 207/772-6587 ⊕ www.vermonttransit.com.

CAR RENTAL

Several car rental options exist at the Portland Jetport; others are dispersed around the South Portland area, just outside the main city limits. *See* Car Rental *in* Smart Travel Tips for national rental agency phone numbers.

CAR TRAVEL

Congress Street leads from I–295 into the heart of Portland; the Gateway Garage on High Street, off Congress, is a convenient place to leave your car downtown. North of Portland, U.S. 1 brings you to Freeport's Main Street, which continues on to Brunswick and Bath. East of Wiscasset you can take Route 27 south to the Boothbays, where Route 96 is a good choice for further exploration. To visit the Pemaquid region, take Route 129 off U.S. 1 in Damariscotta; then pick up Route 130 and follow it down to Pemaquid Point. Return to Waldoboro and U.S. 1 on Route 32 from New Harbor.

In Portland, metered on-street parking is available at 25¢ per half hour, with a two-hour maximum. Parking lots and garages can be found near the Portland Public Market, downtown, in the Old Port, and on the waterfront; most charge $1 per hour or $8–$12 per day. If you're shopping or dining, remember to ask local vendors if they participate in the Park & Shop program, which provides an hour of free shopping for each participating vendor visited.

EMERGENCIES

In an emergency dial 911.

🚑 Hospitals **Maine Medical Center** ✉ 22 Bramhall St., Portland ☎ 207/871-2196. **Mercy Hospital** ✉ 144 State St., Portland ☎ 207/879-3000.

MAIL & SHIPPING

🏤 **U.S. Post Office** ✉ 125 Forest Ave., Portland ☎ 207/871-8461, open weekdays 7:30-7, Sat. 7:30-5. **U.S. Post Office Station A** ✉ 622 Congress St., Portland ☎ 207/

871-8449, open weekdays 8:30-5, Saturday 9-noon. **U.S. Post Office and postal store** ⊠ 400 Congress St., Portland ☎ 207/871-8464, open weekdays 8-7, Sat. 9-1.

MEDIA

The *Portland Press Herald* is published Monday–Saturday; the *Maine Sunday Telegram* is published on Sunday. The *Portland Phoenix,* published each Thursday, is an essential free weekly for those interested in Portland's many entertainment and arts offerings. For other community listings, *Casco Bay Weekly,* also free and available on Thursday, publishes local happenings and events as well as features of regional interest. *Portland Magazine* and the bimonthly *Port City Life,* cover Portland, while the *Maine Times* extends throughout the state.

WMEA 90.1 is the local National Public Radio affiliate. WCSH, channel 6, is the NBC affiliate; WMTW, channel 8, is the ABC affiliate; and WGME, channel 13, is the CBS affiliate. Channel 10 is the Maine Public Broadcasting affiliate.

Sports & the Outdoors

BICYCLING   For professionally guided bicycle tours, information on trails throughout the state, and safety issues, contact the Bicycle Coalition of Maine. **Bicycle Coalition of Maine** ⌂ 59 Federal St., Portland 04101 ☎ 207/774-2933 ⊕ www.bikemaine.org.

BOATING   For boat rentals, *see* town listings. The Maine Professional Guides Association represents kayaking guides.
Maine Professional Guides Association ⌂ Box 847, Augusta 04332 ☎ 207/549-5631 ⊕ www.maineguides.org. **Maine Association of Sea Kayak Guides and Instructors** ⌂ Box 847, Augusta 04332 ☎ 207/549-5631 ⊕ www.maineseakayakguides.com.

TOURS

Several tour operators arrange specialized group trips throughout the state as well as within Portland.
Maine Family Adventures ⊠ 225 Commercial St., Portland ☎ 800/771-7808 ⊕ www.mainefamilyadventures.com. **Ocean View Tours** ☎ 207/741-2776 or 866/251-3626 ⊕ www.mountainviewtours-online.com.

BUS TOURS   In Portland, the informative trolley tours of Mainely Tours cover the city's historical and architectural highlights from Memorial Day through October. Other tours combine a city tour with a bay cruise or a trip to four lighthouses.
Mainely Tours ⊠ 5½ Moulton St. ☎ 207/774-0808 ⊕ www.mainelytours.com.

WALKING TOURS   Greater Portland Landmarks conducts 1½-hour walking tours of the city from July through September; tours begin at the Convention and Visitors Bureau and cost $8.
Convention and Visitors Bureau ☎ 207/772-5800. **Greater Portland Landmarks** ⊠ 165 State St. ☎ 207/774-5561.

TRAIN TRAVEL

Amtrak runs the Downeaster train service from Boston to Portland, with stops (some seasonal) along the coastal route.
Amtrak ☎ 800/872-7245 ⊕ www.amtrakdowneaster.com.

VISITOR INFORMATION

🖪 **Convention and Visitors Bureau of Greater Portland** ⊠ 305 Commercial St., Portland 04101 ☎ 207/772-5800 or 877/833-1374 ⊕ www.visitportland.com. **Freeport Merchants Association** ⌕ 23 Depot St., Freeport 04032 ☎ 207/865-1212 or 800/865-1994 ⊕ www.freeportusa.com. **Portland's Downtown District** ⊠ 94 Free St., Portland 04101 ☎ 207/772-6828 ⊕ www.portlandmaine.com.**Portland Regional Chamber of Commerce** ⊠ 60 Pearl St., Portland 04101 ☎ 207/772-2811 ⊕ www.portlandregion.com.

THE MID-COAST REGION

FROM BRUNSWICK TO MONHEGAN ISLAND

3

By Sherry
Ballou Hanson

LIGHTHOUSES DOT THE HEADLANDS of the Mid-Coast region, where thousands of miles of coastline wait to be explored. Defined by chiseled peninsulas stretching south from U.S. 1, this area has everything from the sandy beaches and sandbars of Popham Beach to the jutting cliffs of Monhegan Island. If you are intent on hooking a trophy-size fish or catching a glimpse of a whale, there are plenty of cruises available. If you just want to explore deserted beaches and secluded coves, kayaks are your best bet. Put in at the Harpswells, or on the Cushing and Saint George peninsulas, or simply paddle among the lobster boats and other vessels that ply these waters.

Fine museums are brimming with the region's dynamic history. The heyday of shipbuilding produced towering square-rigged clipper ships and trading schooners with two and six masts. Tall ships often visit Maine, sometimes sailing up the Kennebec River for a stopover at Bath's Maine Maritime Museum. Not far away, the Bath Iron Works, on the site of the old Percy and Small Shipyard, still builds the U.S. Navy's Aegis-class destroyers. In Brunswick you can visit the home of General Joshua L. Chamberlain, hero at the pivotal Battle of Little Round Top at Gettysburg. He was a professor at Bowdoin College when he made the fateful decision to join the Union Army. His likeness is preserved in a fine bronze statue erected directly across the street from his home, now a museum.

Each town in the region is unique and offers its own charms and attractions. Brunswick has rows of historic wood and clapboard homes, while Bath is known for its maritime heritage. Wiscasset Harbor has docks where you can stroll and waterfront seafood restaurants where you can enjoy the catch of the day. Boothbay has lots of little stores that are perfect for window shopping, while Pemaquid Point is a great destination for picnics. Thomaston and environs offer scenic drives through fishing villages surrounded by water on all sides. Everywhere you can find down-to-earth people who work hard to make sure you have a good stay.

Exploring the Mid-Coast Region

The Mid-Coast region is as varied and interesting as any area in the country. A car is helpful if you want to go far afield, as the remoter areas are not served by public transportation. No matter where you stay, there are plenty of places to explore within a few miles. Brunswick is only a half hour from the Harpswell Islands. Phippsburg and Georgetown are easily accessible from Bath. You can stop for lunch in Wiscasset and then continue to Boothbay Harbor for an afternoon of shopping. Damariscotta is worth a stop for its seafood restaurants. Take at least a day to explore the Pemaquid Peninsula, where you'll find a famous lighthouse, a museum, and art gallery perched on rocky ledges, and a tranquil beach.

Farther north, Thomaston is a good place to stay if you want to explore the St. George and Cushing peninsulas, and the towns of Tenants Harbor and Port Clyde. Marshall Point Lighthouse is in Port Clyde, as is the departure point for Monhegan Island. The island is a great place to spend a day or two hiking through woods and along spectacular cliffs.

Numbers in the text correspond to numbers in the margin and on the Mid-Coast region map.

If you have 3 days

If you have just three days in the area, plan to spend your nights in **Brunswick** ❶ or **Bath** ❷. From Brunswick, drive south on Route 24, or Route 123, to explore the Harpswells. Here you'll find a small beach and the bronze Fishermen's Memorial. Stop for a haddock sandwich at one of the seafood shacks in the area. In the afternoon, you can arrange a kayaking trip along the coast. Try one of the restaurants in Brunswick for dinner. On Day 2, drive south on Route 209 from Bath to Popham Beach State Park, where the Kennebec and Morse rivers meet the sea. Plan to arrive before 10 AM, as the parking lot fills fast. If you arrive at or near low tide, you can explore miles of tidal flats and walk across to Wood Island. The way the tide seems to come in from different directions across the flats is fascinating to watch. You can hike along the beach to Fort Popham, a Civil War–era fortification that is fun to explore. Bring your lunch, or stop for a clam or lobster roll at one of the shops near the beach. No visit to this area is complete without an introduction to its shipbuilding history. Visit the Maine Maritime Museum in Bath on your third day for a tour of the old shipyard and to see the seafaring art and artifacts that fill this beautiful museum. Stroll through downtown Bath in the afternoon, stopping at Waterfront Park to watch the fishing boats, or sign up for a cruise on the Kennebec River.

If you have 5 days

Follow the itinerary above for the first three days. On your fourth day, drive north on U.S. 1 to visit Reid State Park, where you can climb up the ledges and watch the waves pound into the rocks below. There are several lodgings in Georgetown you can choose from. Heading north on your fifth day, leave U.S. 1 shortly after crossing the bridge at **Wiscasset** ❸ and take Route 27 to **Boothbay** ❹, where you can browse in the antiques shops and art galleries or scan the horizon for whales on one of the many sightseeing cruises. Spend the night at a Boothbay lodging.

If you have 7 days

On Day 6, get up early and drive north on U.S. 1. Take Route 130 to Pemaquid Point, where you can find the beautiful Pemaquid Point Light. Nearby are plenty of places to eat. Stay at one of the country inns around **Damariscotta** ❻. Your last day should be spent exploring the St. George and Cushing peninsulas south of **Waldoboro** ❽. A half-hour's drive will see you to the end of either, where you will find a variety of lodgings overlooking the sea. Route 97 off U.S. 1 goes to Cushing and Friendship. Follow Route 131 out of **Thomaston** ❾ to reach **Tenants Harbor** ❿ and **Port Clyde** ⓫, where you can take a boat to **Monhegan Island** ⓬.

About the Restaurants

Lobsters are the main draw—there are even lobster rolls on the menu at many McDonald's locations. You'll find some of the freshest crustaceans at the local lobster pounds, which are saltwater pools where you can decide which lobster to have for dinner. But lobsters are not the only critters you can find on the menus in the Mid-Coast region. The area is famous for its haddock sandwiches, homemade chowders, and fried clams. Steaks and other dishes will satisfy carnivores. The amount of food may be daunting to light eaters, but many restaurants are happy to serve smaller portions. There is always a sinfully delicious chocolate item on the dessert menu, and Green Mountain Coffee is a local favorite. Breakfast anywhere will usually offer blueberry muffins.

Casual dress is perfectly fine in most restaurants along the coast. Many restaurants accept reservations in summer when business is brisk, so call ahead to check.

About the Hotels

The Mid-Coast offers accommodations ranging from oceanfront cabins to elegant B&Bs to seaside resorts. Many of the most interesting lodgings are former sea captains' or shipbuilders' homes, beautifully restored and furnished with period pieces. From Memorial Day through Labor Day, rates rise, many places require a two-night minimum stay, and reservations are essential.

Some of the pricier accommodations have air-conditioning, cable TV, and Internet access. At the lower end of the scale, you can still find clean, comfortable rooms with basic amenities. Stunning views can crop up in any of the price ranges. They're what Maine is famous for, after all.

WHAT IT COSTS					
	$$$$	$$$	$$	$	¢
RESTAURANTS	over $25	$18–$25	$11–$17	$7–$10	under $7
HOTELS	over $200	$150–$200	$100–$150	$60–$100	under $60

Restaurant prices are for a main course at dinner, excluding tax of 7%. Hotel prices are for two people in a standard double room in high season, excluding service charges and 7% tax.

Timing

If you have heard that there are only two seasons in Maine—July and winter—don't believe it. Most visitors come in summer, when the temperatures typically reach the 80s and occasionally the 90s, to enjoy the long stretches of sun-splashed beaches and whale-watching cruises. But many seasoned travelers prefer to visit during the other seasons. In autumn the humidity is gone, the days are often sunny and warm, and the nights are crisp, dropping into the 40s and 50s. Fall foliage in the Mid-Coast region is spectacular, with brilliant reds and oranges bursting from maple trees and yellows illuminating the birch trees until late October. Fishing and hunting are popular activities, and kayaking and white-water rafting are invigorating under the brilliant blue skies.

Many longtime visitors prefer to return in the winter. You don't have to reserve months ahead if you want a room in your favorite country inn or B&B. You can enjoy skiing and snowmobiling, or just curl up by the fire with a good book. Sea storms can be dramatic in November and December, and you might want to visit your favorite stretch of the

3

Bicycling

The best in the state, the Androscoggin River Bike Path is a paved and marked 2 ½-mile route between U.S. 1 and the Androscoggin River. Along the way you will see great blue herons prowling in the shallows, hawks patrolling above, and maybe even a bald eagle surveying the landscape. The national bird, which was seldom seen in these parts a few years ago, has made a comeback—there are now more than 250 nesting pairs in the state. Park at the Water Street lot, off Mason Street, in downtown Brunswick. There are also two longer bike paths in this region: The Coastal Route, a 187-mi journey, takes you along the rocky coastline. The 60-mi Merrymeeting Tour travels between Bath and Wiscasset.

Beaches

Some of the country's most dramatic beaches are located in Maine. As you drive north, they are apt to be rocky, rather than sandy, but in the southern Mid-Coast region there are two awesome beaches, both unique in their ways. Popham Beach, part of Popham Beach State Park near the town of Phippsburg, stretches for miles. When the tide is low, you can explore the sandbars and tidepools, which are teeming with sea creatures. You can even take a stroll out to Wood Island. On one end of the beach is Fort Popham, a fortress dating from the Civil War, which you can explore. No visit to the Mid-Coast region is complete without a stop at Reid State Park, where you'll find Mile Beach and Half Mile Beach. Climb the rocky ledges at the end of Mile Beach and watch the surf smash into the rocks. This is the best place to watch the waves during a storm.

Lighthouses

There are many lighthouses in the Mid-Coast region, and many are within easy driving distance. The Doubling Point Light and Kennebec River Light on the Kennebec River are accessible from Route 209 in Bath. Squirrel Point Light is also accessible by car: Take Route 127 south from Bath until you reach Steen Road. Turn onto Bald Head Road, where you leave your car and hike for about a mile. Farther north, Pemaquid Point Light stands watch over long rocky ledges. The former lighthouse keeper's cottage is now the Fishermen's Museum, which displays historic photographs, scale models, and artifacts that explore the history of commercial fishing in the area. The surf here can be tremendous, especially during a squall. Marshall Point Lighthouse at Port Clyde has been turned into a museum. Two lighthouses near Tenants Harbor—Tenants Harbor Light and Two Bush Island Light—are visible from land or boat. Cruises from Bath take in almost a dozen lights, including Seguin Light, the tallest lighthouse in Maine. From Boothbay Harbor lighthouse cruises include a view of Ram Island Light.

---

coastline at this time of year to see how those boulders you find atop the cliffs got there.

Spring is also a great time to visit the Mid-Coast region, when the hotels and restaurants are not yet crowded. Although many businesses remain closed until early or mid-May, you won't have trouble finding at least a few antiques shops and art galleries that are open. April temperatures often don't reach above the 40s, but the days gradually warm up in early May.

FROM BRUNSWICK TO WISCASSET

Brunswick & the Harpswells

❶ *10 mi north of Freeport.*

Lovely brick-and-clapboard buildings are the highlight of Brunswick's Federal Street Historic District, which includes Federal Street and Park Row and the stately campus of Bowdoin College. Pleasant Street, in the center of town, has interesting shops. Several food carts operate on the town green, known as the mall. You can sample hamburgers, clam rolls, or that old Maine favorite, steamed hot dogs. The newest vendor sells Thai food.

The 110-acre campus of **Bowdoin College** (✉ Maine, Bath, and College Sts., off east end of Pleasant St.) is an enclave of distinguished buildings separated by pleasant gardens and grassy quadrangles. Writer Nathaniel Hawthorne, poet Henry Wadsworth Longfellow, and Civil War hero Joshua L. Chamberlain attended Bowdoin.

Bowdoin's imposing neo-Gothic Hubbard Hall, on the campus quadrangle, is home to the **Peary–MacMillan Arctic Museum,** where you can find navigational instruments and other artifacts from the first successful expedition to the North Pole. The 1909 journey was headed by two of Bowdoin's most famous alumni, Admiral Robert E. Peary and ship master Donald B. MacMillan. The schooner *Bowdoin,* now the flagship of the Maine Maritime Academy in Castine, was MacMillan's vessel for a later trip to the Arctic. Changing exhibits document conditions in the Arctic. ✉ *Junction Bath Rd. and Upper Maine St.* ☎ *207/725–3416* 💷 *Free* ⊗ *Tues.–Sat. 10–5, Sun. 2–5.*

The **Bowdoin College Museum of Art** is set in a splendid Renaissance Revival–style building designed by Charles F. McKim in 1894. The museum displays small but interesting collections that encompass Assyrian and classical art and works by Dutch, Italian, French, and Flemish old masters; a superb gathering of Colonial and Federal paintings, notably Gilbert Stuart portraits of Madison and Jefferson; and a Winslow Homer Gallery of engravings, etchings, and memorabilia (open in summer only). The museum's collection also includes 19th- and 20th-century American painting and sculpture, with works by Mary Cassatt, Andrew Wyeth, and Robert Rauschenberg. ✉ *Junction Bath Rd. and Upper Maine St.* ☎ *207/725–3275* 💷 *Free* ⊗ *Tues.–Sat. 10–5, Sun. 2–5.*

The **General Joshua L. Chamberlain Museum** displays memorabilia and documents the life of Maine's most celebrated Civil War hero. The general, who played an instrumental role in the Union Army's victory at Gettysburg, was elected governor in 1867. From 1871 to 1883 he served as president of Bowdoin College. Across the street, on the edge of the Bowdoin College campus, a statue was erected in his memory. ✉ *226 Maine St.* ☎ *207/729–6606* 💷 *$4* ⊗ *Late May–mid-Oct., Tues.–Sat. 10–4.*

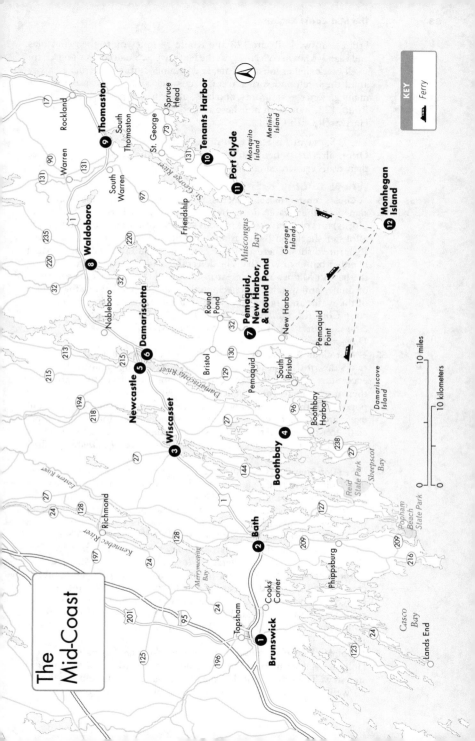

The Mid-Coast

KEY
Ferry

1 Brunswick
2 Bath
3 Wiscasset
4 Boothbay
5 Newcastle
6 Damariscotta
7 Pemaquid, New Harbor, & Round Pond
8 Waldoboro
9 Thomaston
10 Tenants Harbor
11 Port Clyde
12 Monhegan Island

Rockland
Warren
South Warren
South Thomaston
St. George
Spruce Head
Friendship
Nobleboro
Bristol
Round Pond
Pemaquid
South Bristol
New Harbor
Pemaquid Point
Boothbay Harbor
Damariscove Island
Mosquito Island
Metinic Island
Georges Islands
Richmond
Cooks Corner
Topsham
Phippsburg
Lands End

St. George River
Damariscotta River
Eastern River
Kennebec River
Merrymeeting Bay
Muscongus Bay
Sheepscot Bay
Casco Bay
Reid State Park
Popham Beach State Park

0   10 miles
0   10 kilometers

From Brunswick, Route 123 and Route 24 take you to the peninsulas and islands known collectively as the Harpswells. Small coves along Harpswell Neck shelter lobster boats, and summer cottages are tucked away amid the birch and spruce trees. Brunswick and the Harpswells have many galleries, restaurants, and inns, often in unexpected places. Along Route 123, signs with blue herons mark the studios and galleries of the Harpswell Craft Guild.

The U.S. Naval Air Station in Brunswick is home to a squadron of P3 Orion aircraft. When you're driving along the coast, you might see their trails crisscrossing the sky.

Where to Stay & Eat

$$-$$$$
Fodor'sChoice
★
✕ **Cook's Lobster House.** You cross the world's only cribstone bridge (designed so that water flows freely through gaps between the granite blocks) on your way to this famous seafood restaurant, which began as a lobster shack, on Bailey Island. Try the lobster casserole, one of the signature dishes. There are other favorites, including fried clams coated in either batter or crumbs. The delectable haddock sandwich is among the best in Maine. You can eat inside or on the deck. Come for lunch or dinner and watch men checking the lobster pots that dot the surface of the water and the kayakers that fan out across the bay. ⊠ *68 Garrison Cove Rd., Bailey Island* ☎ *207/833–2818* ⊕ *www.cookslobster.com* ⌕ *Reservations not accepted* ☰ *D, MC, V* ☙ *Closed New Year's Day–mid-Feb.*

★ **$$-$$$**
✕ **MacMillan & Company.** A magnificent mahogany bar stretches along two sides of this local favorite. Tiffany-style lamps add to the ambience. Start off with the crabmeat-stuffed mushrooms or the crab cakes, then move on to the excellent prime rib served with a piping hot popover, or the tasty pasta primavera loaded with vegetables. More unusual are the beef tips basted with Jack Daniels. Seafood dishes, especially lobster, are still the favorites, according to owner Ed Rogers. Save room for the special "Sin City" chocolate dessert. ⊠ *94 Maine St.* ☎ *207/721–9662* ☰ *D, MC, V.*

$-$$$
✕ **Sea Dog Brew Pub.** Cross the Androscoggin River to reach the old Bowdoin Mill, a towering yellow brick building. Here you'll find the Sea Dog Brew Pub overlooking the kayakers on the river. People stop by for the hearty sandwiches, fresh seafood, and the famous river driver onion appetizer. Don't miss the crispy calamari salad at the bar. Wash it all down with a microbrew or the root beer made on the premises. There's live entertainment Tuesday through Saturday nights. ⊠ *1 Maine St., Topsham* ☎ *207/725–0162* ⊕ *www.seadogbrewing.com* ☰ *AE, D, MC, V.*

$$
✕ **The Great Impasta.** You can combine your favorite pasta and sauce to create a one-of-a-kind dish at this small storefront restaurant near the bridge to Topsham. The lunch and dinner selections are all tasty, especially the seafood lasagna. This is a popular place, so call ahead to get your name on the waiting list. ⊠ *42 Maine St.* ☎ *207/729–5858* ☰ *D, DC, MC, V.*

$
✕ **Dolphin Chowder House.** This clapboard-covered restaurant at the Dolphin Marina in Harpswell is famous for its fish chowder and lobster stew. The simple but delicious food makes the drive down Route 23 well worth it. Eat in the dining room or order takeout so you can

enjoy the view of Casco Bay. ⊠ *515 Basin Point Rd., South Harpswell* ☎ *207/833–6000* ⊕ *www.dolphinchowderhouse.com* ⊟ *AE, D, MC, V* ☉ *Closed Nov.–May.*

¢–$ ✕ **Fat Boy Drive-In.** Turn on your lights to catch the attention of the servers at this old-fashioned drive-in restaurant. The eatery is renowned for its BLTs made with Canadian bacon. Order one with onion rings and a frappé (try the blueberry). Baskets of fried clams and shrimp are also popular items. ⊠ *111 Bath Rd.* ☎ *207/729–9431* ⊟ *No credit cards* ☉ *Closed mid-Oct.–mid-Mar.*

¢ ✕ **Broadway Deli.** Hearty meals are what you can get at this no-nonsense storefront coffee shop. The mushroom-and-cheese omelet is a good choice for breakfast, and delicious soups and sandwiches round out the lunch menu. The breads are baked on the premises. ⊠ *142 Maine St.* ☎ *207/729–7781* ⊟ *No credit cards.*

¢ ✕ **Wild Oats Bakery.** The scent of freshly baked scones and breads may draw you into this bakery, located in a downtown shopping center. Try the hot soups and chowders and made-to-order sandwiches. ⊠ *149 Maine St.* ☎ *207/725–6287* ⊟ *D, MC, V.*

$$–$$$$ ✕🏠 **Captain Daniel Stone Inn.** This Federal-style inn, built by Captain Daniel Stone in 1819, looks down on the Androscoggin River. In the main house, a grand stairway winds down to the sun-filled lobby. No two rooms are identical, but most have comfortable furnishings such as four-poster beds. Many have whirlpool baths. Excellent service distinguishes the Narcissa Stone Restaurant ($$–$$$). Open all year, the dining room includes a spacious enclosed veranda for spring and summer dining and a double-hearth fireplace to keep things cozy on cooler evenings. Look for entrées such as mariner's stew, which combines lobster, scallops, and shrimp in a seafood broth. Walk to the nearby shops or bicycle along the Androscoggin River Bike Path. ⊠ *10 Water St., 04011* ☎ *877/571–5151 or 207/725–9898* 🖷 *207/725–9898* ⊕ *www.captaindanielstoneinn.com* 🛏 *34 rooms, 4 suites* ♿ *Restaurant, cable TV, no-smoking rooms* ⊟ *AE, D, DC, MC, V* |◯| *CP.*

$$$–$$$$ 🏠 **Log Cabin Inn.** Every room has a view in this luxurious lodging on

Fodor'sChoice   Bailey Island. Among the most popular is the Mt. Washington Room,

★   a second-story hideaway with a full kitchen and private deck with outdoor hot tub and an expansive view of the lobster boats sailing in and out of Mackerel Cove. Take a dip in the pool or enjoy a glass of wine on your private deck. The breakfast room has floor-to-ceiling windows with lovely views. In warm weather there are tables scattered about the patio. On the inn's private beach, you can watch the lobster boats come and go. ⊠ *5 Log Cabin La., Bailey Island 04003* ☎ *207/833–5546* 🖷 *207/833–7858* ⊕ *www.logcabin-maine.com* 🛏 *8 rooms* ♿ *Cable TV, in-room VCRs, pool, beach, bar, shop; no smoking* ⊟ *AE, D, MC, V* ☉ *Closed Nov.–Mar.* |◯| *BP.*

$$–$$$ 🏠 **Brunswick Bed & Breakfast.** Near the shops and restaurants of downtown Brunswick, this gracefully restored Greek Revival house couldn't have a more central location. Crackling fires in the main room and breakfast room keep out the chill during the winter. Eight units grace the main house, with six more in the carriage house. Look for thoughtful touches such as terry robes in the baths. A cottage is available for weekly rentals. Brunswick Town Green and the Tuesday and Friday farmers' market

are across the street. ⊠ *165 Park Row, 04011* ☎ *800/299–4914 or 207/729–4914* ⊕ *www.brunswickbnb.com* 🛏 *12 rooms, 2 suites* ♿ *TV in some rooms, in-room data ports; no pets* ⊟ *AE, MC, V* ⍥l *BP.*

$$–$$$ 🏠 **Captain's Watch Bed & Breakfast.** Built in 1862, the Captain's Watch is the oldest lodging on the Maine Coast. Although much smaller than when it was originally built as the Union Hotel, this property on the National Historic Register retains its distinctive octagonal cupola. History buffs will enjoy the hotel's array of intriguing photos from the days of schooners and steamers. Many of the rooms have pleasant water views. You can arrange to go sailing with Captain Ken Brigham aboard the inn's 38-foot sloop, *Symbion ll.* ⊠ *926 Cundy's Harbor Rd., Harpswell 04079* ☎ *207/725–0979* ⊕ *home.gwi.net/~cwatch* 🛏 *2 rooms, 1 suite* ♿ *Boating, Internet; no a/c, no room phones, no TV in some rooms, no kids under 10* ⊟ *MC, V for deposit only* ⍥l *BP.*

$–$$ 🏠 **Harpswell Inn Bed & Breakfast.** The smell of the salt air greets you each
Fodor$Choice morning at this charming B&B on Lookout Point. The inn was origi-
★ nally the old cookhouse at Look Shipyard, where schooners and brigs were built around the time of the Civil War. Rooms are furnished with antiques, and many have fireplaces and balconies with a view of the sunset over Middle Bay. You can enjoy acres of oak-shaded lawns on the knoll overlooking the ocean. Many shops and restaurants are within walking distance. ⊠ *108 Lookout Point Rd., Harpswell 04079* ☎ *207/833–5509* ⊕ *www.harpswellinn.com* 🛏 *9 rooms, 3 suites* ♿ *Breakfast room; no a/c in some rooms, no phones in some rooms* ⊟ *D, MC, V* ⍥l *BP.*

$$ 🏠 **Bailey Island Motel.** Near the bridge leading to Bailey Island, this clean and comfortable motel serves fresh-baked muffins every morning. Enjoy them in your room or on one of the chairs scattered about the lawn. There's a dock behind the main building where you can launch canoes and kayaks. Owner Chip Black and his cheerful staff love talking about the history of this part of Maine. ⊠ *Rte. 24, Bailey Island 04003* ☎ *207/833–2886* 📠 *207/833–7721* ⊕ *www.baileyislandmotel.com* 🛏 *11 rooms* ♿ *Cable TV, dock; no smoking* ⊟ *MC, V* ⊗ *Closed late Oct.–May* ⍥l *CP.*

Nightlife & the Arts

A six-week concert series at Bowdoin College, the **Bowdoin International Music Festival** (⊠ Bowdoin College ☎ 207/373–1400 ⊕ www.bowdoinfestival.org) runs from late June to early August. The series features performances by students, faculty, and guest artists. The **Maine State Music Theater** (⊠ Bowdoin College ☎ 207/725–8769 ⊕ www.msmt.org) stages Broadway-style shows from mid-June to September. The **Theater Project of Brunswick** (⊠ 14 School St. ☎ 207/729–8584) performs plays for children and adults.

Sports & the Outdoors

The coast near Brunswick is full of hidden coves waiting to be explored. You can kayak along the coast, seeking out secluded beaches and hidden coves and watching gulls and cormorants diving for fish. Stop at Mackerel Cove to watch lobster boats coming in to unload their catch.

★ **H2Outfitters** (✉ Rte. 24, Orr's Island ☎ 207/833–5257 or 800/205–2925 ⊕ www.H2outfitters.com) provides top-notch sea-kayaking instruction for people of all skill levels. The company also rents all the gear you'll need to strike out on your own and leads day and overnight excursions.

The **Androscoggin River Bike Path** (✉ End of Water St.), a 2.5-mi marked and paved pathway, is open from dawn to dusk for joggers, walkers, bikers, and in-line skaters. The course runs along U.S. 1 and the Androscoggin River. Restrooms are available. Dogs are allowed but they must be on a leash and you must clean up after them.

Play 18 holes of golf at the **Brunswick Golf Club** (✉ 246 River Rd. ☎ 207/ 725–8224), a par-72 course.

Shopping

Several good galleries in and around Brunswick sell everything from contemporary paintings to unusual pieces of pottery. If you're in town between May and October, there's a farmers' market on Tuesday and Friday on the town green between Maine Street and Park Row.

Ash Cove Pottery (✉ 75 Ash Cove Rd., Harpswell 04079 ☎ 207/ 833–6004 ⊕ www.mainepotters.com) is worth a trip to see how pottery is fired. This cooperative gallery is open all year. There are two locations for **Georgetown Pottery** (✉ 755 Five Islands Rd., Georgetown ☎ 207/371–2801 ✉ 11 Pleasant St., Brunswick ☎ 207/725–7500 ⊕ www.georgetownpottery.com), the original studio in Georgetown and a gallery in Brunswick. All of the pieces are made on the premises.

Icon Contemporary Art (✉ 19 Mason St. ☎ 207/725–8157) specializes in modern art. **Sebascodegan Artists Cooperative** (✉ 4 Old Orr's Island Rd., Harpswell 04072 ☎ 207/833–5717) displays work by Maine artists. In addition to decorative crafts, **Wyler Craft Gallery** (✉ 150 Maine St. ☎ 207/729–1321) also carries jewelry and clothing.

In the Cook's Corner Shopping Center, **Bookland & Café** (✉ 6 Gurnet Rd. ☎ 207/725–2313 or 207/725–7033) stocks new and used books as well as magazines and newspapers. This is a great place to pick up some freshly baked scones or muffins as well as a selection of sandwiches, soups, and salads. At the tip of Bailey Island, **Land's End Gifts** (✉ Land's End, Bailey Island ☎ 207/833–2313) is a spacious shop overlooking the water. It sells cards, calendars, and collectibles from April through October. The whimsical **Leapin' Lizards** (✉ 56 Maine St. ☎ 207/373–1777 ⊕ www.leapinlizards.biz) stocks products for the mind, body, and spirit. Look for scented candles and other gifts. Psychic readings and healing sessions are also available.

Need a bottle of vintage wine or a wedge of imported cheese? Check out the selection at **Provisions** (✉ 148 Maine St. ☎ 207/729–9288). You can put together a gift basket or stock up for a picnic. **Tontine Fine Candies** (✉ Tontine Mall, 149 Maine St. ☎ 207/729–4462) sells locally made chocolates and other goodies.

en route

U.S. 1 between Brunswick and Wiscasset is a heavily traveled road, especially between 3 and 4 PM, when the shift changes at the Bath Iron Works. It's a good idea to choose an alternate route during these times.

Bath

2 *11 mi northeast of Brunswick, 38 mi northeast of Portland.*

Along Front and Centre streets, in the heart of Bath's historic district, you can find some charming 19th-century Victorian homes. The 1820 Federal-style Pryor House, at 360 Front Street, functions today as a bed-and-breakfast. You can find other examples on Washington Street, such as the 1810 Greek Revival–style mansion at No. 969, covered with gleaming white clapboards, and the Victorian gem at No. 1009, painted a distinctive shade of raspberry. Both are also operated as inns. **Sagadahoc Preservation** (☎ 207/443–2174) conducts guided walking tours of many of the town's private homes and historic buildings from mid-June to early September. Many old ship captains' and shipbuilders' homes are on this tour.

Bath has been a shipbuilding center since 1607. The venerable Bath Iron Works completed its first passenger ship in 1890 and is still building ships today. Currently the company turns out frigates for the U.S. Navy. It's a good idea to avoid U.S. 1 on weekdays from 3:15 to 4:30 PM, when a major shift change takes place. The massive exodus can tie up traffic for miles.

★ In a cluster of buildings that once made up the Percy & Small Shipyard, the **Maine Maritime Museum** examines the world of shipbuilding. A number of impressive ships, including the 142-foot Grand Banks fishing schooner *Sherman Zwicker,* are on display in the port. Exhibits use ship models, paintings, photographs, and historical artifacts to tell the history of the region. From May to November, hour-long tours of the shipyard show you how these massive wooden ships were built. You can watch boatbuilders wield their tools in the boat shop and learn about lobstering and its impact on the local culture. In summer, boat tours sail the scenic Kennebec River. A gift shop and bookstore are on the premises, and you can grab a bite to eat in the restaurant or bring a picnic to eat on the grounds. ⊠ *243 Washington St.* ☎ *207/442–0961* ⊕ *www.bathmaine.com* 💲 *$10* ☉ *Daily 9:30–5.*

FodorsChoice ★ On Georgetown Island, **Reid State Park** (⊠ Rte. 127 ☎ 207/371–2303) has 1½ miles of sand split between three beaches. From the top of Griffith Head, a rocky headland overlooking the park, you can spot the lighthouses on Seguin Island, the Cuckolds, and Hendricks Head. Facilities include showers, restrooms, picnic tables, and a snack bar. In the summer, the parking lots fill by 11 AM on weekends and holidays, so make sure to arrive early. If you're swimming, be aware of the possibility of an undertow. During a storm, this is a great place to observe the ferocity of the waves crashing onto the shore.

Follow Route 209 south from Bath to reach the site of the short-lived Popham Colony, established in 1607. Granite-walled **Fort Popham** (✉ Rte. 209, Phippsburg ☎ 207/389–1335) was built in 1861, for use during the Civil War. It was employed subsequently in the Spanish-American War and World War I. Its history goes back to the Revolutionary War, when a fortification, probably made of wood, was built here to protect nearby settlements. Outside the walls are tables where you can enjoy a picnic lunch.

Fodor'sChoice **Popham Beach State Park** (✉ Rte. 209, Phippsburg ☎ 207/389–1335) ★ has bathhouses and picnic tables. There are no restaurants at this end of the beach, so make sure to pack a picnic. At low tide you can walk to a nearby island and explore tide pools or fish off the ledges. Drive past the entrance to the park and on the right you can see a vista often described as "Million Dollar View." The confluence of the Kennebec and Morse rivers creates an ever-changing pattern of sandbars that shift with the seasons.

Where to Stay & Eat

★ $$$-$$$$ ✕ **Robinhood Free Meetinghouse.** Michael Gagne, one of Maine's best chefs, prepares his classic yet creative cuisine in this 1855 Greek Revival–style meetinghouse. The dining room evokes the past with its cream-color walls, pine floorboards, and cherry Shaker-style chairs. Crisp linens add an elegant touch. You might begin with the artichoke strudel, then move on to the veal saltimbocca or the confit of duck. Finish up with his signature Obsession in Three Chocolates, one of the area's most decadent desserts. The wine list offers a variety of choices to accompany the chef's creations. The service is excellent. ✉ *210 Robinhood Rd., Georgetown* ☎ *207/371–2188* ⊕ *www.robinhood-meetinghouse.com* ▤ *AE, D, MC, V* ☉ *No lunch.*

$$-$$$$ ✕ **Water's Edge Restaurant.** As the name implies, this popular eatery sits right on the water. The former take-out restaurant has become a favorite with locals and visitors alike. The kitchen cooks up some excellent seafood dishes. Specialties include the traditional pan-fried fish, cooked by dipping fish fillets in a mixture of flour and egg and letting them sizzle in a skillet. Other favorites include baked stuffed fish and scallops with crabmeat stuffing topped with Parmesan cheese. Soups and chowders are all made on the premises. ✉ *75 Black's Landing Rd., Sebasco Estates* ☎ *207/389–1803* ▤ *MC, V* ☉ *Closed Sept.–May.*

$$-$$$ ✕ **J.R. Maxwell and Company.** Originally the 1840 Elliott House Hotel, this was for many years the tallest building in Bath. After a complete restoration in 1979, this restaurant took over the space. Famous for its prime rib and seafood entrées, the longtime favorite serves great seafood chowder and steamed clams. The dining room displays half-hull models of several ships built in Bath and an assortment of handsome stained-glass lamp shades. You can enjoy a glass of wine at either of two bars, including the downstairs Boat Builders Pub. ✉ *122 Front St.* ☎ *207/ 443–2014* ▤ *D, MC, V.*

$$-$$$ ✕ **Kennebec Tavern & Marina.** Standing alongside the Kennebec River, Bath's only waterfront restaurant has its own marina, where you can tie up your boat and come in for a delicious lunch or dinner. Specialties in-

clude the smoked cream of tomato soup and the fried calamari. Make sure to try the fried parsnip appetizer—there is nothing like it anywhere. For your entrée, there's no better choice than the pan-blackened catch-of-the-day. The dining room has wonderful views, and the walls are hung with old photos of Bath. If you prefer, you can eat in the bar. ⊠ *119 Commercial St.* ☎ *207/442–9636* ▤ *AE, D, DC, MC, V.*

$$–$$$ ✕ **Mae's Café & Bakery.** Some of the region's tastiest pies, pastries, and cakes are baked in this restaurant, a local favorite since 1977. Works by local artists are hung in the two turn-of-the-century houses joined together. Dine inside or on the front deck, where you can gaze down at the "City of Ships." The satisfying contemporary cuisine includes savory omelets and seafood quiche. All meals can be packed to go. ⊠ *160 Centre St.* ☎ *207/442–8577* ▤ *D, MC, V* ☉ *Closed Jan. No dinner Sun.*

$$–$$$ ✕ **The Osprey.** Traditional Maine fare is served at this excellent restaurant at Robinhood Marina. Open only in summer, the eatery has wonderful views of the boats in the harbor, as well as an osprey nest. Favorite appetizers include the crab cakes and the delicious antipasto. For entrées, sample the seafood Newburg or the pan-braised haddock. ⊠ *Robinhood Rd., Georgetown* ☎ *207/371–2530* ▤ *D, MC, V* ☉ *Closed Columbus Day–Memorial Day.*

$$–$$$ ✕ **Spinney's.** You can see Popham Fort from this waterfront restaurant. Try the tasty lobster rolls or variations made with clams, scallops, crab, or shrimp. Locals say the Popham Platter (every type of seafood you can imagine) and the Wood Island Wreck Platter (shrimp, scallops, and steak hot off the grill) are "wicked good." ⊠ *987 Popham Rd., Phippsburg* ☎ *207/389–1122* ▤ *MC, V* ☉ *Closed late Oct.–Mother's Day.*

$–$$$ ✕ **Beale Street Barbecue.** Ribs—a full slab or a half slab—are the thing in this barbecue joint. For hearty eaters, ask for one of the platters piled high with pulled pork, pulled chicken, or shredded beef. If you can't decide, there's always the massive barbecue sampler. Jalapeño popovers and chili served with corn bread are popular appetizers. Enjoy a beer at the bar while waiting for your table. If you are shopping on Front Street, walk down the covered boardwalk and you'll see this storefront eatery to the left of the large parking lot. ⊠ *215 Water St.* ☎ *207/442–9514* ▤ *MC, V.*

$–$$$ ✕ **Maryellenz Caffe.** All the entrées are cooked to order at this intimate Italian eatery on the Kennebec River. Specialties include grilled shrimp remoulade, lobster tarragon, and pan-seared beef tenderloin medallions. The lobster and artichoke-heart dip is the star among the appetizers. Tiny tables aglow with candles make this a great spot for a romantic dinner. ⊠ *99 Commercial St.* ☎ *207/442–0960* ▤ *MC, V.*

¢–$$ ✕ **Five Islands Lobster Company.** Drive to the end of Route 27 to find this lobster shack, which sits on the dock at Five Islands Marina. On this working wharf you can watch the lobstermen baiting their traps or repairing their boats as you feast on the lobster rolls made fresh daily. The secret of the infamous tarter sauce is dill. After a morning or an afternoon at nearby Reid State Park, you can relax here in the ocean breezes. ⊠ *1447 Five Islands Rd., Georgetown* ☎ *207/371–2990* ▤ *No credit cards* ☉ *Closed Labor Day–early May.*

¢ ✕ **Café Crème.** Changing exhibitions by local artists hang on the walls of this downtown coffee shop. Its prime location, on a corner facing Front

Street, lets you take a break from window-shopping. Come in for a cup of espresso, a blueberry muffin, or one of the delicious house-made scones. Light lunches include freshly prepared salads, stuffed croissants, and quiche. There's also ice cream for the kids. ⊠ *56 Front St.* ☎ *207/443–6454* ▤ *MC, V.*

¢ ✕ **Starlight Café.** Be on the lookout for this bright little eatery, because it's easy to pass right by. It's just downhill from the corner of Lambard and Front streets. Omelets and pancakes are favorites for breakfast, while sandwiches and pizzas are on the menu for lunch. All the breads are baked daily. Make sure to get here before 2 PM, because the café isn't open for dinner. ⊠ *15 Lambard St.* ☎ *207/443–3005* ▤ *No credit cards* ☉ *Closed weekends. No dinner.*

★ **$$$–$$$$** ✕▥ **Sebasco Harbor Resort.** This family resort is spread over 575 acres at the foot of the Phippsburg Peninsula. The owners have retained the resort's old-fashioned feel while making sure all the accommodations are up-to-date. Comfortable guest rooms in the clapboard-covered main building have antique furnishings. Rooms in a building designed to resemble a lighthouse have access to a rooftop viewing platform. These rooms also have wicker furniture and paintings by local artists. The main restaurant, the Pilot House, is known for its innovative takes on classic dishes. Entrées include haddock stuffed with scallops, shrimp, and vegetables. Take a dip in the saltwater pool on the point beside the ocean. ⊠ *Rte. 217* ☐ *Box 75, Sebasco Estates 04565* ☎ *207/389–1161 or 800/225–3819* ☒ *207/389–2004* ⊕ *www.sebasco.com* ⇆ *115 rooms, 23 cottages* ⚖ *3 restaurants, in-room data ports, cable TV, 3-hole golf course, 9-hole golf course, 2 tennis courts, saltwater pool, health club, sauna, dock, boating, bicycles, bowling, Ping-Pong, lounge, recreation room, video game room, shop, playground, Internet, meeting rooms, airport shuttle, no-smoking rooms; no a/c* ▤ *AE, D, MC, V* ☉ *Closed Nov.–mid-May* †⊙† *MAP.*

$$–$$$ ▥ **Edgewater Farm Bed & Breakfast.** Amid 4 acres of gardens, this restored farmhouse dates back to 1800. Throughout the year it's filled with the smells of flowers and country cooking. Rooms are tastefully decorated with handmade quilts and pieces of locally made art. There's no air-conditioning, but the sea breezes make it unnecessary. ⊠ *71 Small Point Rd., Phippsburg 04562* ☎ *207/389–1322* ⊕ *www.edgewaterfarmbedandbreakfast.com* ⇆ *6 rooms* ⚖ *Fans, pool, sauna, Ping-Pong; no a/c, no smoking* ▤ *MC, V* †⊙† *CP.*

★ **$$–$$$** ▥ **The Inn at Bath.** Filled with antiques, this handsome 1810 Greek Revival–style lodging sits in the middle of Brunswick's historic district. Many of the downtown sights, including the local library with its distinctive shaded gazebo, and shops and restaurants are within easy walking distance. The romantic guest rooms are tastefully decorated with works by local artists. Five have wood-burning fireplaces and two have two-person whirlpool tubs. Outside are lovely gardens and a spacious patio. ⊠ *969 Washington St., 04530* ☎ *207/443–4294 or 800/423–0964* ☒ *207/443–4295* ⊕ *www.innatbath.com* ⇆ *8 rooms, 1 suite* ⚖ *In-room data ports, cable TV, in-room VCRs, Internet, meeting rooms, some pets allowed* ▤ *AE, D, MC, V* †⊙† *BP.*

$$–$$$ ▥ **Coveside Bed & Breakfast.** Near the village of Five Islands, this contemporary lodging sits on 5 secluded acres that run along the shore. Every room in the main house and in the cottage has a lovely view of the water. A canoe and several bicycles are available for outings. A dock is perfect for sunbathing or watching the water. Stroll along nearby nature preserves or visit Reid State Park. Gulls, herons, and osprey are frequently sighted here, and you may catch a glimpse of the occasional seal or even a moose. ⊠ *6 Gott's Cove La., Georgetown 04548* ☎ *207/371–2807 or 800/232–5490* ⊕ *www.covesidebandb.com* ⤳ *4 rooms, 1 cottage* ⚓ *Dock, boating, bicycles; no children under 12* ⊟ *AE, D, MC, V* ⊘ *Closed mid-Oct.–late May* ⦿| *BP.*

$$–$$$ ⬚ **The Mooring Bed & Breakfast.** Originally the home of Walter Reid, who donated the land for Reid State Park, this inn has stayed in the same family for generations. It is now owned by Reid's great-granddaughter and her family. The five guest rooms all have air-conditioning and great ocean views. A porch catches the ocean breeze, making it a favorite place to have breakfast. Well-tended gardens grace the grounds, which run along the Kennebec River. The Spanish Room is a great place to retreat with a good book. ⊠ *132 Seguinland Rd., Georgetown 04548* ☎ *207/371–2790 or 866/828–7343* ⊕ *www.themooringb-b.com* ⤳ *5 rooms* ⚓ *Dining room; no smoking* ⊟ *MC, V* ⊘ *Closed mid-Oct.–mid-May* ⦿| *BP.*

$$–$$$ ⬚ **The 1774 Inn.** Listed on the National Register of Historic Places, this Georgian-style mansion dating from before the Revolutionary War has handsome interior detailing and is filled with magnificent antiques. The former McCobb-Hill-Minot House, located on a bend in the Kennebec River, has spacious corner guest rooms in the main house, including two with fireplaces. One room has a deck overlooking the river. A four-bedroom cottage facing the river has its own kitchen, two baths, and four bedrooms. The breakfast menu is likely to include a smoked salmon roulade, vegetable-sausage strata, or cranberry-walnut pancakes, in addition to whole-grain cereals and home-baked muffins and breads. ⊠ *44 Parker Head Rd., Phippsburg 04562* ☎ *207/389–1774* 🖷 *207/389–9076* ⊕ *www.1774inn.com* ⤳ *7 rooms, 1 cottage* ⚓ *Dining room; no room TVs, no children under 12* ⊟ *MC, V* ⦿| *BP.*

$$–$$$ ⬚ **Popham Beach Bed & Breakfast.** Housed in a former Coast Guard station, this casual bed-and-breakfast sits on Popham Beach not far from historic Fort Popham. Sun-filled rooms are comfortably furnished. The nicest quarters include the Library, with two walls lined with books, and the Bunkroom, which overlooks the ocean. Stroll along the shore before partaking in a two- or three-course breakfast in the former mess hall. Beach chairs and umbrellas, picnic tables, and barbecue grills are available for guests. A casual seafood restaurant is close by, and you can order lunch at a small market. ⊠ *4 Riverview Ave., Phippsburg 04562* ☎ *207/389–2409* 🖷 *207/389–2379* ⊕ *www.pophambeachbandb.com* ⤳ *4 rooms, 3 with bath; 1 suite* ⚓ *Fishing; no a/c, no room phones, no room TVs, no children under 15, no smoking* ⊟ *MC, V* ⦿| *BP.*

$–$$$ ⬚ **Kennebec Inn.** This is one of the few B&Bs in the region with a rooftop cupola, where you can have a panoramic view of the Kennebec River and Doubling Point Light. The five-level shipbuilder's house, constructed in 1850, sits on a rise just outside Bath on the road to Phippsburg. This historic property has its original spiral staircase as well as 11-foot walls crowned with plaster moldings and ornate ceiling medallions. Italian marble fireplaces are scattered throughout the house. Every morning you can enjoy a full breakfast in the formal dining room. ⊠ *251 High St., 04530* ☎ *207/443–5324 or 888/595–1564* ⊕ *www. kennebecinn.com* ⌇*4 rooms, 1 suite ♨ Dining room, cable TV; no smoking* ⊟ *D, MC, V* ⫟⊙⫠ *BP.*

$–$$ ⊞ **Pryor House Bed & Breakfast.** An elegant double staircase in the foyer welcomes visitors to this 1820s Federal-style home gazing down on the Kennebec River. It's in the historic district of Bath, so shops and restaurants are nearby. The Tall Chimney Room has a railroad theme, with a working model train that runs around the chimney. There's also a hot tub big enough for two. Nautical themes are reflected in the Washington Room, with its wide pine floorboards and windows overlooking the river, and the Elizabeth Room, decorated in Victorian style in pinks and whites. The owner is an enthusiastic cook and serves up many creative dishes for breakfast. ⊠ *360 Front St., 04530* ☎ *207/443–1146* ⊕ *www. bbonline.com/me/pryorhouse* ⌇*3 rooms ♨ Dining room; no room TVs, no children under 12* ⊟ *AE, D, DC, MC, V* ⫟⊙⫠ *BP.*

Nightlife & the Arts

The **Chocolate Church Arts Center** (⊠ 804 Washington St. ☎ 207/442–8455) hosts folk, jazz, and classical concerts, as well as theatrical performances for adults and children. The gallery space exhibits works in various media by local artists. Classes in watercolors and pastels are available.

Sports & the Outdoors

To cruise the Kennebec or other coastal rivers in the area, contact **Long Reach Cruises** (⊠ 75 Commercial St. ☎ 888/538–6786), which operates excursion and sightseeing tours out of Bath's Waterfront Park. Cruises past some of the region's distinctive sights are the company's specialty, and you can learn all about their history from the narration given by the knowledgable captains and crew. This outfit also heads to Merrymeeting Bay, Harpswell Sound, and Damariscotta Bay. If you want to explore on your own, **Bay Point Sports** (⊠ Rte. 127, Georgetown ☎ 207/ 371–2690 or 888/349–7772 ⊕ eastbaykayaking.com) rents kayaks from April to Labor Day.

Morse Mountain Preserve (⊠ Rte. 216, Phippsburg ☎ No phone), a 600-acre preserve owned by Bates College, has trails through the woods that lead to Sewall Beach. There is a small parking area off the side of the road just after the junction with Route 209. Tranquil **Josephine Newman Sanctuary** (⊠ Bay Point Rd., Georgetown) is a nature preserve on the Georgetown Peninsula. The walking trails are operated by the Maine Audubon Society. Heavy woods surround you, so protect yourself from deer ticks by wearing long pants and sleeves.

An 18-hole championship golf course distinguishes the **Bath Country Club** (⊠ 387 Whiskeag Rd. ☎ 207/442–8411), where you can find a tavern and the biggest pro shop in Maine. The 9-hole **Sebasco Estates Golf Course** (⊠ Rte. 217, Phippsburg ☎ 207/389–1161) sits right on the water.

Shopping

The **Montsweag Flea Market** (⊠ U.S. 1, Woolrich ☎ 207/443–2809) is a roadside attraction with treasure, trash, and everything in between.

It's open on weekends from May to October and also on Friday in summer. There's also a Wednesday antiques market during the summer.

Open year-round, the storefront **Brick Store Antiques** (✉ 143 Front St. ☎ 207/443–2790) displays genuine antiques, no reproductions. It's open evenings for after-dinner browsing. You'll spot an authentic teepee as you approach **Native Arts** (✉ U.S. 1, Woolwich ☎ 207/442–8399), which carries fine crafts made by 50 different Native peoples, from carvings made in Alaska to beadwork produced in South America. Stop in and see the drums and birch bark canoes on display.

Now You're Cooking (✉ 49 Front St. ☎ 207/443–1402 ⊕ www. acooksemporium.com) carries everything you dreamed of for the kitchen, as well as lots of picnic supplies and nifty gadgets. The shop will ship your purchases home for you. **The Front** (✉ 100 Front St. ☎ 207/443–9506) is the place to go if you need a bright summer frock or the perfect necklace. **West Island Gallery** (✉ 37 Bay Point Rd., Georgetown ☎ 207/443–9625) carries contemporary pieces by Maine artists.

en route   Coastal Route 1, which runs between Bath and Wiscasset, takes you across a new bridge that crosses the Kennebec River. Along the way you'll pass Bath Iron Works and its busy yard where destroyers are built. Between the two towns is an eclectic collection of shops. Take home a small statue of St. Francis for your flower garden, or a model ship for your mantle. Traffic on the highway is heavy on weekends, so plan to take your time and enjoy a few stops along the way.

Wiscasset

❸ *10 mi north of Bath, 46 mi northeast of Portland.*

Settled in 1663, Wiscasset sits on the banks of the Sheepscot River. It bills itself as "Maine's Prettiest Village," and when you stroll through town, you understand why. You pass by graceful churches, old cemeteries, and elegant sea captains' homes (many converted into antiques shops or galleries). Pack a picnic and take it down to the dock, where you can watch the fishing boats.

U.S. 1 becomes Main Street, which means traffic often slows to a crawl. Try to arrive early in the morning if you want to find a parking space on Main Street. If they are all taken, turn onto Water Street and you're likely to find a spot.

The **Nickels-Sortwell House,** maintained by the Society for the Preservation of New England Antiquities, is an outstanding example of Federal architecture. Built by Captain William Nickels, a ship owner and trader, the house recalls the prosperity of those times. Tours begin every hour on the hour between 11 and 4. ✉ *121 Main St.* ☎ *207/882–6218* 🎫 *$5* ⊙ *June–mid-Oct., Fri.–Sun. 11–5.*

The 1807 **Castle Tucker** is known for its extravagant architecture, Victorian appointments, and freestanding elliptical staircase. Standing on top of a hill overlooking the Sheepscot River, the structure was built by Judge Silas Lee when Wiscasset was the busiest port east of Boston. It's run by the Society for the Preservation of New England Antiquities. ⊠ *Lee and High Sts.* ☎ *207/882–7364* ✉ *$5* ⊙ *June–mid-Oct., Wed.–Sun. 11–5; tours on the hr 11–4.*

★ The 1852 **Musical Wonder House,** formerly a sea captain's home, is now a museum with a collection of thousands of antique music boxes from around the world. Come and see player pianos and other musical rarities in this grand old home. For an extra fee you can arrange for tours of the main floor or the entire house. ⊠ *18 High St.* ☎ *207/882–7163 or 800/336–3725* ⊕ *www.musicalwonderhouse.com* ✉ *$2* ⊙ *Memorial Day–mid-Oct., daily 10–5.*

At Old Sheepscot Station, the **Wiscasset Waterville & Farmington Railway** celebrates Maine's railroad heritage. You can enjoy train rides and the best selection of Maine railroad books in the state. The railway is run entirely by volunteers. ⊠ *Rte. 218, 5 mi north of U.S. 1, Alna* ☎ *207/ 882–4193* ⊕ *www.wwfry.org* ✉ *Museum free; train $5* ⊙ *Weekends 9–5.*

Where to Stay & Eat

$$–$$$ ✕ **Le Garage.** The best tables at this former service station are on the glassed-in porch overlooking the Sheepscot River and Wiscasset Harbor. Entrées include homemade chicken pie, sea scallops au gratin, and stuffed fillet of sole. The broiled lamb-and-vegetable kebabs are especially tasty. Portions are large, but you can always ask for a half order. Sample something from the wine list while you gaze across the river. The service is excellent. ⊠ *Water St.* ☎ *207/882–5409* ⊟ *MC, V* ⊙ *Closed Jan.*

¢–$ ✕ **Sarah's Café.** This family-friendly restaurant is at the harbor and has lovely views to enjoy. The menu covers a lot of ground, with entrées ranging from Mexican to Italian. There is also the catch of the day and the usual seafood items at market prices. There are various toppings on the hamburgers, such as salsa on the Tex Mex. Lunch and dinner are served all week, breakfast on the weekends. ⊠ *Main St., at the harbor* ☎ *207/882–7504* ⊕ *www.sarahscafe.com* ⊟ *AE, D, MC, V.*

¢ ✕ **Red's Eats.** You've probably driven right past this little red shack on the Wiscasset side of the bridge if you've visited this area. Red's is famous for its hot dogs and onion rings, as well as its lobster and crab rolls. If you spot a kid with an ice cream cone, it probably came from Red's. You can select such old favorites as black raspberry and pistachio. There are a few picnic tables, or pick up your food and walk down to the dock to enjoy the view. Watch out for the sea gulls; they like lobster rolls, too. ⊠ *41 Water St.* ☎ *207/882–6128* ⊟ *No credit cards* ⊙ *Closed mid-Oct.–mid-Apr.*

$–$$$ ✕🏠 **The Squire Tarbox Inn.** Built around 1763, this small country inn is listed on the National Register of Historic Places. The eponymous squire is buried next door in the family plot. Some of the charming guest rooms have fireplaces. Mountain bikes let you explore the surrounding woods, while a rowboat allows you to get a look at the coast. Breakfast includes home-baked croissants and breads, yogurt, and fresh fruit, along with freshly brewed coffee and a variety of teas. The pair of dining rooms have fireplaces to ward off the chill. Look for entrées such as rosemary-roasted rack of lamb and sea scallops in a garlic-butter sauce.

The hosts speak English, German, Italian, and French. ✉ *1181 Main Rd., Wiscasset 04578* ☎ *207/882–7693 or 800/818–0626* 🖷 *207/882–7107* ⊕ *www.squiretarboxinn.com* ☟ *11 rooms* ♿ *Dining room, boating, bicycles; no TVs, no children under 12* ☰ *AE, MC, V* ⊗ *Closed Jan.–Mar.*

$$ 🏨 **Cod Cove Inn.** Every room has a view of the Sheepscot River at this two-story New England–style inn perched on five acres of landscaped grounds. Most guest rooms have a private patio or balcony overlooking the river, and some have gas fireplaces. Continental breakfast includes freshly baked muffins, breads and bagels, fruits and juices, and coffee and tea. ✉ *U.S. 1 and Rte. 27* 🕿 *Box 117, Edgecomb 04556* ☎ *207/882–9586 or 800/882–9586* 🖷 *207/882–9294* ⊕ *www.codcoveinn.com* ☟ *30 rooms* ♿ *Refrigerators, pool, hot tub* ☰ *AE, D, MC, V* ⦿ *CP.*

$–$$ 🏨 **Cod Cove Farm Bed & Breakfast.** This delightful farm, situated on Boothbay Harbor Road just south of U.S. 1, has a distant view of the Sheepscot River. Each of the comfortable rooms has its own theme, such as the Adirondacks Room (with twig furniture and a birch bed) and the Scottish Room (decorated with tartan plaids and lace). In the common areas you can try out Grandmother Urion's Steinway, play games, or just read a good book. The full breakfast may include the signature dish, French toast sundaes. ✉ *Boothbay Harbor Rd.* 🕿 *Box 94, 04556* ☎ *207/882–4299 or 800/293–7718* ⊕ *www.codcovefarm.com* ☟ *4 rooms* ♿ *Breakfast room; no children under 8, no room TVs* ☰ *MC, V* ⦿ *BP.*

★ ☾ **$–$$** 🏨 **Snow Squall Bed & Breakfast.** Built in the early 1850s, this carefully renovated inn is convenient to Wiscasset Village and the harbor. Each guest room is named for a clipper ship built in Maine, including the White Falcon, the Golden Horn, the Flying Eagle, and the Red Jacket. Two rooms have fireplaces. The pair of two-bedroom suites, located in the Carriage House, each have their own entrance. You can walk to art galleries and antiques shops and past some of the region's finest sea captains' homes. ✉ *5 Bradford Rd., 04578* ☎ *207/882–6892 or 800/775–7245* 🖷 *207/882–6832* ⊕ *www.snowsquallinn.com* ☟ *4 rooms, 2 suites* ♿ *Dining room; no TV in some rooms* ☰ *AE, D, MC, V* ⊗ *Closed Nov.–May* ⦿ *BP.*

$ 🏨 **Highnote Bed & Breakfast.** You may hear the owner singing operatic arias when you arrive at this delightful B&B, which will give you a clue as to its unusual name. Antiques fill this one-of-a-kind Victorian abode dating from 1876. You're within walking distance of the harbor and many antiques shops and art studios. Each room is a gallery in itself, hung with works by local artists. Reserve the master bedroom and enjoy a claw-foot tub that has been sunk into the floor. Breakfast is traditionally European, with whole-grain cereals, yogurt and fresh fruit, as well as something that just came out of the oven. A resident horse delights kids in summer. ✉ *26 Lee St., 04578* ☎ *207/882–9628* ⊕ *wiscasset.net/highnote* ☟ *3 rooms* ♿ *No a/c, no room TVs* ☰ *No credit cards* ⦿ *BP.*

$ 🏨 **Marston House.** Two rooms in a carriage house provide a quiet retreat from the hustle and bustle of Main Street, yet they are just a stone's throw from the galleries and shops. Both have private entrances and fireplaces and are simply furnished with Shaker- and Colonial-style pieces. The rooms can be joined to make a suite perfect for families. The inn, which has been serving guests since 1987, has retained its 19th-century character. A hearty continental breakfast is delivered to your room. The owner's antiques business is adjacent to the property, in case you want to browse. ⊠ *101 Main St.* ✆ *Box 517, 04578* ☎ *207/882–6010 or 800/852–4137* 🖶 *207/882–6965* 🛏 *2 rooms* ♿ *Fans; no a/c, no room TVs* ▭ *AE, MC, V* ⊘ *Closed Nov.–Apr.* ✆ *CP.*

$ 🏨 **Wiscasset Motor Lodge.** Set amid the pines, this exceptionally clean and comfortable hotel is convenient to all of the area's attractions. Located between Bath and Wiscasset, it's close to beaches, antiques shops, and flea markets. ⊠ *596 Bath Rd., 04578* ☎ *207/882–7137 or 800/732–8168* ⊕ *www.wiscassetmotorlodge.com* 🛏 *30 rooms* ♿ *Cable TV* ▭ *D, MC, V* ⊘ *Closed Dec.–Mar.* ✆ *CP.*

Shopping

The Wiscasset area rivals Searsport as a destination for antiquing. Shops line Wiscasset's main streets and extend over the bridge into Edgecomb. The **Butterstamp Workshop** (⊠ 55 Middle St. ☎ 207/882–7825) carries handcrafted folk-art pieces made from antique molds. **Marston House American Antiques** (⊠ 101 Main St. ☎ 207/882–6010) specializes in 18th- and 19th-century painted furniture and "smalls" (small objects), homespun textiles, and antique garden accessories and tools.

There are also plenty of studios and galleries with eclectic collections. The **Maine Art Gallery** (⊠ 315 Warren St. ☎ 207/882–7511) presents works by local artists. The **Wiscasset Bay Gallery** (⊠ 67 Main St. ☎ 207/882–7682 ⊕ www.wiscassetbaygallery.com) displays a fine collection of works by 19th- and 20th-century American and European artists. Not to be missed is **Edgecomb Potters** (⊠ 727 Boothbay Rd., Edgecomb ☎ 207/882–9493 ⊕ www.edgecombpotters.com), which specializes in pricey exquisitely glazed porcelain. Open year-round, the shop has one of the best selections in the area. With beautifully glazed kitchen tiles, **Sheepscot River Pottery** (⊠ 34 U.S. 1, Edgecomb 04556 ☎ 207/882–9410 ⊕ www.sheepscot.com) also displays other fine pottery, as well as kitchenware and home accessories. This is the flagship store; three others are found in Damariscotta, Kennebunk, and Portland.

North of the Border (⊠ 605 Bath Rd., Wiscasset ☎ 207/882–5432) has an array of stone and terra-cotta lawn and garden ornaments imported from Mexico. The other odds and ends on display depend on what happened to be shipped north. This roadside spread is open from mid-April to late November. You'll see their brilliant yellow signs in plenty of time to turn into the sprawling parking lot. **Treats** (⊠ 80 Main St. ☎ 207/882–6192) stocks wonderful cheeses and fresh-baked breads, as well as decadent sandwiches for an impromptu picnic at Waterfront Park. The shop also has a fine selection of wines.

THE BOOTHBAY & PEMAQUID PENINSULAS

If you head north from Wiscasset on U.S. 1, you'll reach Route 27 just after crossing the Wiscasset Bridge into Edgecomb. Route 27 brings you into the heart of Boothbay Harbor, a seaside community with a myriad of shops and restaurants. Whale-watching and sightseeing cruises are popular pastimes. Further south along Route 27 is Southport Island, where you can enjoy the ocean scenery and poke into a gallery or two. Route 96 takes you from Boothbay Harbor to East Boothbay, where you can see Ocean Point's rocky ledges and a handful of lobster shacks.

If you bypass Route 27 and continue north on U.S. 1 from Wiscasset, you'll come to Route 130, which leads to the Pemaquid Peninsula. Art galleries, antiques shops, and lobster shacks are found here and there along the country roads that meander through the countryside. At the tip of the point, you can find a much-photographed lighthouse perched on an unforgiving rock ledge. Exploring here reaps many rewards, including views of salt ponds and boat-filled harbors. The twin towns of Damariscotta and Newcastle anchor the region, but small fishing villages such as Pemaquid, New Harbor, and Round Pond give the peninsula its pure Maine flavor.

Boothbay

❹ *13 mi southeast of Wiscasset via U.S. 1 to ME–27.*

When Portlanders want a break from city life, many come north to the Boothbay region, which is made up of Boothbay proper, East Boothbay, and Boothbay Harbor. This part of the shoreline is a craggy stretch of inlets where pleasure craft anchor alongside trawlers and lobster boats. Commercial Street, Wharf Street, Townsend Avenue, and the By-Way are lined with interesting shops and ice-cream parlors. You can browse for hours in the trinket shops, crafts galleries, clothing stores, and boutiques that line the streets around the harbor. Excursion boats leave from the piers off Commercial Street. Boats to Monhegan Island are also available. Drive out to Ocean Point in East Boothbay for some incredible scenery.

A pair of lighthouses are among the sights around Boothbay Harbor. **Burnt Island Light** was built in 1821. The lighthouse can best be seen on harbor cruises but it can also be viewed from the mainland on the west side of the harbor near the northern end of Southport Island. To catch a glimpse of it, follow Route 27 south from Boothbay Harbor. **Cuckolds Light** lies less than a mile off the southern tip of Southport Island. The fog signal was built in 1892, and the light was added in 1907 to prevent heavy shipping traffic entering the harbor from running aground.

☾ At the **Boothbay Railway Village,** about 1 mi north of Boothbay, you can ride 1½ mi on a coal-fired, narrow-gauge steam train that takes you through a model of a century-old New England village. Here you'll find more than 50 antique automobiles. ⊠ *Rte. 27* ☎ *207/633–4727* ⊕ *www. railwayvillage.org* 🗐 *$7* ⊙ *Memorial Day–Columbus Day, daily 9:30–5.*

☾ The **Department of Marine Resources Aquarium** has a shark you can pet, tide pools where you can see marine creatures up close, and tanks with rare blue lobsters. Bring a picnic lunch and enjoy the views of Boothbay Harbor. ⊠ *194 McKown Point Rd., Boothbay Harbor* ☎ *207/633–9559* ⊕ *www.maine.gov/dmr* 🗐 *$5* ⊙ *Memorial Day–late Sept., daily 10–5.*

YOU GOTTA LOTTA MOXIE, KID!

It's difficult to get very far in Maine without running into Moxie—the nation's oldest soft drink. You'll recognize it by its bright orange label. It comes in bottles and cans and is sold in just about every supermarket and convenience store in Maine.

Moxie was invented by Dr. Augustin Thompson of Union, Maine, who introduced the stuff in 1884. Moxie's big claim to fame is that it's the only brand name in the dictionary that is associated with a human quality: "energy, pep,

courage, determination." If you drink it, you'll know why.

Dr. Thompson touted his gentian-root-based drink as a medicine guaranteed to cure just about any illness, including "softening of the brain." He eventually had to drop those claims when the Pure Food & Drug Act was enacted. Despite this, Moxie has continued to prosper. And how does it taste? It tastes awful.

—Stephen Allen

Where to Stay & Eat

$$–$$$ ✕ **McSeagull's.** Lobster bisque is one of the specialties at this casual eatery on a dock overlooking the harbor. There's also a wide selection of soups, chowders, salads, and sandwiches. ✉ *14 Wharf St., Boothbay Harbor* ☎ *207/633–5900* ▭ *MC, V* ☺ *Closed Columbus Day–Memorial Day.*

$–$$$ ✕ **Lobster Dock.** Dine inside or out at this waterfront restaurant, built on the site of the Reed Shipyard, which operated here from the late 1800s to the early 1900s. Specialties of the house include the area's only hot lobster roll. Start off with the baked Brie or seafood chowder, then move on to the yellowfin tuna, rack of lamb, or slow-roasted prime rib. No meal is complete without a slice of the homemade pie. Pets are welcomed on the outside deck. ✉ *49 Atlantic Ave., Boothbay Harbor* ☎ *207/633–7120* ⊕ *www.thelobsterdock.com* ▭ *MC, V* ☺ *Closed Oct.–May.*

$$ ✕ **Type A Café.** There's a large table if you can't wait to eat your meal, but this little eatery mostly packs meals to-go for a seaside picnic or a cruise around the harbor. The gourmet shop, which uses mostly organic products, has such fare as roasted local hens and pork chops with apricots and wild rice. There's a long list of sandwiches and wraps and a good selection of wines. You can also grab a cup of gourmet coffee. ✉ *29 McKown St., Boothbay Harbor* ☎ *207/633–2020* ▭ *AE, MC, V* ☺ *Closed Mar., closed Sun.*

$–$$ ✕ **Lobstermen's Co-op.** Crustacean lovers will find something to satisfy their craving at this dockside working lobster pound. Needless to say, you won't find fresher lobster anywhere else. Eat in the dining room or outside where you can watch the lobstermen at work. For landlubbers, there are also hamburgers and sandwiches on the menu. The restaurant is on the pier near the Fisherman's Memorial. ✉ *99 Atlantic Ave., Boothbay Harbor* ☎ *207/633–4900* ▭ *D, MC, V* ☺ *Closed mid-Oct.–mid-May.*

¢–$$ ✕ **Ebb Tide.** Open all year, this friendly seaside restaurant is easy to spot because of its red-and-white awnings. Many original wooden booths in the dining room have views of the harbor. The establishment is known for its fish sandwiches, shrimp baskets, and lobster dinners. They also serve a good grilled cheese sandwich. Everything on the menu can be packed for takeout. Many people stop by in the afternoon for a cup of coffee and a piece of pie; the walnut pie, made on the premises, is especially delicious. ⊠ *46 Commercial St., Boothbay Harbor* ☎ *207/ 633–5692* ⊟ *No credit cards.*

$$$–$$$$ ✕⌂ **Spruce Point Inn.** Escape the hubbub of Boothbay Harbor at this sprawling resort spread over 15 beautifully landscaped acres. There are plenty of activities here, from a game of tennis to a dip in one of the pools. Guest rooms in the main inn are comfortable, and most have fireplaces, whirlpool baths, and a view of the ocean. A full-service spa offers massages and other treatments. The formal dining room serves dishes such as fillet of sole stuffed with crabmeat, shallots, and asagio and chèvre cheese. A nearby fog horn blows in inclement weather. ⊠ *88 Grandview Ave.* ✑ *Box 237, Boothbay Harbor 04538* ☎ *207/633–4152 or 800/553–0289* 🖷 *207/633–7138* ⊕ *www.sprucepointinn.com* ⇨ *21 rooms, 41 suites, 7 cottages* ⌂ *2 restaurants, microwaves, cable TV, 2 tennis courts, pool, saltwater pool, massage, spa, dock, lounge, meeting rooms; no a/c in some rooms* ⊟ *AE, D, DC, MC, V* ⊘ *Closed late Oct.–mid-May.*

$$$–$$$$ ⌂ **Linekin Bay Resort.** All your meals are included when you stay at this all-inclusive resort, so the only thing you have to worry about is whether you'll spend the day hiking in the 15 acres of wooded land or fishing at the edge of the harbor. There are 20 small sailboats available for guests, and sailing instruction is available. You can fish from the dock, swim in the heated saltwater pool, or challenge a friend to a game of basketball or Ping-Pong. The no-frills rooms are perfect for people who like the outdoors. Open only to guests, the dining room has lobster bakes twice a week. ⊠ *92 Wall Point Rd., Boothbay Harbor 04538* ☎ *207/ 633–2494* 🖷 *207/657–7261* ⊕ *www.linekinbayresort.com* ⇨ *37 cabins* ⌂ *Restaurant, pool, tennis court, dock, boating, fishing, basketball, Ping-Pong; no a/c, no room phones, no room TVs* ⊟ *MC, V* ⊘ *Closed late Sept.–mid-June* ⟦◯⟧ *FAP.*

$$$ ⌂ **The Anchor Watch Bed & Breakfast.** The bright and spacious rooms at this hillside B&B are named for the boats that delivered mail to Monhegan Island in the early 20th century. Comfortable beds are piled high with colorful quilts and each room has a balcony with a view of the ocean. The inn is only a few minutes from the harbor, yet it feels completely out of the way. Breakfasts may include the owners' specialty, baked cheese omelets. Other favorites are blueberry blintzes with raspberry sauce and baked French toast topped with orange-honey butter. ⊠ *9 Eames Rd., Boothbay Harbor 04538* ☎ *207/633–7565* ⊕ *www.anchorwatch.com* ⇨ *5 rooms* ⌂ *Dining room; no a/c in some rooms, no children under 8* ⊟ *MC, V* ⟦◯⟧ *BP.*

$$$ ⌂ **The Greenleaf Inn.** Built in 1849, this tastefully restored B&B is filled with antiques and wicker furniture. There are great ocean views from many of the rooms. Guests congregate in the sunroom, on the wraparound porch, or in the hot tub that overlooks the harbor. After breakfast you

can take your coffee out on the deck and watch the cruise boats set off in search of whales. ⊠ *65 Commercial St., Boothbay Harbor 04538* ☎ *207/633–7346 or 888/950–7724* 🖷 *207/633–2642* ⊕ *www. greenleafinn.com* ↘ *7 rooms* ♨ *Cable TV, in-room VCRs, hot tub, library* ⊟ *AE, D, MC, V* ⋈ *BP.*

$$–$$$ ⚏ **Admiral's Quarters Inn Bed & Breakfast.** Open all year, this renovated 1830 sea captain's house is ideally situated for exploring Boothbay Harbor. Many shops, galleries, and restaurants are within easy walking distance. Fresh baked goods greet you upon your return. All rooms have fireplaces, and some have private decks overlooking the water. On rainy days you can relax by the cozy woodstove in the sunroom. ⊠ *71 Commercial St., Boothbay Harbor 04538* ☎ *207/633–2474 or 800/ 644–1878* 🖷 *207/633–5904* ⊕ *www.admiralsquartersinn.com* ↘ *2 rooms, 5 suites* ♨ *Cable TV, Internet; no children under 12* ⊟ *AE, D, MC, V* ⋈ *BP.*

$$–$$$ ⚏ **Five Gables Inn.** This beautifully restored Victorian inn is the last of the turn-of-the-century hotels that once welcomed guests in the Boothbays. The gabled roof and beautiful gardens give this hillside lodging a distinctive look. The guest rooms tucked underneath the eves have the most charm, though the ceilings may be too low for tall people. All rooms have period furnishings, including four-poster beds. Some have fireplaces, and all but one have views of the islands scattered around Linekin Bay. The broad veranda overlooking the bay has plenty of comfy chairs from which you can enjoy the view along with your breakfast or afternoon tea and cookies. ⊠ *Murray Hill Rd., East Boothbay 04544* ☎ *207/ 633–4551 or 800/451–5048* ⊕ *www.fivegablesinn.com* ↘ *16* ♨ *Fans; no a/c, no room TVs, no children under 12* ⊟ *MC, V* ⊘ *Closed mid-Oct.–Memorial Day* ⋈ *BP.*

$$–$$$ ⚏ **Hodgdon Island Inn.** Every room in this restored 1810 sea captain's house has a view of a quiet cove, and two open out onto a shared sun deck. Sunsets from here, or from the porch where you're served afternoon tea or lemonade, are spectacular. Artwork from New England and the Caribbean graces the walls. The location, five minutes from Boothbay Harbor, puts you within walking distance of a lobster pound and a botanical garden. ⊠ *374 Barters Island Rd., Boothbay 04537* ☎ *207/ 633–7474* 🖷 *207/733–0571* ⊕ *www.hodgdonislandinn.com* ↘ *8 rooms* ♨ *Fans, pool; no a/c, no room phones, no room TVs* ⊟ *D, MC, V* ⋈ *BP.*

$$–$$$ ⚏ **Linekin Bay Bed & Breakfast.** If you are looking for a quiet retreat, consider this charming B&B. The bright sunroom, ringed by lovely gardens, is where guests tend to gather for a full breakfast in the morning or for delicious desserts in the afternoon. All rooms have hardwood floors and handsome fireplaces. Bathrooms are stocked with products such as Tom's of Maine toothpastes. ⊠ *531 Ocean Point Rd., East Boothbay 04544* ☎ *207/633–9900 or 800/596–7420* ⊕ *www.linekinbaybb.com* ↘ *4 rooms* ♨ *Dining room, cable TV, in-room VCRs; no children under 12* ⊟ *MC, V* ⋈ *BP.*

$$–$$$ ⚏ **Ocean Point Inn.** Less than 7 mi from Boothbay Harbor, this lodging at the end of Ocean Point lets you enjoy some spectacular scenery. Choose a rustic cottage or a room in the main building or the old farmstead. Some are warmed by wood-burning fireplaces. The inn has one of the area's largest outdoor heated pools and direct access to the bay that makes it perfect for rowing and kayaking. You can stroll along the shore and watch lobstermen bringing in their catch. ⊠ *Shore Rd., East Boothbay 04544* ☎ *207/633–4200 or 800/552–5554* ⊕ *www.oceanpointinn.com* ⇒ *61 rooms, 7 cottages* ⚘ *Restaurant, refrigerators, cable TV, pool, boating, hiking* ⊟ *AE, D, MC, V* ⊗ *Closed mid-Oct.–Memorial Day.*

$$–$$$ ⬚ **Tug Boat Inn.** This inn offers a variety of accommodations in the heart of Boothbay Harbor. Guest rooms are simple, but have nice touches like colorful quilts and cheery wallpaper. Most have balconies overlooking the harbor. The restaurant, facing the water, is shaped like the prow of a ship. Besides seafood, it also serves excellent steaks. The Tug Boat has the area's only piano bar with live music. A light continental breakfast is included in the rate. ⊠ *80 Commercial St., Boothbay Harbor 04538* ☎ *207/633–4434 or 800/248–2628* ⊕ *www.tugboatinn.com* ⇒*64 rooms* ⚘*Restaurant, piano bar; no-smoking rooms* ⊟ *AE, D, MC, V* ⊗ *Closed late Nov.–mid-Apr.*

$–$$$ ⬚ **Welch House.** This 1889 shipbuilder's house sits high on a hill near
Fodor'sChoice Boothbay Harbor. Antiques, artworks, and bric-a-brac from the owner's
★ travels around the world adorn the rooms. From the shared third-floor deck, you can take in the 180-degree views of the water. Breakfast on the lower deck usually includes one of the chef's specialties, which might mean caramel-apple and pecan-crusted French toast. The location puts you a few minutes' walk from the center of town. ⊠ *36 McKown St., Boothbay Harbor 04538* ☎ *207/633–3431 or 800/279–7313* ⊕*www.welchhouse.com* ⇒*14 rooms* ⚘ *Cable TV, in-room VCRs, some pets* ⊟ *MC, V* ⊗ *Closed Dec.–Mar.* ⭘ *BP.*

$–$$ ⬚ **Harborage Inn.** Built in 1875, this historic home has served as an inn since the 1920s, making it the oldest guest lodging in the area. All the pretty guest rooms reflect the heritage of the Maine Coast, and are decorated with nautical antiques. Wraparound porches lined with flower boxes look out onto the water. ⊠ *73 Townsend Ave., Boothbay Harbor 04538* ☎ *207/633–4640* ⊕ *www.harborageinn.com* ⇒ *5 rooms, 4 suites* ⚘ *Cable TV, microwaves, refrigerators* ⊟ *AE, D, MC, V* ⊗ *Closed Jan.–Mar.* ⭘ *CP.*

$–$$ ⬚ **Topside.** If you want a glimpse of the harbor, this 19th-century sea captain's house perched on a hillside has views from every room. The front lawn is a great place to watch the activities on the harbor below. From here you can walk to dozens of antiques shops, art galleries, and restaurants. Rooms are divided between the main house, and two annexes called the Windward House and the Leeward House. The rooms in the main house are decorated in a comfortable beach-house style. The cottages are a bit more rustic. ⊠*60 McKown St., Boothbay Harbor 04538* ☎*207/633–5404 or 877/486–7466* 🖷*207/633–2206* ⊕*www.topsideinn.com* ⇒ *21 rooms* ⚘ *Fans, cable TV, some pets allowed; no a/c* ⊟ *D, MC* ⊗ *Closed late Oct.–mid-Apr.* ⭘ *BP.*

Sports & the Outdoors

When you are ready to escape the pleasant hustle and bustle of Boothbay Harbor, rent a kayak and explore the harbor to your heart's content. To get a bit farther away, sign up for one of the sightseeing or whale-watching cruises from the piers on Commercial Street. You can also catch a ride on a lobster boat and help haul the traps.

BOATING On Pier 8, **Balmy Day Cruises** (✉ 62 Commercial St., Boothbay Harbor ☎ 207/633–2284 or 800/298–2284 ⊕ www.balmydaycruises.com) offers day trips to Monhegan Island and tours of the harbor. A guided tour of the Burnt Island Lighthouse is available. Cruises run from mid-April to mid-October. Setting sail from Pier 6, **Boothbay Whale Watch** (✉ Pier 6, Boothbay Harbor ☎ 207/633–3500 or 800/942–5363 ⊕ www.boothbaywhalewatch.com) conducts whale-watching tours and sunset cruises from June to mid-October.

On Pier 1 you can find **Cap'n Fish's Boat Trips** (✉ Pier 1, Boothbay Harbor ☎ 207/633–3244 or 800/636–3244 ⊕ www.capnfishsboats.com), which runs regional sightseeing cruises, including puffin-watching adventures. You can also join lobster-hauling and whale-watching rides, trips to Damariscove Harbor and Pemaquid Point, and excursions up the Kennebec River to Bath. Cruises run from late May to late October. For trips lasting from two to five days, head to Pier 1. Cruises operated by **Gypsy Soul** (✉ Pier 1, Boothbay Harbor ☎ 207/592–9243 or 866/464–2789) let you explore quiet coves and look for porpoises, puffins, and whales. Enjoy delicious cuisine on deserted islands and rock to sleep with the motion of the sea.

GOLF Play 18 holes at the **Boothbay Country Club** (✉ 33 Country Club Rd., Boothbay Harbor ☎ 207/633–6085), a par-72 course only five minutes from downtown Boothbay Harbor. Afterward you can stop at the on-site bar and grill.

HIKING Explore 20 mi of groomed trails crisscrossing more than 1,000 acres of natural habitat at the **Boothbay Region Land Trust** (✉ 1 Oak St., Boothbay ☎ 207/633–4818); hikes range from easy to difficult. Located about a mile from Boothbay Center, the **Coastal Maine Botanical Garden** (✉ Barters Island Rd., Boothbay ☎ 207/633–4333 ⊕ www.mainegardens.org) has 128 acres of tidal frontage that are open to hikers. When it is completed in 2006, this will be the biggest botanical garden in Maine.

KAYAKING **Tidal Transit Ocean Kayak Co.** (✉ 18 Granary Way, Boothbay Harbor 04538 ☎ 207/633–7140 ⊕ www.kayakboothbay.com) has equipment to rent and offers guided tours of the coastline. The company is open from Memorial Day to late September.

Shopping

Fodor'sChoice Windchimes and streamers greet you at the door of **Enchantments** (✉ 10
★ Boothbay House Hill, Boothbay Harbor ☎ 207/633–4992), a spiritual retreat filled with magical gifts. You can find extraordinary cards, carvings, mobiles, and jewelry. **Gleason Fine Art** (✉ 31 Townsend Ave., Boothbay Harbor ☎ 207/633–6849 ⊕ www.gleasonfineart.com) showcases a range of artworks—regional and national, 19th-century and contemporary—in a large and airy gallery overlooking the water. The upscale **House of Logan** (✉ 20 Townsend Ave., Boothbay Harbor ☎ 207/633–2293) stocks casual and formal attire for men and women.

McKown Square Quilts (✉ 14-B Boothbay House Hill Rd., Boothbay Harbor ☎ 207/633–2007) displays handmade quilts and fiber art in seven rooms. **Mung Bean** (✉ 37 Townsend Ave., Boothbay Harbor ☎ 207/633–5512) is open until 9:30 PM in summer so it's perfect for after-dinner browsing. You'll find pottery and wood carvings, jewelry and collectibles, and fruit preserves made in Maine. No trip to Boothbay Harbor is complete without a stop at **Orne's Candy Shop** (✉ 11 Commercial St., Boothbay Harbor ☎ 207/633–2695 ⊕ www.ornescandystore.com), a must for anyone with a sweet tooth.

For antiques visit **The Palabra Shop** (✉ 53 Commercial St., Boothbay Harbor ☎ 207/633–4225 ⊕ www.palabrashop.com). **A Silver Lining** (✉ 17 Townsend Ave. ☎ 207/633–4103) has a large selection of original jewelry, as well as older pieces from estates. Beautiful housewares and attractive clothing for the kids can be found at the **Village Store & Children's Shop** (✉ 20 Townsend Ave., Boothbay Harbor ☎ 207/633–2293).

Newcastle

⑤ *18 mi north of Boothbay Harbor via Rte. 27 and U.S. 1.*

The town of Newcastle, between the Sheepscot and the Damariscotta rivers, was settled in the early 1600s. The earliest inhabitants planted apple trees, but the town later became an industrial center, home to several shipyards and a couple of mills. The oldest Catholic church in New England is St. Patrick's, and the church still rings its original Paul Revere bell to call parishioners to worship. Newcastle's charming B&Bs put you close to everything on the Boothbay and Pemaquid peninsulas.

Where to Stay & Eat

$$$–$$$$ ✕🏠 **Newcastle Inn.** A riverside location and an excellent dining room make this country inn a classic. All the guest rooms are filled with antiques and decorated with sumptuous fabrics; some rooms have fireplaces and whirlpool baths. On pleasant mornings, breakfast is served on the back deck overlooking the river. The dining room ($$$$), which is open to the public by reservation, serves five-course meals. The emphasis is on local seafood. ✉ *60 River Rd., Newcastle 04553* ☎ *207/563–5685 or 800/832–8669* 📠 *207/563–6877* ⊕ *www.newcastleinn.com* 🛏 *15 rooms, 3 suites* ♿ *Restaurant, pub, some room TVs, fireplaces, hot tubs; no room phones, no children under 12* 🖃 *AE, MC, V* 🍽 *BP.*

$$ 🏠 **The Flying Cloud.** Each room here is named for a legendary port of call made by the *Flying Cloud*, a clipper ship that was christened in 1851. The main house elegantly combines the original 1790 Cape Cod–style house with an 1840 Greek Revival–style addition. You can enjoy your morning cup of coffee on the deck while you watch lobster boats in the harbor on the Damariscotta River. The sumptuous full breakfast is a great way to start the day. Many area attractions are close by, including the hiking trails at the Great Salt Bay Preserve. ✉ *45 River Rd., 04553* ☎ *207/563–2484* 📠 *207/563–7879* ⊕ *www.theflyingcloud.com* 🛏 *4 rooms, 1 suite* ♿ *Internet; no a/c, no room TVs, no smoking* 🖃 *AE, MC, V* 🍽 *BP.*

$$ ⊞ **Tipsy Butler Bed & Breakfast.** The view from the porch of this 1845 hillside home is of the twin villages of Damariscotta and Newcastle. The large guest rooms have separate sitting areas and are tastefully decorated with period furnishings. The out-of-the-way location assures privacy, but you are only a five-minute walk from many shops and restaurants. ⊠ *11 High St., 04553* ☎ *207/563–3394* ⊕ *www.thetipsybutler.com* ⇨ *4 rooms* ⚭ *Cable TV, in-room VCRs; no smoking* ▭ *MC, V* ⏐◉⏐ *BP.*

Damariscotta

❻ *6 mi east of Newcastle via U.S. 1.*

The Damariscotta region comprises several communities along the rocky coast. The town of Damariscotta, which sits on the water, is filled with attractive shops and several good restaurants. Bremen, which encompasses more than a dozen islands and countless rocky outcrops, offers numerous sporting activities. Nobleboro was settled in the 1720s by Colonel David Dunbar, sent by the British to build the fort at Pemaquid. Neighboring Waldoboro is situated on the Medomak River and was settled largely by Germans in the early 1770s. You can still visit the old German Meeting House, built in 1772. The peninsula stretches south to include Bristol, Round Pond, South Bristol, New Harbor, and Pemaquid.

One of the oldest houses in Damariscotta, the **Chapman-Hall House** was completed in 1754 by Nathaniel Chapman. Unlike nearby houses that have been remodeled, it closely resembles the original design. Tours are given in July and August. ⊠ *Main St. at Church St.* ☎ *No phone* ▭ *Free* ⊙ *Mid-June–mid-Sept., Tues.–Sun. 1–5.*

On U.S. 1, the Damariscotta River Association administers the **Glidden Oyster Shell Middens,** which includes a hiking trail with views of the Damariscotta River. ⊠ *U.S. 1* ☎ *207/563–1393* ⊕ *www.draclt.org* ▭ *Free.*

Where to Stay & Eat

$$–$$$ ✕ **Backstreet Landing Restaurant.** Chef Stephen Richards does everything with lobster—except boil it. He leaves that to others, serving up eclectic dishes instead such as the Lobster Trio, consisting of a baked lobster tail, a lobster knuckle, and a lobster cake. You can also try haddock every way but fried. Locally cultivated oysters are a favorite appetizer, and the cider-brined pork loin is an outstanding entrée if you're not in the mood for seafood. The restaurant is on the tidal marshes directly behind Main Street. ⊠ *17 Elm St.* ☎ *207/563–5666* ⚭ *Reservations essential* ▭ *D, MC, V.*

$$–$$$ ✕ **Damariscotta River Grill.** Whether you eat in the dining room or outside on the deck, you'll have a lovely view of the water at this downtown restaurant. Lobster is popular, as are the scallops and the Italian seafood stew, but you can still get a good steak. There's also a popular Sunday brunch. ⊠ *155 Main St.* ☎ *207/563–2992* ⚭ *Reservations essential* ▭ *MC, V.*

$$–$$$ ✕ **King Eider's Pub & Restaurant.** The classic pub bills itself as having the finest crab cakes in Maine. Other specialties of the house include lobster Courvoisier and house-made ravioli. With exposed brick walls and low wooden beams, it's a cozy place to enjoy your favorite ale. There is also seating on the deck. Stop by in the evening for live entertainment. ⊠ *2 Elm St.* ☎ *207/563–6008* ⌂ *Reservations essential* ▭ *D, MC, V.*

$–$$$ ✕ **Salt Bay Café.** Seafood devotees and those who hanker for meat or vegetarian fare will all like this downtown restaurant. On the menu you can find such delicious dishes as fettuccine Florentine, seafood Alfredo, and filet mignon cooked to perfection. Not to be missed are the scallops Mediterranean. Everything on the menu is made from scratch, from the soups to the desserts. A fireplace keeps the place toasty on winter nights. ⊠ *88 Main St.* ☎ *207/563–3302* ⌂ *Reservations essential* ▭ *MC, V.*

¢–$ ✕ **Paco's Tacos.** Step down the alley behind Sheepscot River Pottery for a made-to-order meal in this brightly painted basement restaurant. Open all year, it serves delicious tacos and other simple Mexican fare. Side dishes such as refried beans and guacamole are also tasty. ⊠ *Off Main St.* ☎ *207/563–5355* ▭ *MC, V* ⊘ *Closed Sun.*

$–$$$ ▦ **Oak Gables.** Nestled on 11 acres of the original Freeman Estate, this year-round facility looks out on an old apple orchard and some rapids of the Damariscotta River. There are several rooms in the main house, as well as two apartments and a separate cottage with a full kitchen. The boathouse has a deck where you can sit right above the water. ⊠ *36 Pleasant St., 04543* ☎ *207/563–1476 or 800/335–7748* ⊕ *www.oakgablesbb.com* ⇥ *3 rooms, 2 apartments, 1 cottage* ⌂ *Some kitchens, pool, Ping-Pong; no a/c* ▭ *MC, V* ⎮○⎮ *BP.*

Nightlife & the Arts

Musicals and plays are staged at the **Lincoln County Community Theater** (⊠ 2 Theater St. ☎ 207/563–3424 ⊕ www.lcct.org). The theater also stages concerts and screens movies throughout the year. Good acoustics make the **Waldo Theatre** (⊠ 916 Main St. ☎ 207/832–6060 ⊕ www.waldotheatre.org) a great place to attend a musical or concert.

Sports & the Outdoors

To rent a sea kayak, or to sign up for lessons, visit **Sea Spirit Adventures** (⊠ 47 Main St. ☎ 207/563–5732 ⊠ 56 Greenland Cove Rd., Bremen ☎ 207/529–4732 ⊕ www.seaspiritadventures.com). Great local excursions include Muscongus Bay and the Damariscotta River.

In the Sheepscot River Valley, **Sheepscot Links** (⊠ 822 Townhouse Rd., Whitefield 04353 ☎ 207/549–5750) is a 9-hole course open to the public. It's in Whitefield, north of U.S. 1. In Walpole, **Wawenock Country Club** (⊠ Rte. 129, Walpole 04573 ☎ 207/563–3938) is just minutes from Damariscotta. Open in late May, the country club includes a public-access course and driving range.

Shopping

Create your own necklace or bracelet from new and vintage beads at **Aboca Beads** (⊠ 157 Main St. ☎ 207/563–1766), in the Damariscotta

Center. If plants are your passion, **Bramble's** (✉ 157 Main St. ☎ 207/ 563–2800) carries gardening tools, topiaries, and pots. You can browse to your heart's content through the shelves at **Maine Coast Book Shop & Café** (✉ 158 Main St. ☎ 207/563–3207). Enjoy a cup of coffee and a blueberry muffin at the adjoining café.

You never know what you can find at **Reny's** (✉ Main St. ☎ 207/563– 5757). Sometimes there's merchandise from L. L. Bean or a coat from a famous designer. This bargain chain has outlets in many Maine towns, but this is its flagship store. The barnlike **Stable Gallery** (✉ Water St. ☎ 207/563–1991) stocks paintings and prints by more than 100 artists. In the Damariscotta Center, **Yuletide & Candles** (✉ 157 Main St. ☎ 207/ 563–6332) is filled with candles and Christmas decorations.

Pemaquid, New Harbor & Round Pond

❼ *17 mi south of Damariscotta via U.S. 1 to Rte. 129 to Rte. 130.*

Route 130 brings you to Pemaquid Point, where you can find the famous lighthouse. If you are going to New Harbor or Round Pond, take a left onto Route 32 where it intersects Route 130 just before Pemaquid Point. You come to New Harbor in about 4 mi, and Round Pond about 6 mi beyond that. Just north of New Harbor on Route 32 is the Rachel Carson Salt Pond Preserve.

At the **Colonial Pemaquid Restoration,** set on a small peninsula jutting into the Pemaquid River, English mariners established a fishing and trading settlement in the early 17th century. The excavations at Fort William Henry, begun in the mid-1960s, have turned up thousands of artifacts from the settlement, including the remains of an old customs house, a tavern, a jail, a forge, and several homes. Some older items are from earlier Native American settlements. The state operates a museum that displays many of these artifacts. The Colonial Pemaquid Tavern is on this site, as are a picnic area and restrooms. ✉ *Rte. 130, New Harbor* ☎ *207/677–2423* 🎟 *$2* ☉ *Memorial Day–Labor Day, daily 9:30–5.*

★ Route 130 terminates at the **Pemaquid Point Light,** which looks as though it sprouted from the ragged, tilted chunk of granite that it commands. The former lighthouse keeper's cottage is now the Fishermen's Museum, which displays historic photographs, scale models, and artifacts that explore commercial fishing in Maine. Also here is the Pemaquid Art Gallery, which mounts exhibitions from July to August. Restrooms, picnic tables, and barbecue grills are all available. Next door to this property is the Sea Gull Shop, with a dining room, gift shop, and ice-cream parlor. *Museum* ✉ *Rte. 130 (Bristol Rd.)* ☎ *207/677–2494* 🎟 *$1* ☉ *Memorial Day–Columbus Day, Mon.–Sat. 10–5, Sun. 11–5.*

From the quarter-acre tide pool known as **Rachel Carson Salt Pond Preserve,** author Rachel Carson gathered most of the material for her book *The Edge of the Sea.* The land, donated to the Nature Conservancy in 1966, is home to many of the creatures who live in the tidal zone. The preserve is just north of New Harbor. ✉ *Rte. 32* ☎ *207/677–2423.*

Where to Stay & Eat

★ **$$** ✕ **Round Pond Lobstermen's Co-op.** Lobster doesn't get any fresher or any cheaper than what's served at this no-frills dockside takeout. The best deal in town is the nightly dinner special: a one-pound lobster, steamers, corn-on-the-cob, and a bag of chips. Regulars often bring their own beer, wine, bread, and salads. Settle in at a picnic table and take in the view over dreamy Round Pond Harbor. ✉ *32 Round Pond Rd., Round Pond* ☎ *207/529–5725* ☐ *MC, V.*

☾ **$$$–$$$$** ✕☐ **The Bradley Inn.** When you think of a country inn, you probably picture something like the Bradley Inn. Within walking distance of Pemaquid Point Light, this former rooming house was originally built as a private residence for sea captain John Bradley. The lovingly restored building now has guest rooms that are comfortable and uncluttered; some have fireplaces, and those on the third floor have ocean views. Nautical knickknacks and works by local artists decorate the rooms in the Main Inn, the Carriage House, and the Garden Cottage. The Bradley Inn has one of the region's best dining rooms ($$$–$$$$). The menu changes nightly, but always emphasizes fresh local foods. You can eat in the dining room or outside on the deck. The pub has piano music on weekends during the summer. ✉ *3063 Bristol Rd., New Harbor 04554* ☎ *207/677–2105 or 800/942–5560* ☐ *207/677–3367* ⊕ *www. bradleyinn.com* ↪ *12 rooms, 4 suites* ↻ *Restaurant, fans, bicycles, boccie, croquet, lounge, piano bar, babysitting, Internet, meeting rooms; no a/c, no TV in some rooms* ☐ *AE, MC, V* ❡❡ *BP.*

$$–$$$ ☐ **The Inn at Round Pond.** Once a stagecoach stop, this 1830s mansard-roofed Colonial sits on the eastern shore of Pemaquid Peninsula. At this restful retreat you won't be bothered by ringing telephones or blaring televisions. The trio of tastefully appointed suites—the Foster Suite, the Prentice Suite, and the Monhegan Suite—have separate sitting rooms decorated with original works by local artists. All have harbor views. A full country breakfast is served each morning. ✉ *1442 Rte. 32, Round Pond 04564* ☎ *207/529–2004* ⊕ *www.theinnatroundpond.com* ↪ *3 suites* ↻ *No in-room phones or TVs, no children under 12* ☐ *AE, D, MC, V* ☾ *Closed Columbus Day–Memorial Day* ❡❡ *BP.*

$$–$$$ ☐ **Tibbets Farm.** Just below the Bristol Dam, this circa-1772 farmhouse sits on the Pemaquid River. The elegant B&B is decorated with country French and American antiques. Enjoy breakfast in the dining room or outside on the porch overlooking the water. You're just minutes away from Pemaquid Light and the sightseeing and whale-watching cruises around Boothbay Harbor. ✉ *1242 Bristol Rd., Bristol 04539* ☎ *207/ 563–1619* ⊕ *www.tibbetsfarmbedandbreakfast.com* ↪ *1 room, 1 suite* ↻ *Dining room, kitchens; no a/c in some rooms, no room phones, no rooms TVs, no children under 14* ☐ *No credit cards* ☾ *Closed Dec.–Apr.* ❡❡ *BP.*

$$ ☐ **Unique Yankee Bed & Breakfast.** Spectacular views of the Gulf of Maine and the sound of crashing surf greet you at this hilltop B&B. The building sits on Christmas Cove, named when explorer Captain John Smith anchored here one Christmas Eve in the early 1600s. Since that time the cove has been a snug harbor for watercraft of all kinds. The rooms have amenities such as fireplaces and hot tubs. ✉ *53*

Coveside Rd., South Bristol 04568 ☎ *207/644–1502 or 866/644–1502* 🖷 *207/644–1503* ⊕ *www.parpac.com/uniqueyankeeofmaine* ⟋ *4 rooms* ⚴ *Microwaves, refrigerators, cable TV; no a/c, no smoking* ☰ *MC, V* ⟙ *BP.*

$–$$ **Sunset Bed & Breakfast.** This cottage dating from the 1850s has a view of the bay from the front porch. The guest rooms are upstairs under the eves, and have skylights that let in lots of sun. The homespun decor includes colorful quilts piled on the beds. You can walk to nearby Christmas Cove and watch the swing bridge open to allow boats to pass. The full breakfast includes breads and muffins, granola and cereals, and fresh fruit in season. ✉ *16 Sunset Loop, South Bristol 04568* ☎ *207/644–8849* ⊕ *www.sunsetbnb.com* ⟋ *2 rooms with shared bath* ⚴ *Fans; no a/c, no room TVs, no smoking* ☰ *No credit cards* ⊙ *Closed Oct.–Apr.* ⟙ *BP.*

$ **Hotel Pemaquid.** Step back in time at this beautifully restored 1888 inn located less than 500 feet from the lighthouse at Pemaquid Point. The main building is Victorian in style; cottages and bungalow units have a more contemporary feel. The carriage-house suite is ideal for honeymooners or others seeking a romantic retreat. Relax on the big wraparound porch or enjoy a fire in the stone fireplace. Antiques decorate the comfortable rooms. ✉ *3098 Bristol Rd., New Harbor 04554* ☎ *207/677–2312* ⊕ *www.hotelpemaquid.com* ⟋ *28 rooms, 6 suites, 2 cottages, 1 apartment* ⚴ *No-smoking rooms; no a/c, no room phones* ☰ *No credit cards* ⊙ *Closed mid-Oct.–mid-May.*

$ **Mill Pond Inn.** A quiet residential street brings you to this circa-1780 inn, which sits on a mill pond across the street from Damariscotta Lake. Loons, otters, and bald eagles reside at the lake, and you can arrange to see them up close on an excursion in the owner's 17-foot antique lapstrake boat. The rooms are warm and inviting, though you may find it hard to tear yourself away from the hammocks-for-two overlooking the pond. ✉ *50 Main St., off Rte. 215 N, Nobleboro 04555* ☎ *207/563–8014* ⊕ *www.millpondinn.com* ⟋ *6 rooms, 1 suite* ⚴ *Boating, bicycles, horseshoes, pub; no a/c, no room phones, no room TVs, no kids under 12, no smoking* ☰ *No credit cards* ⟙ *BP.*

Nightlife & the Arts

Open year-round, the **Round Top Center for the Arts** (✉ U.S. 1, Damariscotta ☎ 207/563–1507 ⊕ www.roundtoparts.org) has a gallery with exhibits that rotate monthly and a performance hall that stages classical, folk, operatic, and jazz concerts.

Sports & the Outdoors

Pemaquid Beach Park (✉ Rte. 130, New Harbor ☎ 207/677–2754) has a sandy beach that's popular with families. There's a snack bar, changing facilities, and picnic tables overlooking John's Bay.

You can take a cruise to Monhegan with **Hardy Boat Cruises** (✉ Shaw's Wharf, New Harbor ☎ 207/677–6026). On the sightseeing cruises you can spot seals and puffins. At **Salt Water Charters** (✉ Round Pond Harbor ☎ 207/677–6229 ⊕ www.saltwater-charters.com), the fishing vessel *Paige Elizabeth* takes passengers on sightseeing cruises.

Shopping

Of the villages on Pemaquid Peninsula, Damariscotta has boutiques and galleries. New Harbor and Round Pond have crafts stores and antiques shops as well as artisans' studios. Antiques shops also dot the main thoroughfares through the region.

The **Granite Hall Store** (✉ Backshore Rd., Round Pond ☎ 207/529–5864) has penny candy, wicker baskets, and cards on the first floor and antiques and books on the second. Order ice-cream cones through a window on the side. It's open May to mid-October. The work of more than 50 Maine artisans is displayed in the 15 rooms of the **Pemaquid Craft Co-op** (✉ 2545 Bristol Rd., New Harbor ☎ 207/677–2077). Stop by from May to mid-October.

THE CUSHING & ST. GEORGE PENINSULAS

These two peninsulas bring to life the state's seafaring traditions. The town of Waldoboro has a beautiful downtown filled with houses that combine several architectural styles. Sea captains were intrigued by what they saw during their travels and came back with ideas for their own homes. Thomaston, another seaside town, is known for the clapboard houses lining its streets.

On a rocky part of the coast, Tenants Harbor has a lobstering tradition that is still strong today. The harbor is full of boats that go out once or twice daily to retrieve crustaceans from the ocean floor. You can grow familiar with their distinctive chug-chug as they enter and leave the harbor. Artists favor this area, and you can browse in many of their studios. Port Clyde is the jumping-off point to Monhegan Island, but has some sights of its own. Marshall Point Lighthouse is within walking distance of the town landing.

Waldoboro

8 *10 mi northeast of Damariscotta.*

Veer off U.S. 1 onto Main Street or down Route 220 or 32, and you can discover a seafaring town with a proud shipbuilding past. Waldoboro's Main Street is lined with houses representing numerous architectural styles, including Cape Cod, Queen Anne, Stick, Greek Revival, and Italianate.

Fawcett's Toy Museum delights adults and children with collectible toys, from Betty Boop and Popeye to Charlie Brown and Mickey Mouse. There's also original comic art. ✉ 3506 U.S. 1 ☎ 207/832–7398 ✍ $3 ☉ *Memorial Day–Columbus Day, Thurs.–Mon. 10–4; Columbus Day–Christmas Eve, weekends noon–3:30.*

Friendship is the birthplace of the distinctive Friendship Sloop, and you can visit the **Friendship Museum** to see exhibits on this popular sailing ship, as well as local historical artifacts. Dating from 1857, the building first served as a one-room schoolhouse. ✉ *Hatchet Cove Rd. and Rte. 220, Friendship* ☎ *207/832–4337* ✍ *Free* ☉ *July–Labor Day, Mon.–Sat. 1–4, Sun. 2–4.*

Between 1893 and 1968, painter Andrew Wyeth painted his famous Christina pictures in the **Olson House.** Reproductions of many of these enigmatic portraits are hung throughout this historic house, now part of the Farnsworth Museum. ⊠ *384 Hathorn Point Rd., Cushing* ☎ *207/ 354–0102* ⊕ *farnsworthmuseum.org* 🎫 *$4* ⊙ *Memorial Day–Columbus Day, daily 11–4.*

Several buildings make up the **Waldoborough Historical Society Museum,** including the one-room Boggs Schoolhouse, built in 1857; the Town Pound, built in 1819; and a barn filled with artifacts such as hooked rugs, antique toys, tools, clothing, and housewares. ⊠ *Main St. and Rte. 220* ☎ *No phone* 🎫 *Free* ⊙ *July–Labor Day, daily 1–4:30.*

One of the oldest churches in Maine, the **Old German Church** was built in 1772. It originally sat on the eastern side of the Medomak River, then was moved across the ice to its present site in 1794. Inside you can find box pews and a 9-foot-tall chalice pulpit. ⊠ *Rte. 32* ☎ *No phone* ⊙ *July and Aug., daily 1–3.*

Where to Stay & Eat

$–$$ ✕ **Moody's Diner.** Settle into one of the well-worn wooden booths or snag a counter stool at this old-style diner known for its home cooking. Breakfast is served all day at this local landmark where coffee is still only 70 cents. Don't miss the legendary walnut pie. ⊠ *1885 U.S. 1* ☎ *207/ 832–7785* ⊟ *D, MC, V.*

★ ♺ $–$$ 🏨 **Harbor Hill Bed & Breakfast.** From the terrace of this B&B you can gaze down at the offshore islands near the town of Friendship. Should you get the urge to see the coastline from a different vantage point, there are five boat launches nearby. Piles of stones rounded by surf and little dishes of shells and sea glass pop up in unexpected places in this cozy inn. Rooms have exposed beams and lots of natural wood. Should you need more room, there's a two-bedroom apartment with a private deck. Books and artworks are everywhere, since the owner is a docent at the Farnsworth Art Museum. Breakfasts have a Scandinavian flair, with lots of whole-grain cereals. ⊠ *Town Landing Rd., Friendship 04547* ☎ *207/ 832–6646* ➥ *3 rooms, 1 apartment* ♣ *Fans, some kitchens, some microwaves, some pets allowed; no a/c, no room TVs* ⊟ *No credit cards* ⊙ *Closed late Oct.–May* ⦿⃝ *BP.*

$ 🏨 **Outsiders Inn Bed & Breakfast.** If you are looking for a quiet retreat that is convenient to the sights, consider the Outsiders Inn. The original homestead was built by Zenas Cook in 1830, and the current owners have preserved much of the charm with period furnishings and decorations. Rooms, some with private baths, are comfortably furnished. A full breakfast with home-baked specialties is served every morning. You can rent kayaks from the on-site outfitter. At the end of your day, take a stroll to the harbor. ⊠ *Box 521A, Harbor Rd., Friendship 04547* ☎ *207/832–5197* ➥ *3 rooms, 1 cottage* ♣ *Breakfast room, boating; no a/c, no room TVs* ⊟ *MC, V* ⦿⃝ *BP.*

$ 🏨 **Payson Farm Bed & Breakfast.** This house, built by the Payson family in 1810, was originally part of a 100-acre property. It now has 45 acres crisscrossed by hiking trails. A charming spiral staircase leads to the second floor, where many of the ceilings are redwood—unusual in this part of the country. Guest rooms are full of rich woods and are decorated with works by local artists. The inn uses all natural fabrics and cotton bedding, so the rooms are ideal for people with allergies. The owner loves to cook, so look for something delicious for breakfast. ☒ *73 Pleasant Point Rd., Cushing 04563* ☎ *207/354–0440* 🖷 *207/354–0440* ⤶ *2 rooms, 1 suite* ♨ *Dining room; no a/c, no room TVs* ☱ *No credit cards* ⍾ *BP.*

$ 🛏 **Roaring Lion Bed & Breakfast.** Tin ceilings, hand-carved woodwork, and other Victorian-era architectural details highlight this friendly B&B. Built in 1905, the house has two fireplaces and a large screened porch where guests tend to congregate. One of the country-style guest rooms has a fireplace. The location is convenient to the Olson House and other local sights. ☒ *995 Main St., 04572* ☎ *207/832–4038* 🖷 *207/832–7892* ⊕ *www.roaringlion.com* ⤶ *4 rooms, 1 with bath* ♨ *No a/c; no room phones, no room TVs* ☱ *No credit cards* ⍾ *BP.*

Nightlife & the Arts
The **Waldo Theatre** (☒ 916 Main St. ☎ 207/832–6060), a Greek Revival–style movie house with an art deco interior, stages concerts, plays, and other live performances.

Shopping
The **Waldoboro 5 & 10** (☒ 17 Friendship St. ☎ 207/832–4624) is the oldest continually operated five-and-ten in the country. It has an old-fashioned soda fountain that serves sandwiches, soups, and ice cream. There's even a penny candy counter that's popular with the kids.

Thomaston

❾ *10 mi northeast of Waldoboro, 72 mi northeast of Portland.*

This is a delightful town, full of beautiful sea captains' homes and dotted with antiques and specialty shops. A National Historic District encompasses parts of High, Main, and Knox streets. Thomaston is the gateway to the two peninsulas, so you will be looking at water on both sides as you arrive.

Past visitors to Thomaston may recall the Maine State Prison, which loomed over the town for decades. Happily, the prison has closed and been replaced by a beautiful open park.

Check out more than 100 boats at the **Maine Watercraft Museum.** This is an in-the-water display of classic crafts that are indigenous to the area. You can learn about shipbuilding and even ride in one of these beauties. ☒ *4 Knox St.* ☎ *207/354–0444* ☉ *May–Sept.*

Built in 1930, **Montpelier** is a replica of the late-18th-century mansion of Major General Henry Knox, a commander in the Revolutionary War and secretary of war in George Washington's cabinet. Antiques, including many Knox family possessions, fill the interior. Architectural appointments include an oval room and a double staircase. Call ahead to reserve space on the half-hourly tours. ☒ *U.S. 1 and Rte. 131* ☎ *207/354–8062* ⊕ *www.generalknoxmuseum.org* ⌦ *$6* ☉ *Memorial Day–late Sept., Tues.–Sat. 10–4.*

Where to Stay & Eat

$$–$$$ ✕ **Harbor View Restaurant.** The location couldn't be more perfect for this waterfront restaurant in Thomaston. Seafood is the specialty here, and it comes in all forms. Mussels in cream sauce is a popular choice, as are the crab rolls, steamed clams, and boiled or baked stuffed lobsters. This is the kind of place where you can order everything from escargot to fish-and-chips. Eat in the dining room or outside on the patio. ⊠ *Public Landing* ☎ *207/354–8173* ⊕ *www.harborviewrestaurant.com* ⌂ *Reservations essential* ⊟ *MC, V.*

$$–$$$ ✕ **Thomaston Café & Bakery.** A changing selection of works by local artists adorns the walls of this small café. Entrées, prepared with locally grown ingredients, include seared fresh tuna on soba noodles, lobster ravioli with lobster sauce, and filet mignon with béarnaise sauce. ⊠ *154 Main St.* ☎ *207/354–8589* ⊟ *MC, V* ⊗ *No dinner Sun.–Thurs.*

$–$$$ ✕ **Waterman's Beach Lobster.** You can eat inside or out at this seaside restaurant in South Thomaston. Lobster and clam rolls are among the many favorites that draw people to this popular spot. There's a private beach where you can stroll while you wait for your dinner, so bring your binoculars to get a closer look at the lobster boats. You'll want to try the freshly baked pies made from old family recipes. ⊠ *359 Waterman Beach Rd., off Rte. 73, South Thomaston* ☎ *207/596–7819 or 207/594–7518* ⊟ *No credit cards* ⊗ *Closed Oct.–mid-June.*

$–$$ ▦ **Weskeag Inn.** Built in the 1830s, this charming B&B is near the reversing falls in the village of South Thomaston. Anglers line the banks in search of stripers in spring, and sun-worshippers swim or float on inner tubes in summer. Watch the herons, egrets, and osprey; sometimes even eagles come here to catch their dinner. Guest rooms are bright and tastefully decorated with period antiques; make sure to ask for one with a view of the water. ⊠ *Rte. 73, South Thomaston 04858* ☎ *207/596–6676* ⊕ *www.midcoast.com/~weskeag* ⇆ *6 rooms, 4 with baths, 1 suite* ⌂ *Cable TV, Internet* ⊟ *No credit cards* ⚏ *BP.*

$ ▦ **Chestnut Tree Bed & Breakfast.** Maine's fleet of windjammers and the Farnsworth Art Museum in Rockland are close to this restored 1850s Colonial-style house. Each of the comfortably furnished guest rooms has a private bath. Coffee and tea are served each afternoon in the lounge, where you can play board games or a hand of cards. ⊠ *12 Wadsworth St., 04861* ☎ *207/354–0089 or 866/745–3723* ⊕ *www.bbonline.com/me/chestnuttree* ⇆ *4 rooms* ⌂ *Cable TV* ⊟ *No credit cards* ⊗ *Closed mid-Oct.–mid-May* ⚏ *BP.*

Shopping

The **Maine State Prison Showroom Outlet** (⊠ Main St. ☎ 207/354–2535) carries furniture and other wooden items fashioned by prisoners. Browse the comprehensive selection of books and original art at **The Personal Book Shop** (⊠ 144 Main St. ☎ 207/354–8058).

Tenants Harbor

❿ *13 mi south of Thomaston.*

Tenants Harbor is a quintessential coastal town—its harbor is dominated by lobster boats, its shores are rocky and slippery, and its downtown streets are lined with clapboard houses, a church, and a general store. It's a favorite with artists, and galleries and studios welcome browsers. The fictional Dunnet Landing of Sarah Orne Jewett's classic *The Country of the Pointed Firs* (1896) is based on towns in this region.

Where to Stay & Eat

$-$$$ ✕ **Sul Mare.** This country trattoria serves authentic regional Italian cuisine such as risotto primavera, made with seasonal vegetables, fresh rosemary, and asiago cheese. The chef's specialties include wood-grilled shrimp with Tuscan olive oil, cannellini beans, tomato, and basil. About 200 yards from the water in Tenants Harbor, Sul Mare couldn't ask for better views. There's take-out service, too. ⊠ *13 River Rd.* ☎ *207/372–9995* ⌕ *Reservations essential* ⊟ *DC, MC, V* ☉ *Closed for lunch Nov.–Apr.*

$$-$$$$ ✕⊡ **East Wind Inn & Meeting House.** Built as a sail loft in 1830, this comfortably old-fashioned inn has a wraparound porch with a dreamy view of the island-studded harbor. Some of the guest rooms in the Meeting House, a converted sea captain's house, are warmed by fireplaces. A grand piano graces the great room. The inn's restaurant ($$–$$$) emphasizes local seafood and a take-out restaurant on the wharf serves lighter fare. ⊠ *21 Mechanic St., 04860* ☎ *207/372–6366 or 800/241–8439* ⊟ *207/ 372–6320* ⊕ *www.eastwindinn.com* ⌕ *18 rooms, 12 with bath; 3 suites; 4 apartments* ⌂ *2 restaurants, some microwaves, cable TV, meeting rooms, some pets allowed; no a/c* ⊟ *AE, D, MC, V* ☉ *Closed Dec.–Apr.* ⏐◉⏐ *BP.*

$-$$ ✕⊡ **The Craignair Inn.** Drive all the way to the end of the road to find
Fodor$Choice this lodging dating from 1928. Sitting on 4 acres right on the water, it
★ was originally built to house granite workers from nearby quarries. The annex was the chapel where the stonecutters and their families worshiped. Rooms are comfortably furnished with antique furniture, and the beds are piled high with colorful quilts. Most rooms have views of the water. Chef Brian Krum wins awards for his creative cuisine served in the inn's dining room. You might want to start with the steamed great eastern mussels and move on to baked stuffed haddock. ⊠ *5 3rd St., Spruce Head 04859* ☎ *207/594–7644 or 800/320–9997* ⊟ *207/596–7124* ⊕ *www.craignair.com* ⌕ *21 rooms, 13 with bath* ⌂ *Cable TV; no a/c* ⊟ *D, MC, V.*

Shopping

The **Port Clyde Arts & Crafts Society Gallery** (⊠ Rte. 131, Tenants Harbor ☎ 207/372–0673) showcases members' works in a colorful garden.

Port Clyde

⑪ *2 mi south of Tenants Harbor via Rte. 131.*

The fishing village of Port Clyde sits at the end of the St. George Peninsula. The road leading to Port Clyde meanders along the St. George River, passing meadows and farmhouses. Shipbuilding was the first commercial enterprise here, and later the catching and canning of seafood. You can still buy Port Clyde sardines. Port Clyde's boat landing is home to

LIGHTING THE WAY

THERE ARE MORE THAN 60 LIGHTHOUSES *strung along the coast of Maine, and 16 of these are in the Mid-Coast region. Ever wonder what makes them so bright? You need the right kind of lens to magnify the light. Resembling giant beehives, the original Fresnel lenses used in these lighthouses were made of prisms that redirected light from a lamp into a concentrated beam.*

The first Fresnel lens was made in France in 1822 by French physicist Augustine Fresnel. Most lenses that were placed in lighthouses along the coasts of Europe and North America were handmade and shipped unassembled from France. The largest of these lenses, called a first-order lens, could be as much as 12 feet tall. Rings of glass prisms arranged above and below the center drum were intended to bend the light beam. Later designs incorporated a bull's eye into the center of the lens, that acted like a magnifying glass to make the beam even more powerful. A Fresnel lens captured all but 17% of the available light, whereas an open flame, even with reflectors behind it, lost 83% of its light.

You can see some of the smaller original lenses in museums in Maine, but you can also see a first-order lens in the Mid-Coast area in the lighthouse on Seguin Island, 10 mi from shore. You can go by boat from the Maine Maritime Museum. The Seguin Light is the only first-order lens in Maine, and one of two remaining lenses still in use north of Virginia. The lens is wonderful to see, shining with 282 prisms.

The Seguin Island Light was commissioned by George Washington in 1795, and is one of the oldest lighthouses in the United states. Most of the original lenses used in lighthouses in this part of the country were mounted on mercury bases that were designed to rotate; these lenses were later replaced because of the danger of

mercury poisoning. The lens at Seguin is a fixed light, meaning that it does not rotate. It used no mercury, so it could be kept in place. Ships can see this beacon 20 mi out to sea. Today the lens reflects the light of a 1,000-watt bulb. Before electricity, incandescent oil vapor was used.

The order of a Fresnel lens is determined by its distance from the flame, and the first-orders lenses were routinely installed in the larger seacoast lighthouses. Smaller lenses in the range of sixth order were used in smaller lighthouses such as those at breakwaters. You can see a fourth-order lens still in use at the Owl's Head Light at the entrance to Rockland Harbor.

Early Fresnel lenses were fairly standard in size and shape, but that posed problems as more and more lighthouses were built along the coasts. The captain of a ship could not tell one light from another in the dark and stormy night, so he didn't know what headland or ledge he was approaching. The lenses eventually were designed to have different personalities that made them easily identifiable. Many lights became known for their distinctive flash patterns. Seguin Island Light is a fixed white light, whereas the Pemaquid Point Light is a white light that flashes every six seconds. Monhegan Island Light, visible from Port Clyde, has a white light that flashes for 2.8 seconds every 30 seconds. In Phippsburg, Pond Island Light shines a white beam with 6-second intervals of white and dark.

the *Elizabeth Ann* and the *Laura B*, the mail boats that serve nearby Monhegan Island. Several artists make their homes in Port Clyde, so check to see if their studios are open while you are visiting.

The 1895 keeper's house at the **Marshall Point Lighthouse** has been turned into a museum containing memorabilia from the town of St. George (a few miles north of Tenants Harbor). The setting has inspired Jamie Wyeth and other noted artists. You can stroll the grounds, have a picnic, and watch boats sail in and out of Port Clyde. The lighthouse is about 1 mi from the Port Clyde boat landing. ✉ *Marshall Point Rd., Port Clyde* ☎ *207/372–6450* 🔖 *Free* ⊙ *June–Sept., weekdays 1–5, Sat. 10–5; May and Oct., weekends 1–5.*

At Owls Head Light State Park, the beautifully maintained **Owls Head Light** (✉ Rte. 73, Owls Head ☎ 207/941–4014) has shown the way since 1825. On West Penobscot Bay, the local landmark indicates the entrance to Rockland Harbor. The grounds are open to the public, but not the lighthouse or keeper's house. This lighthouse still has its original Fresnel lens in place, in use since it was installed in 1856.

On the way to Rockland, stop at the **Owls Head Transportation Museum** (✉ Rte. 73, Owls Head ☎ 207/594–4418 ⊕ www.owlshead.org) to see a collection of antique aircraft, automobiles, motorcycles, carriages, bicycles, and engines. Open throughout the year, the museum schedules exciting antique auto and airplane shows. See a full-size replica of the Wright Brothers' Kitty Hawk Flyer.

Where to Stay & Eat

$–$$$ ✕ **Miller's Lobster Company.** Enjoy a lobster at this restaurant overlooking beautiful Wheeler's Bay. Known for its lobster rolls and steamed clams, Miller's also serves a good steamed hot dog. Eat in the dining room or outside on the deck. ✉ *38 Fuller Rd., Spruce Head* ☎ *207/594–7406* 🚫 *No credit cards* ⊙ *Closed Labor Day–late June.*

¢–$ ✕ **Dip Net Diner.** On a summer day you can grab a crab roll or a slice of pizza here before taking a boat to Monhegan Island or hiking to Marshall Point Lighthouse. Lobster doesn't get any fresher than those cooked right beside the sea where they are caught. Eat inside or order takeout. ✉ *1 Cold Storage Rd.* ☎ *207/372–6307* 🚫 *No credit cards* ⊙ *Closed Labor Day–Memorial Day.*

$ ✕🏨 **Ocean House.** Little has changed at the Ocean Hotel since it first opened for business in the 1820s. Most of the furniture is original, including some of the wrought-iron beds. From the rooms there are excellent views of the harbor. On the walls hang several Jamie Wyeth paintings, and the hotel often hosts the artist himself, who drops by for dinner. Breakfast is available, and a specialty of the house is blueberry pancakes. The hotel is within walking distance of the boat dock, the general store, the post office, and the lighthouse. ✉ *At Monhegan Island boat landing, Box 66, 04855* ☎ *207/372–6691 or 800/269–6691* ⊕ *www.oceanhousehotel.com* 🛏 *10 rooms, 8 with bath* ⚫ *Restaurant; no a/c, no room TVs* 🚫 *No credit cards* ⊙ *Closed Nov.–Apr.*

Shopping

In Port Clyde Village, **Klatfish Gallery** (⊠ Rte. 131, Port Clyde ☎ 207/ 372–8631) carries works by a dozen local artists, including Leo Brooks, Lawrence Goldsmith, and Emily Muir. If you need to stock up on anything before heading out to Monhegan Island, the dock-side **Port Clyde General Store** (⊠ Cold Storage Rd. ☎ 207/372–6543), sells food, drinks, and gas. The store is open throughout the year.

Monhegan Island

⑫ *East of Pemaquid Peninsula, 10 mi south of Port Clyde.*

Remote Monhegan Island, with its high cliffs fronting the sea, was known to Basque, Portuguese, and Breton fishermen well before Columbus discovered America. About a century ago, Monhegan was discovered again by some of America's finest painters, including Rockwell Kent, Robert Henri, A. J. Hammond, and Edward Hopper, who sailed out to paint its open meadows, savage cliffs, wild ocean views, and fishermen's shacks. Tourists followed, and today three excursion boats dock here (*see* Boat Travel *under* The Mid-Coast A to Z *at the end of this chapter*). The village bustles with activity in the summer, when many artists open their studios. You can escape the crowds on the island's 17 mi of hiking trails, which lead to the lighthouse and to the cliffs. Bring a picnic if you're visiting during the day, as restaurants can be packed at lunch.

The **Monhegan Museum,** housed in an 1824 lighthouse and the adjacent assistant keeper's house, has wonderful views of Manana Island. Inside, informative displays depict island life and local flora and fauna. ⊠ *White Head Rd.* ☎ *No phone* ☒ *Donations accepted* ☉ *July–mid-Sept., daily 11:30–3:30.*

Where to Stay & Eat

$$$-$$$$ 🏨 **Island Inn.** This three-story inn, which dates from 1807, has a commanding presence on Monhegan Island's harbor. The waterfront rooms are the nicest, with views of the sunset over stark Manana Island. Avoid the meadow-view rooms, which have the distinct disadvantage of being over kitchen vents. The property includes a small café and a dining room that serves breakfast, lunch, and dinner. ⊠ *1 Ocean Ave., 04852* ☎ *207/ 596–0371* 🖷 *207/594–5517* ⊕ *www.islandinnmonhegan.com* 🛏 *30 rooms, 15 with bath; 4 suites* ☖ *Restaurant, café; no a/c, no room phones, no room TVs* ▭ *MC, V* ☉ *Closed Columbus Day–Memorial Day* ❍ *BP.*

$-$$$ 🏨 **Shining Sails Bed & Breakfast.** Near the ocean, this B&B has the finest accommodations on Monhegan Island. Rooms are light and airy, and are kept cheery with fresh flowers. Most have private decks with ocean views. A common room with a wood-burning stove is filled with games. ⊠ *Monhegan Island, 04852* ☎ *207/596–0041* ⊕ *www.shiningsails. com* 🛏 *2 rooms, 5 apartments* ☖ *Some kitchens; no a/c, no room phones, no room TVs* ▭ *D, MC, V* ❍ *CP.*

THE MID-COAST A TO Z

To research prices, get advice from other travelers, and book travel ar-rangements, visit www.fodors.com.

AIR TRAVEL

The Portland Jet Port is convenient to the Mid-Coast region, being half an hour from Brunswick via the Maine Turnpike or Interstate 295. Car-riers include American, Continental, Delta, Independence, United, and US Airways. Two hours from the Mid-Coast region, Manchester Inter-national Airport, in New Hampshire, is served by Air Canada, Delta, Continental, Northwest, Southwest, United, and US Airways. Bangor International Airport is also about two hours away but be aware that there are frequent cancellations at this small airport. Carriers serving the airport are American, Continental, Delta, and Northwest.

🚩 **Bangor International Airport** ⊠ 287 Godfrey Blvd., Bangor ☎ 207/947-0384 ⊕ www.flybangor.com. **Manchester International Airport** ⊠ 1 Airport Dr., Manches-ter, NH 03103 ☎ 603/624-6539 ⊕ www.flymanchester. **Portland Jet Port** ⊠ 1001 West-brook St., Portland 04102 ☎ 207/874-8877 ⊕ www.portlandjetport.org.

BIKE TRAVEL

There are two major bike routes in the Mid-Coast region. The Coastal Route tour goes all the way from Brunswick to Ellsworth, a distance of 187 mi, along the rocky coastline. Some stretches are along heavily trav-eled roads. You can do a mostly level 5-mi round-trip ride along this route in Brunswick. You begin on Water Street at the west end of the Androscoggin River Pathway. There are restrooms along the way and shady spots to rest along the river.

The 60-mi Merrymeeting Tour, traversing small hills and one major climb, originates in Bath and travels round-trip to Wiscasset. Along the way you can see the Kennebec River and Merrymeeting Bay, famous for its variety of birds, including several types of ducks.

Many rural roads are also great for biking. These roads are narrow, though, and many experience heavy traffic in summer.

BOAT TRAVEL

Port Clyde, a fishing village at the end of Route 131, is the point of departure for the *Laura B.*, the mail boat that runs to Monhegan Is-land. It's operated by the Monhegan Boat Line. In summer the *Balmy Days* sails daily between Boothbay Harbor and Monhegan Island. Boats operated by Hardy Boat Cruises leave daily from Shaw's Wharf in New Harbor.

🚩 *Balmy Days* ☎ 207/633-2284 or 800/298-2284. **Hardy Boat Cruises** ☎ 207/677-2026 or 800/278-3346. **Monhegan Boat Line** ☎ 207/372-8848.

BUS TRAVEL

Catch a bus between Boston and Portland with Concord Trailways. Ver-mont Transit Lines services the Brunswick area.

🚩 Concord Trailways ☎ 800/639-3317 ⊕ www.concordtrailways.com. **Vermont Tran-sit Lines** ☎ 207/729-5301.

CAR TRAVEL

Travelers visiting the Mid-Coast region in summer and early fall may encounter fog. It's best to leave headlights on. Fog may stay around all day, or it may burn off by late morning. Winter driving in Maine can be challenging when snow and ice coat the roads. "Black ice" is a special hazard along the coast, as the road may appear clear but is actually covered by a nearly invisible coating of ice. Four-wheel-drive vehicles are recommended for driving in winter. Always carry warm clothing and blankets, as well as food and drinking water in case of an emergency.

You can call the Maine State Police to report a problem or to get updates on the weather.

🚗 **AAA** ☎ 800/222-4357. **Maine State Police** ☎ 207/871-7755 for problems, 1-800/675-7453 for weather updates ⊕ www.state.me.us/dps/msp.

EMERGENCIES

In an emergency, dial 911.

🏥 Hospitals **Mid-Coast Hospital** ✉ 123 Medical Center Dr., Brunswick ☎ 207/729-0181. **Miles Memorial Hospital** ✉ 35 Miles St., Damariscotta ☎ 207/563-1234. **St. Andrews Hospital** ✉ 6 St. Andrews La., Boothbay Harbor ☎ 207/633-2121.

LODGING

If you want to stay in the area for a week or longer, consider renting a cottage or a cabin. Many people come back year after year. Your Island Connection has accommodations ranging from one-room apartments to houses that sleep 10 or more.

If you want to camp in the area, contact the Maine Office of Tourism or the Maine Camping Guide.

🏕 **Maine Office of Tourism** ☎ 888/624-6345 ⊕ www.usa.visitmaine.com. **Maine Camping Guide** ☎ 207/782-5874 ⊕ www.campmaine.com. **Your Island Connection** ☎ 207/833-7779 or 207/833-7705 ⊕ www.mainerentals.com.

MEDIA

The *Times Record,* which covers the Bath-Brunswick region, publishes weekdays, with a weekend entertainment section on Thursday. A number of weekly newspapers provide local coverage and entertainment listings including the *Coastal Journal* (Brunswick to Waldoboro), the *Wiscasset Newspaper,* the *Boothbay Register,* and the *Lincoln County News* and the *Lincoln County Weekly* (Wiscasset through Waldoboro).

WMEA 90.1 is the local National Public Radio affiliate. WCSH, channel 6, is the NBC affiliate; WMTW, channel 8, is the ABC affiliate; and WGME, channel 13, is the CBS affiliate. Channel 10 is the Maine Public Broadcasting affiliate.

TRAIN TRAVEL

The closest Amtrak comes to the Mid-Coast region is Portland.

🚆 Train Information **Amtrak** ✉ 100 Thompsons Point Rd., Portland ☎ 800/872-7245 or 207/828-3939 ⊕ www.transport me.org ⊕ www.amtrak.com.

VISITOR INFORMATION

🎞 **Boothbay Harbor Region Chamber of Commerce** ⊠ Box 356, 04538 ☎ 207/633–2353 ⊕ www.boothbayharbor.com. **Chamber of Commerce of the Bath/Brunswick Region** ⊠ 45 Front St., Bath 04530 ☎ 207/443–9751 ⊠ 59 Pleasant St., Brunswick 04011 ☎ 207/725–8797 ⊕ www.midcoastmaine.com. **Convention and Visitors Bureau of Greater Portland** ⊠ 245 Commercial St., Portland 04101 ☎ 207/772–5800 ⊕ www.visitportland.com. **Damariscotta Region Chamber of Commerce** ⊠ Box 13, Damariscotta 04543 ☎ 207/772–5800 ⊕ www.damariscottaregion.com. **Freeport Merchants Association** ⊠ 23 Depot St., Freeport 04032 ☎ 207/865–1212 or 877/865–1212 ⊕ www.visitportland.com. **Greater Portland Chamber of Commerce** ⊠ 60 Pearl St., Portland 04101 ☎ 207/772–2811 ⊕ www.portlandregion.com. **Maine Tourism Association** ⊠ U.S. 1 [I–95, Exit 17], Yarmouth 04347 ☎ 207/846–0833 ⊕ www.mainetourism.com.

PENOBSCOT BAY

4

LEARN ALL ABOUT LIGHTHOUSES
at the Maine Lighthouse Museum ⇨*p.131*

LINGER OVER A LAVISH SUNDAY BRUNCH
at Marcel's in the Samoset Resort ⇨*p.140*

DO THE ISLAND HOP
on a ferry to Islesboro ⇨*p.151*

GET SWAMPED BY A LOBSTER BOAT
during the annual Lobster Boat Races ⇨*p.162*

HAGGLE OVER A VINTAGE FIND
at the Searsport Antique Mall ⇨*p.164*

By Stephen and Neva Allen

Few could deny that Penobscot Bay is one of the most dramatically beautiful regions in Maine. Its 1,000-mi-long coastline is made up of rocky granite boulders, wild and often undeveloped shore, a sprinkling of colorful towns, and views of the sea and shore that are a photographer's dream.

The second largest estuary in New England, Penobscot Bay stretches 37 mi from Port Clyde in the south to Stonington, the little fishing village at the tip of Deer Isle, in the north. The bay begins where the Penobscot River ends, near Stockton Springs, and terminates in the Gulf of Maine, where it is 47 mi wide. It covers an estimated 1,070 square mi and is home to more than 1,000 islands, rocks, and ledges, big and small.

Residents who live along the coast will tell you that the bay presents a different face and a different color nearly every day of the year. Some days, it's as blue and placidly flat as a mirror. Other days, especially in winter before a storm, it's black, angry, and crashing, with 5-foot waves and cresting whitecaps.

The bay was formed over time by a series of glacial retreats, the most recent of which occurred 12,000 years ago. The earliest inhabitants of the bay area were Native Americans, who first set up encampments here around 1,000 BC. The word "penobscot" is believed to be a derivative of the original Algonquin Indian word meaning "waters of descending ledges." Descending rock ledges can, in fact, be seen along the Penobscot River.

The bay area was essentially the territory of the Native Americans until the early 1600s, when the French and English began to vie for control. In the American colonial wars, the natives generally favored the British, and this ultimately led to their numbers diminishing. Today, the only Penobscot Indian settlement in the area is at Old Town on an island in the Penobscot River, northwest of Bangor.

By the 1760s, colonial settlements along the bay were growing into towns to support the budding shipbuilding, commercial shipping, granite quarrying, fishing, and lobstering industries. Initially, shipbuilding was the primary moneymaker here. In the 1800s, during the days of the great tall ships, or Down Easters as they were often called, more wooden ships were built along Penobscot Bay than in any other place in America. This golden age of billowing sails and wooden sailing ships did not last long, however. It came to an end with the development of the steam engine. Ships propelled by steam-fed pistons were faster, safer, more reliable, and could hold more cargo. By 1900, sailing ships were no longer a viable commercial venture in Maine.

As you will see when you travel this coast, however, the great tall ships have not disappeared. They have simply been reincarnated—as recreational boats, known as windjammers. Today, there are—once again—more tall ships along Penobscot Bay than anywhere else in the country.

Exploring Penobscot Bay

The only route for exploring this region is the historic two-lane U.S. 1, which winds all the way along Penobscot Bay—from Rockland to Bucksport and farther.

4

If you have

3 days

Numbers in the text correspond to numbers in the margin and on the Penobscot Bay and Rockport & Camden maps.

On the morning of your first day, visit the Farnsworth Museum in **Rockland** ❶ with its wonderful collection of paintings by the Wyeth family. Then drive up to **Camden** ❹, one of the most charming towns along the coast, and take a two-hour excursion on a windjammer high-masted sailing ship. Consider staying at the Lord Camden Inn, in the heart of the downtown, or at one of the many delightful B&Bs in the residential area. On Day 2, drive up to **Belfast** ❼, where you can wander around the downtown area and have lunch at Darby's. In the afternoon, drive north on U.S. 1 to Moose Point State Park, halfway between Belfast and Searsport. Go for a hike on one of the trails by the sea, then continue to **Searsport** ❽ to spend the night at one of the many fine B&Bs, such as the Watchtide Inn. A good choice for dinner would be a favorite of the locals, Anglers Restaurant. Spend your last day browsing through Searsport's many antique and collectibles shops.

If you have

5 days

Begin your itinerary in **Rockland** ❶. Start with a morning visit to the Farnsworth Museum and its wonderful collection of paintings by the Wyeth family. Then head to Rockland's Maine State Ferry Terminal. Take the ferry (with your car) to **Vinalhaven Island** ❷ and spend the day exploring and watching the lobster boats and fishermen down by the harbor. Have dinner and stay overnight at the Tidewater Motel, which is right on the waterfront (be sure to make advance reservations). On Day 2 take the ferry back to Rockland and drive north to **Camden** ❹ where you can explore the shops and galleries, try the excellent restaurants, and stay the night in a charming B&B. Spend your third day and night on an overnight sail on one of the romantic windjammer ships (you will need to arrange this ahead of time). On your fourth day, drive to **Belfast** ❼, where you can walk down the colorful main street with its interesting shops, and explore the harbor. For an authentic Maine dinner, take U.S. 1 across the bridge on the way to Searsport and turn right on Mitchell Avenue to reach Young's Lobster Pound. Stay overnight at the Belfast Harbor Inn nearby. On your last day, drive to **Searsport** ❽ and spend the morning exploring the Penobscot Marine Museum with its wonderful exhibits on the history of Penobscot Bay.

Although the distance from Rockland to Bucksport is only 45 mi, the going is slow: this is an old highway, and the summer months bring heavily congested traffic. There are some impressive coastal views along the drive, but don't expect to see the ocean continuously. The water is blocked for a good part of the way by woods, which are beautiful in their own right. Driving the entire distance without stopping should take about two hours, but you'll probably want to stop along the way and spend a day or two in some of the more colorful towns. If you're driving at night, be wary of moose crossing the road. If you hit one, it will be tough on the moose—but it will be worse on you.

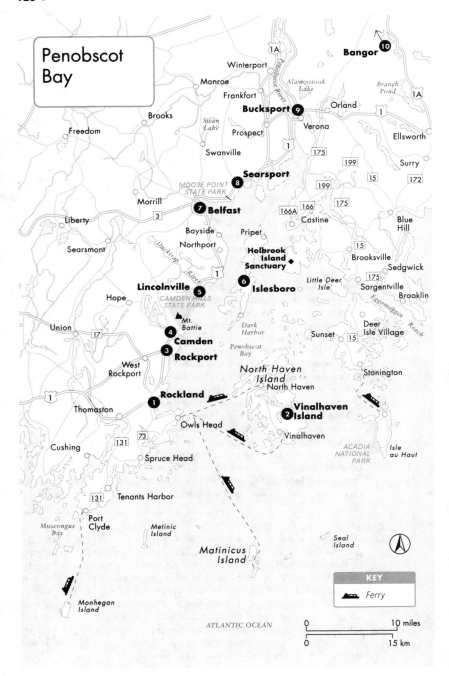

Penobscot
Bay

Bangor ❿

Winterport

Monroe

Frankfort

Brooks

Freedom

Bucksport ❾

Prospect

Swanville

Morrill

Liberty

Searsmont

Swan
Lake

Alamoosook
Lake

Branch
Pond

Orland

Verona

Ellsworth

Surry

Searsport ❽

MOOSE POINT
STATE PARK

Belfast ❼

Bayside

Northport

Pripet

Holbrook
Island
Sanctuary

Castine

Blue
Hill

Brooksville

Sedgwick

Sargentville

Brooklin

Lincolnville ❺

Hope

CAMDEN HILLS
STATE PARK

Mt.
Battie

Camden ❹

Rockport ❸

Union

West
Rockport

Islesboro ❻

Little Deer
Isle

Dark
Harbor

Deer
Isle Village

Sunset

Stonington

Rockland ❶

Thomaston

Owls Head

Cushing

Spruce Head

North Haven
Island
North Haven

Penobscot
Bay

Vinalhaven
Island ❷

Vinalhaven

ACADIA
NATIONAL
PARK

Isle
au Haut

Tenants Harbor

Port
Clyde

Muscongus
Bay

Metinic
Island

Matinicus
Island

Seal
Island

Monhegan
Island

ATLANTIC OCEAN

0   10 miles

0   15 km

KEY
🚢 Ferry

There is no train service or public transportation in the Penobscot Bay area, but there is a luxury bus service, Concord Trailways (*see* Bus Travel *under* Penobscot Bay A to Z), which runs from Bangor to Logan Airport in Boston. It sends down (and up) two buses a day, which stop at all the major towns along the coast.

Exploring the Penobscot Bay coast by water is also a possibility. Ferries travel back and forth to islands such as Islesboro and Vinalhaven, and romantic windjammer cruises sail from Camden and Rockland to various islands or town destinations.

About the Restaurants

Seafood is the name of the game along Penobscot Bay. "Lobstah" is, of course, a staple on most menus and it comes cooked in a myriad of ways: whole lobster dinners (boiled or steamed in the shell), broiled lobster tails, fried lobster, lobster stew, and lobster rolls, which you can even find at McDonald's.

Dining establishments, in keeping with the nature of the area, are generally informal, and casual dress is almost always acceptable. Most restaurants are open for lunch and dinner, and some are open for breakfast. From June through August, reservations are always a good idea, particularly at the more popular or smaller restaurants.

For a truly authentic Maine experience, try one of the lobster pounds in Lincolnville or Belfast. For something a little more upscale, there are a few outstanding gems to be tried, notably Primo's, in Rockland; Marcel's, at the Samoset Resort in Rockport; and the Rhumb Line, in Searsport. Reservations (and a jacket for men) are essential at these establishments.

About the Hotels

Large luxury hotels are few and far between in this region; motels, B&Bs, and campgrounds are more the norm. Accommodations are generally modest, but many of them sit right on the edge of the ocean. A good share of the B&Bs are in historic Federal or Colonial-style homes that date back to the 1850s and are filled with period antiques. Please note that while many of the smaller accommodations and B&Bs—as well as some of the restaurants and many of the museums—are not air-conditioned, ocean breezes usually keep things amply cool.

If you're planning to come between mid-May and mid-October, reservations are recommended at least a month in advance. Additional information about B&Bs in Maine, as well as a reservation service, can be found online at ⊕ www.bbonline.com/me.

WHAT IT COSTS					
	$$$$	**$$$**	**$$**	**$**	**¢**
RESTAURANTS	over $25	$18–$25	$11–$17	$7–$10	under $7
HOTELS	over $200	$150–$200	$100–$150	$60–$100	under $60

Restaurant prices are for a main course at dinner, excluding meal tax of 7%. Hotel prices are for two people in a standard double room in high season, excluding service charges and 7% hospitality tax.

TIMING The high season in Penobscot Bay starts in the middle of May and goes until mid-October. Crowds are a little thinner just after the public schools open in early September and just before they close in mid-June. Though many residents enjoy the long cold winters, most visitors avoid them. The Camden Snowbowl, with its 11 downhill ski trails, is one of the few attractions to entice visitors in the wintery months. Many of the motels, B&Bs, restaurants, and other businesses along U.S. 1 close for the winter.

ROCKLAND AREA

The name "Rockland" defines this area's history. If you set fishing aside, rock cutting—specifically granite and limestone—was once the principal occupation of the area. In fact, numerous government buildings across the United States were built using granite blocks from Rockland and other nearby quarries. Just outside the town of Rockland, a large cement factory on U.S. 1 serves as a reminder of this rocky past.

Rockland

❶ *4 mi northeast of Thomaston, 14 mi northeast of Tenants Harbor.*

The town of Rockland is considered the gateway to Penobscot Bay. It's the first stop on U.S. 1 that offers a glimpse of the often sparkling and island-dotted blue bay. Though it was once a place to pass through on the way to tonier ports like Camden, Rockland—which celebrated its 150th birthday in 2004—now attracts attention on its own, thanks to the renowned Farnsworth Museum, the increasingly popular summer Lobster Festival, and the North Atlantic Blues Festival.

Rockland's Main Street Historic District, with its Italianate, Mansard, Greek Revival, and Colonial Revival buildings, is on the National Register of Historic Places. Specialty shops and galleries line the main street, and restaurants and inns continue to open. Even with its growing popularity as a summer destination, however, Rockland is still a large fishing port and the commercial hub of this coastal area. You can find plenty of working boats moored alongside the yachts and windjammers, and the town retains some of its working-class flavor, although it's fading.

Rockland Harbor is the berth of more windjammer ships than any other port in the United States. The best place in Rockland to view these beautiful vessels as they sail in and out of the harbor is the mile-long granite breakwater, which bisects the outer portion of Rockland Harbor. To get there, go north on U.S. 1, turn right on Waldo Avenue, and turn right again on Samoset Road. The breakwater is at the end of this short road.

At the end of the breakwater is a late-19th-century light, the **Rockland Breakwater Lighthouse,** a popular subject for photographers. A wooden lighthouse was first erected here in 1888, but it was moved four times before 1895. The current stone light tower, which is only 18 feet high, was erected between 1900 and 1902. The lighthouse had a keeper until 1963, but is now automated.

The city of Rockland is planning to open a new visitor center, the **Gateway Center,** in spring 2005. The building, on Park Drive near the waterfront, will also house the Maine Lighthouse Museum. ⊠ *1 Park Dr.* ☎ *207/506–0376* ⊕ *www.mainelighthousemuseum.com.*

★ ♻ **The Maine Lighthouse Museum** (formerly known as the Shore Village Museum) contains the largest collection of lighthouse memorabilia and Coast Guard lighthouse artifacts in the world, including an extensive collection of Fresnel lenses. You can hear the moaning of a foghorn and the clanging of a buoy bell, and see the whirling of a light behind a Fresnel lens. The museum also houses a large collection of model ships and life-saving gear. Lighthouse souvenirs are available in the store. The museum is planning to open in its new location in the Gateway Center on Park Drive in spring 2005. Until that time it will be in its old location at 104 Limerock Street. ⊠ *Until spring 2005: 104 Limerock St. After spring 2005: 1 Park Dr.* ☎ *207/594–3301* ⊕ *www.mainelighthousemuseum. com* 💷 *Donation suggested* ⊙ *June–mid-Oct., daily 10–4; mid-Oct.–June by appointment.*

Fodor'sChoice ★ The **Farnsworth Art Museum and Wyeth Center** is one of the most important small museums in the country. The **Wyeth Center** is devoted to Maine-related works of the famous Wyeth family: N. C. Wyeth, an accomplished illustrator whose works were featured in many turn-of-the-century books; his son Andrew, one of America's best-known painters, and Andrew's son James, also an accomplished painter who lives nearby on an island. Some works from the personal collection of Andrew and Betsy Wyeth include *The Patriot, Adrift, Maiden Hair, Dr. Syn, The Clearing,* and *Watch Cap.* Also on display are works by Fitz Hugh Lane, George Bellows, Frank W. Benson, Edward Hopper (his paintings of old Rockland are a highlight), Louise Nevelson, and Fairfield Porter. Works by living Maine artists are shown in the **Jamien Morehouse Wing.** The **Farnsworth Homestead,** a handsome circa-1852 Greek Revival dwelling that is part of the museum, retains its original lavish Victorian furnishings. There is a museum store next to the Morehouse Wing (*see* Shopping). The museum also operates the **Olsen House** (⊠ Hathorn Point Rd., Cushing), which is depicted in Andrew Wyeth's famous painting *Christina's World.* ⊠ *16 Museum St.* ☎ *207/596–6457* ⊕ *www. farnsworthmuseum.org* 💷 *$9 for the museum and the Olsen House; $4 for the Olsen House only* ⊙ *Mid-May–June and mid-Oct.–Dec., Tues.–Sun. 10–5; July–mid-Oct., Wed.–Fri. 10–7, Sat.–Tues. 10–5; Jan.–mid-May, hrs vary, call ahead.*

The **Owls Head Transportation Museum** and the **Owls Head Lighthouse** are only 3 mi south of Rockland. For complete information on these sights *see* the Port Clyde section in Chapter 3.

Where to Stay & Eat

$$–$$$$ Fodor'sChoice ★ ✕ **Primo.** This restaurant has won so many awards it would be impossible to list them all here. The co-owners are chef Melissa Kelly and pastry chef Price Kushner. Their cuisine combines fresh Maine ingredients with Mediterranean influences. The menu, which changes weekly, may include wood-roasted black sea bass, local crab-stuffed turbot, or diver-harvested-scallop and basil ravioli. They grow much of their own food

in an extensive organic garden. To try some of Melissa and Price's delicious recipes at home, log on to their Web site. ⊠ *2 S. Main St.* ☎ *207/ 596-0770* ⊕ *www.primorestaurant.com* ⌲ *Reservations essential* ⊟ *AE, D, DC, MC, V* ⊘ *Closed Dec.–Apr.*

★ **$$–$$$** ✕ **Amalfi.** A well-chosen and affordable wine list and excellent service have made this storefront bistro a hit with locals and visitors alike. Chef-owner David Cooke serves delicious Mediterranean cuisine, influenced by the culinary traditions of France, Spain, Italy, Greece, and Morocco. The menu changes seasonally but may include the house paella with chorizo, or duck risotto. Ask about the oysters and the Chocolate Soup. ⊠ *421 Main St.* ☎ *207/596–0012* ⊕ *www.amalfi-tonight.com* ⊟ *AE, MC, V* ⊘ *Closed Mon. No lunch.*

$$–$$$ ✕ **Café Miranda.** At this cozy little bistro with a brick oven and open kitchen, the huge menu changes daily to include fresh seasonal ingredients. Chef-owner Kerry Alterio has come up with creative ideas to reflect the cuisines of Italy, Thailand, Mexico, Armenia, and other countries. You could make a full meal just from the 20 or so imaginative appetizers. The many entrées may include crispy panfried soft-shell crabs with red bean ragout and yellow jasmine rice, or scallops and Italian sausage with cherry peppers and arugula greens. ⊠ *15 Oak St.* ☎ *207/594–2034* ⊕ *www.cafemiranda.com* ⌲ *Reservations essential* ⊟ *MC, V* ⊘ *No lunch.*

$$-$$$ ✕ **Grapes Restaurant.** Located on the public landing pier at Harbor Park, Grapes' main attraction is the fabulous view. In warm weather, you can sit out on the patio and watch the windjammers go by. Seafood and Italian are the specialties here, and some of the specials include lobster fettucini Alfredo, Murphy's pasta, which is topped with a ripe Gorgonzola cheese, and lobster stew. ⊠ *275 Main St.* ☎ *207/594–9050* ⊟ *MC, V* ⊘ *Closed Apr.–Oct.*

$$–$$$ **The Landings Restaurant & Marina.** If you'd like a traditional Maine lobster dinner with a view, try the Landings. It's right on the dock, next to the marina. They serve lobster prepared in a variety of ways, plus other seafood dinners, steak, poultry, and pasta. If the restaurant is crowded, you can order food at the bar. ⊠ *1 Commercial St.* ☎ *207/596–6563* ⊟ *D, MC, V* ⊘ *Closed Mon.*

$–$$$ ✕ **China Coast.** At lunchtime, the China Coast offers the popular "All You Can Eat Buffet," with a selection of 40 dishes. At dinner you need to order from the menu, which includes Szechuan, Hunan, Mandarin, and Cantonese fare. Spicy hot dishes are clearly marked. If you're with a group, the traditional Chinese Family Dinners are a bargain. ⊠ *Harbor Plaza Mall, 235 Camden St.* ☎ *207/594–1038* ⊟ *D, MC, V.*

$–$$$ ✕ **Rockland Cafe.** This downtown place may not look like much from
FodorsChoice the outside, but it's probably the most popular restaurant in town—es-
★ pecially among the locals. It's open for breakfast, lunch, and dinner and is famous for the size of its breakfasts. The restaurant can be a real bargain if you go for the all-you-can-eat, family-style lunch or dinner. At dinner, the seafood combo of shrimps, scallops, clams, and fish is excellent, or there's the classic liver and onions. ⊠ *441 S. Main St.* ☎ *207/ 596-7556* ⊕ *www.rocklandcafe.com* ⊟ *AE, D, MC, V.*

¢–$$ ✕ **Kate's Seafood Restaurant.** Kate's is a small and unassuming place. The decor is simple, the food is modest but inexpensive, and the service is quick—the locals love it. The menu includes fried clams, steamers, Maine shrimp, lobster rolls, and crab rolls. ⊠ *1 U.S. 1, 1 mi south of Thomaston* ☏ *207/594–2626* ▭ *MC, V* ⊙ *Closed Mon. and mid-Oct.–Apr.*

¢–$$ ✕ **Market on Main.** This is essentially an Italian-American food market with wonderful cheeses, gourmet pantry items, and wines. Open for breakfast, lunch, and dinner, their international deli offers interesting dishes such as falafel with yogurt and cucumber, or fried Szechuan dumplings made with turkey and bok choy. While there is a space for sit-down dining, they also have a large selection of heat-and-serve foods for takeout. Locally, this place is known as MOM's. That ought to tell you something. ⊠ *315 Main St.* ☏ *207/594–0015* ⊕ *www.marketonmain. net* ▭ *MC, V.*

$–$$ ✕▦ **Navigator Motor Inn.** The Navigator is right across the street from the Maine State Ferry terminal, making it extremely convenient if you're planning to head out on one of the island ferries. The rooms are rather plain, but they all have refrigerators, and many of them have balconies overlooking the bay. The Oceanside Seafood & Steakhouse ($–$$$), with its simple blue-and-tan decor, offers—not surprisingly—seafood and steak. The broiled scallops with bacon is a good choice, as are the baby back ribs, and the chicken teriyaki. ⊠ *520 Main St., 04841* ☏ *207/594–2131 or 800/545–8026* 🖷 *207/594–7763* ⊕ *www.navigatorinn.com* ⇗ *81 rooms* ⚹ *Restaurant, lounge, refrigerators* ▭ *AE, D, MC, V.*

$–$$ ✕▦ **Trade Winds Motor Inn.** This large motel is near the Maine State Ferry terminal. Many of the rooms have balconies overlooking the harbor and marina. The restaurant seats up to 150 people and offers dishes such as steamed mussels, pecan-encrusted halibut, or Maine shrimp in a garlic cream sauce over pasta. ⊠ *2 Park Dr., 04841* ☏ *207/596–6661 or 800/834–3130* 🖷 *207/596–6492* ⊕ *www.tradewindsmaine. com* ⇗ *138 rooms, 4 suites* ⚹ *Restaurant, cable TV, indoor pool, gym* ▭ *AE, D, MC V.*

★ $$–$$$$ ▦ **Berry Manor Inn.** Built in 1898, this inn is in a historic residential neighborhood. Originally, it was the residence of Charles H. Berry, a prominent Rockland merchant. The large guest rooms are elegantly furnished with antiques and reproduction pieces. All rooms have fireplaces; TVs are available upon request. A guest pantry is stocked with sweets. The inn is within walking distance of downtown and the harbor. ⊠ *81 Talbot Ave., 04841* ☏ *207/596–7696 or 800/774–5692* 🖷 *207/596–9958* ⊕ *www.berrymanorinn.com* ⇗ *12 rooms* ⚹ *In-room data ports, some in-room hot tubs, library, meeting room; no room TVs, no smoking* ▭ *AE, MC, V* ℗ *BP.*

$$–$$$$ ▦ **Captain Lindsey House.** This charming inn is aptly named—it's filled with artifacts and treasures from all over the world, much as a sea captain's home would have been in the early 1800s. The spacious rooms are furnished with antiques and reproductions. All of the beds have European-style down comforters. Special discounts are given to windjammer customers; ask for details when you make your reservation. The Water Works Pub and Restaurant is right next door. ⊠ *5 Lindsey St., 04841* ☏ *207/596–7950 or 800/523–2145* ⊕ *www.lindseyhouse.com* ⇗ *9 rooms* ▭ *AE, D, MC, V.*

★ **$$–$$$$** ⊡ **Limerock Inn.** This inn is literally in the center of town (Limerock is the street that bisects Rockland into two halves), so you can easily walk to the Farnsworth Museum or any of the other downtown attractions. The house is built in the Queen Anne–Victorian style, and among the meticulously decorated rooms is one called Island Cottage, which features a whirlpool tub and doors that open onto a private deck overlooking a garden. The Grand Manan room has a fireplace, a whirlpool tub, and a four-poster king-size bed. Room TVs are available upon request. ⊠ *96 Limerock St., 04841* ☎ *207/594–2257 or 800/546–3762* ⊕ *www. limerockinn.com* ⇝ *8 rooms* ⚲ *In-room data ports; no room phones, no room TVs, no smoking.* ⊟ *D, MC, V* ⏐⏐ *BP.*

For additional B&B listings in the Rockland area, contact **Historic Inns of Rockland** (⊕ www.historicinnsofrockland.com).

Nightlife & the Arts

While there is not much in the way of nightlife in Rockland, the **Black Bull Tavern** (⊠ 420 Main St. ☎ 207/593–9060) does offer live entertainment throughout the summer. The tavern has large picture windows offering a view of downtown Rockland, and weather permitting, you can drink and dine at sidewalk tables. Tin ceilings and pleasant mustard and mahogany furnishings give the Bull an authentic pub feel. The menu includes specials such as chicken, broccoli and sundried tomato penne, and Jack Daniels–marinated sirloin tips. The **Time Out Pub** (⊠ 275 Main St. ☎ 207/593–9336) is known as the home of the blues even though they have live music only on Monday nights. The menu includes typical pub grub: sandwiches, burgers, etc. The **Waterworks Pub & Restaurant** (⊠ 5 Lindsey St. ☎ 207/596–2753) was formerly a garage for the town waterworks. It features live music and dancing Wednesday through Saturday. The menu includes burgers and other pub-style food.

FESTIVALS The relatively new **Maine Boats and Harbors Show** (MBHS ☎ 800/565–4951 ⊕ www.maineboats.com) is steadily gaining popularity. The show, at Harbor Park, features boats in the water, boats on land, marine ware, nautical-but-nice art, and lots of booths offering seafood. MBHS takes place in mid-August (call for exact dates). Admission is $10.

★ ⟳ Rockland's annual **Lobster Festival** (☎ 207/596–0376 or 800/562–2529 ⊕ www.mainelobsterfestival.com), in early August, is nearly 60 years old and has become the biggest local event of the year. People come from all over the country to sample lobster in every possible form: steamed, fried, chowder, lobster rolls, you name it. During the few days of the festival, tons of lobsters (10 tons in the most recent year) are steamed in the world's largest lobster cooker—you have to see it to believe it. In addition, there's shrimp in its many forms, steamed clams, and Maine mussels. The festival, held in the Harbor Park, includes a parade, entertainment, craft and marine exhibits, food booths—and of course, the crowning of the Lobster Festival Sea Goddess.

More than a dozen well-known blues artists gather for the **North Atlantic Blues Festival** (☎ 207/593–1189 ⊕ www.northatlanticbluesfestival.com), a two-night show in July. The show officially takes place at Harbor Park, but it also includes a Blues Club Crawl through downtown Rockland,

WINDJAMMER EXCURSIONS

NOTHING DEFINES THE MAINE COASTAL EXPERIENCE *more than a trip on a sailing windjammer ship. Most of the windjammers are berthed in either Rockland or Camden, and you can get information on all of them by contacting one of two windjammer organizations: The Maine Windjammer Association (800/807–9463;* ⊕ *www.sailmainecoast.com); or Maine Windjammer Cruises (207/236–2938 or 888/692–7245;* ⊕ *www.mainewindjammercruises.com). They both offer three- to eight-day cruises from Camden, Rockland, and Rockport. Prices are about $180 for an overnighter, and range from $395 to $875 for a three- to six-day cruise, all meals included.*

Here is a selection of some of the best windjammer cruises in the area. Most of the ships are of the schooner type.

Camden-Rockport Angelique, *Yankee Packet Co., 207/236–8873. Appledore, which can take you out for just a day-sail, 207/236–8353. Mary Day, Coastal Cruises, 207/236–2750. Olad, Downeast Windjammer Packet Co., 207/236–2323. Yacht Heron, 207/236–8605 or 800 599–8605.*

Rockland American Eagle, *North End Shipyard, 207/594–8007. Nathanial Bowditch, 207/273–4062. Summertime, 800/562–8290. Victory Chimes, 207/265–5651. Wendameen, 207/594–1751.*

which gives this staid old Maine town the atmosphere of New Orleans. Admission is $25 for adults and $5 for children 6–12.

The **Rockland Harborfest Jazz and Art Festival** (☎ 207/596–3076), a traditional end-of-summer one-night musical event, takes place in mid-September at Harbor Park. There's entertainment, food, arts and crafts, tours of windjammer ships at the dock, and kids' activities. In 2004 Dave Brubeck and his sons were among the performers. The highlight of the festivities is the annual Bay Chamber Concert Jazz Gala.

Sports & the Outdoors

AERIAL TOURS **Maine Atlantic Aviation** (☎ 207/596–5557 or 800/780–6071 ⊕ www.maineatlanticaviation.com) offers plane and helicopter tours of the coast. Enjoy lighthouse or island tours—or name your own destination.

BOAT RENTALS & TOURS **Bay Island Yacht Charters** (✉ 117A Tillison Ave. ☎ 207/596–7550 or 800/421–2492) has a sailing school and day rentals for motor or sailboats. **Coastal Passages** (☎ 207/593–9093) conducts daily boat trips from Rockland's Middle Pier. Among the variety of trips you can choose from are: lobster-hauling, seal-watching, mackerel-fishing, or a sunset lighthouse cruise. Prices range from $10 to $25.

A windjammer excursion can be the highlight of your trip. Windjammers docked in Rockland include *Wendameen* (one-night cruises), *American Eagle, Heritage, Isaac Evans, J&E Riggin, Nathaniel Bowditch,* and *Simplicity.* Prices are about $180 for an overnighter, and range from $395 to $875 for a three-to-six-day cruise, all meals included. For more information about any of these boats, or for general information about windjammers, contact the **Maine Windjammer Association** (☎ 800/807–9463 ⊕ www.sailmainecoast.com).

FISHING **Snow Marine Park** (⊠ Mechanic St., off Rte. 73 in Rockland's southend) is the best spot in the area for shore fishing. They have a float from which you can fish. There are public toilets in the park and places to eat nearby, but no equipment rentals or bait shop. The mile-long **Rockland Breakwater** is also a popular shore-fishing spot, mostly for mackerel.

Shopping

Puffin's Nest Clothing & Gifts (⊠ 464 Main St. ☎ 207/594–2660) offers a wide variety of made-in-Maine clothing and gifts, including T-shirts, sweatshirts, hats, buoy bells (the quintessential Maine gift), candles, jams, and jellies. They also have stores in Damariscotta and Port Clyde. **Second Read Books & Coffee** (⊠ 328 Main St. ☎ 207/594–4123) is a wonderful place for book lovers. They have a huge selection, the staff is friendly, and you can enjoy coffee and a homemade pastry while browsing. **Planet Toys** (⊠ 318 Main St. ☎ 207/596–5976) is Maine's largest toy store. Their well-chosen motto is, "You're never too old to play." **The Wine Seller** (⊠ 315 Main St. ☎ 207/594–2621 ⊕ www.fruitothevine.com) has a large selection of domestic and imported wines and can prepare gift baskets. They're closed Sunday. The **Farnsworth Museum Store** (⊠ 352 Main St. ☎ 207/596–6457) sells jewelry, books, and prints of the museum's paintings. **Que Pasa on Main** (⊠ 405 Main St. ☎ 207/594–6112) is an interesting little shop that is filled with imports, candles, charms, and other gifts.

GALLERIES There are more art galleries in this little working-class town than you would expect. Most are located on Main Street; some of the best are listed below. (Keep in mind that Main Street was originally called Elm Street and some of the older businesses still use Elm Street as their address.)

The **Caldbeck Gallery** (⊠ 12 Elm St. ☎ 207/594–5935 ⊕ www.caldbeck.com) displays contemporary Maine works by artists such as William Thon, Lois Dodd, Alan Bray, and Dennis Pinette. **Harbor Square Gallery** (⊠ 374 Main St. ☎ 207/594–8700) has roomfuls of Maine-related arts and crafts. **Elan Fine Arts** (⊠ 8 Elm St. ☎ 207/596–9933 ⊕ www.elanfinearts.com) displays works by contemporary American artists. **The Gallery** (⊠ 357 Main St. ☎ 207/596–0084) specializes in marine paintings.

Vinalhaven

★ ❷ *East of Rockland via Maine State Ferry on U.S. 1.*

Penobscot Bay is home to more than 1,000 islands. While most of them have infrequent ferry service, or are totally uninhabited, Vinalhaven is relatively accessible—*relatively* being the key word here. There are six ferry trips per day to and from Vinalhaven in summer—that's it, no exceptions. If you miss the last ferry back, or if there simply is not enough room for your car on the last ferry, you will have to spend the night on the island and chances are you'll be sleeping in your car if you don't have room reservations. That said, Vinalhaven is an interesting day or overnight trip as long as you heed the ferry schedule.

The largest inhabited island in Maine, Vinalhaven has a year-round population of about 1,200. It's nearly 8 mi long and 5 mi wide and is mostly wooded. At one time, there was a booming granite industry on the island, but the quarries are now used mostly for swimming or fishing. Many island residents work in the lobster-harvesting business. Thanks to the state government, they even have a special season when they can gather lobsters while those on the mainland cannot (to compensate them for living in such a grim and harsh environment, not unlike the Aran Islands of Ireland).

The Maine State Ferry Terminal, which offers the six trips a day to and from Vinalhaven, is right in the center of Rockland, on U.S. 1, across from the Navigator Motor Inn. The ferry runs throughout the year (except on major holidays), but the times change somewhat from the end of October through December, so you might want to call first. Ferry service to Northhaven and to Mantinicus, a small island 23 mi from Rockland, is also available.

The village of Vinalhaven is small and easy to explore. There is a designated walking path on the north side of Main Street which runs from the ferry terminal to the center of town. Within a 1 mi radius of the ferry dock you will find two town parks and a nature conservancy area. There is only one road on the island, so it's pretty easy to find your way around. Biking the island can be fun though there are no designated bike paths and the road can be a little rough outside the village. There is no public transportation on the island.

You can learn about the island's quarrying history at the **Historical Society Museum.** This small museum has photographic displays of the strenuous work of cutting granite, as well as artifacts from the Civil War. ⊠ *High St.* ☎ *207/863–4410* ⊕ *www.midcoast.com/~vhhissoc* ☉ *Mid-June–early Sept., daily* ▣ *Donations accepted.*

To cool off, take a dip in the cool, clear waters of a quarry. Swimming is free, but there are no lifeguards or changing facilities. Two options close to the ferry terminal are: **Lawson's,** 1 mi on North Haven Road; and **Booth Quarry,** 1½ mi on East Main St.

off the
beaten
path

NORTH HAVEN ISLAND – North Haven is appropriately just north of Vinalhaven across a small stretch of sea, 12 mi from the mainland. This is the smaller of the two islands, but it's home to some large summer residences of the rich if not famous. There is one general store, a small restaurant, and a small B&B on the island. The year-round population is only about 330. The Maine State Ferry runs between North Haven and Rockland three times a day throughout the year (except for major holidays).

MANTINICUS ISLAND – This is one of Maine's most remote, inhabited islands. It's 23 mi from the mainland; more than two hours by ferry (from the Maine State Ferry Terminal in Rockland). During the off-season, the ferry runs only once a month; in June, July, and August, it runs once a week. **Tuckanuck Lodge** ($–$$) (☎ 207/366–3830) is the only place to stay on the island.

For information on ferry service to all the islands from Rockland, contact the **Maine State Ferry Service** at Rockland Harbor. ⌂ *Box 645, Rockland, ME 04841* ☎ *207/596–2202 or 800/491–4883.*

Where to Stay & Eat

$$–$$$ ✕ **The Harbor Gawker.** This mariner-theme restaurant, decorated with old wooden lobster traps and fishing gear, has been in business for 30 years. The fare, seafood of course, is abundant and tasty. Lobster dinners and the ever-popular lobster rolls are recommended. ⊠ *Main St., Vinalhaven* ☎ *207/863–9365* ⊙ *Closed Sun. and mid-Nov.–mid-Apr.* ☰ *MC, V.*

$$–$$$$ ⌂ **The Tidewater Motel.** This little motel is one of the few places to stay on Vinalhaven, and it's the only one right on the waterfront and near the ferry dock. The 19-room facility is actually built on a bridge overlooking the harbor, and all rooms have wonderful views. If you want a real treat, get up early enough to watch the lobster boats leave around 5 AM. They usually come back sometime between 3 and 5 PM the same day. ⌂ *Box 546* ⊠ *Carver St., Vinalhaven 04863* ☎ *207/863–4618* ⊕ *www.tidewatermotel.com* ⇨ *19 rooms* ⌂ *Some kitchens, cable TV, canoes, bicycles; no a/c, no pets, no smoking* ☰ *AE, D, MC, V* ⎮⊙⎮ *CP.*

$–$$ ⌂ **Our Place Inn.** On North Haven Island, this is a classic 19th-century farmhouse with five rooms in the main house and three separate but self-contained cottages. The inn is 2 mi from town but only a short walk from Pulpit Harbor. Three of the rooms in the main house have private baths. The cottages are small but all have private baths and kitchenettes. For something different, request to stay in the lighthouse room. ⌂ *Box 704* ⊠ *Crabtree Point Rd., North Haven 04853* ☎ *207/867–4998.* ⊕ *www.ourplaceinn.com* ⇨ *5 rooms, 3 with bath; 3 cottages* ⌂ *Cable TV, some kitchenettes, bicycles; no a/c in some rooms, no smoking* ☰ *MC, V* ⎮⊙⎮ *CP.*

$–$$ ⌂ **Payne Homestead.** The Payne Homestead is at the Moses Webster House, a French Victorian home that was built in 1873 by the owner of a granite quarry. It is listed on the National Register of Historic Places, and opened as a B&B in 1995. The rooms, with their large windows and brass and wood furnishings, display the quiet and refined elegance typical of the original home. ⊠ *Box 216, Atlantic Ave., Vinalhaven 04863* ☎ *207/863–9963* ⊕ *www.paynehomestead.com* ⇨ *5 rooms, 1 with bath* ⌂ *No a/c, no room phones, no room TVs* ☰ *MC, V.*

AROUND ROCKPORT, CAMDEN & LINCOLNVILLE

Rockport

❸ *4 mi north of Rockland on U.S. 1.*

Heading north on U.S. 1, you come to Rockport before you reach the tourist mecca of Camden. The most interesting part of Rockport, the

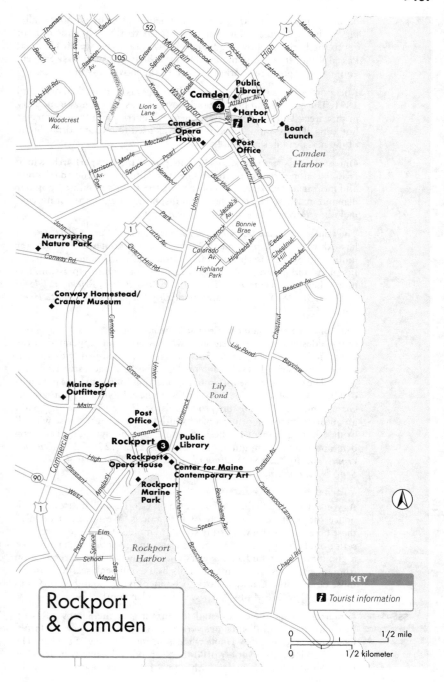

Rockport & Camden

harbor, is not right on U.S. 1, so many people drive by without realizing it's here. But the colorful harbor area is worth a short detour. To get to the harbor, follow the first ROCKPORT sign you see off U.S. 1 at Pascal Road. If you saw the movie *In the Bedroom* with Sissy Spacek, you may recognize the harbor—much of the movie was filmed here.

Rockport—originally called Goose River—was part of Camden until 1891. The cutting and burning of limestone was once a major industry in this area. The stone was cut in nearby quarries and then burned in hot kilns. The resulting lime powder was used to create mortar. Some of the massive kilns are still here.

One of the most famous sights in Rockport is the **Rockport Arch,** which crosses Union Street at the town line. It was first constructed of wood and mortar in 1926, was demolished in 1984, then rebuilt by popular demand in 1985. The arch has been displayed in a number of movies, including *Peyton Place* and *In the Bedroom.*

The **Center for Maine Contemporary Art** (formerly Maine Coast Artists) has exhibited work by some of Maine's best—and newest—artists for more than 50 years. The exhibits, in four galleries, range from traditional art and photography to various forms of artistic expression. Exhibits change on a rotating basis. ⊠ *162 Russell Ave., Rockport 04856* ☎ *207/236–2875* ⊕ *www.artsmaine.org* ⊲ *$3* ⊗ *Tues.–Sat. 10–5, Sun. 1–5.*

The **Conway Homestead and Cramer Museum,** built around 1770, is one of the oldest houses in the region. It was restored and is operated by the Camden-Rockport Historical Society. The house is filled with authentic furnishings and household items from the 18th and early-19th centuries. The Cramer Museum contains collections of photos and paintings of Mid-Coast Maine in the early 1900s. Some exhibits and photographs change annually. The museum grounds also include an 18th-century barn; an outdoor Victorian privy; a blacksmith's shop; a sugar house with all of its 1820 equipment for boiling maple sap into syrup; an herb garden; and the museum gift shop. ⊠ *U.S. 1* ☎ *207/236–2257* ⊕ *www. crmuseum.org* ⊲ *$5* ⊗ *July and Aug., Mon.–Thurs. 10–4; June and Sept. by appointment.*

Where to Stay & Eat

As you drive through the Rockport area on U.S. 1, you'll notice an abundance of small, independently owned motels. We have not detailed these here because they are truly standard motels, which merit little description. However, these places are clean and relatively inexpensive—a good choice for budget travelers and anyone without a reservation (though even these places may be fully booked in peak season). For details, contact the **Camden-Rockport-Lincolnville Chamber of Commerce** (☎ 207/236–4404 ⊕ www.visitcamden.com).

$$$–$$$$
Fodor'sChoice
★

× **Marcel's.** This fine continental restaurant is at the Samoset Resort. You can enjoy tableside preparation of a classic rack of lamb, Châteaubriand, or Steak Diane while admiring the view of the bay. The menu also includes a variety of Maine seafood and a fine wine list. The lavish Sunday brunch buffet, with some of the finest seafood along the coast, is famous and attracts many locals as well as visitors. ⊠ *220 Warrenton St., off U.S. 1, Rockport* ☎ *207/594–2511* ⚓ *Reservations essential* 🏛 *Jacket required* ⊟ *AE, D, MC, V* ⊙ *No lunch.*

$$–$$$ ✕ **The Helm Restaurant.** This restaurant offers French and American cuisine accompanied by excellent views and simple surroundings. Among the specialties on the French side are bouillabaisse, coq au vin, and coquille St. Jacques. On the American side, there's locally caught seafood, charbroiled steaks, and homemade soups and chowders. The huge salad bar is popular with the locals. Specials include baked stuffed haddock, and the complete Maine Shore Dinner, which comes with lobster, chowder, steamed clams, and corn. The full menu is available for takeout. ⊠ *U.S. 1* ☎ *207/236–4337* ⊙ *Closed Tues.* ⊟ *MC, V.*

¢–$$$ ✕ **McMahon's Rockport Grille.** This little place is popular for its homemade soups, such as seafood chowder, and its quirky lunches, such as sloppy joes and roasted red potatoes. For dinner, they offer an excellent prime rib, king or queen cut, and they have live music on weekends in summer. ⊠ *U.S. 1* ☎ *207/236–4431* ⊟ *AE, D, MC, V.*

$–$$ **The Offshore Restaurant.** Seafood is the specialty here but the large menu also includes steak, pot roast, liver, and chicken. The restaurant is bright and airy and there is a lovely view of the bay from the large windows. ⊠ *U.S. 1* ☎ *207/596–6804* ⊟ *AE, D, MC, V.*

$$–$$$$ ✕🏨 **Samoset Resort.** This 230-acre, all-encompassing, oceanside resort
Fodor'sChoice on the Rockland-Rockport town line offers luxurious rooms and suites,
★ all with a private balcony or patio, and an ocean or garden view. The spacious rooms are decorated in deep green and burgundy tones. *Golf Digest* called the resort's 18-hole championship golf course "The Top Ranked Resort Course in New England," and "The Seventh Most Beautiful Course in America." There are three dining options within the resort. The flagship restaurant, Marcel's, features French and American cuisine, as well as specials from the sea. The menu includes chicken and scallops Chambord, rack of lamb for two, Châteaubriand for two, Steak Diane, and blueberry duck breast. They also have an extensive and impressive wine list. Reservations are essential here, and men must wear a jacket. For a less formal affair, try the Breakwater Cafe, which offers basic New England fare, such as homemade chowder and lobster rolls, and outdoor seating when the weather is nice. The Clubhouse Grille, which caters to the golf crowd, serves casual food, which you can enjoy inside or on the porch. ⊠ *220 Warrenton St., Rockport 04856* ☎ *207/ 594–2511 or 800/341–1650* 🖶 *207/594–0722* ⊕ *www.samoset.com* 🛏 *156 rooms, 22 suites* ⚭ *3 restaurants, in-room data ports, some minibars, cable TV with movies and video games, 4 tennis courts, 2 pools (1 indoor), 18-hole golf course, putting green, pro shop, health club, hot tub, massage, sauna, dock, racquetball, lounge, babysitting, children's programs (ages 3–12), playground, dry cleaning, laundry service, concierge, Internet, business services, meeting rooms, airport shuttle; no smoking* ⊟ *AE, D, MC, V.*

$$–$$$ 🏨 **The Country Inn at Camden-Rockport.** This all-suite inn has 47 country-style rooms in the main building and 11 private cottage suites (available May through October only). All rooms have private decks; some also include fireplaces and Jacuzzis. One of the cottage suites is pet-friendly. ⊠ *40 Commercial St. (U.S. 1), 04856* ☎ *207/236–2725* ⊕ *www.*

countryinnmaine.com ⌨ *47 rooms, 11 cottages △ Minibars, cable TV with video games and movies, indoor pool, gym, shop, laundry service, Internet, meeting rooms, some pets allowed ⊟ AE, D, MC V ⑩ CP.*

$–$$$ ⊡ **Island View Inn.** The best thing about this inn is the spectacular view of the ocean. All of the bright and airy rooms have ocean views, balconies, and the spacious grounds make for enjoyable walks. The rooms are decorated in shades of turquoise and yellow, and there are charming quilts on all the beds. ⊠ *904 Commercial St. (U.S. 1), 04856* ☎ *207/ 596–0040 or 866/711–8439* 🖷 *800/589–4009* ⊕ *www. islandviewinnmaine.com* ⌨ *15 rooms △ In-room data ports, refrigerators, cable TV, outdoor pool ⊟ AE. D, MC, V.*

$–$$ ⊡ **Claddagh Motel & Suites.** Hosts Alex and Sioban Gilmore offer Irish hospitality in a coastal Maine setting. The main building resembles a New England–style clapboard house with white paint and green awnings. Rooms are in a small wing in the back. Potted flowers and plants add extra charm to this small motel. ⊡ *Box 988* ⊠ *U.S. 1, 04856* ☎ *207/ 594–8479 or 800/871–5454.* ⊕ *www.claddaghmotel.com* ⌨ *13 rooms, 6 suites △ Some refrigerators, cable TV, in-room VCRs, outdoor pool; no smoking, no a/c ⊟ AE, D, MC, V ⊘ Closed Dec.–Feb.* ⑩ *CP.*

$ ⊡ **White Gates Inn.** This family-run inn is nestled in a quiet rural setting, surrounded by huge oak trees and spacious lawns and gardens. The hosts, Charlie and Ann Emerson, live on the property. All rooms are on the ground level, and many are rustic in nature with knotty pine paneling and old-fashioned Maine quilts. ⊠ *700 Commercial St. (U.S. 1), 04856* ☎ *207/594–4625* ⊕ *www.whitegatesinn.com* ⌨ *15 rooms △ Cable TV ⊟ AE, MC, V* ⑩ *CP.*

¢–$ ⊡ **Schooner Bay Motor Inn.** This inn is about a mile from the Rockport Harbor (about halfway between Rockport and Camden). The rooms are simple but clean and relatively inexpensive. ⊠ *337 Commercial St. (U.S. 1), 04856* ☎ *207/236–2205 or 888/308–8855* ⊕ *www. sbaymotorinn.com* ⌨ *23 rooms △ In-room data ports, cable TV; no smoking ⊟ AE, D, MC, V ⊘ Closed Nov.–Mar.* ⑩ *CP.*

The Arts

The **Bay Chamber Concerts** (⊠ Box 228, 04856 ☎ 207/236–2823 ⊕ www. baychamberconcerts.org) features major artists performing classical, jazz, dance, and world music. Some recent performers have included Dave Brubeck and his sons, the Vermeer String Quartet, Joseph Silverstein, and Regina Carter. Concerts are held Thursday and Friday nights during July and August, at the historic Rockport Opera House (6 Central Street). There are additional, though less frequent, concerts throughout the year.

Sports & the Outdoors

Maine Sport (⊠ U.S. 1 ☎ 207/236–7120 or 800/722–0826 ⊕ www. mainesport.com) rents bikes, camping and fishing gear, canoes, kayaks, cross-country skis, ice skates, and snowshoes. It also conducts kayaking clinics.

FISHING   The **Rockport Marine Park** lies at the foot of Rockport Harbor and has several floats from which you can fish. Facilities include a boat ramp, picnic tables, nearby places to eat, and public toilets.

Shopping

The state of Maine is famous for the number of handmade goods it offers, and **Maine Gathering** (✉ 21 Main St. ☎ 207/236–9004 ⊕ www. mainegathering.com) sells a ton of them. Items for sale range from handmade arts and crafts to hand-dipped chocolates to the state's largest collection of Passamaquoddy and Penobscot Indian baskets.

For a unique, only-in-Maine gift, try **Bald Mountain Maple** (✉ 555 Commercial St. ☎ 207/236–2717 ⊕ www.mainegold.com). There are few things as tasty as Maine maple syrup products, and they have endless variations here. Shipping is available.

en route You do not have to return to U.S. 1 to reach Camden from Rockland. Instead, just follow the harbor route (Calderwood Lane) right up into Camden. You'll pass an attractive collection of residential houses between the two towns.

Camden

🔵 *8 mi north of Rockland, 5 mi south of Lincolnville.*

More than any other town along the Penobscot Bay, Camden is the perfect picture-postcard of a Maine coastal village. Not surprisingly, the town is crowded with visitors from June through September; but don't let that scare you away, Camden is worth it. Just come prepared for busy traffic on the town's main street (U.S. 1), and be sure to make accommodation reservations well in advance. You'll also want to make restaurant reservations whenever possible.

"Where the Mountains Meet the Sea," the longtime publicity slogan for Camden-Rockport-Lincolnville, is an apt description, as you will discover when you look up from the harbor. The town is famous not only for geography but also for its large fleet of windjammers—relics and replicas from the age of sailing—with their romantic histories and great billowing sails. At just about any hour during the warm months, you're likely to see at least one windjammer tied up in the harbor. The excursions, whether for an afternoon or a week, are best from June through September.

One of the biggest and most colorful events of the year in Camden is **Windjammer Weekend,** which usually takes place at the beginning of September and includes the single largest gathering of windjammer ships in the world, plus lots of good eats. ☎ *207/374–2993 or 800/807–9463.*

Downtown Camden has some of the best shopping in the region. The district's compact size makes it perfect for exploring on foot: shops, restaurants, and galleries line Main Street (U.S. 1), as well as side streets and alleys around the harbor. Keep in mind, Camden is one of the most popular destinations on the Maine coast, so don't expect to find a quiet little town.

The residential area of Camden is quite charming and filled with many fascinating old period houses from the time when Federal, Greek Revival, and Victorian architecture were the rage among the wealthy.

Many of them now are B&Bs. You might want to explore the area on foot if you have the time. The chamber of commerce, at the public landing (207/236–4404) can provide you with a walking map of the historical district.

★ ☾ ▵ Although their height may not be much more than 1,000 feet, the hills in **Camden Hills State Park** are lovely landmarks for miles along the low, rolling reaches of the Maine coast. The 5,500-acre park contains 25 mi of hiking trails, including the easy Nature Trail up Mount Battie. Hike or drive to the top for a magnificent view over Camden and island-studded Penobscot Bay. There is a campground here. ✉ U.S. 1 ☎ 207/236–3109 for park or camping information.

need a break?

Down by the harbor you can find a number of independent fast-food stands that offer clam chowder, fried fish, and lobster rolls. For something sweet, try **Boynton-McKay** (✉ 30 Main St. ☎ 207/236–2465), an 1890s ice-cream parlor that serves ice cream made the old-fashioned way, as well as modern-day smoothies.

Merryspring Nature Park is a 66-acre retreat with herb, rose, rhododendron, hosta, and children's gardens as well as 4 mi of walking trails. ✉ Conway Rd., off U.S. 1 ☎ 207/236–2239 ⊕ www.merrysprings.org ☞ Free ☉ Daily dawn–dusk.

Where to Stay & Eat

★ $$$ ✗ **Atlantica Restaurant.** The Atlantica, which is owned and operated by Ken and Del Paquin, is in a historic clapboard building right on the water's edge. The lower deck is cantilevered over the water offering a romantic setting with great views. The decor inside is a combination of white walls and contemporary paintings. Fresh seafood with French and Asian accents is the specialty here. Favorites include pan-roasted split lobster tails with lemon butter, lobster stuffed with scallops, and the seldom-found skate with brown butter. ✉ Bayview Landing ☎ 207/236–6011 or 888/507–8514 ⊕ www.atlanticarestaurant.com ☞ Reservations essential ☰ AE, MC, V.

★ $–$$$ ✗ **Cappy's Chowder House.** Cappy's has been around for so long (more than two decades) it's become somewhat of a Camden institution. As you would expect from the name, Cappy's "chowdah" is the thing to order here—it's been written up in the New York Times and in Bon Appetit magazine—but there are plenty of other seafood specials to choose from. Don't be afraid to bring the kids—this place has many bargain meals, and Cappy loves kids. ✉ 1 Main St. ☎ 207/236–2254 ⊕ www.cappyschowder.com ☞ Reservations not accepted ☰ MC, V.

$–$$$ ✗ **Quarterdeck Bar & Grill.** This neighborhood grill with its brick oven and two full bars, offers broiled seafood, pasta specials, and homemade desserts. When the weather is good, you can dine on the deck and enjoy the harbor views. They even have live music out there in summer. ✉ 21 Bay View St. ☎ 207/236–3272 ☰ MC, V.

$–$$$ ✗ **Waterfront Restaurant.** Come here for a ringside seat on Camden Harbor. The best view, when the weather cooperates, is from the deck. The fare is primarily seafood, but they also serve beef, chicken, and salads. Lobster and crabmeat rolls are highlights at lunch. ✉ 40 Bay View St.

A CHILD OF PENOBSCOT BAY . . .

T WAS A WARM AUGUST NIGHT IN 1912 when the young Rockland poet Edna St. Vincent Millay appeared at the White Hall Inn. She was there to read her poem "Renascence," to an audience of inn guests and employees.

All I could see from where I stood

Was three long mountains and a wood;

I turned and looked another way,

And saw three islands in a bay.

(Edna St. Vincent Millay, "Renascence")

The woman who was to become one of America's most famous poets was born in 1892 in the unlikely city of Rockland, a working town of seamen and stonecutters. Like many artists before her, she became famous almost by accident. At the age of 20, she entered the same poem, "Renascence," in a poetry contest. The poem only took fourth place, but it was enough to bring her attention from academics, and she was awarded a scholarship to the prestigious Vassar College.

She continued writing and winning awards, and eventually she was awarded a Pulitzer Prize for her poetry. She was reknowned for her beauty and spent most of her adult life leading a rather wild existence in Greenwich Village, in New York City.

Eventually, she married a man much older than herself, Eugen Boissevain, who became her manager and supporter. A heavy smoker, she died in 1950 at the age of 58. She had written in one of her most famous poems that she was a person who had burnt her candle at both ends, and she lamented that it "would not last the night."

☎ 207/236–3747 ⊕ www.waterfrontcamden.com ⌧ Reservations not accepted ☐ AE, MC, V.

$$ ✕ Sonny G's. One of the few Italian restaurants in Camden, Sonny's is an informal, family-dining kind of place. You can recognize the restaurant from a block away; just look for the bright red awning. The decor inside is classic Italian red and white. The résumé of chef Kurk Wheeler includes cooking at the famous Spago's. The cuisine here is traditional Italian; the specials include shrimp scampi, steak pizzailo, and chicken cacciatore. ⌧ 31 Elm St. ☎ 207/236–4477 ☐ MC, V ⊙ Closed Sun. No lunch.

¢–$ ✕ Camden Deli. This little place is as popular with the locals as it is with the visitors. If you simply *must* have that pastrami-on-rye with a nice pickle, this is the place to go. You can even sit on the rooftop deck and watch the boats in the harbor while you're enjoying your pastrami. ⌧ 37 Main St. ☎ 207/236–8343 ⊕ www.camdendeli.com ☐ AE, D, MC, V.

★ $$–$$$$ ✕ Hartstone Inn. This downtown 1835 Mansard-roofed Victorian home has been turned into an elegant and sophisticated retreat and a fine culinary destination. No detail has been overlooked, from soft robes, down comforters, and chocolate truffles in the guest rooms to china, crystal, and silver in the dining room. The specialty is a five-course prix-fixe menu. The inn also hosts seasonal food festivals and off-season cooking classes. ⊠ *41 Elm St., 04843* ☎ *207/236–4259 or 800/ 788–4823* 🖷 *207/236–9575* ⊕ *www.hartstoneinn.com* ⟿ *6 rooms, 6 suites* ⟳ *Restaurant, in-room data ports, cable TV; no smoking.*

$$–$$$ ✕⬚ **The Whitehall Inn.** One of Camden's best-known inns, the Whitehall is an 1834 white clapboard sea captain's home just north of town. The Millay Room, off the lobby, preserves memorabilia of the poet Edna St. Vincent Millay, who grew up in the area and who read her poetry here. The sparsely furnished rooms have dark-wood bedsteads, white bedspreads, and claw-foot tubs. The dining room, which serves traditional and creative American cuisine as well as many seafood specialties, is open to the public for dinner. ⊠ *52 High St., 04843* ☎ *207/236– 3391 or 800/789–6565* 🖷 *207/236–4427 seasonal* ⊕ *www.whitehallinn.com* ⟿ *50 rooms, 45 with bath* ⟳ *Restaurant, tennis court, shuffleboard; no a/c, no phones in some rooms, no room TVs* ⊟ *AE, MC, V* ☉ *Closed mid-Oct.–mid-May* ⦿l *BP.*

$$$$ ⬚ **The Inn at Sunrise Point.** This luxury inn has been widely recognized for its spectacular setting and service. The main house and cottages are right on the ocean, resulting in beautiful ocean views from nearly all of the rooms. Amenities such as plush robes and oversized tubs and showers are standard; some rooms include romantic wood-burning fireplaces and Jacuzzis. ⊠ *Rte. 1,* ⬚ *Box 1344 04843* ☎ *207/236–7716* ⊕ *www. sunrisepoint.com* ⟿ *3 rooms, 4 cottages, 2 suites* ⟳ *Room TVs with VCRs, some minibars* ⊟ *MC, V* ⦿l *BP.*

$$$–$$$$ ⬚ **Camden Harbour Inn.** Built in 1874, this white clapboard inn has a panoramic view of Camden's colorful harbor. At the time it was built, many tourists came to the inn via steamship from Boston and were brought up to the inn by horse-drawn carriages. Today the attractive rooms are decorated with hand-picked flowers or, perhaps, a basket of one of Maine's most famous products, apples. Each room is filled with period antiques. Some have decks or balconies, some have fireplaces, and many have clawfoot bathtubs. ⊠ *83 Bay View St., 04843* ☎ *207/236–4200 or 800/236– 4266* ⊕ *www.camdenharbourinn.com* ⟿ *22 rooms* ⟳ *Cable TV, some in-room data ports* ⊟ *AE, D, MC, V* ☉ *Closed Nov.–Apr.* ⦿l *BP.*

$$$–$$$$ ⬚ **Camden Riverhouse Hotel, Camden Riverhouse Mill, Camden Riverhouse Inn.** This is an unusual collection of three different accommodations, all centrally located and all on the same property. The hotel and historic mill offer comfortable rooms with modern amenities; the inn offers onebedroom suites with full kitchens and living rooms. All of the accommodations are simple but clean; some of the suites have fireplaces. ⊠ *11 Tannery La., 04843* ☎ *207/236–0500 or 800/755–7483* ⊕ *www. camdenmaine.com* ⟿ *46 rooms, 8 suites* ⟳ *In-room data ports, kitchenettes, microwaves, refrigerators, cable TV, indoor pool, gym, hot tub, Internet* ⊟ *AE, D, MC, V* ⦿l *CP.*

★ $$$–$$$$ ⬚ **Lord Camden Inn.** This is an excellent location if you want to be in the very center of town, near the harbor. The exterior of the building is red brick with bright blue-and-white awnings. The colorful interior is furnished with restored antiques and paintings by local artists. Despite being downtown, the inn offers plenty of ocean views from the upstairs rooms, and some of the rooms have lovely old-fashioned, four-poster beds. There's no on-site restaurant but you can find plenty of dining options within walking distance. ⊠ *24 Main St., 04843* ☎ *207/236–4325 or 800/336–4325* ⊕ *www.lordcamdeninn.com* ⇆ *37 rooms* ⚲ *In-room data ports, cable TV, some microwaves, some refrigerators, meeting rooms* ▤ *MC, V* ⚮ *BP.*

$$$–$$$$ ⊞ **Norumbega.** This is probably the most unusual-looking B&B you'll
FodorsChoice ever see. Think Addams Family meets Count Dracula in a wacky cas-
★ tle of a home. This gray-stone castle was built in 1886 by local busi-
nessman and inventor (of duplex telegraphy) Joseph Stearns. Before
building his home, he spent a year visiting the castles of Europe and adapt-
ing the best ideas he found. He named his home after the original 17th-
century name for what is now Maine, "Norumbega." Stearns and his
family lived in his castle by the sea until his death in 1895. The man-
sion was converted into a B&B in 1984. It has been named by the *Maine
Times* as the most photographed piece of real estate in the state. Many
of the antique-filled rooms have fireplaces and private balconies, which
overlook the bay. ⊠ *63 High St., 04843* ☎ *207/236–4646 or 800/
363–4646* ⊕ *www.norumbegainn.com* ⇆ *13 rooms* ⚲ *In-room data
ports, cable TV; no a/c* ▤ *AE, D, MC, V* ⚮ *BP.*

★ $$–$$$$ ⊞ **The Windward House.** Built in the Greek Revival style, this picturesque
house dates back to 1854. All of the rooms have oversized beds, as well
as private baths, and the home is only a block from the harbor. If you
can get it, the Quarterdeck room has the best view. Newlyweds—or ro-
mantics—should inquire about the Romance Package. ⊠ *6 High St.,
04843* ☎ *207/236–9656 or 877/492–9656* 🖷 *207/230–0433* ⊕ *www.
windwardhouse.com* ⇆ *5 rooms, 3 suites* ⚲ *In-room data ports, some
in-room hot tubs, cable TV, in-room VCRs* ▤ *AE, D, MC, V* ⚮ *BP.*

$–$$$$ ⊞ **Beloin's on the Maine Coast.** Beloin's sits on a natural sea ledge on the
edge of the ocean, so it offers spectacular views and easy shore access.
There are nine rooms in the motel, five one-bedroom shore cottages,
and two two-bedroom shore cottages, all with views. They also have a
private beach, picnic tables, and grills. Camden Hills State Park is
nearby. ⊠ *254 Belfast Rd. (U.S. 1), 04843* ☎ *207/236–3262* ⊕ *www.
beloins.com* ⇆ *9 rooms, 7 cottages* ⚲ *Some kitchenettes, cable TV, some
pets allowed; no a/c* ▤ *D, MC, V.*

$$–$$$ ⊞ **The Belmont Inn.** This attractive inn, with its wraparound porch, is in
a quiet, off-the-main-street location, yet is only a five-minute walk from
the harbor. The rooms are large, bright, and airy and are decorated in
either a Federal, French, or country style. All rooms have private baths
and air-conditioning; a few have gas-fired fireplaces. ⊠ *6 Belmont Ave.,
04843* ☎ *207/236–8053 or 800/238–8053* ⊕ *www.thebelmontinn.
com* ⇆ *6 rooms* ⚲ *No room TVs, no room phones, no smoking* ▤ *AE,
MC, V* ⚮ *BP.*

★ $$–$$$ ⊞ **Camden Maine Stay.** This 1802 clapboard inn is listed on the National
Register of Historic Places. The grounds are classic and inviting, from
the flowers lining the granite walk in summer to the snow-laden bushes
in winter. The fresh and colorful rooms contain Eastlake and other pe-
riod furniture; six have fireplaces. The property is within easy walking
distance of shops and restaurants. ⊠ *22 High St., 04842* ☎ *207/236–
9636* 🖷 *207/236–0621* ⊕ *www.camdenmainestay.com* ⇆ *5 rooms, 3
suites* ⚲ *Cable TV, Internet; no room phones, no smoking* ▤ *AE, MC,
V* ⚮ *BP.*

$$ ⬚ **Cedar Crest Motel.** This white clapboard complex is on the crest of a hill with a nice view of Mount Battie. The rooms are bright and airy, and the spacious restaurant is well known for its hearty breakfasts. ⊠ *115 Elm St., 04843* ☎ *207/236–4839 or 800/422–4964* ⊕ *www. cedarcrestmotel.com* ⟿ *37 rooms* ⚲ *Restaurant, some refrigerators, cable TV, outdoor pool, playground, laundry facilities* ⊟ *AE, D, MC, V* ⊘ *Closed Oct.–mid-May.*

$–$$ ⬚ **Towne Motel.** In high-price Camden, this is one of the few affordable places to stay within easy reach of the colorful harbor. You won't find many frills here, but you will find simple, clean rooms with private baths and air-conditioning. There is one handicapped-friendly room and one room with a full kitchen. ⊠ *68 Elm St. (U.S. 1), 04843* ☎ *207/236– 3377 or 800/656–4999* ⊕ *www.camdenmotel.com* ⟿ *18 rooms* ⚲ *Cable TV* ⊟ *AE, D, MC, V* ⦿ *CP.*

$–$$ ⚠ **Camden Hills State Park Camping.** The 107-site camping area, open from mid-May to mid-October, operates on a first-come, first-served basis. The entrance to the park and the campground is 2 mi north of Camden off U.S. 1. ☎ *207/236–3109* ✉ *$20 nightly for out-of-state, $15 for in-state, 14-day maximum* ⚲ *Flush toilets, hot showers, playground.*

For additional B&B listings, contact Camden Maine Bed & Breakfast Inns (⬚ Camden's Premier Inns, Box 553, Camden, ME 04843 ⊕ www. camdeninns.com).

Nightlife

Gilbert's Publick House (⊠ 12 Bay View St. ☎ 207/236–4320) is the favorite drinking place of the windjammer crowd and other boat people. They offer live music, dancing, pub food, and some local brews.

Sports & the Outdoors

Maine Sport Outfitters. (⊠ U.S. 1, 2 mi south of Camden ☎ 207/236– 8797 or 800/722–0826) rents bicycles, kayaks, and canoes. They also offer sea kayak tours and family canoe trips.

Brown Dog Bikes (⊠ 46 Elm St. ☎ 207/236–6664 ⊕ www.browndogbike. com) delivers rental bikes to area lodging.

SAILING & BOATING
★ ☾ General information on sailing and boating in the Penobscot Bay can be found at www.sailmaine.com. For the voyage of a lifetime, you and your family should think seriously about a **windjammer trip.** The following windjammers leave from Camden Harbor, most are of the schooner type: *Olad* (☎ 207/236–2323 ⊕ www.maineschooners.com); *Lazy Jack* (☎ 207/230–0602 ⊕ www.schoonerlazyjack.com); *Windjammer Surprise* (☎ 207/236–4687 ⊕ www.camdenmainesailing.com); and *Shantih II* (☎ 207/236–8605 or 800/599–8605 ⊕ www. woodenboatco.com). Prices range from $395 to $875 for a three-to-six-day cruise, all meals included—and often that means a lobster bake on a deserted beach somewhere.

For other types of boat rentals, the *Betselma* (⊠ Camden Public Landing ☎ 207/236–4446) offers one- and two-hour powerboat trips.

SKI AREAS
★ ☾ The Maine Coast isn't known for skiing, but the **Camden Snow Bowl** (⊠ Hosmer Pond Rd. ☎ 207/236–3438, 207/236–4418 snow phone

⊕ www.camdensnowbowl.com) has a 950-foot-vertical mountain with 11 trails accessed by one double chair and two T-bars. The complex also includes a small lodge with a cafeteria, a ski school, and ski and toboggan rentals. Activities include skiing, night skiing, snowboarding, tubing, tobogganing, and ice-skating—plus magnificent views over Penobscot Bay. The North American Tobogganing Championships, a tongue-in-cheek event open to anyone, is held annually in early February.

★ There are 16 km (10 mi) of cross-country skiing trails at **Camden Hills State Park** (⊠ U.S. 1 ☎ 207/236–0849).

Shopping

Camden is a shopper's paradise with lots of interesting places to spend money. Most of the shops and galleries are along Camden's main drag, U.S. 1, so you can easily complete a shopping tour on foot. Keep in mind that U.S. 1 has three different names within the town limits—it starts as Elm Street, then changes to Main Street, then becomes High Street. So don't let the addresses listed below throw you off. Start your shopping tour at the Camden Harbor, turn right on Bay View, and walk to Main/High Street.

ABCD Books (⊠ 23 Bay View St. ☎ 207/236–3903 or 888/236–3903) has a discriminating selection of quality antiquarian and rare books. **Ducktrap Bay Trading Co.** (⊠ 37 Bay View St. ☎ 207/236–6259 ⊕ www.ducktrapbay.com) offers decorative wildlife carvings, bronze sculptures, scrimshaw etchings, marine art, ship models and prints, and original Maine art. **Owl and Turtle Bookshop** (⊠ 8 Bay View St. ☎ 207/236–4769 ⊕ www.owlandturtle.com) has been here for 35 years and sells books, CDs, cassettes, and cards. The two-story shop has rooms devoted to marine and children's books. **Bayview Gallery** (⊠ 33 Bay View St. ☎ 207/236–4534 ⊕ www.bayviewgallery.com) specializes in original art, prints, and posters, almost all with Maine themes. **Maine Gold** (⊠ 12 Bay View St. ☎ 702/236–2717) sells authentic Maine maple syrup. **Planet World** (⊠ 10 Main St. ☎ 207/236–4410) has unusual gifts—including books, toys, and clothing—from Maine and other parts of the world. **Lily, Lupine & Fern** (⊠ 43 Main St. ☎ 207/236–9600) sells a nice selection of beer and fine wines, plus gourmet foods and cheese. They also dish up New York deli–style sandwiches. **Maine Gathering** (⊠ 21 Main St. ☎ 207/236–9004) is a premier showplace for Maine crafts and Native American arts and crafts. **Small Wonder Gallery** (⊠ Public Landing ☎ 207/236–6005 ⊕ www.smallwondergallery.com) offers original watercolors, wood engravings, metal sculptures, etchings, tiles, porcelain, and prints.

Lincolnville

⑤ *6 mi north of Camden via U.S. 1.*

Looking at a map, you may notice there are two parts to Lincolnville: Lincolnville Beach on U.S. 1, and the town of Lincolnville Center a little inland on Route 73. The area of most interest—where you can find the restaurants and the ferry to Islesboro—is Lincolnville Beach. This is a tiny area; you could be through it in less than a minute. Still, it does have a little history going all the way back to the Revolution, and there are even a few small cannons on the beach that were intended to repel the British in the War of 1812, though they were never used. Lincolnville is 6 mi north of Camden, which makes it a great place to stay if rooms in Camden are fully booked, or if you just want someplace a little quieter.

It's hard to believe you would actually find a winemaker in chilly Maine, but there is an excellent one in this area. **Cellar Door Winery** (✉ Youngtown Rd. ☎ 207/763–4478) offers free tours of their facility from 11 to 5 daily, year-round. No reservations are required, but a call ahead of time is a good idea. To get to the winery, go out Route 52 from U.S. 1 and turn right on Youngtown Road.

off the
beaten
path

ISLAND PICNICS – How does a picnic on a deserted island sound? Island Picnics can provide just that aboard the *Katy D.* They furnish all the fixings, including the lobster, which is cooked right on the island. ✉ *2478 Atlantic Hwy.* ☎ *207/236–6001* ⊕ *www. islandpicnics.com.*

Where to Stay & Eat

★ **$$–$$$** ✗ **Chez Michel.** This little restaurant sits right on U.S. 1 and offers nice views of the bay. The menu consists of French and American cuisine, with an emphasis on steak and seafood. Owner-chef Michel Hetuin's bouillabaisse is the specialty. ✉ *U.S. 1, Lincolnville Beach* ☎ *207/789–5600* ⚐ *Reservations essential* ⊟ *AE, D, DC, MC, V* ☉ *No lunch weekdays.*

$–$$$ ✗ **Lobster Pound Restaurant.** If you're looking for the real Maine, you've
FodorsChoice come to the right place. This summertime favorite is right on the beach, ★ off U.S. 1—you can't miss it. The place is huge so you won't have to wait long for a table. They have seating for 260 inside the restaurant and 40 on the patio. Plus there is a 70-seat picnic area if you're willing to take your food to go. Lobster and seafood are, of course, the reason to come here though they also offer turkey and steak. The traditional meal is a Shore Dinner, which includes fish, clam, or lobster chowder; steamed mussels or clams; a fresh boiled lobster; and corn on the cob. The restaurant sits right on the coast, so you can admire the passing sailboats as you dine. ✉ *U.S. 1, Lincolnville Beach* ☎ *207/789–5550* ⊕ *www.midcoast.com/~lobstrlb* ⊟ *AE, D, MC, V* ☉ *Closed Nov.–Apr.*

$–$$$ ✗ **Whale's Tooth Pub & Restaurant.** This pub and restaurant is in an old brick building on the main road. The restaurant serves steamed lobsters and mussels, fried calamari, broiled scallops, and other seafood specials. Prime rib, charbroiled steaks, and pasta dishes are also on the menu. The interior is reminiscent of an Old English pub, and there is a deck for days when the weather is good. ✉ *U.S. 1* ☎ *207/789–5200* ⊕ *www. whalestoothpub.com.*

$$–$$$ ✗🛏 **Youngtown Inn and Restaurant.** Inside this white Federal-style farm-
FodorsChoice house you'll find a French-inspired country retreat and a well-respected ★ French restaurant ($$$–$$$$). The country location, which is closer to Lincolnville than Lincolnville Beach, guarantees quiet, and the inn is a short walk from the Fernald Neck Preserve on Lake Megunticook. Simple, airy rooms open to decks with views of the rolling countryside. Four have fireplaces. The restaurant, open to the public for dinner, serves en-

trées such as rack of lamb and breast of pheasant with foie gras mousse. ⊠ *Rte. 52 at Youngtown Rd., 04849* ☎ *207/763–4290 or 800/291–8438* 🖷 *207/763–4078* ⊕ *www.youngtowninn.com* 🛏 *5 rooms, 1 suite* ⚭ *Restaurant, cable TV; no smoking* ⊟ *AE, MC, V* ⊠| *BP.*

$$$$
FodorsChoice
★

🏨 **Inn at Ocean's Edge.** This beautiful white inn on 7 acres has one of the loveliest settings in the area, with heavy forest on one side and the ocean on the other. The inn looks as if it has been here for decades, but the original building was only built in 1999 and the upper building in 2001. The rooms are styled simply but with old-fashioned New England elegance. Every room has a king-size bed, an ocean view, a fireplace, and a whirlpool for two. There is an English-style pub with a fireplace and a fine array of brews on-site. ⊠ *U.S. 1, Lincolnville* ⍟ *Box 704, Camden 04843* ☎ *207/236–0945* 🖷 *207/236–0609* ⊕ *www.innatoceansedge.com* 🛏 *26 rooms, 1 suite* ⚭ *In-room data ports, cable TV, in-room VCRs, gym, pub, meeting room; no smoking* ⊟ *MC, V* ⊠| *BP.*

$$$–$$$$

🏨 **Victorian by the Sea.** With a quiet waterside location well off U.S. 1, the Victorian Inn feels as if it's a world away from all the hustle and bustle of town. Most rooms and the wraparound porch have magnificent views over island-studded Penobscot Bay. Romantic touches include canopied brass beds, braided rugs, white wicker furniture, and floral wallpapers. Six guest rooms have fireplaces; four more fireplaces are in common rooms, including the glass-enclosed breakfast room. ⊠ *33 Sea View Dr., Lincolnville* ⍟ *Box 1385, Camden 04843* ☎ *207/236–3785 or 800/382–9817* 🖷 *207/236–0017* ⊕ *www.victorianbythesea.com* 🛏 *5 rooms, 2 suites* ⚭ *No a/c in some rooms, no room TVs, no smoking* ⊟ *AE, MC, V* ⊠| *BP.*

$–$$$

🏨 **Black Horse Inn.** This inn looks like a beautiful New England country home. There's even an old-fashioned horse and carriage out in front—the horse, of course, being a statue. The standard rooms here are simple but elegant, many of them with four-poster beds. The four luxurious suites all include a Jacuzzi, wet bar, refrigerator, and complimentary bottle of champagne. The breakfast room is bright and airy and overlooks the sea. ⊠ *U.S. 1, Lincolnville* ⍟ *P.O. Box 1093, Camden 04843* ☎ *207/236–6800 or 800/374–9085* 🛏 *21 rooms, 4 suites* ⚭ *Cable TV, pool, outdoor hot tub* ⊟ *AE, D, MC, V* ⊠| *CP.*

Shopping

Maine's Massachusetts House Galleries (⊠ U.S. 1 ☎ 207/789–5705) displays regional art, including bronzes, carvings, sculptures, and landscapes and seascapes in pencil, oil, and watercolor. The **Windsor Chairmakers** (⊠ U.S. 1 ☎ 207/789–5188 or 800/789–5188) sells custom-made handcrafted beds, chests, china cabinets, dining tables, highboys, Shaker furniture, and chairs. You can even go to the back of the shop and watch the furniture being made. It's open seven days a week, from 9 until 5.

Islesboro

❻ *3 mi east of Lincolnville via Islesboro Ferry (terminal on U.S. 1).*

★ If you would like to visit one of Maine's islands but don't have much time, Islesboro would be your best choice. The island is only 3 mi, a 20-

minute ferry ride, off the mainland. You can take your car with you. The drive from one end of the island to the other (on the island's only road) is lovely. It takes you through Warren State Park, a nice place to stop for a picnic and the only public camping area on the island. There are two stores on the island where you can buy supplies for your picnic: the Island Market is a short distance from the ferry terminal on the main road; and Durkee's General Store is 5 mi farther north at 863 Main Road. Next to the island's ferry terminal are the Sailor's Memorial Museum and the Grindle Point Lighthouse, both worth a brief look.

The permanent year-round population of Islesboro is about 625, but it swells to around 3,000 in summer. Most of the people who live on the island full-time earn their living in one way or another from the sea. Some of them work at the three boatyards on the island, others are fishermen, and still others run small businesses. Seasonal residents may include some more familiar faces: John Travolta and his wife, Kelly Preston, have a home here, as does Kirstie Alley.

The **Islesboro Ferry** departs from Lincolnville Harbor, a few hundred feet from the Lobster Pound Restaurant. Try to head out on one of the early ferries so you have enough time to drive around and get back. If you miss the last ferry, you'll have to stay on the island overnight. The ferry runs back and forth nine times a day from April through October and seven times a day from November through March. There are fewer runs on Sunday. As of this writing, the round-trip cost for a vehicle and one passenger is $23.50, slightly more with additional passengers, less if you leave the vehicle behind. ☎ 207/789-5611. *Call for schedules.*

Where to Stay & Eat

★ $$-$$$ ⊞ **Dark Harbor House.** This stately Georgian-Revival house, with its large veranda overlooking Dark Harbor, was built in 1896 for a successful Philadelphia banker. It was just one of many summer mansions erected for wealthy vacationers around the turn of the twentieth century. Many of the attractively decorated New England–style rooms have fireplaces, as well as four-poster canopied beds. Breakfast and dinner are served either in the oval dining room or on the enclosed sunporch. The house is listed on the National Register of Historic Places. ⌂ *Box 185, Islesboro 04848* ⊠ *Dark Harbor, 04848* ☎ *207/734-6669* ⊕ *www.darkharborhouse.com* ⇌ *11 rooms* ⚐ *Dining room; no a/c, no room phones, no room TVs* ⊟ *MC, V* ⊗ *Closed Nov.–Mar.* ⍥ *MAP.*

en route   A brief detour off U.S. 1, a few miles south of Belfast on your way up from Lincolnville, will take you through **Bayside**, a delightful little Victorian resort village by the sea. Small old houses are clustered in a truly beautiful setting. The **Northport Golf Course** is also in this area.

BELFAST TO BANGOR

The farther you get up the coast and away from Camden, the less touristy the area becomes, and the more you see of the real Maine. Traffic jams and overpacked restaurants give way to a more relaxed and casual atmosphere, and locals start to treat you like a potential neighbor.

As you drive north on U.S. 1, you pass through the charming coastal towns of Belfast, Searsport, and Bucksport. Bangor is 20 mi inland. If you're driving up U.S. 1 on a "coastal trip," you can probably leave Bangor off your itinerary. If you want to fly in, however, Bangor International Airport is the quickest point of access to northern Penobscot Bay, Bar Harbor, Mount Desert Island, and Acadia National Park.

Belfast

➐ *10 mi north of Lincolnville, 46 mi northeast of Augusta.*

A number of Maine coastal towns, such as Wiscasset and Damariscotta, like to think of themselves as the prettiest little town in Maine, but Belfast has equal claim to this title. It has a full variety of charms: a beautiful waterfront; an old and interesting main street climbing up from the harbor; a delightful array of B&Bs, restaurants, and shops; and a friendly population. The downtown even has old-fashioned street lamps, which set the streets aglow at night. The only thing Belfast does not have is traffic jams.

The economy of Belfast (which was originally to be named Londonderry) has seen many changes over the years. In the 1800s, Belfast was a shipbuilding center and home to many ship captains. Starting in the early 1900s, a shoe factory, a chicken-processing plant, and a sardine-packing factory were the primary employers. The first two disappeared about 30 years ago, and the sardine-packing plant packed up in 2002. The biggest employer in Belfast now is MBNA, the credit card giant, although tourism is also becoming a viable industry.

In the mid-1800s, Belfast was home to a number of wealthy business magnates. Their mansions still stand along High Street, offering some excellent examples of Greek-Revival and Federal architecture. The **Belfast Chamber of Commerce Visitor Center** (⊠ 17 Main St., at the harbor ☎ 207/338–3808) can provide you with a free walking tour brochure that describes the various historic homes and buildings, as well as the old business section in the harbor area.

The Belfast Historical Society & Museum is housed in an old Federal-style brick building dating back to 1835. The museum contains many paintings, photographs, and artifacts relating to the maritime history of the town. ⊠ *10 Market St., near the courthouse* ☎ *207/338–9229* ☼ *Thurs. and Sun. 1–4.*

★ ⓒ The **Belfast & Moosehead Lake Railroad** offers a great old-fashioned steam engine train excursion from Belfast to the little town of Waldo to the southwest (two hours round-trip). The train leaves the Belfast station on the waterfront at 12:30 PM every Wednesday through Sunday. ⊠ *44 Front St., near the harbor* ☎ *800/392–5500* ⊕ *www.belfastrailroad.com* ☼ *June–Nov.*

Where to Stay & Eat

★ **$$–$$$** ✕ **Bay River Bistro.** This is one of Belfast's most elegant restaurants. In a restored historic building, it's a great spot for a special occasion. The restaurant is operated by the same people who own the nearby White

House B&B. The decor is refined and tasteful, with a fireplace in the corner. Some of the specials are pan-seared bay scallops in a saffron cream sauce, lobster cakes with Cajun aioli sauce, and roast duck with a raspberry sauce. All the European-style pastries and desserts are made on the premises. ⊠ *39 Main St.* ☎ *207/338–5888* ⊕ *www.bayrivermarket. com* ⊟ *AE, D, DC, MC, V* ⊙ *Closed Sun.*

$$–$$$ ✕ **Twilight Cafe.** This is a delightful little gourmet place right in the middle of downtown. The restaurant is set in an art gallery, so you have plenty to look at while you are waiting for your dinner. When the weather is nice, you can dine on the patio in the back. Pecan-crusted lobster cakes with pumpkin ginger crème fraîche is a specialty of the house, as are veal chops with mushrooms, and bouillabaisse. ⊠ *72 Main St.* ☎ *207/338–0937* ⊴ *Reservations essential* ⊟ *AE, MC, V* ⊙ *Closed Sun. No lunch.*

★ **$–$$$** ✕ **The Maine Chowder & Steak House.** This large, popular restaurant has been standing watch over the bay for a long time. It's an excellent place for seafood. Ask for a table by a window—the view, particularly at sunset, is spectacular. Lobster, prepared any way you like it, is a specialty, as is the chowder. Favorites include the Lazy Man's Lobster (they crack the shells for you), and the Chowder House Mariner's Platter. ⊠ *139 Searsport Ave. (U.S. 1) between Belfast and Searsport* ☎ *207/338–5225* ⊟ *AE, D, MC, V.*

$–$$$ ✕ **Weathervane.** This is part of a chain of popular seafood restaurants in New England. The restaurant is large, so you shouldn't have to wait long for a table. The food and service are usually good, although things can seem a little rushed in summer. The restaurant sits right on the edge of Belfast Harbor, overlooking the bay, and tugboats are parked outside. The large menu features seafood, pasta, and steaks. A popular menu choice is the Lazy Man's Lobster (they do all the shell-cracking work for you). Fresh seafood is also available to go. ⊠ *1 Main St., Public Landing, at base of Main St.* ☎ *207/338–1777* ⊕ *www.weathervaneseafoods. com* ⊟ *AE, D, MC, V.*

$–$$$ ✕ **Young's Lobster Pound.** The place looks more like a corrugated steel
Fodor'sChoice fish cannery than a restaurant, but this is pure Maine. Young's sits right
★ on the edge of the water, across the river from the Belfast Harbor (cross Veterans Bridge to get here). When you first walk in, you'll see tanks and tanks and tanks of live lobsters of varying size. The traditional meal here is the Shore Dinner: fish or clam chowder; steamed clams or mussels; a 1½ -pound boiled lobster; corn on the cob; and rolls and butter. Order your dinner at the counter then find a table inside, or on the deck. They'll call you when your order is ready. ⊠ *2 Fairview St., go north over U.S. 1 Veterans Bridge, turn right on Mitchell Ave.* ☎ *207/338–1160* ⊟ *AE, D, MC, V* ⊙ *Closed Labor Day–Easter.*

$–$$ ✕ **Darby's Restaurant and Pub.** Darby's is a charming old-fashioned restaurant and bar that seems to have been in Belfast forever and is very popular with the locals. Tin ceilings and a friendly bar create a comfortable atmosphere for the creative casual fare served here. The eclectic menu lists hearty soups and sandwiches as well as dishes with an international flavor. A couple of examples are Darby's monsoon curry, pad thai, and seafood à la Greque. ⊠ *155 High St.* ☎ *207/338–2339* ⊟ *AE, D, MC, V.*

$–$$ ✕ **Dockside Family Restaurant.** One of the best things about this restaurant is its convenience. It's on the main street, less than a block from the harbor. Despite the location, not many of the tables have a view, but Dockside has been here a long time, and the food, especially the seafood, is good. The decor is plain and simple and the emphasis is on family dining, so feel free to bring the whole gang. Don't miss out on the lobster stew; they're famous for it. ⊠ *30 Main St.* ☎ *207/338–6889* ▤ *AE, D, MC, V* ☉ *Closed Mon.*

$–$$ ✕ **Dos Amigos.** This popular Mexican restaurant is much larger than it looks from the outside. It has multiple rooms, which are nearly always filled with people enjoying good food and drinks at reasonable prices. The Smoked Duck Quesadilla is excellent, as are the margaritas. ⊠ *U.S. 1, Northport* ☎ *3 mi south of Belfast, 207/338–5775* ▤ *AE, D, MC, V* ⌂ *Reservations essential* ☉ *No lunch.*

★ **¢–$$** ✕ **Oriental Plaza.** For many years, this was a very popular—mostly with the locals—Chinese restaurant in a little shopping center in Belfast. But in May 2004, they moved to a better and bigger location, on U.S. 1 halfway between Belfast and Searsport. They serve Chinese, American, and Philippine cuisine and are open for breakfast, lunch, and dinner year-round. There's a Chinese lunch buffet daily and a dinner buffet every Wednesday. General Tao's Chicken and the Pupu Platter for two are popular items on the dinner menu. ⊠ *176 Searsport Ave. (U.S. 1)* ☎ *207/338–4444* ▤ *AE, MC, V.*

$ ✕ **Bay Wrap.** This is a good place if you're just looking for a quick and refreshing bite. The small but popular establishment offers an unusual and original variety of wraps. The Wraptor, roast turkey with tarragon-garlic aioli on a bed of greens, tomatoes, and onions, is delicious. The restaurant is downtown, one block off the main street. ⊠ *20 Beaver St.* ☎ *207/338–9757* ▤ *MC, V.*

★ **$$–$$$** ✕▥ **Comfort Inn.** This is the largest motel in the Belfast-Searsport area, and every room overlooks the bay. The spacious rooms are simple but functional in design. The second- and third-floor rooms have private balconies, and the ground-floor rooms have patios. Many people who live in the area feel that the adjoining restaurant, Ocean's Edge ($$–$$$), is the best restaurant around. Food, service, price, and atmosphere all seem to be right. The menu offers a variety of fare, including the lavish Fisherman's Feast, which comes with lobster, crab, clams, scallops, and fish; and the excellent charbroiled filet mignon Oscar, which is topped with asparagus. ⊠ *159 Searsport Ave., U.S. 1 between Belfast and Searsport, 04915* ☎ *207/338–2090 or 800/303–5098* ⊕ *www.comfortinnbelfast.com* ⤵ *83 rooms* ⌂ *Restaurant, cable TV, indoor pool, hot tub, sauna, Internet* ▤ *AE, D, MC, V* ⅋ *CP.*

$–$$$ ✕▥ **Belfast Bay Meadows Inn.** This shingled cottage on 5 meadowed acres overlooking the bay is a relatively new arrival to the Belfast B&B scene. The rooms are bright and airy and decorated in pastel shades, with old-fashioned New England quilts on the beds. Some of the rooms even have their own fireplaces. The inn has a lovely restaurant, named after its accomplished chef, Oliver. One of Oliver's specials is scallop cakes with blood orange salsa. ⊠ *192 Northport Ave., 04915* ☎ *207/338–5715 or 800/335–2370* ⊕ *www.baymeadowsinn.com* ⤵ *19 rooms* ⌂ *Restaurant, cable TV* ▤ *AE, D, MC, V* ⅋ *BP.*

★ $$–$$$ 🖼 **Jeweled Turret Inn.** Turrets, columns, gables, and magnificent wood-work embellish this inn, originally built in 1898 as the home of a local attorney. The inn is named for the jewel-like stained-glass windows in the stairway turret. The gem theme continues in the den, where the ornate rock fireplace is said to include rocks from every state in the Union. Elegant Victorian pieces furnish the rooms: the Opal Room has a marble bath with whirlpool tub in addition to a French armoire and a four-poster bed. ⊠ *40 Pearl St., 04915* ☎ *207/338–2304 or 800/696–2304* ⊕ *www.jeweledturret.com* ⇨ *7 rooms* ♿ *No a/c in some rooms, no room phones, no room TVs, no smoking* ⊟ *AE, MC, V* ⏹ *BP.*

★ $$–$$$ 🖼 **The White House.** This 1840 landmark by Maine architect Calvin Ryder is considered to be one of the most sophisticated examples of Greek-Revival architecture in New England. An eight-sided cupola tops the house; inside are ornate plaster ceiling medallions, Italian marble fireplaces, an elliptical flying staircase, and intricate moldings. Crystal chandeliers, oriental rugs, antiques, and reproduction pieces elegantly decorate the spacious rooms. You can relax in the English garden, in the gazebo, or under the enormous copper beech tree. The people who own this also operate the elegant Bay River Bistro restaurant in downtown Belfast. ⊠ *1 Church St., 04915* ☎ *207/338–1901 or 888/290–1901* 🖷 *207/338–5161* ⊕ *www.mainebb.com* ⇨ *4 rooms, 2 suites* ♿ *Some cable TV, some in-room VCRs; no smoking.* ⊟ *D, MC, V* ⏹ *BP.*

$–$$ 🖼 **Belfast Harbor Inn.** This motel-type inn is ideally situated on U.S. 1 between Belfast and Searsport with 6 acres of oceanfront property. Every room has a beautiful view of the sea across the spacious lawn. The upstairs rooms have private balconies; the lower ones have patios. There is also a nice bridal suite with a king-size bed. The rooms are basic but attractive, and the complimentary continental breakfast is more generous than most, with a lot of fresh fruit and homemade pastries. ⊠ *91 Searsport Ave. (U.S. 1), 04915* ☎ *207/338–2740 or 800/545–8576* ⊕ *www.belfastharborinn.com* ⇨ *61 rooms* ♿ *Cable TV, outdoor pool* ⊟ *AE, D, MC, V* ⏹ *CP.*

$–$$ 🖼 **Colonial Gables Oceanfront Village.** Colonial Gables is on 10 ocean-front acres on U.S. 1 between Belfast and Searsport. The motel and private cottages all offer spectacular ocean views and access to a private sandy beach. The motel rooms are simple but attractive. Cottages have fully equipped kitchenettes and private porches. Activities include nightly campfires on the beach. ⊠ *U.S. 1, 04915* ☎ *207/338–4000 or 800/937–6246* ⊕ *www.colonialgables.com* ⇨ *43 cottages, 13 rooms* ♿ *Some kitchenettes; no a/c in some rooms, no phones in some rooms, no TVs in some rooms* ⊟ *AE, D, MC, V* ⊗ *Closed Nov.–Apr.*

$–$$ 🖼 **Londonderry Inn.** This charming, fully restored farm house was originally built in 1803. The name is appropriate since "Londonderry" was the first name proposed for the town of Belfast. The property includes gardens, fruit trees, a small pond, and tons of bird feeders, which means you might get a peek at some of Maine's wild turkeys here. Several of the rooms have four-poster beds and old-fashioned New England quilts. The formal living room has a fireplace and cozy leather furniture. In the library, you can find more than 200 videos for your evening's diversion. Complimentary beverages and dessert are served in the early evening. ⊠ *133 Belmont Ave. (Route 3), 2 mi from downtown Belfast,*

04915 ☎ 207/338–2763 or 877/529–9566 ⊕ www.londonderry-inn. com ⟿ 5 rooms ⚙ Cable TV, in-room VCRs, refrigerators; no smoking ⊟ AE, D, MC, V ⅋◎⦀ BP.

Nightlife & the Arts

Logos Pub & Grill (⊠ 121 Main St. ☎ 207/338–0300) is a friendly downtown pub with live music on Friday and Saturday. They also operate a comedy club in summer. **The Lookout Pub** (⊠ 37 Front St. ☎ 207/338–8999) offers a 40-foot "Lobster Bar," pub food, gourmet lobster rolls, some of the best burgers in town, and 17 draft beers on tap. They also have pool tables and dancing with live music on the weekends.

The **Colonial Theater** (⊠ 163 High St. ☎ 207/338–1930) is a wonderful old-fashioned movie palace with an elephant on the roof. **Belfast Maskers** (⊠ 43 Front St. ☎ 207/338–9668 ⊕ www.belfastmaskers.org) is a small theater company with its own theater down by the waterfront. Liv Ullman and Margot Kidder have both been hosts here.

Sports & the Outdoors

AERIAL TOURS **Coastal Helicopters** (⊠ 26 Airport Rd., Belfast Airport ☎ 207/338–3755 ⊕ www.950B.com ⊟ MC, V) offers helicopter tours of the coast, where you can see lighthouses, windjammers, and islands. Helicopters are also available for charter to look at coastal real estate.

BOAT TOURS **Belfast Bay Cruises** (⊠ Railroad pier at the harbor ☎ 207/338–1063 ⊕ www.belfastbaycruises.com) offers bay cruises, sometimes with sightings of seals and porpoises. The cruises stop at historic Castine for lunch. A lobstering cruise, on which you'll learn how lobsters are caught, is also available.

From June to September, the **Kathryn B.** (⊠ *Atlantic Coast Schooner Co., 391 Hatchet Mountain Rd., Hope, 04847 ☎ 207/763–4255 or 800/500–6077*) windjammer ship offers three- and six-day cruises along the Penobscot Bay coast from Belfast Harbor. The three-day cruises board either Sunday or Wednesday night and sail the next morning. The six-night cruises board on Sunday and sail the next morning. All meals are included.

Gafia Sailing Charters (🖅 *Box 146, Belfast, ME 04915* ⊠ *Belfast City Landing ☎ 207/323–4800 ⊕ www.sailbelfast.com*) offers day cruises or overnight charters aboard their yacht *Gafia*, a 46-foot cutter ("Gafia" is an acronym for "Get Away From It All"). They also offer a lunch-on-an-island cruise or a lobster dinner cruise.

CURLING **Belfast Curling Club** (⊠ 211 Belmont Ave. (Rte. 3), 3 mi west of Belfast ☎ 207/338–9851) is just about the only place in Maine where you can see curling, and they love visitors. Activities take place throughout the week, November through March. Call for times.

GOLF **Northport Golf Club** (⊠ Bluff Rd. Northport, 4 mi south of Belfast off U.S. 1 ☎ 207/338–2270) has a 9-hole, par-72 layout that was built in 1916. The yardage is 6,087; there is a pro shop and snack bar.

KAYAKING **Water Walker Sea Kayak** (⊠ 152 Lincolnville Ave. ☎ 207/338–6424 ⊕ www.touringkayaks.com) provides guided sea kayak trips among the islands of Penobscot Bay. Paddlers of all levels are welcome. Instructions, rentals, and sales also are available. The owner, Ray Wirth, is an area schoolteacher. **Belfast Kayak Tours** (⊠ Belfast City Pier ☎ 207/382–6204 ⊙ Memorial Day–mid-Sept.) provides a two-hour fully outfitted kayak excursion that includes paddle and safety lessons.

PARKS **Belfast City Park** (⊠ High St., 1 mi east of downtown) has a playground, tennis courts (lighted at night), a baseball diamond, and an outdoor swimming pool with lockers and showers. Use of the park is free, and since it's right on the edge of the sea, it's a wonderful place for a picnic.

Shopping

Belfast is an easy town in which to shop. Nearly all of the interesting little stores are centered around the intersection of Main and High streets. **The Green Store** (⊠ 71 Main St. ☎ 207/338–4045), sells nothing but environmentally friendly products from lightbulbs to clothing. **Colburn Shoe Store** (⊠ 79 Main St. ☎ 207/338–1934 or 877/338–1934) is worth a visit simply because it's the oldest shoe store in America. At one time, the making of shoes was a major industry in Belfast. **The Phoenix Loft Gallery** (⊠ 157 High St. ☎ 207/338–0087 ⊕ www.phoenixloftgallery.com) has an interesting collection of regional and local artists. The **Fertile Mind Book Shop** (⊠ 105 Main St. ☎ 207/338–2498) has all kinds of reading matter, much of it about Maine. At the **Parent Gallery** (⊠ 92 Main St. ☎ 207/338–1553 ⊕ www.nealparent.com), a talented father and daughter have their painting and photographic works displayed. **Coyote Moon** (⊠ 54 Main St. ☎ 207/338–5659) sells things for the body, soul, and mind. **The Purple Baboon** (⊠ 31 Front St. just off Main near the harbor ☎ 207/338–6505) is an unusual shop that sells gifts, collectibles, and souvenirs. The **Shamrock, Thistle & Rose** (⊠ 48 Main St. ☎ 207/338–1864 ⊕ www.shamrockthistlerose.com) sells clothing, jewelry, art, and music from Ireland, Scotland, and England. **All About Games** (⊠ 78 Main St. ☎ 207/338–9984) sells any kind of game you could want, including a "Maine" version of Monopoly.

SHOPPING EN ROUTE One of the first places you come to after you cross the U.S. 1 bridge, heading north toward Searsport, is **Perry's Nuthouse** (⊠ 17 Searsport Ave. [U.S. 1] ☎ 207/338–1630). Perry's has been here since 1927, and the building dates back to 1850. The delicious treats for sale include nuts from around the world, homemade fudge, local honeys, and Maine maple syrup. Native American handicrafts are also available.

Mainely Pottery (⊠ 181 Searsport Ave., [U.S. 1] ☎ 207/338–1108 ⊕ www.mainelypottery.com) offers outstanding pottery from 30 Maine potters. **Yankee Trader Gift Shop** (⊠ 169 Searsport Ave. [U.S. 1] ☎ 207/338–2475) offers a wide variety of gifts, many of them made in Maine.

Festivals & Events

Belfast Bay Festival (☎ 207/338–5719 ▣ Free) is the biggest event of the summer in Belfast. It takes place in mid-July and includes a parade, a midway, lots of food—including a down home barbecue—and fireworks. It all takes place in Belfast's City Park on Northport Avenue.

Arts in the Park (⊕ www.belfastmaine.org/artsinthepark ✉ Free) takes place in mid-July down by the harbor, and features the works of more than 70 Maine-area artists.

Belfast Summer Nights (☎ 207/338–8448) features a variety of interesting live music events every Thursday evening, from 5:30 to 7:30, for 11 weeks during the summer. It takes place at the park down by the harbor and is free of charge.

en route

Heading north from Belfast on U.S. 1, you will go over a modern bridge with probably the greatest view (especially at sunrise or sunset) of any bridge in Maine: the beautiful Belfast harbor, filled with sailing ships. Beneath you runs the Passagassawakeag River. Don't try to pronounce it—rumor has that it's an Indian word meaning: You can't pronounce this.

Moose Point State Park (✉ U.S. 1 between Belfast and Searsport ☎ 207/548–2882) is ideal for easy hikes and picnics overlooking Penobscot Bay.

Searsport

❽ *6 mi northeast of Belfast, 57 mi northeast of Augusta.*

Searsport is well known as the Antique Capital of Maine, and with good reason: the Antique Mall alone contains 70 separate dealers. But antiques are not the town's only point of interest; Searsport also has a rich history of shipbuilding and seafaring.

In the early to mid-1800s, there were 10 shipbuilding facilities in Searsport. The population of the town was about 1,000 people larger than it is today because of the ready availability of jobs. By the mid-1800s, Searsport was home to more than 200 sailing ship captains, more than any other town in America, according to the Penobscot Marine Museum. It was commonly said then that when a captain took a cargo to Hong Kong, if he walked down the main street, he was more likely to meet someone from Searsport than from China.

Except for a few rotting pilings down at the waterfront, the shipbuilding industry is gone now. It all disappeared after the invention of the steam engine and the growth of the steamship business. Steamships were larger, could carry more cargo, and were more efficient and safer. But thanks to those old shipyards, Searsport still has the second deepest port on the coast of Maine, after Portland. If you read the Tom Clancy novel *The Hunt for Red October*, or saw the movie, you may recall that the men on the stolen submarine were looking on a sea chart for a little-used deepwater port on the Atlantic Coast where they could hide out submerged and undetected. They found it at "Searsport."

need a break?

For a delicious selection of homemade pastries and coffee, stop in at **Coastal Coffee** (✉ 25 Main St.) right in the heart of downtown, open 6 AM–2 PM.

CloseUp

A VANISHED INDUSTRY

I N THE MID-1800S, THERE WAS A MAJOR INDUSTRY IN MAINE *that gave work to thousands of men each winter. The product of this industry was so valuable that it was shipped around the world in the great tall-masted schooners. The industry no longer exists, although the product does. Can you guess what this profitable product and industry was? Believe it or not, it was ice. During Maine's freezing cold winter months, loggers and farmers who couldn't do their normal work would go out to Maine's freshwater rivers and lakes and cut ice from the frozen waters. Using string lines, the men would section the ice off into 2-by-4-foot rectangles. Then they would use one-handled saws to cut the ice into blocks, weighing about 200 pounds each. The blocks of ice would be loaded onto horse-drawn sleds and taken to an ice house. Finally, the ice would be loaded aboard a schooner for transport. They packed the ice in straw and sawdust to help insulate it, but they still lost about 20% to melt. The other 80% could be sold for a generous profit all over the world. On the way back, they could even sell the dried-out straw. There are pictures and examples of tools left from the ice industry on display at the Penobscot Marine Museum, in Searsport.*

The seafaring history of Searsport can best be observed at Maine's largest maritime museum, the Penobscot Marine Museum. It's also evident in the many former sea captains' homes along U.S. 1, many of which have been converted to bed-and-breakfasts. Searsport's downtown area is only a block long and can easily be explored in less than an hour.

★ The **Penobscot Marine Museum** is dedicated to the history of Penobscot Bay and the maritime history of Maine. The exhibits, artifacts, souvenirs, and paintings are displayed in a unique setting of seven historic buildings, including two sea captains' houses, and five other buildings in an original seaside village. The various exhibits provide fascinating documentation of the region's seafaring way of life. The museum's outstanding collection of marine art includes the largest gathering in the country of works by Thomas and James Buttersworth. Also of note are photos of local sea captains; a collection of China-trade merchandise; artifacts of life at sea (including lots of scrimshaw); navigational instruments; tools from the area's history of logging, granite cutting, fishing, and ice cutting; treasures collected by seafarers from around the globe; and models of famous ships. The museum also has a rotating exhibit every year on a different theme. Two recent themes have been "Pirates!" and "Lobstahs!" Next to the museum, you can find the Penobscot Marine Museum Store, where you can buy anything nautical. ⊠ *5 E. Main St. (U.S. 1)* ☎ *207/548–2529* ⊕ *www.penobscotmarinemuseum. org* ⊠ *$8* ⊙ *Memorial Day–mid-Oct., Mon.–Sat. 10–5, Sun. noon–5.*

off the beaten path

SEARS ISLAND – This is the largest uninhabited island off the coast of Maine, measuring some 940 acres. The forested island is about a mile long and a half-mile wide and is home to a variety of wildlife, plants, and birds. Although you cannot drive on the island—you have to walk across a causeway to get here—a paved road bisects the island, making it an excellent place for a hike or a picnic. The 9-mi shoreline perimeter also makes an excellent hike. You might even see seals sunning themselves on the rocks. Camping is not allowed. ⊹ *Take U.S. 1 north from Searsport and turn right on Sears Island Rd.* ⊠ *Free.*

Where to Stay & Eat

★ **$$$–$$$$** ✕ **The Rhumb Line.** This upscale restaurant in an 18th-century sea captain's home delivers fine dining, with formally attired waitstaff and excellent food. Specials include pan-seared peppered swordfish with Vidalia onion picalilly, horseradish-crusted salmon with remoulade sauce, and grilled rack of lamb with blackberry mint vinegar. ⊠ *200 E. Main St.* ☎ *207/548–2600* ⊕ *www.therhumblinerestaurant.com* ⚐ *Reservations essential* ▭ *MC, V* ⊙ *No lunch.*

$–$$$ ✕ **The Chocolate Grille.** The Grille is the largest restaurant in the Searsport area, so you almost never have to wait for a table. The menu includes sandwiches, burgers, pizza, and delicious desserts. Dinner specials include chicken with wild mushrooms and marsala, garlic-and-herb-stuffed prime rib, and pan-seared duckling. The large bar is a popular spot for meeting friends or watching sports events. As to the name of the restaurant, the owner says he wanted to combine the two most popular words in dining: *grille* and *chocolate.* ⊠ *1 E. Main St. (U.S. 1)* ☎ *207/548– 2555* ⊕ *www.chocolategrille.com* ▭ *AE, D, MC, V.*

$–$$ ✕ **Anglers.** This little restaurant has been around for a long time and has a large local following. It can be a little hard to get into on a busy night, but it's worth the wait. The service is friendly—this is the kind of place where the waitresses call you "Hon"—the prices are reasonable, and the seafood is good. ⊠ *U.S. 1, 1 mi north of downtown* ☎ *207/548–2405* ⚐ *Reservations essential* ▭ *D, MC, V.*

$–$$ ✕ **The Mariner.** This cozy little spot is in the very heart of downtown. The simple atmosphere is publike, with good drinks and good, inexpensive food. In summer, lobster and crabmeat rolls are on the menu, along with the year-round selections of burgers, sandwiches, and of course, lobster stew. Dinner entrées include fried jumbo shrimp and fried haddock. ⊠ *23 E. Main St.* ☎ *207/548–6600* ▭ *MC, V.*

$$–$$$ ⊡ **Watchtide . . . By the Sea.** This lovely inn was built in 1794, and the

Fodor's Choice ★

first owner of the property was Henry Knox, George Washington's Secretary of War. Since then, it has been a favorite of many visitors, among them Eleanor Roosevelt, who stayed here many times. The house is listed on the National Register of Historic Places, as the College Club Inn. All of the rooms are furnished in New England style, some with brass beds, most with quilts, and some with fireplaces. There is also a honeymoon suite with a Jacuzzi and a fireplace. The sumptuous breakfast is served on a beautiful sunporch overlooking the sea. ✉ *190 W. Main St. (U.S. 1), 04974* ☎ *207/548–6575 or 800/698–6575* ⊕ *www.watchtide.com* ☞ *5 rooms* ♿ *Gift shop; no room phones, no room TVs, no smoking* ⊟ *AE, D, MC, V* ⦿ *BP.*

★ $–$$ ⊞ **Carriage House Inn.** This stately Victorian mansion is listed on the National Register of Historic Places. A rambling white clapboard home, it was built in 1874 by one of Searsport's many clipper ship captains, John McGilvery. Later, it became the home of the impressionist painter Waldo Pierce. Pierce was close friends with Ernest Hemingway, whom he met in the ambulance corp, and the two met here often. One can only imagine what their conversations in the lavish library must have been like. The house is filled with heirlooms from the 19th-century era of the great clipper ships, and there is a solid stone fireplace in the downstairs den. ✉ *120 E. Main St., 04974* ☎ *207/548–2289* ⊕ *www. carriagehouseinmaine.com* ☞ *3 rooms* ♿ *Library; no a/c, no room phones, no room TVs, no smoking* ⊟ *AE, D, MC, V* ⦿ *BP.*

★ $–$$ ⊞ **Homeport Inn.** This 1861 inn, a former sea captain's home on U.S. 1, provides an opulent Victorian environment that might put you in the mood to rummage through the nearby antiques and treasure shops. The back rooms on the first level have private decks and views of the bay, which you can walk down to. Families often stay in the housekeeping cottages, which are even nearer to the bay. ✉ *121 E. Main St., 04974* ☎ *207/548–2259 or 800/742–5814* ⊕ *www.homeportbnb.com* ☞ *10 rooms, 7 with bath; 3 cottages* ♿ *Some pets allowed in cottages; no a/c, no room phones, no room TVs, no smoking.* ⊟ *AE, D, MC, V* ⦿ *BP.*

$–$$$ ⊞ **Inn Britannia.** Each of the rooms here is named after a place in England—such as London, the Cotswolds, Warwick, and Dover—and they are all decorated in an elegant modern British style, with lots of bright colors. Some of the rooms have fireplaces, and some have four-poster beds. In addition to the beautiful gardens, the inn has the only Backyard Wildlife Habitat on Maine's Mid-Coast that has been certified by the National Wildlife Foundation. ✉ *132 W. Main St. (U.S. 1), 04974* ☎ *207/548–2007 or 866/466–2748* ⊕ *www.innbritannia.com* ☞ *8 rooms* ♿ *Cable TV, some pets allowed; no a/c, no room phones, no TV in some rooms, no smoking* ⊟ *D, MC, V* ⦿ *BP.*

¢–$ ⊞ **Light's Motel.** This is a basic budget motel. The rooms are small but clean, and there is a good restaurant, Angler's, right next door. ✉ *215 E. Main St. (U.S. 1), 04974* ☎ *207/548–7299* ☞ *14 rooms* ⊟ *D, MC, V.*

★ $ ⛺ **Searsport Shores Ocean Camping.** This campsite sits right on the edge of the ocean, and offers spectacular views from most of its sites. It has 120 sites on 40 acres for RVs and tents. Also offered are attractive gardens, nature trails, art classes, and activities for the kids. ✉ *216 W. Main St. (U.S. 1), 04974* ☎ *207/548–6059* ⊕ *www.campocean.com* ♿ *Flush toilets, partial hookups, drinking water, guest laundry, showers, fire pits, picnic tables, public telephone, play area, private beach, kayak rentals, lobster bakes, gift shop* ⊟ *D, MC, V* ☉ *Closed Nov.–Apr.*

Festivals & Events

The **Lobster Boat Races** are an annual series of events that take place in the major fishing communities (eight of them) up and down the Penobscot Bay. The race in Searsport, the final one of the season, is one of the best. The original intention of the races was to give lobstermen an annual way to blow off a little steam and to show off their boats and abilities. Thanks to the American spirit of obsessive competition, however, some boatmen in recent years have had high-powered lobster boats constructed specifically for these races. They'll burn up an expensive engine and swamp other nearby boats just to win the competition and a $50 trophy. "Bragging rights," it's called. But hey, it's all in the spirit of fun, and for observers, it's a lot of fun. The Searsport race usually takes place the last Sunday in August at the town pier at the end of Steamboat Avenue. Just look for the posters around town. There's no charge to watch the race, and everyone—especially the boatmen—turns it into a big party.

Sports & the Outdoors

FISHING The Searsport Town Landing, at the end of Steamboat Avenue, provides several floats where you can fish for mackerel or, occasionally, stripers. Kids like to do a little crabbing with bait at the end of a line here as well. Shore fishing can be done at the Sears Island Causeway, at the end of Sears Island Road, off U.S. 1. **Penobscot Bay Outfitters** (⊠ 118 Nickerson Rd. ☎ 207/338–1883 ⊕ www.seaduck.net) offers fishing charters on the bay.

GOLF The **Searsport Pines Golf Course** (⊠ 240 Mt. Ephraim Rd. ☎ 207/548–2854) is a 9-hole public course just west of town. They also have a pro for golf lessons.

Shopping

The **Penobscot Marine Museum Store** (⊠ 40 E. Main St. ☎ 207/548–0334 ⊕ www.penobscotmarinemuseum.org) is right next to the museum and has a large collection of pottery, paintings, books, and ship paraphernalia. The store is closed from November through April. **The Grasshopper Shop** (⊠ 37 E. Main St. ☎ 207/548–2244) is devoted to clothing, jewelry, and Maine-made gifts. **Cronin & Murphy Fine Art** (⊠ 36 E. Main St. ☎ 207/548–0073) features 20th-century paintings, art, pottery, and mission furniture. **Left Bank Books** (⊠ 21 E. Main St. ☎ 207/548–6400) is a relatively new arrival to the Searsport shopping scene. It's in a historic old brick building that was the home of Searsport's first bank back in 1840. Although the shop is small, it displays 6,000 books in the categories of fiction, nonfiction, biography, history, travel, and children's fare. **Bluejacket Shipcrafters** (⊠ 160 E. Main St. ☎ 207/548–9970 ⊕ www.bluejacketinc.com) is the largest model ship company in the United States.

Boat lovers should stop at **Hamilton Marine** (⊠ 155 E. Main St. ☎ 207/548–6302 or 800/639–2715 ⊕ www.hamiltonmarine.com). The store sells anything and everything related to boats, from the traditional bronze hardware to the latest in electronics. They also have a large collection of marine books, gifts, and maps. **Penobscot Books & Gallery** (⊠ 164 W. Main St. ☎ 207/548–6490) carries nearly 40,000 books, but specializes in books about fine art and architecture. From U.S. 1 you can't miss this place—it's huge and yellow. The store is closed on Monday.

More than 70 craft dealers show their wares at **Silkweeds Country and Victorian Gifts** (⊠ 191 E. Main St. [U.S. 1] ☎ 207/548–6501), which is part of a chain. The store is large and specializes in Christmas goodies among other things. The many varieties of homemade fudge are delicious. If you are looking for some live lobsters to cook up on your own and a nice wine to go with them, you cannot go wrong at Searsport's privately owned large and varied market, **Tozier's** (⊠ 220 E. Main St. ☎ 207/548–6220). They have lobsters in the tank, sandwiches made to order, excellent pizza, and a fine variety of wines.

ANTIQUES   In Searsport, shopping usually implies antiques. In summer there's a large number of flea market–type stalls all along U.S. 1 a mile or so north of downtown.

The biggest collection of antiques is in the **Searsport Antique Mall** (⊠ 149 E. Main St. [U.S. 1] ☎ 207/548–2640), which has more than 70 dealers. In the very heart of town, **Captain Tinkham's Emporium** (⊠ 34 E. Main St. ☎ 207/548–6465) offers antiques, collectibles, old books, magazines, records, paintings, and prints. Hundreds of teddy bears and antiques can be found at **Cranberry Hollow** (⊠ 157 W. Main St. ☎ 207/548–2647). The owner even makes custom bears from old fur coats. **Pumpkin Patch Antiques** (⊠ 15 W. Main St. ☎ 207/548–6047) displays such items as quilts, nautical memorabilia, and painted and wood furniture from about 20 dealers. It's open April through Thanksgiving or by appointment.

en route   As you head north on U.S. 1 from Searsport, a detour at the little town of Stockton Springs will take you to the **Fort Point State Park & Lighthouse** (⊠ Cape Jellison ☎ 207/567–3356). This lovely park sits on a peaceful peninsula jutting into the bay. This is a delightful place for a picnic and there are many nice walks through the woods. The 1837 lighthouse is open by appointment only.

Maine is famous for its blueberries, one of the most important crops in the state. In August and September, you can pick your own blueberries at **Staples Homestead** (⊠ 1194 Cape Jellison Rd., Stockton Springs ☎ 207/567–3393). This farm has been in the same family since 1838. Call first for directions.

The **Old Winterport Commercial House** (⊠ 114 Main St. [U.S. 1], Winterport ☎ 207/223–5854 ⊕ www.antiquesandreusables.com), on the road from Searsport to Bucksport, is worth a stop. They have 3,200 square feet of American and European furniture, antiques, and curios.

Bucksport

 9 mi north of Searsport via U.S. 1.

The narrow but long Waldo-Hancock suspension bridge, spanning the Penobscot River, welcomes visitors to Bucksport. The bridge was built in 1931 and, at this writing, was in the process of being replaced. If you look to your left as you cross the bridge, you can see the huge and sprawling International Paper Co., the largest employer in the area. Tours of the factory are available. For more information call 207/469–1700.

Bucksport was founded in 1763 by Jonathan Buck. Buck was a Puritan who hated witchcraft and actually sentenced a local woman, who was thought to be a witch, to death. Legend has it that before she was hanged, she cast a curse upon him, saying that he would never escape her presence, even in his grave.

Buck died in 1795 and was buried in a cemetery east of Bucksport. A monument to honor the founder of the town was erected at the gravesite in 1852. As the monument weathered, an image in the shape of a woman's leg began to form under his name. You can see her leg on his stone to this day.

🐾 **Fort Knox State Park** is not the Fort Knox with all the gold in it, but it is worth a visit. The largest fort in Maine, Fort Knox was built between 1844 and 1869 when the British were disputing the borderline between Maine and New Brunswick. The fort was intended to protect the Penobscot River Valley from British naval attack. The fort never saw any actual fighting but it was used for troop training and garrison during the Civil War and the Spanish-American War. Visitors are welcome to explore the fort's passageways and many rooms. Guided tours are available during the summer season. ⊠ *Rte. 174, take Waldo-Hancock Bridge south across river, turn right at Rte. 174, follow signs* ☎ *207/469–6553* ⊕ *www.fortknox.maineguide.com* 💰 *$3* ⊙ *May–Oct., daily 8:30–dusk.*

Where to Stay & Eat

$$ ✕ **MacLeod's Restaurant.** There are not many places to eat in Bucksport, so MacLeod's, right across the street from the Best Western motel, is probably your best option. The menu is impressive for a small-town place, and includes dishes such as raspberry roasted duck and a seafood dinner called the Captain's Boat. ⊠ *51 Main St.* ☎ *207/469–3963* ⊟ *D, MC, V* ⊙ *No lunch.*

$–$$ 🏨 **Jed Prouty Best Western Motor Inn.** This riverfront motel is 1 mi from Fort Knox State Park. Rooms are basic but clean and comfortable. There is no restaurant in the motel, but MacLeod's is right across the street. ⊠ *52 Main St., 04416* ☎ *207/469–3113* 🖷 *207/469–3113* ⊕ *www.bestwestern.com* ⮡ *40 rooms* ⚒ *In-room data ports, minibars, cable TV, no-smoking rooms* ⊟ *AE, D, MC, V.*

en route Halfway between BuUcksport and Ellsworth, an abandoned chicken barn has been converted into **The Big Chicken Barn Books & Antiques** (⊠ 1768 Bucksport Rd. [U.S. 1] ☎ 207/667–7308 ⊕ www.bigchickenbarn.com). Antiques, collectibles, and thousands of books cover 21,000 square feet of retail space. It's worth a stop; it's even worth a detour.

Bangor

10 *133 mi northeast of Portland, 20 mi northwest of Bucksport off U.S. 15, 46 mi west of Bar Harbor.*

The second largest city in Maine, Bangor is about 20 mi from the coast and is the unofficial capital of northern Maine. Back in the 19th century, its most important product and export was lumber from the state's vast North Woods. Bangor's location right on the Penobscot River helped to make it the largest lumber port in the world. Today, a 31-foot-tall statue of the legendary lumberman Paul Bunyan stands in front of the Bangor Auditorium.

Lumber is no longer at the heart of Bangor's economy, but Maine's second city (after Portland) has thrived in other ways. Because of its airport, Bangor has become a gateway to Mount Desert Island, Bar Harbor, and Acadia National Park. The downtown area is small, but still you can find a number of interesting shops there. For serious shopping, head for the Bangor Mall, out on Hogan Road.

Bangor is also home to author Stephen King, who lives in an old Victorian house notable for its bat-winged iron gate, on West Broadway. King and his wife, Tabitha, are active members of the community and contribute generously to local charities, the arts, and education.

The **Maine Discovery Museum** opened in 2001 as the largest children's museum in the state. It has three floors of interactive and hands-on exhibits. Kids can explore Maine's ecosystem in Nature Trails, travel to foreign countries in Passport to the World, and walk through Maine's literary classics in Booktown. ⊠ *74 Main St.* ☎ *207/262–7200* ⊕ *www.mainediscoverymuseum.org* ⊠ *$5.50* ☉ *Tues.–Thurs. and Sat. 9:30–5, Fri. 9:30–8, Sun. 11–5.*

The **Bangor Museum & Center for History** offers a history of Bangor in exhibits and photos. Some of the more interesting exhibits are those of period clothing, a re-creation of a Victorian parlor, and some Native American artifacts. ⊠ *6 State St.* ☎ *207/942–1900* ⊕ *www.bangormuseum.org* ⊠ *Free* ☉ *Tues.–Fri. 10–4, Sat. noon–4.*

The **Cole Land Transportation Museum** chronicles the history of transportation in Maine through historical photographs and more than 200 vehicles. ⊠ *405 Perry Rd.* ☎ *207/990–3600* ⊕ *www.colemuseum.org* ⊠ *$5* ☉ *May–mid-Nov., daily 9–5.*

Where to Eat

$–$$$$ ✕ **Weathervane.** This large seafood restaurant is part of a well-known chain in New England. The fried lobster, stuffed haddock, and Lazy Man's Lobster are favorites. ⊠ *710 Wilson St., Brewer, across the bridge from Bangor* ☎ *207/989–4232* ☰ *AE, D, MC, V.*

$$–$$$ ✕ **Thistle's.** Paintings by local artists adorn the walls in this bright storefront restaurant. The diverse menu includes entrées such as Argentinian steak with chimichurri sauce, pickled ginger salmon picatta, and roast duckling. Musicians often perform during dinner. ⊠ *175 Exchange St.* ☎ *207/945–5480* ☰ *MC, V* ☉ *Closed Sun.*

★ **$-$$$** ✕ **Guinness & Porcelli's.** You'll find Italian fare and Irish hospitality at this popular dinner spot. The restaurant is easy to find since it's right on the main drag (U.S. 1A) as you enter town. One of the specials is veal shiitake saltimbocca. ⊠ *735 Main St.* ☎ *207/947–2300* ⚐ *Reservations essential* ☱ *AE, D, MC, V* ⊘ *No lunch.*

$-$$ ✕ **Momma Baldacci's Italian Restaurant.** This large restaurant was started about 40 years ago by the grandparents of Maine's governor (at this writing), John Baldacci. The Baldacci family still runs the restaurant and it has a huge local clientele. The fare is Italian-American; the two most popular dishes are homemade lasagna and veal parmigiana. ⊠ *12 Alden St.* ☎ *207/945–5813* ⚐ *Reservations essential* ☱ *AE, D, MC, V.*

Where to Stay

Large chain hotels with standard rooms and amenities in Bangor include the **Holiday Inn** (⊕ www.ichotelsgroup.com), **Ramada Inn** (⊕ www.bangorramada.com), and **Motel 6** (⊕ www.atmotel6.com). Hotels near the airport include: the **Four Points Sheraton** (⊕ www.fourpoints.com), which is connected to Bangor International Airport via a skywalk; the **Fairfield Inn by Marriott** (⊕ www.fairfieldinn.com); and the **Days Inn** (⊕ www.daysinn.com).

$$-$$$$ 🏨 **The Lucerne Inn.** This is one of the most famous and respected inns in

Fodor'sChoice New England. Nestled in the mountains, the Lucerne overlooks beau-
★ tiful Phillips Lake. The inn was established in 1814, and in keeping with that history, every room is furnished with antiques. The rooms all have a view of the lake, a wood-burning fireplace, and a whirlpool tub; some have wet bars, refrigerators, and balconies as well. There's a golf course directly across the street. The inn's restaurant is nearly as famous as the inn and draws many of the local people for its lavish Sunday Brunch Buffet. The traditional dinner among guests is the boiled Maine lobster. The inn is 15 minutes outside of Bangor. ⊠ *Rte. 1A, 15 min east of Bangor* ⛫ *R.R. 3, Box 540, Dedham 04429* ☎ *207/843–5123 or 800/325–5123* 🖷 *207/843–6138* ⊕ *www.lucerneinn.com* ➴ *31 rooms, 4 suites* ⚐ *Restaurant, cable TV, fireplaces, whirlpools, pool, lounge, meeting rooms, no-smoking rooms* ☱ *MC, V* � CP.*

$-$$ 🏨 **Best Western Black Bear Inn.** This hotel is close to the University of Maine at Orono, as well as the Bangor Mall. The rooms are large and airy with king-size beds. Some of the rooms have balconies. ⊠ *4 Godfrey Dr., 04473, Exit 51 off I–95 going north* ☎ *207/866–7120* ⊕ *www.blackbearinnorono.com* ➴ *68 rooms* ⚐ *Cable TV, gym, sauna, meeting rooms, some pets allowed* ☱ *AE, D, MC, V* ⦿ CP.

$-$$ 🏨 **Best Western White House Inn.** Right beside I–95, this motel sits on 40 acres of land and is family-owned. All of the rooms are large, bright, and airy. Some have fireplaces, and a few on the third floor have cathedral ceilings; ask about them. ⊠*155 Littlefield Ave., 04401, Exit 44 off I–95* ☎*207/862–3737 or 800/937–8376* ⊕*www.bestwestern.com/whitehouseinnbangor* ➴ *66 rooms* ⚐ *Cable TV, refrigerators, pool, sauna, lounge, laundry services, Internet, some pets allowed* ☱ *AE, D, MC, V* ⦿ CP.

$-$$ 🏨 **The Charles Inn.** This hotel has a great location in an old building on West Market Square, right downtown. The somewhat small rooms are furnished in an elegant, Victorian-like style, many with four-poster canopied beds. The hotel has a free airport car service, which transports you to and from the airport in a gray limousine. ⊠ *20 Broad St., 04401* ☎ *207/992–2820* ⊕ *www.thecharlesinn.com* ⌁ *32 rooms* ⌂ *Cable TV, some pets allowed* ☐ *D, MC, V* ⦿ *CP.*

Festivals & the Arts

The **Bangor Symphony Orchestra** (⊠ 44 Central St. ☎ 207/942–5555 or 800/639–3221) performs at the Bangor Opera House from September through mid-May. The **Penobscot Theatre Company** (⊠ 131 Main St. ☎ 207/942–3333 ⊕ www.ptc.maineguide.com) stages live classic and contemporary plays from October to May. From mid-July to mid-August, the company hosts the **Maine Shakespeare Festival** on the riverfront. Admission to the festival is $17 for adults, $9 for children under 12.

Fodor'sChoice   **The American Folk Festival** (☎ 207/992–2630 or 800/916–6673 ⊕ www.
★ americanfolkfestival.com), formerly known as the National Folk Festival, is the biggest event of the summer, attracting thousands of people. The three-day, multistage event takes place on the waterfront and includes traditional folk performers from around the country. Events include a rich array of music and dance performances, workshops, storytelling, parades, craft exhibits, and tons of food. Music may include blues, gospel, jazz, bluegrass, country-western, Cajun, mariachi, honky-tonk, and zydeco. Some of the craft exhibits include pottery, blacksmithing, quilting, musical instrument making, boat building, and wood carving, as well as a variety of crafts from the Native American groups in Maine. The festival is held at the end of August, and admission is free.

Golf

The **Bangor Municipal Golf Course,** a public club, has both an 18-hole course and a 9-hole course. Both courses are fairly flat and easy to walk. Fees are $27 for 18 holes, $13 for nine. Golf carts are available for an additional fee. ⊠ *278 Webster Ave.* ☎ *207/941–0232* 🖷 *207/947–3157.*

The **Penobscot Valley Country Club** has an 18-hole golf course designed by Donald Ross. Facilities include a dining room, grill room, snack bar, and pro shop. Guests are allowed to play the course, with or without a sponsor, up to four times per calendar year. Guest fees are $60 without a golf cart, $75 with. ⊠ *Orono, I–95 north to Exit 50, follow signs* ☎ *207/866–2060* ⊕ *www.penobscotvalleycc.com* ⊙ *Closed mid-Oct.–mid-Apr.*

Shopping

The **Bangor Mall** (⊠ Hogan Rd., Exits 48A and 49 off I–95 ☎ 207/947–7333 ⊕ www.bangormall.com) has the best shopping in the area. Anchor stores include Filene's, JCPenney, Sears Roebuck, and Dick's Sporting Equipment. Ruby Tuesdays in the mall is a good place for lunch.

PENOBSCOT BAY A TO Z

To research prices, get advice from other travelers, and book travel arrangements, visit www.fodors.com.

AIRPORTS

Bangor International is the major airport in the Penobscot Bay area. You can access the airport from I–95.

🔢 **Bangor International Airport** ✉ 287 Godfrey Blvd., Bangor ☎ 207/947-0384 or 866/359-2264 ⊕ www.flybangor.com.

AIRPORT TRANSFERS There is no public transportation available from the airport, but there are plenty of taxis. Major car rental companies at the airport include Avis, Budget, Hertz, and National.

🔢 **Avis** ☎ 207/947-8383 ⊕ www.avis.com. **Budget** ☎ 207/945-9429 ⊕ www.budget. com. **Hertz** ☎ 207/945-5519 ⊕ www.hertz.com. **National** ☎ 207/947-0158 ⊕ www. nationalcar.com.

CARRIERS American, Delta, Northwest, and US Airways service Bangor International to and from the key cities of Boston, Albany, Philadelphia, Baltimore, and Portsmouth, as well as St. John in Nova Scotia, Canada.

🔢 **American Airlines** ☎ 800/433-7300 ⊕ www.aa.com. **Delta** ☎ 800/221-1212 ⊕ www.delta.com. **Northwest** ☎ 800/225-2525 ⊕ www.nwa.com. **US Airways** ☎ 800/ 428-4322 ⊕ www.usairways.com.

BUS TRAVEL

The Penobscot Bay area has virtually no public transportation, but there are small taxi companies in each town. The bay area does have a luxury (snacks, drinks, movies) bus service, Concord Trailways, which runs two buses a day from the University of Maine, at Orono, to Logan Airport in Boston, with a stop in Portland, and two buses a day starting from the same point but going down coastal U.S. 1 to Boston and Logan Airport. The bus stops at all major towns along the way. There is also a bus terminal in Bangor where you will find Greyhound and Vermont Transit bus lines, both of which have three buses a day heading south to such destinations as Portland, Boston, and New York City.

🔢 **Concord Trailways** ✉ 1039 Union St. ☎ 207/945-4000. **Greyhound Bus Lines** ✉ 158 Main St. ☎ 207/872-5000. **Vermont Transit Lines** ✉ 158 Main St. ☎ 207/945-3000.

CAR TRAVEL

Major roads going near or through the Penobscot Bay area are U.S. 1 and, for faster travel, Interstate 95. Historic U.S. 1 is a two-lane highway. Despite its narrowness, it is a fairly good road in summer. If you are coming up I–95 and want to get off to begin your coastal tour in the Penobscot Bay area, take the Augusta exit and follow the signs to U.S. 1.

In winter the Maine Department of Transportation keeps most major roads plowed and graveled. However, you should always drive with caution in snowy conditions and carry a survivor kit, including water, extra food, warm blankets, a flashlight, and a cell phone.

🔢 **Maine State Police** ☎ 800/452-4664. **Maine Turnpike Authority** ☎ 800/698-7747. **Road Conditions** 207/624-3595 or 511 from a cellular phone.

EMERGENCIES

In an emergency, dial 911.

🔢 **24-Hour Medical Care Eastern Maine Medical Center** ✉ 489 State St., Bangor ☎ 207/973-7000. **St. Joseph Hospital** ✉ 360 Broadway, Bangor ☎ 207/262-1000. **Waldo County General Hospital** ✉ 130 Northport Ave., Belfast ☎ 207/338-2500 or 800/649-2536. **Penobscot Bay Medical Center** ✉ U.S. 1, Rockport ☎ 207/596-8000.

MEDIA

Each major town along the Penobscot Bay has its own traditional weekly newspaper (Courier Publications in Rockland owns many of them), but the major daily along the coast is the *Bangor Daily News*. You can also usually find the *Portland Telegram, Boston Globe, New York Times,* and *USA Today* at major supermarkets or convenience stores.

You can access all of the major networks, such as NBC (WLBZ channel 2), CBS (WABI channel 6), and ABC (WMTW channel 8) along the coast, and most hotels and motels are equipped with cable. You can access National Public Radio (90.9 FM), and Voice of Maine (103.9 FM). If you like music from the Big Band era, try 105.5 on your FM dial.

VISITOR INFORMATION

🚩 **Rockland-Thomaston Area Chamber of Commerce** ☎ 800/562-2529 ⊕ www.therealmaine.com. **Camden-Rockport-Lincolnville Chamber of Commerce** ☎ 800/223-5459 ⊕ www.camdenme.org. **Belfast Area Chamber of Commerce** ☎ 207/338-5900 ⊕ www.belfastme.org. **Searsport Chamber of Commerce** ☎ 207/548-0173 ⊕ www.searsportme.com. **Greater Bangor Convention & Visitors Bureau** ✉ 519 Main St., Box 1443 04401 ☎ 207/947-0307 ⊕ www.bangorregion.com.

THE BLUE HILL PENINSULA

5

GO TO SLEEP WITH AN OCEAN VIEW
at the Castine Inn ⇨*p.177*

TRAWL FOR POTTERY TREASURES
at the galleries in Blue Hill ⇨*p.181*

WATCH THE BOATS
from a lighthouse tower
at First Light Bed & Breakfast ⇨*p.180*

COUNT BLUE HERONS & BALD EAGLES
at the Holbrook Island Sanctuary ⇨*p.184*

LEARN THE ART OF THE BLACKSMITH
at Haystack Mountain School of Crafts ⇨*p.186*

By Lelah Cole If you want to explore art galleries, savor some exquisite meals, or simply enjoy a slower pace of life, you should be quite content on the Blue Hill Peninsula. The area is not at all like its coastal neighbors, as very little of it has been developed. There aren't any must-see attractions to top your to-do list, so you are left to investigate the area on your own terms, seeking out the artists, restaurants, or views that interest you most.

The peninsula, approximately 16 mi wide and 20 mi long, juts out into Penobscot Bay. Not far from the mainland are the islands of Deer Isle, Little Deer Isle, and Stonington. A twisting network of roads rolls over fields and around coves, linking the towns of Blue Hill, Brooksville, Sedgwick, and Brooklin. This is a place to meander as you take in views of open fields reaching to the water's edge or, around the next bend, a tree-shaded farmhouse with an old stone wall marking the property line. No wonder painters, photographers, sculptors, and other artists are drawn to the area. You can find more than 20 galleries on Deer Isle and Stonington, and at least half as many on the mainland.

Although the area lacks the mountains, lakes, ponds, and vast quantity of trails of neighboring Mount Desert Island, you can still find local vendors who will rent bicycles and, beyond the peninsula, an archipelago of uninhabited islands known as Merchant's Row is a favorite spot for sea kayakers. Exploring the area on bicycle or boat will give you a more complete picture than if you stick to the car. And if you want to explore more of the region, Acadia National Park (*see* Chapter 6) is an easy day trip.

With small inns, charming bed-and-breakfasts, and outstanding restaurants scattered across the area, the Blue Hill Peninsula may just convince you to leave the rest of the coastline to the tourists.

Exploring the Blue Hill Peninsula

To explore the Blue Hill Peninsula thoroughly, you should have a car, a good map, and a relaxed schedule. Be prepared to get lost, and don't worry if you do. The roads can be confusing to those unfamiliar with the area, as they crisscross, overlap, branch off in odd directions, and sometimes seem to run parallel to themselves. If you are traveling north through the state on U.S. 1 and Route 3, you can reach the peninsula from Route 175, just east of Bucksport. If you're traveling south, your best bet is to follow Route 172 where it branches off near Ellsworth.

Deer Isle, Little Deer Island, and Stonington are accessible by bridge. Route 15 leads you on to Little Deer Isle and Deer Isle. When you reach the village of Deer Isle the road splits, with Route 15 following a more or less direct route to Stonington, while Route 15A, reaches the same destination but meanders along the island's western edge. Neither route has particularly great views. For those wishing to travel on to Isle au Haut, home to a part of Acadia National Park, ferry service is the only way to get there.

5

Numbers in the text correspond to numbers in the margin and on the Blue Hill Peninsula map.

If you have
3 days

If you have three days on the Blue Hill Peninsula, plan to stay in **Blue Hill** ②. Visit the town's shops and galleries during your first morning, then take the afternoon to tour neighboring **Sedgwick** ③, home to the world-famous Wooden Boat School, and **Brooksville** ⑤, where you can find the Sow's Ear Winery. On Day 2, spend the morning climbing Blue Hill Mountain, where you have 360-degree views of the entire Blue Hill Peninsula, then head to Castine for the rest of the day. Take the walking tour of the village, making sure to see historic homes like the Ives House and local landmarks like the Abbott School and the Unitarian Church. On your last day, explore **Deer Isle** ⑥ and **Stonington** ⑦, where you can learn about the region's rocky past at the Deer Isle Granite Museum and Settlement Quarry.

If you have
5 days

If you have five days, follow the above itinerary, then on your third and fourth nights, stay in **Deer Isle** ⑥ or **Stonington** ⑦. On Day 4, take a guided sea kayak tour, then have dinner in Deer Isle. On Day 5, take the ferry to **Isle au Haut** ⑧, hiking the trails that lead through Acadia National Park.

Perhaps the most unique way to explore the peninsula is by sea kayak. With the mainland so undeveloped and with so many islands to explore, it's an ideal way to take in spectacular scenery at every turn, observe marine mammals and birds, and get away from civilization for a while.

About the Restaurants

Eateries on the Blue Hill Peninsula tend to fall into one of two categories: expensive restaurants where you can expect expertly prepared cuisine, or more casual places where you can grab a sandwich, burger, or crab roll. The fine-dining establishments tend to offer more organic foods than you might expect to find elsewhere. You can always count on finding freshly caught seafood, but many restaurants on the peninsula proudly promote their locally grown produce and locally raised meats. This emphasis is not just about eating healthier foods; it's also about supporting local farmers and fishermen.

About the Hotels

You won't find high-rise hotels on the Blue Hill Peninsula. Instead, the countryside is dotted with inns, B&Bs, and small but distinguished hotels. Be prepared to find that your room lacks a TV or a phone. Without these amenities, you can slip away from your day-to-day life. Many accommodations also do without air-conditioning. Although summer days can still get quite warm, ocean breezes will cool your room off at night, providing what locals call "free air-conditioning."

WHAT IT COSTS				
	$$$$	$$$	$$	$	¢
RESTAURANTS	over $25	$18–$25	$11–$17	$7–$10	under $7
HOTELS	over $200	$150–$200	$100–$150	$60–$100	under $60

Restaurant prices are for a main course at dinner, excluding tax of 7%. Hotel prices are for two people in a standard double room in high season, excluding service charges and 7% tax.

Timing

Because it is relatively undiscovered, the Blue Hill Peninsula does not have what you would call a high season. The best time to visit is from late May or early June to October (the Blue Hill Peninsula Chamber of Commerce does not open until Memorial Day weekend, and the Deer Isle–Stonington Chamber of Commerce begins its season in mid-June). There are few lodging options, so it's a good idea to reserve rooms well in advance. Outside of these months you will find that many restaurants and hotels have closed for the season. During the summer months, galleries open their doors, concerts enliven the evenings, and a handful of festivals draw locals and visitors alike. Check with the local chambers of commerce for schedules of events.

BLUE HILL & ENVIRONS

Blue Hill and Castine are the most visited towns in the Blue Hill Peninsula, but they manage to retain an off-the-beaten-path charm. For villages with an even more secluded feel, visit Brooklin, Brooksville, and Sedgwick.

Castine

❶ *30 mi southeast of Searsport.*

A summer destination for more than 100 years, Castine is a well-preserved seaside village rich in history. Although a few different Native American tribes inhabited the area before the 1600s, French explorer Samuel de Champlain was the first European to record its location on a map. The French established a trading post here in 1613, naming the area Pentagoet. A year later, Captain John Smith claimed the area for the British. The French regained control of the peninsula with the 1667 Breda Treaty, and Jean Vincent d'Abbadie de St. Castin obtained a land grant in the Pentagoet area, which would later have his name. Castine's strategic position on Penobscot Bay and its importance as a trading post meant there were many battles for control until 1815. The Dutch claimed the area in 1674 and 1676, and England made it a stronghold during the Revolutionary War, but they lost it with America's victory. In the 19th century, Castine was an important port for trading ships and fishing vessels. The Civil War and the advent of train travel brought its prominence as a port to an end, but by the late 1800s, some of the nation's wealthier citizens discovered Castine as a pleasant summer retreat.

5

Flower Festival In June the fields and roadsides of the Blue Hill Peninsula are decorated with the blues, pinks, and purples of one of Maine's most popular flowers, the lupine. Although the flower thrives throughout coastal Maine, nowhere else is it more celebrated than here. The Deer Isle–Stonington Lupine Festival, held the third Saturday in June, showcases everything you can do with the buds. Events at the fair include a bean cook-off, a rummage sale and bazaar, and an art show. There's also food and live music. A map indicating prime viewing spots is available from area businesses.

Gallery Hopping If you're visiting the Blue Hill Peninsula area to collect antiques or find new artwork, you might want to pick up a copy of the annual *Arts Guide,* which showcases shops and galleries on Deer Isle–Stonington and the Blue Hill Peninsula. Make sure to see the Haystack Mountain School of Arts, which has tours every Wednesday at 1 PM, as well as interesting evening lectures. You can find galleries in and around downtown Deer Isle that exhibit oil and watercolor paintings, photography, and sculpture. Stonington has a few galleries, as does the village of Blue Hill. As you drive along the peninsula's winding roads, you can find studios selling everything from pottery to handmade paper.

Federal- and Greek Revival–style architecture, spectacular views of Penobscot Bay, and a peaceful setting make Castine an ideal spot to spend a day or two. Well worth exploring are its lively harbor front, two small museums, and the ruins of a British fort. For a nice stroll, park your car at the landing and walk up Main Street toward the white Trinitarian Federated Church, which has a tapering spire. Among the white clapboard buildings that ring the town common are the Ives House (once the summer home of the poet Robert Lowell), the Abbott School, and the Unitarian Church, capped by a whimsical belfry. The Maine Maritime Academy is also here, and its training ship often can be seen in port. Historical markers are posted throughout town, making it ideal for a self-guided walking tour. You can also pick up a map detailing the historic sites at most local businesses.

The **Castine Historical Society Museum** has changing exhibits that portray Castine's tumultuous history, highlighting the Native American tribes that lived here and its rise as a trading port. Look for the town's Bicentennial Quilt, created in 1996 to celebrate the town's 200th birthday. ⊠ *Court St., Town Common* Ⓓ *Box 238, 04421* ☎ *207/326–4118* ▦ *Free* ☉ *July 1–Labor Day. Tues.–Sat. 10–4, Sun. 1–4.*

The **Wilson Museum** is made up of four historic structures. The main building houses anthropologist-geologist John Howard Wilson's collection of prehistoric artifacts from around the world, including rocks, minerals, and other intriguing objects. The **John Perkins House** is a restored Colonial-era house originally built on what is now Court Street, in

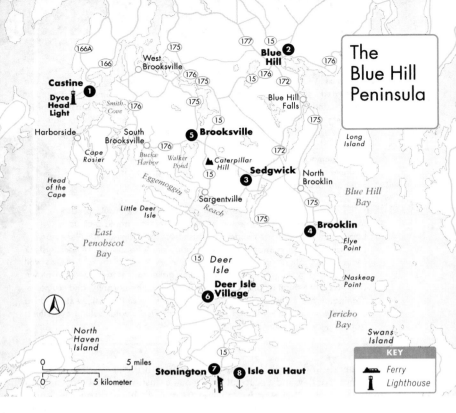

The Blue Hill Peninsula

1763, and enlarged in 1774 and 1783. The house fell into disrepair until the 1960s, when the Castine Scientific Society had the house taken down piece by piece and reassembled it here on the grounds of the Wilson Museum. Inside you can find Perkins family heirlooms and 18th- and early-19th-century furnishings. The kitchen and four front rooms appear as they did in 1783. The **Blacksmith Shop** holds demonstrations showing all the tricks of this old-time trade. Inside the **Hearse House** you can see the summer and winter hearses that serviced Castine more than a century ago. ✉ *107 Perkins St.* ☎ *207/326-9247* ⊕ *www. wilsonmuseum.org* ⊠ *Museum, Blacksmith Shop, and Hearse House free; John Perkins House $5* ☉ *Museum late May–late Sept., Tues.–Sun. 2–5; John Perkins House, Blacksmith Shop, Hearse House July and Aug., Sun. and Wed. 2–5.*

Where to Stay & Eat

$–$$$ ✕ **Dennett's Wharf.** Originally built as a sail rigging loft in the early 1800s, this longtime favorite is a good place for fresh seafood. The waterfront restaurant also serves burgers, sandwiches, and other light fare. There are several microbrews on tap, including the tasty Dennett's Wharf Rat Ale. Eat in the dining room or outside on the deck. ✉ *15 Sea St.* ☎ *207/ 326-9045* ⊟ *MC, V* ☉ *Closed Columbus Day–May.*

$$–$$$$ ✕⌂ **Castine Inn.** Originally built in 1898, the Castine Inn is a delight-
Fodor'sChoice ful place to stay. Most of the guest rooms are rather simple, but they
★ are bright and airy, and have views of the ocean. A seascape mural cov-
ers the walls of the dining room ($$$$), where chef Tom Gutow serves
an excellent prix-fixe menu. You might try an appetizer of Penobscot
Bay crab cakes with mustard vinaigrette and herb mayonnaise, fol-
lowed by the pork with spinach, chard, and fingerling potatoes. The staff
is happy to suggest the correct wine pairings for each course. After din-
ner, relax outside in the garden or unwind in the English-style pub. ⊠ *33
Main St., 04421* ☎ *207/326–4365* 🖷 *207/326–4570* ⊕ *www.castineinn.
com* ⌂ *Reservations essential* ⇩ *15 rooms, 4 suites* ⌂ *Restaurant,
sauna, pub; no a/c, no room phones, no room TVs, no children under
8, no smoking* ▤ *MC, V* ⊘ *Closed Nov.–late Apr.* ⑩ *BP.*

$$–$$$$ ✕⌂ **Pentagoet Inn.** With period lithographs in the common rooms,
claw-foot tubs in the bathrooms, and a cozy pub, the owners of this
inn strive to create an air of romance. Guest rooms are in the main inn,
a Queen Anne–style building with a three-story turret and numerous
gables, or a nearby 18th-century sea captain's home. The most mem-
orable is Room 3, which has a balcony covered with flowers and views
of town. With tables in the dining room or on a porch, the restaurant
($$$) specializes in fresh fish. You might try the Stonington crabcake
appetizer, followed by the seared duck on a Belgian endive salad. The
perfect finale is profiteroles with vanilla ice cream and chocolate
ganache sauce. Enjoy a full breakfast in a room adjacent to the gar-
den, and freshly baked cookies each afternoon. ⊠ *26 Main St., 04421*
☎ *800/845–1701 or 207/326–8616* 🖷 *207/326–9382* ⊕ *www.
pentagoet.com* ⇩ *16 rooms* ⌂ *Restaurant, pub; no a/c, no room
phones, no room TVs, no smoking* ⌂ *Reservations essential* ▤ *MC,
V* ⊘ *Closed late Oct.–May* ⑩ *BP.*

$–$$$ ✕⌂ **Manor Inn.** Bordering a 95-acre forest with trails that lead all the
way to the bay, this 1895 inn resembles an English manor house. Rooms
are individually decorated—four have fireplaces and one has a private
porch. Some bathrooms have marble tubs and walk-in showers. The dining room ($$–$$$), which offers eclectic international cuisine empha-
sizing local ingredients, can accommodate gatherings of up to 200
people. It overlooks the expansive lawn and side gardens. The pub
serves lighter fare. Yoga classes are held in a fully equipped studio three
times a week. ⊠ *15 Manor Dr., off Battle Ave., 04421* ☎ *207/326–4861*
🖷 *207/326–0891* ⊕ *www.manor-inn.com* ⇩ *13 rooms, 1 suite* ⌂ *Restaurant, pub, some pets allowed (fee), no-smoking rooms; no a/c in some
rooms, no TV in some rooms* ▤ *AE, D, DC, MC, V* ⑩ *BP.*

Sports & the Outdoors

At Dennett's Wharf, **Castine Kayak Adventures** (⊠ 15 Sea St. ☎ 207/326–
9045) operates tours with a registered Maine guide. Walk through the
restaurant to the deck, where you can sign up for a half day of kayaking along the shore, or a full day of kayaking by ship wrecks, reversing
falls, and islands in Penobscot Bay. The steam launch *Laurie Ellen* (⊠ Dennett's Wharf ☎ 207/326–9045 or 207/266–2841) is the only wood-fired,
steam-powered passenger steam launch in the country. Climb aboard
for a trip around Castine Harbor and up the Bagaduce River.

Shopping
Four Flags (⌧ 19 Water St. ☎ 207/326–8526) has nautical charts, prints of old maps, and other souvenirs. **Compass Rose Bookstore & Café** (⌧ 3 Main St. ☎ 207/326–9366) carries books, music, and games. The coffee shop has cookies and a self-serve lunch. **Leila Day Antiques** (⌧ 53 Main St. ☎ 207/326–8786) specializes in interesting antiques, colorful quilts, and nautical accessories.

M&E Gummel Chairworks (⌧ 600 The Shore Rd. ☎ 207/326–8122 ⊕ www.gummelchairworks.com) crafts authentic benchmade Windsor chairs. The **McGrath-Dunham Gallery** (⌧ 9 Main St. ☎ 207/326–9175 ⊕ www.mcgrathdunhamgallery.com) sells paintings, sculpture, and pottery.

en route   As you approach the village of Castine, you'll notice a large sign on the right side of the road that reads: BRITISH CANAL 1779. Just before the sign, turn right and follow the road to the **Back Shore.** This large pebble beach is a favorite local hang out. It's the perfect place to enjoy a picnic by the ocean.

Blue Hill

❷ *19 mi east of Castine.*

Snuggled between 943-foot Blue Hill Mountain and Blue Hill Bay, the village of Blue Hill is perched dramatically over the harbor. Originally known for its granite quarries, copper mines, and shipbuilding, today the town is popular with people who love its pottery. You can find a plethora of galleries, shops, and studios along its streets. Blue Hill is also a good spot for shopping, as there are numerous bookstores and antiques shops. The Blue Hill Fair (⊕ www.bluehillfair.com), held Labor Day weekend, is a tradition in these parts, with agricultural exhibits, food, rides, and entertainment.

☾ Focusing on how pollution affects marine mammals, the **Marine Environmental Research Institute** has programs for all ages, including interesting lectures and guided walks along the beach. A weekly story hour for kids includes crafts projects, usually directed by a local artist. Children can hold small sea creatures from a "touch tank," including green crabs, sea stars, whelks, and periwinkles. Two viewing tanks house lobsters, rock crabs, anemones, and other small sea creatures. ⌧ *55 Main St.* ☎ *207/374–2135* ⊕ *www.meriresearch.org.*

need a break?   With 50 different types of bread, each made by hand, **Pain de Famille** (⌧ 7 Main St. ☎ 207/374–3839), is a good place to stop if you're packing a picnic or putting together a midday snack. The shop also sells a selection of vegetarian sandwiches and pizza—made with homemade crust, of course.

Jonathan Fisher was the first permanent minister of Blue Hill. The **Parson Fisher House,** which he built from 1814 to 1820, provides a fascinating look at his many accomplishments and talents, which included writing and illustrating books, painting, farming, and building furniture.

Also on view is a wooden clock he crafted while a student at Harvard; the face holds messages about time written in English, Greek, Latin, Hebrew, and French. The site is on the National Register of Historic Places. ⊠ *Rte. 15/176, west of intersection with Rte. 172* ☎ *No phone* 🗺 *$5* ⊙ *July–mid-Sept., Mon.–Sat. 1–4.*

Now housing the Blue Hill Historical Society, the **Holt House,** was built in 1815 by Jeremiah Thorndike Holt, grandson of one of the first European settlers to the area. Today, the property is in the process of being furnished with period antiques while society members collect and maintain documents and other memorabilia important to the town. Visitors will find reproductions of the home's original stenciled decorations and a kitchen with a restored fireplace and the original iron pot hooks. ⊠ *Water and Main Sts.* ☎ *No phone* ⊙ *July and Aug., Tues. and Fri. 1–4, Sat. 10–1.*

Where to Stay & Eat

$$$ ✕ **Arborvine.** Crackling fireplaces, period antiques, exposed beams, and
Fodor'sChoice hardwood floors covered with Oriental rugs create an elegant and com-
★ forting atmosphere in each of the four candle-lit dining rooms in this renovated Cape Cod–style house. You might begin with a salad of mixed greens, sliced beets, and sliced pears with blue cheese crumbled on top. For your entrée, choose from among dishes like medallions of beef and goat cheese with fingerling potatoes, or pork tenderloin with sweet cherries in a port wine reduction. Be sure to save room for a dessert, such as lemon mousse or wonderfully creamy cheesecake. A take-out lunch menu is available at the adjacent Moveable Feasts deli. ⊠ *Tenney Hill, Main St.* ☎ *207/374–2119* ▤ *MC, V* ⊙ *Closed Mon. and Tues. Sept.–June. No lunch.*

¢–$$ ✕ **Marlintini's Grill.** Locals go to Marlintini's for specialties like the fried haddock sandwich, which is perfectly crispy. The restaurant also has a selection of other sandwiches and seafood. Originally in downtown Blue Hill, Marlintini's moved to a larger location west of the village in 2004. The brightly painted walls are adorned with colorful paintings. ⊠ *Rte. 15* ☎ *207/374–2500* ▤ *MC, V.*

$$–$$$ ✕🏠 **Captain Merrill Inn.** This Federal-style mansion, built during the 1800s, has charming guest rooms that overlook Main Street. Many have hardwood floors and windows that let in lots of light. More modern rooms in an annex include an apartment with a private entrance and a view of Blue Hill Bay. A kitchenette makes it good for families. The restaurant ($$–$$$$) serves lobster cooked nine different ways, as well as a variety of other seafood, chicken, and beef entrées. ⊠ *1 Union St., 04614* ☎ *207/374–2555* ⊕ *www.captainmerrillinn.com* 🛏 *6 rooms, 1 suite, 1 apartment* ♢ *Restaurant, kitchenette; no a/c in some rooms, no phones in some rooms, no TV in some rooms, no smoking* ▤ *AE, D, MC, V* ⊙ *Restaurant closed mid-Oct.–June.*

★ **$$$** 🏠 **Blue Hill Inn.** This rambling inn dating from 1830 is a comfortable place to relax after exploring nearby shops and galleries. Original pumpkin pine and painted floors set the tone for the mix of Empire and early-Victorian pieces that fill the two parlors and guest rooms, several of which have working fireplaces. One of the nicest rooms is No. 8, which has exposures on three sides and views of the flower gardens and apple trees.

Two rooms have antique claw-foot tubs perfect for soaking. The spacious Cape House Suite (available after the rest of the inn has closed for the season) has a bed as well as two pullout sofas, a full kitchen, and a private deck. The inn has a bar that offers 100 different types of wine. Here you can enjoy appetizers before you head out to dinner or specialty coffees and liquors when you return. ⊠ *40 Union St., 04614* ☎ *207/374–2844 or 800/826–7415* 🖷 *207/374–2829* ⊕ *www. bluehillinn.com* ⇨ *11 rooms, 1 suite* ♢ *Bar, Internet; no room phones, no room TVs, no children, no smoking* ⊟ *AE, MC, V* ☉ *Closed Nov.–mid-May* ⏹ *BP.*

$$–$$$ ▦ **First Light Bed & Breakfast.** In the quiet village of East Blue Hill, this bed-and-breakfast sits right on the water's edge. The tower of a lighthouse is open to guests and has chairs and a telescope for viewing passing boats by day, and stars at night. Rooms are individually decorated to reflect their names. The Seaside Garden Room, which has views of McHeard's Cove and Blue Hill Bay, shares a bath with the Maine Room, overlooking a stream and a salt pond. The Lighthouse Suite, on the main floor of the tower, has a great view of Blue Hill Bay and distant mountains. When the tide is low, you can walk down to the shore. When it's high, enjoy the views from a seaside seating area. The inn is just before the green metal bridge that leads to East Blue Hill. ⊠ *821 East Blue Hill Rd., East Blue Hill 04629* ☎ *207/374–5879* ⊕ *www. firstlightbandb.com* ⇨ *2 rooms with shared bath, 1 suite* ♢ *Dining room, refrigerators; no a/c, no room phones, no room TVs* ⊟ *No credit cards.*

$–$$ ▦ **Heritage Motor Inn.** On a hill northeast of town, this well-kept motel has some simple, comfortable rooms, and some views of the harbor. Two two-level suites with full kitchens were added in 2004. ⊠ *60 Ellsworth Rd., 04614* ☎ *207/374–5646* ⊕ *www.bhheritagemotorinn.com* ⇨ *18 rooms, 2 suites* ♢ *Cable TV; no smoking* ⊟ *MC, V* ☉ *Closed late Oct.–May.*

Nightlife & the Arts

In Kneisel Hall, the **Kneisel Hall Chamber Music Festival** (⊠ 137 Pleasant St. ☎ 207/374–2203) has concerts on Sunday afternoons and Friday evenings in summer. The first Saturday of every month, a **Contra Dance** is held at the Blue Hill Town Hall (⊠ Main and Union Sts.). Similar to square dancing, contra dancing involves two couples dancing specific patterns.

Sports & the Outdoors

The Osgood Trail provides hikers with breathtaking views as it leads up **Blue Hill Mountain** (⊠ Mountain Rd., Blue Hill). The dirt path meanders through the woods, over rocky ledges, and up stone steps. A second trail is accessible to hikers as well as all-terrain vehicles. A fire tower at the top offers 360-degree views of Blue Hill Peninsula. The tower is no longer maintained, so use caution. Maps of hiking trails in the area are available at **Blue Hill Heritage Trust** (⊠ 101 Union St., Blue Hill ☎ 207/374–5118 ⊕ www.bluehillheritagetrust.org), which maintains the Osgood Trail.

You can rent sea kayaks, canoes, and bicycles at **The Activity Shop** (⊠ 61 Ellsworth Rd., Blue Hill ☎ 207/374–3600). Pick them up at the shop, or have them delivered. **Rocky Coast Outfitters** (⊠ Grindleville Rd., Blue

Hill ☎ 207/374–8866) has sea kayaks, canoes, and bicycles by the day or by the week. Delivery is available.

Shopping

Rackliffe Pottery (⊠ 126 Ellsworth Rd., Blue Hill ☎ 207/374–2297) sells colorful pottery made with lead-free glazes. You can choose among water pitchers, tea-and-coffee sets, and sets of canisters. **Rowantrees Pottery** (⊠ 9 Union St. ☎ 207/374–5535) has an extensive selection of dinnerware, tea sets, vases, and decorative items. The shop makes many of the same pieces it did 60 years ago, so if you break a favorite item, you can find a replacement.

★ **Blue Hill Bay Gallery** (⊠ 11 Tenny Hill ☎ 207/374–5773 ⊕ www. bluehillbaygallery.com) sells oil and watercolor paintings of the local landscape. Bird carvings and other items are also available. The gallery is open daily from Memorial Day to Labor Day and on weekends from mid-May to Memorial Day and from Labor Day to mid-October. **Handworks Gallery** (⊠ 48 Main St. ☎ 207/374–5613) carries unusual crafts made by local artists such as bookshelves and clothes trees fashioned from bark-peeled tree branches, wooden boxes, jewelry, dishes, and other

★ items. **Jud Hartmann Gallery** (⊠ Main and Pleasant Sts. ☎ 207/359–2544 ⊕ www.judhartmanngallery.com) displays bronze sculptures of Iriquois and Abenaki Native Americans. Some sculptures are busts, while others depict a scene. Oil and watercolor paintings by other artists are also on display.

L. Balombini (⊠ 54 Main St. ☎ 207/374–5142 ⊕ www.lbalombini.com) uses wire, buttons, and other materials to create whimsical sculptures of people, fish, and other creatures. **Leighton Gallery** (⊠ 24 Parker Point Rd. ☎ 207/374–5001 ⊕ www.leightongallery.com) shows oil paintings, lithographs, watercolors, and other contemporary art. Many pieces are abstract. Outside, granite, bronze, and wood sculptures are displayed in a gardenlike setting under apple trees and white pines. **Liros Gallery** (⊠ 14 Parker Point Rd. ☎ 207/374–5370 ⊕ www.lirosgallery.com) exhibits oil and watercolor paintings, hand-colored engravings, and wood cuts of birds and flowers.

In an old red barn, the **Blue Hill Wine Shop** (⊠ Main St. ☎ 207/374–2161), carries more than 1,000 different wines. It's west of the intersection of Routes 172 and 176. For natural-wood toys, handblown-glass vases, and other crafts, visit the **Faerie Ring** (⊠ 27 Water St. ☎ 207/374–2545 ⊕ www.thefaeriering.com). **New Cargoes** (⊠ 49 Main St. ☎ 207/374–3733) sells cookware, glassware, tea towels, clothing, quilts, and other products, many of them made in Maine. **North Country Textiles** (⊠ 38 Main St. ☎ 207/374–2715 ⊕ northcountrytextiles.com) specializes in fine woven shawls, throws, baby blankets, place mats, and pillows in subtle patterns and color schemes.

en route   Offering kayakers some of the strongest currents around, **Reversing Falls** is worth a stop as you travel along Route 175 from Blue Hill to Brooklin. Water flowing in and out of Salt Marsh Pond from Blue Hill Bay eddies under the Stevens Bridge. See it by foot or by kayak. ⊠ *Rte. 175, south of Blue Hill.*

CloseUp

YOUR OWN MAINE CLAMBAKE

F YOU INQUIRE AROUND THE CAMDEN HARBOR, you'll find there are a few windjammers and boats (Lively Lady Too is one of them) that will take you to an uninhabited island for a real Maine clambake on the beach. Traditionally, everything is buried in the sand, a fire is built over the spot, then it's all dug up when it's ready to eat. If you really like the idea of a Maine clambake, however, you don't have to wait until you visit Maine to enjoy one. Here's how you can do it at home, right on your stovetop.

A Maine Clambake

Ingredients:

2 boiled lobsters (1 to 1¼ pounds each)

Scallops and fish (optional)

4 ears of corn

2 cans new potatoes

2 cans onions

1 dozen clams

2 bottles clam juice

Spinach or kale (in place of the more traditional seaweed)

In a large soup pot, layer the ingredients as follows: Put the corn in the bottom of the pan and cover with a layer of spinach or kale. Put the potatoes in a single layer on top of that and cover with another layer of spinach or kale. Continue this process with the remaining ingredients as follows: fish, spinach, onions, spinach, lobsters, spinach, clams. Pour the clam juice over everything, put the lid on, and let simmer for 15–20 minutes. Serve with bread, tossed salad, and white wine.

—Stephen Allen

Sedgwick, Brooklin & Brooksville

Winding through the hills, the roads that lead to the small villages of Sedgwick, Brooklin, and Brooksville take you past rambling farmhouses, beautiful ocean coves, and blueberry fields with the occasional mass of granite. It's a perfect Sunday drive, no matter what day of the week it happens to be.

❸ Incorporated in 1798, **Sedgwick** runs along much of Eggemoggin Reach, the body of water that separates the mainland from Deer Isle, Little Deer
❹ Island, and Stonington. The village of **Brooklin**, originally part of Sedgwick, established itself as an independent town in 1849. Today, it is home to the world-famous Wooden Boat School, a 64-acre oceanfront campus offering courses in woodworking, boat building, and seamanship.
❺ The town of **Brooksville**, incorporated in 1817, is almost completely surrounded by water, with Eggemoggin Reach, Walker Pond, and the Bagaduce River marking its boundaries.

Gardens filled with brightly colored poppies, as well as lovely perennials, are the attraction at the **Blue Poppy Garden** (⊠ 1000 Reach Rd., Sedgwick ☎ 207/359–2739 ⊕ www.bluepoppygarden.com). A nature trail winds through the woods past native plants identified by small signs. There's a dining room that serves lunch and afternoon tea in July and August. At the gift shop you can purchase blue poppy plants and seeds. The gardens are open mid-May to mid-October.

A few miles south of Brooklin, Naskeag Point Road leads to a broken-shell beach called **Naskeag Point.** From here you can take in views of the small islands in Jericho Bay as you picnic under the apple trees. A bench remembers "all the fishermen who brave the sea." This area, famous for being the site of the 1778 Battle of Naskeag, has a long history. An ancient Nordic coin was discovered on the beach. To find Naskeag Point Road, turn at the Brooklin General Store.

To taste locally produced fruit wines, visit the **Sow's Ear Winery** (⊠ Coastal Rd., Brooksville ☎ 207/326–4649). Owner Tom Hoey grows the apples for his cider and the rhubarb for his rhubarb wine, and uses locally grown blueberries and cranberries for his berry wines.

Where to Stay & Eat

$–$$$ ✕ **Café Out Back.** Popular among people who tie up their boats in Buck's Harbor, this eatery is behind the Buck's Harbor Market. It's a casual place with a checkerboard-tile floor and green tables. A dinner here can be as simple as pizza or as extravagant as duck with fois grois. You'll also find steaks, sandwiches, and pasta dishes on the menu. The restaurant has a reasonably priced wine list and a deck for outdoor dining. ⊠ *Rte. 176 and Cornfield Hill Rd. South Brooksville* ☎ *207/326–8683* ▤ *MC, V* ☉ *July and Aug., daily; Sept.–June, Thurs.–Sun.*

★ $$–$$$$ ✕▦ **Oakland House Seaside Resort.** Set between Eggemoggin Reach and a private pond, this relaxing retreat sits on more than 50 acres of shorefront property. Open since 1889, the resort accommodations range from comfortable guest rooms furnished in arts-and-crafts style to more rustic cottages with fireplaces. Ask for Room 7, which has a sitting area and ocean views on three sides. The resort's well-known restaurant offers a five-course menu that changes daily. Dinner might begin with seared tuna with wasabi vinaigrette followed by lobster bisque and prime rib. Every Thursday you can join a lobster picnic. The resort has hiking trails leading through the woods, including one that ends at a peak overlooking Pumpkin Island Lighthouse and beyond. A dock, available for boaters, was a stop for steamboats during the early 1900s. Weeklong artist workshops are held throughout the season, including painting and photography. ⊠ *435 Herrick Rd., Brooksville 04617* ☎ *207/359–8521* ▤ *207/359–9865* ⊕ *www.oaklandhouse.com* ⊲ *10 rooms, 7 with bath; 15 cottages* ⚭ *Restaurant, kitchenettes, boating, beach, recreation room, business services; no a/c, no room phones, no room TVs* ▤ *MC, V* ☉ *Closed mid-Oct.–late May* ⓞ *BP, MAP.*

$$–$$$ ✕▦ **The Lookout.** As its name suggest, this small inn dating from the 1790s overlooks Blue Hill Bay. Many of the comfortably furnished rooms have views of the ocean. It's common to find a soccer or volleyball game going on in the large field that leads down to the beach, where seaside lobster bakes are held twice a week. The 40-seat restaurant has three dining rooms, including one on a porch facing the ocean. It serves breakfast and dinner Tuesday through Sunday. The dinner menu fea-

tures American fare like filet mignon, roast duckling, and rack of lamb. ✉ *Flye Point Rd., Brooklin 04616* ☏ *207/359–2188* ⊕ *www.acadia. net/lookout* ⚱ *Reservations essential* ➳ *9 rooms, 4 with bath; 7 cottages* ⚲ *Restaurant, some pets allowed; no a/c, no room TVs, no room phones, no smoking* ▭ *AE, D, MC, V* ☺ *Inn closed mid-Oct.–June. Cottages closed Nov.–Apr.* ⎡◉⎤ *BP.*

★ $ ✕⎡⎤ **Brooklin Inn.** A comfortable yet elegant atmosphere distinguishes this B&B in downtown Brooklin. There are plenty of homey touches like hardwood floors and an upstairs deck. The sunny rooms have attractive bureaus and beds piled with cozy quilts. The restaurant offers meals made from scratch and specializes in fresh fish and locally raised beef, poultry, and lamb. You can also find soups, salads, and desserts worth saving room for. In summer you can dine on the enclosed porch. An Irish pub downstairs showcases local musicians most Saturday nights. ✉ *Rte. 175, Brooklin 04616* ☏ *207/359–2777* ⊕ *www. brooklininn.com* ➳ *5 rooms, 2 with shared baths* ⚲ *Restaurant; no a/c, no room phones, no room TVs* ▭ *AE, D, DC, MC, V.*

$–$$$ ⎡⎤ **Hiram Blake Camp.** Established in 1916, this camp sits on Cape Rosier. The waterside cottages, with one to three bedrooms, have exposed wood beams, separate sitting areas, full kitchens, and screened porches. There are miles of hiking trails, a pebble beach, and plenty of open areas for children to play. You can take one of the camp's kayaks to nearby Spectacle Island. The restaurant serves a set menu each night, but you can always call ahead to order lobster. The dining room, which is lined with bookshelves, has long wooden tables that encourage family-style dining. ✉ *220 Weir Cove Rd., Harborside 04642* ☏ *207/326–4951* ⊕ *www.hiramblake.com* ➳ *15 cabins* ⚲ *Restaurant, beach, boating, recreation room; no a/c, no room phones, no room TVs* ▭ *No credit cards* ☺ *Closed late Sept.–June* ⎡◉⎤ *MAP.*

Nightlife & the Arts

A popular way to spend Monday evenings is to attend a street dance sponsored by a steel drum band called **Flash! In The Pans** (☏ 207/374–5247 ⊕ www.peninsulapan.org). The energetic group performs every other week from late June to early September at the Buck's Harbor Market in South Brooksville. There are also performances in Castine, Blue Hill, and Sedgwick. Proceeds from the dances benefit area schools, fire departments, and ambulance crews.

Sports & the Outdoors

The 1,230-acre **Holbrook Island Sanctuary** (✉ 172 Indian Bar Rd., Brooksville ☏ 207/326–4012) protects the region's fragile ecosystem. You have a good chance of spotting a blue heron, osprey, or bald eagle. Open from 9 AM to sunset, the park has nine hiking trails, a gravel beach with splendid views, and a picnic area. You can get a trail map at the parking areas.

At Buck's Harbor Marina, the 44-foot cruising ketch *Perelandra* (✉ Coastal Rd., South Brooksville ☏ 207/326–4279 ⊕ www. windroseaway.com) sails from Buck's Harbor Marina daily. A maximum of six people can cruise around Penobscot Bay and the nearby islands.

The family-run **Pine Ridge Golf Center** (⌂ Rte. 15, ½ mi from Caterpillar Hill, Sedgwick ☎ 207/359–6788) has a 19-hole miniature golf course and a driving range.

Shopping

In downtown Brooklin, **Naskeag Antiques & Artisans** (⌂ Rte. 175 ☎ 207/359–4619) specializes in antique furniture and quilts. Other items like scarves, hats, and bags are also available. **Sedgwick Antiques** (⌂ Rtes. 172 and 175, Sedgwick ☎ 207-359–8834) buys and sells antiques year-round.

---

en route

As you travel south toward Deer Isle, scenic Route 15 passes through Sedgwick before taking you over the graceful suspension bridge that crosses Eggemoggin Reach. The picnic area at **Caterpillar Hill,** on the mainland about 1 mi south of the junction of Routes 15 and 175, has a fabulous view of Penobscot Bay dotted with hundreds of deep-green islands. You can even see across the bay to the Camden Hills, southwest of the Blue Hill Peninsula. With good reason, this spot is known as Million Dollar View.

DEER ISLE & STONINGTON

Separated from the Blue Hill Peninsula by Eggemoggin Reach, Deer Isle and Stonington are significantly off the beaten path. The area was first settled in 1755 by farmers, but today is primarily devoted to fishing. That's why the annual Fishermen's Day, held in late July, is so popular. Coast Guard demonstrations, rowboat races, and a codfish relay race mark the celebration. An Independence Day festival includes a "fish and fritter fry" on the Stonington pier and fireworks over Stonington Harbor.

Deer Isle Village

❻ *16 mi south of Blue Hill.*

Around Deer Isle Village, thick woods give way to tidal coves. Stacks of lobster traps populate the backyards of shingled houses, and dirt roads lead to secluded summer cottages. This region is prized by artists, and studios and galleries are plentiful.

For picnics, bird-watching, or launching kayaks and canoes, visit **Mariners Memorial Park,** overlooking secluded Long Cove. There is a half-mile walking loop and a small perennial and shrub garden maintained by the Evergreen Garden Club. ⌂ *Fire Rd. 501, off Sunshine Rd., Deer Isle* ☎ *No phone* ▨ *Free* ☉ *Daily, dawn–dusk.*

A mixture of hard- and soft-wood trees, including birch, oak, maple, and white pine, make an excellent habitat for songbirds at **Shore Acres Preserve** on the eastern edge of Deer Isle. On a 1½-mi walking trail you can see native plants like juniper, blueberry, cranberry, as well as mushrooms, mosses, and ferns. You might even spot a fox, a red squirrel, or a hawk. ⌂ *Greenlaw District Rd., off Sunshine Rd., Deer Isle* ☎ *No phone* ▨ *Free* ☉ *Daily dawn–dusk.*

Enjoy miles of woodland and shore trails at the **Edgar M. Tennis Preserve,** where you can look for hawks, eagles, and ospreys, and wander among old apple trees, fields of wild flowers, and ocean-polished rocks. ⊠ *Tennis Rd., off Sunshine Rd., Deer Isle* ☎ No phone 📧 *Free* ☉ *Daily dawn–dusk.*

Famous landscape architect Frederick Law Olmsted once owned **Barred Island Preserve.** His grandniece, Carolyn Olmsted, donated it to the Nature Conservancy in 1969. The island is accessible only at low tide. The mile-long trail leading to the island offers great views of Penobscot Bay. Pick up a brochure at the Deer Isle/Stonington Chamber of Commerce for a map of the islands you can see from the area. The parking area fills quickly, so make sure to arrive early. ⊠ *Goose Cove Rd., Deer Isle* ☎ No phone 📧 *Free* ☉ *Daily dawn–dusk.*

Haystack Mountain School of Crafts offers two- and three-week-long courses for people of all skill levels in such crafts as blacksmithing, basketry, printmaking, and weaving. Artisans from around the world present evening lectures throughout the summer. You can attend the lectures or take a tour of the facility at 1 PM on Wednesday. In autumn, shorter courses are available to New England residents. The school is off Route 15, about 6 mi from Deer Isle Village. ⊠ *89 Haystack School Dr., Deer Isle* ☎ *207/348–2306* ⊕ *www.haystack-mtn.org* 📧 *Free* ☉ *June–Sept.*

Exhibiting works by area artists through the summer, the gallery of the **Deer Isle Artists Association** is open daily. ⊠ *6 Dow St., off Rte. 15, Deer Isle* ☎ *207/348–2330* ☉ *Late June–Aug., daily 1–5.*

Where to Stay & Eat

★ **\$\$–\$\$\$** ✕ **Sisters Restaurant.** Just beyond the bridge to Little Deer Isle, this restaurant makes good use of locally caught seafood. The entrées are prepared with flair; crab cakes are served with a whole-grain mustard sauce, tuna is rubbed with ancho-chili powder and dressed with a melon salsa, and a blueberry reduction tops a beef tenderloin that is wrapped in bacon and stuffed with Gorgonzola butter. The open dining room offers some views of Eggemoggin Reach and has a relaxed atmosphere—you're likely to find some people dressed up, and some with windblown hair who just tied up their boat at the dock. ⊠ *Rte. 15, Little Deer Isle* ☎ *207/348–6115* ▭ *AE, D, MC, V* ☉ *Closed Labor Day–mid-June.*

\$\$\$–\$\$\$\$ ✕▢ **Goose Cove Lodge.** A country lane leads to this spectacular oceanfront property, where cottages and suites are scattered through the woods and along a sandy beach. Most of the guest rooms have fireplaces to keep out the chill. At low tide you can walk across a sandbar to the beautiful Barred Island Preserve. Reservations are essential at the superb restaurant (\$\$–\$\$\$). The expertly prepared contemporary American fare includes at least one vegetarian entrée. On Monday nights in July and August you can join a lobster feast on the beach. ⊠ *300 Goose Cove Rd.* ✍ *Box 40, Sunset 04683* ☎ *207/348–2508 or 800/728–1963* 🖷 *207/348–2624* ⊕ *www.goosecovelodge.com* ⌨ *2 rooms, 7 suites, 13 cottages* ⚑ *2 restaurants, beach, boating, hiking; no a/c, no room phones, no room TVs, no smoking* ▭ *D, MC, V* ☉ *All but 3 units closed mid-Oct.–mid-May* ⦿ *BP.*

★ **$$–$$$** ✕⊡ **Pilgrim's Inn.** A four-story gambrel-roof house, this inn dates from about 1793. Wing chairs and Oriental rugs fill the library; a downstairs taproom has a huge brick fireplace and pine furniture. Individually furnished guest rooms overlook a mill pond and harbor. Three cottages—the Rugusa Rose, Ginny's One, and Ginny's Two—are perfect for families. The dining room ($$$–$$$$) is rustic yet elegant with exposed beams, hardwood floors, and French oil lamps. Try an appetizer of ouzo-flamed gulf shrimp with black olives and feta or a warm salad of spinach, smoked mussels, goat cheese, and pine nuts. For the main course, you can try traditional boiled Maine lobster, or go for something entirely different like sautéed venison with shiitake mushrooms. Be sure to save room for desserts like the mocha mousse. ⊠ *20 Main St., 04627* ☎ *207/348–6615 or 888/778–7505* 🖷 *207/346–6615* ⊕ *www.pilgrimsinn.com* ➾ *12 rooms, 3 cottages* ⚑ *Restaurant, bicycles, some pets allowed; no a/c, no room phones, no room TVs, no smoking* ⊟ *AE, D, MC, V* ☉ *Closed mid-Oct.–mid-May* ⃓◐⃒ *BP.*

$ ⊡ **Eggemoggin Landing.** Just over the bridge in Little Deer Isle, this motel has comfortable rooms with views of the water. The guest rooms are simple, but the beds are as comfortable as you'd find anywhere. The on-site marina, where you can dock your boat, rents a 40-foot trimaran and 36-foot powerboat. The facility specializes in overnight kayak tours. All your equipment and your meals are delivered to your destination so all you have to do is the paddling. ⊠ *Rte. 15, Little Deer Isle 04650* ☎ *207/348–6115* 🖷 *207/348–2738* ⊕ *www.acadia.net/eggland* ➾ *20 rooms* ⚑ *Cable TV, bicycles, boating; no a/c, no smoking* ⊟ *AE, D, MC, V* ☉ *Closed Oct.–May* ⃓◐⃒ *CP.*

Sports & the Outdoors

One- and two-person canoes and kayaks are available at **Finest Kind Canoe & Kayak Rentals** (⊠ Center District Rd., near Rtes. 15 and 15A, Deer Isle ☎ 207/348–7714 ⊕ www.finestkindenterprises.com). The company offers free delivery and pickup. It also rents mountain bikes by the day or by the week. The staff at **Granite Island Guide Service** (⊠ 66 Dunham Point Rd. ☎ 207/348–2668 ⊕ www.graniteislandguide.com) lead kayaking and canoe trips in summer, and snowshoeing and cross-country skiing excursions in winter.

Shopping

Blue Heron Gallery (⊠ 22 Church St. ☎ 207/348–2940 ⊕ www.blueherondeerisle.com) sells work by the artists from the Haystack Mountain School of Crafts. Meet the exhibiting artists at receptions from 3 to 5 PM every other Sunday in June and August. Purchase a handmade quilt from **Dockside Quilt Gallery** (⊠ 33 Church St. ☎ 207/348–2849 or 207/348–7712 ⊕ www.docksidequiltgallery.com). If you don't see anything you like, you can always commission a custom-designed quilt. **Turtle Gallery** (⊠ 61 N. Deer Isle Rd. ☎ 207/348–9977) exhibits contemporary painting and sculpture.

Harbor Farm (⊠ 29 Little Deer Isle Rd., Little Deer Isle ☎ 207/348–7737) carries wonderful products for the home, such as pottery, linens, and folk art. **Nervous Nellie's Jams and Jellies** (⊠ 598 Sunshine Rd. ☎ 800/777–6825) sells jams and jellies and operates a café. There's also an out-

CloseUp

STONINGTON GRANITE

ALTHOUGH YOU CAN SEE ALMOST NO SIGN OF IT TODAY, *the granite industry used to be a vital part of Stonington's economy. The first quarry was established in the 1860s, when the area known as Green's Landing had a population of approximately 300 people. From 1869 to 1969, area granite was used to build the Brooklyn Bridge, the Boston Museum of Fine Arts, the Smithsonian Institution, and other well-known sites. Demand was so high during the late 1800s that the town welcomed a wave of immigrants from Italy and Sweden, swelling the population to more than 5,000 people.*

In 1897 Green's Landing split from Deer Isle and became known as Stonington. Since no bridge connected the area to the mainland until 1939, the community had to be completely self-sufficient. The boom was short-lived, however. With the rediscovery of concrete in the early 20th

century, the granite industry ground to a sudden halt. Although one quarry reopened in the 1960s to fashion the granite blocks used in the Kennedy Memorial, it was unable to remain profitable. Today, Stonington's year-round population totals less than 1,200. The only remaining active quarry is on Crotch Island, just off the coast of Stonington. Its granite is shipped to Rhode Island, where it is cut for countertops and building facades.

–Lelah Cole

door sculpture garden. **Old Deer Isle Parish House Antiques** (⊠ 7 Church St. ☎ 207/348–9964) is a great place for poking around in piles of old kitchenware, glassware, books, and linens.

Stonington

➐ *7 mi south of Deer Isle.*

Stonington is rather isolated, which has helped retain its small-town flavor. The boutiques and galleries lining Main Street cater mostly to out-of-towners, but the town remains a fishing community at heart. The principal activity is at the waterfront, where boats arrive overflowing with the day's catch. The sloped island that rises to the south is Isle au Haut, which contains a remote section of Acadia National Park; it's accessible by mail boat from Stonington.

The tiny **Deer Isle Granite Museum** documents Stonington's quarrying tradition. The museum's centerpiece is an 8- by 15-foot working model of quarrying operations on Crotch Island and the town of Stonington at the turn of the last century. ⊠ *Main St.* ☎ *207/367–6331* ☒ *Free* ☉ *Memorial Day–Labor Day, Mon.–Sat. 10–5, Sun. 1–5.*

Once a busy mine employing hundreds of men, **Settlement Quarry** has been closed since the 1980s. It's worth a visit for its panoramic views of the island and its easy walking trails. ⊠ *Off Oceanville Rd.*

> **off the beaten path**
>
> **OFF-SHORE ISLANDS** – Many of the uninhabited islands near Deer Isle and Stonington are open for public use. One of the most popular is Green Island, which has an old quarry that is perfect for swimming. Some are for day use only, while others allow overnight camping. All of these islands operate on a "leave no trace" basis, meaning that you can stay on marked trails, and carry out what you carry in. For more information, contact **Island Heritage Trust** (⊠ Main St. ✑ Box 42, Deer Isle 04627 ☎ 207/348–2455) or the **Maine Island Trail Association** (⊠ 328 Main St. ✑ Box C, Rockland 04841 ☎ 207/596–6456 ⊕ www.mita.org).

Where to Stay & Eat

$–$$ ✕ **Fisherman's Friend.** For an extensive list of seafood specials, stop by this family-style restaurant. Look for crabmeat and clam rolls, fried clam and shrimp baskets, and other seafood platters. Pies and other desserts are made on the premises. The decor isn't fancy—this is a paper-place-mat kind of place. ⊠ *40 School St.* ☎ *207/367–2442* ☰ *D, MC, V* ☽ *Closed late Oct.–Apr.*

★ **$–$$** ✕ **Lily's.** Homemade baked goods, delicious sandwiches, and fresh salads are on the menu at this eatery. Try the Italian turkey sandwich, which has slices of oven-roasted turkey and Jack cheese on homemade sourdough bread. The dining room's glass-top tables let you gaze at the shells and various treasures inside. A produce stand behind the restaurant sells some of the same organic foods used by the chefs here. ⊠ *Rte. 15 and Airport Rd.* ☎ *207/367–5936* ☰ *MC, V.*

¢–$$ ✕ **Harbor Café.** This downtown restaurant is open year-round, so you can always stop by for staples like hamburgers, hot dogs, and sandwiches. In summer there's also salmon, halibut, lobster, and other seafood available at dinner. In the morning you're likely to sit next to fishermen who stop here before heading out for a day's work. ⊠ *Main St.* ☎ *207/367–5099* ☰ *MC, V.*

$$ ▦ **Inn on the Harbor.** From the front, this inn made up of four century-old Victorian buildings is as plain and unadorned as the town in which it is located. But in the rear is an expansive deck over the harbor—a pleasant spot for morning coffee or afternoon cocktails. Rooms on the harbor side have lovely views, and some have fireplaces and private decks. Those facing the street side can be noisy at night. One room is wheelchair accessible. ⊠ *45 Main St.* ✑ *Box 69, 04681* ☎ *207/367–2420 or 800/942–2420* ₰ *207/367–5165* ⊕ *www.innontheharbor.com* ☝ *12 rooms, 2 suites* ♘ *Coffee shop, in-room data ports, cable TV; no a/c, no children under 12, no smoking* ☰ *AE, D, MC, V* ⑩ *CP.*

¢–$ ▦ **Boyce's Motel.** This downtown motel offers simply furnished guest rooms with wall-to-wall carpeting. It also has apartment-style accommodations with full kitchens, separate sitting areas, and decks with views of the harbor. ⊠ *44 Main St., 04681* ☎ *207/367–2421 or 800/224–2421* ₰ *207/367–0937* ⊕ *www.boycesmotel.com* ☝ *4 rooms, 7 apartments* ♘ *Some kitchens, some pets allowed; no a/c* ☰ *AE, D, MC, V.*

¢ ⚠ **Old Quarry Campground.** This oceanfront campground offers both open and wooded campsites with raised platforms for tents, table, chairs, and fire rings. Carts are available to tote your gear to your site. Another property, Sunshine Campground, is on Deer Isle. ⚐ *Flush toilets, drinking water, guest laundry, showers, public telephone, general store, swimming (ocean)* ⌁ *10 tent sites* ⌂ *130 Settlement Rd., off Oceanville Rd., 04681* ☎ *207/367–8977* 🖷 *207/367–0937* ⊕ *www. oldquarry.com* ⊠ *$26–$32* ▭ *MC, V* ⊙ *Closed Nov.–Apr.*

Nightlife & the Arts

In the Stonington Opera House, **Opera House Arts** (⌂ School St. ☎ 207/367–2788 ⊕ www.operahousearts.org) hosts live theater, music, and dance events. You can spot this boxlike building from the pier.

Sports & the Outdoors

Old Quarry Ocean Adventures (⌂ 130 Settlement Rd. ☎ 207/367–8977 ⊕ www.oldquarry.com) rents bicycles, canoes, and kayaks and offers guided tours of the bay. Captain Bill Baker's three-hour boat tours take you past Stonington Harbor on the way to the outer islands. You can see Crotch Island, which has the area's only active stone quarry, and Green Island, where you can take a dip in a water-filled quarry. Tours cover the region's natural history, the history of Stonington, and the history of the granite industry. Sunset cruises are also available.

Shopping

In downtown Stonington, a handful of shops and restaurants are found along Main Street. Art and antiques are for sale at the **Clown** (⌂ 6 Thurlow's Hill ☎ 207/367–6348), as well as specialty foods and a good wine selection. Facing the harbor, **Dockside Books & Gifts** (⌂ 62 West Main St. ☎ 207/367–2652) stocks an eclectic selection of books. **Isalos** (⌂ 26 Main St. ☎ 207/367–2700 ⊕ www.isalosart.com), named for the Greek word for "waterline," sells paintings and photography by area artists.

Isle au Haut

❽ *14 mi south of Stonington.*

Isle au Haut thrusts its steeply ridged back out of the sea south of Stonington. French explorer Samuel D. Champlain discovered Isle au Haut—or "High Island"—in 1604, but heaps of shells suggest that native populations lived on or visited the island prior to his arrival. The island is accessible only by mail boat, but the 45-minute journey is well worth the effort. As you pass between the tiny islands of Merchants Row, you might see terns, guillemots, and harbor seals. The ferry makes two trips a day between Stonington and the Town Landing from Monday to Saturday, and adds a Sunday trip from mid-May to mid-September. In summer (mid-June to mid-September) the ferry also stops at Duck Harbor, located within Acadia National Park. The ferry will not unload bicycles, kayaks, or canoes at Duck Harbor, however.

Except for a grocery store and a natural foods store, Isle au Haut does not have any opportunities for shopping. The island is ideal for day-trippers intent on exploring its miles of trails. You could also stay a night or two, enjoying the low-key accommodations and delicious home-made meals.

★ Half of Isle au Haut is part of beautiful **Acadia National Park.** More than 18 mi of trails wind through quiet spruce woods, along beaches and sea-side cliffs, and over the spine of the central mountain ridge. The park's small campground, with five lean-tos, is open from mid-May to mid-October and fills up quickly. Reservations are essential. You can access Acadia National Park from the Town Landing. If you turn right when you arrive at the dock, the ranger station is a short walk or bike ride away. Public restrooms are here, as is the trailhead for the Duck Har-bor Trail. Be sure to check out the display of vertebrae and a jawbone from a whale. ⊠ *Isle au Haut* ☎ *207/288–3338* ⊕ *www.nps.gov/acad.*

Where to Stay & Eat

$$$$ ⊞ **Bel's Inn.** Around the corner from Town Landing, this small inn has two simply decorated rooms with big bureaus and comfortable beds. The full breakfast served each morning includes homemade bread. Steak and pork chops are often served at dinner, and you can always splurge on lobster. ⊠ *612 Seaside Harbor* ⊕ *Box 61, 04645* ☎ *207/335–2201* ⊕ *www.isleauhaut.net* 🛏 *2 rooms with shared bath* ⋄ *Restaurant; no room phones, no room TVs, no a/c, no smoking.* ⊟ *No credit cards* ⊗ *Closed late Oct.–mid-May* ⋈ *FAP.*

$$$$ ⊞ **The Inn at Isle au Haut.** This sea captain's home from 1897 retains its architectural charm. On the eastern side of the island, the seaside inn has views of sheep roaming around distant York Island and Cadillac Mountain. Comfortable wicker furniture is scattered around the porch, where appetizers are served when the weather is good. Downstairs, the dining room has original oil lamps and a model of the sea captain's boat (which sank just offshore). Breakfast includes granola and a hot dish—like a spinach, tomato, and cheese frittata—that changes daily. Dinner is an elaborate five-course meal usually incorporating local seafood. One night a week the inn has a lobster bake on the shore. The first-floor Cap-tain's Quarters, the only room with a private bath, has an ocean view, as do two of the three upstairs rooms. All have colorful quilts and frilly canopies. ⊠ *78 Atlantic Ave.* ⊕ *Box 78, 04645* ☎ *207/335–5141* ⊕ *www.innatisleauhaut.com* 🛏 *4 rooms, 1 with private bath* ⋄ *Din-ing room, bicycles; no a/c, no room phones, no room TVs, no smoking* ⊟ *No credit cards* ⊗ *Closed Oct.–May* ⋈ *FAP.*

$$$$ ⊞ **The Keeper's House.** Hidden by thick woods, this converted lighthouse keeper's home is an ideal spot to unwind. The ecofriendly inn has a re-verse-osmosis system that purifies the drinking water and solar-power and wind-power generators. There's no electricity in the guest rooms, however, so in the evening you can dine by candlelight and read by kerosene lantern. The spacious rooms are filled with painted wood fur-niture and decorated with local crafts. Breakfast features pancakes, granola with fresh fruit, eggs Benedict with smoked salmon, and other delicious dishes. Dinner emphasizes locally raised meats and freshly caught fish, like the haddock used for the delicious seafood stew. The inn also packs bag lunches you can take when exploring the trails of Acadia Na-tional Park. ⊠ *Lighthouse Rd.* ⊕ *Box 26, 04645* ☎ *207/460–0257* ⊕ *www.keepershouse.com* 🛏 *4 rooms, 2 with shared bath; 1 cottage*

⚘ *Dining room, bicycles, hiking; no a/c, no room phones, no room TVs* ⊟ *No credit cards* ⊘ *Closed mid-Oct.–mid-May* ⦿*| FAP.*

Sports & the Outdoors

There's no place to rent bicycles on Isle au Haut. If you want to bike around the island, head to **Old Quarry Ocean Adventures** (⊠ 130 Settlement Rd., Stonington ☎ 207/367–8977 ⊕ www.oldquarry.com). The mainland company can transport you and your bikes to Isle au Haut.

THE BLUE HILL PENINSULA A TO Z

To research prices, get advice from other travelers, and book travel arrangements, visit www.fodors.com.

AIR TRAVEL

Although Trenton's Hancock County–Bar Harbor Airport is near the Blue Hill Peninsula, only one commuter airline—Colgan Air, a subsidiary of US Airways, flies here. Most travelers prefer Bangor International Airport, an hour's drive from the peninsula. American, Continental, Delta, Midwest Express, Northwest, and US Airways fly into Bangor. Direct flights are available to and from Boston, New York, Philadelphia, Cincinnati, Detroit, and Albany.

🛪 **Bangor International Airport** ⊠ 287 Godfrey Blvd., Bangor ☎ 207/947–0384 ⊕ www.flybangor.com. **Hancock County–Bar Harbor Airport** ⊠ Rte. 3, Trenton ☎ 207/667-7329 ⊕ www.bhbairport.com.

BIKE TRAVEL

The Blue Hill Peninsula's winding roads rarely have adequate bike lanes, so be on your guard when exploring the region. Although there are a few bike rental shops in the area, your best bet is to take your own bike if you're going to Isle au Haut or Acadia National Park.

EMERGENCIES

In an emergency, dial 911.

🛈 Police In Stonington, call ☎ 207/667-7575 for police emergencies.

🛈 24-Hour Medical Care **Blue Hill Memorial Hospital** ⊠ 57 Water St., Blue Hill ☎ 207/374-2836 ⊕ www.bhmh.org. **Island Medical Center** ⊠ Airport Rd., near Rte. 15, Stonington ☎ 207/367-2311.

LODGING

🛈 **Island Vacation Rentals** ☎ 207/367-5095 ⊕ www.deerisleproperties.com. **Sargent's House Rentals** ☎ 207/367-5156 ⊕ www.sargentsrentalsinc.com. **Peninsula Properties** ☎ 207/374-2428 ⊕ www.peninsulapropertyrentals.com. **Slaven Realty** ☎ 207/374-0900.

MEDIA

NEWSPAPERS & MAGAZINES The weekly *Castine Patriot* provides news and features for the villages of Castine and Penobscot. *The Weekly Packet* serves Blue Hill, Brooklin, Brooksville, Sedgwick, and Surry. News about Deer Isle, Stonington, and Isle au Haut can be found in the weekly *Island Ad-Vantages*. The *Bangor Daily News* is the regional daily newspaper.

TELEVISION & RADIO Community radio station 89.9 FM in Blue Hill has eclectic programming, playing country, classical, folk, jazz, and reggae. The local National Public Radio affiliate is 90.9 FM. Channel 2 is the NBC affiliate, channel 7 is the ABC affiliate, and channel 5 is the CBS affiliate. Channel 12 is the Maine Public Broadcasting affiliate.

SPORTS & THE OUTDOORS

HIKING The Blue Hill Peninsula does not offer a lot of hiking trails, but local organizations such as the Blue Hill Heritage Trust and the Deer Isle Conservation Commission have tried to establish new trails and expand existing ones. To find out which outer islands are open to the public for day or overnight use, contact the Maine Island Trail Association.
🖪 **Blue Hill Heritage Trust** ⌂ Box 222 ✉ 101 Union St., Blue Hill 04614 ☎ 207/374–5118 ⊕ www.bluehillheritagetrust.org. **Deer Isle Conservation Commission** ⌂ Box 627, Deer Isle 04627 **Maine Island Trail Association** ⌂ Box C ✉ 328 Main St., Rockland 04841 ☎ 207/596–6456 ⊕ www.mita.org.

TRAIN TRAVEL

Portland is the closest city to the Blue Hill Peninsula with train service. Amtrak's "Downeaster" connects Portland to Boston with several stops in southern Maine and New Hampshire. From Portland, it takes approximately three hours to reach the peninsula.
🖪 **Amtrak** ☎ 800/872-7245 ⊕ www.amtrak.com.

VISITOR INFORMATION

🖪 **Blue Hill Peninsula Chamber of Commerce** ✉ 28 Water St., Blue Hill 04614 ☎ 207/374-3242 ⊕ www.bluehillpeninsula.com. **Deer Isle–Stonington Chamber of Commerce** ✉ Rte. 15, Deer Isle 04627 ☎ 207/348-6124 ⊕ www.deerisle.com.

MOUNT DESERT ISLAND & ACADIA NATIONAL PARK

6

WATCH THE SUNRISE FROM 1,532 FEET
on the peak of Cadillac Mountain ⇨*p.213*

SEIZE THE KODAK MOMENT
at Bass Harbor Head Light ⇨*p.213*

INDULGE IN SPECIALTY TAPAS
at Havana restaurant in Bar Harbor ⇨*p.203*

STOP AND SMELL THE AZALEAS
at Asticou Azalea Garden ⇨*p.217*

BOOK A ROOM WITH A VIEW
at the Asticou Inn ⇨*p.218*

SET SAIL ON A TOUR
out of Northeast Harbor ⇨*p.219*

By Lelah Cole **WITH SOME OF THE MOST DRAMATIC AND VARIED SCENERY ON THE MAINE COAST,** Mount Desert Island attracts more than 2 million visitors each year and has been a popular summer destination for more than a century. The island, much of which belongs to Acadia National Park, measures approximately 12 mi long and 9 mi across. Samuel de Champlain, the first European explorer to discover the area, named the island the "Isle de Monts Desert." Today Mount Desert Island (often pronounced "dessert") is Maine's most popular tourist attraction. The rocky coastline rises starkly from the ocean, appreciable along the scenic drives. Trails for hikers of all skill levels lead to the rounded tops of the mountains, providing views of Frenchman Bay, Blue Hill Bay, and beyond. Ponds and lakes beckon you to swim, fish, or boat. Ferries and charter boats provide spectacular views and a new perspective of the island, as well as a chance to explore the outer islands. A network of carriage roads lets you explore Acadia National Park's wooded interior, filled with birds and other wildlife.

Mount Desert Island has four different townships, each with its own personality. The town of Bar Harbor is on the northeastern corner of the island, and includes Bar Harbor, Hulls Cove, Salsbury Cove, and Town Hill. The town of Mount Desert comprises the southeastern corner of the island and parts of the western edge, and includes Mount Desert, Somesville, Hall Quarry, Beech Hill, Pretty Marsh, Northeast Harbor, Seal Harbor, and Otter Creek. As its name suggests, the town of Southwest Harbor is on the southwestern corner of the island, although the town of Tremont is at the southernmost tip of the west side. This area includes the villages of Southwest Harbor, Manset, Bass Harbor, Bernard, and Seal Cove. Bar Harbor is a major tourist center, with plenty of accommodations, restaurants, and shops. Less congested are smaller towns such as Northeast Harbor, Southwest Harbor, Bass Harbor, and the outlying islands.

After a full day of sightseeing and exploring, you can relax in a comfortable seaside room, watch the sunset from the top of Cadillac Mountain, or dine at one of the island's numerous eateries. Whatever your interests, Mount Desert Island and Acadia National Park can provide days—and even weeks—of enjoyment.

Exploring Mount Desert Island & Acadia National Park

Shaped like an upside down "U," Mount Desert Island is relatively easy to navigate. It may, however, take longer to reach some of the more distant points than you might expect. Somes Sound, the only fjord on the eastern coast of North America, runs up the middle of the island, requiring drivers at the ends of the "U" to drive quite a long distance to reach a town that is actually quite close as the crow flies. Beyond the geographical barriers, summer traffic can slow your progress and make finding a parking space nearly impossible. To combat this problem, Acadia National Park has created a free bus system called the Island Explorer. The system, which operates during the high season, links the island's villages and campgrounds. These propane-propelled buses are kinder to the environment than most cars, and are air-conditioned and outfitted with bike racks.

To truly explore Mount Desert Island, you must leave your car behind. Acadia's Park Loop Road provides an excellent overview of the island, but to get a feel for the the island's natural beauty, you should seek as many opportunities as you can for hiking, biking, and boating.

About the Restaurants

With some of the nation's wealthiest families making Mount Desert Island their summer residence, a handful of restaurants cater to those seeking an upscale dining experience. These restaurants offer carefully prepared dishes, extensive wine lists, and impressive service. Like most of the coast, the area is also home to many restaurants specializing in hamburgers and other typical American fare. You won't see fast-food chains, but you will find good food at reasonable prices.

Many area restaurants carry locally produced microbrews on draft or by the bottle. If you like pale ales, brown ales, or stouts, you should be able to find something to tempt the palate.

About the Hotels

As one of the most popular summer vacation spots in the country, Mount Desert Island offers a range of accommodation options to suit every budget. Whether you are looking for campgrounds, bed-and-breakfasts, or resort hotels, there are lodging options to meet your needs. While Bar Harbor is the most well known community on the island, the other villages offer accommodations that are equally—or even more—enticing. If you prefer to be close to shopping and nightlife, Bar Harbor is your best choice. For a quieter lodging experience, opt for one of the other villages.

If you drive along Route 3, you can spot a number of roadside motels and cabin-style accommodations that fall into lower price categories. Some bed-and-breakfasts can also be quite reasonable. Those looking to stay in a sprawling resort hotel or a beautifully appointed seaside inn should be prepared for prices in the top categories. The high-season rates go into effect during the second half of June and don't drop again until after Labor Day. Those traveling in the spring or during autumn will find room rates often dip significantly. Winter rates will always be the lowest.

WHAT IT COSTS					
	$$$$	$$$	$$	$	¢
RESTAURANTS	over $25	$18–$25	$11–$17	$7–$10	under $7
HOTELS	over $200	$150–$200	$100–$150	$60–$100	under $60

Restaurant prices are for a main course at dinner, excluding tax of 7%. Hotel prices are for two people in a standard double room in high season, excluding service charges and 7% tax.

Timing

Memorial Day and Labor Day mark the official beginning and end of high season on Mount Desert Island. The reality, however, is that there is no reason you have to visit during this narrow window. Temperatures

Numbers in the text correspond to numbers in the margin and on the Mount Desert Island and Bar Harbor maps.

6

If you have
3 days

If you have three days on Mount Desert Island, stay in **Bar Harbor ❸–❾**. There's plenty of things in this popular resort town to keep you occupied on your first day—from bustling boutiques to interesting museums. On Day 2, stop at the Hulls Cove Visitor Center to pick up information about special events, then head to Acadia National Park. A drive around **Park Loop Road ⓫** is a great way to learn the lay of the land. Stop along the way—a lot of the scenic overlooks have informational signs you may find interesting. Finish up the Park Loop Road journey by driving to the top of **Cadillac Mountain ⓯** to enjoy the sunset. On Day 3, rent a bike and explore the network of carriage roads that crisscross the island. Take in the spectacular view of **Jordan Pond ⓮** from the observation deck of the Jordan Pond House, a restaurant known for its massive popovers with lots of strawberry jam. For the afternoon's entertainment, hike the South Bubble Mountain (easier) or Penobscot Mountain (more challenging).

If you have
5 days

Follow the three-day itinerary above. On Day 4, drive to **Northeast Harbor ㉑**, the summer home of many of the country's wealthiest families. Take in the Asticou Azalea Garden and Thuya Gardens. On your last day, take a sightseeing cruise in the morning. In the afternoon, head to Bass Harbor Head Lighthouse, taking in **Somesville ㉒** and **Southwest Harbor ㉓** along the way.

---

often begin to rise in April or May. The crowds are smaller during these months, but you may have to contend with minor irritants such as ice and snow on the trails through Acadia National Park.

By September, the heat and humidity of the summer begin to taper off, making it one of the most enjoyable months to visit. Autumn foliage peaks between the end of September and the middle of October, enhancing the already spectacular views. Although many seasonal businesses close their doors after Columbus Day, the island does not shut down entirely. You can still find some good restaurants and a small number of lodging options throughout the winter months.

Regardless of when you decide to visit, you will enjoy your visit to the island more if you book your accommodations in advance. Although it's possible to find last-minute accommodations during the summer months, it may take several phone calls before you locate a room. If you have a particular type of lodging in mind, it's best to book as far in advance as possible. Accommodations tend to fill up especially quickly on holiday weekends. From November to April, your challenge shifts from finding an open room to finding an open hotel. You'll definitely want to call ahead.

GATEWAYS TO MOUNT DESERT ISLAND

Ellsworth and Trenton are unlikely to be focal points during your vacation, but you can't avoid them if you're traveling to Mount Desert Island. Ellsworth is a good place to pick up supplies for your journey, and Trenton has a small airport with commuter flights to Boston and Rockland. Perhaps Trenton's best offering is the view you see when crossing the bridge to the island. On clear days, the sunlight sparkles off the ocean, and the bald peaks of Acadia's mountains stand out starkly against the rich forests of conifers and evergreens. The beauty of it is overwhelming.

Ellsworth

❶ *140 mi northeast of Portland, 28 mi south of Bangor.*

Ellsworth is the storm's eye through which all vehicles traveling to Mount Desert Island must pass. As such, the few short miles of U.S. 1 that pass through the city can be fraught with frustration during the summer months. Traffic can back up for miles as cars wait to pass through the four traffic lights along High Street. Despite the congestion, Ellsworth is a good spot for refueling—literally and figuratively. With two supermarkets, several good restaurants, and a range of shops, the city offers just about anything you need. The main shopping strips are along High Street (where you can find two malls) and Main Street (home to attractive brick buildings that house some distinctive shops).

At the 130-acre **Stanwood Homestead Museum & Bird Sanctuary** you can look for birds along the trails and visit the 1850 Stanwood House Museum, a Cape Cod–style house. Cordelia Stanwood, born in 1856, was one of Maine's earliest ornithologists. ⊠ *Rte. 3* ☎ *207/667–8460* 🎦 *Free* ☉ *Trails daily sunrise–sunset; museum mid-May–mid-Oct., daily 10–4.*

Between 1824 and 1828, Col. John Black built **Woodlawn,** an elegant Georgian mansion. Inside are an especially fine elliptical flying staircase and period artifacts from the three generations of the family that lived here. Outside, you can wander through several different gardens. The formal garden, enclosed by a lilac hedge, features flowers that were popular in the 19th century, including iris, daylilies, and phlox. A millstone lies inside the garden, a donation from the Ladies Club of Mount Desert Island, which insisted it be recovered from a shipwreck off Baker's Island in 1895. The garden's urn remains from the original design. The site also features a community garden that provides residents with an opportunity to grow their own vegetables and flowers with guidance from area master gardeners. Woodlawn has 17 acres of grounds and 2 mi of walking trails that Col. Black used as a bridle path. ⊠ *Surrey Rd.* ☎ *207/667–8671* ⊕ *www.woodlawnmuseum.org* 🎦 *$8; free access to gardens and grounds* ☉ *May and Oct., Tues.–Sun. 1–4; June–Sept., Tues.–Sat. 10–5 and Sun. 1–4.*

6

Carriage Roads

Roads and cars often go hand in hand, but this is not always true in Acadia National Park. Between 1913 and 1940, John D. Rockefeller Jr. designed and funded the construction of more than 40 mi of carriage roads. Rockefeller, a summer resident of Mount Desert Island, wanted to maintain a way for horse-drawn carriages to safely travel the island after the arrival of automobiles. Today, the carriage roads provide hours of enjoyment to walkers, joggers, and bikers. The roads wind through fields and forests, past lakes, ponds, and swamps, and around hills and mountains. You can admire the Canadian mayflowers and young, curled ferns in the spring; nibble at blueberries that grow among the granite boulders in summer; collect the fallen crimson leaves of sugar maples in autumn; or enjoy the solitude of the winter landscape on snowshoes or cross-country skis. The network of roads offers excursions of varying length and difficulty, so be sure to pick up a map to plan your best routes.

Gorgeous Gardens

When Beatrix Farrand, one of the country's first well-known female landscape gardeners, was preparing to retire in the 1950s, she offered her own estate to Bar Harbor as a public park. Since she had designed plant-filled retreats for everywhere from the College of the Atlantic to the White House, she assumed the town would jump at the chance. But the town politely declined her offer, saying that the property taxes for the site would be too high. She decided to dismantle the garden, and gave her friends a year to come collect any plants they desired. Her friend Charles Savage, also a landscape designer, retrieved several of Farrand's rhododendrons and azaleas, and used them when he created the Asticou Azalea Garden and Thuya Gardens in Northeast Harbor. Some of her beloved blooms remain in the gardens today.

On the Water

With its dramatic coastline, Mount Desert Island is a great spot for sea kayaking. There are shops all over the island that are happy to provide you with gear, offer expert instruction, and give tips on possible routes. Along the way you'll see cormorants and other birds, and you might catch a glimpse of harbor seals. If you're an angler, stop by the Hulls Cove Visitor Center to find out which species thrive in the dozens of ponds and lakes scattered around the island. Some are popular in the warmer months, while others are better for ice fishing. You can rent canoes in Bar Harbor and other towns. Most of the lakes and ponds have well-marked public access points, making boating even easier. If you are planning on using a motorized watercraft anywhere besides the ocean, check with the park rangers first—many lakes and ponds don't allow motor boats or restrict the size of the engine.

Where to Stay & Eat

The city of Ellsworth is about a half-hour drive from most of the attractions on Mount Desert Island. Despite its relatively close proximity to such natural beauty, Ellsworth doesn't have a great deal of charm. A few accommodations are available, but aren't likely to be much cheaper than those on the island.

$$–$$$ ╳ **Turriglios Italian Restaurant.** Tucked away on a side street, this Italian restaurant has a following among the locals. The menu offers traditional fare such as fettuccini Alfredo and stuffed manicotti, as well as more unusual entrées such as *aragosta alla pescatora,* a medley of lobster, scallops, shrimp, and mussels tossed with linguine and a mildly spicy marinara sauce. There's also a good wine list. ⊠ *Franklin and Main Sts., Ellsworth* ☎ *207/667–0202* ⊟ *MC, V* ☉ *Closed Mon.*

$–$$ ╳ **Cleonice.** You can find a satisfying selection of tapas at this Mediterranean-style restaurant, as well as entrées for lunch and dinner. The menu includes items such as baby spinach salad with goat cheese, bacon, and hazelnuts and a paella that is chock full of scallops, crab, mussels, chicken, and Spanish sausage. ⊠ *112 Main St.* ☎ *207/664–7554* ⊟ *AE, MC, V.*

¢–$$ ╳ **Jordan's Snack Bar.** This take-out restaurant with a roll-up-your-sleeves atmosphere has some of the best fried clams around. Locals will wait more than an hour on opening day to order the delicious fried seafood. There are also burgers and fries on the menu. Choose between the indoor seating area and the outdoor picnic tables. To find this place, turn left where U.S. 1 splits from Route 3 and continue for about a mile. ⊠ *200 Down East Rd., Ellsworth* ☎ *207/667–2174* ⊟ *MC, V* ☉ *Closed Nov.–early Mar.*

¢–$$ ╳ **Riverside Café.** The only thing better than the food at this popular eatery is the staff's camaraderie. The employees are fast, friendly, and frequently banter back and forth across the restaurant. Open early for breakfast, the café offers everything from French toast and blueberry pancakes to omelets and breakfast burritos. On Sunday, the menu expands to include raspberry-stuffed French toast and pumpkin pancakes with maple cream. For lunch you can choose between sandwiches, quiches, and salads. The breads, muffins, and biscuits are all baked on the premises. Works by a different area artist are displayed each month. ⊠ *151 Main St.* ☎ *207/ 667–7220* ⊟ *AE, MC, V* ☉ *No dinner.*

¢–$ ╳ **Frankie's Café.** This small eatery serves up fresh sandwiches, wraps, and soups to eat in or take out. There are also a few hot dishes that rotate daily, including stuffed ravioli, fajitas, lasagna, and quiche. Frankie's has a gift shop offering a number of items with British flair, including teas, teapots, and teakettles. Brilliant! ⊠ *40 High St.* ☎ *207/ 667–7701* ⊟ *MC, V.*

$$–$$$ ⌂ **Comfort Inn.** Open throughout the year, this chain hotel has simply decorated rooms with some nice touches like hair driers and irons. It sits adjacent to the L. L. Bean factory outlet and several eateries. ⊠ *130 High St., 04609* ☎ *207/667–1345* ⊕ *www.comfortinn.com* ⇴ *63 rooms* ♿ *Some microwaves, some refrigerators, cable TV, exercise room* ⊟ *AE, D, MC, V* ┃◎┃ *CP.*

Nightlife & the Arts

A local landmark, the **Grand Auditorium** (⊠ 165 Main St. ☎ 207/667–9500 ⊕ www.grandonline.org) opened as a movie theater in 1938. It fell into disrepair, sitting vacant from the '50s to the '70s. The theater reopened in 1975 with a concert by Noel Paul Stookey, and since then has staged plays, concerts, and films.

Sports & the Outdoors

Bar Harbor Bicycle Shop (✉ 193 Main St. ☎ 207/667–6886 ⊕ www. barharborbike.com) rents both recreational and high-performance bikes.

Shopping

One of the best sporting goods stores in the state, **Cadillac Mountain Sports** (✉ 34 High St. ☎ 207/667–7819 ⊕ www.cadillacmountainsports.com) has developed a following among locals and visitors alike. A branch of the original store in Bar Harbor, this location carries top-quality bicycles, canoes, kayaks, cross-country skis, and a selection of hiking and camping equipment. If you need a pair of hiking boots, some running shoes, a bike helmet, or a warmer jacket, this is the place to stop. The **Grasshopper Shop** (✉ 124 Main St. ☎ 207/667–5816) sells fun and unique gifts. You can find books, candles, linens, jewelry, and women's clothing and shoes. Most of the lower level is dedicated to items for children.

With a selection of organic and natural foods, **John Edward's Market** (✉ 158 Main St. ☎ 207/667–9377) is a pleasant alternative to the supermarket when you're stocking up on supplies. Downstairs is a wine cellar and an art gallery that showcases works by area artists. The fluorescent lighting is a bit harsh, but the art—and the wine—are worth investigating. You can find everything for your kitchen at **Rooster Brother** (✉ 29 Main St. ☎ 207/667–8675), including nonstick cookware and bamboo steamers, as well as wines, cheese, and freshly ground coffee.

Trenton

❷ *5 mi south of Ellsworth via Rte. 3.*

Like Ellsworth, Trenton is a town that everyone traveling to Mount Desert Island must pass through. The town offers little in the way of dining or lodging options, but it does have the closest airport to the island, which is filled with private jets in summer. Sightseeing flights by plane or glider are popular. Carroll's Supermarket usually has the cheapest gas around—and often the longest lines at the pumps.

In its fields and woods, the **Acadia Zoo** shelters about 45 species of wild and domestic animals, including reindeer, alligators, wolves, and a moose. A converted barn serves as a rain-forest habitat for monkeys, birds, reptiles, and other Amazon creatures. Shows are scheduled throughout the day. ✉ *446 Bar Harbor Rd.* ☎ *207/667–3244* ⊕ *www. acadiazoo.com* ✎ *$8* ☉ *May–Dec., daily 9:30–dusk.*

About 8 mi from Route 3, the seaside **Lamoine State Park** offers a quiet respite from the crowds on Mount Desert Island. During the day you can stroll along the pebble beach, eat lunch on one of the picnic tables, or pull your boat up to the dock. The state park officially closes in winter, but remains accessible for hikers and cross-country skiers. ✉ *23 State Park Rd., Lamoine* ☎ *207/667–4778 or 207/941–4014* ⊕ *www. acadiamagic.com.*

Sports & the Outdoors

The **Bar Harbor Golf Course** (✉ Rtes. 3 and 204, Trenton ☎ 207/667–7505) is a 9-hole golf course open to the public. If you want to practice your swing, **Vokes Golf Range** (⊠ Bar Harbor Rd. ☎ 207/667–9519) has a driving range. There's also a miniature golf course for the kids.

🖑 **Seacoast Fun Park** (⊠ Bar Harbor Rd. ☎ 207/667–3573) has go-karts, two short waterslides, and a miniature golf course.

BAR HARBOR

160 mi northeast of Portland, 22 mi southeast of Ellsworth on Rte. 3.

A resort town since the 19th century, Bar Harbor now serves visitors to Acadia National Park with inns, motels, and restaurants. Most of its grand mansions were destroyed in a fire that devastated the island in 1947, but many of those that survived have been converted into businesses. Shops are clustered along Main, Mount Desert, and Cottage streets. Take a stroll down West Street, a National Historic District, where you can see some fine old houses.

❸ **Bar Harbor Historical Society Museum.** The museum displays photographs of Bar Harbor from the days when it catered to the very rich. Other exhibits document the great fire that devastated the town in 1947. ⊠ *33 Ledgelawn Ave.* ☎ *207/288–3807 or 207/288–0000* 🎫 *Free* ⊘ *June–Oct., Mon.–Sat. 1–4.*

❹ **Abbe Museum.** The only museum devoted solely to Maine's Native American heritage, the Abbe Museum houses a collection of artifacts that spans 10,000 years. Open since 2001, the museum has permanent and changing exhibitions. ⊠ *26 Mount Desert St.* ☎ *207/288–3519* ⊕ *www.abbemuseum.org* 🎫 *$5* ⊘ *Feb.–Dec., daily 9–5* ⊘ *Closed Jan.*

🖑 ❺ **George B. Dorr Museum of Natural History.** This small museum at the College of the Atlantic has wildlife exhibits, a hands-on discovery room, interpretive programs, and summer field studies for children. ⊠ *105 Eden St.* ☎ *207/288–5395 or 207/288–5015* ⊕ *www.coa.edu/nhm* 🎫 *$4* ⊘ *Mid-June–Labor Day, Mon.–Sat. 10–5. Labor Day–mid-Nov. and mid-Jan.–mid-June, Fri. and Sun. 1–4, Sat. 10–4.*

❻ **Ethel Blum Gallery.** This art museum at the College of the Atlantic hosts exhibits throughout the year on painting, sculpture, photography, and other media. ⊠ *105 Eden St.* ☎ *207/288–5015* 🎫 *Free* ⊘ *Late Sept.–May, Weekdays 9–4; June–late Sept., Tues.–Sat. 10–4.*

🖑 ❼ **Bar Harbor Whale Museum.** Learn about the history of whaling, the anatomy of whales, and how biologists are working to gain more information about these massive creatures at this interesting museum. All proceeds from the gift shop benefit Allied Whale, a nonprofit organization that conducts marine mammal research. ⊠ *52 West St.* ☎ *207/288–1054* 🎫 *Free* ⊘ *June, daily noon–8; July and Aug., daily 9–9; Sept. and Oct., daily 10–8.*

🖑 ❽ **Mount Desert Oceanarium.** You'll find a lobster hatchery and exhibits on the fishing and sea life of the Gulf of Maine at this interesting complex. ⊠ *Rte. 3, Bar Harbor* ☎ *207/288–5005* ⊕ *www.theoceanarium.com* 🎫 *$9* ⊘ *Mid-May–late Oct., Mon.–Sat. 9–5.*

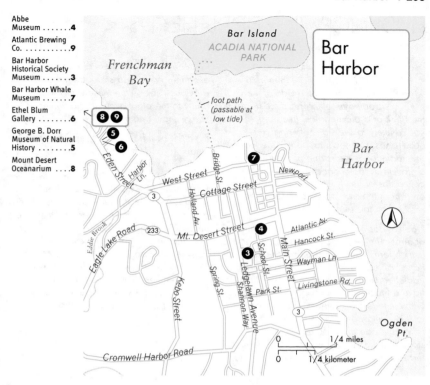

9 Atlantic Brewing Company. Near Bar Harbor in the village of Town Hill, this microbrewery has free tastings. Tours at 2, 3, and 4 PM last approximately 45 minutes. A barbecue restaurant is also on the premises. ⊠ *Knox Rd., turn at Town Hill Country Store, Town Hill* ☎ *207/288–2337* ⊕ *www.atlanticbrewing.com* 🖃 *Free* ⊙ *Open May–late Oct., daily 10–5.*

Where to Eat

★ **$$$$** ✕ **George's.** Fine linens grace the tables, and original art fills the walls of the four small dining rooms in this charming old house. It may be difficult to choose among the entrées, but you won't go wrong with the lobster strudel with chanterelle ragout or the charcoal-grilled swordfish with salsa served over couscous. Whatever you pick, remember to save room for dessert. The restaurant always has 10 to 12 wines by the glass. Jazz musicians perform nightly during the summer months. ⊠ *7 Stephen's La.* ☎ *207/288–4505* ⊕ *www.georgesbarharbor.com* 🖃 *AE, D, DC, MC, V* ⊙ *Closed Nov.–mid-June.*

★ **$$–$$$$** ✕ **Havana.** Soft jazz playing in the background sets the tone at this storefront restaurant on the edge of downtown Bar Harbor. The pumpkin-color walls and wood floors lend an air of sophistication. The Latin-influenced menu emphasizes local ingredients and changes weekly. Specializing in tapas, the menu may include crab-and-roasted-corn cakes

CloseUp

FIDDLING WITH FIDDLEHEADS

AS YOU HEAD TOWARD MOUNT DESERT ISLAND, *it's common to see vendors on the side of the roadways selling produce from the back of a pickup truck. In spring, you're likely to see signs offering* CLEAN FIDDLEHEADS. *Unknown to many Americans, the fiddlehead fern is one of nature's true delicacies. Fiddleheads are the tightly coiled tips of newly emerging fronds, and are about the size of two or three quarters stacked on top of each other.*

Fiddleheads come from different varieties of ferns. The best fiddleheads come from ostrich ferns, which, unlike most ferns, have hairless casings. You can also eat the fiddleheads from cinnamon ferns but they have a fuzzier casing. You shouldn't fiddle with some ferns, however. The bracken fern is similar to the ostrich fern, but it's hairy and can give you quite a stomachache. It can be difficult to identify ferns, but if you are determined to forage,

you can identify the type of fern by examining the dead stalks from the previous year. Often these stalks will hold firmly to the plant even after a winter of heavy snow and ice.

Even the best fiddleheads require a good cleaning, and should be thoroughly cooked. If you pick some fiddleheads, be sure to boil them for 10 to 15 minutes. The best method is to boil them for about 7 minutes in one pot, then discard the water and boil them in fresh water until they are tender. Fiddleheads have a distinct flavor that aficionados say is somewhere between asparagus and spinach. Many area restaurants will offer them as a side dish, toss them with pasta, or add them to other dishes. Be sure to give them a try if you are visiting during springtime.

or grilled swordfish marinated in ginger and lime and finished with a scallion vinaigrette. There's also a phenomenal wine list. ⊠ *318 Main St.* ☎ *207/288–2822* ⊕ *www.havanamaine.com* ⚑ *Reservations essential* ⊟ *MC, V* ⊗ *Closed Sun.–Tues. late Oct.–mid-May.*

$$$

Fodor'sChoice

★

✕ **The Burning Tree.** Local art adorns the walls in the two dining rooms and on the porch at this restaurant in Otter Creek. The ever-changing menu emphasizes freshly caught seafood. Entrées include pan-sautéed monkfish, Cajun-style lobster, and crab au gratin. Delicious dishes such as chicken pot roast hold their own on the menu. There are always two or three vegetarian choices. ⊠ *Rte. 3, Otter Creek* ☎ *207/288–9331* ⊟ *D, MC, V* ⊗ *Closed Tues. and mid-Oct.–late May.*

★ **$$–$$$**

✕ **Mache.** Painted with muted earth tones and decorated with flickering candles, this restaurant's low-key ambience allows for the food to take center stage. The menu changes weekly, but always begins with freshly baked bread. Choose from appetizers such as seared scallops and fiddlehead ferns tossed with penne and Alfredo sauce. Entrées include a seared salmon filet with ginger and basil, and pan-fried tofu with apricots. There's also a cheese course featuring local blue cheese and chèvre. Choose from a short but thoughtfully selected wine list and be sure to save room for one of their homemade desserts—the lemon tart is excellent. ⊠ *135 Cottage St.* ☎ *207/288–0447* ▤ *MC, V* ⊘ *Closed Mon.*

$$–$$$ ✕ **Rupununi.** Sit on the patio of this relaxed, American-style bar and grill, and watch the world go by. Serving up burgers, steaks, and salads, it has something for everyone on the menu. You can also choose from a reasonably priced selection of wines and beers from six different microbreweries. ⊠ *119 Main St.* ☎ *207/288–2766* ⊕ *www.rupununi. com* ▤ *AE, D, DC, MC, V* ⊘ *Closed Nov.–Apr.*

$–$$$ ✕ **Donohue's Eatery & Spirits.** Varnished wooden booths add to the cozy atmosphere at this downtown restaurant. Try the baby spinach salad with sesame-ginger vinaigrette dressing or the tasty wraps. Local musicians play on the weekends, or you can grab the microphone on the weekly karaoke night. You'll also find locally brewed beers on tap. ⊠ *30 Cottage St.* ☎ *207/288–3030* ▤ *MC, V* ⊘ *Closed Nov.–Apr.*

$–$$$ ✕ **Galyn's.** Open throughout the year, this casual eatery serves items such as a Cajun pork sandwich or a chicken foccacia sandwich for lunch. For dinner, the emphasis switches to steak and seafood, with options such as garlic shrimp tossed with linguine and lots of lobster dishes. The Indian pudding is delicious. ⊠ *17 Main St.* ☎ *207/288–9706* ⌙ *Reservations essential* ▤ *AE, D, MC, V.*

$–$$$ ✕ **McKay's Public House.** Low lighting and glowing candles set the right mood for relaxed but elegant dining. The pub menu includes familiar favorites such as fish-and-chips, but also more unusual options such as lamb burgers, corned beef and cabbage, and bangers and mash. The restaurant also emphasizes fresh seafood, offering crab cakes, porcini halibut, seared scallops, and other dishes. Key lime pie, crème brûlée, cheesecake, and other desserts will tempt your palate. Reservations are a good idea. ⊠ *231 Main St.* ☎ *207/288–2002* ▤ *AE, MC, V.*

$$ ✕ **Eden Vegetarian Café.** You'll find artfully prepared vegetarian meals at this restaurant near the harbor. Start with an appetizer of baby bok choi kimchee, chilled melon gazpacho, or grilled artichoke with a citrus-bernaise sauce. Choose from entrées such as rigatoni with roasted garlic, broccoli, fresh tomatoes, and pesto. Vegetables here are organic and come from local farms. ⊠ *78 West St.* ☎ *207/288–4422* ▤ *D, MC, V.*

$–$$ ✕ **Thrumcap.** Dark-wood paneling and gleaming floors exude elegance at this casual café. You can select dishes from their prix-fixe menu, such as shrimp and boursin ravioli, grilled marinated quail with plum sauce, and coconut-fried lobster with tropical-fruit salsa. If you can't decide on a wine, try a "mini-flight"—two half glasses of two different wines. ⊠ *123 Cottage St.* ☎ *207/288–3884* ▤ *MC, V* ⊘ *Closed Sun. and Nov.–May.*

Where to Stay

$$$$ ✕▥ **Harborside Hotel & Marina.** One of Bar Harbor's newest lodgings, this Tudor-style hotel has a prime location next to the harbor. The guest rooms are elegantly decorated in soft yellows and greens; the baths are tiled in marble. Most rooms have balconies, many have water views. Suites have high-definition TVs and surround sound stereo, and penthouse suites have a full kitchen, dining room, hot tub, and fireplace. The inn's restaurant, the Pier, is open to the public for lunch and dinner and specializes in fresh seafood, including lobster and jumbo scallops. At this writing, the adjacent Bar Harbor Club was planning to finish its spa, tennis court, and saltwater pool in 2005. ⊠ *55 West St., 04609* ☎ *207/288–5033 or 800/328–5033* ⊕ *www.theharborsidehotel.com* ⇨ *187 rooms* ⌂ *3 restaurants, some in-room data ports, some kitchens, tennis court, 2 pools (1 saltwater), health club, spa, dock, laundry service, meeting rooms; no-smoking rooms* ⊟ *AE, D, DC, MC, V* ⏿ *CP.*

$$$–$$$$ ✕⊡ **Bar Harbor Inn.** Originally established in the late 1800s as a men's drinking club, this waterfront inn has rooms spread out over three buildings on well-landscaped grounds. Most rooms have gas fireplaces and balconies with great views. Rooms in the Oceanfront Lodge have private decks overlooking the ocean. Should you need more room, there are also some two-level suites. The elegant waterfront restaurant, the Reading Room, serves mostly Continental fare. Look for Maine specialties such as lobster pie and Indian pudding. There's live music nightly. The inn is a short walk from town, so you're close to all the sights. ⊠ *Newport Dr., 04609* ☎ *207/288–3351 or 800/248–3351* ⎙ *207/288–5296* ⊕ *www.barharborinn.com* ⌖ *Dinner reservations essential* ⇨ *138 rooms, 15 suites* ⌂ *2 restaurants, in-room safes, refrigerators, cable TV, in-room DVD players, pool, gym, business services, meeting room; no smoking* ⊟ *AE, D, DC, MC, V* ⊘ *Closed late Nov.–late Mar.* ⏿ *CP.*

$$$–$$$$ ✕⊡ **Bluenose Inn–Bar Harbor Hotel.** This resort is perched on the top of a hill overlooking Frenchman Bay. All the comfortable guest rooms have gas fireplaces, and most have excellent views. Executive chef Frederic Link presides over the Rose Garden ($$$$), which features fine seafood and beef entrées on the three-course prix-fixe and five-course tasting menus. To start, try the strudel filled with asparagus or the Maine lobster bisque. North Atlantic salmon, Maine lobster, rack of lamb, pan-seared venison steak, and other entrées are popular. Finally, choose from desserts such as a warm apple tart, vanilla-bean crème brûlée, or flourless chocolate cake. After touring Acadia National Park, you can relax in the hot tub or steam room or swim a few laps in the indoor or outdoor pool. ⊠ *90 Eden St., 04609* ☎ *800/445–4077 or 207/288–3348* ⎙ *207/288–2183* ⊕ *www.bluenoseinn.com* ⌖ *Dinner reservations essential* ⇨ *97 rooms, 1 suite* ⌂ *2 restaurants, in-room safes, refrigerators, cable TV, in-room DVD players, 2 pools (1 indoor), hot tub, steam room, gym, lounge, gift shop, Internet* ⊟ *AE, D, DC, MC, V* ⊘ *Closed Nov.–late Apr.*

$$–$$$ ✕⊡ **Two Cats.** Fresh, organic ingredients are emphasized at this colorful eatery. Eat in the dining room or outside on the pleasant patio. The chefs grow their own herbs and bake their own breads, biscuits, and muffins. (Try them with the delicious strawberry butter.) For breakfast, try the raspberry almond pancakes, or the "summer scramble"—eggs with scallions, tomatoes, and cheese. For dinner, the menu includes barbecued ribs, rainbow trout, and sage-rubbed grilled vegetables. Two Cats also has several comfortable rooms upstairs with hardwood floors, and antique four-poster beds. A gourmet breakfast from the restaurant is included in the rate. ⊠ *130 Cottage St., 04609* ☎ *800/355–2808 or 207/288–2808* ⊕ *www.2catsbarharbor.com* ⇨ *1 room, 1 suite, 1 studio* ⌂ *Restaurant, some kitchens* ⊟ *MC, V* ⏿ *BP.*

★ $$$$ ⊡ **Balance Rock Inn.** This grand summer cottage built in 1903 commands a prime waterfront location. An expansive lawn and gardens full of annuals lead down to the ocean. Even if your room doesn't have an ocean view, you can enjoy it from a wicker chair on the porch. Rooms are spacious and meticulously furnished with reproduction pieces—four-poster and canopy beds in guest rooms, crystal chandeliers and a grand piano in common rooms. All rooms have whirlpool tubs, and some have fireplaces. A buffet-style breakfast is served each morning. ⊠ *21 Albert Meadow, 04609* ☎ *207/288–2610 or 800/753–0494* ☒ *207/288–5534* ⊕ *www.barharborvacations.com* ⇨ *6 rooms, 3 suites* ♿ *In-room data ports, cable TV, in-room DVD players, pool, gym, bar, concierge* ☰ *AE, D, MC, V* ⊗ *Closed late Oct.–early May* ⎮◎⎮ *BP.*

★ **$$$$** ⌂ **Bass Cottage Inn.** Completely renovated in 2004, this elegant and refreshing inn, dating from 1885, respects its Victorian history—without the stuffy Victorian decor. All rooms have their own character—each was designed by the owner with a family member or friend in mind. Light-colored walls, hardwood floors, and gas fireplaces give them a comfortable, contemporary feel. While the inn does not have ocean views, it is a short walk from most Bar Harbor attractions. Wine and hors d'oeuvres are served each evening, and a full gourmet breakfast is available in the atrium each morning. You can relax on the sun porch, in the parlor, or in the reading room in front of the fireplace. The club-style lounge is filled with puzzles and games. Appointments with a licensed massage therapist are available. ⊠ *14 The Field, 04609* ☎ *866/782–9224 or 207/288–1234* ⊕ *www.basscottage.com* ⇨ *10 rooms* ♿ *Cable TV, in-room DVD players, Internet; no-smoking rooms* ☰ *AE, MC, V* ⊗ *Closed early Dec.–mid-May* ⎮◎⎮ *BP.*

$$$–$$$$ ⌂ **Nannau.** For a taste of 19th-century Bar Harbor, stay at this 1904 seaside estate, listed on the National Register of Historic Places. The lodging is secluded among towering evergreens a mile from downtown Bar Harbor. The shingle-style house is comfortably furnished with period furniture, fabrics, and wallpapers. All rooms have ocean views; two have fireplaces. The 4-acre property borders Compass Harbor and a section of Acadia National Park. ⊠ *396 Main St.* ⌂ *Box 710, 04609* ☎ *207/ 288–5575* ⊕ *www.nannau.com* ⇨ *3 rooms, 1 suite* ♿ *No a/c, no room phones, no room TVs, no smoking* ☰ *MC, V* ⊗ *Closed Nov.–June* ⎮◎⎮ *BP.*

$$$–$$$$ ⌂ **Ullikana.** Inside the stucco-and-timber walls of this traditional Tudor **Fodor's**Choice cottage, antiques are juxtaposed with contemporary country pieces; vi★ brant color with French country wallpapers; and abstract art with folk creations. The combination not only works—it shines. Rooms are large; many have fireplaces, and some have decks. Breakfast is an elaborate multicourse affair. The refurbished Yellow House across the drive has six additional rooms decorated in traditional Old Bar Harbor style. ⊠ *16 The Field, 04609* ☎ *207/288–9552* ☒ *207/288–3682* ⊕ *www.ullikana. com* ⇨ *16 rooms* ♿ *No a/c in some rooms, no room phones, no room TVs, no smoking* ☰ *MC, V* ⊗ *Closed Nov.–May* ⎮◎⎮ *BP.*

$$$ ⌂ **Bar Harbor Grand Hotel.** Modeled after the Rodick House, a hotel built in the late 1800s, this contemporary hotel evokes the Victorian era. Comfortable guest rooms have thoughtful additions such as coffeemakers and refrigerators. Meal plans at another hotel, the Bar Harbor Inn, can be arranged. ⊠ *269 Main St., 04609* ☎ *888/766–2529 or 207/288–5226* ⊕ *www.barharborgrand.com* ⇨ *70 rooms* ♿ *Refrigerators, cable TV, in-room DVD players, pool, hot tub, Internet, laundry, gift shop, no-*

smoking rooms ⊟ AE, DC, MC, V ⊘ Closed mid-Nov.–mid-Apr.
†⊚† CP.

$$ ⊞ **Cromwell Harbor Motel.** Less than a mile from downtown Bar Harbor, this clean and pleasant motel is set amid pretty gardens. From here you can walk to a quiet section of Acadia National Park. ⊠ *359 Main St., 04069* ☎ *207/288–3201 or 800/544–3201* ⊕ *www.cromwellharbor. com* ⌁ *26 rooms* ⌂ *Some microwaves, some refrigerators, cable TV, pool, no-smoking rooms* ⊟ AE, D, MC, V.

$$ ⊞ **Seacroft Inn.** It's an easy walk to Bar Harbor or the Shore Path from this rambling, multigabled inn. The property has seven efficiency units, including one two-bedroom unit that is a good choice for families. A breakfast basket is delivered to your room each morning. ⊠ *18 Albert Meadow, 04609* ☎ *207/288–4669 or 800/824–9694* ⊕ *www.seacroftinn. com* ⌁ *6 rooms, 1 2-bedroom unit* ⌂ *Refrigerators, microwaves, cable TV* ⊟ MC, V ⊘ Closed mid.-Nov.–Apr. †⊚† CP.

$ ⊞ **Eden Village Motel & Cottages.** Children can learn to fish at the pond on this 25-acre property, 5 mi from downtown Bar Harbor. Although the furnishings are not new, the rooms certainly are comfortable and most have views of the top of Cadillac Mountain. A back porch that extends the length of the building has picnic tables and grills. Cottages vary in size, but all have working fireplaces, barbecue grills, and screened porches. A mile-long nature trail passes by blueberry bushes, and cherry and apple trees. ⊠ *986 Rte. 3, 04609* ☎ *207/288–4670* ⊕ *www. edenvillage.com* ⌁ *10 rooms, 11 cottages* ⌂ *Some kitchenettes, boating, fishing, no-smoking rooms; no a/c in some rooms* ⊟ DC, MC, V ⊘ Closed mid-Oct.–mid-May.

Nightlife & the Arts

The **Arcady Music Festival** (☎ 207/288–3151) schedules classical concerts at locations around Mount Desert Island throughout the year. The **Bar Harbor Music Festival** (⊠ 59 Cottage St. ☎ 207/288–5744) hosts jazz, classical, and pop concerts by young professionals from July to early August.

★ The art deco–style **Criterion Theater** (⊠ 35 Cottage St. ☎ 207/288–3441) stages concerts, plays, and other live performances. Movies are screened at **Reel Pizza Cinerama** (⊠ 33-B Kennebec Pl. ☎ 207/288–3811).

If you want to shoot some pool or throw some darts, try the **Carmen Verandah** (⊠ 119 Main St. ☎ 207/288–2766 ⊕ www.carmenverandah. com). The upstairs bar has live music and dancing. **Geddy's Pub** (⊠ 19 Main St. ☎ 207/288–5077) hosts local musicians early in the evening and DJs spinning later at night.

At the **Lompoc Café & Brewpub** (⊠ 30 Rodick St. ☎ 207/288–9513) you can play a game of boccie in the delightful garden.

Sports & the Outdoors

Bicycling
Acadia Bike Rentals (⊠ 48 Cottage St. ☎ 207/288–9605 or 800/526–8615) rents mountain bikes good for negotiating the trails in Acadia Na-

tional Park. The **Bar Harbor Bicycle Shop** (⊠ 141 Cottage St. ☎ 207/288–3886 or 800/824–2453) rents bikes by the half or full day.

Birding

Down East Nature Tours (✑ Box 521, Bar Harbor 04609 ☎ 207/288–8128) leads excursions for individuals and small groups. You can learn the basics of birding, including how to identify a particular species.

Boating

Acadia Outfitters (⊠ 106 Cottage St. ☎ 207/288–8118) rents canoes and sea kayaks. **Coastal Kayaking Tours** (⊠ 48 Cottage St. ☎ 207/288–9605 or 800/526–8615) conducts tours of the rocky coastline led by registered guides. **National Park Sea Kayak Tours** (⊠ 39 Cottage St. ☎ 207/288–0342 or 800/347–0940) leads guided kayak tours.

The **Bar Harbor Ferry** (⊠ Bar Harbor Inn Pier ☎ 207/288–2984 ⊕ www.barharborferry.com) travels between Bar Harbor and Winter Harbor, home to Acadia National Park's Schoodic Peninsula. Along the way you'll have great views of the mountains and see a few lighthouses. The free bus shuttle from the ferry terminal takes you to Winter Harbor, Schoodic Point, Birch Harbor, and Prospect Harbor. You can bring a bike along.

Ⓒ If you are curious about what's lurking in the deep, set sail on **The Seal** (⊠ Bar Harbor Inn Pier ☎ 207/288–3483 ⊕ www.divered.com). While "Diver Ed" explores the sea bottom with his underwater video camera, you can see what he finds on an LCD screen on the boat. Kids can get a close-up look at the creatures he brings back on to the boat.

The four-masted schooner *Margaret Todd* (⊠ Bar Harbor Inn Pier ☎ 207/288–4585 ⊕ www.downeastwindjammer.com) operates 1½- to 2-hour tours three times a day from mid-May to October. The schooner *Rachel B. Jackson* (⊠ Harborside Hotel & Marina ☎ 207/288–2216) offers three day cruises and one sunset cruise.

Golf

One of Maine's best courses, the **Kebo Valley Golf Club** (⊠ Eagle Lake Rd. ☎ 207/288–3000 ⊕ www.kebovalleygolfclub.com) is a classic links-style 18-hole course. Peak season greens fees are $75. You can
Ⓒ play 9 or 18 holes of miniature golf at **Pirates Cove Adventure Golf** (⊠ Rte. 3 ☎ 207/288–2133).

Rock Climbing

On an island with steep rock faces, mountain climbing is—not surprisingly—a popular outdoor activity. The **Acadia Mountain Guides Climbing School** (⊠ 198 Main St. ☎ 207/288–8186 or 888/232–9559 ⊕ www.acadiamountainguides.com) has private and group instruction for rock and ice climbing. In summer the school sponsors weeklong camps for teens. The **Atlantic Climbing School** (⊠ 24 Cottage St. ☎ 207/288–2521 ⊕ www.acadiaclimbing.com) offers instruction for climbers of all skill levels. It can tailor its climbs for families or groups.

Whale Watching

Acadian Whale Adventures (⊠ 55 West St. ☎ 207/288–9800 ⊕ www.barharborwhales.com) has three different whale-watching cruises: just whales, whales and lighthouses, or whales and puffins. The *Acadian Whale*

Watcher (⊠ Main and Cottage Sts. ☎ 207/288–9794 or 800/421–3307) runs 3½-hour whale watching cruises from June to mid-October. **Bar Harbor Whale Watch Co.** (⊠ 1 West St. ☎ 207/288–2386 ⊕ www.whalesrus.com) operates the catamaran *Friendship V,* for whale watching, and the *Katherine,* for lobster fishing and seal watching.

Shopping

The **Alone Moose** (⊠ 78 West St. ☎ 207/288–4229) has interesting artwork made with materials such as clay, pottery, wood, and fiberglass. The **Birdsnest Gallery** (⊠ 12 Mount Desert St. ☎ 207/288–4054) sells paintings and sculpture. The **Eclipse Gallery** (⊠ 12 Mount Desert St. ☎ 207/288–9048) carries handblown glass, ceramics, art photography, and wood furniture.

Fodor'sChoice **Island Artisans** (⊠ 99 Main St. ☎ 207/288–4214) sells basketry, pottery,
★ fiber work, and jewelry created by Maine-based artisans. **Native Arts Gallery** (⊠ 99 Main St. ☎ 207/288–4474 ⊕ www.nativeartsgallery.com) sells Native American silver and gold jewelry.

☺ Paint your own pottery or piece together your own mosaic at **All Fired Up** (⊠ 101 Cottage St. ☎ 207/288–3130 ⊕ www.acadiaallfiredup.com). It can take three to four days to get pottery returned during summer months, and up to a week during the rest of the year. **Ben and Bill's Chocolate Emporium** (⊠ 66 Main St. ☎ 207/288–3281) is a chocolate lover's nirvana. The shop also has more than 20 flavors of ice cream, including the popular KGB (Kahlua, Grand Marnier, and Bailey's). Do *not* be fooled into trying the lobster ice cream.

One of the best sporting goods stores in the state, **Cadillac Mountain Sports** (⊠ 28 Cottage St. ☎ 207/288–4532 ⊕ www.cadillacmountainsports.com) has developed a following of locals and visitors alike. You can find top-quality climbing, hiking, and camping equipment. In winter you can rent cross-country skis, ice skates, and snowshoes. For one-hour photo developing, visit **First Exposure** (⊠ 156 Main St. ☎ 207/288–5868). The shop also stocks camera equipment.

Michael H. Graves Antiques (⊠ 10 Albert Meadow ☎ 207/288–3830) specializes in maps and books focusing on Mount Desert Island. **Songs of the Sea** (⊠ 47 West St. ☎ 207/288–5653) specializes in folk music. It sells handcrafted Irish and Scottish instruments.

ACADIA NATIONAL PARK

4 mi northwest of Bar Harbor.

With more than 30,000 acres of protected forests, beaches, mountains, and rocky coastline, it's no wonder Acadia National Park attracts millions of visitors each year. The park holds some of the most spectacular and varied scenery on the eastern seaboard: a rugged coastline of surf-pounded granite and an interior graced by sculpted mountains, quiet ponds, and lush deciduous forests. Cadillac Mountain, the highest point of land on the eastern coast, dominates the park. Although it's rugged, Acadia National Park also has graceful stone bridges, horse-drawn car-

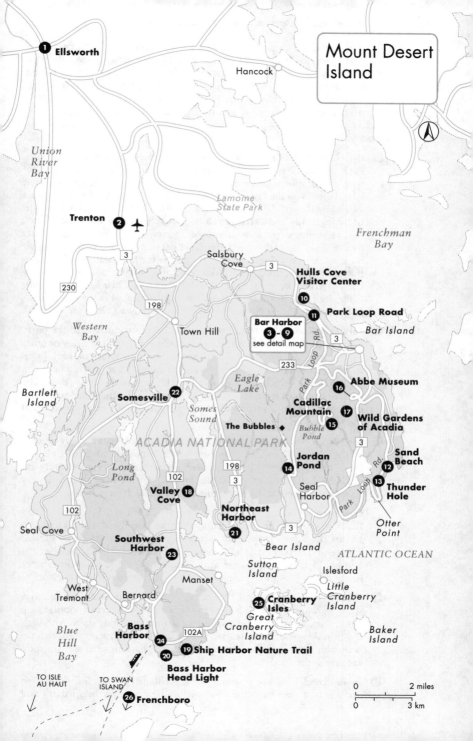

riages, and the elegant Jordan Pond Tea House. The 27-mi Park Loop Road provides an excellent introduction, but to truly appreciate the park, you must get off the main road and experience it by walking, biking, sea kayaking, or taking a carriage ride on the carriage trails. If you get off the beaten path, you can find places in the park that you can have practically to yourself, despite the summer crowds.

What to See

⑩ Hulls Cove Visitor Center. At the Hulls Cove entrance to Acadia National Park, northwest of Bar Harbor on Route 3, the Hulls Cove Visitor Center is a great spot to get your bearings. A large relief map of Mount Desert Island gives you the lay of the land and you can watch a free 15-minute video about everything the park has to offer. Pick up guidebooks, maps of hiking trails and carriage roads, schedules for naturalist-led tours, and recordings for drive-it-yourself tours. Don't forget the *Acadia Beaver Log,* the park's free newspaper detailing guided hikes and other ranger-led events. Junior ranger programs for kids, nature hikes, photography walks, tidepool explorations, and evening talks are all popular. The visitor center is off Park Loop Road. ⊠ *Park Loop Rd., Hulls Cove* ☎ *207/288–3338* ⊕ *www.nps.gov/acad* ☉ *Visitor center mid-June–Aug., daily 8–6; mid-Apr.–mid-June, Sept., and Oct., daily 8–4:30.*

★ ⑪ Park Loop Road. This road provides the best introduction to the park. You can drive around it in an hour, but allow at least half a day or more to explore the many sites along the way. Traveling south on Park Loop Road toward Sand Beach, you'll reach a small ticket booth where you pay a $20-per-vehicle entrance fee, good for seven consecutive days. The fee is not charged from November 1 to April 30. Traffic is one-way from the Route 233 entrance to the Stanley Brook Road entrance south of the Jordan Pond House.

⑫ Sand Beach. This small stretch of pink sand is one of the few sandy beaches on the island. A lifeguard is on duty from Memorial Day through Labor Day. Although people do swim here, the water temperature rarely exceeds 55°F. Restrooms and changing facilities are available. You may recognize this beach from the movie *The Cider House Rules.*

Ocean Trail. This 2 mi trail runs alongside Park Loop Road from Sand Beach to Otter Point. (This section of Park Loop Road is also known as Ocean Drive, and is the only section open to vehicle traffic in winter.) The easily accessible trail has some of the best scenery in Maine: the cliffs and boulders of pink granite at the ocean's edge, the twisted branches of the dwarf Jack pines, and ocean views that stretch to the horizon.

⑬ Thunder Hole. The ocean "thunders" into this natural seaside cave, spraying water all the way up to the viewing area. This is a popular stop along Park Loop Road, especially on stormy or windy days. Although the closest view of this attraction is reached by a stairway, a wheelchair-accessible path provides fairly good views. A parking area and gift shop are across the road.

⑭ Jordan Pond. The water source for the village of Seal Harbor, Jordan Pond is best seen from the observation deck next to the Jordan Pond

House Restaurant. Rising above the water are the Bubbles, two mountains of similar size and shape. Maps and other items are available at the information booth beside the restaurant. Many people leave their cars in the overflow parking lots north of the restaurant's parking lot when setting off on biking or hiking trips along the carriage roads that converge here.

⑮ Cadillac Mountain. At 1,532 feet, this is the first place in the country to see the sun's rays from the beginning of October to the beginning of March. Dozens of visitors make the trek to see the sunrise or, for those less-inclined to get up so early, sunset. From the smooth summit you have an awesome 360-degree view of the jagged coastline that runs around the island. Decades ago a train took visitors to a hotel at the summit. Today a small gift shop and some restrooms are the only structures at the top.

⑯ Abbe Museum at Sieur de Monts Spring. The original Abbe Museum (a larger museum has since opened in Bar Harbor) has exhibits on the history of the Abbe people who once inhabited this area. The museum is on the National Register of Historic Places. ⊠ *Sieur de Monts Spring exit from Rte. 3 or Park Loop Rd.* ☎ *207/288–3519* ⊕ *www. abbemuseum.org* ⬚ *$2* ☉ *Memorial Day–mid-Oct., 10–4.*

⑰ Wild Gardens of Acadia. Adjacent to Sieur de Monts Springs, several gardens display well-labeled plants that are representative of the island's many habitats. ⊠ *Sieur de Monts Spring exit from Rte. 3 or Park Loop Rd.* ☎ *207/288–3400* ⬚ *Free.*

⑱ Valley Cove. A parking area tucked away near the end of Fernald Point Road leads to a carriage road accessing scenic Valley Cove. Along Somes Sound, Valley Cove offers hiking trails that lead to Acadia and Flying mountains. ⊠ *Fernald Point Rd.*

⑲ Ship Harbor Nature Trail. Located on the southwestern side of the island, just beyond Seawall, this mostly flat, mile-long trail winds through the woods and along the seashore. The nearby Wonderland Trail offers a similar walk. ⊠ *Rte. 102, Seawall* ⬚ *Free.*

★ ⑳ Bass Harbor Head Light. Originally built in 1858, this lighthouse is one of the most photographed in Maine. The light, now automated, marks the entrance to Blue Hill Bay. The grounds and residence are Coast Guard property, but two trails around the facility provide excellent views. ⊠ *Rte. 102, Bass Harbor* ☉ *9–sunset* ⬚ *Free.*

Where to Stay & Eat

Unlike some national parks, Acadia National Park does not have its own hotel. Those wishing to stay inside the park need to camp at one of its campgrounds.

$$–$$$ ✕ **Jordan Pond House.** Oversize popovers with strawberry jam or homemade ice cream are a century-old tradition at this restaurant overlooking Jordan Pond. Dine outside on the tea lawn or the brick patio, or inside an enclosed porch or dining room. The lunch menu emphasizes sandwiches and salads, while the dinner menu includes seafood as well as beef and chicken. With two satellite parking lots, the restaurant makes an ideal base for hiking or biking along the nearby carriage roads. You can also use the adjacent boat launch for canoeing or kayaking on Jordan Pond. The gift shop sells bottled water, juices, and sodas from 9 to 9. ⊠ *Park Loop Rd.* ☎ *207/276–3316* 🖃 *AE, D, MC, V* ⊙ *May–late Oct.*

¢ ⚠ **Blackwoods Campground.** One of only two campgrounds located inside Acadia National Park, Blackwoods is open throughout the year. Reservations for a stay between May and October can be made four months in advance. ⊠ *Rte. 3, Otter Creek* ☎ *800/365–2267* ⊙ *Year-round.*

¢ ⚠ **Seawall Campground.** On the quiet side of the island, this campground offers space on a first-come, first-served basis, starting at 8 AM. Seawall is open from late May to late September. ⊠ *Rte. 102A, Manset* ☎ *207/244–3600* ⊙ *Closed late Sept.–late May.*

Sports & the Outdoors

The best way to see Acadia National Park is to get out of your vehicle and explore by foot, bicycle, or boat. There are more than 40 miles of carriage roads that are perfect for walking and biking in the warmer months and cross-country skiing and snowshoeing in the winter. There are more than 115 mi for hiking, numerous ponds and lakes for canoeing or kayaking, two beaches for swimming, and steep cliffs for rock climbing.

Bicycling

The more than 40 mi of carriage roads that crisscross the island are open to bicycles. Originally designed and funded by John D. Rockefeller to facilitate carriage travel after automobiles were introduced, these well-maintained gravel roads provide a range of terrains for bikers of all levels. Even during the busiest months you can find quiet stretches where you can get close-up looks at the native ferns, mosses, and trees. You may also spot chipmunks, birds, or even deer. Although the carriage roads are marked at most intersections, it's a good idea to carry a map. With so many side roads and loops, it is easy to extend or shorten your trip.

The two most popular places to start your ride are Eagle Lake and Jordan Pond. Eagle Lake has a small parking lot that fills up quickly, so don't be surprised if you have to park on the roadside. The 6-mi carriage road around Eagle Lake is popular with families. It meets up with other carriage roads along the way. Jordan Pond has a larger parking lot and a number of different trails. You may want to bike from Eagle Lake to Jordan Pond, where you can stop for tea and popovers at Jordan Pond House Restaurant. Perhaps the most challenging route is the Around the Mountain Trail, an 11-mi loop with an extended climb up the northwest side of Parkman Mountain. Other places to start your ride—with less parking—are the Gate House and Parkman Mountain in Northeast Harbor.

Remember that horses and carriages still use these roads. It is best to yield to horses when they approach and to warn the rider when approaching from behind. You can pick up trail maps at the Hulls Cove Visitor Center. Although it is not nearly as peaceful, you can bike along

Park Loop Road. You must follow the traffic during the one-way section between the Route 233 entrance and the Stanley Brook Road entrance. If you want to bike the entire loop, ride clockwise. Biking is not allowed on any of the hiking trails.

Boating

Mount Desert Island has numerous lakes and ponds that attract canoers and kayakers. Motorboats are permissible, but Eagle Lake, Jordan Pond, Lower Hadlock Pond, and Upper Hadlock Pond have a 10-horsepower limit. Motor boats are most often seen on the ocean, which gives you a great view of this and neighboring islands. Public launching areas are available at each town pier.

Cross-Country Skiing

When the snow falls on Mount Desert Island, the more than 40 mi of carriage roads used for biking and hiking during the rest of the year are transformed into a cross-country skiing paradise. With so few visitors on the island during this time of year, you can ski or snowshoe for miles without seeing anyone else. Be sure to bring a carriage road map with you. Snowshoe tracks are usually to the right or between the ski trails.

Fishing

Several lakes and ponds throughout Acadia National Park attract anglers. Maine residents 16 and older and non-Maine residents 12 and older must have a license to fish in fresh waters. Fishing licenses can be purchased at town halls and at some stores. Fishing licenses are not required for ocean fishing.

Hiking

Acadia National Park maintains more than 115 mi of hiking paths, from easy strolls around lakes and ponds to rigorous treks with climbs up rock faces and scrambles along cliffs. Although most hiking trails are on the east side of the island, the west side also has some scenic trails. Perhaps one of the most notorious climbs is the Precipice Trail, which involves climbing over boulders and up ladders to navigate steep paths and narrow ledges. This trail is usually closed until early or mid-August while the endangered peregrine falcons raise their young. For those looking for this type of climb, the Beehive Trail, just before Sand Beach, provides similar terrain. For those wishing for a long climb, try the trails leading up Cadillac Mountain or Dorr Mountain. Another option is to climb Parkman, Sargeant, and Penobscot mountains.

The trail up South Bubble Mountain is popular for families. The climb is not too difficult, and children enjoy trying to push an enormous boulder known as Bubble Rock off the mountain. The Beech Hill Mountain Trail has an old fire tower at the top that kids find appealing. On the west side of the island, the trail up St. Sauveur does not provide much of a view, but you can connect to the Valley Peak Trail, which provides excellent views of Somes Sound Fjord, Northeast Harbor, and the outer islands. The Hulls Cove Visitor Center and area bookstores have trail guides and maps and will help you match a trail with your interests and abilities. You can park at one end of any trail and use the free shuttle bus to get back to your starting point.

Horseback Riding

Acadia National Park does not have its own horseback riding program, but you can arrange for carriage rides or board your horses at **Wildwood Stables** (✉ Park Loop Rd., Seal Harbor ☎ 207/276–3622 or 859/356–7139 ⊕ www.acadia.net/wildwood). With more than 40 mi of carriage roads, the park is an excellent place to ride your horse at a slow, comfortable pace. The stables, which do not rent horses, are a half-mile south of the Jordan Pond House Restaurant.

Rock Climbing

Acadia National Park has plenty of rock faces to challenge both novice and advanced climbers. Otter Cliffs and Champlain Mountain are popular for face climbing, and Gorham Mountain offers good boulder climbing.

Snowmobiling

Once the snow falls, most of Park Loop Road closes to cars and snowmobiles take over. Except for a few well-marked places, snowmobiles are not allowed on the carriage roads. The speed limit for snowmobiles is 35 mph.

Swimming

The Park has two beaches that are perfect for swimming, Sand Beach and Echo Lake Beach. Sand Beach, along Park Loop Road, has changing rooms, restrooms, and a lifeguard on duty from Memorial Day to Labor Day. The water temperature here rarely reaches above 55°F. Echo Lake Beach, on the western side of the island just north of Southwest Harbor, has much warmer water. There are changing rooms, restrooms, and a lifeguard on duty throughout the summer.

AROUND MOUNT DESERT ISLAND

While Bar Harbor is the best-known village on Mount Desert Island, there's plenty to see and do around the entire Island. Take a scenic drive along Sargeant Drive for spectacular views of Somes Sound—the only fjord on the East Coast. Visit the villages of Northeast Harbor, Somesville, and Southwest Harbor, each with its own unique character. The west side of the island—also known as the "back side" or the "quiet side"—has its own restaurants and accommodations. To get a unique perspective of the island, take a cruise. Away from the crowds and traffic, you'll have plenty of time to discover some of the island's less-obvious charms.

Northeast Harbor

㉑ *12 mi south of Bar Harbor via Rtes. 3 and 198 or Rtes. 233 and 198.*

The summer community for some of the nation's wealthiest families, Northeast Harbor is a quiet place to stay. The village has one of the best harbors on the coast, and fills with yachts and powerboats during peak season. It's a great place to sign up for a cruise around Somes Sound or to the Cranberry Islands. Other than that, there isn't much to hold your attention for long. There's a handful of restaurants, boutiques, and art galleries on the downtown streets.

With many varieties of rhododendrons and azaleas, the Japanese-style **Asticou Azalea Garden** is spectacular from the end of May to the middle of June. Even when the pink, white, and blue flowers are not in full bloom, you can find plenty to admire. Originally designed by Charles Savage, the gardens contain many plants from landscape gardener Beatrix Farrand's Bar Harbor garden. ⊠ *Rtes. 198 and 3,* ⊕ *www.asticou. com/gardens.html* ☜ *$1* ⊙ *Daily.*

The official repository for the records of the Town of Mount Desert, the **Northeast Harbor Library** hosts an always-changing exhibit in the Patterson Room. ⊠ *1 Joy Rd.* ☎ *207/276–3333* ⊙ *Mon.–Sat. 10–5.*

Hidden atop a hill on Peabody Drive, **Thuya Gardens** was once the summer home of Boston architect Joseph Henry Curtis. Today the site is a peaceful and elegant spot to take in formal perennial gardens. Designed by Charles Savage and named for the property's majestic white cedars, *Thuja occidentalis,* the garden is filled with colorful blooms throughout the summer. Walk the immaculately groomed grass paths or enjoy the view from a well-placed bench. You'll find delphiniums, daylilies, dahlias, heliotrope, snapdragons, and many more. If you have time, take a look inside the Curtis home, which has a large collection of books compiled by Savage. To get to the gardens, park in the small lot near the Asticou Inn and climb the footpath across the road. Alternately, continue down Peabody Drive and make a left on Thuya Drive. ⊠ *Peabody Dr.* ☎ *207/276–5130* ⊕ *www.asticou.com/gardens.html* ☜ *$1* ⊙ *Daily.*

Where to Stay & Eat

$$$–$$$$ ✕ **Abel's Lobster Pound.** You can watch the sun set and the cooks steam your lobster from the panoramic windows of this restaurant, situated a stone's throw from Somes Sound. If you want a slight variation on the famed crustacean, try the Lobster Newberg. ⊠ *Rte. 198, south of junction of Rtes. 198 and 233, Mount Desert* ☎ *207/276–5827* ▤ *MC, V* ⊙ *Closed Labor Day–mid-June.*

$–$$$ ✕ **Colonel's Delicatessen.** Known around town simply as "The Colonel's," this restaurant serves up simple fare for breakfast, lunch, and dinner. In front, the bakery turns out delicious breads, rolls, croissants, turnovers, and muffins, as well as cookies, cakes, whoopie pies, and other sumptuous desserts. Make sure to try one of the glazed donut twists, with or without chocolate drizzled over the top. The adjacent deli offers a range of premium meats. At the restaurant in the rear, you can eat in the dining room or take your food outside to the deck. The kitchen serves up seafood specials, as well as burgers and pizza. You can also have your meal wrapped up for takeout. ⊠ *143 Main St.* ☎ *207/276–5147* ▤ *No credit cards* ⊙ *Closed mid-Oct.–mid-May.*

$–$$$ ✕ **The Docksider.** As its name suggests, this roll-up-your-sleeves restaurant sits just above the Northeast Harbor Marina. If you're looking for a lobster dinner with a minimum amount of fuss, this is the place. There are also hamburgers and other quick bites. Finish off with an ice-cream cone or a milk shake. Eat inside, on the deck, or take it with you. ⊠ *14 Sea St.* ☎ *207/276–3965* ▤ *MC, V* ⊙ *Closed mid-Oct.–May.*

$–$$$ ✕ **151 Main Street.** This café serves up crab cakes and a wide range of seafood options. There are also tasty pizzas, salads, and other light fare.

Be prepared to wait to be seated during peak months. The service can be slow, but the atmosphere is pleasant, with hardwood floors and large windows overlooking Main Street. ☒ *151 Main St.* ☎ *207/276–9898* ⊟ *AE, MC, V* ⊘ *Closed Oct.–May.*

★ $$$$ ✕⊡ **Asticou Inn.** Established in 1883, this grand inn overlooking Northeast Harbor has some of the best views you'll find. The attractively furnished guest rooms have hardwood floors, hand-braided rugs, and brass beds. The restaurant ($$–$$$$) is open to the public for breakfast and dinner, as well as lunch in July and August. You can eat in the dining room or outside on the deck overlooking the harbor. The baked stuffed lobster is among the most popular dishes, but the kitchen also does great things with salmon, halibut, and swordfish. The extensive wine list includes more than 100 wines. The inn is close to Acadia National Park's hiking trails and carriage roads. ☒ *15 Peabody Dr., 04662* ☎ *800/258–3373* ⊕ *www.asticou.com* ⤳ *24 rooms, 24 suites* ⚫ *Restaurant, tennis court, pool, meeting rooms; no a/c in some rooms, no room TVs* ⊟ *MC, V* ⊘ *Closed mid-Oct.–mid-May* ⦿ *EP.*

$$$$ ⊡ **Kimball Terrace Inn.** Overlooking Northeast Harbor, this lodging offers clean, comfortable accommodations. Many of the guest rooms have views of the marina or the surrounding mountains. A short distance from the center of the village, the inn is close enough to walk to shops and galleries, but far enough away to feel a bit secluded. Adjacent to the inn, the Main Sail serves breakfast, lunch, and dinner. Dine inside or out on the deck. ☒ *Huntington Rd., 04662* ☎ *800/454–6225 or 207/276–3383* 🖷 *207/276–4102* ⊕ *www.kimballterraceinn.com* ⤳ *70 rooms* ⚫ *Restaurant, pool, lounge, shop, meeting rooms* ⊟ *AE, D, MC, V.*

$$$–$$$$ ⊡ **Maison Suisse Inn.** A bit removed from the hustle and bustle of Main Street, this inn dates to the late 1800s. Surrounded by gardens, the main building has sunny common areas where guests congregate. The guest rooms, each individually decorated, are filled with antiques, and some have beautiful silk-screened wallpaper. Rooms 4 and 5 have private porches. An annex called Peregrine Lodge has five additional rooms, each with a fireplace. One suite with full kitchen is perfect for families. Breakfast is included in the rates. ☒ *144 Main St., 04662* ☎ *800/624–7668 or 207/276–5223* 🖷 *207/276–5223* ⊕ *www.maisonsuisse.com* ⤳ *11 rooms, 5 suites* ⚫ *Some kitchens, cable TV, no-smoking rooms; no a/c* ⊟ *AE, MC, V* ⊘ *Closed late Oct.–May* ⦿ *BP.*

$$–$$$ ⊡ **Harbourside Inn.** Built in 1888 by noted architect Fred Savage, this hillside inn is tucked into the edge of the woods. It's easy to get to Acadia National Park, as trails begin in the backyard. A unique collection of maps hangs in the public rooms, including one of the United States dating back to 1860. Rooms have hardwood floors, Oriental rugs, and flowers plucked from the surrounding gardens. Some 19th-century furnishings add to the period feel. Most baths have marble sinks and wonderful tubs for soaking. Room 8 has a delightful enclosed outdoor seating area with a porch swing, wicker furniture, and a teak lounge chair. A continental breakfast features homemade blueberry muffins on the porch. ☒ *Harborside Rd., 04662* ☎ *207/276–3272* ⊕ *www.harboursideinn.com* ⤳ *11 rooms, 3 suites* ⚫ *Some kitchenettes; no a/c, no room TVs, no smoking* ⊟ *No credit cards* ⊘ *Closed mid-Sept.–mid-June.* ⦿ *CP.*

Sports & the Outdoors

Only a few miles from Northeast Harbor, **Seal Harbor Beach** (⊠ Rte. 3, Seal Harbor) gives those daring enough to brave the cold water a chance to swim in the ocean. There's ample parking across the street, where you can also find public restrooms.

The small **Northeast Harbor Bike Shop** (⊠ 118 Main St. ☎ 207/276–5480) rents bikes for half- and full-day excursions. Repair work is also done on the premises.

Open from mid-May to mid-November, the **Northeast Harbor Golf Club** (⊠ 15 Sargeant Dr. ☎ 207/276–5335) has an 18-hole course originally built in 1895. Peak-season greens fees are $85. The club may close to the public during holiday weekends.

A number of different charter companies operate tours out of Northeast Harbor. The desk near the harbormaster's office has information about the different companies. Boat charters and tours usually begin on Memorial Day weekend and run through Columbus Day, but schedules vary depending on the weather. Call ahead if you're visiting at the beginning or the end of the season.

The 33-foot sloop *Blackjack* (⊠ Northeast Harbor ☎ 207/276–3056) operates four tours every day except Sunday. The ship can comfortably hold as many as six passengers. The 33-foot sloop *Chamar* (⊠ Northeast Harbor ☎ 207/276–3993 or 207/266–4699) runs two narrated tours each day. The 15-mi loop varies depending on weather conditions, but it usually passes through Somes Sound and Southwest Harbor. Along the way you can see seals and osprey. Full- and half-day charters are available. The boat can accommodate two to six passengers.

The beautiful *Poor Richard* (⊠ Northeast Harbor ☎ 207/276–3785) specializes in lobster picnics on outer islands. It also offers nature cruises to see seals and other creatures. *The Sea Princess* (⊠ Northeast Harbor ☎ 207/276–5352) offers two different nature cruises, a sunset dinner cruise, and a trip around Somes Sound. These naturalist-narrated tours will introduce you to the wildlife you may encounter in the inland waters. The nature cruises include a stop at Little Cranberry Island, where you will have time to visit the Islesford Historical Museum (*see* full listing in the Outer Islands section of this chapter). The sunset cruise stops here for dinner at the Islesford Dock Restaurant.

Departing from Northeast Harbor or Southwest Harbor, the *Delight* (Available in summer only ☎ 207/244–5724) takes you on tours or transports you to other ports. Specializing in photography charters, **MDI Water Taxi** (☎ 207/244–7312) can transport you to an outer island or provide private charter services for sightseeing tours. The boat departs from Northeast Harbor or Southwest Harbor.

Cranberry Isles Mail Boat Ferry Service (⊠ Northeast Harbor ☎ 207/244–3575) is the easiest way to travel to Little or Great Cranberry Island. The boat departs from the Northeast Harbor marina and stops at both islands every day throughout the year. In summer the boat makes six daily round-trip journeys. The company also has boats available for excursions around the area. The **Islesford Ferry** (☎ 207/276–3717) makes daily trips to Baker's Island. Operating only in summer, it departs from Northeast Harbor or Southwest Harbor.

Shopping

You won't find Northeast Harbor's main street lined with T-shirt and souvenir shops. Instead, the town has many upscale stores selling jewelry, clothing, and fine art.

A smaller version of the Bar Harbor shop, **Island Artisans** (✉ 119 Main St. ☎ 207/276–4045 ⊕ www.islandartisans.com) sells work by area artists, including pottery, tiles, jewelry, and clothing. The **Kimball Shop** (✉ 135 Main St. ☎ 207/276–3300) carries fine china, glassware, and cookware. There are also soaps and candles that make nice gifts.

For unique jewelry made from seaglass, visit **Lisa Hall Seaglass Jewelry** (✉ Sea St. ☎ 207/244–0400 ⊕ www.lisahalljewelry.com). You can find unique ornaments at **Shaw Jewelry** (✉ 100 Main St. ☎ 207/276–5000 ⊕ www.shawjewelry.com). These pieces are designed by more than 100 nationally recognized artists.

en route   The best way to see Somes Sound—the only fjord on the East Coast of North America—is to take the scenic **Sargeant Drive,** which branches off Route 198. A long stretch of the roadway is edged by granite cliffs on one side and the shore on the other. Along the way you can take in views of Valley Cove and Hall Quarry. In summer you can watch sailboats and large yachts cruising the fjord. In winter the ice masses that form on the cliffs create a spectacular show. The road is a bit narrow and is closed to buses, campers, and other large vehicles.

Somesville

 7 mi northwest of Northeast Harbor via Rtes. 198 and 102.

Most visitors pass through Somesville on their way to Southwest Harbor, but this well-preserved village, the oldest on the island, is more than a stop along the way. Originally settled by Abraham Somes in 1763, this was once a bustling commercial center with shingle, lumber, and wool mills; a tannery; a varnish factory; and a dye shop. Today, Route 102, which passes through the center of town, takes you past a row of white clapboard houses with black shutters and well-manicured lawns. Designated a historic district in 1975, Somesville has one of the most photographed spots on the island: a small house with a foot bridge that crosses an old mill pond.

A few miles off Route 102, the **Beech Hill Farm** grows several acres of organic produce for area markets. Operated by the College of the Atlantic, the vegetable and flower garden are open to the public three days a week. ✉ *307 Beech Hill Rd.* ☎ *207/244–5204* ⊙ *July–Oct., Tues., Thurs., and Sat. 9–6.*

Operated by the Mount Desert Island Historical Society, the **Somesville Museum** has exhibits depicting the community's long history. You can also purchase a booklet with a self-guided walking tour of the village here. ⊠ *2 Oak Hill Rd.* ☎ *207/244–5043* ⊕ *www.mdihistory.org* ✉ *$1* ⊙ *Mid-June–Sept., Tues.–Sat. 10–4.*

Maintained by Acadia National Park, the **Pretty Marsh Picnic Area** is 4 mi from Somesville. This secluded spot is well suited for a picnic lunch, an afternoon barbecue, or a lobster bake. There are fire pits, picnic tables, and restrooms. ⊠ *Rte. 102A, Pretty Marsh* ✉ *Free* ⊙ *May–Oct.*

★ Open since 1964, the **Seal Cove Auto Museum** has around 100 immaculately maintained vehicles from the "Brass Era," which ran from the beginning of auto production until about 1915. There are also 35 antique motorcycles. You can find gasoline, steam, and electric vehicles and some interesting rarities. Each car has a sign detailing its history. This one-of-a-kind museum is worth a visit, even if you don't normally go for antique cars. ⊠ *Rte. 102, Seal Cove* ☎ *207/244–9242* ⊕ *www.sealcoveautomuseum.org* ✉ *$5* ⊙ *June 1–Sept. 15, daily 10–5.*

Where to Stay & Eat

¢ ⚠ **Mount Desert Campground.** Near the village of Somesville, this campground has one of the best locations imaginable. It lies at the head of Somes Sound, the only fjord on the East Coast. The campground prefers tents, so vehicles longer than 20 feet are not allowed. Many sites are along the waterfront, and all are tucked into the woods for a sense of privacy. Restrooms and showers are placed sensibly throughout the campground and are kept meticulously clean. Canoes and kayaks are available for rent, and there's a dock with access to the ocean. The Gathering Place has baked goods in the morning and ice cream and coffee in the evening. ⚲ *Flush toilets, drinking water, showers, fire pits, food service, swimming (ocean)* ⊠ *516 Sound Dr., Mount Desert 04660* ☎ *207/244–3710* ⊕ *www.mountdesertcampground.com* ⊙ *Mid-June–mid-Sept.* ▤ *MC, V.*

Nightlife & the Arts

Across the road from the Somesville Fire Station, the **Acadia Repertory Theatre** (⊠ Rte. 102 ☎ 207/244–7260 ⊕ www.acadiarep.com) produces plays throughout the summer. This small, informal theater is an excellent place to spend a summer evening.

Sports & the Outdoors

At the south end of Echo Lake, **Echo Lake Beach** (⊠ Rte. 102) has a sandy beach where many people brave the icy waters. Lifeguards are on duty in summer. Look for the sign just before you reach Southwest Harbor.

Long Pond (⊠ Pretty Marsh Rd.) is the largest body of fresh water on the island. It's a great spot for canoeing, kayaking, and swimming.

Several feet from Long Pond, the largest pond on Mount Desert Island, is **National Park Canoe & Kayak Rentals** (⊠ Pretty Marsh Rd. ☎ 877/378–6907 or 207/244–5854 ⊕ www.acadia.net/canoe). You can be in the water in minutes.

Shopping

Port in a Storm Bookstore (⊠ Rte. 102 ☎ 207/244–4114) stocks a well-chosen selection of books. The atmosphere is conducive to browsing, with soaring ceilings and comfy chairs.

Southwest Harbor

② *5 mi south of Somesville via Rte. 102 S.*

On what is known as the "quiet side" of the island, Southwest Harbor has fewer attractions than other towns. It can still be quite busy in summer, however. This working port is home to well-known boat- building companies, a major source of employment in the area. To reach the harbor from Route 102, make a left onto Clark Point Road.

The **Mount Desert Oceanarium** has exhibits on the fishing and sea life of the Gulf of Maine, a live-seal program, and hands-on exhibits such as a touch tank. ⊠ *Clark Point Rd.* ☎ *207/244-7330* ⊕ *www. theoceanarium.com* ⊠ *$9* ⊙ *Mid-May–late Oct., Mon.–Sat. 9–5.*

The **Wendell Gilley Museum** showcases bird carvings by Gilley, has carving demonstrations and workshops, and exhibits wildlife art. Bird carvings are to scale, and include the ruffed grouse, upland sandpiper, American goldfinch, Atlantic puffin, and the loon. ⊠ *4 Herrick Rd.* ☎ *207/244-7555* ⊕ *www.wendellgilleymuseum.org* ⊠ *$5* ⊙ *July and Aug., Tues.–Sun. 10–5; June, Sept., and Oct., Tues.–Sun. 10–4; May, Nov., and Dec., Fri.–Sun. 10–4.*

Sponsored by the Southwest Harbor/Tremont Chamber of Commerce, **Oktoberfest** has become a rite of autumn. Visit with the brewers, sample new foods, and enjoy music and entertainment. ☎ *800/423–9264 or 207/244–9264* ⊕ *www.acadiachamber.com.*

Where to Stay & Eat

★ **$$$–$$$$** ✕ **Fiddler's Green.** Perhaps the most difficult part of dining at this harborside restaurant is selecting just one entrée. It's hard to choose between dishes such as pan-seared yellowfin tuna with wasabi-and-tamari sauce or scallops with asparagus, spinach, tomato, pancetta, and grilled polenta. Everything here is fresh, including the locally grown organic produce. The desserts—including vanilla-bean crème brûlée and Grand Marnier bundt cake—make for hard decisions. Choose a bottle from a wine list that regularly includes 130 selections, and has as many as 180 at the height of summer. ⊠ *411 Main St.* ☎ *207/244-9416* ⚑ *Reservations essential* ⊙ *Open Memorial Day–June and Sept.–Columbus Day, Thurs.–Sun; July and Aug., Tues.–Sun.*

$$–$$$$ ✕ **Red Sky.** Whether you're dressed for a night on the town or have just tied your boat up at the pier, you feel comfortable at this downtown restaurant. Start with a salad of locally grown greens topped with chunks of blue cheese, caramelized pears, and balsamic vinaigrette, or the baby lamb chops with a bittersweet-chocolate-and-mint vinaigrette. For an entrée you can choose from delicious dishes like lobster risotto with asparagus and porcini mushrooms, and maple-glazed baby back ribs. The restaurant has more than 40 wines by the bottle and 10 wines by the glass. Save room for the cheese course. ⊠ *146 Seawall Rd.* ☎ *207/244-0476* ⚑ *Reservations essential.*

$$$ ✕ **Deck House Restaurant.** A beautiful view of Southwest Harbor isn't the only reason to come to this harborside restaurant. Shortly after 8 PM, the servers sing, dance, and play musical instruments when they aren't serving you your dinner. All guests pay a $7 show fee. ⊠ *Great Har-*

bor Marina ☎ *207/244–5044* ⚛ *Reservations essential* ⊘ *Closed mid-Sept.–mid-June.*

$–$$$ ✕ **Beal's Lobster Pier.** You can watch lobstermen hauling in their catch at this working lobster pound. Lobster, clams, and other seafood make up most of the menu. You can eat your meal outside on the picnic tables. If you want to organize your own lobster bake, you can order the critters to-go. ⊠ *182 Clark Point Rd.* ☎ *207/244–7178* ⊕ *www.bealslobster.com* ⊟ *AE, MC, V* ⊘ *Closed mid-Oct.–mid-May.*

$$ ✕ **Seaweed Café.** This unpretentious little restaurant serves natural and organic seafood with an Asian touch. You can order sushi and sashimi, as well as a variety of noodle dishes, all beautifully presented. Flowers on each table give the dining room a romantic feel. ⊠ *146 Seawall Rd.* ☎ *207/244–0572* ⚛ *Reservations essential* ⊟ *No credit cards* ⊘ *Closed Sun.–Tues., and Jan.–Apr. No lunch.*

$–$$ ✕ **Eat-A-Pita.** Fresh vegetables are the focus of the menu at this downtown eatery. Offering four kinds of pita bread, a hefty list of crisp veggies, and other fillings, this restaurant is a good bet for lunch. Try a whole-wheat pita stuffed with chickpeas, tomatoes, leaf lettuce, cucumbers, shredded carrots, alfalfa sprouts, green onions, bell peppers, and marinated chicken drizzled with honey-mustard dressing. At night, the restaurant turns into Café 2, which features salmon, lamb, and other heartier fare. ⊠ *326 Main St.* ☎ *207/244–4344* ⊟ *MC, V* ⊘ *Closed mid-Oct.–May.*

$–$$ ✕ **Little Notch Pizzeria.** Delicious pizzas are on the menu at this eatery. Try a pie with prosciutto, ricotta, and artichoke hearts. The restaurant also serves salads, sandwiches, and other light fare, as well as delicious breads. ⊠ *340 Main St.* ☎ *207/244–3357* ⊘ *Open year-round.*

$$$–$$$$ ⊡ **Claremont Hotel.** Built in 1884, the Claremont calls up memories of the long, leisurely vacations of days gone by. The inn commands a view of Somes Sound. Croquet is taken seriously here—a tournament is held on the lawn the first week in August. Rooms are simply—some would say sparsely—decorated; cottages are more rustic. Breakfast and dinner are served in the waterfront dining room, where the menu changes weekly. It's popular, so make sure to call ahead. In summer lunch is served at the Boat House, at a dock where you can tie up your boat and come ashore. ⊠ *Clark Point Rd.* ⌂ *Box 137, 04679* ☎ *207/244–5036 or 800/244–5036* ⊟ *207/244–3512* ⊕ *www.theclaremont.com* ↪ *30 rooms, 2 suites, 14 cottages* ⚛ *Restaurant, tennis court, dock, bicycles, croquet; no a/c, no room TVs, no smoking* ⊟ *No credit cards* ⊘ *Hotel closed mid-Oct.–mid-June; cottages closed Nov.–mid-May* ❙⊙❙ *BP, MAP.*

$$–$$$$ ⊡ **Lindenwood Inn.** If you're looking for something other than Victoriana, try the accommodations at this harborside inn. The sunny rooms are decorated with art from around the world. Room 5 has a fireplace and a private balcony, and the penthouse has a deck with an outdoor hot tub. A separate bungalow has a downstairs bedroom, a sleeping loft, and a kitchen. ⊠ *118 Clark Point Rd.* ⌂ *Box 1328, 04679* ☎ *800/307–5335 or 207/244–5335* ⊕ *www.lindenwoodinn.com* ↪ *5 rooms, 3 suites, 1 bungalow* ⚛ *Pool, hot tub; no smoking* ⊟ *AE, MC, V* ❙⊙❙ *BP.*

$$–$$$ ⊡ **Harbour Cottage Inn.** Elegant but casual, this lodging is close to the harbor. Built in 1870 as part of the island's first summer hotel, the inn has tastefully decorated rooms that are named after different kinds of boats. All have private bathrooms, most with steam showers or whirl-

pool tubs. A carriage house is also available. The nearby oceanfront property, Pier One, has four suites and one cottage rented by the week. Guests have use of several bicycles and the 150-foot-long pier. ⊠ *9 Dirigo Rd., 04679* ☎ *888/843–3022 or 207/244–5738* ⊕ *www.harbourcottageinn. com* ⇨ *8 rooms, 3 suites* ⚓ *Dock, bicycles, bar, no-smoking rooms; no a/c in some rooms* ⊗ *Closed Nov.–mid-Apr.* ¶⊙| *BP.*

$$–$$$ 🖼 **Kingsleigh Inn.** It's the details that make the difference at this inn in Southwest Harbor. In your guest room you'll find fresh flowers, bottles of port, and divine homemade chocolate truffles, and in the bath there are fluffy robes and slippers. Originally built in 1904, the inn is decorated with period furnishings. Guest rooms have atmospheric additions like ceiling fans. Several rooms have balconies with harbor views. The third-floor suite has hardwood floors, a wood-burning fireplace, and a telescope for stargazing or watching boats travel in and out of the harbor. You can relax by the fireplace in the living room or take in the fresh sea air from the wraparound porch. ⊠ *373 Main St., 04679* ☎ *207/ 244–5302* 🖨 *207/244–7691* ⊕ *www.kingsleighinn.com* ⇨ *8 rooms, 1 suite* ⚓ *Fans; no a/c in some rooms, no room phones, no room TVs, no smoking* 🖃 *MC, V* ⊗ *Closed Nov.–Apr.* ¶⊙| *BP.*

$$ 🖼 **Island House.** This B&B on the quiet side of the island has two simple and bright rooms in the main house and one suite in the carriage house. Perfect for families, the carriage-house room has a living area and a kitchenette. ⊠ *121 Clark Point Rd.* ⌑ *Box 1006, 04679* ☎ *207/ 244–5180* ⊕ *www.islandhousebb.com* ⇨ *2 rooms, 1 suite* ⚓ *Kitchenette; no a/c, no room phones, no room TVs, no children under 5, no smoking* 🖃 *MC, V* ¶⊙| *BP.*

$–$$ 🖼 **Moorings Inn & Cottages.** Nothing is fancy here except the jaw-dropping view of Somes Sound. The main house, which dates back to the late 18th century, is decorated with period antiques. The rooms in the main house are more charming, but those in a newer wing have sliding-glass doors leading to private decks. The homey cottages have the most privacy. ⊠ *135 Shore Rd., Manset* ⌑ *Box 744, Southwest Harbor 04679* ☎ *800/596–5523 or 207/244–5523* ⊕ *www.mooringsinn.com* ⇨ *13 rooms, 5 cottages, 1 apartment* ⚓ *Some kitchenettes, some microwaves, some refrigerators, bicycles, boating; no a/c, no room phones, no room TVs* 🖃 *No credit cards* ⊗ *Closed mid-Oct.–mid-May.* ¶⊙| *CP.*

¢   🖼 **Smuggler's Den Campground.** Whether you're camping in a tent or sleeping in a recreational vehicle, this campground has everything you need. Located in a wooded area, the campground has amenities such as basketball and volleyball courts and a heated pool. There are hot showers, a coin laundry, and a camp store for any last-minute needs. The simple cabins can accommodate up to five people. Campsites are available for any length of time, while cabins are rented by the week. ⚓ *Flush toilets, full hookups, drinking water, showers, fire pits, picnic tables, public telephone, general store, play area, swimming (heated pool)* ⊠ *Rte. 102, 04679* ☎ *877/244–9033 or 207/244–3944* 🖨 *207/244–4072* ⊕ *www.smugglersdencampground.com* 🖃 *MC, V.*

Sports & the Outdoors

Southwest Cycle (⊠ 370 Main St. ☎ 207/244–5856) rents bicycles by the day or week.

Acadia Adventures Sea Kayak Tours (⊠ 19 Clark Point Rd. ☎ 207/244–0680) runs morning and afternoon tours in two-person sea kayaks. Tours are tailored for all different skill levels. **Manset Yacht Service** (⊠ Shore Rd., Manset ☎ 207/244–4040) charters powerboats and sailboats. If you want to explore on your own, **Mansell Boat & Marine** (⊠ Rte. 102A, Manset ☎ 207/244–5625) rents small powerboats and sailboats.

The **Maine State Sea Kayak Guide Service** (⊠ 254 Main St., Southwest Harbor ☎ 877/481–9500 or 207/244–9500 ⊕ www.mainestatekayak. com) offers half-day sea kayak tours for up to six people. Tours are tailored to suit both beginning and experienced paddlers. Specializing in photography tours, **MDI Water Taxi** (☎ 207/244–7312) can transport you to the outer islands. The boat departs from the docks at Southwest Harbor or Northeast Harbor.

Next to the Coast Guard Station, **Masako Queen Deep Sea Fishing Company** (⊠ Clark Point Rd. ☎ 207/244–5385), has half-day fishing trips and full-day deep-sea fishing excursions. Each passenger is assigned a lobster trap, and can keep any legal lobsters caught in that trap. Fish for mackerel, bluefish, codfish, and more. These trips fill up fast, so reservations are recommended.

If you want to hit the links, there's a 9-hole golf course at **Causeway Club** ⊠ *Fernald Point Rd., Southwest Harbor* ☎ *207/244–7220.*

Shopping

Aylen & Son (⊠ 320 Main St. ☎ 207/244–7369) sells fine jewelry using stones from local, national, and international sources. All pieces are in sterling silver or 18-karat gold. Dedicated to making art affordable to everyone, **Gallery West** (⊠ 336 Main St. ☎ 207/244–9899 ⊕ www. gallerywest.net) has paintings, sculpture, and other works of art. **MDI Sportswear** (⊠ 366 Main St. ☎ 207/244–3121) sells clothing, sandals, and athletic footwear. You can find a superb selection of wines, olives, and cheeses at **Sawyer's Specialties** (⊠ 353 Main St. ☎ 207/244–3317).

Bass Harbor

㉔ *4 mi south of Southwest Harbor via Rte. 102 or Rte. 102A*

Bass Harbor is a tiny lobstering village with a relaxed atmosphere and a few accommodations and restaurants. If you're looking to get away from the crowds, consider using this hardworking community as your base. Although Bass Harbor does not draw as many tourists as other villages, the Bass Harbor Head Light in Acadia National Park is one of the region's most popular attractions. From here you can hike on the Ship Harbor Nature Trail or take a ferry to Frenchboro.

Where to Stay & Eat

$–$$$$ ✕ **Seafood Ketch.** You can watch lobster boats sail in and out of the harbor while you enjoy fresh seafood on the deck or in the dining room at this family-owned restaurant. If you're looking for fried clams or steamed lobster dinners with all the fixings, you can find them here. ⊠ *McMullin Ave.* ☎ *207/244–7463* ▭ *D, MC, V* ☉ *Closed Nov.–Apr.*

¢–$$ ✕ **Thurston's Lobster Pound.** On the peninsula across from Bass Harbor, Thurston's Lobster Pound is easy to spot because of its bright yellow awning. You can buy fresh lobsters to-go or sit at outdoor tables. Order everything from a grilled cheese sandwich to a boiled lobster served with clams or mussels. Side dishes such as corn, potato salad, and coleslaw cost extra. ⊠ *Steamboat Wharf and Bernard Rds., Bernard* ☎ *207/244–7600* ✆ *Closed Columbus Day–Memorial Day.*

¢–$ ✕ **Freya's.** Roll up your sleeves at this family-style restaurant, where meals arrive in plastic baskets. Sit in the dining room or at a picnic table along the wharf, taking in views of the harbor filled with lobster boats. Try a lobster roll—perfectly cooked and served in a buttery grilled roll—with french fries on the side. There are also burgers and other casual fare. Freya's has live entertainment on Thursday nights in August. ⊠ *Shore Rd.* ☎ *207/244–9101.*

$$–$$$ ▣ **Bass Harbor Gables.** For all the comforts of home, consider one of the two-level apartments or the cottage at this lodging near the water. The upstairs rooms of both apartments have ocean views. North Gables, the smaller of the two, has a cozy living room, a full kitchen, and two bedrooms. Grand Gables has hardwood floors and a spiral staircase leading to a master bedroom with cathedral ceilings and two other bedrooms. The cottage has a separate living room with a pullout sofa, a full kitchen, and sliding-glass doors opening out to two decks with views of the water. ⊠ *Shore Rd., 04653* ☎ *207/244–3699* ⊕ *www.bhgables.com* ⇨ *2 apartments, 1 cottage* ♻ *Cable TV, in-room DVD/VCR players; no a/c, no room phones* ⊟ *No credit cards* ✆ *Closed Nov.–Apr.*

$–$$ ▣ **Bass Harbor Inn.** If you're looking for someplace away from the crowds, consider this lodging near the harbor. Originally built in 1870, the inn has a relaxed atmosphere. Many of the bright and airy rooms lead out to sunny decks. The third-floor studio has cathedral ceilings, a kitchenette, and views of the ocean. ⊠ *Shore Rd., 04653* ☎ *207/244–5157* ⊕ *www.acadiavacations.com* ⇨ *6 rooms, 1 studio* ♻ *No a/c, no room TVs, no room phones* ⊟ *AE, MC, V* ⊙| *CP.*

Sports & the Outdoors

At Little Island Marina, **Island Cruises** (⊠ Shore Rd. ☎ 207/244–5785) offers a lunch cruise to Frenchboro and an afternoon nature cruise through Blue Hill Bay. These popular cruises are scheduled from mid-June to late September. The **Maine State Ferry Service** (☎ 207/244–3254) operates a ferry carrying both passengers and vehicles to Swans Island and Frenchboro.

Shopping

E. L. Higgins (⊠ Bernard Rd., Bernard ☎ 207/244–3983 ⊕ www.antiquewicker.com) carries antique wicker, furniture, and glassware.

THE OUTER ISLANDS

If your schedule permits, take the time to visit one or more of the islands off Mount Desert Island. You're likely to see seals and other wildlife, as well as unobstructed views of Mount Desert Island's mountains. Each island has its own unique character, and some offer more amenities than others. Expect to explore on foot or by bicycle.

Cranberry Isles

25 *1–5 mi south of Mount Desert Island via boat.*

Off the southeast shore of Mount Desert Island lie the five Cranberry Isles—Great Cranberry, Islesford (also frequently called Little Cranberry), Baker Island, Sutton Island, and Bear Island. Ferry trips to Great Cranberry, Islesford, and Baker Island are a great way to escape the crowds on Mount Desert Island. Consider bringing a bike to Great Cranberry and Islesford. Be sure to look for the beautiful lighthouse on Bear Island, located just before the entrance to Northeast Harbor.

Of the Cranberry Islands, Islesford has the closest thing to a village. You can find a cluster of houses, a church, a market, and a fishermen's co-op near the ferry dock. The **Islesford Historical Museum,** run by Acadia National Park, has displays of ship models, dolls, tools, and other artifacts that document the island's history. ⊠ *Islesford* ☎ *207/244-9224* ⊡ *Free* ⊗ *Mid-June–late Sept., daily 10–noon and 12:30–3.*

The **Great Cranberry Historical Society** has a collection of artifacts from the island that include baskets, photographs, and even old report cards. ⊠ *Great Cranberry* ☎ *207/244-9055* ⊕ *www.gcihs.org* ⊡ *Free* ⊗ *Late June–mid-Sept., Mon.–Sat. 10:30–4.*

Baker Island, the remotest of the Cranberry Isles, looks almost black from a distance because it is covered by a thick spruce forest. The Islesford Ferry from Northeast Harbor conducts a 4½-hour narrated tour, during which you are likely to see ospreys, cormorants, and harbor seals. Because Baker Island has no natural harbor, you ride in a fishing dory to get to shore.

Where to Stay & Eat

$–$$$ ✕ **Islesford Dock Restaurant.** You can't ask for a better seaside atmosphere than at this restaurant. Overlooking the harbor, this casual eatery has great views of the ocean and Mount Desert Island. You can dine on traditional seafood fare, or opt for steaks or sandwiches. In summer it's open for lunch from Tuesday to Saturday and for dinner throughout the week. ⊠ *Islesford* ☎ *207/244-7494* ⚑ *Reservations essential* ⊟ *D, MC, V* ⊗ *Closed Labor Day–mid-June.*

Sports & the Outdoors

Sailing from Northeast Harbor, the **Beal & Bunker Mail Boat Ferry Service** (☎ 207/244–3575) serves Great Cranberry, Islesford, and Sutton Island. The **Cranberry Cove Boating Company** (☎ 207/244–5882 ⊕ www.barharborferry.com) runs from Southwest Harbor to Great Cranberry, Islesford, and Sutton Island. Baker Island is reached by the cruise boats operated each summer by the **Islesford Ferry Company** (☎ 207/276–3717) from Northeast Harbor.

Explore the Cranberry Isles in two-person kayaks from **Joy of Kayaking** (⊠ Islesford ☎ 207/244–4309). Life jackets, laminated maps, and compasses are provided. Make sure to reserve a day or two ahead.

Shopping

Established in 1987, **Islesford Artists** (⌧ Islesford ☎ 207/244–3145) displays works by island artists.

Frenchboro

㉖ *8 mi south of Bass Harbor via boat.*

The popular catchphrase "You can't get there from here" applies to the island of Frenchboro. You *can* get to Frenchboro, but only on certain days of the week. The ferry service runs two round-trip voyages to Frenchboro on Friday, and one-way voyages on Wednesday, Thursday, and Sunday. Some charter services will also take you to Frenchboro. Although a bed-and-breakfast recently opened on the island, you might be better off just spending the day. Frenchboro is not the place to visit if you're looking for streets lined with galleries and boutiques. But if you want to see an authentic fishing community, this is the place.

You can find local memorabilia at the **Frenchboro Historical Society Museum.** The museum has a gift shop with locally made crafts and a cookbook compiling recipes from island residents. Stop here to pick up a map detailing the island's walking trails. ⌧ *Frenchboro* ☎ *207/334–2932* ☺ *Memorial Day–Labor Day, noon–5.*

If you're traveling in the region around the beginning of August, check out the annual **Frenchboro Lobster Festival.** A tradition for half a century, the festival is always held the second Saturday of August. Round-trip ferry service is available.

Where to Stay & Eat

$–$$$ ✕ **Lunt's Deli.** A popular spot among visitors to the island, this dockside restaurant serves up lobster rolls, seafood chowder, sandwiches, and salads. ⌧ *Frenchboro Dock* ☎ *207/334–2922* ☺ *July 5–Labor Day.*

Sports & the Outdoors

The **Maine State Ferry Service** (⌀ Bass Harbor ☎ 207/244–3254 or 800/491–4883 ⊕ www.state.me.us/mdot/opt/ferry/ferry.htm) operates round-trip passenger ferry service between Frenchboro and Bass Harbor from April to October.

MOUNT DESERT ISLAND & ACADIA NATIONAL PARK A TO Z

To research prices, get advice from other travelers, and book travel arrangements, visit www.fodors.com.

AIR TRAVEL

Although Trenton's Hancock County–Bar Harbor Airport offers the closest airport to the Mount Desert Island region, only one commuter airline, Colgan Air (operated by US Airways Express), services the airport. Most people prefer Bangor International Airport, an hour's drive from the island. American, Continental, Delta, Midwest Express, Northwest, and US Airways fly into Bangor. Direct flights are available to and from Boston, New York LaGuardia, Philadelphia, Cincinnati, Detroit, and Albany.

🖪 **Bangor International Airport** ✉ 287 Godfrey Blvd., Bangor ☎ 207/947-0384 ⊕ www.flybangor.com. **Hancock County–Bar Harbor Airport** ✉ Rte. 3, Trenton ☎ 207/667-7329 ⊕ www.bhbairport.com.

BIKE TRAVEL

Although Acadia National Park is a bicycle-friendly area, traveling along the island's major thoroughfares can be challenging. Bike lanes are narrow or nonexistent on many stretches of road, leaving bikers the choice of biking in roadside gravel, which can be soft when wet, or sharing the road with vehicle traffic. In summer, when traffic is heavy and many drivers are distracted by the scenery, it's a good idea to avoid the main roads.

BUS TRAVEL

The free Island Explorer shuttle service circles the entire island from the end of May to September, with limited service continuing through mid-October. Buses are equipped with racks for stowing bicycles and service the major campgrounds, Acadia National Park, and Trenton's Hancock County–Bar Harbor Airport. Concord Trailways operates shuttle service from Bangor International Airport to Bar Harbor, with stops along the way in Bangor and Ellsworth. Vermont Transit runs between Bangor and Bar Harbor. If the bus isn't delayed by traffic, it takes about an hour. Downeast Transportation operates buses from Ellsworth to various locations on Mount Desert Island. Greyhound Bus Lines services Bangor. West's Coastal Connection is a public bus operated by the Maine Department of Transportation. You can take the bus from the Bangor International Airport to Ellsworth, where you can transfer to another bus to the island.

🖪 **Concord Trailways** ☎ 207/942-8686 or 888/741-8686 ⊕ www.concordtrailways.com. **Downeast Transportation** ☎ 207/667-5796. **Greyhound Bus Lines** ☎ 800/231-2222 ⊕ www.greyhound.com. **Island Explorer** ☎ 207/667-5796 ⊕ www.exploreacadia.com. **Vermont Transit** ☎ 207/772-6587 or 800/451-3292 ⊕ www.vermonttransit.com. **West's Coastal Connection** ☎ 800/596-2823 ⊕ www.state.me.us.

CAR TRAVEL

From the gateway towns of Ellsworth and Trenton, Route 3 leads to Mount Desert Island. When you reach the island, Route 3 continues to Bar Harbor. Route 102 heads toward Somesville and Southwest Harbor. In summer, traffic can slow considerably, especially in the afternoon. If Northeast Harbor is your first destination when arriving on the island, take Route 102 to Somesville, then turn onto Route 198.

In Acadia National Park, the 27-mi Park Loop Road is accessible from Hulls Cove (Visitor Center entrance), Otter Creek (Sieur de Monts Spring entrance), and Seal Harbor (Jordan Pond House entrance). You can also access Park Loop Road from Bar Harbor (Cadillac Mountain entrance).

EMERGENCIES

In case of an emergency, call 911.

🖪 Hospitals **Eastern Maine Medical Center** ✉ 489 State St., Bangor ☎ 207/973-8000. **Maine Coast Memorial Hospital** ✉ 50 Union St., Ellsworth ☎ 207/664-5311 ⊕ www.

mainehospital.org. **Mount Desert Island Hospital** ✉ 10 Wayman La., Bar Harbor ☎ 207/288–5081. **Northeast Harbor Clinic** ✉ Kimball Rd., Northeast Harbor ☎ 207/ 276–3331. **Southwest Harbor Medical Center** ✉ 45 Herrick Rd., Southwest Harbor ☎ 207/ 244–5513.

LODGING

Several companies can help you find vacation rental accommodations, from in-town cottages to secluded estates.

The Davis Agency ✉ 363 Main St., Southwest Harbor 04679 ☎ 207/244–3891 ⊕ www.davisagencyrealty.com. **Janet Moore Real Estate** ✉ 12B Main St., Northeast Harbor 04662 ☎ 207/276–4292 ⊕ www.moore-realestate.com. **The Knowles Company** ✉ 1 Summit Rd., Northeast Harbor 04662 ☎ 207/276–3322 ⊕ www.knowlesco.com. **Maine Island Properties** ⌂ Box 1025, Mount Desert 04660 ☎ 207/244–4348 ⊕ www. maineislandproperties.com. **Mount Desert Properties** ⌂ Box 536, Bar Harbor 04609 ☎ 207/288–4523 ⊕ www.barharborvacationhome.com.

MEDIA

Daily newspapers serving the region include the *Bangor Daily News,* published Monday through Saturday. Weekly papers include the *Bar Harbor Times, Ellsworth American, Ellsworth Weekly,* and the *Islander.*

Community radio station WERU 89.9 FM in Blue Hill has eclectic programming featuring reggae, jazz, blues, oldies, folk, and other music. WMEH 90.9 is the local National Public Radio affiliate. WLBZ, channel 2, is the NBC affiliate. WVII, channel 7, is the ABC affiliate. WABI, channel 5, is the CBS affiliate. WMEB, channel 12, is the Maine Public Broadcasting affiliate.

Sports & the Outdoors

FISHING Maine residents 16 and older and non-Maine residents 12 and older must have a license to fish in fresh waters. Fishing licenses may be purchased at town halls and at some stores. Fishing licenses are not required for ocean fishing.

Bar Harbor Municipal Office ✉ 93 Cottage St., Bar Harbor ☎ 207/288–4098. **Mount Desert Municipal Office** ✉ Sea St., Northeast Harbor ☎ 207/276–5531. **Southwest Harbor Town Office** ✉ Main St., Southwest Harbor ☎ 207/244–5404. **Tremont Town Office** ✉ Bernard Rd., Tremont ☎ 207/244–7204.

KAYAKING The Maine Professional Guides Association represents kayaking guides. **Maine Professional Guides Association** ⌂ Box 847, Augusta 04332 ☎ 207/549– 5631 ⊕ www.maineguides.org.

TOURS

Acadia National Park Tours operates a 2½-hour bus tour of Acadia National Park, narrated by a naturalist, from May to October, and 2½-hour narrated trolley tours. Bar Harbor Taxi & Tours conducts half-day historic and scenic tours of the area. Downeast Nature Tours leads small-group tours highlighting the island's flora and fauna.

Acadia Air, at Hancock County Airport between Ellsworth and Bar Harbor, rents aircraft and flies seven aerial sightseeing routes from spring to fall. A Step Back in Time uses Victorian-costumed guides to lead walking tours that highlight the 1890s in Bar Harbor. Tours leave from 48 Cottage Street.

Acadia Air ☎ 207/667-5534. **Acadia National Park Tours** ☎ 207/288-3327. **Bar Harbor Taxi & Tours** ☎ 207/288-4020. **Downeast Nature Tours** ☎ 207/288-8128. **A Step Back in Time** ☎ 207/288-9605.

TRAIN TRAVEL

Portland is the closest city to the Mount Desert Island region with train service. Amtrak's "Downeaster" connects Portland to Boston with several stops in southern Maine and New Hampshire. It takes approximately three hours to reach Mount Desert Island by car from the train station.

Amtrak ☎ 800/872-7245 ⊕ www.amtrak.com.

VISITOR INFORMATION

Acadia Information Center ⊠ 1201 Bar Harbor Rd., Trenton ☎ 207/667-8550 ⊕ www.acadiainfo.com. **Acadia National Park** ⌂ Box 177, Bar Harbor 04609 ☎ 207/288-3338 ⊕ www.nps.gov/acad. **Bangor Convention & Visitors Bureau** ⊠ 115 Main St., Bangor 04401 ☎ 207/947-5205 or 800/926-6673 ⊕ www.bangorcvb.org. **Bangor Region Chamber of Commerce** ⊠ 519 Main St., Bangor 04401 ☎ 207/947-0307 ⊕ www.bangorregion.com. **Bar Harbor Chamber of Commerce** ⊠ 93 Cottage St. ⌂ Box 158, Bar Harbor 04609 ☎ 207/288-3393, 207/288-5103, or 800/288-5103 ⊕ www.barharborinfo.com. **Ellsworth Area Chamber of Commerce** ⊠ 163 High St., Ellsworth ☎ 207/667-5584 ⊕ www.ellsworthchamber.org. **Mount Desert Chamber of Commerce** ⊠ Sea St., Northeast Harbor ☎ 207/276-5040. **Mount Desert Island Information Center** ⊠ Rte. 3, Thompson Island ☎ 207/288-3411. **Southwest Harbor/ Tremont Chamber of Commerce** ⊠ Main St. ⌂ Box 1143, Southwest Harbor 04679 ☎ 207/ 244-9264 or 800/423-9264 ⊕ www.acadiachamber.com.

WAY DOWN EAST

7

BE MYSTIFIED BY REVERSING FALLS
while enjoying a seafood dinner
at Tidal Falls Lobster Restaurant ⇨*p.235*

BRING A PICNIC BASKET
to the quietest part of
Acadia National Park ⇨*p.240*

SURROUND YOURSELF WITH NATURE
at Oceanside Meadows Inn ⇨*p.242*

VIEW THOUSANDS OF PUFFINS
on a cruise to Machias Seal Island ⇨*p.251*

STAND IN AWE OF THE LANDSCAPE
at Cutler Coast Public Reserved Land ⇨*p.255*

POSE WITH A CANDY-STRIPED LIGHTHOUSE
at Quoddy Head State Park ⇨*p.256*

By Mary Ruoff **SLOGANS SUCH AS "THE REAL MAINE"** ring truer Way Down East. The raw, mostly undeveloped coast in this remote region is more accessible than it is further south. Pleasure craft don't crowd out lobster boats and draggers in small harbor towns the way they do in other coastal towns. Even in summer here you're likely to have rocky beaches and shady hiking trails to yourself. The slower pace is as calming as a sea breeze.

One innkeeper relates that visitors who plan to stay a few days often opt for a week after learning more about the region's offerings, which include two national wildlife refuges, more than half a dozen state parks and public preserves, and increasingly, conservancy-owned public land. Cutler's Bold Coast, with its dramatic granite headlands, is protected from development. Waters near Eastport have some of the world's highest tides. Lakes perfect for canoeing and kayaking are sprinkled inland. Rivers snake through marshland as they near the many bays. Boulders are strewn on blueberry barrens. Rare plants thrive in coastal bogs and heaths. Dark-purple-and-pink lupines line the roads in late June.

The Downeast Heritage Center, which opened in Calais in 2004, helps visitors learn about the wilderness areas Way Down East. It's just one example of how ecotourism is offering economic hope in a region that remains one of the poorest in the state. Residents often work a series of seasonal jobs, and many hope to siphon tourist dollars, as you might guess from the signs beckoning you to stop at homestead galleries, roadside stands, and quiet inns.

Exploring Way Down East

Way Down East covers roughly a fourth of the state's coast, at least as the crow flies. A car is essential for exploring this vast swath of land. U.S. 1, usually following the coast slightly inland, is the main transportation spine. Except for Grand Lake Stream, an upcountry fishing mecca, towns highlighted are along this highway or nearby on the area's many bays and peninsulas. The inland countryside is sprinkled with lakes and rolling with hills, so consider returning via an inland route.

About the Restaurants

Aside from a Dunkin' Donuts in Calais and a McDonald's in Machias, there are no fast-food chains Way Down East. If you don't have time to stop, you can grab a sandwich or slice of pizza at most convenience stores. Your only choice for a sit-down meal is often one of the many family establishments serving breakfast, lunch, and dinner. All of these places have massive menus heavy on the seafood, and it's not all fried. Save room for the desserts, often made right on the premises. Upscale dining establishments serving more creative cuisine are scattered throughout the region. Don't be surprised if you find that the best restaurant is in the inn where you're staying.

About the Hotels

In the villages and along the back roads you can find wonderful bed-and-breakfasts run by innkeepers eager to share Down East's laid-back charms. Some are cozy places where you might feel you're staying in a friend's country house, while others are grand mansions where the rooms are filled with antiques. Don't write off anything called a cottage; many in this region are luxurious. All charge less than you might think; upscale establishments that would command $150 a night or more in Bar Harbor often have rooms for less than $100. What you won't find Way Down East are chain hotels though there are some inexpensive roadside motels, most of them in larger towns.

WHAT IT COSTS					
	$$$$	$$$	$$	$	¢
RESTAURANTS	over $25	$18–$25	$11–$17	$7–$10	under $7
HOTELS	over $200	$151–$200	$101–$150	$61–$100	under $60

Restaurant prices are for a main course at dinner, excluding 7% tax. Hotel prices are for two people in a standard double room in high season, excluding service charges and 7% tax.

Timing

Reservations are recommended in July and August, although it's usually possible to find last-minute rooms. The exception is during one of the popular summer festivals, when you may find hotels are booked solid, even in neighboring towns. Temperatures in summer average about 70°F during the day. Nights are cool, so be sure to bring a light jacket. Fog is likely this time of year—and more common than in the south—so come prepared to appreciate its haunting beauty. Many establishments are open from Memorial Day to Columbus Day. Winter sports outfitters are almost nonexistent, but folks trickle in for winter getaways—the scenery never disappoints.

EASTERN HANCOCK COUNTY

As you drive east from Ellsworth, Mount Desert Island rises across Frenchman Bay. Eastern Hancock County attracts people who come to visit Acadia National Park and busy Bar Harbor, but want a respite from the crowds. With dramatic seaside scenery, tucked-away fishing villages, and artists in droves, lots of folks come just to stay put.

Hancock

❶ *9 mi east of Ellsworth.*

A small triangular green with a Civil War monument marks the center of Hancock. Not far away are the summer cottages at Hancock Point where stunning views await, especially at sunset, across Frenchman Bay. You can pick up items for an impromptu picnic in Hancock or across the bridge in Sullivan, where there are more mountain-framed views.

Lamoine State Park is a quiet preserve at the end of the Schoodic Peninsula. You can walk along the rocky beach or down a mile-long trail with Mount Desert Island looming in the background. There's a boat launch and fishing pier, a picnic area with grills, and 62 campsites without hookups. ⊠ *23 State Park Rd., Lemoine* ☎ *207/667–4778 or 207/941–4014* ⊕ *www.state.me.us/doc/parks/programs* 🖃 *$3* ☉ *Daily.*

Numbers in the text correspond to numbers in the margin and on the Way Down East and Campobello Island maps.

If you have 3 days

Head to the **Schoodic Peninsula** ❷, where you can explore the tide pools on the surf-beaten ledges of Acadia National Park. Then amble about the downtown area of tranquil Winter Harbor—bustling Bar Harbor across the bay seems a world away. There are more shops to discover all around Schoodic Peninsula, where many artists have galleries beside their homes. Spend the night at a small inn in Gouldsboro, Corea, or Prospect Harbor. On Day 2, travel north to **Milbridge** ❹, where you can enjoy the Milbridge Historical Museum, with displays on the town's shipbuilding heyday. In **Cherryfield** ❺, follow the Narraguagus River while checking out the impressive Victorian homes. Next, tour historic Ruggles House in **Columbia Falls** ❻. Continuing north, take the road to **Jonesport** ❼. When you arrive, cross the bridge to **Beals Island** ❼ for a late afternoon hike at Great Wass Island Preserve. Spend the night in Jonesport, or nearby in **Machias** ❽. The next day, take a morning puffin cruise from Jonesport.

If you have 5 days

Follow the three-day itinerary above. On Day 4, drive to **Lubec** ❿ and cross the bridge to New Brunswick's **Campobello Island** ⓫. Tour the Roosevelt Cottage at Roosevelt Campobello International Park and, if tides allow, walk out to East Quoddy Head Light. Then head to West Quoddy Head Light in Lubec to hike along the shore. Stay overnight in Lubec or on Campobello Island. On Day 5, visit Cottage Garden & Shoreline Nature Center in Lubec. Returning south on U.S. 1, visit the Burnham Tavern Museum in Machias. If time allows, take in the town's other historic sites or travel down to Roque Bluffs State Park for a hike.

If you have 6 days

Follow the five-day itinerary above. On Day 6, head to **Calais** ⓭ on U.S. 1, a gorgeous drive hugging the St. Croix River. Stop at the St. Croix Island International Historic Site, which overlooks the island where the French first settled in North America. Then visit the Downeast Heritage Center on the waterfront, with exhibits on the region's natural resources and history. Enjoy an afternoon hike at Moosehorn National Wildlife Refuge. Spend the night in Calais or back in Eastport.

Where to Stay & Eat

★ **$$–$$$** ✕ **Tidal Falls Lobster Restaurant.** This lobster stand overlooks one of New England's best known reversing falls, a phenomenon created when the current "reverses" from the bay to the harbor. White water roils from an hour before to an hour after low tide, but the falls always put on a good show. The menu eschews fried foods, opting instead for dishes such as steamed mussels. Look for sides such as garlic bread and mesclun salad. You can eat outdoors or inside a screened room. Bring your own wine (glasses and openers are provided). ⊠ *Tidal Falls Rd.* ☎ *207/422–*

6457 ⊘ *Closed mid-Sept.–mid-June. No lunch Mon.–Wed. June 21–Labor Day. Grounds open daily.*

$–$$$ ✕ **Ruth & Wimpy's.** Identifiable by the giant statues of "Wilbur the Lobster" and a trio of clams, this is a popular stop for families. Eat in the large dining room, outside on the deck, or in the screened-in area beside a wood-fired cooker. The menu includes more than 25 lobster dishes, including fried lobster, lobster Newburg, and lobster with haddock. You can also get steamed lobsters, clams, and mussels to go at the rustic lobster shack. ⊠ *U.S. 1* ☎ *207/422–3723* ▭ *D, MC, V* ⊘ *Mid-Dec.–Mar.*

$$$ ✕▣ **Le Domaine Inn.** In the French country–style dining room ($$$$), the owner serves classic dishes such as *coquille St. Jacques* (scallops with a ginger infused cider glaze) and *ris de veau pané à l'Anglaise* (veal sweetbreads with capers). The French cuisine is accompanied by the more than 5,000 bottles in the wine cellar. Le Domaine is known primarily for its food, but the French-influenced guest rooms are also inviting. They open onto private decks overlooking the perennial gardens, a pond, and the trails that meander through the property's 100 acres. A pair of suites have fireplaces to keep out the chill. The owner's mother was from Provence, so the decor feels quite authentic. ⊠ *1513 U.S. 1, 04640* ☎ *207/422–3395 or 800/554–8498* 🖷 *207/422–3916* ⊕ *www.ledomaine.com* ⇱ *3 rooms, 2 suites* ⚏ *Restaurant, ceiling fans, hiking, some pets allowed (fee); no room TVs* ▭ *AE, D, MC, V* ⊘ *Closed late Oct.–May. Restaurant closed Mon. June–mid-Oct. No lunch* ¶⦵ *CB.*

★ $$–$$$ ✕▣ **Crocker House Inn.** Set amid towering fir trees, this shingle-style lodging was built in 1884. The inn holds comfortable rooms decorated with authentic antiques and country-style furnishings. The accommodations in the Carriage House are perfect for families. The inn's restaurant ($$$–$$$$) draws diners from Bangor and beyond with dressed-up versions of traditional New England fare. The signature dish is scallops sautéed in white wine and topped with garlic, lemon, mushrooms, scallions, and tomatoes. ⊠ *967 Point Rd., 04640* ☎ *207/422–6806 or 877/715–6017* 🖷 *207/422–3105* ⊕ *www.crockerhouse.com* ⇱ *11 rooms* ⚏ *Restaurant, hot tub, bicycles, some pets allowed; no room TVs, no smoking* ▭ *AE, D, MC, V* ⊘ *Closed Jan.–mid-Mar. Closed Mon.–Thurs. late Mar., Apr., Nov. and Dec. No lunch* ¶⦵ *BP.*

★ $–$$ ▣ **Island View Inn.** Built around the beginning of the 19th century, this spacious shingled house is filled with furnishings from its days as a summer cottage. Steps lead from the manicured lawn to a private beach, where the views extend directly across Frenchman Bay to Mount Desert Island. Padded rocking chairs line the wraparound porch. The largest guest rooms have separate sitting areas; all open onto shared porches. The massive living room has an antique game table and built-in seats beside a fieldstone fireplace. ⊠ *12 Miramar Ave., Sullivan 04664* ☎ *207/422–3031* ⊕ *www.maineus.com/islandview* ⇱ *7 rooms* ⚏ *Dining room, boating, croquet, some pets allowed; no a/c, no room phones, no room TVs, no smoking* ▭ *D, MC, V* ⊘ *Closed mid-Oct.–mid-May* ¶⦵ *BP.*

Downeast Fisheries Trail

This informative trail points out sights that tell the story of fishing past and present. There's lots to learn about, such as weir fishing (a technique using nets attached to poles that Native Americans taught European settlers); sardine canning, the lifeblood of many towns in the early 20th century; and lobstering and salmon farming, major parts of today's economy. A nicely designed pocket pamphlet, available at Washinton County chambers of commerce, leads people on the trail. So far, 4 of the 14 sites are marked with interpretive panels. Many towns in Washington County are on the Downeast Fisheries Trail, and Milbridge, Lubec, and Eastport have more than one stop.

7

Puffin Cruises

Set sail from Cutler or Jonesport on a cruise to Machias Seal Island, the state's largest puffin colony. Many people come Way Down East just to visit this treeless, rocky isle 10 mi off the coast, a summer home puffins share with scores of other seabirds, including razorbills, common terns, arctic terns, common murres, black guillemots, and common eiders. With clownish ways and a "stuffed toy" look—white breasts beneath jet-black coats, goggle-like eyes, and blue bands on red-orange beaks—thousands of puffin steal the show. Canada and the United States dispute ownership of the migratory bird sanctuary, but tour operators cooperate with the Canadian Wildlife Service to control access. Weather can prevent boat landings, as there is no pier, but if you go ashore, you can walk on grassy paths to closetlike blinds where four people can stand comfortably as puffins court, clatter, and nuzzle. You might want to bring a sweater, temperatures in July and August can drop to 50°F.

Sea Kayaking

Since much of the coastline of Way Down East remains undeveloped, it's no surprise that paddlers—novice and experienced—love it here. The glacier-carved topography makes this a top kayaking destination. Many fjordlike bays offer stunning scenery on both sides of the boat. Islands near the mainland entice paddlers to explore. Pink granite ledges are common in the southern half of the region. North of Jonesport the coast changes, and these smooth rocks are replaced with jagged stones. Here you can see where Native Americans left their mark on the landscape: this region is home to what some consider the most significant petroglyph sites on the East Coast. Two of these ancient art collections are easy to reach by sea kayak. Paddle out to see carvings of a caribou, a walrus, and humans adorned with antlered headdresses.

$ 🏠 **Three Pines.** This impeccable saltbox on Sullivan Harbor is connected to the owner's home by a covered walkway. You can enjoy your breakfast on the screened porch, in the dining room, or in your room. A path along the shore looks toward Cadillac Mountain, while trails traverse the wooded 40 acres. ⊠ *274 East Side Rd., 04640* ☎ *207/460–7595* ⊕ *www.threepinesbandb.com* 📠 *2 rooms* ♺ *Dining room, bicycles, canoe, some pets allowed; no a/c, no room phones, no smoking* 🚫 *No credit cards* ⊠ *BP.*

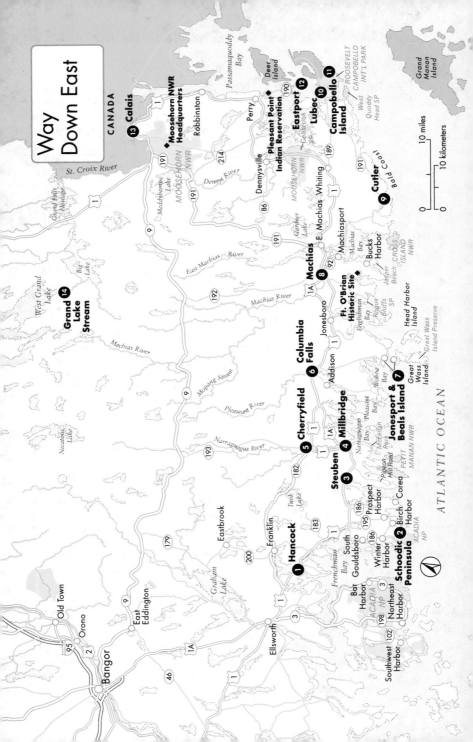

Way Down East

CANADA

ATLANTIC OCEAN

Nightlife & the Arts

The **Pierre Monteux School for Conductors** (⌧ Off U.S. 1 ☎ 207/422–3931) presents orchestral and chamber concerts from mid-June through mid-August.

Sports & the Outdoors

You can paddle on open water in Frenchman Bay or follow the shores of Taunton Bay on kayak excursions with **Hancock Point Kayak Tours** (⌧ 58 Point Rd. ☎207/422–6854). The company also arranges overnight kayaking and backpacking trips, and cross-country skiing and snowshoe trips.

Shopping

FOOD In August, buy pints of fresh blueberries or pick them yourself at **Hog Bay Berries** (⌧ 207 Hog Bay Rd., Franklin ☎ 207/565–3584 ⊕ www.hogbayberries.com). You can also buy blueberry pies and jams. Touting freshly made "good foods to go" such as Thai peanut noodles, Provençal roasted vegetables, and organic chicken cooked on a rotisserie, color-splashed **Mano's Market** (⌧ 1513 U.S. 1 ☎ 207/422–6500) also has a café and stocks wine, cheese, and packaged specialty foods. The **Sullivan Harbor Farm Smokehouse** (⌧ U.S. 1 ☎ 800/422–4014 ⊕ www.sullivanharborfarm.com) cold-smokes salmon and other seafood in the traditional Scottish manner. Load up for a picnic—insulated bags are available.

GALLERIES Acclaimed regional artist Philip Barter's boldly hued paintings of Down East scenes dominate at **Barter Family Gallery** (⌧ 318 South Bay Rd., Franklin ☎ 207/442–3190 ⊕ www.barterfamilyartgallery). This playful gallery near Sullivan also showcases sculpture and woolen rugs by talented family members. Heron dinnerware is one of the specialties, but there's much more to see at **Hog Bay Pottery** (⌧ 245 Hog Bay Rd., Franklin ☎207/565–2282 ⊕www.hogbay.com). The shop sells the owners' pottery and handwoven wool rugs. He fires his wood-burning kiln twice a year.

Walkways connect Japanese-style pavilions at **Lunaform** (⌧ 66 Cedar La., Sullivan ☎ 207/422–0923), which makes large, hand-turned concrete urns and planters for gardens and homes. Human figures fuse with animals and the natural world in Russell Wray's sculpture, etchings, and engravings, sold at **Raven Tree Gallery** (⌧ 536 Point Rd. ☎ 207/422–8273), which also carries the artist's jewelry. There's a toy-stocked playhouse for kids at **Spring Woods Gallery** (⌧ 19 Willowbrook La., Sullivan ☎ 207/422–3007 ⊕ www.springwoodsgallery.com), which carries the owners' paintings and prints of local scenes. Housed in the lower level of the Sullivan Town Office, **Sullivan Harbor Gallery** (⌧ U.S. 1, Sullivan ☎ No phone) displays work by local artisans.

en route Heading north on U.S. 1, the **Schoodic National Scenic Byway** starts at the Hancock-Sullivan bridge, where work began in 2004 on a facility that will detail the region's history, culture, and natural resources. The byway turns south on Route 186 en route to the Schoodic section of Acadia National Park, but you don't have to wait until then for awesome views of Cadillac Mountain across Frenchman Bay. One of the best is 1½ mi north of the bridge.

On the **State Route 182 Maine Scenic Byway,** overhanging trees create a tunnel of color come fall. From U.S. 1, take Route 182 to Franklin, a quaint town where the 13-mi scenic drive begins. Take in the scenery at Tunk Lake, about 6 mi from Franklin. The byway ends in Cherryfield, where you can return to U.S. 1.

Schoodic Peninsula

2 *23 mi southeast of Hancock, 32 mi east of Ellsworth.*

The landscape of Schoodic Peninsula makes it easy to understand why the overflow from Bar Harbor's wealthy summer population settled in Winter Harbor. The craggy coastline, the towering evergreens, and views over Frenchman Bay are breathtaking year-round. A drive through the community of Grindstone Neck shows what Bar Harbor might have been like before most of it was destroyed in the Great Fire of 1947. Artists and artisans have opened galleries in and around Winter Harbor. Anchored at the foot of the peninsula, Winter Harbor was once part of Gouldsboro, which wraps around it.

The Schoodic Peninsula is also home to several smaller coastal villages. The largest of these is **Birch Harbor.** Near Birch Harbor you can find **Prospect Harbor,** a small fishing village nearly untouched by tourism. There's also **Corea,** where there's little to do besides watch the fishermen at work, wander along stone beaches, or gaze out to sea—and that's what makes it so special.

FodorsChoice   The only section of **Acadia National Park** that sits on the mainland is at
★   the southern side of the Schoodic Peninsula. A few miles east of Winter Harbor, the park has a scenic 6-mi one-way loop that edges along the coast and yields views of Grindstone Neck, Winter Harbor, and Winter Harbor Lighthouse. At the tip of the point, huge slabs of pink granite lie jumbled along the shore, thrashed unmercifully by the crashing surf, and jack pines cling to life amid the rocks. The Fraser Point Day-Use Area at the beginning of the loop is an ideal place for a picnic. Work off your lunch with a hike up Schoodic Head for the panoramic views up and down the coast. A bus called the Island Explorer takes passengers from Prospect Harbor, Birch Harbor, and Winter Harbor and drops them off anywhere in the park. ⊠ *Rte. 186* ☎ *207/288–3338* ⊕ *www. nps.gov/acad* ☞ *$10 per car.*

Where to Stay & Eat

★ **$$$–$$$$** ✕ **Bunker's Wharf.** On a narrow harbor that opens onto the ocean, this restaurant and lobster pound sits near Acadia National Park. Enjoy the views from the stone patio or from the large windows in the blond-wood dining room. Some seats in the bar face the water. The setting—quintessential Maine—isn't all that keeps locals coming back. The restaurant is also known for generous portions and scrumptious fare, from fried clams on a baguette at lunch to baked haddock with foccacia-bread stuffing at dinner. The Sunday brunch menu includes lobster stew. ⊠ *260 East Schoodic Dr., Birch Harbor* ☎ *207/963–2244* ▤ *MC, V* ⊗ *Closed Nov.–mid May.*

★ **\$\$\$–\$\$\$\$** ✕ **Mama's Boy Bistro.** With a lovely bar constructed from mahogany and ash, this bistro may be Way Down East's fanciest dining spot. The building, with soaring gables and a stone hearth, is typical of this part of the state. There is balcony seating overlooking an open kitchen, where you can watch the chefs prepare entrées such as grilled sablefish and beef tenderloin with a Gruyère cheese and red onion tart. A honey-and-basil syrup and candied pistachios top the goat-cheese cheesecake. ⊠ *10 Main St., Winter Harbor* ☎ *207/963–2365* ⊕ *www. mamasboybistro.com* ☰ *AE, D, MC, V* ⊙ *Closed Mon. in season. Closed mid-Oct.–mid-May. No lunch.*

\$\$–\$\$\$ ✕ **Fisherman's Inn.** The house specialty, lobster pie, is one of the many seafood dishes on the menu at this casual eatery founded in 1947. Beef, chicken, and vegetarian dishes are also available. An appetizer of cheese spread and salmon pâté comes from a local smokehouse run by the couple that owns the restaurant. They've made some changes, such as the addition of water-view windows, but they've kept the dark-wood booths that give the place a sense of history. ⊠ *7 Newman St., Winter Harbor* ☎ *207/963–5585* ☰ *D, MC, V* ⊙ *Closed mid-Oct.–late May.*

\$–\$\$\$ ✕ **Chase's Restaurant.** The orange booths may remind you of a fast-food joint, but this family restaurant has a reputation for serving good, basic fare. In this region, that means a lot of fish. There are large and small fried seafood dinners and several more expensive seafood platters. It's also open for breakfast. ⊠ *193 Main St., Winter Harbor 04693* ☎ *207/ 963–7171* ☰ *MC, V.*

\$–\$\$ ✕ **West Bay Lobsters in the Rough.** Lobsters and steamers, accompanied by corn on the cob, coleslaw, or baked beans, are among the dishes served in this casual eatery. Save room for the freshly baked blueberry pie. Eat in the greenhouse, at the outdoor tables, or have meals packed up to take on a picnic. ⊠ *West Bay Rd., Prospect Harbor* ☎ *207/963–7021* ☰ *AE, D, DC, MC, V* ⊙ *Closed Nov.–May. No lunch.*

¢–\$ ✕ **Downeast Deli.** This downtown delicatessen's pizzas topped with smoked fish and sandwiches made with Williams of Vermont and Block & Barrel meats are all amply proportioned. The prices, however, aren't oversized. The second-floor dining area overlooks the harbor; a stream meanders past the picnic area. Local arts and crafts such as hand-cast bells are sold at a market held here on weekends from July through Labor Day. You can buy beer and wine to go. ⊠ *27 Main St., Prospect Harbor* ☎ *207/963–2700* ☰ *MC, V* ⊙ *Closed Sun. Sept.–late May.*

¢ ✕ **J. M. Gerrish Provisions.** The store that opened here in the early 1900s was where locals and visitors alike went for ice cream. The new owners kept the original name and part of the old marble counter, but transformed the space into a café and specialty foods store. The menu has soups, salads, and savory sandwiches such as turkey and cheddar topped with peach salsa. Provisions include local organic produce and wine. And yes, you can still buy an ice-cream cone. ⊠ *352 Main St., Winter Harbor* ☎ *207/963–2244* ☰ *AE, D, MC, V* ⊙ *Closed Oct.–mid-May.*

\$\$–\$\$\$ ⌂ **Elsa's Inn on the Harbor.** With Prospect Harbor Point Light in the distance, all the guest rooms at this lodging have wonderful water views. You can watch fishermen come and go from a rocker on the porch or a window seat in the parlor. A family that's lived on the peninsula for more than six generations transformed their ancestral home into an inn, adding amenities such as good-size baths. One room has a whirlpool, and all have terry robes and down duvets. ✉ *179 Main St., Prospect Harbor 04669* ☎ *207/963–7571* ⊕ *www.elsasinn.com* ➲ *6 rooms* ⚘ *Ceiling fans, some pets allowed, some room TVs; no a/c, no room phones, no smoking* ⊟ *MC, V* ⦿⎮ *BP.*

$$–$$$

FodorsChoice
★

🏨 **Oceanside Meadows Inn.** This place is a must for nature lovers. Trail maps guide you through a 200-acre preserve dotted with woods, streams, salt marshes, and ponds. Inspired by the moose, eagles, and other wildlife that thrive here, the innkeepers created the Oceanside Meadows Innstitute for the Arts & Sciences, which holds lectures, musical performances, art exhibits, and other events in the restored barn. Furnished with antiques, country pieces, and family treasures and scented with flowers from the gardens, the inn has sunny, inviting living rooms with fireplaces and a separate guest kitchen. Guest rooms are spread among two white clapboard buildings fronting a private beach shaded by granite ledges. Breakfast is an extravagant multicourse affair that may include chilled strawberry soup. ✉ *202 Corea Rd., Prospect Harbor 04669* ☎ *207/963–5557* 🖷 *207/963–5928* ⊕ *www. oceaninn.com* ➲ *12 rooms, 3 suites* ⚘ *BBQ, beach, croquet, hiking, horseshoes, concert hall, Internet, meeting rooms, some pets allowed (fee); no smoking, no a/c, no room TVs* ⊟ *AE, D, DC, MC, V* ⊗ *Closed Nov.–Apr.* ⦿⎮ *BP.*

$$

🏨 **Black Duck Inn.** The comfortable common areas and guest rooms at this B&B are tastefully decorated with antiques, including the owner's toy collection. The walls are decorated with works by artists who've stayed here. A beachstone fireplace is the focal point of the cozy den. The first-floor guest room has a separate entrance and a private deck. If you're traveling with a small group, the two-bedroom suite is a great value. Two tiny cottages are perched on the harbor. Salt marshes and a small bay are tucked along trails on the inn's 12 acres. ✉ *36 Crowley Island Rd., Corea 04624* ☎ *207/963–2689 or 877/963–2689* 🖷 *207/963–7495* ⊕ *www.blackduck.com* ➲ *2 rooms, 1 suite, 2 cottages* ⚘ *No a/c, no room phones, no room TVs, no children under 7, no smoking* ⊟ *D, MC, V* ⊗ *Closed Nov.–Apr.* ⦿⎮ *BP.*

$–$$

🏨 **Bluff House Inn.** Combining the service of a hotel with the ambience of a B&B, this modern two-story inn on a secluded hillside has expansive views of Frenchman Bay. You can see its granite shores from the inn's wraparound porches. The dining room, open only to guests, serves light food and beer and wine in the late afternoon and evening. There's a picnic area with grill (a lobster pot is available for those who want to boil their own dinner). A stone fireplace warms one of the knotty pine lounge areas. The individually decorated guest rooms have furnishings from around the state. ✉ *57 Bluff House Rd., Gouldsboro 04607* ☎ *207/963–7805* ⊕ *www.bluffinn.com* ➲ *8 rooms, 1 apartment* ⚘ *Dining room; no a/c, no room TVs, no smoking* ⊟ *AE, D, DC, MC, V* ⦿⎮ *CP.*

$–$$

🏨 **Sunset House Bed & Breakfast.** From the porch of this homey lodging, you can look out over a tidal cove, then turn your gaze to the freshwater pond where you can swim or canoe. The third floor, with three rooms sharing a bath and kitchen, is a good choice for families. The full breakfast includes delicacies such as smoked salmon. ✉ *54 Clinic Rd., Goulds-*

boro 04670 ☎ *207/963–7156 or 800/233–7156* 🖷 *207/963–5859* ⊕ *www.sunsethousebnb.com* ⤳ *7 rooms, 4 with bath* ⚓ *Pond, boating; no a/c in some rooms, no room TVs, no children under 5, no smoking* ⊟ *D, MC, V* ⦿⧾ *BP.*

$ ⊡ **The Pines.** This motel's location, right at the beginning of the Schoodic Point Loop, makes it a good choice. All of the guest rooms have beds piled with hand-stitched quilts. The comfortable cabins sleep from four to six people and have separate seating areas and kitchenettes. ⬠ *Box 406* ⊠ *17 Main St. (Rte. 186), Winter Harbor 04693* ☎ *207/963–2296* ⊕ *www.ayuh.net* ⤳ *3 rooms, 4 cottages, 2 cabins* ⚓ *Snack bar, some kitchenettes, some microwaves, some cable TV, playground; no a/c* ⊟ *MC, V.*

Nightlife & the Arts

Afternoon and evening musical performances are part of the **Schoodic Arts Festival** (☎ 207/963–2569 ⊕ www.schoodicarts.org), which takes place at venues throughout the peninsula during the first two weeks of August. Schoodic Steel, a community steel pan band, drums up a lot of excitement at its evening performance on the last weekend of the festival. An art show is held on the first Saturday.

Free musical concerts and lectures on topics such as Maine's lobster fishery and the Ice Age's impact on the region are held at **Oceanside Meadows Innstitute for the Arts & Sciences** (⊠ Corea Rd., Prospect Harbor ☎ 207/963–5557) from late June through September. The Innstitute is housed in a restored barn at Oceanside Meadows Inn, whose owners founded the organization.

Schoodic Arts for All presents local musicians at the 1904 **Hammond Hall** (⊠ 427 Main St. ☎ 207/963–2569 ⊕ www.schoodicarts.org). Classical and jazz music is featured during the Hammond Hall Renaissance Concert Series, held the second Friday of the month from May to October. Local musicians take the stage for Last Friday Coffee House on the last Friday of the month throughout the year.

Sports & the Outdoors

MooseLook Guide Service (⊠ 150 Corea Road, Prospect Harbor ☎ 207/963–7223 ⊕ www.mooselookguideservice.com) rents canoes, kayaks, and bikes and leads canoeing and kayaking trips.

Departing from Bunker's Wharf, **Robertson Sea Tours Adventures** (⊠ 260 East Schoodic Dr., Birch Harbor ☎ 207/546–3883 ⊕ www.robertsonseatours.com) takes up to six passengers out on a lobster boat. You can cruise among the islands of Frenchman Bay or look for puffins on Petit Manan Island. The boat sails Wednesday to Saturday from June to September.

You can see the ocean from every green at the 9-hole **Grindstone Neck Golf Course** (⊠ 106 Grindstone Ave., Winter Harbor ☎ 207/963–7760 ⊕ www.grindstonegolf.com), one of Maine's oldest courses.

Shopping

The wines sold at **Bartlett Maine Estate Winery** (⊠ U.S. 1, Gouldsboro ☎ 207/546–2408 ⊕ bartlettwine.com) are produced from locally grown apples, pears, blueberries, and other fruit. Ask the vintners what foods to pair them with while sampling different wines in the tasting room. It's open Memorial Day to Columbus Day. A pioneering organic grower on West Bay, **Darthia Farm** (⌂ Rte. 186, Gouldsboro ☏ 207/963–7771 or 800/285–6234 ⊕ www.darthiafarm.com) operates a store from June through September where you can buy produce and herbs, along with preserves, handspun yarn, and knitted items. Kids love the farm animals and the hayrides on Tuesday and Thursday in August. Salmon pâté and smoked salmon, mussels, and cheese are among specialty foods sold at **Grindstone Neck of Maine** (⌂ Rte. 186, Winter Harbor ☏ 207/963–7347 or 866/831–8734 ⊕ www.grindstoneneckofmaine.com), which gives tours of its smokehouse. Load up for a picnic—coolers provided for a deposit. Along with mostly organic local produce, **Winter Harbor Farmers Market** (⌂ 10 Main St., Winter Harbor ☏ 207/288–4737) sells goat cheese, beef and chicken, hand-spun yarn, knitted items, and maple syrup and preserves. The market operates on Tuesday mornings from late June to early September.

Glass wildlife sculptures, flowers, goblets, and beads are for sale at **Gypsy Moose Glass Co.** (⌂ 20 Williamsbrook Rd., Gouldsboro ☏ 207/963–2674 ⊕ www.oceaninn.com/gypsymoose), whose owner gives glass-blowing demonstrations. It's open March to December. One of the area's premier artisans, **Lee Art Glass Studio** (⌂ Main St., Winter Harbor ☏ 207/963–7004) carries fused-glass tableware and other items.

Stoneware sinks, tile, and dishware are the mainstay at **Maine Kiln Works** (⌂ Rte. 186, West Gouldsboro ☏ 207/963–5819 ⊕ www.waterstonesink.com), but hand-crafted wood items such as dogsleds and rowing shells are also hung from the ceilings. Watch the potter hard at work in this former general store. It's open late May through mid-October, or by appointment. Born in Winter Harbor, M. Louise Shaw worked as an artist and graphic designer in Connecticut for many years and now sells her oils and watercolors of local scenes at the small but charming **Maloué Gallery** (⌂ 355 Main St. ☏ 207/963–2193).

Hand-cast bronze doorbells are among the items sold at **U.S. Bells** (⌂ Rte. 186, Prospect Harbor ☏ 207/963–7184 ⊕ www.usbells.com). You are often able to tour the foundry. In two buildings fronted by gardens, **Winter Harbor Antiques** (⌂ 424 Main St., Winter Harbor ☏ 207/963–2547) stocks antiques, handmade baskets, and local arts and crafts.

Step back in time at **Winter Harbor 5 & 10** (⌂ 349 Main St., Winter Harbor ☏ 207/963–7927), a tried-and-true dime store with a big selection of local T-shirts and sweatshirts.

WASHINGTON COUNTY

Towns in the southwestern corner of Washington County seem more like one community than those off at the ends of necks and peninsulas farther Down East. Though it's less well known as a destination, Washington County's wildlife refuge, charming architecture, salmon-filled river, and historical museum make this a path to beat.

Steuben

③ *17 mi north of Hancock via U.S. 1.*

Steuben is the first town in Washington County if you're heading north on U.S. 1. The town is on the east side of the highway, largely hidden by the trees. If you don't have time to stop, at least take a drive through the hamlet (there's a second turnoff if you miss the first one). Settled in the 1760s, Steuben was named by an aide-de-camp to General George Washington, and his 1785 Federal-style manse still stands on a hill across from the town center.

Steuben has a lost-in-time feel. The 1850s Greek Revival Steuben Union Church beside the village green is a classic. The handsome Henry D. Moore Parish House next door, built in 1910, is a public library.

Visitors are welcome at **Petit Manan National Wildlife Refuge**, a 2,166-acre sanctuary of fields, forests, and rocky shorefront at the tip of a penin-sula. The wildlife viewing and bird-watching are renowned. In August the park is a popular spot for picking wild blueberries. You can explore the refuge on two walking trails; the shore trail looks out on sand-color Petit Manan Lighthouse, Maine's second tallest light. Parking is limited, so arrive early. ✉ *Pigeon Hill Rd.* ☎ *207/546–2124* ⊕ *www.petitmanan. fws.gov* ✉ *Free* ☉ *Daily.*

Where to Stay & Eat

$–$$ ✕ **Country Charm.** A welcome surprise along the road to Petit Manan National Wildlife Refuge, this restaurant serves tasty regional fare. Its out-of-the-way location doesn't deter locals, who come for the hearty breakfasts or the salad bar. The facade is nondescript, but the dining room has considerable charm. ✉ *326 Pigeon Hill Rd.* ☎ *207/546–3763* ▤ *MC, V* ☉ *Closed Mon. Sept.–June.*

Shopping

Functional and decorative burl bowls, carved birds, and free-form fur-niture are found at **Carbone Sculpture Studio & Gallery** (✉ 460 Pigeon Hill Rd. ☎ 207/546–2170). Most of Ray Carbone's works are in wood, but there are stone and bronze pieces. Some are displayed in the sunny garden.

Milbridge

④ *22 mi north of Hancock via U.S. 1.*

Lumbering spurred the shipbuilding that thrived here in the 1800s, and Milbridge is still a major commercial center. As you enter the town, you pass a large Christmas wreath wholesaler and a blueberry packager's headquarters.

The town may be small, but it has 75 mi of coastline spread about sev-eral peninsulas and bays that are waiting to be explored. You can hike along the shore and enjoy views of the islands dotting Narraguagus Bay at the 10-acre **McClellan Park**. Rounded boulders swath the shore, and smaller stones form a gray- and black-hued beach near the waterfront picnic area. A dozen campsites accommodate tents and small to medium recreational vehicles. For more information on camping, contact the town office. ⊠ *Wyman Rd.* ☎ *207/546–2422* ⊕ *www.milbridgemaine.com* ⊗ *Memorial Day–Columbus Day.*

The facade of the **Milbridge Historical Museum** may lack period charm, but the interior more than makes up for it. Permanent exhibits document maritime industries past and present: shipbuilding, sardine canning, weir fishing, and lobstering. There are also displays about blueberry production. Changing exhibits occupy about a third of the display space, and the meeting room doubles as an art gallery—local artists are on a waiting list. ⊠ *83 Main St.* ☎ *207/546–4471* ⊕ *www. milbridgehistoricalsociety.org* ☜ *Free* ⊗ *June–Sept., weekends 1–4; July and Aug., Tues., and weekends 1–4.*

Where to Stay & Eat

$ ☶ **My Sweeties' Bed & Breakfast.** Don't be deterred if the facade is unfinished—inside this B&B you'll find homey accommodations. The four rooms are done up in different themes, such as the Captain's Room and the Lighthouse Room. The handsome dining room, where breakfast is served, has lovely oak wainscoting and a built-in hutch. ⊠ *51 Main St., 04658* ☎ *207/546–3717 or 866/665–2560* ⊕ *www.mysweeties.net* ☜ *4 rooms, 2 with bath* ⚭ *Some pets allowed; no a/c, no smoking* ☐ *MC, V* ⦿ *BP.*

Nightlife & the Arts

The town's largest annual event is the **Milbridge Days Celebration** (☎ 207/ 546–2422 ⊕ www.milbridgemaine.com), held each year on the last weekend of July. There's a blueberry pancake breakfast, clam-and-lobster bake, parade, crafts show, and most famously, a codfish relay race.

There's only one screen at **Milbridge Theatre** (⊠ 26 Main St. ☎ 207/546– 2038), but it's a large one and the price is right—$4.50. The owner of the only movie theater between Ellsworth and Calais is likely to greet you in the little lobby—he hasn't missed a show since opening the place in 1978. If you're lucky, you'll catch one of the player-piano performances. The theater is open daily Memorial Day through early January and weekends in April and May.

Sports & the Outdoors

Departing from Milbridge Marina in a six-passenger lobster boat, **Robertson Sea Tours Adventures** (☎ 207/546–3883 ⊕ www. robertsonseatours.com) runs sightseeing excursions and lobster dinner cruises (you can haul a few of the captain's traps), and puffin-watching trips to Petit Manan Island. Prices start at $40 per person. The company operates from late May to September.

Shopping

You can buy more than local produce at the **Milbridge Farmers' Market** (⊠ Main St. ☎ 207/546–2395), including soap, cheese, spices, and maple syrup. In a parking lot facing Main Street, the market operates from 9 to noon on Saturday from June to mid-October.

en route | As an exhibit at the Milbridge Historical Museum explains, coastal farmers built **salt marsh dikes** in the 1800s to drain the wetlands and free more land for crops. Their labor-intensive work is still visible along Route 1A half a mile north of the Narraguagus River Bridge. The Pleasant River south of U.S. 1 in Addison is also a good place to spot these altered landscapes, with low ridges and pools where dirt was removed for the dikes. Note that if you take Route 1A from Milbridge, you will reconnect with U.S. 1 before Addison, but you'll miss the lovely architecture of Cherryfield.

Cherryfield

5 *6 mi north of Milbridge via U.S. 1.*

Up the Narraguagus River from Milbridge, Cherryfield was a lumbering center in the 1800s. The river was once lined with lumber mills. Now this stretch is a lovely waterway overlooked by a gazebo in a small town park. The industry's legacy remains in the surprising number of ornate Victorian homes, unusual for a small New England village. The town has 52 buildings on the National Historic Register in such styles as Colonial Revival, Greek Revival, Italianate, and Queen Anne. The historic district runs along U.S. 1 and the handful of side streets. You can pick up a guide to the area at a convenience store on the corner of U.S. 1 and Main Street. Don't miss the **William M. Nash House,** on the River Road. This lavishly embellished Second Empire mansion perched high on a hill was considered as a location for one of the *Addams Family* movies.

Today, Cherryfield is known as the "Blueberry Capital of the World." Maine's two largest blueberry plants sit side by side on Route 193. To see the area's **wild blueberry barrens,** head north past the factories and take a right onto Ridge Road. The best way to explore this hilly landscape is by bicycle.

Where to Stay & Eat

$ ▢ **Ricker House Bed & Breakfast.** An 1803 Federal home in the historic district, Ricker House has two guest rooms overlooking the river. Both are nicely furnished with antiques—one has a chaise lounge and a four-poster bed. Both have separate sitting areas, but you can also relax in the downstairs sunroom. In business since 1985, the owners have loaded up notebooks with itineraries for exploring the nearby lakes, rivers, and towns. ✉ *49 Park St., Cherryfield 04622* ☎ *207/546–2780* ⬲ *2 rooms with shared bath* ⚘ *No a/c, no room phones, no room TVs, no smoking* ▭ *No credit cards* ⊙ *Closed Dec.–Apr.* ◉❙ *BP.*

COLUMBIA FALLS TO MACHIAS

It's hard to tell where one bay ends and another begins among the points and peninsulas of this section of Way Down East. Above Jonesport the granite shores become more jagged. Fishing villages here retain their centuries-old culture even as more tourists trickle in.

Columbia Falls

❻ *41 mi east of Ellsworth, 78 mi west of Calais.*

Founded in the late 18th century, Columbia Falls is a pretty village along the Pleasant River. True to its name, a waterfall tumbles into the river in the center of town. Once a prosperous shipbuilding center, Columbia Falls still has a number of stately homes dating from that era. U.S. 1 used to pass through the center of town, but now it passes to the west. It's worth driving through even if you don't have time to stop.

★ Judge Thomas Ruggles, a wealthy lumber dealer, store owner, postmaster, and Justice of the Court of Sessions, built **Ruggles House** in 1818. The house's distinctive Federal architecture, flying staircase, palladian window, and intricate woodwork were crafted over three years by Massachusetts wood-carver Alvah Peterson using a penknife. ⊠ *146 Main St.* ☎ *207/483–4637* ⊕ *www.ruggleshouse.com* ⊠ *$5* ⊙ *June–mid-Oct., Mon.–Sat., 9:30–4:30, Sun. 11–4:30.*

Where to Stay & Eat

$–$$$ ✕ **White House.** Deep-fried, sautéed, or broiled seafood dinners are the draw at this longtime favorite. If you love lobster but don't want to do all the work, the "lazy man's lobster" is shelled for you. Specials such as chicken enchiladas bolster the traditional fare. The corned beef hash served at breakfast is beloved by locals. Don't look for a white building—the restaurant is covered in shingles. Inside are blueberry-color booths and photographs of the local blueberry and cranberry harvest. ⊠ *U.S.1, Jonesboro* ☎ *207/434–2792* ⊟ *AE, D, MC, V.*

$–$$ ▦ **Dream Catcher.** A double sleigh and huge trunk adorn the wraparound porch at this hilltop lodging. The parlor has charming touches like a marble fireplace and pocket doors. Upstairs the mansard roof adds some atmosphere to the spacious guest rooms. The accommodations have a New York or Irish theme, so look for family mementos such as sports pennants and old family photos among the antique furnishings. The New York room can be enlarged to make a suite. ⊠ *898 U.S. 1* ⊟ *Box 157, 04623* ☎ *207/483–0937* ⊕ *www.dreamcatcherbnb.net* ⇱ *3 rooms* 𝄴 *Some pets allowed (fee); no a/c, no room phones, no room TVs* ⊟ *No credit cards* ⊙⊙ *BP.*

$ ▦ **Pleasant Bay Bed & Breakfast.** This Cape Cod-style inn takes advantage of its riverfront location. Stroll the nature paths on the 110-acre property, which winds around a peninsula and out to Pleasant Bay—you can even take one of the inn's llamas along for company. A screened porch and deck overlook the Pleasant River. The county-style rooms, all with water views, are decorated with antiques. A two-room suite has a private deck. A full breakfast is served before 8 AM, while a continental breakfast is available for late risers. ⊠ *386 West Side Rd.* ⊟ *Box 222, Addison 04606* ☎ *207/483–4490* ▤ *207/ 483–4653* ⇱ *3 rooms, 1 with bath; 1 suite* 𝄴 *Some refrigerators; no a/c, no room phones in some rooms, no TV in some rooms, no smoking* ⊟ *MC, V* ⊙⊙ *BP.*

WILD FOR BLUEBERRIES

THERE'S NO NEED TO INQUIRE about the cheesecake topping if you dine out in August when the wild blueberry crop comes in. Anything but blueberries would be unthinkable.

Way Down East, wild blueberries have long been a favorite food—and a key ingredient in cultural and economic life. Maine produces about half the commercial harvest—some 80 million pounds annually, up from 20 million in the early 1980s—with Canada supplying virtually all the rest. Washington County yields 65 percent of Maine's total crop, which is why the state's largest blueberry processors are here: Cherryfield Foods and Jasper Wyman & Son were founded shortly after the Civil War.

Wild blueberries, which bear fruit every other year, thrive in the region's cold climate and sandy, acidic soil. Undulating blueberry barrens stretch for miles in Deblois and Cherryfield—"the Blueberry Capital of the World"—and are scattered throughout Washington County. Look for tufts among low-lying plants along the roadways. In spring, fields shimmer as the small-leafed plants turn myriad shades of mauve, honey orange, and lemon yellow. White flowers appear in June, and fall transforms the barrens into a sea of red, attracting the foliage crowd.

Amid Cherryfield's barrens, a plaque on a boulder lauds the late J. Burleigh Crane for helping advance an industry that's not as wild as it used to be. Honey bees have been brought in to supplement native pollinators. Fields are irrigated. Barrens are burned and mowed to rid plants of disease and insects, reducing the need for pesticides. Most fields are owned by large corporations, though there are still 500 or so small growers.

About 60% of Maine's crop is now harvested with machinery. That requires moving boulders, so the rest continues to be harvested by hand with blueberry rakes. Made at Jonesport's Hubbard Rake Company, blueberry rakes resemble large forks that pull the berries off their stems. A good raker can earn between $250 and $300 a day. Years ago, year-round residents did the work. Today migrant workers make up two-thirds of the labor force, which balloons to 8,000 in August.

Blueberries get their dark color from anthocyanin, believed to provide their antioxidant power. Wild blueberries have more of these antiaging, anticancer compounds than their cultivated cousins. Like cranberries, another native plant, they are also thought to fight urinary tract infections. Smaller and more flavorful than cultivated blueberries, wild ones are mostly used in packaged foods. Only 1% of the state's crop—about 750,000 pints—is consumed fresh, mostly in Maine. Look for fresh berries (sometimes starting in late July and lasting until early September) at roadside stands, farmers' markets, and supermarkets.

–Mary Ruoff

Sports & the Outdoors

Blueberry barrens border the 9-hole **Barren View Golf Course** (⊠ U.S. 1, Jonesboro ☎ 207/434–6531 📠 207/434–7651 ⊕ www.barrenview. com), which also has a driving range.

Shopping

Next door to historic Ruggles House, **Columbia Falls Pottery** (⊠ 150 Main St. ☎ 207/483–4075 ⊕ www.columbiafallspottery.com) carries owner April Adams's hand-thrown earthnware pottery. Her work is decorated with local flora (blueberry, columbine, and bunchberry are popular), ships, and lighthouses.

Yes, the deep-blue geodesic dome housing **Wild Blueberry Land** (⊠ U.S. 1 ☎ 207/483–2583) is supposed to resemble a giant blueberry. In addition to foods filled with blueberries, the shop has displays about the local cash crop. A retired manager of the state blueberry research farm and his wife run this unusual shop. It's open from June to mid-October.

Jonesport & Beals Island

❼ *12 mi south of Columbia Falls, 20 mi southwest of Machias.*

The birding is superb around Jonesport and Beals Island, a pair of fishing communities joined by a bridge over the harbor. A handful of stately homes are tucked away on Jonesport's Sawyer Square, where Sawyer Memorial Congregational Church's exquisite stained-glass windows are illuminated at night. But the towns are less geared to travelers than those on the Schoodic Peninsula. Lobster traps are still piled in the yards throughout both towns. Lobster boat races near Moosabec Reach are the highlight of the community's annual Independence Day celebration.

At the tip of Beals Island, **Great Wass Island Preserve** (⊠ Beals Island ☎ 207/729–5181) is a 1,540-acre preserve where you can find stunted pines and raised peat bogs. Trails lead through the woods and emerge onto the undeveloped coast, where you may spot gray seals as you make your way among the rocks and boulders. Admission is free.

Where to Stay & Eat

$–$$ ✕ **Tall Barney's.** Salty accents add plenty of flavor at this down-home restaurant. Reserved for fishermen, the "liar's table" near the entrance is about as legendary as the namesake. The menu tells of Tall Barney, a brawny fisherman who left truly tall tales in his wake. Your server may be among his multitudinous descendants. Lobstermen arrive when the place opens at 4 AM, and tourists show up somewhat later. The menu includes five types of seafood stew, "tall" and "small" burgers, and oversized desserts such as "no bakes" (a candylike chocolate cookie—a local favorite). ⊠ *52 Main St.* ☎ *207/497–2403* ▭ *MC, V.*

★ $$ ▣ **Harbor House on Sawyer Cove.** The two spacious rooms on the third floor of this harbor-front building have big windows overlooking the water. Both have separate sitting areas and are tastefully furnished with Victorian flourishes such as cabbage-rose wallpaper and handwoven rugs. Breakfast is served on the enclosed porch. You can relax on the lawn, which is flanked by beach roses. Don't miss the telegraph office in an original storefront, now the inn's antique shop. ⊠ *27 Sawyer Sq.* ⬠ *Box 468, Jonesport 04649* ☎ *207/497–5417* 🖨 *207/497–3211* ⊕ *www. harborhs.com* ⬐ *2 rooms* ⬩ *Cable TV, Internet; no a/c, no room phones, no children under 12* ⊟ *D, MC, V* ⚬ *BP.*

Sports & the Outdoors

In business since 1940, **Norton of Jonesport** (☎ 207/497–5933 ⊕ www. machiassealisland.com) takes passengers on day trips to Machias Seal Island, where thousands of puffins nest. Arctic terns, razorbill auks, common murres, and many other seabirds also nest on the rocky island. Trips, which cost $60 per person, are offered from late May through early September. Mistake Island is a highlight of trips offered by **Coastal Cruises** (☎ 207/497–3064). A six-passenger boat traverses island-strewn waters dotted with salmon farms. On the island, a boardwalk leads to 72-foot Moose Peak Light. Prices start at $40 per person. The season runs from late June to early September.

Shopping

Years ago, many Down East fishermen hunted sea ducks to help feed their families, and the area's decoy-carving tradition lives on at **Nelson Decoys** (⊠ 13 Cranberry La. ☎ 207/497–3488), whose owners carve and paint wood eiders, puffins, and other waterfowl. The couple's store, in an old elementary school, also carries works by other Maine artists, including watercolor paintings and sea glass sculptures. Relax in rustic rockers while reading a local history book, and check out the owners' personal decoy collection.

Antique ship bells, old maritime prints, and authentic sextants, compasses, and ship wheels are among the treasurers at **Jonesport Nautical Antiques** (⊠ Main and Cogswell Sts. ☎ 207/497–2900 ⊕ www. nauticalantiques.com).

Machias

❽ *20 mi northeast of Jonesport.*

Machias lays claim to being the site of the first naval battle of the Revolutionary War. Despite being outnumbered and outarmed, a small group of Machias men under the leadership of Jeremiah O'Brien captured the armed British schooner *Margaretta.* That battle, fought on June 12, 1775, is now known as the "Lexington of the Sea." The town's other claim to fame is its wild blueberries. On the third weekend in August, the annual Machias Wild Blueberry Festival is a community celebration complete with parade, crafts fair, concerts, and plenty of blueberry dishes.

★ The **Burnham Tavern Museum,** housed in a building dating from 1770, details the colorful history of Job Burnham and other early residents of the area. It was in this tavern that the men of Machias laid the plans that culminated in the capture of the *Margaretta* in 1775. Period furnishings show what life was like in colonial times. ⊠ *Rte. 192* ☎ *207/ 255–4432* ⊕ *www.burnhamtavern.com* ⬠ *$5* ⊙ *Mid-June–early Sept., weekdays 9–5; mid-Sept.–mid-June, by appointment.*

Built in 1810, the **Nathan Gates House** houses the Machiasport Historical Society. The museum contains an extensive collection of old photographs, period furniture, housewares and tools, and other memorabilia. There's also a genealogical library. The Marine Room highlights the area's seafaring and shipbuilding past. A model school room and post office occupy the adjacent Cooper House, a utilitarian building constructed in 1850. ⊠ *Rte. 92, Machiasport* ☎ *207/255–8461* ⌦ *Free* ☉ *Late June–early Sept., Tues.–Sat. 12:30–4:30.*

Dating from the late 18th century, the **O'Brien Cemetery** is the final resting place for many of Machias's earliest settlers. It's in Bad Little Falls Park. ⊠ *Rte. 92, Machias.*

At the head of Machias Bay, **Fort O'Brien State Historic Site** looks toward the waters where a naval battle was waged in 1775. This was an active fort during the Revolutionary War, the War of 1812, and the Civil War. ⊠ *Rte. 92, Machiasport* ☎ *207/941–4014* ⊕ *www.state.me.us/doc/parks* ☉ *Memorial Day–Labor Day.*

Down East's rock- and fir-bound shores give way to a crescent-shape pebble beach at **Roque Bluffs State Park.** Just beyond the beach you can find a freshwater pond that's ideal for swimming. The park has changing areas, restrooms, a picnic area with grills, and a playground. Miles of trails traverse woods, apple orchards, and blueberry fields. The trail head is just before the park entrance at Roque Bluffs Community Church. ⊠ *Schoppee Point Rd., Roque Bluffs* ☎ *207/255–3475 or 207/941–4014* ⊕ *www.state.me.us/doc/parks* ⌦ *$2* ☉ *May 15–Oct. 15 daily.*

off the beaten path

JASPER BEACH – There is no sand here, just sea-polished stones that fascinate with their colors—heather, ochre, and bluish tones abound. This secluded spot is on Howard Cove in the village of Buck's Harbor, 9½ mi south of Machias. When naming the beach, folks were misled by the red volcanic rhyolite stones whose color resembles jasper. There's a bluff on one end and a salt marsh nearby. ⊠ *Rte. 92, Buck's Harbor.*

Where to Stay & Eat

$$$ ✕ **Artist's Café.** In an old house across from the University of Maine, this restaurant has garnered a strong local following. The white-wall dining rooms provide a simple backdrop for the eye-catching works by local artists and the palate-pleasing works by the chefs. The menu changes weekly, but a beloved appetizer called Horses Standing Still—hand-rolled Thai dumplings filled with chicken and shrimp and served with a dipping sauce—is almost always available. There are always four entrées, including a vegetarian dish. You might find the Mex, a spicy stack of tortillas. Lunch has the same Italian, French, and Thai influences. ⊠ *3 Hill St.* ☎ *207/255–8900* ▭ *MC, V* ☉ *Closed mid-Oct.–mid-Apr. No lunch Sat. except July and Aug.*

$–$$ ✕ **A.J.'s Bar & Grill.** Pubs are rare in these parts, so locals come to order a Guinness Stout or a locally brewed Sea Dog Ale. The menu includes burgers, wraps, and steaks, as well as more unusual offerings such as *poutine*, a French-Canadian dish consisting of french fries drowned in gravy and covered with chunks of cheese curds. Pale wood and cathedral ceilings make the large rooms seem larger yet. If you shoot some pool, you can get a close look at the animal heads mounted on the walls. Food is served until 1 AM, but the music can get loud later in the evening. ⊠ *21 Main St.* ☎ *207/255–3107* ⊟ *MC, V* ⊗ *Closed Sun. Oct.–May.*

$–$$ ✕ **Blue Bird Ranch.** Family restaurants dominate Way Down East, and this is a favorite of people throughout the region. The Blue Bird Ranch is known for its homestyle cooking and reasonable prices. The dining rooms are large and the staff is chipper. The menu includes everything from Cobb salad to fish stew. ⊠ *3 E. Main St.* ☎ *207/255–3351* ⊟ *AE, D, DC, MC, V.*

$ ✕ **Riverside Inn & Restaurant.** A bright yellow exterior invites a stop at this delightful inn perched on the banks of the Machias River. Inside you can find hammered tin ceilings and lots of hand-carved wood. The spacious guest rooms have antique furnishings and colorful quilts. The two-bedroom suite has a private balcony and a full kitchen. The restaurant ($$–$$$) has maintained its excellent reputation. The chef brings a special flair to traditional dishes such as London broil, as well as local dishes such as hake cakes and sautéed shrimp and scallops. Ask for a table in the intimate sunroom. ⊠ *U.S. 1* ⊙ *Box 373, East Machias 04630* ☎ *207/255–4134 or 888/255–4344* ⊟ *207/255–0577* ⊕ *www. riversideinn-maine.com* ⇨ *2 rooms, 2 suites* � ⌂ *Restaurant, cable TV; no a/c, no room phones, no smoking* ⊟ *AE, MC, V* � ⌶⦿⌶ *BP* ⊗ *Closed Jan.–early Feb.; restaurant closed Mon.–Wed. mid-Feb.–May and Mon. June–Dec. No lunch.*

$$ 🏠 **Captain Cates Bed & Breakfast.** The main portion of this Victorian home was built in 1875. On a bright morning or afternoon, you can relax in the lovely sunroom or on the covered swing on the front lawn, overlooking a wide stretch of the Machias River. Rooms are furnished with antiques, and most have water views. ⊠ *307 Port Rd., Machiasport 04655* ☎ *207/255–8812* ⊟ *207/255–6705* ⊕ *www.captaincates.com* ⇨ *6 rooms with shared baths* � ⌂ *No a/c, no room phones, no room TVs, no smoking* ⊟ *No credit cards* ⌶⦿⌶ *BP.*

$–$$ 🏠 **Machias Motor Inn.** This inn is on the tidal Machias River, and many of the clean, comfortable rooms have decks overlooking the water. Snowmobile trails are nearby. Helen's Restaurant serves breakfast, lunch, and dinner, and is known in these parts for its excellent pies. ⊠ *20 E. Main St., 04654* ☎ *207/255–4861 or 207/255–4862* ⊕ *www. machiasmotorinn.com* ⇨ *34 rooms, 1 suite* � ⌂ *Restaurant, cable TV, some kitchenettes, some microwaves, some refrigerators, meeting room, some pets allowed (fee), no-smoking rooms* ⊟ *AE, D, MC, V.*

$ 🏠 **Broadway Inn.** On a residential street near downtown Machias, this inn has rooms that are named for favorite New England authors such as Robert Frost and Edith Wharton. Furnished with antiques such as an oaken bed and an unusual pair of wood wing chairs, the guest rooms are clean and comfortable. ⊠ *14 Broadway St., 04654* ☎ *207/255–8551* ⊟ *207/255–0604* ⊕ *www.lighthousehg.com* ⇨ *3 rooms, 1 with bath* �A *No a/c, no room phones, no room TVs, no smoking* ⊟ *MC, V* ⌶⦿⌶ *BP.*

★ $ 🖼 **Micmac Farm.** You can launch a kayak or canoe on the Machias River at this wonderfully secluded 50-acre property. Grouped along the river are three spacious pine cabins with kitchenettes and decks. The historic cape house has an antiques-filled parlor and a "keeping room" that looks much as it did when the home was built in 1776. The guest room off the parlor is a modern addition with river-view deck and a whirlpool bath. ⊠ *47 Micmac La., Machiasport 04655* ☎ *207/255–3008* ⊕ *www.micmacfarm.com* ⇆ *1 room, 3 cabins* ⌂ *Some refrigerators, some kitchenettes, some room TVs, some pets allowed, no-smoking rooms; no a/c, no room phones* ☰ *MC, V* �) *Closed late Oct.–mid May* ¶◯ *CP (B&B only).*

Nightlife & the Arts

Although small, the **Art Galleries at the University of Maine** (⊠ 9 O'Brien Ave. ☎207/255–1200) have a strong selection of paintings by John Marin and other regional artists. Two galleries showcase rotating exhibitions of works from the permanent collection. Don't miss the William Zorach sculpture just outside the front door.

Sports & the Outdoors

Sunrise Canoe & Kayak (⊠ Hoytt Rd., Machias ☎ 207/255–3375 or 877/ 980–2300 ⊕ www.sunrisecanoeandkayak.com) offers sea-kayaking day trips to petroglyphs carved on slate ledges in Machias Bay. Many are between 1,500 and 3,000 years old. The company also outfits canoes and leads overnight sea-kayaking and canoe trips, including trips on the Machias River. If you prefer to go it alone, there are bike and canoe rentals.

With ocean views from most of its 9 holes, the small but challenging **Great Cove Golf Course** (⊠ 387 Great Cove Rd., Roque Bluffs ☎ 207/ 434–7200) has a club house and driving range.

Shopping

Abstract designs in bold purples, blues, and tangerines are for sale at **Connie's Clay of Fundy Pottery** (⊠U.S. 1, East Machias ☎207/255–0173). The owner gives demonstrations in the attached studio and invites visitors to relax on the deck. Art of all kinds can be found at the congenial **Woodwind Gallery** (⊠ 62 Dublin St. ☎ 207/255–3727). Exhibitors range from a self-taught watercolor painter to a leading pastel artist. This gallery is also headquarters of the Maine Black Fly Breeders Association, a tongue-in-cheek group that sells funny souvenirs.

Stock up on fresh fruits and vegetables at **Machias Valley Farmers' Market** (⊠ U.S. 1 ☎ 207/483–2260), held early May through October on Saturday from 8 to noon. The market is occasionally open on a Wednesday or a Friday.

Cutler

❾ *13 mi south of East Machias via Rte. 191.*

There's not a shop or boutique in this fishing hamlet—Cutler's natural beauty is what makes it worth exploring. Puffin cruises depart from the protected harbor, which opens like a keyhole onto the ocean and is known as Little River because of its shape. The Bold Coast, as the towering headlands flanking the harbor entrance are called, has some of Maine's best shoreline trails.

★ The beautiful coastal trails at **Cutler Coast Public Reserved Land** are likely to take your breath away. The 12,000-acre state preserve north of Cutler Harbor includes 4½ mi of undeveloped Bold Coast, as the headland between Lubec and Cutler is known. While much of Maine's coast is chiseled with large bays and coves, here a wall of steep cliffs—some 150 feet tall—juts below ledges partially forested with spruce and fir. Look for whales, seals, and porpoises while taking in views of cliff-ringed Grand Manan Island and the Bay of Fundy. Climb down the log ladders to reach the pebble beaches. Revealing the area's unusual terrain, the two hiking trails loop inland, passing peat bogs, salt marshes, blueberry barrens, swamps, and meadows. The trail from the parking area to the coast is 1½ mi; the longer hiking trails are 6 and 10 mi long. There are three primitive campsites at the preserve, which is 17 mi south of Cutler. ⊠ *Rte. 191* ☎ *207/827–1818* ⊕ *www.state.me.us/doc/parks* ▧ *Free* ☉ *Daily.*

Two-hundred and forty-seven acres make up the Maine Coastal Heritage Trust's **Western Head Preserve,** which flanks the coast south of Cutler Harbor. The pristine park is known for its awesome views. Along the steep cliffs, wind and salt spray have sculpted spruce and fir trees into odd, stunted shapes. There are several beaches, and cranberries, iris, and juniper grow from rock ledges. ⊠ *End of Destiny Bay Rd.* ☎ *207/ 729–7366* ⊕ *www.mcht.org* ▧ *Free* ☉ *Daily.*

Where to Stay & Eat

$$ ✕▥ **Tide Run Harborside Inn.** Looking across the harbor to the town wharf, this lodging is a great spot to watch the fishing boats coming and going. This home dating from 1873 has loads of charm: pressed-tin ceilings, brick hearths, painted ceiling beams, and wide plank floors. Tastefully decorated rooms have soft featherbeds. Guests gather in the living room and on the screened porch. The restaurant ($$–$$$) uses locally caught fish and organic produce. Look for dishes such as crabmeat-stuffed haddock with champagne-cream sauce and seafood stew splashed with Pernod. ⊠ *212 Destiny Bay Rd., 04626* ☎ *207/259–3800* ⊕ *www. tiderun.com* ⇨ *3 rooms* ⚭ *Restaurant, cable TV; no a/c, no room phones, no smoking* ▤ *MC, V* ☉ *Closed Nov.–Apr.; restaurant closed Sun. and Mon.* ⑩ *BP.*

$ ▥ **Little River Lodge.** Built in the 1880s to house guests arriving by steamship, this hotel no longer has its elegant three-story tower. The interior retains a sense of grandeur, however, with lovely woodwork and fireplaces in the living and dining rooms. Guest rooms are decorated with nautical antiques, maritime art, and rare books. If you are intent on exploring the area, the innkeepers are happy to pack you a picnic or bag lunch. ⌂ *Box 251* ⊠ *Rte. 191, 04626* ☎ *207/259–4437* ⊕ *www. cutlerlodge.com* ⇨ *5 rooms, 2 with bath* ⚭ *Dining room; no a/c, no room phones, no smoking* ▤ *No credit cards* ⑩ *BP* ☉ *Closed mid-Oct.–Apr.*

Sports & the Outdoors

It's a 45-minute trip to Machias Seal Island, a favored nesting place for puffins and many other seabirds. **Bold Coast Charter Co.** (☎ 207/259–

4484 ⊕ www.boldcoast.com) takes visitors to the island from May to August. Capt. Andrew Patterson also gives scenic tours of the Bold Coast and Down East islands, with lots of opportunities to spot marine life. Trips begin at $35 per person.

Shopping

Picturesque labels, including one of Cutler's harbor, adorn the canned mussels, clams, lobster meat, chowders, and bisques packed in small batches at **Look's Gourmet Seafood** (⊠ Rte. 191, between Cutler and Machias ☎ 207/259–3341). Baked beans and Indian pudding, New England favorites, are sold here, as are a variety of sauces and dips.

en route | After dipping to Cutler from Machias, Route 191 loops toward Lubec. Mounded, treeless terrain is found along this lonely stretch. Heaths and bogs form a subarctic ecosystem where rare plants thrive in the acidic soil.

COBSCOOK & PASSAMAQUODDY BAYS

Distances can be confusing in this part of the region. It's only a mile or so by boat from Lubec, on Cobscook Bay, to Eastport, facing Passamaquoddy Bay, while the circuitous land route is nearly 40 mi. The area's huge tides are as high as 28 feet, and the largest whirlpool in the Northern Hemisphere, called "Old Sow," swirls off Eastport. Canadian islands, including Campobello, can be seen directly across the water. In summer you can take the ferry from Campobello to Canada's Deer Island and on to Eastport. Or take the "Quoddy Loop," ferrying to the Canadian mainland from Deer Island and returning by land.

Lubec

🔟 *28 mi east of Machias.*

Lubec is the first town in the United States to see the sunrise. The village is perched at the end of a narrow strip of land, so you often can see water in three directions. Abandoned smokehouses once used for sardines are clustered on the piers along Water Street, awaiting restoration. Lubec is a popular destination for outdoor enthusiasts, as there are plenty of opportunities for hiking and biking. It's a good base for day trips to New Brunswick's Campobello Island, reached by a bridge—the only one to the island—from downtown Lubec.

★ The easternmost point of land in the United States, **Quoddy Head State Park,** is marked by candy-stripe West Quoddy Head Light. In 1806 President Thomas Jefferson signed an order authorizing construction of a lighthouse on this site. You can't climb the tower, but the former lightkeeper's house has a museum with a video showing the interior. The museum also has displays on Lubec's maritime past and the region's marine life. A gallery displays lighthouse art by locals. A mystical 2-mi path along the cliffs here yields magnificent views of Canada's cliff-clad Grand Manan island. Whales can often be sighted offshore. The 483-acre park has a picnic area. ⊠ *S. Lubec Rd. off Rte. 189* ☎ *No phone* 🖻 *$2* ⊙ *May 15–Oct. 15.*

One of Maine's great gardens is at **Cottage Garden & Shoreline Nature Center.** Winding paths lead through perennial and rose gardens, as well as sections with rhododendrons, dwarf conifers, and shrubs. The nature center, in a shingled building, has videos and exhibits about the area's natural wonders, from the whales that inhabit the nearby waters to the tundra created by peat land bogs. Owned by a couple who lives on the property, the garden has a gift shop where you can purchase her artwork and his birdhouses and garden benches. ⊠ *N. Lubec Rd., off Rte. 189* ☎ *207/733–2902* ☜ *Free* ⊙ *June–Aug., daily dawn–dusk.*

Where to Stay & Eat

$–$$ ✕ **Phinney's Seaview.** The name of this window-lined restaurant, on a hill overlooking Johnson Bay, sums up its best asset. Long lines form outside in summer for tables in the white-and-blue bead-board dining room or outside on the deck. Don't miss the seafood platter, which includes haddock, scallops, shrimp, and clams. ⊠ *Rte. 189* ☎ *207/773–4844* ▭ *AE, D, MC, V* ⊙ *Closed late Oct.–early Apr.*

$–$$ ✕ **Uncle Kippy's.** There isn't much of a view from the picture windows, but locals don't mind—they come here for the satisfying seafood. There's one large dining room with a bar beside the main entrance. The menu includes seafood dinners and combo platters. It's also open early for breakfast. ⊠ *Rte. 189* ☎ *207/733–2400* ▭ *MC, V* ⊙ *Closed Mon.*

¢ ✕ **Atlantic House Coffee Shop.** From this restaurant's two small decks you can gaze past the old smokehouses to the Lubec Narrows. Enjoy old-fashioned favorites such as chicken pot pie, or opt for a sandwich or slice of pizza. For a sweet treat there's ice cream, doughnuts, and yummy pastries made on the premises. It also sells breakfast sandwiches. ⊠ *52 Water St.* ☎ *207/733–0906* ▭ *No credit cards* ⊙ *Closed Nov.–Apr.*

$ ✕▣ **Home Port Inn.** A Colonial-style house perched high atop a hill, this grand lodging dating from 1880 has generously sized guest rooms, some with water views. All are furnished with family antiques, including several stately beds. Warm up by the fireplace in the large cherry-red living room's two sitting areas. The elegant restaurant ($$–$$$), one of the best in town, opens onto a deck overlooking Cobscook Bay. The menu emphasizes seafood, but the steak au poivre is a favorite among the locals. Lobster is served in a casserole with drawn butter, sherry, and bread crumbs, or in a salad with artichoke hearts and a creamy tarragon dressing. ⊠ *45 Main St., 04652* ☎ *207/733–2077 or 800/457–2077* ⊕ *www.homeportinn.com* ⇨ *7 rooms* ♨ *Restaurant; no a/c, no room phones, no room TVs, no smoking* ▭ *AE, D, MC, V* ⊙ *Closed mid-Oct.–Apr.* ¶◎¶ *CP.*

$–$$ ▣ **Lighthouse Inn.** Sitting where Lubec Narrows meets Johnson Bay, this three-story inn looks toward Mulholland Point Lighthouse. Rooms vary in size and shape and have a mix of old and new furnishings; all but one have a water view. The adjacent Chowder House serves several different types of chowder, from corn to clam. The desserts are made on the premises. It's open for dinner from late May through October and serves lunch in July and August. ⌂ *Box 308* ⊠ *7 Water St., 04652* ☎ *207/733–4300* 🖷 *917/369–1242* ⊕ *www.lighthouseinnmaine.com* ⇨ *9 rooms* ♨ *Café, fans, cable TV; no smoking* ▭ *MC, V* ⊙ *Closed Nov.–mid-May* ¶◎¶ *CP.*

$–$$ 🏠 **Peacock House.** Five generations of the Peacock family lived in this white clapboard house before it was converted into an inn. With a large foyer, library, and living room, the 1860 sea captain's home has plenty of places where you can relax. Minglers are drawn to the sunroom, which opens to the deck and has a bar where you can help yourself to a complimentary glass of sherry. The best of the rooms has a separate sitting area and a gas fireplace. ☒ *27 Summer St., 04652* ☎ *207/733–2403 or 888/305–0036* ⊕ *www.peacockhouse.com* ⇆ *5 rooms, 2 suites* ⚅ *Some cable TV, some in-room VCRs; no a/c, no room phones, no TV in some rooms* ⊟ *MC, V* ⊙ *Closed Nov.–Apr.* ⏏ *BP.*

Nightlife & the Arts

Offering free classical and jazz performances, the **Mary Potterton Memorial Concert Series** (☒ Church and Main Sts. ☎ 207/733–2316 ⊕ www.summerkeys.com) has performances on Wednesday evenings from June to August at the Congregational Christian Church. The series is sponsored by SummerKeys, which offers music classes in the summer.

Shopping

Pick up a six-pack—of smoked salmon kabobs—at **Bold Coast Smokehouse** (☒ 224 County Rd. ☎ 207/733–8912 or 888/733–0807 ⊕ www.boldcoastsmokehouse.com). Other offerings include trout pâté and salt-cured salmon from Scandinavia. Buy local produce at **Lubec Farmers' Market** (☒ 106 Main St. ☎ 207/733–4760). You can also find smoked salmon, freshly baked bread, and locally made pottery and crafts. It's open from mid-June through mid-October on Sunday from 9 to 1. Loaded with local souvenirs such as moose T-shirts, **Puffin Pines Country Gift Store** (☒ U.S. 1, Whiting ☎ 207/733–9782) also has a well-stocked information center.

Try before you buy at **Seaside Chocolate** (☒ 72 Water St. ☎ 207/733–2575 or 800/282–7220 ⊕ www.seasidechocolate.com), in the second floor of an old cannery. Watch as the same scrumptious chocolates that are sold in gift stores all over the region are made in small batches. Bonbons have caramel-nougat centers; needhams, with shredded coconut and potato filling, are a Maine tradition. Find leather-bottomed slippers with lighthouse designs and whimsical socks with shells or other bits of nature on the cuffs at **Water Street Fiberarts Studio** (☒ 67 Water St. ☎ 207/733–4869). Other unique textiles in this downtown shop include silk brocade pillows and pointy-toe Christmas stockings, ornamented wool hats, and girls' dresses. The shop is open May through December, or by appointment.

On the road to West Quoddy Head Light, **West Quoddy Gifts** (☒ S. Lubec Rd. ☎ 207/733–2457 ⊕ www.westquoddygifts.com) stocks gifts depicting this and other area lighthouses. The store also carries T-shirts and sweatshirts with its own designs. It's open mid-April through late December.

en route   Fingers of land extend into Whiting Bay and Broad and Burnt coves at the 888-acre **Cobscook Bay State Park** (☒ U.S. 1, Dennysville ☎ 207/726–4412 ⊕ www.state.me.us/doc/parks/programs), a great place to spend the afternoon. You won't be disappointed if you arrive at low tide—the islands rising from the mud flats after the water has receded have an ethereal beauty. A short hiking trail to a rock crest with views of Whiting Bay links with a longer trail.

Campobello Island, Canada

⓫ *28 mi east of Machias.*

A popular excursion from Lubec, New Brunswick's Campobello Island has two fishing villages, Welshpool and Wilson's Beach. The only bridge is from Lubec, but in summer a car ferry shuttles passengers from Campobello Island to Deer Island, where you can continue on to the Canadian mainland. U.S. citizens don't need a passport to enter Canada, but should have a photo ID and proof of citizenship, such as a birth certificate. Stop at the information booth after passing customs for an update on tides—specifically, when you will be able to walk to **East Quoddy Head Lighthouse** (⊠ End of Rte. 774, Wilson's Beach). On a tiny island off the northern end of Campobello, this distinctive lighthouse is marked with a large red cross and is accessible only at and around low tide.

★ A joint project of the American and the Canadian governments, **Roosevelt Campobello International Park** is crisscrossed with interesting hiking trails. Eagle Hill Bog has a wooden walkway and signs identifying rare plants. Neatly manicured Campobello Island has always had a special appeal for the wealthy and famous. It was here that President Franklin Roosevelt and his family spent summers. The 34-room Roosevelt Cottage was presented to Eleanor and Franklin as a wedding gift, and the wicker-filled structure looks essentially as it did when the family was in residence. ⊠ *Rte. 774, Welshpool, Campobello Island, New Brunswick, Canada* ☎ *506/752-2922* ☒ *Free* ☉ *House open Memorial Day–Columbus Day, daily 10–6; grounds daily.*

Many visitors to Campobello Island don't venture beyond Roosevelt Campobello International Park, but for those who do much awaits at the adjacent **Herring Cove Provincial Park.** There's a golf course, 76 campsites with electric hookups, playgrounds, and six trails, including a carriage road that traverses log bridges and spruce forests. Don't miss the mile-long black sand beach at the namesake cove, with sea-smoothed stones in mesmerizing hues at low tide. ⊠ *Herring Cove Rd., off Rte. 774* ☎ *506/752-7010* ☒ *Free* ☉ *Daily.*

Where to Stay & Eat

$–$$ ✕ **Sweet Time Bakery.** Grab some freshly baked goodies or stop for breakfast, lunch, or dinner at this popular eatery in Welshpool. Sandwiches, salads, and seafood dishes are on the menu. For breakfast try Cindy's Pic, with eggs, toast, fish cakes, and chow-chow, a sweet green tomato relish. ⊠ *1001 Rte. 774, Welshpool* ☎ *506/752-2428* ☱ *No credit cards* ☉ *Closed Dec. 24–Jan. 1.*

★ **¢–$$** ✕ **Family Fisheries.** Seafood lovers know that fried fish doesn't have to be greasy. That's why people keep heading across the bridge to eat at this family restaurant on Wilson's Beach. The freshest seafood is delivered to the restaurant and the adjoining fish market. Order fried haddock, scallops, shrimps, or clams alone or as part of a seafood platter. Lobster and clams are cooked outside. Eat in the large dining room or

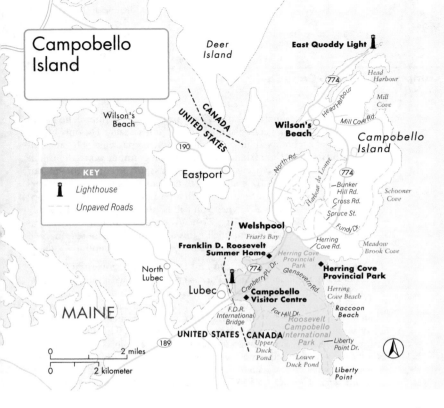

in a screened room beside the playground. ✉ *1977 Rte. 774, Wilson's Beach* ☎ *506/752–2470* 🖃 *MC, V* ⊘ *Closed Mon.–Wed. late Oct.–mid-Nov.; closed late Nov.–May.*

¢–$ ✕🏠 **Lupine Lodge.** Next to Roosevelt Campobello International Park, this inn was originally a Roosevelt cousin's summer home. One of three log buildings houses a water-view restaurant ($–$$) warmed by a two-sided fireplace. The menu includes specialties such as seafood omelets. Rooms are the same cedar-walled sleeping quarters used years ago. Some have huge baths with original tile and claw-foot tubs. ✉ *610 Rte. 774, Welshpool, New Brunswick E5E 1A5* ☎ *506/752–2555* 🖷 *506/752–9885* ⊕ *www.lupinelodge.com* ⬚ *11 rooms* ⟁ *No a/c, no room phones, no room TVs, no smoking* 🖃 *MC, V* ⊘ *Closed late Oct.–mid-May.*

★ $$–$$$$ 🏠 **Owen House.** Built in 1835 by an admiral, this handsome seaside home has an unusual two-sided staircase. A spinning wheel and horsehair couch are among the many furnishings dating back to the 19th century. Quilts add a homey touch. Relax in the two sitting rooms, admire local art in the gallery, or stroll about the expansive lawn. Breakfast is shared around the dining room table. ✉ *11 Welshpool St., Welshpool, New Brunswick E5E 1G3* ☎ *506/752–2977* ⊕ *www.owenhouse.ca* ⬚ *9 rooms, 5 with bath* ⟁ *Dining room, meeting room; no a/c, no room*

MAINE FISHERMEN'S CHOWDER

MOST RECIPES FOR FISHERMEN'S chowder call for milk. But as one fisherman from Stonington, Maine said: "Milk is for sissies, kid." The following is a recipe for a real Fisherman's Chowder.

Ingredients: 2 pounds Maine firm fish, such as haddock or cod, cut in bite-size pieces

1 pound scallops

1 dozen fresh clams or 2 cans chopped clams and their juice

1 bottle clam juice

1 quart chicken stock

1 tablespoon chopped garlic

1 tablespoon thyme

1 package dried onion soup mix

1 large can new potatoes

1 small can tomato sauce

1 cup white wine

1/4 cup flour

Tabasco sauce

In a large soup pot, combine stock and clam juice with garlic, thyme, dried soup, potatoes, and tomato sauce. Heat until boiling. Reduce heat and add fish, scallops, and clams. Mix flour with a little water and add to pot. Simmer for 10 minutes, then add white wine, and Tabasco sauce as desired. Serve with homemade hot bread and a large salad.

—Stephen Allen

phones, no room TVs, no children under 6, no smoking ▦ MC, V ⊙ Closed late Oct.–mid-May ⦿ BP.

Sports & the Outdoors

Spot whales and other creatures from a 20-passenger lobster boat operated by **Island Cruises** (✉ 1 Head Harbour Wharf Rd., Wilson's Beach ☎ 506/752–1107 or 888/249–4400). It operates daily from July to September. Cruises cost $40 and depart from Head Harbour Wharf.

Eastport

12 39 mi north of Lubec, 102 mi east of Ellsworth.

Connected by a granite causeway to the mainland at Pleasant Point Reservation, Eastport has wonderful views of the nearby islands. Known for its diverse architecture, the town was one of the nation's busiest seaports in the early 1800s. In the late 19th century, 14 sardine canneries operated here. The industry's decline in the 20th century left the city economically depressed, but now the town has set its sights on salmon. The weekend after Labor Day, the Maine Salmon Festival attracts large crowds with boat tours of salmon pens, architecture and cemetery tours, arts and crafts shows, and dinners featuring the local delicacy.

Get downtown early to secure a viewing spot for Maine's largest Independence Day parade. Canadian bagpipe bands make this an event not to be missed. The day culminates with fireworks over the bay. On the second weekend in August, locals celebrate Sipayik Indian Days at the Pleasant Point Reservation. This festival of Passamaquoddy culture includes canoe races, dancing, drumming, and traditional dancing.

Anchoring downtown Eastport is the **National Historic Waterfront District,** which extends from the Customs House down Water Street to Bank Square and the Peavey Library. Spanning such architectural styles as Federal, Victorian, Queen Anne, and Greek Revival, the district was largely built in the 19th century. A canon sits on the lawn at the Romanesque Revival library, one of the many interesting structures. Take the waterfront walkway to watch the fishing boats and freighters. The tides, among the highest in the world, fluctuate as much as 28 feet. That explains the ladders and steep gangways necessary to access boats.

The **Quoddy Maritime Museum** has a changing local history exhibit and the large concrete model used for a tidal power project aborted soon after it was begun in the 1930s. The gift shop is a craft cooperative where you can buy painted furniture, fabrics, and jewelry. ⊠ *69–71 Water St.* ☎ *207/853–2358* ▢ *Free* ⊙ *Memorial Day–mid-Sept., daily 10–5.*

Housed in a former bank, the **Tides Institute & Museum of Art** exhibits works depicting the Passamaquoddy Bay area from the 1800s through the present. With tall windows letting in lots of light, the main room is ideal for viewing photos of fishermen and a dreamy painting of Grand Manan Island's towering cliffs. Occasional exhibits will show photography, etchings, and block prints produced by the institute. ⊠ *43 Water St.* ☎ *207/853–4047* ⊕ *www.tidesinstitute.org* ▢ *Free* ⊙ *Mid-June–mid-Sept., Tues.–Sun. 10–5; late Sept.–early June, Wed.–Sat. 10–5.*

As you enter town, the yellow trim on **Raye's Mustard Mill** makes it hard to miss. This is the only remaining stone mill in the U.S., producing only stone-ground mustard. This historic property once served the sardine-packing industry. You can tour the mill and purchase mustards made on the premises at its Pantry Store. A small café serves light fare at lunch and sweet treats throughout the day. ⊠ *83 Washington St.* ☎ *207/ 853–4451 or 800/853–1903* ⊕ *www.rayesmustard.com* ▢ *Free* ⊙ *Jan.–May, 8:30–5; June–Dec., daily 9–4:30.*

From the short trail that begins behind Washington County Technical College, **Shakford Head State Park** (⊠ Deep Cove Rd. ☎ 207/941–4014 ⊕ www.state.me.us/doc/parks ▢ Free ⊙ Daily) has wonderful views over Passamaquoddy Bay to Campobello and Grand Manan islands. From here you can see the pens for Eastport's salmon-farming industry. Side trails lead to a pebble beach and a rock promontory with caves and arches at its base. Retrace your steps or return on a loop trail around the undeveloped peninsula that's home to this 90-acre park.

Route 190 leads through **Pleasant Point Reservation,** home to members of the Passamaquoddy, or "People of the Dawn." This group lived in the area long before the arrival of European settlers. A museum explains their culture with photos and artifacts such as woven grass baskets. The highlight is a 17-foot birch bark canoe. ⊠ *Rte. 190* ☎ *207/853–4001* 📠 *Free* ⊙ *Weekdays 8:30–11 and noon–4.*

Where to Stay & Eat

$–$$$ ✕ **WaCo Diner.** You can find out about everything happening in and around Eastport at this favorite local spot. Beyond the old-fashioned counter and booths there's a modern dining room with fireplace overlooking the water and a deck that's open in warmer weather. Lobster rolls, haddock sandwiches, and fish-and-chips are some of the most popular dishes, and there's no scrimping on the ice cream served with the homemade pies. ⊠ *47 Water St.* ☎ *207/853–4046* 🍴 *AE, D, DC, MC, V* ⊙ *Closed Dec.–Mar. No dinner Mon., Tues., and Thurs.*

★ **$–$$** ✕ **Eastport Chowder House.** Just north of downtown Eastport, this expansive waterfront eatery sits on the pier next to where the ferry docks. Built atop an old cannery foundation, it has original details such as wood beams and a stone wall. Eat in the downstairs pub, upstairs in the dining room, or on the large deck. This place is packed in summer, when families turn out for fried and baked seafood dishes. The house specialties include a smoked fish appetizer and seafood pasta in a wine-and-cheese sauce. End your meal with something sweet from the ice-cream shop. ⊠ *167 Water St.* ☎ *207/853–4700* 🍴 *D, MC, V* ⊙ *Closed late Oct.–early May.*

$–$$ ✕ **La Sardina Loca.** The name of this Mexican restaurant, which means "The Crazy Sardine," is a tip of the sombrero to Eastport's fish-canning days. Illuminated Santas and other odd decorations cover the walls and dangle from the ceilings—above you hangs an upside-down Christmas tree. Margaritas are served in mason jars. The menu is typical Mexican fare, though crabmeat enchiladas in season and the herring appetizer add a Down East touch. There's a small bar in one corner and occasional live music. ⊠ *28 Water St.* ☎ *207/853–2739* 🍴 *AE, D, MC, V* ⊙ *Closed Mon. and Tues. No lunch.*

¢ ✕ **Rosie's Hot Dog Stand.** Frankfurters, french fries, onion rings, and chili are on the menu at this hot dog stand on the Eastport Breakwater. Opened in the 1960s, it is an Eastport institution. ⊠ *Eastport Breakwater* ☎ *No phone* 🍴 *No credit cards* ⊙ *Closed Oct.–Apr.*

$–$$ 🏨 **Motel East.** These rooms with a view also happen to be a good value. All the spacious accommodations at this three-level waterfront motel on the edge of downtown look across Passamaquoddy Bay to Campobello Island. Furnishings such as wingback chairs are a step above those found at most motels. Rooms have kitchenettes and balconies or terraces. A small garden and picnic area overlook the water. The adjacent cottage has a deck and its own yard. ⊠ *23A Water St., 04631* ☎☎ *207/853–4747* 🌐 *www.eastportme.info* 🛏 *14 rooms* ♨ *Cable TV, some refrigerators, some microwaves, some kitchenettes, some no-smoking rooms, some pets allowed (fee); no a/c* 🍴 *AE, D, DC, MC, V.*

$ 🏨 **Kilby House.** Seaman Herbert Kilby built this Queen Anne home between downtown and the ferry stop in 1887. Adjoining sitting rooms are dominated by a fireplace and grand piano, and dark mahogany and walnut antiques are found throughout the rest of the inn. The master bedroom has a graceful four-poster bed. Other rooms are smaller, but light-color walls keep them from feeling cramped. ⊠ *122 Water St., 04631*

☎ *207/853–0989 or 800/853–4557* ⊕ *www.kilbyhouse.com* ⇖ *5 rooms, 3 with bath* ♧ *No a/c, no room phones, no children under 12, no smoking* ⊟ *MC, V* ♟ *BP.*

$ ⊡ **Miliken House.** Many of the furnishings and mementos that add so much charm to this 1846 home come from the family of the original occupant, who owned a wharf. Two blocks from the waterfront, the house has an arched double parlor with matching marble fireplaces and intricate woodwork. Elegant second-floor rooms have marble-topped dressers and ornately carved headboards. Third -floor rooms are smaller, but don't have that cramped feeling. Breakfast may include blueberry crêpes or buttermilk pancakes with blueberry sauce. ⊠ *29 Washington St., 04631* ☎ *207/853–2955 or 888/507–9370* ⊕ *www.eastport-inn.com* ⇖ *6 rooms* ♧ *Some pets allowed; no a/c, no room phones, no smoking, no TV in some rooms* ⊟ *MC, V* ♟ *BP.*

$ ⊡ **Weston House.** A Federal-style home built in 1810, this antiques-filled inn in downtown Eastport overlooks Passamaquoddy Bay. The Weston Room epitomizes the home's comfortable elegance, with crimson walls, tasteful works of art, and a fireplace decorated with a fleur-de-lis and flanked with small pillars. Naturalist John James Audubon slept in the room decorated with bird prints and his books. The three rooms share two baths, but they allow plenty of privacy. The deck and patio lead to a large garden with fanciful sitting areas. A lavish breakfast is served in the formal dining room, one of several spacious common rooms. ⊠ *26 Boynton St., 04631* ☎ *207/853–2907 or 800/ 853–2907* ⊕ *www.westonhouse-maine.com* ⇖ *3 rooms with shared baths* ♧ *Cable TV; no a/c, no room phones, no smoking* ⊟ *No credit cards* ♟ *BP.*

FodorśChoice
★

¢–$ ⊡ **Todd House.** This pre–Revolutionary War home has changed little over the years. Latched plank doors, wood floors, hearth, and a two-sided "good morning" staircase are all original. Antiques and artifacts add to the feeling of having stepped back in time. Two parlors downstairs have been converted into guest rooms with a shared bath. Two upstairs rooms also share a bath, while a pair of large, modern rooms in an addition have private baths. ⊠ *1 Capen Ave., 04631* ☎ *207/853–2328* ⇖ *6 rooms, 2 with bath* ♧ *Cable TV, some kitchenettes; no a/c, no room phones, no smoking* ⊟ *No credit cards* ♟ *CP.*

Nightlife & the Arts

A summer concert series and plays by a community theater company are performed from May through October at **Eastport Arts Center** (⊠ Dana and Water Sts. ☎ 207/853–2358). The center is housed in a former Masonic hall built in 1877.

Presentations on history, culture, and geography are held in a waterfront room at **CommonSpace At-The-Commons** (⊠ 51 Water St. ☎ 207/853–4123). A signboard in front announces upcoming talks.

Sports & the Outdoors

Operated by a family that's plied local waters for five generations, **Eastport Windjammers/Harris Whale Watching & Fishing** (⊠ 104 Water St. ☎ 207/853–2500 or 207/853–4303 ⊕ www.eastportwindjammers. com) offers whale-watching and sunset cruises on the 50-passenger

Sylvina W. Beal, a schooner built in 1911. You can help hoist the red sails on the windjammer, which docks downtown. Deep-sea fishing trips are available on the 35-passenger *Quoddy Dam.* The *Halie Matthew,* which will set sail in 2005, will offer overnight cruises. Eastport Windjammers operates from June to mid-October. Day cruises are $25 to $35, and reservations are recommended.

Tour Eastport in a 1947 bus once used to transport sardine workers with **Scenic Island Tours** (✉ 37 Washington St. ☎ 207/853–4831). Passengers don Mexican hats and disembark at a lovely spot by the sea to enjoy lunch, which is towed behind the bus in the matching trailer.

Shopping

Bird lovers flock to **Crow Tracks** (✉ 11 Water St. ☎ 207/853–2336), a gallery that sells the owner's vividly painted carvings of all sorts of fowl, including some on driftwood. Giant bowls and vases catch your eye at **Earth Forms** (✉ 5 Dana St. ☎ 207/853–2430), but there are many more manageable sizes as well. The friendly owner uses his own constantly changing glaze recipes to create cleverly banded designs. The shop is open March to December. Displaying works by artists who live in the area, **Eastport Gallery** (✉ 52 Water St. ☎ 207/853–4166 ⊕ www.eastportgallery. com) is open mid-June to mid-October.

Adirondack-style furnishings on the veranda draw people to the **45th Parallel** (✉ U.S. 1, Perry ☎ 207/853–9500 ⊕ www.fortyfifthparallel.com). This large store stocks a fun mix of antiques, jewelry, nautical decorations, and home furnishings. It's open May to December. **Joe's Basket Shop** (✉ Rte. 190, Pleasant Point ☎ 207/853–2840) has fancy and coarse baskets and other items made by members of the Passamaquoddy tribe. **Quoddy Wigwam** (✉ U.S. 1, Perry ☎ 207/853–4812) sells handcrafted moccasins and other Native American crafts. Bowls made from tree burls, trunks, and branches are found at the **Shop-At-The Commons** (✉ 51 Water St. ☎ 207/853–4123). There are also story quilts and other items.

Selling nautical supplies since 1818, the nation's oldest ship chandlery, **S. L. Wadsworth & Son** (✉ 42 Water St. ☎ 207/853–4343) is still run by the same family. An interesting pamphlet details its history. Check out the nautical maps and old photos of Eastport's waterfront. Load up on farm-fresh eggs, locally grown produce, and fresh flowers at **Sunrise County Farmers' Market** (✉ Washington St. ☎ 287/853–4750). The market is held on Thursday from 11 to 2, from the end of June through October.

en route Much of U.S. 1 to Calais is a **scenic drive** that cruises along the St. Croix River, which enters Passamaquoddy Bay in Robbinston. The river often resembles the elongated bays along the coast, and can be just as breathtaking. Don't miss the overlook in Robbinston across from a Greek Revival mansion. Keep an eye out for the 12 granite milestones between Robbinston and Calais, erected in the late 1800s by a wealthy Calais lumberman, abolitionist, author, and diplomat who liked to pace his horses between the river city and his summer estate.

GRAND LAKE STREAM REGION

Flowing through a valley along the U.S.-Canadian border, the St. Croix River enters Passamaquoddy Bay about 12 mi south of Calais. This is the gateway to the Grand Lake Stream region, a remote watershed of cove-lined lakes and flowages world-famous for fishing. Outdoor recreation opportunities abound in this area.

Calais

⑬ *28 mi north of Eastport via Rte. 190 and U.S. 1, 98 mi east of Bangor on Rte. 9.*

The St. Croix River is tidal from Passamaquoddy Bay to Calais. Tides here can surge more than 30 feet, the highest in the continental United States. St. Croix Island was the site of North America's first French settlement, and its 400th anniversary was the cause of much celebrating in 2004. A shipbuilding and lumbering center in the 1800s, Calais struggled economically in the late 20th century, but tourism is beginning to change the tide. The opening of the Downeast Heritage Center on the revitalized waterfront was part of the settlement commemorations. The city is developing a riverfront park, and one of the nation's oldest wildlife refuges is nearby.

St. Stephen, in New Brunswick, shares a busy border crossing with Calais. Traffic delays at the bridge can last 40 minutes in summer, but walking from downtown to downtown takes only a few minutes. U.S. citizens don't need a passport to enter Canada but should have a photo ID and proof of citizenship.

Fodor'sChoice Consider launching a trip Way Down East at the **Downeast Heritage Cen-**
★ **ter.** Housed in a three-level brick-and-glass building on the waterfront, the center has information about the region's natural wonders. You can use touch screens to search out places of interest. Exhibits tell about the history of the Passamaquoddy Indians and early French settlement. There's a touch tank filled with sea creatures, a waterfront walk, and a birding workshop. ⊠ *39 Union St.* ☎ *207/454–7878 or 877/454–2500* ⊕ *www.downeastheritage.org* 🖃 *$6* ☽ *Memorial Day–Labor Day, daily 9–5; Labor Day–Memorial Day, Tues.–Sat. 11–3.*

Treat yourself to free samples at the **Chocolate Museum,** in downtown St. Stephen, New Brunswick. The museum tells the story of one of Canada's leading candy companies, Ganong Bros., the first in North America to sell chocolates in heart-shape boxes. Housed in Ganong's original factory, the museum has interactive exhibits and a delightful collection of candy boxes. Acadian heroine Evangeline, Ganong's marketing symbol for years, is carved in chocolate. You can buy hand-dipped chocolates at the store next door. ⊠ *71 Milltown Blvd., St. Stephen, New Brunswick* ☎ *506/466–7848* ⊕ *www.chocolatemuseum.ca* 🖃 *$5* ☽ *Mar.–June 14 and Sept.–Nov., weekdays 9–5; June 15–Aug., Mon.–Sat. 9–6:30, Sun. 1–5.*

Statues of French settlers and Passamaquoddy Indians grace the path at the mainland section of **St. Croix Island International Historic Site,** 8 mi south of downtown Calais. It looks out at the site of France's first settlement in the New World. An accompanying text tells the story of the Indians who came to the aid of French settlers after ice floes trapped them on the island. A pavilion shelters a model of the 1604 settlement based on a drawing by Samuel Champlain, who explored this region. ⊠ *U.S. 1* ☎ *207/288–3338* ⊕ *www.nps.gov/sacr* ☜ *Free* ☉ *July–Sept., daily 8–6.*

One of Down East's best birding spots is the **Moosehorn National Wildlife Refuge.** Spread over 20,000 acres, the refuge is home to game birds, songbirds, shorebirds, wading birds, and waterfowl. An observation deck on U.S. 1 overlooks platforms where bald eagles and osprey nest. Look for moose and other wildlife along 60 mi of roads and trails used for biking, hiking, and cross-country skiing. Several lakes and streams are open to fishing. ⊠ *Charlotte Rd., Baring* ☎ *207/454–7161* ⊕ *moosehorn.fws.gov* ☜ *Free* ☉ *Daily.*

Where to Stay & Eat

$$–$$$$ ✕ **Chandler House.** Tables covered with red tablecloths are scattered among several rooms in this old homestead. Soft lighting gives the place a homey feel. Not everything on the extensive menu is fried. Many of the fish and seafood entrées are cooked in white wine or topped with sauces flavored with dill or pine nuts. Fish-and-chips and other smaller entrées are available at lunch. ⊠ *9 Chandler St.* ☎ *207/454–7922* ▤ *AE, D, MC, V* ☉ *Closed Mon. mid-Sept.–May.*

$–$$ ✕ **Bernardini's.** The woodwork in this popular storefront Italian restaurant was salvaged from a Catholic church slated for demolition. The owners say the recipe for the spicy spaghetti sauce was handed down by an ancestor who moved here from Italy. Veal is a specialty—try it lightly breaded, sautéed with mushrooms, or topped with crabmeat, asparagus, and hollandaise sauce. You can order smaller-size portions of pasta for lunch. ⊠ *257 Main St.* ☎ *207/454–2237* ▤ *MC, V* ☉ *Closed Sun.*

¢ ✕ **Border Town Subz.** Near the waterfront, this take-out place is owned by a mother-daughter team who are renowned for their more than 25 varieties of subs. You can eat your sandwich here or take it with you. The "turkey deluxe" is a top seller; as is "grandpa's chili." ⊠ *313 Main St.* ☎ *207/454–8562* ▤ *MC, V* ☉ *Closed Sun.*

$ ✕▦ **Redclyffe Shore Motor Inn.** Overlooking the St. Croix River and Passamaquoddy Bay, this lodging has generously sized rooms with water views. The restaurant ($–$$$) is in a landmark 1862 Victorian Gothic with ornate gingerbread trim. The menu includes steak-and-seafood combos as well as veal, chicken, and duck dishes. ⊠ *U.S. 1* ☜ *Box 40, Robbinston 04671* ☎ *207/454–3270* ☏ *207/454–8723* ⊕ *www.redclyffeshoremotorinn.com* ⇱ *16 rooms* ♿ *Refrigerators, cable TV, shop, Internet, some no-smoking rooms; no a/c in some rooms* ▤ *AE, D, MC, V* ☉ *Motel closed Nov.–Apr., restaurant closed mid-Jan.–Apr. No lunch.*

¢ ✕ **Heslin's.** On the St. Croix River, this lodging has basic rooms, as well as cottages and cabins. Many of the rooms face the water. The lovely restaurant ($$–$$$) has picture windows to ensure that every table has wonderful views. Try the lobster pie or the shrimp and scallops flavored with brandy and mustard. ✉ *26 Brogan Rd., 04619* ☎ *207/454–3762* 📠 *207/454–0148* 🌐 *www.mainerec.com* *11 rooms, 5 cabins, 5 cottages* *Cable TV, some refrigerators, some microwaves, some kitchenettes, some no-smoking rooms* 💳 *D, MC, V* ⏲ *Closed mid-Oct.–mid-May. No lunch.*

$ **Greystone Bed & Breakfast.** Opened in 2004, Calais's only B&B is in a gracious Greek Revival home near the center of town. The double parlor has Corinthian columns, black marble fireplaces, and French windows. Sip your coffee on the three-sided porch. Guests rooms are furnished with antiques and some newer pieces. ✉ *13 Calais Ave., 04619* ☎ *207/454–2848* 🌐 *www.greystonecalaisme.com* *2 rooms* *Cable TV; no a/c, no room phones, no smoking* 💳 *MC, V* ⏲ *Closed Nov.–May* 🍽 *BP.*

Sports & the Outdoors

Lobstering takes place on the tidal St. Croix River, and you can help haul in traps on boat tours to nearby islands. Kids love to toss back the sea urchins and starfish that come up with the traps.

On St. Croix River cruises with **Up Close Tours** (✉ U.S. 1, Robbinston ☎ 207/454–2844 days, 207/454–2285 nights 🌐 www.upclosetours.com), the captain, a former teacher, uses fruit to represent the planetary bodies when explaining the region's high tides. The river's maritime past and present are also discussed. The six-passenger boat departs from the Robbinston boat landing June through September. Trips cost $30 per person. Overnight trips on the St. Croix River are offered by **Sunrise Canoe & Kayak** (✉ Hoytt Rd., Machias ☎ 207/255–3375 or 877/980–2300 🌐 www.sunrisecanoeandkayak.com). These guided trips are especially nice in fall. Prices start at $418 per person for a four-day trip. Cruises with **Eastport Windjammers/Harris Whale Watching & Fishing** (✉ 15 Union St. ☎ 207/454–8562 or 207/853–2500 🌐 www.eastportwindjammers.com) depart from the waterfront behind the State Visitor Information Center. Tickets are $32.

The 9-hole golf course at **St. Croix Country Club** (✉ U.S. 1 ☎ 207/454–8875) has views of the St. Croix River. Large trees make this course challenging.

Shopping

Maine-made handcrafts, from sweetgrass baskets to bath salts to driftwood mirrors, are sold at **Chmerto's** (✉ 283 Main St. ☎ 207/454–3300). You can also pick up locally produced jams and chocolates. Fill your picnic basket with local fruits and vegetables at **Sunrise County Farmers' Market** (✉ 15 Union St. ☎ 207/853–4750). The market is open June through October, Tuesday 11–3.

Grand Lake Stream

14 *50 mi northwest of Eastport, 108 mi east of Bangor.*

This tiny community, on Grand Lake Stream between West Grand Lake and Big Lake, was once one of the largest tannery centers in the world.

Today it's renowned for fishing, especially for land-locked salmon and smallmouth bass. It's also known for the Grand Laker, a square-end wood canoe built specifically for use on the often windy lakes in this region. Along the Canadian border, outdoors lovers will find lakes and rivers for swimming, boating, and fishing; trails for hiking; and plenty of places to spot wildlife.

The **Grand Lake Stream Historical Society & Museum** is in a homestead dating back to when this area was one of the country's tanning centers. The home and barn are filled with artifacts from the town's early days. Here you can learn more about the Grand Lake canoes. ⊠ *U.S. 1* ☎ *207/796–5562* 🖵 *Free* ☉ *Mid-May–mid-Sept., Sun. 2–4.*

Where to Stay & Eat

$$$$ ▥ **Leen's Lodge.** Rustic cabins varying in size from one to four bedrooms are nestled on 23 wooded acres on West Grand Lake. All have woodstoves or fireplaces and big windows to take in the views. A country-style breakfast and a hearty, home-style dinner are served in a central lodge, where you can also find a TV, card tables, books, and games. The lodge can arrange guided fishing trips, wildlife or photographic trips, and other excursions. Boat rentals are available. ⊠ *368 Bonney Brook Rd.* 🖆 *Box 40, 04637* ☎ *207/796–2929 or 800/995–3367* ⊕ *www.leenslodge.com* ⬎ *10 cabins* 🖧 *Some kitchenettes, beach, boating, hiking, recreation room, some pets allowed; no a/c, no room phones, no room TVs* ⊟ *AE, MC, V* ☉ *Closed Nov.–Apr.* ⫙⊙⫙ *MAP.*

$$$$ ▥ **Weatherby's.** Nicknamed "the fishermen's resort," Weatherby's is ideal for anglers who want to be in the center of the action. The cottages, each with a fireplace, surround the main lodge. Breakfast and dinner are served in the dining room, and boxed lunches are provided for guests exploring the area. ⊠ *112 Millford Rd.* 🖆 *Box 69, 04637* ☎ *207/796–5558* ⊕ *www.weatherbys.com* ⬎ *15 cottages* 🖧 *Some pets allowed (fee); no a/c; no room phones, no room TVs* ⊟ *D, MC, V* ☉ *Closed Nov.–Apr.* ⫙⊙⫙ *FAP.*

Nightlife & the Arts

On the last full weekend of July, the two-day **Grand Lake Stream Folk Arts Festival** (☎ 207/796–8199 ⊕ www.thecclc.org) attracts thousands of visitors. Bluegrass and folk music are performed, and there are canoe and antique quilt exhibits. Admission is $5 for both days.

Sports & the Outdoors

The **Grand Lake Stream Guides Association** (⊠ Grand Lake Stream ☎ No phone ⊕ www.grandlakestreamguides.com) maintains more than 25 launch sites at area lakes. Guides lead fishing and wildlife trips in Grand Laker canoes.

Shopping

Shamel Boat & Canoe Works (⊠ 42 Tough End Rd. ☎ 207/796–8199) specializes in Grand Laker canoes. Watch the owner make these traditional cedar canoes by hand.

WAY DOWN EAST A TO Z

To research prices, get advice from other travelers, and book travel arrangements, visit www.fodors.com.

AIR TRAVEL

Hancock County–Bar Harbor Airport, 13 mi from the town of Hancock, is served by US Airways Express. Many visitors to this region use Maine's two major commercial airports in Bangor and Portland. Bangor International Airport is 98 mi from Calais and 35 mi from Hancock. Portland International Jetport is 228 mi from Calais and 163 mi from Hancock. Bangor International Airport is served by American, Continental, Delta, Northwest, and US Airways. Portland International Jetport is served by American, Continental, Delta, Independence Air, Northwest, United, and US Airways.

🛪 **Portland International Jetport** ⊠ 1001 Westbrook St., Portland ☎ 207/874-8877 ⊕ www.portlandjetport.org. **Bangor International Airport** ⊠ 287 Godfrey Blvd., ☎ 207/947-0384 ⊕ www.flybangor.com. **Hancock County-Bar Harbor Airport** ⊠ 143 Caruso Dr., Trenton ☎ 207/667-7329 ⊕ www.bhbairport.com.

BIKE TRAVEL

Narrow roads without bike lanes are the rule in this region, but you can find some beautiful routes on the long fingers of land that stretch toward the ocean as well as on the inland side of U.S. 1, where you can see plenty of lakes. Most land owned by logging companies is not open for cycling.

BOAT & FERRY TRAVEL

East Coast Ferries provides ferry service between Eastport and Deer Island and Deer Island and Campobello from late June to mid-September. Ferries run on Atlantic time, which is one hour ahead of Eastern time. Bar Harbor Ferry provides passenger service between Bar Harbor and Winter Harbor from mid-May to early October.

🛥 **East Coast Ferries** ☎ 506/747-2159 ⊕ www.eastcoastferries.nb.ca. **Bar Harbor Ferry** ☎ 207/288-2984 ⊕ www.barharborferry.com.

BUS TRAVEL

West's Coastal Connection provides bus service between Calais and Bangor via Ellsworth, stopping at towns en route on U.S. 1.

🚌 **West's Coastal Connection** ☎ 207/546-2823 or 800/596-2823 ⊕ www.westbusservice.com.

CAR TRAVEL

U.S. 1 is the primary coastal route in this region, with smaller roads leading to towns along the coast. Route 182 between Franklin and Cherryfield, a pleasant inland route, is a Maine Scenic Byway. The Schoodic National Scenic Byway follows U.S. 1 through Sullivan, then turns south on Route 186 on its way to the Schoodic Peninsula. Route 1A shaves several miles off a coastal trip north of Milbridge but bypasses historic Cherryfield. The most direct route to Lubec is Route 189, but Route 191 between East Machias and West Lubec is a scenic coastal drive through Cutler. Coastal U.S. 1 winds its way to Calais, but the quickest route from Bangor is Route 9, known as the "Airline." Route 191 is a scenic route from the Calais area back Down East. From Machias take Route 192 to Route 9.

Headquartered in Machias, Maine State Police Troop J patrols Washington and Hancock counties.

AAA Northern New England ☎ 800/222-4357 ⊕ www.aaanne.com. **Maine State Police Troop J** ☎ 207/255-6125 ⊕ www.state.me.us/dps/msp.

EMERGENCIES
In case of an emergency dial 911.

Hospitals **Down East Community Hospital** ⊠ Court St., Machias ☎ 207/255-3356. **Calais Regional Hospital** ⊠ 22 Hospital La., Calais ☎ 207/454-7521.

LODGING
Cabins and campgrounds are common Way Down East. Black Duck Properties specializes in rental properties on the Schoodic Peninsula. Hearts of Maine has waterfront listings from Steuben to Eastport, with the largest concentration in the Machias and Jonesport areas. The Maine Campground Association provides information on private campgrounds.

Black Duck Properties ⬠ Box 39, Corea 04624 ☎ 207/963-2689 ⊕ www.acadia. net/blackduck. **Hearts of Maine** ⊠ 5 Ocean Whisper Dr., Addison 04606 ☎ 207/483-4396 ⊕ www.heartsofmaine.com. **Maine Campground Association** ☎ 207/782-5874 ⊕ www.campmaine.com.

MEDIA
The *Bangor Daily News* is published weekdays. Other weekly newspapers in the region include the *Calais Advertiser,* the *DownEast Times* (Calais), *Downeast Coastal Press* (Cutler), *Machias Valley News Observer,* and the twice-monthly *Quoddy Tides* (Eastport).

WMEH 90.0 and WMED 89.7 are the local National Public Radio affiliates. WLBZ, channel 2, is the NBC affiliate. WVII, channel 7, is the ABC affiliate. WABI, channel 5, is the CBS affiliate. WMEB, channel 12, or WMED, channel 13, is the Maine Public Broadcasting affiliate.

Sports & the Outdoors
BOATING The Maine Professional Guides Association represents kayaking guides.

Maine Professional Guides Association ⬠ Box 847, Augusta 04332 ☎ 207/549-5631 ⊕ www.maineguides.org.

FISHING For information about fishing and licenses, contact the Maine Department of Inland Fisheries and Wildlife.

Maine Department of Inland Fisheries and Wildlife ⊠ 284 State St., Augusta 04333 ☎ 207/287-8000 ⊕ www.mefishwildlife.com.

HIKING Conservation groups and state and federal wildlife agencies teamed up to publish "Cobscook Trails," a pocket-size booklet with detailed information about hiking and walking trails around Cobscook Bay and the Bold Coast between Lubec and Cutler.

Cobscook Trails Project ⊠ Box 49, Whiting 04691 ☎ 207/733-5509 ⊕ www.qrlt.org.

TRAIN TRAVEL

There is no rail service Way Down East. Amtrak's Downeaster operates between Boston and Portland.

🚂 **Amtrak** ☎ 800/872-7245 ⊕ www.amtrak.com.

VISITOR INFORMATION

Many chambers in the region distribute free copies of the pamphlet "Maine's Washington County: Just Off the Beaten Path." It's several cuts above the usual tourist promotion booklet.

🚂 **Campobello Island Tourism Association** ⊠ 1977 Rte. 774, Wilson's Beach, New Brunswick E5E1J7 Canada ☎ 506/752-2419. **Cobscook Bay Chamber of Commerce** ⌂ Box 42, Whiting 04691 ☎ 207/733-2201. **Eastport Area Chamber of Commerce** ⊠ 23 Water St. ⌂ Box 254, Eastport 04631 ☎ 207/853-4644 ⊕ www.eastport.net. **Grand Lake Stream Chamber of Commerce** ⌂ Box 124, Grand Lake Stream 04637 ⊕ www. grandlakestream.com. **Greater East Grand Lake Chamber of Commerce** ⌂ Box 159, ⊠ Danforth 04424 ☎ 207/448-7788 ⊕ www.eastgrandlake.org. **Machias Bay Area Chamber of Commerce** ⊠ 12 E. Main St. ⌂ Box 606, Machias 04654 ☎ 207/255-4402 ⊕ www.machiaschamber.org. **Schoodic Peninsula Chamber of Commerce** ⌂ Box 381, Winter Harbor 04693 ☎ 207/963-7658 ⊕ www.acadia-schoodic.org. **Sunrise County Economic Council** ⌂ Box 679, Machias 04654 ☎ 207/255-0983 ⊕ www.sunrisecounty.org.

INDEX